WASTE MANAGEMENT

Planning, Evaluation, Technologies

DAVID C. WILSON
Harwell Laboratory

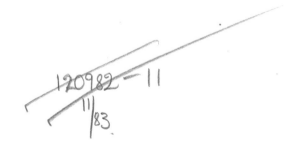
CLARENDON PRESS OXFORD 1981

Oxford University Press, Walton Street, Oxford OX2 6DP

OXFORD   LONDON   GLASGOW
NEW YORK   TORONTO   MELBOURNE   WELLINGTON
KUALA LUMPUR   SINGAPORE   JAKARTA   HONG KONG   TOKYO
DELHI   BOMBAY   CALCUTTA   MADRAS   KARACHI
NAIROBI   DAR ES SALAAM   CAPE TOWN

Published in the United States
by Oxford University Press, New York

British Library Cataloguing in Publication Data
Wilson, David C.
    Waste management.
    1. Refuse and refuse disposal
    I. Title
    628.4'4   TD791   80–41812
    ISBN 0–19–859001–6

Printed and bound in Great Britain
at The Pitman Press, Bath

To my mother and father

PREFACE

For many years, disposal of the wastes produced by an industrialized society was characterized by the maxim, 'Out of sight, out of mind'. Gradually this attitude has begun to change, and much progress has been made over the past decade. It is increasingly recognized that the goal of a cleaner environment can only be achieved by integrated control of all types of pollution and of all wastes, whether they be discharged to air, to water, or to land. In addition, with growing shortages of energy and materials, waste is now seen as a potential resource, and the challenge of economically exploiting that potential is beginning to be taken up in earnest.

This book then is directed at the subject of waste management. For our purposes, 'waste' is defined loosely as any unwanted residual material which cannot be discharged, directly or after suitable treatment, to the atmosphere or to a receiving water. We are thus concerned with all solid and semi-solid wastes, and with some liquid wastes. In order to focus the discussion, attention is directed primarily at municipal solid wastes, but the principles and technologies can equally be applied to other types of waste.

The technologies available for the disposal, treatment, separation, or reclamation of municipal wastes have burgeoned in recent years. When this fact is added to increasing pressures on resources—of land, materials, energy, environmental quality, and finance—and to the local political difficulties in establishing *any* facility to handle wastes, it is clear that waste management is becoming an increasingly thorny problem for the public, the planners, and the decision makers alike. The purpose of this book is twofold:

(a) To present a systems approach to the problem of planning for waste management, and to consider in detail the comparative evaluation of alternative technologies on the two important criteria of economics and the conservation of resources;

(b) To provide a comprehensive, up-to-date, and critical review of the state of the art in waste management technology. The use of the methods developed for quantitative evaluation enable some 30 representative options to be compared on a consistent basis, thus allowing an assessment of the most promising technologies for the future.

The book begins with a general introduction to the problem of waste management. International data are presented on types and quantities of waste generated, on the composition of household waste, and on the current use of technologies for municipal waste disposal. In addition an overview of available technologies is given.

Part I. Planning and evaluation in waste management

Chapter 2 introduces a simplified and formal conceptual structure of the planning process for waste management. Many difficulties are avoided if the system is properly defined, and much of the chapter is devoted to topics such as legislation, local government finance, and surveying current and forecasting future waste arisings. Emphasis is laid on the separation of the political planning process from the supporting technical analysis. This analysis is often aided by the use of mathematical models to provide an abstraction which one can understand and specify clearly. However, in order to compromise between reality and tractability, these models must focus on some aspects of a problem at the expense of others.

Previous work in planning for waste management has been largely restricted to the application of sophisticated operational research models to strategy evaluation, focusing on the combination of facilities to produce a least-cost plan. These models, reviewed in Chapter 3, are limited by an inability to consider data uncertainty or multiple objectives. The approach developed here (Chapter 4) focuses rather on the prior problem of selecting the best technologies to use. By including in each option all the operations performed on the waste arising from one source, a 'single waste flow model' is defined that will be sufficient for many planning purposes.

In principle, each option is evaluated against each criterion, the results being displayed in tabular form. Attempts are often made to reduce this table to a single performance index for each option against all the criteria, with interpretation reduced to choosing the option with the best index. However, this depends on complete quantification, which for essentially qualitative criteria introduces subjective elements into the analysis. Attention here is rather on the development of quantitative measures of performance on a few criteria, leaving the assessment of intangibles and overall balancing of criteria to the decision maker. The criteria chosen for detailed consideration are those of economics and resource conservation, where the prospects for objective evaluation are best.

Cost estimates for alternative waste management options are often difficult to compare owing to significant differences in assumptions about a process, in the estimating procedure used, or in the operations included. Conventions are proposed in Chapter 5 to alleviate these problems. In addition to processing and the disposal of any residual waste, each option must also include all significant transport steps. Simple models are developed in Chapter 6 to calculate the cost of transporting waste, in collection or bulk haulage vehicles, as a function of the distance travelled. All the component parts of the overall cost estimate are subject to considerable uncertainty. To determine the most critical parameters on which the estimate depends, and to allow proper consideration to be paid to their uncertainty, a discounted cash flow model incorporating sensitivity and risk analysis is developed in Chapter 7.

Economics does not always adequately reflect the scarcity of physical resources. The contribution which resource recovery from waste makes to the conservation of energy and materials may be measured conveniently by its implications for primary energy use. Process energy analysis is applied in Chapter 8 to evaluate the primary energy inputs to each option, and the savings implied by the use of the recovered fuel and material products. The results are expressed as two measures of net energy efficiency, differing in whether or not savings from materials recovery are included.

The techniques for economic and energy evaluation are demonstrated in Chapters 7 and 8 by a case study of some 30 options, using the best information available. The uncertainty in the estimates is substantial, and the analysis must therefore be carried out explicitly for any specific application. Nevertheless, certain general conclusions on the status of options may be drawn; the results from the case study provide the quantitative basis for the critical review of technologies in Part II.

Previous studies of waste management planning have often resulted in a 'black box' to produce the optimal plan. The framework developed here aims rather to expose the core of the problem. A number of simple, quantitative tools are developed for use in screening options for waste disposal, treatment, or resource recovery. The final assessment of intangibles and balancing of criteria is left with the planners and the politicians.

Part II. Waste management technology

The second half of the book is devoted to a comprehensive and critical review of the state of the art in waste management technology, as seen in early 1980. Progress in this field has been rapid over the last ten years, and it is currently difficult to find a balanced judgement on the relative merits of the processes, or even to see clearly the relationships between them. It is hoped that this treatise will help to remedy this situation.

The many technologies are rationalized under nine headings, which are dealt with in Chapters 11–19, respectively:
Landfill;
Transfer or treatment prior to landfill;
Incineration;
Separation processes;
Production of a solid refuse-derived fuel (RDF.);
Direct incineration of RDF;
Wet pulping;
Pyrolysis and other thermal processes;
Biological processes.

In addition, Chapter 20 looks briefly at technologies appropriate to the management of potentially hazardous wastes.

Each chapter follows a similar pattern. Particular emphasis is given to the overall objectives of the technology, to the similarities and differences between the various derivative processes, and to the relationships with other technologies. Flowsheets are presented in a standard format to allow easy comparison. The state of development and operating experiences are emphasized. Where there have been significant recent advances in our understanding of the scientific basis of a technology, then these are reviewed in depth: an example is the simple landfilling of wastes.

A unique feature of this book is the emphasis given to collating quantitative information on the technologies. This enables the use of the evaluation techniques developed in Part I to compare some 30 options, selected as typical of the state of the art, on a consistent basis. Some readers may prefer to skip from the qualitative introductory sections at the beginning of each section or chapter directly to the discussion at the end.

The final chapter of the book brings together the general conclusions of Part II, and the results of the evaluations on the criteria of economics and resource conservation, to provide an overall picture of the current state of the art in waste management technology and to speculate on future trends.

Harwell
July 1980

DCW

ACKNOWLEDGEMENTS

Much of the credit for this work must go to the many people who contributed to it over the past six years, through their encouragement, insight, discussion, and sometimes disagreement. Without their help the final product would have been infinitely worse that it actually is; however, the responsibility for the remaining errors and for the opinions expressed are the author's alone.

I am grateful to my many colleagues at the Harwell Laboratory. Mr H. I. Shalgosky, Dr C. Stevens, and Mr D. J. V. Campbell each read all or part of the final manuscript. Dr F. S. Feates, Dr M. D. Hebden, both now with the Department of the Environment, and Dr J. Bromley each deserve special mention, but I would include also the other members of the Environmental Safety and Operations Research Groups.

The work on which Part I of the book is based was performed jointly at the Department of Engineering Science, Oxford University and at Harwell. Dr John Bridgwater of Oxford, now Professor of Chemical Engineering at the University of Birmingham, provided both insight and constant encouragement and spent many hours reading various early drafts of the manuscript. Professor J. C. Friedly of the University of Rochester, New York gave liberally of his time during his visits to Oxford. Professor D. H. Allen of Stirling University generously made available his computer program for discounted cash flow sensitivity and risk analysis which was adapted for use here. Both Professor Allen and Mr S. S. Wilson of Oxford University read a version of the manuscript and provided many useful comments. Among the many other individuals and organizations who contributed through helpful discussion or by providing information were Dr A. V. Bridgwater of the University of Aston in Birmingham; Dr D. R. Davies of Redland Purle Limited; Professor R. S. Berry of the University of Chicago; the Warren Spring Laboratory; and several Local Authorities. Part of the work was made possible by financial support from the United Kingdom Atomic Energy Authority.

I would like to express my thanks to the following individuals or organizations for their kind permission to reproduce copyright material: Andco Incorporated: Figs. 18.6, 18.7; Professor R. S. Berry: Fig. 8.1; Bühler–Miag (England) Limited: Figs. 12.6, 15.1b, c, 19.3; Department of the Environment: Fig. 11.4; Harwell Laboratory: Figs. 11.1, 11.2, 11.3, 12.2, 12.3, 12.5, 12.7, 12.8, 12.11, 13.1, 20.2; Her Majesty's Stationery Office: Quotation from Waste Management Paper No. 3 in section 2.5, Fig. 20.1; Open University: Fig. 11.5; Cleanaway Limited: Fig. 20.5; South Yorkshire County Council: Figs. 12.1, 12.4, 13.6, 14.2, 14.3, 14.7, 14.8, 15.1a, 15.4;

The Stablex Group: Fig. 20.3; Vølund Limited: Figs. 13.2, 13.4; Wimpey Waste Management Limited: Fig. 20.4;

The work of completing this book would have been made much more difficult had it not been for the cheerful way in which my long-suffering typists, Mrs Penny Buffery and Mrs Iris Judd, faced their daunting task. Mr D. J. McGahan courageously helped with the task of proof reading. Last, but by no means least, I must thank my wife Leslie for her support and patience in sharing me with this work over innumerable evenings and weekends, and my daughter Katie for the time off to finish the book.

CONTENTS

1. THE PROBLEM OF WASTE MANAGEMENT

1.1. Introduction

All human activities give rise to residual materials which are not of immediate use where they arise. These residuals may be recycled, reclaimed, or reused; otherwise they constitute waste which will ultimately be released to the environment. The biosphere has the capacity to transform many wastes over time, either into harmless products or into nutrients which can be used again. However, the natural assimilative capacity of the environment can easily be exceeded if wastes, particularly those from man's industrial activities, are not controlled. Indeed, for some wastes such as persistent plastics and chlorinated organic compounds, the environment appears to have little or no assimilative capacity. In such circumstances, pollution and loss of environmental quality will ensue. Careful planning and control of waste management is thus required. A simplified, schematic representation of the flows of materials, services, wastes, and pollution to and from the environment is shown in Fig. 1.1.

Ideally, waste management should be viewed as a unity, with integrated control directed at all three waste receiving media, namely air, water, and land. However, the complexity of such an approach has led to fragmentation, with the various problems being dealt with in a piecemeal fashion, as and when the environmental insult reaches such proportions as to demand immediate action. In many industrialized countries, epidemics of cholera led to control of sewage discharges to rivers as early as the nineteenth century; industrial effluents threatened to kill all life in the American Great Lakes in the 1950s and 1960s; and the problem of urban smog has focused attention on air pollution. As controls over waste discharges to air and to water have become more stringent, so more pressure has been put on the third receiving medium, namely land. This book focuses attention on those wastes which are unsuitable or unacceptable for discharge to the atmosphere or to the aquatic system, and for which disposal to land is the primary option available.

The relationships between the three waste-receiving media must always

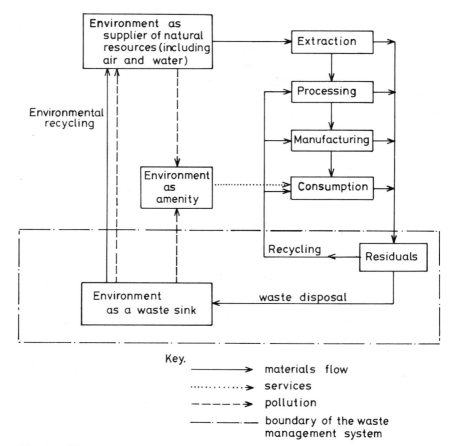

Fig. 1.1. Waste management in an industrial economy.

be borne in mind. The reduction of air pollution by removing particulate materials or acidic gases before discharge produces either a solid or a liquid waste for disposal; the reduction of water pollution normally produces a sludge. Wastes which are not acceptable for discharge to water, including solids, sludges, and some liquids, are normally disposed of on land. Attempts to treat these wastes to make them more acceptable for disposal, for example by incineration, simply shift some of the waste load back to the atmosphere or to water, exchanging one form of pollution for another.

Wastes are often subdivided, by source, by type, or by potential for reuse. One important distinction is between 'scrap' and 'waste'. Scrap may be defined as a residual which can be sold or disposed of advantageously, while waste has a negative value. Home scrap, which is recycled within a factory, and new scrap, which is returned from the manufacturer to the raw material processor for direct recycling, pose few problems. Old scrap arises after the use of a product and may be separated at its source so that it is relatively uncontaminated for collection and processing, or it may be recovered from a central waste treatment plant. The distinction between old scrap and waste is not always clear cut, as changes in technology or the economy may turn one into the other. It follows that waste management must concern itself with old scrap currently being recycled, as well as with the wastes presently produced, and that recovery of resources from waste is always an option.

1.2. Types of waste

All wastes disposed of to land are competing for the same limited reserves of landfill space, and so any subdivision of waste should be regarded with caution. On the other hand, the appropriate method for disposal, treatment, or resource recovery will depend on the properties and composition of the waste. Wastes may be differentiated by their origin, physical form, and detailed composition. A classification of waste, distinguished mainly by source, is shown in Table 1.1, together with an indication of the quantities generated in a number of industrialized countries.

Mining and quarrying wastes, pulverized fuel-ash, and building rubble must generally be used either as an aggregate or hardcore, or be disposed of to local landfill; management problems are associated mainly with the quantities involved, although acid mine tailings pose additional problems. Most farm wastes are returned to the land as a part of good agricultural practice, as is some sewage sludge. Medical and radioactive wastes merit specialized control owing to their particular hazards. Old vehicles have a positive scrap value. Major attention in waste management is thus usually directed at two categories identified in Table 1.1, those of household and commercial (often referred to collectively as municipal), and industrial wastes.

Industrial wastes are very varied. They may be classified by physical form (solid, liquid, and sludge), and by properties (inert and non-flammable, potentially combustible and/or biodegradable, and those which require special care in handling and disposal). Most liquid wastes disposed of to land will be in the third category requiring special care, for otherwise they would probably be suitable for disposal to water. The difficult wastes may be further subdivided by chemical composition or by their specific source, a system of 176 categories having been proposed (Department of the Environment 1976b).

Not all wastes which arise within a factory will be related to the processes in use. Often a significant portion, similar in nature to municipal waste, comes from offices and canteens. Municipal waste is generated at many locations and must be collected, either by the local authority or by a private

Table 1.1

Types of waste and quantities generated

Description	Approximate quantities[1] (million tonnes per year)									
	UK[2]	W. Germany[3]	France[4]	Netherlands[5]	Belgium[4]	Italy[4]	Sweden[4]	Finland[6]	Japan[7]	USA[8]
Municipal wastes (household and commercial)	20	20	12.5	5.2	2.6	21	2.5	1.1	35	150
Industrial wastes:										
similar to municipal		8	32					2.5	13	
production wastes		13	16	1.9						
sludges		7								
hazardous wastes	4–5	3	2	1				0.4		57
Total	50	31	50	3	1	19	1.7		140	270
Pulverized fuel ash	12								13	
Mine wastes	60	80	42							1890
Quarry wastes	50		75							
Wastes from construction and demolition	3	96			6.5			0.3	75	
Agricultural wastes	250	260	220	1		130	32		44	660
Sewage sludge (at 5% solids content)	20	36	6.2	3	3		4	1.4	44	
Medical, surgical, and veterinary wastes										
Radioactive wastes										
Old cars, vehicles and trailers		1.3						0.1		
Tyres	0.2	0.3	0.4							
Residues from waste treatment										

1. The availability of information on quantities is very patchy. The data shown are likely to have been based on extrapolations from very limited survey information, and must therefore be regarded as a rough guide only.
2. UK data for 1974–5 taken mainly from Department of the Environment (1976a) and Department of the Environment and the Welsh Office (1976a). Figures for industrial wastes are extrapolations from preliminary survey data only (Millard 1977; Wilson 1979a). Sewage sludge based on estimate of Bolton and Klein (1971).
3. West German data for 1977 from Umweltbundesamt, Berlin, as quoted by Diering (1979).
4. Data for 1975 (approx.) from Brusset and Rocherolles (1979). Data on industrial waste in France from ANRED, the National Agency for Recovery and Disposal of Waste.
5. Data for the Netherlands in 1977 from Kreiter (1979).
6. Private communication from the Ministry of the Interior, Helsinki.
7. Very approximate quantities for Japan estimated mainly from the data given by Green (1979) for 1976. The estimate of industrial wastes includes 55 million tonnes of slag and 67 million tonnes of acids and alkalis. Quantity of municipal wastes taken from Sakiyama, Takamatsu, and Nishizaki (1979).
8. Lutton, Regan, and Jones (1979).

contractor. Some waste is delivered to local authorities directly, including bulky items unsuitable for normal collection vehicles.

Both the quantity and the composition of municipal waste vary widely from day to day, and according to the season of the year. Considerable differences may be observed not only between countries but also between neighbouring localities and between different types of property within the same town. Representative information on the composition of household wastes worldwide has been compiled in Table 1.2; the availability of information outside the developed, Western world is generally poor. The data in Table 1.2 allow some comments to be made on the use and abuse of information on waste composition:

Any study of waste management must relate to a specific waste composition; there is no substitute for a local analysis.

As waste composition varies so much, and can be expected to change considerably during the operating life of any waste treatment plant, any study for waste management must include an examination of the sensitivity of its results to changes in waste composition.

Care must be taken to obtain a representative sample for analysis, allowing, for example, for variations between houses and apartments. It must also be remembered that municipal wastes include components other than household waste, e.g. commercial and bulky wastes, street sweepings, etc.

Waste will vary considerably in composition from season to season. Analyses should be conducted regularly during the year.

A general trend is apparent in Western countries towards an increase in paper content and a decrease in fine material (ash) content, as oil and gas have replaced solid fuels for domestic heating. It is possible that this trend may be reversed when oil and gas become relatively scarce compared to coal.

The pitfalls in extrapolating historical trends are shown in the data for Birmingham, England, and Stüttgart, West Germany, where a steady trend towards higher paper contents was reversed in the early 1970s.

There is no standard method for analysing wastes. Some of the observed variations in fine materials, vegetable and putrescible matter, rubber, leather and wood, and miscellaneous wastes will be due to differences in the classification of the components in the waste.

In general terms, the paper content of waste is in the range 20–70 per cent in the developed world, and in the range 5–20 per cent in less developed countries. Conversely, vegetable and putrescible contents are in the ranges 15–50 per cent and 50–80 per cent, respectively. Such gross differences obviously affect the types of treatment process which will be feasible.

Metal content is in the range 1–10 per cent, while glass varies between 1

Table 1.2

The composition of domestic waste worldwide (percentage by weight)

Location	Date	Source	Fine material	Paper	Vegetable and putrescible	Textiles	Rubber, leather, and wood	Plastics	Ferrous	Non-ferrous	Glass	Miscellaneous	Moisture[a]	Heating value (MJ/kg)	Waste per capita[c] (Kg/year)
Austria Vienna	1975	Wohlfärter and Striedinger (1979)	9.9*	38.3	18.6	7.6	2.2	6.1		8.1	9.2	*			
Belgium Urban	1976	Devroede (1979)	5	30	40	2	—	5	4.5	0.8	8	4.6			220
Rural	1976		5	15	45	1.5	—	5.5	5.5	0.3	16	6.2			150
Bulgaria	1975	Alter (1977a)	24*	10	54	*	7.0	1.7		1.7	1.6	*			
Canada	1967	Bond and Straub (1973)	5	70	*		10*	*	5		5	5			
Czechoslovakia Prague Summer	1967	Bond and Straub (1973)	6	14	*		39*	*	2		11	28			
Winter	1967	Bond and Straub (1973)	65	7	*		22*	*	1		3	2			
Denmark	1975	Alter (1977a)	19.7*	13.4	41.8	8.1		4.2	6.2		6.6	*			
Finland	1978	Hansen, Tjell, and Christensen (1979)	—	32.9	44.0	1.5	1.6	6.8	4.1		6.1	3.2			
	1978	Private communication	*	55	20	*	*	6	5		6	8*			
France	1977	Thomé-Kozmiensky (1977)	22	34	15	3	—	4	4		9	9		9	200
Gabon	1977	Shin (1979)	*	6	77*	*	*	3	5		9	*			280
Iran Teheran	1978	Nejat (1979)	1.1	17.2	69.8	4.1	—	3.8	1.8		2.1	—			210
Israel	1967	Bond and Straub (1973)	1.9	23.9	*	*	71.3*	*	1.1		0.9	1.9	(52)	5	
Italy	1977	Thomé-Kozmiensky (1979)	21*	18	50	*	*	4	3.1	0.4	4	*			430
Japan	1974	Sakiyama et al. (1979)	9.6	38.1	18.0	—	8.0	12.0	*		*	14.2*	(57)	5.7	350
	1975		6.1	46.2	18.6	*	5.6	12.7	*		*	10.7*	(56)	6.0	
Tokyo	1972	Shiga (1975)	20.1*	38.2	22.7	*	0.5	7.3	4.1		7.1	*	(49)	6.0	

Location	Year	Reference											Moisture	
Norway														
Standard	1974	} Halmø (1976)	3.7	34.1	37.6	3.3	5.5	5.7	3.6		5.5	1.0		180
Svalbard	1976		0.1	12.6	42.7	1.7	3.3	2.1	2.6		36.3	0.7		910
Spain	1978	Aller (1979)	*	18	50	2	*	4	4		3	19		330
Sweden	1977	Thomé-Kozmiensky (1979); Steier (1979)	*	50	15	2	*	8	1		8	10	(30)	
United Kingdom														
Averages	1967	Department of the Environment (1971)	31.0	29.5	15.5	2.1	–	1.1	8.0		8.1	4.7	(25)[b]	8.0–10.5
	1968	} Waste Management Advisory Council (1976)	21.9	36.9	17.6	2.4	–	1.1	8.9		9.1	2.1		
	1973		19	33	18	3.5	–	1.5	10		5	–		
Birmingham														
Autumn	1969	West Midlands County Council private communication (1977)	14.3	46.1	20.6	2.7	–	0.8	6.2		5.4	3.0		
Spring	1970		13.8	50.4	13.6	3.9	–	0.7	6.4		7.4	3.9		
Autumn	1974		17.4	29.3	15.6	5.4	–	0.9	9.6		10.6	11.3		
Spring	1975		20.5	29.4	13.9	7.4	–	1.7	6.3		7.0	9.9		
English mining area														
Smoke control	1970	} Skitt (1972)	29.4	23.6	23.7	0.9	–	0.8	6.5		10.8	4.3		
No smoke control	1970		67.9	3.9	6.2	1.4	–	0.8	6.0		8.4	5.4		
United States														
Averages	1973	US Environmental Protection Agency (1975)	1.5	39.6	27.4	1.6	6.3	4.1	8.9	1.0	10.3	–	(25.2)	800
	1974	Kaiser (1975)	10	43	20	3	5	3	7		9	10		10.6
	1977	Abert (1979a)	–	30	37	3	5	4	8.5	1.5	10	1		
	1977	Thomé-Kozmiensky (1979)	*	50	23	*	*	1	7.5	1.5	9	8*		
West Germany														
Average	1977	Thomé-Kozmiensky (1979)	22	31	16	2	–	4	4.5	0.7	13	7	(25)[b]	8.4
Berlin	1978	Barghoorn and Gössele (1979)	11.0	21.8	31.4	1.8	1.6	6.0	4.3	0.6	19.1	1.4		
Aachen	1976	Hoberg and Schulz (1977)	22.0	30.8	16.6	1.6	–	4.5	6.9		13.5	4.1		
Munich	1974	Furmaier (1979)	23.9	40.6	7.5	3.2	2.8	7.5	5.8	0.3	6.9	1.5		
Tübingen	1974	Tabasaran (1979)	10.7	13.7	44.3	*	5.2	7.6*	4.7		13.8	*	(27.6)	
Stuttgart	1950		57.0	13.8	17.6	–	4.3*	2.3*	2.5		2.5	*		
	1960	} Furmaier (1979)	44.6	23.3	17.2	–	5.1*	2.3	2.8		4.7	*		
	1970		28.0	31.0	18.0	–	4.9	4.1	3.3		8.2	2.5		
	1974	Tabasaran (1979)	6.2	14.7	52.4	*	4.1	6.2*	5.3		9.9	1.2		350

(a) All percentages are calculated on a wet weight basis. Moisture contents are an average over all refuse components. Conversion from wet to dry weight is illustrated in Table 1.3.
(b) Pavoni, Heer, and Hagerty (1975).
(c) In most cases the estimate is based on data in Table 1.1.
* Categories lumped together.

and 20 per cent. This reflects both the gross national product of the country and local attitudes to materials recycling. The lowest percentages appear to be those for Israel, where recycling is a facet of national loyalty.

The pastics content of refuse is increasing, being generally in the range 2–13 per cent. It is currently highest in Japan.

This specific waste composition used throughout this work for illustrative purposes is shown in Table 1.3. It may be considered to be representative of an 'average' waste in the developed, Western world.

Table 1.3

The nominal waste composition used in this work

Constituent	Wet weight (%)	Heat content[a] (MJ/kg)	Moisture[a] content (%)	Dry weight[b] (%)
Fine material	12	6.03	25.0	9.0
Vegetable and putrescible	20	8.45	52.5	9.4
Paper	40	13.44	22.7	30.9
Textiles	3	15.34	25.0	2.2
Rubber, leather and wood	5	17.52	13.6	4.3
Plastics	3	26.95	15.0	2.6
Ferrous metals	7.6			7.2
Aluminium	0.5	1.64	5.0	0.5
Other non-ferrous metals	0.1			0.1
Glass	9	0.19	2.0	8.8
Moisture	–	–	–	25.0
Total average value	100	10.07	24.95	100.0

(a) Heat and moisture content of constituents from Kaiser (1975).
(b) Dry weight percentage figures derived from wet weight percentage and moisture content.

It is clear from Tables 1.2 and 1.3 that in industrialized countries municipal wastes contain much which is suitable for reclamation or reuse. Recovery is aided when materials are separated at source; once they are mixed, separation and upgrading by manual or mechanical means is more difficult, and the quality of the products is lower. Source separation has been successfully used in the past for a wide range of materials, but in Britain, for example, it is now limited mainly to paper, with smaller contributions from metals, glass, and textiles. The decline in the returnable glass bottle and the introduction of stringent hygiene regulations governing the use of food waste as pig fodder have increased the quantity of these materials in waste. The prospects for separation of plastics at source are currently poor owing to the difficulties of separating the various types, although experiments in Japan and West Germany have had some success.

Despite the advantages of separation at source, for the foreseeable future much recoverable material will enter the solid waste stream. Thus attention in this text is directed to the management of that waste, by treatment, reclamation, or disposal. Reference is made primarily to municipal waste, and to industrial wastes of similar composition. The principles discussed apply equally to other industrial wastes, and indeed to all wastes, being disposed of to land.

1.3. Technologies for waste management

An enormous variety of technologies are either available or potentially available for the management of municipal wastes. These technologies may be rationalized under a number of headings:

Processes for final disposal, either of all the waste or of any residue remaining after treatment.

Treatment to achieve volume reduction prior to final disposal.

Separation of the organic from the inorganic fraction of the waste.

Recovery of materials from the inorganic fraction.

Recovery of materials from the organic fraction.

Reclamation of the organic fraction to produce either a fuel or a chemical product.

An expansion of this classification is given in Table 1.4. The major alternatives are outlined briefly in the remainder of this section; a detailed study of waste management technologies is the subject of Part II of the book.

The major technologies currently in use for municipal waste disposal are landfill, perhaps with prior transfer or pulverization, incineration, and composting. A summary of the application of these technologies in a number of industrialized countries is given in Table 1.5.

A note on terminology is appropriate here. The term 'recovery' implies the physical separation of a component such as ferrous metals from the mixed waste, while 'reclamation' implies the chemical transformation of the waste into a new product such as a fuel. For the sake of brevity, the terms 'resource recovery' and 'reclamation' are also used here, interchangeably, as generic descriptions of all such technologies.

1.3.1. Landfill

The only significant method for final disposal of municipal waste is landfill, since even if treatment and resource recovery processes are used they will leave some residue for disposal. Direct landfill of untreated waste can be acceptable if it is properly carried out, and may be used to public benefit in land reclamation. Present operating practices are often unsatisfactory, although in Britain site licensing was introduced during 1977 and the

Table 1.4

A classification of waste management technologies

General aim of the process	Process	Comment
Final disposal	Landfill	A transfer station may be used with distant landfill
	Sea disposal	No longer used for municipal wastes
Treatment to achieve volume reduction prior to landfill	Pulverization	Wet or dry process
	High-density baling	Bales may be self-sustaining or require wiring
	Incineration	Many alternative furnaces available
Energy recovery from unprocessed waste	Incineration	With heat recovery as steam or electricity
	Pyrolysis and other thermal processes	Some variants accept unprocessed refuse (see below)
	Landfill	With collection of methane gas from anaerobic decomposition of the waste
Separation of organic and inorganic fractions	Dry separation	Uses some combination of shredding, air classification, magnetic separation and screening. Many proprietary variations
	Wet pulverization	Uses a rotary drum pulverizer with one or more screens for the output
	Wet pulping	Waste converted to a water slurry, organics pulped and inorganics separated by centrifugal action
Materials recovery from inorganic fraction (or from incinerator residue)	Magnetic separation	Ferrous metals. May be applied to pulverized or unprocessed waste
	Non-ferrous metal separation	Uses eddy current, electrostatic, or heavy media separators
	Glass separation	Uses some combination of screens, jigs, hydraulic classifiers, roll crusher, froth flotation and optical (colour) sorting
Materials recovery from organic fraction	Paper and plastics recovery	From dry separation, by hand picking or air classification
	Paper fibre recovery	Wet pulping was originally aimed primarily at paper recovery. Several other approaches are now being developed
	Composting	Produces humus for use as soil supplement. Many variations using both mechanical high-rate and traditional windrowing methods
	Wallboard production	Using a dried organic fraction or compost
	Annelidic recycling	Uses earthworms to convert organic wastes into a fertilizer (worm castings) and protein (dried earthworms)
Energy (or chemical) recovery from organic fraction		
(a) Combustion	RDF as supplementary boiler	Wide variation in output form of solid refuse-derived fuel (RDF), depending on particle size, moisture content, freedom from inorganic contaminants and separation of paper/plastics from putrescible organics
	RDF as supplementary fuel in cement kiln	Ash incorporated in cement product
	Incineration of RDF	With heat recovery as steam or electricity. RDF may be fired in suspension or in a fluidized bed
(b) Pyrolysis and other thermal processes	Pyrolysis	Thermal decomposition in the absence of oxygen. Products are solid, liquid and gaseous fuels, the relative yields depending on process conditions
	Gasification	Partial oxidation, the heat of reaction being provided by combustion of some of the waste in air or oxygen. Product is a low to medium heating value gas

Table 1.4—cont.

General aim of the process	Process	Comment
	Steam reforming	Reaction with steam, to produce gas rich in carbon monoxide and hydrogen
	Hydrogasification	Pyrolysis in a hydrogen-rich atmosphere to produce a medium heating value gas
	Hydrogenation	Pyrolysis in a hydrogen-rich atmosphere under pressure to produce a liquid fuel
	Wet oxidation	Oxidation of a wet slurry of organic wastes with oxygen at high temperature and pressure. Main product is a solution of low molecular weight acids
(c) Bioconversion	Hydrolysis	Acid or enzyme catalysed hydrolysis of cellulose to produce sugars, which can be fermented to yield e.g. ethanol or single cell protein (yeast). Alkaline hydrolysis could yield organic acids for recovery
	Anaerobic digestion	To produce methane
	Biophotolysis	Sunlight induced intra-cellular enzymatic reduction of water to produce hydrogen gas

situation should improve. In good operating practice, waste is spread and compacted into layers not exceeding 2.5 m in depth, and is covered regularly with inert material, to a depth not less than 15 cm. The compaction and regular covering help to minimize nuisance such as smells, fires, windblown litter, vermin, and insects. Good practice also demands regular pest control and movable screens to control litter. On completion of the site, a final layer of cover is required to a minimum depth of 1 m.

Table 1.5

Current technologies for municipal waste disposal

(percentage by weight disposed of by each method)

Country	Date	Source	Landfill[a]	Incineration	Composting
Austria	1979	b	65	24	11
Belgium (Flanders)	1978	b	62	27	9
Denmark	1979	Pedersen 1979	(32)	66	(2)
England	1977–8	Society of County Treasurers 1979	89	10	<1
France	1975	c	60	29	10
Japan	1979	Sakiyama et al. 1979	52	46	2
Netherlands	1975	c	64	30	6
Sweden	1975	c	65	33	2
Switzerland	1978	b,c	15	70	14
United States of America	1979	d	95	5	–
West Germany	1979	b	71	25	3

(a) Including landfill after pulverization or transfer.
(b) Thomé-Kozmiensky (1979).
(c) Brusset and Rocherolles (1979).
(d) Estimated from total capacity of the 70 operational incinerators in May 1979, 32 000 tonnes per day (Alvarez 1979), assuming operation at full capacity for 250 days per year. Remaining waste landfilled, with small quantity going to new resource recovery plants.

A landfill site is an inelegant biological reactor, in which the waste decomposes over time. The temperature within the landfill will rise, giving a potential fire hazard. In the past, some open dumps burned almost continuously. Settlement will occur as decomposition proceeds, and this will delay use of the reclaimed site. Much recent research has focused on the chemistry and microbiology of landfilled wastes, particularly as they affect the production of highly contaminated aqueous leachate and landfill gas (Chapter 11). Any air present within the waste is normally used up quickly, so that most decomposition takes place anaerobically. The gases produced are thus usually a mixture of methane and carbon dioxide, and may be regarded either as a potential hazard or as a recoverable resource depending on the circumstances. Landfill leachate may cause water pollution if it contaminates either surface or groundwater supplies. Two alternative management strategies may be adopted for leachate control: (i) a site is chosen or engineered so as to provide a significant degree of containment for wastes and leachates. Care is required to prevent the water level within the waste rising to such an extent that leachate escapes laterally, polluting surface streams; and (ii) a site is chosen which allows leachate to migrate away slowly, the concentration of potentially polluting components being significantly attenuated by natural processes. Research in the United Kingdom suggests that for most wastes a properly managed policy of attenuation and dispersion may be environmentally preferable to the superficially safer policy of concentration and containment.

With competition from alternative land uses and increased awareness of the risks of water pollution, landfill sites near urban areas are becoming difficult to establish. Direct haul in collection vehicles is both inconvenient and expensive; increasing use is being made of transfer stations, which allow the waste to pass to a more convenient and economic means of transport whilst the collection vehicle and its crew return to their task. Haulage from transfer stations is most commonly by road, but transport by rail and barge are used, notably in London. The transfer station itself may range from a simple concrete pad on which the waste is tipped and from which it is loaded into open-topped vehicles by a front-end loader, to a sophisticated plant using compactors to load enclosed containers. The latter system makes higher vehicle payloads possible, but in Britain the maximum legal payload is achievable without compaction; the main advantage is that both vehicles and plant are more acceptable for use in an urban area.

Landfill of unprocessed waste is still the dominant method of disposal in most countries of the world (Table 1.5). It is particularly prevalent in the United States of America (95 per cent of all wastes) and England (86 per cent), with levels of 60–70 per cent in other European countries and 50 per cent in Japan. Exceptions, where incineration predominates, include

Switzerland and Denmark. Of the wastes which are landfilled in England, probably about 10 per cent are delivered via transfer stations.

1.3.2. Volume reduction prior to landfill

The scarcity of landfill sites has led to the use of methods for reducing the volume of waste requiring final disposal. Such treatment may also render the waste more acceptable environmentally, thus making more sites available. The three principal methods are pulverization, high-density baling and incineration.

Pulverization or size reduction may be achieved by a dry or a wet process. In the dry process, crushers, shearers or grinders adapted from mineral processing may be used, although hammermills are most common; size reduction is achieved by swing hammers attached to a central shaft which rotates at high speed about either a vertical or a horizontal axis. In the wet process, the waste, together with a controlled addition of water, is tumbled in a large drum which rotates about a horizontal axis, producing self-pulverization of the soft organic materials by the hard objects in the waste. Two fractions are produced: a fibrous, largely organic material, which passes through perforations in the drum, and oversize objects, which pass out of the end of the drum. Both processes have been used extensively in Britain, but their use has declined; it is now about 3 per cent of local authority wastes in England (Society of County Treasurers and County Surveyors' Society 1979).

In high-density baling the waste is compressed into bales of about 1 m³ weighing over 1 t each. Two main variants are available, one producing self-sustaining bales from raw waste and the other wired bales from pulverized waste. Several plants have been built in Europe and the USA since 1975, but significant operational experience has yet to be gained.

Incineration has been used as a means of municipal waste disposal since the last century; its share of the market currently ranges from a low of 5 per cent in the USA and 10 per cent in England, through a moderate 20–30 per cent in many European countries and 46 per cent in Japan, to a high of about 70 per cent in Switzerland and Denmark (Table 1.5). The waste is burnt under controlled conditions to produce a sterile ash and gases which, after cleaning, can be discharged to the atmosphere. Many incinerator furnaces are available, those most commonly used for municipal wastes having a moving metal grate which slowly propels waste through the furnace. Removal of dust from the gases is necessary, an electrostatic precipitator being commonly used. If the concentrations of noxious acidic gases exceed permissible levels, a wet scrubber must be used. Incineration is still being developed, a particularly interesting innovation being the modular incinerator. This is a starved air system, using two combustion chambers, which produces gaseous products claimed to be suitable for discharge without cleaning. The modular design enables local plants to be built, thus saving transport costs.

Each of these methods reduces the volume of the waste in a landfill. These volumes are compared to those achieved with untreated waste in Table 1.6. Recent developments in compactors used on conventional landfills, in particular the introduction of large steel-wheeled machines, have somewhat reduced the advantage of pre-treatment, although accurate measurements of effective density on maturity are not yet available. Treatment makes the landfill site easier to manage. Baled waste may simply be stacked using a fork-lift truck. Accurate placement of the bales is claimed not to be necessary as 'springback' (expansion of the bales) will occur, and gaps will be filled. Pulverized waste is more homogeneous than untreated waste and is thus easier to spread. Both pulverization and baling reduce windblown litter and the volume of cover required, and make the waste unattractive to insects or vermin. Ash from incineration is similar to a mineral waste and is easy to handle.

Table 1.6

The volume occupied by 1 tonne of waste.

An extended discussion is given in Section 11.2. Volumes in a landfill include the necessary cover material. All units are m³

	Source			
Treatment of waste	Loram 1976	Jackson, Renold, and Wilson 1975	Bratley 1977	Section 11.2
Placed in dustbin	7.1	–	8.6	–
In collection vehicle	–	–	3.5	–
In a landfill on maturity:				
Direct landfill	1.53	1.5–1.9	–	–
After pulverization	1.18	1.29	–	–
After baling	1.02	1.03	–	–
After incineration	0.44	0.64	–	–
In a landfill on deposition, with compaction by:				
Tracked machine	–	–	2.1	1.7–2.5
Rubber wheeled machine	–	–	1.5–1.8	1.3–2.0
Steel-wheeled compactor	–	–	1.0–1.6	1.0–2.0

The relative risk of water pollution from the alternative methods is difficult to assess, although current research in Britain is designed to clarify this point. The effect of extreme compaction with a steel-wheeled machine or baled waste on leachate generation is not known, although it has been claimed that little biodegradation is observed after many years. Pulverization speeds up initial decomposition of the waste, giving higher leachate generation initially, but allowing a more rapid maturing of the site. Combined with the more even settlement which results, the site can be re-developed more quickly and this has led to the widespread adoption of pulverization for land reclamation. In the past incinerator ash was assumed to be inert, but recent research suggests a significant threat of water pollution from readily soluble inorganic compounds.

1.3.3. Resource recovery or reclamation

Incineration and pulverization are more adaptable than direct landfill or baling, as they offer more prospects for the recovery of energy or materials. For unprocessed waste, the possibilities are limited to the hand picking of materials or the magnetic extraction of ferrous metals from conveyor belts, and to the collection of the methane which results from the anaerobic decomposition of organic materials in a landfill.

The heat from incineration may be utilized by passing the hot gases through a boiler to raise steam, which is in turn used for heating or electricity generation. A steady market must be found. District heating schemes have peak demand in the winter, although the provision of cooled water for summer air conditioning is possible. In addition, since customers may require a continuous supply, expensive back-up facilities using alternative fuels are often needed. In Britain, although incineration is used quite extensively, there are only five plants generating steam and one generating electricity. Heat recovery is, however, the norm in most European countries and in Japan; it is particularly prevalent in Denmark and Switzerland.

In general, resource recovery requires the initial separation of the waste into organic and inorganic fractions, the former being used as a source of energy or materials and the latter of materials alone. There are three ways of achieving this initial separation:

(i) Dry separation uses some combination of pulverization, air classification, magnetic separation, screening, and ballistic or gravity separation. Many variations have been proposed, depending on the ultimate products required.

(ii) Wet pulverization is readily adapted to separation, as a fibrous organic and a largely inorganic fraction are normally produced.

(iii) In wet pulping, the waste is converted to an aqueous slurry which enters a hydrapulper, where the organics are pulped and inorganics are rejected by centrifugal action.

1.3.4. Recovery of materials

The inorganic fraction of the waste may be processed further to separate ferrous metals, non-ferrous metals, and glass. For non-ferrous metals and glass, equipment is still being developed and several alternative schemes have been proposed. The unit operations include density, electrostatic or eddy-current separation, and froth flotation or colour sorting of glass. The exact products and the quality depend on the flowsheet and methods used for product upgrading. Similar methods may be used to separate materials from incinerator residue, although the yield of aluminium, and to a lesser extent iron, is reduced by oxidation. The residue after processing may be suitable for use as an aggregate, or may simply be landfilled.

The organic fraction of the waste may be processed for materials or energy recovery. Bundles of paper and corrugated board and sheets of plastic may be hand-picked from the incoming waste on a conveyor. With dry separation, most American processes produce a single organic fraction, while European processes produce at least two, namely vegetable wastes and a light paper and plastics product. The latter may be used as a refuse-derived fuel, as a feedstock for paper and plastics recovery, or as a filler for wallboard. The organic slurry from wet pulping may be dewatered for use as a fuel, or processed for recovery of paper fibres.

A further alternative to paper or energy recovery is composting, which involves the four basic steps of waste preparation, digestion, curing, and finishing. Preparation separates organic from inorganic components. Digestion is the critical step, in which the waste is decomposed by aerobic organisms to form humus. The prepared waste may be piled in windrows which are regularly turned, or a high-rate mechanical digester may be used, in which typical retention times are 3–5 days. Curing is necessary to decompose remaining cellulose and lignin in the compost, while finishing upgrades the product, for example by removing remaining inorganics, particularly glass. In recent years, the market for compost as a soil conditioner has declined, although about 10 per cent of municipal wastes are still composted in a few European countries (Table 1.5). A reversal of this decline may be hindered by worries over heavy metals in the compost. However, compost may become increasingly important in arid areas such as the Middle East or South Africa. Alternative uses suggested for compost include those as a fertilizer base, as a filler in wallboard or building block production, as a source of cellulose fibre, or as artificial roughage in cattle feed.

An interesting concept in materials reclamation from organic wastes is annelidic recycling, in which the waste is used as the feedstock for a rapidly growing population of red earthworms. The waste is converted into a rich fertilizer (worm castings) and any surplus worms can be dried and sold as a high-protein supplement to animal feedstuffs. The process originates from Japan, and is being used commercially for wastes from food processing in both Japan and Canada. A similar concept being explored in Spain is the breeding of fly larvae on the putrescible fraction of the waste, for use as a protein supplement.

1.3.5. Energy recovery

The organic fraction of waste may be processed for the reclamation of either energy or chemicals, by combustion or other thermal processes, or by biochemical conversion. Here the generic product is termed a waste-derived fuel (WDF), while the term refuse-derived fuel (RDF) is reserved for solid fuels.

Processed waste or RDF may be fired directly in an incinerator, the heat being used to generate steam or electricity. RDF may be fired wholly or partly in suspension rather than on a conventional grate. An interesting development is the incinerator turbine, in which the hot exhaust gases from a fluidized bed incinerator are used to drive a gas turbine generator.

In order to overcome some of the problems of incineration, notably its high capital cost and the difficulty of using the heat produced continuously, recent work has focused on the use of RDF as a supplementary fuel in conventional boilers; several plants are now producing RDF on a commercial basis. The simplest form of RDF is dry pulverized waste with magnetic metals removed. This product may be upgraded, for example by using air classification to remove further inorganic materials, or by screening to remove in addition putrescible organic materials, leaving mainly paper and plastics in the RDF. The product may be further improved by drying, by size reduction to a fluff, by chemical embrittlement and reduction to a powder in a ball mill, or by forming into pellets or briquettes. Both wet pulverization and wet pulping give initial organic fractions which are more homogeneous than those from dry separation, although dewatering or drying may be required. RDF can be stored, at least for a short time, and can be burned in conventional boilers with little modification, subject to restrictions on ash handling, gas cleaning, and corrosion.

A related method is the use of RDF as a supplementary fuel in cement manufacture, where minimal pre-processing by size reduction and magnetic extraction may be adequate since the ash is incorporated in the product. Thus there is little or no residue for disposal to land. Two experimental schemes have been operated successfully in England and a commercial plant is now beginning operation.

As an alternative to energy recovery via complete combustion, there are a variety of thermal processes which can convert an organic feedstock into a mixture of solid, liquid or gaseous waste-derived fuels, some of which could also be used as feedstocks for chemical synthesis. 'Pyrolysis' is often used as a generic term, but strictly it applies only to thermal decomposition in the absence of oxygen. When the heat for pyrolysis is provided by combustion of part of the waste in air or oxygen, the term 'gasification' is more appropriate. Related thermal processes include steam reforming, hydrogenation, hydrogasification, and wet oxidation. The chemistry of thermal degradation is extremely complex and only partially understood. By manipulating the environmental conditions within the reactor, the yield of any desired product may be optimized. Some 150 processes have been proposed for the reclamation of municipal or other wastes, but currently only one is in use on a small commercial scale. One large demonstration plant in the USA provides a salutary case study of the pitfalls of over-enthusiastic development of a new and untried technology (Section 18.9).

Organic wastes may be decomposed by the action of micro-organisms. Examples include anaerobic decomposition in a landfill site to produce methane and aerobic degradation to yield compost. Anaerobic digestion at an accelerated rate using processed waste as input has been the subject of much recent academic research. Any separation method may be used but wet pulping to produce an aqueous slurry is perhaps the most suitable. Sewage sludge and additional nutrients may be added before digestion. The product gas may be upgraded, by drying and the removal of carbon dioxide, to produce high-purity methane suitable for pipeline distribution. The critical problem is the low conversion, leaving a substantial residue for disposal.

Hydrolysis of the cellulose in waste produces sugar, which can then be fermented to produce, for example, ethanol or single-cell proteins (yeast). The initial hydrolysis may use acid, alkaline or enzyme catalysis. Acid hydrolysis is an old process, but interest was revived by the more recent work of Porteous (1967) and others, who used higher temperatures to increase the rate of reaction.

1.3.6. Processing other wastes

Many of the methods of processing municipal wastes can be used for other wastes. Agricultural wastes, sewage sludge, and residues from food processing may be composted or used for energy recovery, for example by bioconversion. Plastics and rubber tyres have been used as feedstocks for pyrolysis. Considerable attention has been paid to those wastes which require special care in handling or disposal. For the more difficult the options, as outlined in Chapter 20, are:

(a) Modify the production process to reduce waste generation.

(b) Recover the material for reuse.

(c) Destroy the toxicity by:

Thermal processing, with or without energy recovery; several incinerators have been developed specifically for this purpose;

Chemical decomposition, e.g. the oxidation of cyanide;

Biochemical decomposition, e.g. that of phenol or pharmaceutical wastes.

(d) Change the form of the waste so that the toxic component is stable or insoluble. Examples include the precipitation of heavy metals from solution, and the solidification of inorganic sludges by encapsulation in a polymeric lattice.

(e) Dispose finally of the waste or a stabilized form by landfill or at sea. Disposal at sea was once used widely, for municipal as well as other wastes, but it is now strictly limited by international convention to certain difficult wastes, with a complete ban on materials, including mercury, cadmium, and halogenated hydrocarbons, which are concentrated by marine organisms.

Landfill is particularly unsuitable for certain wastes, including flammable materials with a low flashpoint, materials with a strong odour, strong oxidants, acids or alkalis, concentrated persistent toxic substances, and other materials hazardous to the operators. For some inert wastes, landfill is the only option.

1.4. The systems approach

Increasing pressures on resources of land, materials, and energy have combined to make waste management a complex problem at the local, regional, and national levels. The choice of the most suitable method of dealing with wastes and the long-term provision of adequate facilities are major planning problems.

It is increasingly common to talk of a systems approach as necessary when public-sector planning decisions are to be made. The plan must be formulated in the wider context of the system of which it is a part. In essence the systems approach provides an organized framework in which evaluation may be conducted.

This book is divided into two complementary parts. In Part I, the systems approach is applied to planning for waste management. The aim is twofold:

To help the reader gain insight into the problems of waste management;

(i) To help the reader gain insight into the problems of waste management.

(ii) To show how such an approach can enable the planner to reach more reasoned decisions and to present a more coherent policy.

Considerable attention is given to evaluation techniques, and in particular to the comparison of technologies on the criteria of economics and the conservation of resources. Part II presents a comprehensive and critical review of the state of the art in waste management technologies, as seen in 1980. By using the methods developed in Part I, it has been possible to compare the alternative technologies on a consistent basis and to draw conclusions on the most promising options for the future.

Part I. PLANNING AND EVALUATION IN WASTE MANAGEMENT

2. WASTE MANAGEMENT PLANNING

2.1. A framework for planning

Planning any human activity is a complex process. There will usually be a number of external factors which need to be taken into account before the problem can be properly formulated; several conflicting objectives will need to be considered; a number of steps will be involved in generating and evaluating plans. In order to provide a focus for this discussion on waste management, a simplified and formal conceptual structure of the planning process is introduced (Fig. 2.1). The steps in the process may be summarized as:

The system must be defined in order to plan the level of disposal activities. This requires clarification of the external terms of reference and of what is and is not included within the system under consideration; it also requires survey information on wastes arising now and in the future and on the availability of disposal facilities, in particular landfill sites.

The criteria against which the plans are to be assessed must be established.

The available technologies for waste disposal, treatment, or resource recovery must be evaluated and assessed.

Overall strategies for waste management in the area must be formulated using the most promising technologies and potential locations. These alternative strategies must then be evaluated and assessed.

An overall plan must be selected.

One of the main features of the conceptual structure is the separation of the political planning process from the technical analysis required in its support. Whilst this distinction is not always clear in practice, the professional waste disposal officers (here referred to as 'the planners') will generally perform the technical analysis and provide information and advice to the political decision makers.

In any given situation the precise order of the steps in Fig. 2.1 may change, and feedback from steps later in the planning procedure to those earlier will occur. Despite such limitations, this planning structure serves to make explicit the relationship of the various facets of planning, and in particular to emphasize the separation of system definition from technical analysis. The

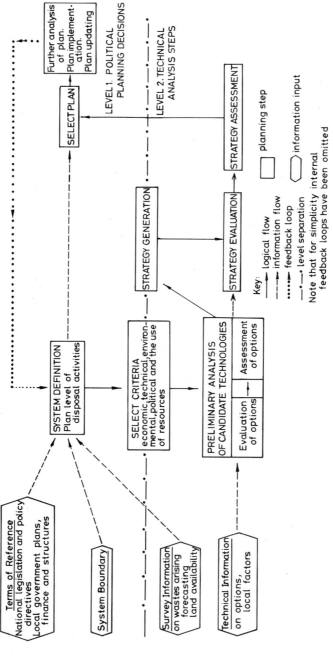

Fig. 2.1. A conceptual structure of the strategic planning process for waste management to land.

more general advice of the Department of the Environment (1976c) on waste disposal planning is consistent with this conceptual structure.

The various aspects of the planning process identified in Fig. 2.1 are now examined in more detail.

2.2. Terms of reference

The terms of reference within which planning for waste management to land is conducted include national legislation and policy directives, and local government plans, finance, and structures. Much may also depend on the local council's political objectives and on social attitudes in the area. The situation in Britain is examined here by way of a case study.

2.2.1. National legislation and policy directives

In Britain, as in many other countries, the legislative requirements on a local authority with regard to waste management are undergoing radical change. The existing situation is controlled by the Public Health Act of 1936, under which an authority has an obligation to collect household waste and discretionary power to collect commercial waste at a reasonable charge, and the powers to dispose of the waste so collected. The Control of Pollution Act of 1974 will, when implemented fully, extend the responsibility of a waste disposal authority to include the adequate disposal of all controlled waste, including household, commercial, and industrial waste, in its area. Thus industrial wastes will become the responsibility of the local authorities for the first time, although this responsibility is not backed by full powers, such as the direction of industrial waste to a particular treatment facility or disposal site. The relationship of the public and private sectors in waste disposal is discussed below.

Several Acts between these two major pieces of legislation affected waste management. In 1967, the Civic Amenities Act required the provision of sites where the public could deposit waste. After a public outcry in 1972 over the indiscriminate dumping of cyanide, the Deposit of Poisonous Wastes Act made such fly-tipping an offence, and introduced a system of notifications to waste disposal and water authorities of the generation and disposal of these and other hazardous wastes.

Local government re-organization took place in London in 1965, in the rest of England and Wales in 1974, and in Scotland in 1975. A two-tier power structure was introduced, the higher being county or metropolitan county councils, or regional councils in Scotland, and the lower district or metropolitan borough councils. All the new councils serve larger areas, with the 1165 old borough and district councils in England outside Greater London being reduced to 45 first-tier and 332 second-tier authorities. In England, the responsibility for waste management is split, with disposal going to the first-tier and collection to the second-tier authorities. In Wales and Scotland both collection and disposal remain the responsiblity of the district councils. A waste disposal authority is thus a county or metropolitan county council in England or a district council in Wales or Scotland.

The major provisions and the state of implementation of the Control of Pollution Act of 1974, as it applies to waste on land, are summarized in Table 2.1. For planning, the most pertinent part of the Act is Section 2, which sets out the legal requirements for the preparation and revision of waste disposal plans. Prior to the implementation of this section in 1978, the Department of the Environment issued guidelines on both waste disposal surveys (1976*b*) and the preparation of waste disposal plans (1976*c*).

Table 2.1

Provisions of the Control of Polution Act 1974 which cover waste management to land

Act Section	Whether implemented (January 1981)	Provision
1	No	Places a duty on disposal authorities to ensure that all arrangements for the disposal of controlled waste are adequate.
2	Yes (as from July 1978, but currently 'on ice' due to financial restrictions on local government)	Places a duty on disposal authorities to conduct waste disposal surveys, to prepare waste disposal plans and to update them. The plan must include (i) Estimates of the kinds and quantities of controlled waste that are to be generated in its area, to be brought into its area, to be disposed of by the authority itself, or to be disposed of by persons other than the authority. (ii) The methods of waste disposal (including resource recovery) to be employed in the area, and the priorities to be accorded during the period to the provision of different methods of disposal. (iii) The sites and equipment which the authority and other persons presently provide, and propose to provide during the period. (iv) The estimated costs of the methods of disposal mentioned in the plan. Provisions are laid down for consultations on the draft plan, for its modification and publication.
3	Yes	Makes it an offence to dispose, or to cause or knowingly permit the disposal, of controlled waste on any land or at any treatment plant unless the site has been licensed for the disposal of such waste.
4	Yes	Covers the interim period for the implementation of, and possible exemptions from, site licensing. Grants exemption from Section 3 for the disposal of household waste within the curtilage of the dwelling. Specifies the considerations to be taken into account by the Secretary of State in granting further exemptions from Section 3.
5–6	Yes	Governs the issue of disposal licences by a waste disposal authority. Site licensing is an additional requirement to normal planning permission. A licence will only be refused if the authority is satisfied that its refusal is necessary for the purpose of preventing water polution or danger to public health. Water authorities and collection authorities must be consulted. Any appropriate conditions may be attached to the licence, and it is an offence to contravene such conditions. The authority will maintain a public register of all current disposal licences.
7	Yes	Governs the variation of licence conditions and the revocation of licences. An authority may only vary the conditions if, in their opinion, the changes are both desirable and unlikely to require unreasonable expenditure by the licence holder. An authority may only revoke a licence if its continuance would cause water pollution, danger to public health or be seriously detrimental to local amenities.
8	Yes	Deals with the transfer and relinquishment of licences.
9	Yes	Imposes a duty on the waste disposal authority to supervise licensed activities. The authority is empowered to carry out any work necessary on a licensed site in the case of an emergency, and to recover any costs so incurred.

Table 2.1—cont.

Act Section	Whether implemented (January 1981)	Provision
10	Yes	Governs appeals to the Secretary of State when an application for a licence or a licence modification is rejected, when conditions are specified or modified, or when a licence is revoked.
11	Yes	Exempts the waste disposal authority from the need to license its own activities. The authority is however required to adopt a resolution specifying the conditions which will be met by each such activity.
12–13	In part	Defines the power of collection authorities. A duty is imposed to collect domestic waste, and commercial waste if so requested. The power to collect industrial wastes, with the consent of the disposal authority, is conferred.
14	No	Governs co-operation between the collection and disposal authorities. Imposes a duty on the collection authority to deliver to the disposal authority, at such places as the latter may direct, all the waste it collects, except for waste paper and any other material to which the disposal authority agrees, which may be disposed of for recycling. Imposes a duty on the disposal authority to dispose of the waste so delivered to it. Such waste belongs to the disposal authority. Payments between the authorities are required: To the disposal authority for handling commercial or industrial waste for which a charge has been levied. To the collection authority for wastes separated for recycling and thus not requiring disposal, and for transport costs when the place of waste delivery is unreasonably far from the collection authority's area.
15	No	Governs waste disposal in Scotland.
16	Yes	Deals with the removal of wastes deposited in breach of licensing provisions.
17	Yes	Controls the disposal of 'special wastes', defined as any controlled waste which is dangerous or difficult to dispose of. Enables the Secretary of State for the Environment to make regulations, which may include powers of direction of special wastes to specified sites. Regulations are due to come into operation in March 1981. These are directed primarily at transportation of wastes, to provide early warning of the illegal 'fly-tipping' of potentially dangerous wastes at unauthorised sites.
18–19	Mainly yes	Gives limited powers with respect to other waste (i.e. not controlled waste). The Secretary of State may include certain agricultural or mining and quarrying wastes under specified sections of the Act in prescribed areas. Disposal authorities have power to collect information or to make plans for the disposal of other wastes.
20	Yes	Enables a disposal authority to reclaim waste and sell the products.
21	Yes	Enables a disposal authority to use waste for the production of heat or electricity. Any electricity generated which is surplus to the needs of the producing installation must be sold to the local Electricity Board.
30	Yes	Defines terms used in Part 1 of the Act. Controlled waste means household, industrial and commercial waste or any such waste. Waste includes 'any substance which constitutes a scrap material or an effluent or other unwanted surplus substance arising from the application of any process; and any substance or article which requires to be disposed of as being broken, worn out, contaminated or otherwise spoiled', but does not include explosive substances. Household waste consists of waste from a private dwelling, and of similar waste arising elsewhere. Industrial waste consists of waste from any factory or premises of a nationalized industry, but excludes waste from any mine or quarry. Commercial waste consists of waste from premises used wholly or mainly for the purposes of trade or business, or the purposes of sport, recreation or entertainment, excluding household and industrial waste, waste from any mine or quarry and waste from premises used for agriculture.

2.2.2. Local government plans

Waste management is only one part of the overall planning of local authorities. In England and Wales the county councils are required to produce structure plans while the district councils may produce local plans. A structure plan should formulate policy and general proposals for the development and other use of land in the area concerned, including measures for the improvement of the physical environment and the management of traffic. Structural matters are those which affect the whole or a significant part of the area or which influence the development of the area in a significant way. Thus the structure plan is an overall statement of policy and strategy over the medium to long term, a period of 15 years being generally recommended. A local plan provides more definitive guidance for development and development control in a much smaller area, such as a small town or part of a larger town. The emphasis of a local plan is thus tactical rather than strategic. Detailed guidance on structure and local plans has been provided by the Department of the Environment and the Welsh Office (1977).

Structure and local plans thus impinge on waste disposal principally with regard to land use. Any proposal to site a waste treatment or resource recovery plant or a landfill site must conform to the general strategy of the structure plan. Provisions made for mineral extraction will control the creation of potential landfill sites. Indeed, the use of waste to reclaim derelict land or worked-out mineral extraction sites may form part of a structure or local plan. In addition, any waste disposal facility is subject to normal planning procedures under which restrictions on the use of the facility may be imposed. For example, the conditions on a landfill site may include precautions against water pollution or provision for the restoration of the land after filling is complete. In order to control noise, the maximum number of vehicles entering a site or the number of working hours per day may be restricted.

2.2.3. Local government finance

The methods of financing both revenue and capital expenditure may have an important influence on the choice of a waste disposal strategy. In Britain, revenue expenditure by local authorities is financed partly by the rates, partly by central government through the rate support grant and partly by charges levied, such as those for the collection and disposal of commercial and industrial waste (Marshall 1974). Central government does not control the total budget but the rate support grant provides a strong sanction if recommended spending levels are exceeded. Waste disposal thus competes with other services for its share of the budget. It is unfortunate that the rationalization of waste disposal into large authorities and the higher standards of operation introduced by the Control of Pollution Act have coincided with a period of public expenditure cuts.

Capital expenditure by local authorities in England and Wales is more stringently controlled by central government (Department of the Environment and the Welsh office 1976b). A limit on total capital expenditure by all authorities is set, and this is divided between three classes of investment.

Key sector services include housing, major transport schemes, education, personal social services, docks and harbours, police, and the administration of justice. For these, central standards and national policy co-ordination are required, and each project must be presented to the appropriate Minister for approval or loan sanction. The Minister must ensure that the total capital expenditure falls within the total allowed for that year. The *subsidiary sector* is covered by a special fund allowing for the purchase of land for certain key sector services. To allow for the variation in land prices through the country, the total funds rather than individual allocations are controlled.

The *locally determined sector* is the residual category of investment and includes all projects which do not fall within the others. Expenditure is controlled by *block borrowing approval* given each year to each authority or group of authorities by the Secretary of State. Separate allocations are made to the London boroughs and the metropolitan counties (the Greater London Council is not subject to control); all other authorities share block allocations made on a county basis. The total sum available is distributed in agreed proportions after deduction of the contribution which the authorities are expected to make from revenue rather than from loans. Total capital expenditure on all services not included in the key sector, but including vehicles, equipment, and furniture required for key sector services, must not exceed the level of this sanction unless it may be met from revenue, capital receipts, or reserve payments. The major services competing for the available capital are roads and transport; local environmental services (including waste collection and disposal, recreation parks and baths, municipal buildings, and cemeteries and crematoria); law, order, and protection services, including the fire service; and education, libraries, and the arts. The total locally determined sector allocation for England and Wales has declined over recent years, with corresponding decreases for local environmental services (Department of the Environment and other Departments 1977, 1978, 1979):

	Total locally determined sector	Local environment services
	(£ million, approx. Nov. 1977 prices)	
1975–6	710	'425
1977–8	450	170
1978–9	536	304
1979–80 (projected)	468	232

Capital expenditure by waste disposal authorities in England is documented by the Society of County Treasurers (SCT) annual statistics (Department of the Environment 1979):

	£ million (actual)	£ million (1977) (see Table 10.1)
1974–5	15.2	23.4
1975–6	25.1	30.6
1976–7	26.1	27.9
1977–8	19.8	18.6
1978–9	19.0	15.6

The decline in real terms between 1975–6 and 1978–9 was nearly 50 per cent.

It is clear that this system imposes a severe constraint on waste disposal. A large facility might require a major proportion of the total funds available to the county area for several years. A large projects pool, set aside before distribution of the total sum in the locally determined sector, was designed to help finance projects costing more than £1 million or over 20 per cent of the total allocation (Department of the Environment and the Welsh Office 1970), but this has now been discontinued. One possible solution is the provision of the facility by a waste disposal contractor with his own funds, charging the authority for the waste delivered. The effect would be expected to be an increase in revenue expenditure, as the charge will cover both the contractor's profit and a commercial rate of return on the investment.

An anomaly of the British system of local government finance may adversely affect the waste disposal service. Although the purchase of land is charged to the service for which it is required, the sale of land has until recently been credited to central funds. This ruling has now been relaxed so that the selling agency may retain 50 per cent of the proceeds. Thus if capital is invested in restoring landfill sites, it can only be offset against part of the receipts from the sale of the land, and this may discourage the use of landfill for land reclamation.

The sanction of capital investments does not imply that central government makes any contribution towards the expenditure. The finance has still to be raised on the money market. The Public Works Loan Board (PWLB) is the agency which lends public money to local authorities. The interest rate is fixed for the length of the loan, and repayments of the capital may be made in instalments or on maturity. Above a certain annual quota an authority will have to pay a higher interest rate. Rather than borrowing the money for each project directly from the PWLB, many authorities operate a central loans pool, which borrows money each year to a maximum of the locally determined sector block sanction, and from which each service borrows the capital it requires. The loans pool may borrow from the PWLB or on the open market. The effect of the loans pool is to average out variations in interest rates. Each year an average rate charged to the borrowing services is calculated, thereby protecting individual projects which might otherwise borrow from the PWLB when rates are high and continue to pay that rate even when current rates are much lower. PWLB rates, on quota loans repayable in equal instalments over 15–25 years, rose from 7–9 per cent in 1970–2 to 13–15 per cent in 1974–80, with peaks of about 17 per cent in January 1975 and October 1976 and 16 per cent in January 1980, and troughs of about 10.5–11.5 per cent in October 1977 and April 1979.

In addition to sanctioning the total capital expenditure by a local authority, the government also specifies the maximum period over which the loan may be repaid. Those relevant to waste disposal are:

60 years for land;

40 years for buildings and civil engineering works;

20 years for machinery, plant, rolling stock, fencing, electrical and mechanical equipment to an industrial specification, and works of renewal and repair;

10 years for vehicles.

Thus the financial appraisal of a local authority investment in, say, an incinerator, may amortize different parts of the capital over periods from 10 to 60 years.

The British system of local government finance may be contrasted to that in the USA. There the federal and state governments play a minor role, and most funds are raised through local taxes or user charges, the latter often being levied on householders for the waste collection service.

The principal means of financing a large project of more than $1 million with a lifetime of more than 10 years is by the issue of bonds for that specific purpose to the public. General obligation bonds are directly underwritten by the issuing municipality, and therefore represent a tax commitment by the residents. Rules exist for the maximum debt of an authority and voter approval for each bond issue is often required. For these reasons, revenue bonds are frequently preferred in which the bond issue is tied to a particular project and is underwritten by the revenues of the project. A third alternative, which releases the local authority from financial commitment, is the pollution control revenue bond. The facility is technically owned by the local government but is leased to a private firm for the exact amount required to service the debt. The bond holder is in effect guaranteed payment by the private corporation. The rationale for this arrangement is that the private firm has access to the tax-free borrowing facilities of the local authority.

Interest rates available to municipalities in the USA have until recently (1980–81) been low, around 5–8 per cent. General obligation bonds generally command the lowest interest rates, with revenue bond and pollution control revenue bond rates about 0.5 per cent higher, and the debt rate (as opposed to equity financing rates) of private corporations about 2.5 per cent higher. More details of the US financing system are given by Resource Planning Associates (1974) or Randol (1975).

2.2.4. The structure of local government

Planning for waste management is frequently discussed at a regional level. Many of the mathematical models used for technical analysis are aimed at producing an optimal plan which is best for the region as a whole. This approach is only helpful if there is a strong central authority which is responsible for the region and has the power to implement its chosen plans. It is thus important to ask if such authorities do exist.

In the USA there is a decentralized system of local government with each small community responsible for providing its own services. The problems of agreeing any regional strategy for waste management will be great, as each community may pursue its own interests and may have the power of veto.

In England, the county councils appear to be strong central planning authorities. However their powers are not absolute, and they are required by the Control of Pollution Act to consult on the waste disposal plan with the water authorities, the district councils (collection authorities), other waste disposal authorities, the private waste disposal industry and the general public.

The water authorities have a statutory duty to protect public water supplies or resources which may be required for drinking purposes. Their approval is crucial for disposal by landfill, which may contaminate water supplies either by surface runoff or by seepage into nearby streams or aquifers. Until recently there has been little knowledge of which geological formations offer the best protection to water supplies. Water authorities have taken a cautious attitude, often imposing stringent conditions on the use of potential sites. Results are now available which offer guidance on landfill selection (Section 11.4), and a more constructive partnership between waste disposal and water authorities may emerge (Department of the Environment and the Welsh Office 1976a).

Other waste disposal authorities need to be consulted to achieve co-ordination with their plans. In practice regional co-operation will be sufficient, the need being greatest around the major conurbations with the least reserves of landfill space. For example, most London waste is currently sent to the surrounding counties. Major accumulations of worked-out mineral extraction sites such as the Bedfordshire brick-pits could become regional landfill facilities. The disposal of the more difficult hazardous wastes must be planned at a regional level to achieve uniform standards of site selection, and to avoid extreme situations where either each county must find its own landfill site, or where all such wastes are transported to just a few national sites (Davies 1975).

The power of the private sector in waste disposal is considerable. Many companies make up the industry, from small firms, involved mainly in transport, to major national companies, covering all waste management activities. In addition to contractors, the industry includes those firms which dispose of their own wastes. Waste disposal authorities have responsibility to ensure the adequate disposal of all waste, but do not have the power of direction over industrial waste. Waste disposal contractors are often subsidiaries of mineral extraction companies, taking over worked-out mineral sites for operation as landfills. In time this trend could have implications for waste disposal authorities as it is conceivable that they could face a private monopoly of landfill sites. The Department of the Environment (1976e) has issued guidelines on the relationship between waste disposal authorities and the private sector and seeks to promote co-operation. Stress is laid on the need to include both public and private sectors and all controlled waste in the waste disposal plan; ideally this is envisaged as involving investment in both sectors and the use of disposal facilities irrespective of ownership and the origin of the waste.

The general public is represented in the debate on waste disposal plans by interested individuals, environmental groups, local community associations, and *ad hoc* groups formed to fight specific proposals. Whatever facility is proposed, be it a landfill site or a theoretically less objectionable resource recovery plant, local opposition may be expected because waste disposal is thought to produce offensive smells and windblown litter. As higher landfilling standards are implemented, public opinion may become less hostile. Growing awareness of resource shortages may lead to the questioning of any strategy based solely on disposal. The environmental cause is readily taken up by local objectors to a landfill site or transfer station. Public opinion will be taken seriously if it can muster political support. Thus an area of marshland overlooked by a select residential area may be a poor prospect for a landfill site. Political objectives are based on social attitudes, and are central in the formulation of the criteria by which alternative plans are assessed. A plan is more likely to be acceptable to the public if their points of view are considered during its preparation.

A preferred plan for a region will not be optimal for every sectional interest group. To implement an optimal regional plan requires a strong central planning authority. Although the English County approximates to such an authority, the power of water, collection, and other waste disposal authorities, and of private industry and local communities, may necessitate an approach in which individual interest groups are explicitly considered. However, to provide a basis for this discussion, the existence of a central planning authority is assumed.

2.3. System boundary

In any planning exercise, it is essential to compare like with like. All the plans to be considered must achieve the same basic purpose. The system boundary requires definition with respect to:

The level of planning;

The operations to be considered;

The types of waste.

There is no unique system boundary, and interactions across the hypothetical boundary, which is defined as a matter of convenience, must be taken into account.

Three levels of planning may be distinguished, namely operational, strategic, and policy. They may be differentiated either by the time scale or by the complexity of the objectives. Operational decisions are short- to medium-term, say up to 5 years ahead, and involve a single well-defined objective. Strategic decisions are long-term, say up to 20 or 25 years ahead, and involve many objectives which are often in conflict even when general policy is known. This is the level of waste management planning of principal concern here. Policy decisions are also long-term, and often form part of the context for planning, being suggested or dictated by central government. For example, a policy statement may set the broad objectives of a strategic planning exercise.

The unit operations of waste management are:

Waste storage at source;

Collection or pick-up;

Haul to the initial discharge point;

Treatment or transfer;

Haul of the residual waste material;

Final disposal to land (or sea).

Fig. 2.2 gives more detail and shows the system boundary proposed and used here. Waste collection for which planning is largely an operational problem is outside the boundary, while disposal, involving strategic decisions on the rational use over the long term of limited resources of land, finance and the assimilative capacity of the environment is within the boundary. This boundary is sufficiently general to include both the public and private sectors of waste management and to allow for different types of waste.

The physical connection between waste collection and disposal occurs where the collection vehicle discharges its load. However, the haul of waste from the collection round to this discharge point is defined as part of the disposal function. How much of this haul should be regarded as part of collection and how much as part of disposal is unclear. For English local authorities, the Control of Pollution Act requires payment from the disposal to the collection authority when the place of waste delivery is 'unreasonably far from the collection authority's area', the interpretation being left to negotiation between the authorities. In London, payments are made for

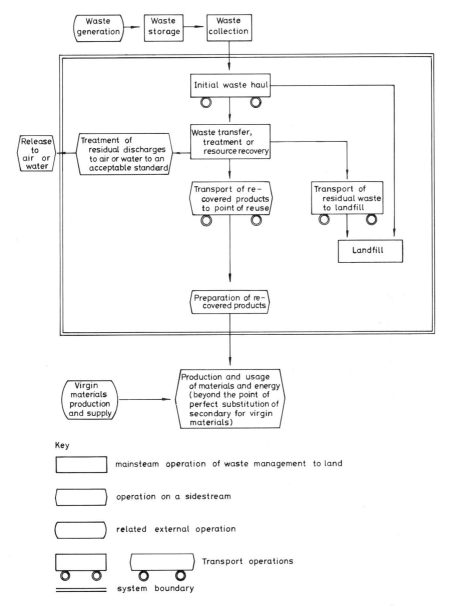

Fig. 2.2. The system boundary for waste management to land as used in this work.

haul distances in excess of 3 miles from an agreed centre of the collection area (Patrick 1975a).

A change in location of the waste discharge point may necessitate operational changes in the organization of collection by, say, altering boundaries and vehicle routing in the pick-up operation, the number of trips made to the discharge point each day, or the assignment of crews to vehicles. Such tactical changes make collection flexible with costs less dependent on haul distance than might be expected, although labour relations play a vital part in implementing changes. A collection authority must be given due warning of changes in delivery points so that planning and negotiations may take place.

Interactions across the system boundary will take place in both directions. Not only do decisons on waste disposal effect collection but certain collection decisions also affect waste disposal, an example being the extent of separate collection of materials for recycling. Such collections may be undertaken by the collection authorities, by voluntary groups such as the Boy Scouts, or by scrap dealers. The demand for such materials is unstable, and these collection activities often follow the market. Sustained separation of materials at source requires institutional changes to stabilize prices. A local authority planning a separate paper collection needs a guaranteed price to justify investing in a baling plant. An interesting experiment in separate collection was the Oxfam project at Kirklees in West Yorkshire, in which each householder was provided with a stand on which were mounted four colour-coded plastic sacks, for newspapers, other paper, textiles, and metal and glass. The materials were sorted by hand and contracts for most products were negotiated (Cunningham and Voglar 1975). However, the scheme was abandoned after a year for financial reasons.

Waste generation will also affect waste disposal. Examples include a trend to more extensive packaging, a decision by manufacturers to standardize the shape of glass containers and reinstitute a system for their return and reuse, a change in the lifetime of consumer durable goods, and policy changes in air or water pollution. The last affects not only waste generation but also the selection of landfill sites and the effluent standards imposed on discharges from a waste treatment plant.

2.4. Survey information

An essential requirement for planning is information on the quantity and types of wastes, both now and in the future, and on the availablity of land. The accuracy and scope of the data required will depend on the subsequent technical analysis performed and so feedback will occur from these later steps in the planning process (Fig. 2.1).

2.4.1. Current waste arisings

A waste disposal survey is a necessary preliminary to the production of a plan. Guidance on its conduct is provided by the Department of the Environment (1976b).

Information on the average quantities of waste will be subject to both sampling and weighing errors. The former occur when a sample survey is necessary, as for example with industrial wastes. Although the accuracy of the total waste estimated for an area from a well-designed survey is good, disaggregation of the figures to estimate production by industry, by sub-area, or by waste type will increase errors because only certain of the categories will have been sampled in depth. Even where a total sample is possible, as with wastes delivered by collection authorities, errors may occur because not all the waste is weighed and estimates have to be made from related variables such as the average load of a vehicle and the number of loads. For certain purposes, volume of the waste is a more appropriate measure than weight and so waste density data must also be found: in many cases the density will vary widely depending on the degree of compaction achieved.

Both waste quantity and waste composition are subject to daily and seasonal fluctuation. Waste disposal facilities must be provided to cope with peak waste output rather than the average, and seasonal variations in the quantities of available materials may have important contractual and economic implications for resource recovery. For collection authority wastes, records should reveal quantity variations, whilst the composition may be obtained by regular sample analyses (Skitt 1972). It is unwise to rely on national average composition data, as local variations can be substantial (Table 1.2). It is generally not possible to predict the composition of industrial waste as it depends largely on the specific production processes in use.

2.4.2. Forecasting waste arisings

Forecasting trends in waste production and composition is a complex subject to which three generic approaches may be distinguished. The simplest is the exploratory calculation, which seeks to find what amount and types of waste would arise in one particular set of circumstances. In contrast, the time-series forecast seeks the most likely result rather than just one possible result. Finally, the cross-section forecast predicts the waste generation of, say, a household from known behaviour of other households.

A common approach begins with current figures of population, waste production per capita, total work force, and waste production per employee. The calculation of these waste production coefficients is subject to considerable error, particularly if local data are not available or results from a sample survey are being used. Future production is calculated by applying fixed arithmetic or exponential growth rates to the four variables. A sophistication of this method of exploratory calculation was developed for household wastes by the Local Government Operational Research Unit (LGORU) (Green 1969). The waste production coefficient is disaggregated into components for each material as determined by a local waste analysis, and trends for each are calculated by applying national economic projections of exponential growth in consumption. The method was tested for Birmingham by Thomson (1979) who found that predictions from earlier observations in his series did not agree with subsequent data. He then used a multiple regression analysis to relate the weight or volume of waste per dwelling per week, or the percentage weight of various components, to time. The results obtained on the historical data are instructive. The amount of paper in the waste rose from around 30 per cent in 1964 to over 40 per cent by 1970, agreeing with the L G O R U growth rate of 5 per cent per annum in paper consumption. However, after 1970 the amount fell, to around 30 per cent by 1974 (Table 1.2). This reversal was presumably due to increased separation of paper at source, encouraged by the rise in waste paper prices which reached a peak in 1974. Apartments, which are not well adapted to separate storage and collection of waste paper, did not show the fall. This illustrates the pitfalls of using fixed growth rates in forecasting and of extrapolating past trends.

Statistics of industrial production may be manipulated by economic input–output models, which show the relationships between different industries and final consumer demands for commodities. Extensions to explicitly include the environment and waste production have been made (Victor 1972) and one such model was used by Stern (1973) for industrial waste forecasting. The model predicts the total, direct and indirect, waste production implied by each unit of final demand (tonne/£) in each industrial classification. Exploratory calculations show how waste production changes in response to certain changes in consumer demand. The major disadvantage of the method is the vast amount of information required.

All these forecasting models rely on the extrapolation of data. The majority use independent estimates of growth rates which are assumed to apply indefinitely. The causal mechanisms which affect waste generation are not explicitly considered, except in a rather cursory manner by L G O R U who applied consumption growth rates to domestic waste components. A more satisfactory approach would seek to develop an understanding of waste generation, to translate this understanding into a series of mathematical relationships, and to estimate the parameters in these from historical data using multiple-regression analysis. Such an econometric model reduces the problem to one of forecasting the explanatory variables which determine waste generation.

The econometric method has been applied to the forecasting of household waste production, relating waste generated to such socioeconomic variables as population, dwelling unit size and character, income level, and cultural characteristics (Grossman, Hudson, and Marks 1974; Hudson, Grossman, and Marks 1975; Jackson, Moar, and Ulph 1975). The use of such methods is currently restricted to cross-section forecasting. Time-series forecasting is much more complicated, involving not only the prediction of changes in each of the explanatory variables, which may be as much of a problem as forecasting waste generation directly, but also a knowledge of the time lags between changes in the explanatory variables and their effect on waste generation. The use of econometric models for exploratory calculation, answering a question such as what would waste production be if average real incomes increased, is relatively straightforward.

The prospects for econometric models in industrial waste forecasting do not appear good because the causal mechanisms of waste production are closely tied to specific technologies. Thus, even if the exact relationships between current waste output patterns and consumer demand may be unravelled by an input–output model, the rapidity of technological changes would make extrapolations unreliable.

The problems of accurately predicting the quantities or types of waste which will arise at any time in the future are formidable. The most realistic and practicable approach is to generate a range of alternative futures which may occur, and to examine the flexibility of proposed plans to cope with this uncertainty. A useful discussion of forecasting in waste disposal is that of Berry (1978).

2.4.3. The availability of land

It is important to know the availability of land for both processing plants and landfill sites at an early stage of planning. The search will be guided by existing land-use plans. For processing plants, siting criteria will be similar to those for other industrial plants. For landfill sites, criteria are rather more comprehensive. The information required on present and potential sites includes availability and location, ultimate capacity, the waste types acceptable, and the likely permitted rates of use. The latter may depend on such factors as site access, traffic constraints, and nuisance to local residents.

Ground or air surveys will reveal potential landfill sites such as derelict land, land in need of upgrading, and mineral workings, available now or when operations cease. However, if a long time horizon for planning of, say, more than 10 years is being considered, these may not represent all the sites. The creation of landfill space from mineral extraction may take less than 10 years from the initial planning stage to availability for waste disposal. For this reason, co-ordination of waste disposal plans and the structure plan provisions for mineral extraction is essential. Careful consideration is required before an initial survey is accepted as proof that long-term landfill is not a feasible waste disposal strategy and that some form of treatment is essential to reduce the volume of waste requiring disposal.

After an initial survey, the list of potential sites may be reduced substantially by considering general planning criteria and site ownership. For example, an abandoned mineral extraction site is not necessarily worked out and an upturn in market demand may bring it back into production. A worked-out site will not necessarily be available for waste disposal, despite the fact that in Britain planning consents for mineral extraction frequently include a requirement to restore the land after use. This requirement was clarified in a letter from the Ministry of Housing and Local Government to the London Brick Company in 1952, concerning their Bedfordshire brick pits. It stated that backfilling should be with suitable materials available at reasonable times and on reasonable terms. The interpretation of 'reasonable terms' is unclear; the Company claim that a reasonable profit is required, while the local authority claim that the Company should pay a reasonable price for the material (Bugler 1975). The result of this impasse is that owners of worked-out mineral sites have an asset which is appreciating in value as landfill space becomes more scarce. Often a waste disposal subsidiary is formed to exploit the assets.

Hydrogeological suitability must also be considered. Before a site can be used a detailed survey will be required, but preliminary assessment by the water authority and a desk geological study will probably reduce the list considerably. The waste types acceptable at a site and limitations on the rate of use will depend on detailed consideration of both hydrogeological and planning factors. A qualitative assessment will be all that is possible at an early stage of planning.

The best estimates of landfill site capacity use aerial photography (Ballam and Collins 1975). For sites in use a simple operational method of estimating site life has been proposed by L G O R U (Roberts 1972), based on regular measurements of the capacity unfilled. The effective landfill capacity may depend on both planning conditions, such as the permitting of hills, and the terms of a site operating licence, such as the proportion of cover material which must be used.

2.5. Selection of criteria

When all the necessary background work has been done and the exact problem has been defined, politicians and planners can set down the objectives of a particular waste management plan (see Fig. 2.1). A broad statement of these objectives constitutes a policy decision, and may form part of the terms of reference for the study. In Britain the Department of the Environment (1976c) states:

The overall objective of a waste disposal strategy is the disposal of waste at the least possible cost to the community with due regard to the safeguarding of the environment and the use of waste as a resource.

This is by no means the only policy which could be adopted. Alternative statements might be to dispose of waste with the least adverse effect on the environment with due regard to the cost to the community; to deal with all wastes in a socially and legally acceptable manner at a reasonable cost; or to maximize the conservation of resources with due regard to the cost.

Whatever policy is adopted, it is necessary to translate the broad statement into precisely defined criteria against which alternative technological options and disposal plans are assessed. A set of criteria will normally encompass economic, technical, environmental, and political objectives, and that of resource conservation. Possible subdivisions of each category are suggested in Table 2.2. The selection and definition of criteria is dynamic, with feedback occurring from later stages of the planning process. For example, the definitions may be revised or the emphasis given to criteria

Table 2.2

Criteria for the assessment of waste management plans

Economic
Capital costs
Land costs
Operating costs
Revenues:
  Extent of market commitment
  Stability of markets
Net cost per tonne
Net present cost
Sensitivity of costs to market or other fluctuations
Uncertainty in cost estimates, i.e. financial risk
Financing arrangements

Technical
Adequacy of the technology:
  Feasibility
  Operating experience
  Adaptability to local conditions
  Reliability
  Interdependence of components (can system operate if one component fails?)
  Safety
Potential for future development
Flexibility to cope with changes in:
  Waste quantities
  Waste composition
  Source separation of materials
Dependence on outside systems:
  e.g. vulnerability to strikes

Environmental
Public health
Water pollution
Air pollution:
  Dust
  Noxious gases
  Odours
Quality and quantity of residual wastes
Noise
Traffic
Aesthetics

Table 2.2—cont.

Political
Equity between communities or interest groups
Flexibility in location of facilities
Public acceptance
Number of jobs created
Employee acceptance

Use and conservation of resources
Products recovered:
  Market potential
Net effect on primary energy supply:
  Energy requirements
Net effect on supply of materials:
  Raw materials usage
Land usage:
  Volume reduction
  Land reclamation
Water requirements

---

may be altered when practical implications rather than initial abstractions are considered.

2.6. Technical analysis

Technical analysis for waste management planning is aimed at investment appraisal. The problem is, given an expected pattern of wastes arising, to decide what kind of facilities should be built, together with their location, capacity, and time for implementation. Each answer constitutes a possible waste disposal plan. The analysis may usefully, if somewhat arbitrarily, be broken into the evaluation and assessment of the alternative technologies for waste processing, the generation of strategies, and the evaluation and assessment of these strategies.

The preliminary analysis of technologies which may be used for waste disposal, treatment, reclamation, or resource recovery evaluates each against the criteria and assesses their overall performance, selecting those worthy of further study. Evaluation is used here to imply measurement against each criterion in turn, while assessment is the process of making the selection balancing all the criteria. The preliminary analysis requires for each technology considerable information, which will depend on the assessment criteria, but would typically include capital and operating costs, materials balances, energy usage, environmental impact and technical data on the state of development, and the time until it is generally available. At present, the frequent lack of such data handicaps waste management planning. Furthermore, much of the information needs to be revised in the light of local factors including land availability, prices and markets, capital spending limits, and planning regulations.

Strategy generation assembles alternative strategies from the most promising technologies and potential locations, a step requiring feedback to the decision makers. Examples of possible strategies are:

(i) Dispose of all waste in local landfills;

(ii) Dispose of all waste in large landfills, and use road or rail transfer where appropriate;

(iii) Utilize central waste treatment plant or plants, with the appropriate technology chosen from incineration, incineration with heat recovery, or physical sorting to produce a solid, refuse–derived fuel.

Strategy evaluation seeks to develop from each strategy a 'best' or 'optimal' plan. The suggested policy objective for waste disposal authorities in Britain (Section 2.5) implies the use of such an approach with the single objective of least cost to the community, subject to constraints regarding protection of the environment and the use of waste as a resource. The optimization may be repeated using several criteria, producing, for each strategy, a set of plans and performance indices. Strategy assessment is required to sift this information, to allow consideration of other criteria not easily quantified or optimized, and to interpret the 'optimal' plans of strategy evaluation in the light of the assumptions made.

2.7. Plan selection and implementation

Technical analysis provides information for politicians to make a decision. Plan selection may be integrated with, or may simply use, the results of strategy assessment. The selection of a strategic plan does not represent the end of the planning process. Much remains to be done in turning the strategic plan into a series of operational plans and in implementing the necessary decisions. As the planning becomes more detailed, many of the steps of Fig. 2.1 may need to be repeated, for example establishing the optimum design capacity of a plant with more confidence. Implementation of the plan needs to be monitored (Schwarz and Collins 1974) and regular updating will be required. While recognizing the necessity for this work, the present concern is with the initial formulation, assessment, and selection of a strategic plan.

2.8. Discussion

While the structure of the waste management planning process presented in Fig. 2.1 may be seen as an abstraction, this formalization of planning into a series of interrelated steps is important. Opinions may differ on the precise order of the steps, or on how far this ideal structure corresponds to a particular real situation. However, the value of the structure remains, in that it makes explicit the steps required and emphasizes their interrelationships. The separation of political planning from technical analysis is to be noted particularly.

Technical analysis is often aided by the use of models. Previous work in waste management has been largely restricted to the application of sophisticated operational research models. This is just one of many possibilities and is not necessarily the best; its unquestioned use has brought modelling into disrepute.

A model provides a simplified and generalized view of what are seen as the important characteristics of a real situation. It is an abstraction from reality which is used to gain clarity and to reduce the variety and complexity of the real world to a level one can understand and specify clearly. Its value lies in exploration of the behaviour of a system in circumstances where it is impossible, for technical, economic, political, or moral reasons, to experiment. The model provides a systematic means by which the planner can explore the effects of alternative objectives, or the consequences of alternative courses of action, measured as far as possible on a fair basis, thus allowing expert judgement to be brought to bear. It might be relatively easy to formulate an accurate verbal description of a problem and to translate it into the more precise language of mathematical symbols, but such a model would be very complex, and probably could not be solved exactly. At whatever level modelling is carried out, simplification is necessary in order to achieve a compromise between reality and tractability. In these circumstances it is essential that the planner has an understanding of the assumptions made in the model. The role of any model must always be one of suggesting plans for further study, and not as a direct planning tool. The purpose is not to *supplant* expert judgement as a 'black box' approach would imply, but to *supplement* it.

A model covering all aspects of waste management planning would be hopelessly complicated, but there are five principal sub-areas identified in Fig. 2.1 where mathematical modelling techniques may be usefully employed:

   (i) Forecasting waste arisings;
   (ii) Evaluation of candidate technologies;
  (iii) Assessment of candidate technologies;
  (iv) Strategy evaluation;
   (v) Strategy assessment.

A balanced approach to planning would look at each in detail. In practice, however, simplifying assumptions are usually made in all but one or two, in order that sufficient attention may be paid to these. In the past attention has concentrated primarily on strategy evaluation; this work is examined in detail in the next chapter. The following chapter looks at an alternative, more pragmatic approach based on the evaluation and assessment of technologies. The remainder of Part I is then concerned with developing methods of evaluating alternative technologies against particular important criteria.

3. STRATEGY EVALUATION

3.1. Introduction

In the past, mathematical modelling has been proposed as an aid to waste management planning primarily for strategy evaluation. It is therefore appropriate to begin by critically reviewing this literature and assessing the potential contribution of models for strategy evaluation. The aim is to identify the role of such models and to highlight their limitations.

Strategy evaluation is one of the steps in the planning process identified in the last chapter. The basic principle is to select from an overall strategy the optimal plan for waste management, specifying what technologies are to be utilized, where and when the plants are to be built and with what capacity.

Strategy evaluation seeks to combine technologies in such a way as to produce the 'best' plan against a given criterion, most commonly that of least cost, subject to certain constraints. In operational research, this is an allocation model which assigns wastes from sources to sinks and determines the flows. The immediate result is thus a set of waste allocations from each source and to each sink. This presupposes an established network of facilities and care is required in adaptation of the model to strategic planning, where information is required on what facilities should be provided for use in the future.

Compromise is necessary between the reality with which the planning problem is represented and the ease with which the resultant model may be solved. A complex model may not be amenable to exact solution, and many studies have focused attention on solving the model rather than on relating results to the original planning problem. Often it is more helpful to use a relatively simple model, for example by solving for a number of different strategies and comparing the results.

In this chapter, each aspect of strategy evaluation is examined in turn, noting the issues raised, the modelling approach generally adopted, and any exceptions. This enables those aspects of the problem which have not been treated adequately to be highlighted and the assumptions inherent in the models to be exposed. It is important that the planner be conversant with these assumptions, so that waste management may be formulated effectively for modelling purposes. More extensive reviews of strategy evaluation are also available (Wilson 1977a, 1977b).

The next section discusses the formulation of the planning problem in such a way that a model for strategy evaluation, which is just one step in the overall process, may be utilized. The available models are then classified in terms of their treatment of certain technical points. At the end of the chapter a case study is examined and the future potential of such models is examined.

3.2. Formulation

Strategy evaluation is just one step in the planning process shown in Fig. 2.1. To use a model of strategy evaluation as a tool for waste management planning requires information from each of the preceding steps. If attention is focused on just one step of technical analysis, simplification in the treatment of the other steps is inevitable. It is thus necessary to consider strategy evaluation in the context of the overall planning process.

3.2.1. System boundary

Most models of strategy evaluation regard the initial haul of waste in a collection vehicle as part of waste disposal (Fig. 2.2). Individual collection tasks are aggregated into source areas, with each represented as a single point of waste generation. The more source points used, the more accurate is the representation of waste generation. In a few cases initial haul is not included within the system boundary, and transfer stations then serve as the point sources (Pathak 1974; Anderson and Nigam, model 1, 1967).

Wastes may be classified by their source, physical state, or handling characteristics. Most models restrict their scope to solid wastes collected by a local authority, including household and perhaps some commercial wastes. Exceptions include Hekimian (1972) and the University of Louisville (1970) who include industrial wastes without differentiation from household wastes; Haddix (model 1, 1975) who separates commercial and industrial wastes from household wastes only by their initial haul costs; Anderson and Nigam (1967) who include household solid and liquid (sewage) wastes; and Panagiotakopoulos (1976) who presents a theoretical framework for the integrated planning of waste management to air, land, and water. Differentiation of wastes within a model by their properties would be a significant extension of scope, but progress has been limited. Crosby and Renold (1974) included hazardous, biodegradable, and inert wastes in a study of landfill site selection in which the more polluting wastes were limited to those sites offering less risk of water pollution. Pathak (1974) distinguished organic from inorganic wastes, restricting the applicability of some processing options. Models which include resource recovery should be sensitive to changes in waste composition, but such detail is beyond the scope of current models.

3.2.2. Survey information

Most strategy evaluation exercises have laid little emphasis on data collection. Information on wastes arising will always be uncertain, but the common approach of estimating a waste coefficient (as waste per capita or per employee) from a small sample survey, or even by analogy with a 'national average' and scaling up to the population, is not satisfactory. The smaller the areas used as waste generation points in the model, the more difficult it is to estimate the waste at each point. The problem is most severe in the case of industrial waste, as local variations mean that only a total survey could produce reasonable results for each small area.

Forecasting wastes arising over time is grossly simplified in most models. The typical approach applies fixed growth rates to both waste coefficients and to population or employment figures, and was seen in section 2.4.2 to be unsatisfactory.

At a preliminary stage of planning, land availability is necessarily uncertain. As such, the related questions of facility location and availability are principal topics of investigation in several models, the model often being run several times for closely related strategies. Geological information is used in some studies (Crosby and Renold 1974; Clayton and Huie 1973). The capacity of landfill sites is also required for models, and again this information is uncertain.

3.2.3. Selection of criteria

The objective in most models for strategy evaluation is that of minimizing cost. In environmental and social terms, the strategies and plans are assumed to be of equal benefit. Extensions to this economic criterion are discussed later.

3.2.4. The preliminary analysis of candidate technologies

This step of the planning process is reduced for models of strategy evaluation to a need for more information, notably on the costs of each technology. Little attention is devoted to its collection. Exceptions, where empirical work on relating facility costs to waste throughput is reported, include Pathak (1974), Dawson (1970), and Clayton and Huie (1973). A specific study should use local costs, particularly for variable factors such as labour and the value of recovered products.

Costs which are incurred in different periods are generally reduced for comparison to a net present value. The choice of discount rate may affect the optimal solution critically. Inflation is considered in a few cases, but the assumption of constant costs in real terms is more common. The LGORU models (Parker and Portlock 1974) increase wage costs relative to other costs at a fixed annual exponential rate.

The additional information required on each technology depends on the criteria used. Basic data include the reduction achieved in the weight or volume of waste requiring disposal, and the design capacity of the facilities.

3.2.5. Summary

The problem of planning for waste management is generally simplified in models of strategy evaluation to the following form:

(i) Wastes are allocated from sources to sinks, minimizing total system cost subject to certain constraints.

(ii) The decision variables to be found are the waste flows from each source to each sink, in each period.

(iii) Wastes of specified quantity and type arise at the point sources, and variations over time are defined.

(iv) Collection vehicles transport waste from the point sources to initial waste discharge points, and the cost of this transport as a function of time or distance is given.

(v) A set of initial waste discharge points is postulated. These may already exist or be potential sites. For each the location may be either fixed or variable.

(vi) At each discharge point a specific technology is assumed. For each technology the cost as a function of waste throughput, a waste reduction factor, and the standards of the operation must be specified. In addition, restrictions on the capacity of the facility may be imposed, either in total or as a maximum or a minimum throughput in each period.

(vii) If transport is needed from the initial discharge point to a final disposal site for all or part of the waste, the method of transport must be specified and a cost function provided.

(viii) A set of final disposal sites is postulated. The same considerations apply to these as to the initial discharge points. Indeed, some landfill sites will serve both functions.

The other aspects of waste planning are reflected in the strategy evaluation model primarily as data inputs. The model is deterministic, producing the optimal solution corresponding to a given set of fixed data. However, many of the data used are uncertain and some account of this must be taken before confidence can be placed in the results.

3.3. A classification of models

There are several areas where simplification may be made in strategy evaluation. Each of these is now dealt with in turn, noting the assumptions which may be made, generally in order of increasing complexity. Some compromise between the reality and tractability of a model is inevitable. In Table 3.1 the models are classified by their type, treatment of time, and approximation of the cost function. In addition, the coverage of each is summarized in terms of its choice of technology, algorithm or mathematical solution procedure, capacity constraints, sensitivity analysis, implementation, and other points of interest.

3.3.1. The type of model

Models may be distinguished by the principal question addressed. The primary distinction is between the location-allocation model, which seeks the optimal locations for facilities, and the selection-allocation model, which seeks to select facilities from a set of fixed locations. The former is apparently the more general, but this is achieved at the expense of additional simplifying assumptions. The models are limited to locating a fixed number of facilities of a single type, achieving optimization of the number by comparing several solutions, and precluding the consideration of mixed strategies such as central incineration in a city combined with local landfill in outlying areas. In addition these location-allocation models do not include transhipment facilities, time as an explicit variable, or capacity constraints (see later sections). For such reasons, the selection-allocation model is the more common. Its solution is better developed and so there is greater freedom to represent other aspects realistically, while in practice free choice in the location of facilities for waste treatment or disposal is uncommon.

Selection-allocation models may be subdivided according to the use for which they were developed. For example, if the aim is to develop an optimal system, existing facilities may be ignored (e.g. Baker 1963). If it is to optimize the use of the present system, potential facilities need not be considered, while the extension of a present system requires the inclusion of both potential and existing facilities (Helms and Clark 1971). Some models are directed specifically at questions of investment timing and phasing of plant capacity (e.g. Vasan, model B, 1974).

The capacity-expansion model focuses attention on this last point of phasing the capacity of a plant to meet a growing demand. The models generally consider a simple one-source/one-sink system in isolation, applying the earlier work of Manne (1967). An exception is Rao (1975) who developed two alternative algorithms for one source and several sinks, in which he allowed a choice of facility type. Solution methods for many sources and many sinks are not well developed (Erlenkotter 1975).

It may be noted from Table 3.1 that several authors have produced models of more than one type. In addition, some have developed models of strategy evaluation alongside other aspects of waste management such as collection (e.g. Marks and Liebman 1970; Schultz 1967). Usually the various models are not integrated to form a single planning package. The exception

Table 3.1
Classification of models

Static

Type of model	Model	Date	Choice of technology	Algorithm 1	Algorithm 2	Capacity	Sensitivity analysis	Implementation	Notes
Location-allocation models	Wersan, Quon, and Charnes 1	1971		A	H			S	
	Schultz 2[a]	1967		A			N	S	
	LGORU 1[b]	1969			N			M*	1
	Merced County study[c]	1971		A	H			S*	
Selection-allocation models (i) Constant unit cost	Kuhner and Heiler 1	1973	TS+		LP	L	X	S	5
	LGORU 2[b]	1974	TS+		LP	S	√	L	
	University of Louisville	1970			LP/I	C		M*	2
	Anderson and Nigam 2	1967		A	B	S		S	
	Marks and Liebman 2	1967	TS+	A	LP	C		M	2
	Wersan et al. 2	1970	TS	A	LP	C		S	2
	Berkeley Group[d]	1971		A	H			L	3
	Hardy and Grissom	1976		(A)	B			S	3
	Panagiotakopoulos	1976	TS+	A	H	C		S	4
(ii) Piecewise-linear cost function	Baker	1963	TS	A	T	C		M	
	Schlottmann	1977	RR		LP	S		L	
(iii) Fixed charge type cost function	Morse and Roth	1970	TS	A	T		√	M	
	Helms and Clark	1971			W	S	√	S	
	Harvey and O'Flaherty	1972			MIP		√	S*	
	Marks and Liebman 1[g]	1970	TS	A	B	C	√	M	
	Rossman	1971	TS+	A	B	C	√	M	
	Vasan A	1974	TS	A	B	D	√	M*	
	Haddix 1	1975	TS	A	B	C	√	M*	7
	Haddix and Wees[h]	1975	RR		B		√	M*	
(iv) Direct use of concave cost functions	Dawson	1970	TS+	A	H	S	X √	L	5
	Clayton and Huie	1973		A	H			S	9
	Pathak	1974	RR	A	B			M	

Dynamic step by step optimization

Type of model	Model	Date	Choice of technology	Algorithm 1	Algorithm 2	Capacity	Sensitivity analysis	Implementation	Notes
Selection-allocation models (i) Constant unit cost	Collins and Haugen[e]	1973	TS	A	LP	L	X	S	
	Hekimian	1972	TS	A	H/I	S	√	L	5
(iii) Fixed charge type cost function	Esmaili	1972	TS+	A	H/I	S		M	
	US EPA Solid Waste Allocation Model (SWAM)[j]	1973	TS+		W	C		S	*
	Vasan B	1975	TS+	A	H	D		M	7
Capacity expansion models	Nigam 2	1970		A	An/H		√	S	

Dynamic optimization over time

Type of model	Model	Date	Choice of technology	Algorithm 1	Algorithm 2	Capacity	Sensitivity analysis	Implementation	Notes
Selection-allocation models (i) Constant unit cost	Crosby and Renold	1974			LP	C	√	L*	
	LGORU 3[b]	1974	TS+		LP	S	X	M*	
	Thomson	1979			LP	L	X	M	
(ii) Piecewise-linear cost function	Fuertes et al.[f]	1974	TS+		MPSX		√	M	6
(iii) Fixed charge type cost function	Skelly Shields	1968	TS+		W	L	√	M	
		1972	TS+	A	B	C	√	M	
	Kuhner and Heiler 2	1973	TS+		MPSX	L	√	S	
	Schneider et al.	1974	TS+		MPSX	L			
	Kuhner and Harrington[i]	1973	RR	A	MPSX (H)	L	N	L*	6 / 8
	Mitre Corporation[k]	1976	RR		W	C		M*	10
Capacity expansion models	Schultz 3[a]	1967			An	D		S	
	Harrington	1969			LP	S	√	S	
	Nigam 1	1970		A	An	D	√	S	
	Rao	1975	TS+	A	H	L	√	S	

Key to Table 3.1—Classification of Models

Primary categories
Type of model (Section 3.3.1)
Treatment of time (Section 3.3.3)
Cost function (Section 3.3.4)

Secondary categories
Choice of technology: Notes the inclusion of transhipment facilities in model formulation (Section 3.3.2):

Blank	Simple allocation from sources to sinks only
TS	Admits transhipment facilities
TS+	Allows transhipment with gains and therefore consideration of volume/weight reductions
RR	Markets for products of a resource recovery facility are explicitly modelled

Algorithm: in column 1 an A indicates that algorithm development was a theme of the work. Column 2 notes features of algorithms used:

An	Analytical solution
LP	Linear programming
MIP	Mixed integer–linear programming
MPSX	MIP using IBM's MPSX package (International Business Machines Corporation 1973)
T	Trial and error
H	Heuristic
W	Uses the heuristic algorithm of Walker (1968, 1973, 1976)
B	Branch and bound
I	Includes iteration on unit costs

Capacity: treatment of capacity constraints (Section 3.3.6):

Blank	No capacity constraints used
C	Fixed capacity constraints on all facilities, including upper limits on plant throughput
S	Fixed capacity constraints on final waste sinks only
L	Additional constraints on lower capacity (minimum throughput) used
D	Discrete capacity levels only are considered for intermediate facilities

Sensitivity analysis: (Section 3.3.7):

Blank	None
√	Some done—see Table 3.2
X	Several similar strategies evaluated in order to explore sensitivity to sink location and availability
N	See notes

Implementation: the size of problem to which the model has been applied (defined in terms of numbers of sources and, more critically, of sinks, i.e. intermediate plus final disposal facilities):

Blank	Model not implemented
S	Small-scale problem, with less than 10 sinks and up to 30 sources
M	Medium-scale problem, with 10–30 sinks and 10–100 sources
L	Large-scale problem, with more than 30 sinks and/or more than 100 sources
*	Indicates a model applied during an actual solid waste management planning process (i.e. application not just to demonstrate the model)

Notes
1. Produces penalty cost contours around optimal sink locations. Uses the conjugate gradient algorithm of Powell (1964).
2. Transportation routing models.
3. Selects a given number of sinks from a set.
4. Selects waste treatment methods for an integrated waste management system, considering flows of all wastes to air, water, and land.
5. Superimposes transhipment facilities onto a source–sink allocation after optimization.
6. Considers the implications of a decentralized political system (Section 3.3.8).
7. Three separate models differing in treatment of capacity constraints.
8. Use heuristics to generate several 'good' solutions near the optimum.
9. The cost of a given strategy is found by allocating sources to the nearest sink, with transport costs for rural area determined from a heuristic routing algorithm.
10. A package of models allowing trade-off between model sophistication (particularly the treatment of time and resource recovery facilities) and the degree of aggregation of sources and sinks.

References
Generally sufficient information in the table. Exceptional cases are:
(a) Schultz (1967, 1969).
(b) Nice and Selby (1969) and Parker and Portlock (1974) (LGORU: Local Government Operational Research Unit).
(c) Engineering Science Inc. and Grunwald, Crawford, and Associates (1971).
(d) Golueke and McGauhey (1971), El-Shaieb (1968).
(e) Collins and Haugen, unpublished report (1973), and Watson (1974).
(f) Fuertes (1973), Fuertes, Hudson, and Marks (1974) and Hudson, Grossman, and Marks (1975).
(g) Marks and Liebman (1970, 1971).
(h) Haddix and Wees (1975) and Haddix, model 2 (1975).
(i) Weston (1971) and Walker, Aquilina, and Schur (1974).
(j) Kühner and Harrington (1973, 1974, 1975a,b) and Kühner (1974).
(k) Mitre Corporation (1976) and Berman (1973a, 1976).

is the work of L G O R U (Parker and Portlock 1974) which is examined later as a case study.

3.3.2. Choice of technology

A model for strategy evaluation may be simplified by restricting the types of technology admitted. Four classes of technology may be distinguished, in order of increasing model complexity:

(i) In the simplest case, waste is allocated directly from a source to a final disposal site.

(ii) Transhipment occurs when waste may be allocated from a source to a final disposal site by way of a transfer station or other facility which does not alter the waste flow.

(iii) Transhipment 'with gains' allows the inclusion of a processing facility which alters the weight or volume of waste requiring final disposal.

(iv) Resource recovery facilities produce at least two outputs, a waste for final disposal and a product for sale. Market outlets for the products are introduced as additional final sinks with their own cost functions and capacity constraints.

It is possible to include a technology in a simpler formulation of the model by making additional assumptions. For example, markets for recovered products are explicitly modelled in only a few cases (Table 3.1), and models of transhipment or transhipment with gains may be reduced to simple allocation type by prior assignment of the facility to a fixed disposal site (L G O R U model 1, in Nice and Selby 1969; Helms and Clark 1971).

3.3.3. Time

The simplest way of considering time in strategy evaluation is the static model, which is solved for one period only. This period may be the current year, a representative year from the time horizon (Rossman 1971) or the complete time horizon (Dawson 1970). The static model may be extended by analysing different periods of the time horizon (University of Louisville 1970; L G O R U model 1, in Brookes and Green 1968). One stage further on is dynamic step-by-step optimization, in which the model is solved independently in successive periods. The only really satisfactory approach is a dynamic model with optimization over time, in which trade-offs are allowed between costs and benefits at different times. The difficulties of implementing this approach, particularly the long computer calculation times, have led to the simpler methods being more popular (Table 3.1). The choice of time horizon in models varies, with periods of up to 30 years fairly common. The sensitivity of the solutions to the time horizon was investigated by Shields (1972).

3.3.4. Facility costs

The cost of any waste disposal facility, be it for waste treatment, resource recovery, or disposal, consists of three components: a capital cost to set it up, an overhead cost to keep it open, and a variable operating cost which depends on waste throughput. The general form assumed for the cost of a facility is a concave function of waste throughput (Fig. 3.1. (a)), equivalent to a declining unit cost or economy of scale function (Fig. 3.2. (a)). Thus the larger a plant or disposal site, the less the cost per tonne. Empirical evidence for this type of function has been obtained for existing operations (Dawson 1970). Unfortunately this cost function is unsuitable for direct use in a model, and the approximation used determines the ease with which the model may be solved. There are four common approaches:

(i) The simplest assumes constant unit costs (Fig. 3.1. (b), 3.2. (b)), and this allows the use of linear programming, for which solution procedures are well developed. However, it also implies a knowledge of the waste throughput *prior* to the model allocation from source to sinks. The throughput implied is that at which the straight line intersects the curve in either figure (marked as W^0). This limitation may be alleviated by iteration on the unit costs until a self-consistent result is achieved (University of Louisville 1970; Hekimian 1972).

(ii) A piecewise-linear approximation uses two or more linear segments to represent the function (Fig. 3.1. (c)), implying stepwise unit costs (Fig. 3.2. (c)). Solution may be achieved by modifications of standard linear programming procedures (Fuertes, Hudson and Marks 1974) or by iteration, using a procedure analogous to that mentioned above to match assigned costs and allocated waste loads (Baker 1963).

(iii) A fixed charge cost function consists of two parts—a fixed charge or capital cost, which is incurred only if the facility is used, and a variable portion, which depends on waste throughput and is usually linear (Fig. 3.1. (d)), although piecewise-linear approximations may be used (Walker, Aquilina, and Schur 1974). The equivalent unit cost curve has the correct general shape (Fig. 3.2. (d)). The fixed cost introduces into the representation a discrete variable, which takes the value of 0 if the facility is not built or 1 if it is. This results in a mixed integer-linear program. A number of such models lay emphasis on the development of algorithms (Table 3.1). The fixed charge function is not an ideal representation of facility costs. The simple form shown in Fig. 3.1. (d) implies that the fixed cost is independent of facility size. Clearly this is not the case in practice.

(iv) In certain circumstances it may be possible to use the concave cost function directly. Pathak (1974) developed a suitable algorithm, but this converged to an optimal solution only very slowly. The concave cost function may also be used directly in procedures which allocate sources to

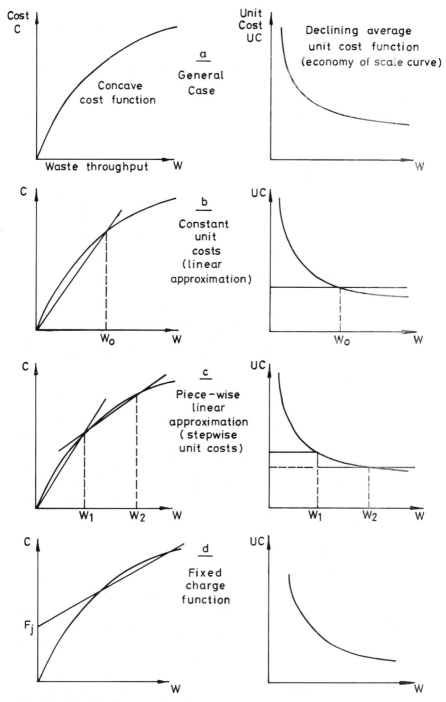

Fig. 3.1. Total facility cost functions.

Fig. 3.2. Corresponding average unit cost functions.

sinks *before* the facility cost is considered, the exact waste load thus being known. Such a method can only produce an approximate solution, and results in spurious accuracy as a facility will not in practice be built to such an exact capacity. Models using this approach include Clayton and Huie (1973), Dawson (1970), and L G O R U model 1 (Nice and Selby 1969).

3.3.5. Transport costs

In general the unit cost of waste transport per tonne–kilometre or per tonne–minute is considered fixed, irrespective of the quantity shipped. The primary variable is either distance or time, with the latter measured directly or via distance and the average vehicle speed. There are four common methods for estimating the distances between two points. The road distances are measured, crow-fly distance is used (the Euclidean or L_2 metric), an empirical relation is developed relating road distances to crow-fly distances, or a rectangular L-shaped travel path is assumed (the L_1 metric), this being most common in American urban studies.

A constant unit cost for waste transport is generally assumed. An alternative view, particularly applied to bulk transfer vehicles, is that the daily cost is constant, so that the cost per tonne will decrease in steps as the number of daily trips increases (L G O R U models, Nice and Selby 1969; Anderson and Nigam, model 1, 1967).

For initial haul in a collection vehicle, the separation of waste collection and disposal often assumed implies that the cost of collection is independent of the haul distance. A few models include collection costs directly in the objective function. Schultz (1967, 1969) and Clayton and Huie (1973) simply add in a time for waste pick-up. The L G O R U models (Nice and Selby 1969; Parker and Portlock 1974) express total collection plus haul cost as a function of haul distance, using deterministic parameters taken from existing collection practice. This does not admit the reorganization of collection rounds and overstates the dependence of costs on haul distance. Transport cost functions are examined in Chapter 6.

3.3.6. Capacity of facilities

The capacities of proposed waste disposal facilities are among the major variables in the planning process. In practice, a new facility is built to a certain design capacity, away from which its unit cost of operation will rise. The design must incorporate some redundancy or excess capacity to cope with equipment mantenance, unscheduled down-time, daily and seasonal fluctuations in waste output, and any expected increases in wastes arising over the plant's operating life. Landfill sites also have a total capacity, which even after a survey will not be known with certainty, and for which the best use over time is sought.

It has already been seen that all strategy evaluation models allocate wastes from sources to sinks. The decision variables are the flows from each source to each sink. The design capacity of a sink does not enter the model formulation directly. The model will give the total waste allocations, to each sink in each period, which correspond to the minimum cost. Capacity constraints may be used to restrict the amount of these assignments. The model as such gives no direct information on what design capacity is appropriate. With assignments to each sink, the planner has information on which to base his choice of capacities. The major output from a waste allocation model, which is being used for strategic rather than for operational planning, is thus not the detailed allocation pattern but information so that the planner can formulate practical plans worthy of further study. The allocation pattern gives spurious detail and must *not* be used as an operational plan when implementing a strategic plan.

The choice of design capacity is guided by the aggregate of waste allocations from all sources to a particular sink. These allocations are chosen by the model in such a way as to minimize total cost. However, the cost functions used to relate total facility costs to the waste throughput do not adequately reflect the realities of the decision as to facility capacity. Each point on the concave cost function (Fig. 3.1. (a)) corresponds to a plant built to an *exact* capacity and operating at that capacity. When a model allocates fluctuating quantities of waste to a given sink, the costs used in each period correspond to fully utilized plants of *different* capacity. These costs are not necessarily appropriate to the more realistic situation of a single plant of adequate capacity operating at different levels of utilization. It follows that the solution produced by the model may not be that of minimum cost, or may not even be practical. This reinforces the previous conclusion that it is only by the careful use of capacity constraints, and with a healthy suspicion of the detailed allocation patterns arising from the solution, that a model can suggest promising plans worthy of further study.

There are several ways in which capacity constraints have been used. The treatment adopted in a particular model is noted in Table 3.1. Common approaches include constraints on the total capacity of landfills and constraints on the annual throughput of processing plants. Some authors apply both upper and lower limits to plant capacity in an attempt to even out the assigned waste load at, or about, the design capacity. This capacity may be chosen beforehand, or may be determined by an initial run of the model without constraints, the design capacity being set, for example, at the waste allocation in the first period (Skelly 1968). A set of discrete capacity levels, each corresponding to an increment in design capacity and using a different cost function, from which the capacity of intermediate facilities must be chosen, is a concept introduced in a few cases. It may well be more in accord with reality than the more common assumptions of unlimited capacity, or of a single cost function appropriate up to a certain maximum capacity, but it has been used largely as a matter of computational convenience. Insights into the choice of capacity can be obtained from sensitivity analysis on capacity constraints, as discussed below.

The capacity of facilities is a vital element in the planning decision and this is the aspect with which strategy evaluation models are least able to cope. The consequences for the use of such models is far reaching. A model cannot by itself select the appropriate design capacities of facilities, it can at best provide enough information to allow the planner to formulate plans for further study.

3.3.7. The effects of parameter variability

The operational research models used in strategy evaluation are deterministic, that is they assume that the parameters are known with certainty. In fact, as noted earlier, all the data for the model are uncertain. An optimal plan for one set of fixed parameters is of little use. Several techniques can be used to provide estimates of the robustness of a given plan as parameters change.

The simplest is sensitivity analysis, which explores the effect of single changes in the values of parameters. The extent of sensitivity analysis among strategy evaluation models is noted in Table 3.1, and in more detail in Table 3.2. The parameters explored are grouped roughly into three categories:

    (i) Those stochastic variables which are fed into the model as data, including wastes arising, landfill capacities, facility and transport costs, and vehicle speeds.

    (ii) Those parameters which are either generated by, or may be elucidated by, the model. The capacities of facilities may be explored by systematically varying the constraints for both the upper and lower bounds on the capacity, while the size of the study area may be used to elucidate the benefits of a regional approach.

    (iii) Those economic variables which are implicit in the evaluation procedures. These include the time horizon, the discount rate, and economic shadow prices used to reflect environmental protection.

In addition, several authors explore the sensitivity of the solution to the location or availability of certain sinks by repeating the model for several closely related strategies. This is noted in Table 3.1.

Sensitivity analysis is much helped in practical application by 'dual variables' or 'shadow prices' from a programming model (Hillier and Lieberman 1967). Unfortunately only a linear, or near-linear, model yields duals with useful economic interpretations. A dual is associated with each constraint equation used in the model, and if it is non-zero the constraint is binding. The value of the dual indicates the economic benefit of relaxing the constraint value by one unit. For example, the dual associated with an upper limit on the annual throughput of a facility shows the marginal benefit of increasing the capacity of the facility by one unit. A related parameter is the

Table 3.2

The extent and scope of sensitivity analysis, showing the parameters whose effect on system performance is explored by the different authors

Model		Stochastic variables						Parameters — Model parameters				Economic parameters		
		Use of dual variables	Wastes arising/forecasting	Landfill capacities	Facility costs	Transport costs	Vehicle speed	Upper bounds on intermediate plant capacity	Lower bounds on intermediate plant capacity	Region size	Time horizon	Discount rate	Use of economic shadow prices	Explicit environmental constraints
Clayton and Huie	1973									X				
Crosby and Renold	1974	X											X	
Fuertes et al.[f]	1974	X	X[1]	X[1]					X[1]					
Harrington	1969	X												
Harvey and O'Flaherty	1972				X	X								
Hekimian	1972									X				
Kühner and Heiler	1973		X											
Marks and Liebman 1[g]	1970	X			X		X	X						X
Morse and Roth	1970												X	
Nigam 1	1970		X					X						
Nigam 2	1970		X											
Rao	1975				X								(X)	
Rossman	1971		X	X	X									
Shields	1972						X					X		
Skelly	1968	(X)	X											

1. Lists dual variables generated by the model.
References: sufficient information in the table in most cases. In other cases, letters refer to the key for Table 3.1.

opportunity cost, which gives the penalty incurred by allocating one unit of waste to a sink not in the optimal solution. This may be used, for example, to indicate the most economical alternative if a given sink is not available. Since both dual variables and opportunity costs indicate marginal costs, caution is necessary to ensure that their limits of validity are not exceeded.

Three major factors limit the usefulness of sensitivity analysis. Firstly, the objective function is often very flat near the optimum, so that the sensitivity to quite large changes in a parameter is small. Kühner and Harrington (1973) (Kühner 1974) generated several good solutions near the optimum which have significantly different configurations. Secondly, sensitivity analysis is essentially a technique for studying changes in single parameters. Two small changes together may have a greater effect than the sum of the two sensitivities would suggest. Simultaneous changes in two or more variables may be investigated directly by the use of stochastic modelling (Charnes and Cooper 1963; Hillier and Lieberman 1967; Tintner and Sengupta 1972). Finally, sensitivity analysis does not provide information on the likelihood of a given change. Risk analysis could be used instead, with parameters entered not as deterministic values but as probability distributions. The output from the model would no longer be a single least cost but rather a probability distribution. Neither stochastic modelling nor risk analysis appear to have been used in strategy evaluation.

3.3.8. Extensions of the objective function

A strategy evaluation model seeks to develop a plan which gives the optimal performance against one criterion. In practice there will be more than one criterion in a planning decision, and so any advance beyond that of least financial cost is welcome. Unfortunately, a mathematical function cannot generally be optimized with respect to more than one objective at the same time. For this reason, formal models of strategy assessment are scarce. Before looking at possible approaches, it is useful to examine the extent to which some of the alternative criteria listed in Table 2.2 have been incorporated within the standard framework of a least-cost model for strategy evaluation.

One way of introducing alternative criteria is to impose additional constraints, such as financial constraints on capital expenditure in each period (Skelly 1968; Kühner and Heiler 1973; Panagiotakopoulos 1976), or traffic constraints (Anderson and Nigam 1967; Marks and Liebman, model 2, 1970; EPA SWAM model, Walker et al. 1974; Mitre Corporation 1976; Berman 1973a, 1976). Another is to use shadow prices to reflect social costs more accurately than is done by market prices. Shadow prices have been applied to environmental protection (Morse and Roth 1970; Crosby and Renold 1974), to reflect the benefits foregone when land is used for waste disposal (Kühner and Heiler, model 2, 1973), and to the decision to close down an existing facility or to upgrade it to meet more stringent operating standards (Kühner and Heiler, model 1, 1973; Kühner 1974). It could be said that sensitivity or risk analysis introduce an additional criterion, that of flexibility to cope with an uncertain future.

Three approaches to more formal assessment are found in the literature. The first two were developed specifically to address the problem of implementing a regional plan for solid waste management in a decentralized political system.

The simplest produces a trade-off curve of minimum cost against another objective, by systematically varying the value of the second, introduced as a constraint on the least-cost problem. The method was developed by Fuertes, Hudson and Marks (1974) (Fuertes 1973) with a second objective of maximum equity between communities. Equity was measured indirectly, increasing as the waste shipment in ton–miles decreases, either in total or across political boundaries. The significance of this measure was questioned by Kühner and Harrington (1975b), who pointed out that its relevance was to the regional planner, as it does not allow an appraisal of equity for the decision maker of each individual community. Nevertheless the trade-off curve, showing in this case the cost of increasing equity, could be valuable in extending the scope of strategy evaluation models.

Kühner and Harrington (1973, 1974, 1975a, 1975b) (Kühner 1974) defined interest groups in the region, and evaluated separately the costs and benefits as seen by each. A set of solutions is identified, for each of which no group can be made better off without making another group worse off. This technique of Paretian Environmental Analysis, developed by Dorfman and Jacoby (1972) (Dorfman 1972), permits explicit consideration of the trade-off between interest groups. The model still minimizes the total system cost, but identifies in addition 'efficient' solutions near to the minimum-cost solution which are significantly different as viewed by each individual interest group. This approach represents the most comprehensive attempt yet to extend the power and scope of strategy evaluation models.

The third approach is the most fundamental. Strategies are evaluated against several criteria and their overall performance is then assessed. The techniques used are complex, and are examined in the next chapter. The only application has been by Hekimian (1972).

Strategy evaluation models do not at present provide a satisfactory treatment of the many conflicting objectives which need to be considered in practice. Thus they cannot tell the planner which plan to select but can only guide him as to how plans perform, within the limitations of the model, against a single objective. It is for the planner to judge performance on the other criteria and to make the overall assessment.

3.4. A case study of a strategy evaluation model

The approach of the Local Government Operational Research Unit (LGORU) in England has been chosen for discussion in some detail for several reasons. As indicated earlier it is the one attempt at combining several strategy evaluation models into an integrated package for waste management planning, and this might be expected to produce a more powerful tool. It is possibly the model with the most extensive application, but it is also one of the least well documented. A qualitative description is given by Parker and Portlock (1974), while the only technical report is an early paper by Nice and Selby (1969).

Each study begins by gathering information, principally on collection methods and landfill availability. The initial model determines the optimum number and locations of a particular type of facility. These locations are then used as a guide to finding practical sites, which in turn are evaluated using a static model of linear programming type. Transfer stations and relay collection (in which there is more than one vehicle per team of collectors) may be evaluated by superimposing them on a given strategy to see if they lower the total cost. Practical strategies are evaluated using a simple dynamic transportation model to optimize the use of facilities over time. The results are usually presented as a series of maps showing the allocation of collection zones to facilities in each period.

Each step is quite simple and involves a number of assumptions. The initial study of landfill availability decides whether some form of volume reduction is a necessary part of any strategy. As the time horizon of L G O R U studies is around 25 years and new landfill space may be created through mineral extraction over, say, 10 years, there is an obvious danger that volume reduction methods will be recommended when they are not in fact required.

The plant location model suffers from a number of disadvantages. A simple trade-off is sought between the transport costs from collection rounds to the facility sites, and the costs of operating facilities at the capacities implied by the quantities of waste assigned. Only one type of treatment or disposal facility may be included in a strategy; each facility must dispose of all the waste which it accepts, implying that the costs of an incinerator, for example, must include the cost of transport and disposal of the residue at a predetermined landfill site; time variations or capacity constraints on the facilities may not be considered. In addition, the collection cost model tends to overstate the rise in combined collection and haul (or transport) costs as the distance from a collection round to the facility site increases (Section 6.2). This will lead to a bias towards a larger number of facilities. For example, the South Hampshire study (Brookes and Green 1968) recommended the construction of six incinerators in a relatively small area. Costs for systems with three to nine incinerators lay within 2.4 per cent of each other, while only 0.75 per cent separated systems with four to nine incinerators. These differences are within the expected error limits and are thus of little significance. Configurations with only one to two incinerators were ruled out by the high transport costs for outlying areas and the exclusion of mixed landfill and incineration strategies. No analysis of the incremental returns on investment in additional incinerators was attempted.

The other models in the L G O R U planning package are both of linear programming type. They suffer from the usual problems of assuming a unit cost for each facility, and hence its capacity, before allocations are made, and an inadequate treatment of the capacities of facilities which is exacerbated by the absence of capacity constraints. Sensitivity analysis does not feature in any of the published applications of the method. The results from the L G O R U models are subject to the same caveat as other models, namely they provide information on which strategic plans may be based rather than providing detailed operational planning information. Unfortunately the results are presented as maps, showing allocations for each period. This gives a spurious accuracy to the results, discouraging their constructive use in formulating strategic plans and creating an image of the model as a black box for producing optimal plans.

3.5. The future development of strategy evaluation models

This review has shown that, despite much activity, no completely satisfactory approach has been found for strategy evaluation. The complexity of the real situation is such that some compromise between model accuracy and tractability is inevitable. For some aspects, modelling is satisfactory, although its implementation may pose difficulties in solving the model. Examples include the treatment of complex facilities, of time, and of capital cost. For other aspects, more serious difficulties were encountered, which may be summarized as:

(i) There is a two-fold problem associated with the choice of appropriate design capacities for facilities. First, no direct information is given by the model, which simply indicates the aggregate allocations to each sink for each period. Secondly, these assignments may not be correct due to inconsistencies in the use of the facility cost function. The result is that the model cannot be used as a direct planning tool, it is merely a method of generating plans for further study.

(ii) The models are appropriate to a situation where all the parameters are known with certainty, while waste management is characterized by uncertain data. This problem may be alleviated to some extent ,by analysis of parameter variability, but the techniques for this are currently restricted in scope.

(iii) The adequate treatment of more than one objective is not possible in a strategy evaluation model. The cost of a plan is just one piece of information to be used in a planning decision.

Each of these difficulties is of a fundamental character and will not be solved by experience alone. Together they restrict models to a limited role of screening alternatives and suggesting plans for further study, for which simple models suffice. Too much attention in the past has been paid to solving complex mathematical models with little attempt to relate the results to reality. While some additional work on applying the results is desirable, we are forced to the conclusion that models for strategy evaluation currently offer little scope for further development as practical aids to waste management planning.

4. A PRAGMATIC APPROACH TO PLANNING

4.1. Introduction

An alternative approach to technical analysis in planning for waste management is to build on the preliminary analysis of technologies, rather than on strategy evaluation, as the basis for an overall planning tool. This is essentially a much simpler approach; each technology is evaluated against each criterion, and those which perform best in the evaluation exercise are assessed. One of the criticisms made in the last chapter was that strategy evaluation was only meaningful if a detailed analysis of technologies had been made, and this was in general not the case. In fact, if each technology is defined to include all the operations performed on the wastes arising from a single source, as shown in Fig. 2.2, then strategy evaluation has been effectively subsumed. This 'single waste-flow model' is thus not only *necessary*, but also it will often be *sufficient* for planning purposes. The need for a strategy evaluation model may be reduced or eliminated if a region can be divided into smaller areas with limited interaction, each of which may be regarded as a single waste arising. Such subdivision is possible in the presence of, for example:

Natural barriers such as rivers or mountains;

A concentration of population and industry into well-separated towns;

Existing facilities with fixed catchment areas.

This pragmatic approach to planning is sufficiently flexible to include several waste types from the same source. However, for illustration, this discussion is confined to those wastes collected by a local authority. Once the principle has been established, the scope can be broadened.

The preliminary analysis of technologies for waste disposal is one application of the techniques of project evaluation or investment appraisal. In order to establish the most useful and promising lines for development of the single waste-flow model, it is first necessary to look at both the general methods of project evaluation and their previous application in waste management.

4.2. Methods of project evaluation

4.2.1. Principle

Project evaluation essentially lists the possible courses of action and the assessment criteria, measuring the performance of each option against each criterion and assessing which is the preferred alternative. The initial results of the evaluation may conveniently be displayed in a tabular form or matrix, in which each row represents an option and each column a criterion, the corresponding entry showing the performance. The individual evaluations may be quantitative, semi-quantitative, or qualitative. Even the criteria for which evaluations are quantified may be difficult to compare if different measures are used, for example cost in pounds sterling and water pollution potential in kilograms of biological oxygen demand.

The many variants of project evaluation differ in the number of criteria, the order of steps in the evaluation sequence, and the assessment procedure. Assessment is aimed at helping the decision maker interpret the matrix, but how far assessment should proceed is a matter of debate. One may identify various steps (which do not necessarily have to follow this sequence):

(i) The evaluations of each option against each criterion may be ranked in the order of increasing performance against that criterion.

(ii) This ordinal ranking may be extended to give a cardinal ranking in which option 1 is say, three times as good as option 2, when measured against that particular criterion.

(iii) The cardinal scores against each criterion may be normalized to a common numerical basis, such as score out of 10.

(iv) The criteria may be ranked, or arranged in order of importance.

(v) This ranking may be quantified by the assignment of relative weights to the criteria.

(vi) By combining the normalized scores of each option against each criterion with the relative weights of each criterion, a single numerical score or index of performance for each option may be obtained. The decision is reduced to the trivial level of selecting that option with the best overall score.

Each step in assessment involves assumptions, and some discussion of these is necessary.

The ordering of options against a single criteria is straightforward, although it must be remembered that the only numerical property of ordinal numbers is to make a list. The adoption of either a cardinal or normalized score for each option against each criterion has pitfalls. Fully quantitative evaluations are required for all the criteria. Problems may be encountered when measuring, say, the risk to a public water supply. Costs and benefits for a given criterion may not be commensurate. For example, with a criterion of public health an option might decrease rodent and fly nuisance but increase smells. Changes in costs and benefits over time are difficult to reflect in a single measurement unless monetary units are used. In addition, for normalization it is necessary to define the zero and maximum values, and the appropriate form (e.g. linear or logarithmic) of the performance scale. It is clear that assigning numerical scores for many criteria introduces a subjective element. One approach is to use committees of experts or decision makers to assign scores. Techniques for using their options and achieving consensus between their conflicting points of view have been developed (Klee 1972; Morris 1974, 1977).

The ordering or weighting of criteria also introduces subjective elements, and again one may appeal to experts or decision makers. There are at least two serious problems with the more sophisticated approach of weighting. A significant school of thought sees it as a potentially dangerous technique. For example, Kazanowski (1968) accepts weighting where there is a single autocratic decision maker, as when a company gives cash rewards for cost-saving suggestions from its employees, or in bi-partite negotiations. However, when there are many decision makers, who may be accountable to the general public, he sees weighting as 'self-delusive and fallacious'. If some person or group does not agree with a decision, then the weights used will be challenged. Thus instead of facilitating a consensus for action, the weighted evaluation may stimulate the formation of opposing factions that prevent the reaching of such a consensus.

A second problem concerns the usual assumption that weights may be assigned to criteria independently of the quantification of project performance against the criteria. Nash, Pearce, and Stanley (1975a) point out that this implies constant marginal rates of substitution between effects on each criterion, irrespective of the quantities involved, and conclude that it is hard to think of any assumptions under which these weightings could be meaningful. The problem may be sidestepped by first evaluating the performance and then deriving the weights. The consequences for assessment would be significant as any revision of the performance scores would necessitate a revision of the weights.

The final assessment step is the combination of the numerical scores of each option, k, against each criterion, i, with the relative weights of the criteria. Alternatives for combining weights, w_i with scores S_{ki} include:

(i) The linear additive model:

$$S_k = \sum_i w_i S_{ki} \tag{4.1}$$

(ii) The addilog model:

$$S_k = \sum_i w_i \log (S_{ki}) \tag{4.2}$$

(iii) The multiplactive model:

$$S_k = \prod_i (S_{ki})^{w_i} \qquad (4.3)$$

where S_k is the overall performance index for option k.

It is clear that there is no unique way of determining the index. Its value, and thus the choice of the preferred option, can be altered by changing the numbers and definitions of criteria, by redefining the scales used for quantifying performance scores against each criterion, by changing the weights, or by using a different model for combining the individual scores and weights. Each model assumes that the criteria used are independent, a condition which rarely holds in practice.

There is no objective way in which any particular assessment scheme can be proven to be better than another. When an analyst comes to test his model, he is testing it, not against an objective reality, but against his own preconceived ideas of what he expected the answer to be. This observation has led to allegations that the technique is one of justification rather than evaluation, using figures to give quantitative respectability to what is simply a subjective judgement (Kazanowski 1968).

The involvement of committees of decision makers, planners, or experts in scoring and weighting is an attempt to circumvent this problem, and to substitute the subjective preferences of the public or certain proxy bodies for those of the analyst. However, these committees are usually employed simply to determine scores and weights. They are not used at the final stage of project selection. The selected system is presented to the decision makers as that which their own preferences have indicated as best. Consensus is sought not on the policy decision but on certain mechanistic steps in the assessment exercise. Moreover, many of the techniques for reaching consensus explicitly reject committee debate and political bargaining (e.g. Hekimian 1972). The use of any model to *select* a project should be treated with suspicion. These formal techniques could be viewed as an attempt to remove the decision from the hands of the politicians, justified presumably because the techniques used for revealing their subjective preferences and for reaching consensus are an improvement on the normal political process. However, the power of the analyst remains considerable. The choice of model for combining the scores and weights is his, and different choices could lead to a different project being selected. The implications for democracy of such a system are serious.

4.2.2. Alternative techniques

The literature contains many techniques for project evaluation (Lichfield, Kettle, and Whitbread 1975). A false dichotomy is generally assumed between the so-called matrix techniques, exemplified by cost–effectiveness analysis (Kazanowski 1968) and the goals-achievement matrix (Hill 1968), and the twin methods of financial appraisal and cost–benefit analysis (Mishan 1975). In fact, these latter may be viewed as special cases of the general approach outlined here, with, in the first case, just one criterion, that of financial return to the project developers, and in the second the reduction of the matrix to a single performance score for each project in terms of money.

Cost–benefit analysis may thus be compared to a matrix method which produces an overall performance index. The value judgement which under-pins either is that the decision should reflect individuals' preferences, although they differ on how this is to be achieved. Cost–benefit analysis attempts to measure all costs and benefits by reference to individual preferences as revealed in the market, while matrix methods make use of the preferences of elected representatives to evaluate performance and to weigh the various criteria. The problems with either approach are analogous. Both require quantitative measurement of performance against each criterion, but in cost–benefit analysis all the measurements must be in monetary units. The indirect measurement of intangible costs and benefits has made some progress, for example in the use of property values to measure the costs of noise pollution (Pearce 1975), but much remains to be done. The problems of combining individual scores and weights in the matrix method have a counterpart in cost–benefit analysis, where the preferences of each indi-vidual must be aggregated to represent society as a whole. Several schemes have been suggested, and the choice between them is controversial (Nash, Pearce, and Stanley 1975b; Mishan 1975). The advantage of the matrix method over cost–benefit analysis is that it is more comprehensive, con-sidering non-market effects explicitly.

This comparison of techniques considered only a matrix method produc-ing a single performance index for each option. The matrix approach is much more flexible than this, offering a simple and clear means of presenting the results of a multicriterion evaluation. Not all the develop-ments of the method have used weighting. For example, Kazanowski (1968), who produced a standard methodology for cost–effectiveness analysis, limited assessment to the ranking of criteria, after a preliminary screening of options to eliminate those which fail to meet a standard of either maximum cost or minimum effectiveness. This approach avoids many of the pitfalls associated with weighting, and preserves the important distinction between the political planning decision and the technical analysis made in its support.

4.3. Project evaluation in waste management planning

The evaluation and assessment of candidate technologies for waste disposal, treatment, and resource recovery have received limited attention. Most authors have confined themselves to financial appraisal, considering only the financial costs and benefits accruing to the project operator. Many of these appraisals are partial in scope, omitting significant operations made on the waste (Fig. 2.2).

In Britain, the Department of the Environment (1976a) has issued guidelines on the evaluation of options. The method recommended is based on cost–benefit analysis, but amounts in practice to a largely financial appraisal from the viewpoint of the local authority. Listing of intangible effects is advocated, leaving it to be decided if they justify rejection of the cheapest alternative. This is equivalent to a matrix evaluation, with the financial criterion quantified and heavily weighted relative to the other qualitative criteria. A difference in net present cost between two options of £500 000 appears large, but if, say, 10 000 people feel that they each require just £6 a year to compensate them for the loss of view or amenity caused by the cheaper option, then on a cost–benefit criterion of least social cost the ranking is reversed (assuming a 10 per cent discount rate over 20 years). There has been some attempt to measure intangible costs within a cost–benefit framework. For example, Schmalensee, Ramanathan, Ramm, and Smallwood (1975) used property prices to measure the social costs of a landfill site, but their results were disappointing as no significant effects were found.

A matrix approach to project evaluation has also been used. Popovich, Duckstein, and Kisiel (1973) applied the cost–effectiveness methodology of Kazanowski (1968) to three waste management options for a city in Arizona. The criteria used were arranged in order of importance and weighting was not used. Most evaluations were qualitative. McDonald (1976) developed a methodology for comparing the environmental impacts of different landfill sites. Weights were assigned to the criteria, but no attempt was made to reduce the results to a single performance index for each site.

Other workers have used weighting procedures leading to composite performance indices. Klee (1971) discussed a decision problem concerning the best means of dismantling and disposing of redundant wooden railway wagons. He developed a technique based on a pairwise comparison of options, called Decision Alternative Ratio Evaluation (D A R E), which was used to determine both the performance scores of the options on each criterion and the relative weights of the criteria.

Wenger and Rhyner (1972) applied a similar method to the selection of a solid waste disposal option, using a stochastic procedure in which the value of each weight and score pair ($w_i S_{ki}$ in the linear additive model, equation 4.1) was selected by a random number, from a uniform range with error limits of ±50 per cent. The results were presented as the average index value of S_k, together with its 95 per cent confidence limits. If the overall performance indices of two alternatives overlap, then no justification for preferring one or the other is provided. This is an extension of the single-index matrix models, and attempts to overcome some of the problems of weighting.

Hekimian (1972) applied a formal assessment procedure, with the cost of each plan, as determined by a strategy evaluation model, just one of his seven criteria. The method was split into two phases, the first screening out options which failed to meet minimum performance standards of flexibility and implementation, and the latter involving a sophisticated committee system of assessment with political bargaining specifically excluded.

A variation is the use of two performance indices, based on system cost and system effectiveness, rather than one. The results are then presented as a two-dimensional trade-off map, permitting some comparison of cost versus effectiveness. The approach is similar to that of Fuertes, Hudson, and Marks (1974) for trading-off system cost versus equity in a strategy evaluation model (Section 3.3.8). The problems in producing the single effectiveness index are, however, almost as great as those with a combined performance index.

A major study to quantify the social and environmental costs of solid waste management was carried out in the Fresno area of California by the Aerojet-General Corporation and Engineering Science Inc. (1969). 19 separate 'conditions' or operations on the solid waste were identified and the performance of each was determined against 13 'environmental bad effects' of solid wastes and against 12 'ancillary effects' of alternative waste management systems. The individual performance scores were determined by a combination of committee scoring and weighting. The scores for each condition and for each waste type were then combined into an overall performance score for each of 18 municipal–industrial waste management systems and 4 agricultural systems. The results were presented as a diagram showing the trade-off between system cost and the improvement in effectiveness over the present system. The procedure is complex and, although commissioned as a prototype 'how-to-do-it' exercise, no similar approach has since been attempted.

Drobny, Qasim, and Valentine (1971) applied cost–effectiveness to waste-water treatment plant for military camps. The scoring and weighting procedure used a paired comparison method, and the final results for 15 systems measured on 8 effectiveness criteria were presented as an effectiveness versus unit cost of treatment trade-off diagram. Huang, Dalton, *et al.* (1975) proposed a similar procedure, incorporating preliminary feasibility screening, for selecting an option for resource recovery from solid waste. Committees are used for scoring and weighting and the use of separate scoring of each option against each criterion in each period is advocated. No guidance is given, however, on combining the scores for different periods. Suloway (1976) presents the results of a similar evaluation which led to the selection of a plant to produce refuse-derived fuel as the preferred option for Chicago.

The Mitre Corporation (Berman 1973*b*) produced a methodology for screening options prior to the use of their strategy evaluation model (Berman 1973*a*). This involved a trade-off between cost and effectiveness, the latter measured in terms of the volume of waste requiring landfill disposal. Options which did not perform best on either criterion of minimum cost or minimum volume of residue were eliminated.

4.4. Developing a single waste-flow model

All project evaluation techniques can be seen as variations of a multi-criterion evaluation of options. Assessment may be limited to displaying the matrix to best effect so that the decision makers may more easily interpret it. The criteria may be ranked in order of importance or the options ranked by performance on each criterion. Alternatively, assessment may produce a single performance index for each option against all the criteria, with interpretation reduced to choosing the option with the best index. A special case is cost–benefit analysis, where the index is in monetary units. The derivation of a single index depends on the quantification of all performance scores and criteria weights, which in turn introduces subjective elements to the analysis. Sophisticated procedures are necessary to canvass the opinions of decision makers or others on what numbers should be assigned. In addition, other problems were identified above, notably the lack of an objective way of testing the validity of the model. The major disadvantage in this method of assessment is that the distinction is lost between the political planning process and the technical analysis required in its support.

For such reasons, assessment is here confined to displaying the results of the evaluation to best effect. Attention is focused rather on the evaluation and, in particular, on the quantification of performance against certain criteria. The existence of such measures of performance has been seen to be a necessary precondition for easy assessment.

There are many criteria to be considered in assessing options and plans for waste management, and some of these were listed in Table 2.2. Five broad categories were distinguished, namely economic, technical, environmental, political, and that of the use and conservation of resources, each of which poses problems. Qualitative evaluation is straightforward, but quantitative measurement of performance is more difficult. For the less tangible technical, environmental, and political criteria, prospects for quantitative evaluation are presently rather poor. Therefore, in the remainder of Part I, attention will be concentrated on the other two criteria, rationalizing and extending the scope of present methods of economic evaluation and measuring, perhaps for the first time, the resource implications of options for waste management.

5. THE ECONOMICS OF WASTE PROCESSING

5.1. Introduction

The decision to implement any particular technology as a method of disposal, treatment, or reclamation for solid wastes must be based on a sound economic evaluation of the alternatives. The principles of such an evaluation are developed in the next three chapters. The discussion begins here with the economics of the technology itself, and continues with transport costs, the treatment of uncertainty in cost and revenue estimates, and the application of the methods to a case study; this examines some 30 options which are identified in Part II of the book as representative of the current state of the art in waste management technology. Unless otherwise stated, all costs quoted refer to the first half of 1977.

Much has been written on the economics of waste management, but there is little agreement on either the costs or even the relative cost rankings of the various processes. Information on existing operations is limited owing to the recent development of much treatment and reclamation techology; even when available its interpretation is made difficult by variations in the age of plant, in accountancy practice and in standards of operation. More generally, information is based on development or design studies, which by their nature often tend to be optimistic. For example, a demonstration pyrolysis plant at Baltimore, Maryland, which uses the Monsanto Landgard system, was estimated in 1972 to cost $14.7 million (Buss 1973). Scale-up problems were encountered and air emission standards not met. In 1975 the replacement cost of the plant was quoted as $28 million (Sussman 1975), and in fact the project was abandoned by its developers early in 1977.

In this chapter, attention is focused on those aspects of the economic evaluation of technologies where differences in the approach or in the assumptions may lead to significant variations in the results. A number of conventions are proposed to facilitate both the comparison of economic analyses and their use in planning a waste management system.

5.2. Historical cost data

The best source of cost data should be records of current operations, but, as no two operations are identical, it is difficult to use the data unless considerable detail is available. For example, one needs to know the age of the plant, the standards of the operation, and the accounting conventions. Often the records are incomplete. To overcome some of the problems associated with single observations, data may be collected on many similar operations and statistical analysis performed. This is useful for the technologies which are in widespread use, i.e. landfill, pulverization, transfer, and incineration.

An example of such work is that of Dawson (1970). He related the overall unit costs of transfer, incineration, and landfill operations to the weight of waste handled, and, for the first case, to bulk haulage distance. The data were obtained by postal survey in the San Francisco area, with a sample size between 18 and 32 in each case. The estimating equations tested the hypothesis that the unit costs decrease as waste throughput increases. Although the explanatory power of the equations was low, ranging from 43 to 75 per cent, statistically significant coefficients were obtained, providing evidence for economy of scale.

Statistics on waste disposal in England are now being compiled annually by the Society of County Treasurers and County Surveyors' Society (1976, 1979). The returns for 1975–6 are summarized in Figs 5.1 (a)–(d), which show the variation of the total expenditure by each county (including capital charges) with the weight of waste disposed of by each of the four principal methods.

It is traditional in the waste disposal industry to quote costs per unit of waste, e.g. £/tonne. The hypothesis that the unit cost is constant, irrespective of the quantity of waste handled, was tested by linear regression analysis (Table 5.1); as can be seen in Fig. 5.1, there is considerable scatter about the best-fit lines. The scatter may be measured by the coefficient of determination, R^2, which expresses the variation explained by the given regression line ($R^2 = 1$ for a perfect fit). R^2 ranges from 0.37 for transfer stations, through 0.49 for landfill and 0.75 for pulverization, to 0.97 for incineration. Although the explanatory power of the linear hypothesis is not always good, statistically significant unit costs are obtained. The uncertainty on the unit cost b is measured by the standard deviation s. There is a 95 per cent chance that the unit cost will be within the range £$b \pm 2s$ (Fig. 5.1 and Table 5.1).

However, these average unit costs are of limited use in planning. Not only do they mask considerable variations between counties, but also the original data were aggregated on a county basis so that, for example, information on economy of scale in individual operations is lost. The unit costs include capital repayments on the average historic cost of plants in operation, a

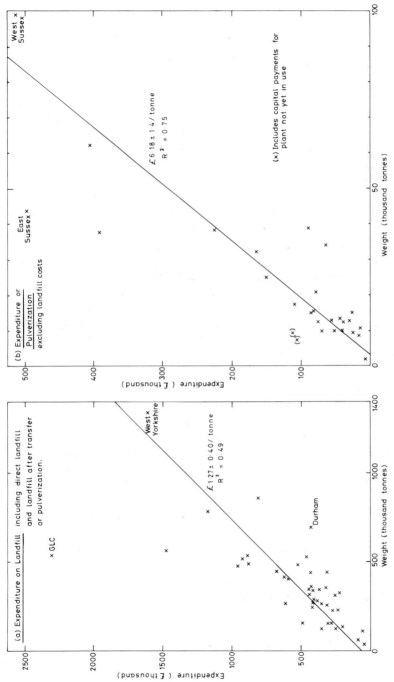

Fig. 5.1. Expenditure on waste disposal by English counties in 1975–6.

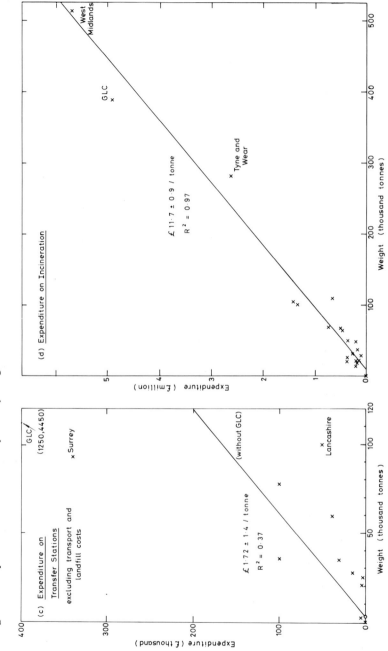

Fig. 5.1. Expenditure on waste disposal by English counties in 1975–6—cont.

figure which is lower than the average replacement cost. On this basis, the average cost of incineration, for example, was £11.7/tonne, with a 95 per cent confidence limit of ±£0.9/tonne (Fig. 5.1d).

This example serves to illustrate a more general point; the numerical value of a cost figure depends on the purpose for which it is intended to be used, and a cost derived from one purpose cannot be directly used for another. Among the possible purposes of a cost estimate, one may include:

National statistics, to give a nationwide average for the cost of an activity;
Accounting, to account for the expenditure of funds or to control costs;
Planning, to compare the costs of alternative methods of waste management.

The concern here is primarily with the last application, in strategic planning.

5.3. Methods of economic evaluation

5.3.1. Annual cost versus discounted cash flow

There are two basic alternative methods for calculating the cost of an activity, namely the annual or accountancy cost and discounted cash flow. These are now examined in turn.

Table 5.1

Regression analysis of the 1975–6 waste disposal statistics.
Data are taken from the Society of County Treasurers (1976) survey of the 46 English counties. The model estimated in each case was:

expenditure = $a + b$ (weight disposed)

The constant term a was not significantly different from zero in any case

Disposal method	Average unit cost b (£/t)	Standard deviation s (£/t)	t-statistic for b[1]	Coefficient of determination R^2	Number of observations[2]
Landfill[3]	1.27	0.20	6.5**	0.49	45
Pulverization[4]	6.18	0.71	8.8**	0.75	27
Transfer[5]	1.72	0.71	2.4*	0.37	12
Incineration[6]	11.7	0.45	26**	0.97	21

1. Shows that b is significantly different from zero at the 95 per cent (*) or 99.9 per cent (**) level.
2. The point (0,0) is included in each case.
3. Includes direct landfill and landfill after transfer or pulverization.
4. Excludes cost of landfill. Two observations excluded from the analysis because they included capital payments or debt charges for plant not yet in use.
5. Excludes cost of transport and landfill. The observation for the Greater London Council (1.25 million tonnes, £4.45 million) is excluded as it dominates the analysis, giving b = £3.6/t, R^2 = 0.994.
6. The high coefficient of determination for incineration depends critically on just three counties (W. Midlands, GLC, and Tyne and Wear) with more than 200 000 t/a. If these are removed, b = £10.3/t and R^2 = 0.74.

To calculate the annual or accountancy cost, the costs and revenues for one year only are considered. Capital costs are included either as an annuity payment or as depreciation and interest charges. Variations used in the waste management literature have included the use of straight-line depreciation with either equity or bond financing to calculate the annual capital charge (Abert, Alter, and Bernheisel 1974; Sussman 1976); the calculation of initial capital costs in the year of start-up by escalating the costs incurred during each year of construction at the rate of inflation, common in US literature, and including interest charges during construction (Sussman 1976); and the use of different capital recovery rates for different components of the capital cost (Midwest Research Institute 1973).

In discounted cash flow analysis (DCF), all costs and revenues, including capital costs, are entered directly in the year in which they occur. To allow easy comparison of different investments, an internal rate of return may be calculated, or the costs and benefits may be discounted back to the start of the project to yield a net present value (NPV):

$$NPV = \sum_{n=0}^{N} \frac{C_n}{(1+r)^n} \tag{5.1}$$

where C_n is the net cash flow in year n, N is the lifetime of the project in years, and r is the discount rate.

For use in waste management, where a local authority has a statutory obligation to dispose of waste, the results may be calculated as a net present cost (NPC) or, more conveniently, as the equivalent cost per tonne of waste. The latter may be calculated from the equivalent annual cost (EAC) for each year of the project's operating life:

$$NPC = EAC \left[\sum_{n=(N_1+1)}^{N} \frac{1}{(1+r)^n} \right] = EAC\, (a_{rN} - a_{rN_1}) \tag{5.2}$$

where N_1 is the construction period in years. Tabulations of a_{rN}, the present value in year 0 of an annuity of 1 per annum for N years, are available (Merrett and Sykes 1963).

In a comparative evaluation, the project with highest net present value, or lowest net present cost, will normally be preferred. However, if capital expenditure is restricted, projects cannot necessarily be ranked in the order of least net present cost.

For use in planning, DCF methods have many advantages over the more conventional accountancy cost. This is particularly so when, quite apart from the effects of inflation, the annual costs are likely to vary over time, for example:

When a sequence of landfill sites is being compared with a treatment plant of longer life;

If major items of equipment need replacement during the lifetime of the plant;

When changes in the rate of waste production are expected.

The use of DCF by waste disposal authorities in the UK has been recommended by the Department of the Environment (1976a). DCF need not be difficult to apply in practice; the principles are simple and the arithmetic can easily be performed using a pocket calculator.

5.3.2. The discount rate

If equivalent results are sought from DCF and annual cost calculations, it is necessary that the discount rate be equal to the interest rate at which the capital may be borrowed. However, for investment appraisal in the public sector a social discount rate is more commonly used. There are two approaches to determining this rate (Walsh and Williams 1969).

The social opportunity cost (SOC) discount rate is set equal to the real rate of return on marginal low risk projects undertaken by private industry; the rationale is that this is what the money would earn if it were not invested in the public sector. The optimal amount of public investment is then determined by accepting projects which give a return higher than the SOC rate and rejecting those which do not. In Britain, all public sector investments are evaluated using the Treasury test discount rate, which is set periodically as the SOC; a rate of 10 per cent was used from 1969 to 1978, but this has now been reduced to 5 per cent (UK Parliament 1978). Note that in practice the test discount rate is used, not to decide on the amount of public expenditure, but to choose between alternative ways of doing the same thing or to determine the composition of an investment programme within a budget constraint (Rees 1973).

The alternative approach uses the rate of social time preference (STP) as the social discount rate. This is based on the amount of consumption necessary in the future to compensate society as a whole for the sacrifice of consumption now. The determination of this rate is difficult, but it is generally accepted to be lower than the SOC rate, with a figure of 3–5 per cent commonly suggested.

Both the SOC and STP discount rates have disadvantages when used with projects which have long lives. Neither takes account of the preferences of future generations (Nash 1973). Further, positive discount rates are based on the expectation of economic growth, so that future generations will be better off than this one. For goods which are becoming more scarce with time, including non-renewable resources such as land, minerals, or oil, and amenities such as clean water or a beautiful view, this expectation does not hold. The difficulty may be overcome either by using different discount rates for different goods (Price 1973; Institution of Chemical Engineers 1976) or by using economic shadow (or accounting) prices for specific items whose relative value is expected to increase through time (Walsh and Williams 1969; Arrow 1976).

In evaluating projects in a local authority, there are at least four alternatives when choosing a discount rate. These are listed below, together with the values appropriate in the first half of 1977:

The interest rate at which the authority may borrow—about 13 per cent;

A commercial rate of return—about 25 per cent;

A social opportunity cost (SOC) rate—about 10 per cent;

A social time preference (STP) rate—about 3–5 per cent.

The two social discount rates are real rates of return, required over and above any return necessary to keep pace with inflation. The others are nominal rates, which reflect expectations of future inflation in addition to private investment grants, business taxation, and attitudes to risk (Whipple 1975). If a nominal rate of return is used as the discount rate r in Equation 5.1, the cash flows C_n for each year of the project must include increases expected due to inflation. The use of a real rate of return allows cash flows to be evaluated at current costs, and so avoids the need to predict inflation.

The UK Treasury test discount rate of 10 per cent appropriate in 1977 implied, at a time when annual inflation was about 15 per cent, a nominal discount rate of about 27 per cent, which was much higher than the actual cost of capital of around 13 per cent. This discrepancy was the reason for the reduction in test discount rate to 5 per cent at the beginning of 1978. It should be noted that, even in real terms, a private company will usually require a higher rate of return than the test discount rate in order to allow for its payment of taxes.

As different discount rates are appropriate in different circumstances, it is recommended that results should be presented for a range of values. This has the additional benefit of showing the variations of project viability in a fluctuating capital market. To avoid the problems of forecasting inflation, the discount rate should be a real rate of return.

5.3.3. The time horizon

It is essential that all the waste management options being compared in a particular study should refer to the same period. A waste treatment or reclamation plant may have an expected life of 10–25 years: to compare this with a local landfill site with a life of just a couple of years is meaningless. Rather, the local landfill should be evaluated as an interim measure, to be followed by, say, a transfer station serving three more distant landfill sites one after the other. When these two new options are compared by DCF analysis over, say, 20 years, the treatment or reclamation plant might well prove to be the cheaper alternative.

The choice of a suitable time horizon for comparison of projects is important. In Britain 10 years is suggested (Department of the Environment

1976c), but this is shorter than the expected life of a processing plant, typically taken as 20 years (Department of the Environment 1976a). Here a time horizon of 23 years will be used, comprising a construction period of 3 years and a life of 20 years. The effect of assumed project lifetime on the comparative evaluation of options should be explored.

5.3.4. Cost–benefit analysis

It could be argued that, in evaluating options for waste management, a local authority should aim to minimize the cost to society as a whole rather than the financial cost to itself. Such an approach is in fact recommended by the Department of the Environment (1976a), and it is of interest to look briefly at those areas, apart from the inclusion of intangible costs, where the two measures may diverge.

Cost–benefit analysis (CB A) does not include transfer payments between members of a society, such as the payment of rates, or the receipt of investment grants from central government. Each is relevant to a financial appraisal, and their inclusion is recommended by the Department of the Environment (1976a).

The measurement of financial costs in CB A uses the concept of opportunity cost, or the foregone benefits of the best alternative project. It is being used increasingly in financial appraisal, where the practice of current cost accounting enters the replacement, rather than the historic, cost of capital items. Particular problems arise with the opportunity costs of land, labour, and capital. In each case the market price is suggested for use in waste disposal planning (Department of the Environment 1976a). If derelict land has no alternative use then its opportunity cost is zero, although competition from the private sector for landfill space would give it a market value. If a local authority is using a private facility, the rent paid is the financial cost and may be higher than the social opportunity cost. In an area of high unemployment, the social opportunity cost of a new job may be less than the market wage if the labour may be recruited from the unemployment pool. If there are strict limits on capital spending within a local authority, the opportunity cost of using capital for one service, say waste disposal, rather than another, say the fire service, may be higher than its financial cost.

Waste disposal may produce materials and energy for sale or may reclaim land. The market prices for these commodities may not represent their true value to society. If they do not, CB A should use an economic shadow price for the commodity. In practice the determination of a shadow price is difficult; sometimes it may not be certain whether it is greater or less than the market price. Consider the example of using landfill as a method of reclaiming land for agricultural use. The benefit to society of the reclaimed land is theoretically equal to its market price, which should reflect both the scarcity value of the land and the discounted value of the food it will produce. It could be argued that home-produced food has a shadow price higher than its market price due either to subsidized imports or to world-wide scarcity. Farmland is being used to build new homes, and the value of new land created from a non-productive site may be felt to be worth a premium. Against this has to be set alternative uses for the site, such as a quarry for water recreation.

At the present time, one cannot estimate shadow prices with confidence. As a result, the approach adopted here is to use a financial appraisal, examining the sensitivity of the evaluation to various shadow prices for recovered products or land.

5.4. Capital cost estimates

There are many problems in obtaining realistic estimates for the capital costs of facilities for waste disposal, treatment, or resource recovery. A very wide range of cost estimates may be found in the literature for what appear to be similar plants. This may be illustrated by two examples taken from Part II, in both of which the estimates have been corrected to apply to a 300 tonne per day plant at first-half 1977 prices:

    (1) Pulverization plants in the UK: 24 plants built 1967–77 for local authorities. Range of corrected costs £340 000–£2 700 000. Mean cost £1 100 000; standard deviation £900 000.

    (2) Plants producing an 'American' refuse-derived fuel by dry separation of waste: 27 estimates. Range £1.1–£7.4 million. Mean cost £3.8 million; standard deviation £1.7 million.

This enormous variability in capital cost estimates may be attributed to four main sources, namely differences in design conception, in operating standards, in costs specific to a site, and in cost estimating procedures.

5.4.1. Influence of design conception—an illustration

The influence of design conception on the capital cost of a plant is well illustrated by examining in some detail the second example above, namely the production of a solid refuse-derived fuel (RDF) by dry physical separation of the waste. Distinction is made between 'American' RDF, in which the fuel product contains most of the organic materials, and the paper-rich product produced by most European processes (Chapters 14, 15). A typical flow-sheet for the production of an American RDF is shown in Fig. 5.2. A great many process variations have been proposed, and, as noted above, the range of capital costs is enormous.

An important study by Smith (1975) of the US Environmental Protection Agency attempted to clarify matters by producing normalized estimates for four independent designs. The plants were standardized to the basic flowsheet shown in Fig. 5.2, with the addition of hand picking of paper from

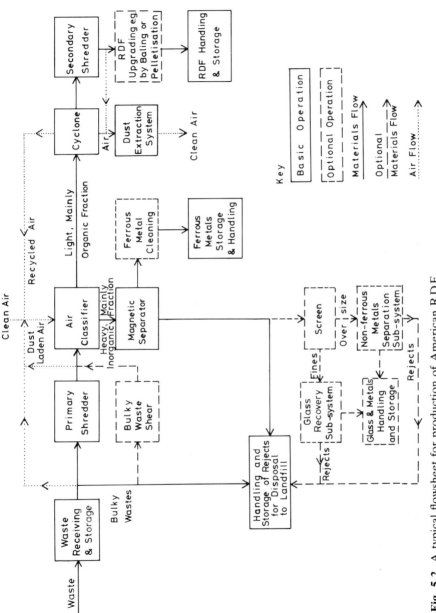

Fig. 5.2. A typical flowsheet for production of American RDF.

the conveyor belt feeding the primary shredder. The products were thus hand-picked paper, American RDF, and ferrous metals. The normalized capital costs, corrected for factors specific to the site and for some assumptions made in the estimation, still show considerable variation (see Table 15.2). The largest difference in direct costs was $6.2 million (Jan. 1974) between the General Electric Company (GEC) and National Center for Resource Recovery (NCRR) designs, and this may be explained largely in terms of different design conceptions for essentially the same process requirements. Major differences may arise from:

(i) The number of process lines. A number of duplicate lines give greater plant reliability. When spare lines or capacity are provided, the plant is said to possess redundancy. Some redundancy is required to cope with plant down-time, and to accommodate daily and seasonal changes in waste output and a growth in waste production through time. The amount of redundancy provided has a critical effect on capital cost, with an additional process line in the GEC design accounting for $3–4 million of the cost difference.

(ii) Variations in handling and storage facilities for the incoming waste. The waste may be tipped onto a concrete floor from which it is moved to conveyors by a front-end loader, it may be tipped directly onto an underground conveyor, or it may be tipped into an underground bunker from which it is removed by overhead crane. If weekend or year-round working is required, sufficient storage must be available to cope with holiday periods when no waste is collected. Storage for 2–4 days is thus required (Scott and Holmes 1974). The provision of overhead cranes and an underground bunker with 2 days capacity added $1 million to the GEC design relative to that of the NCRR.

(iii) Product storage facilities. The GEC design incorporates two live-bottom silos for RDF storage, at a cost of over $1 million, while the NCRR design makes no such provision. Some interruption in delivery of products to their users must be expected, and a minimum capacity of one day's output is probably necessary.

(iv) Building design. The GEC design uses one large two-storey factory, while the NCRR use a number of small single storey buildings with only half the total floor space, giving a cost saving of around $1 million.

5.4.2. Differences in operating standards

The capital investment to meet air emission standards is large, and the consequences of over-optimism in the equipment performance. can be serious. Similarly, standards of dust-extraction and noise suppression vary widely. In addition, if a plant is designed for remote handling of solid waste, the increased capital costs are substantial. For example, a transfer station may simply involve loading the waste from a concrete pad into open vehicles with a front-end loader, or it may be a fully enclosed operation in which the waste is tipped directly onto conveyors, from which it is loaded by compactors into enclosed containers. The more sophisticated plant might cost about ten times as much as the simple operation.

5.4.3. Costs specific to a site

Comparison of capital estimates is complicated further by significant local variations in land, site preparation, and construction costs. Land is sometimes included and sometimes excluded, often entering the operating cost as a lease payment. Site preparation may require new access facilities, special foundations, or the demolition of existing structures. The effects of such variations on capital costs are best documented for landfill sites, where additional site works may include site grading, the diversion of surface waters, or the installation of liners and leachate collection systems to protect groundwater supplies from possible contamination (Chapter 11). In the USA, regional differentials in construction costs may give direct capital costs of 75–115 per cent of the national average (Smith 1975).

5.4.4. Cost estimating procedures

Capital cost estimation is well documented in the chemical engineering literature (Peters and Timmerhaus 1968; Miller 1973; Holland, Watson, and Wilkinson 1974; Institution of Chemical Engineers 1977). Most methods use correlations with historical data. Since there has been little prior experience with waste processing, such correlations must be used with care. The largest class of procedures begin with an estimate of the delivered equipment cost (DEC) and apply multiplying factors to obtain the total fixed cost, C_{FC}, of the plant. The simplest example uses a single factor, f_L, termed the Lang factor, for the complete plant (Lang 1948):

$$C_{FC} = f_L \, (\text{DEC}) \qquad (5.3)$$

Lang factors vary between plants, but typical values for the chemical industry are 3.10 for solids processing, 3.63 for mixed solids–fluids processing and 4.74 for fluid processing (Holland *et al.* 1974).

A rather more sophisticated method breaks the Lang factor into a number of other factors φ_1, φ_2, φ_3, so that:

$$C_{FC} = \varphi_1 \varphi_2 \varphi_3 \, (\text{DEC}) \qquad (5.4)$$

where φ_1 is the installation factor, φ_2 the direct cost factor (which may be broken down further as the sum of factors for process piping, instrumentation, building, utilities, and services), and φ_3 the indirect cost factor, which is the sum of factors for architectural and engineering fees, contractors' overheads, and contingency (Holland *et al.* 1974). This method is typical of that currently used in estimation for waste processing plant. Variations may involve direct estimation of some components and use of the above factors for others.

5.4.5. Potential pitfalls in capital cost estimation

It is instructive to examine some of the problems which may be encountered in practice. For illustration, reference is made to the paper of Stuckenbruck and King (1977), who examined the economics of two resource recovery options. One is an American R D F system, similar to that in Fig. 5.2, which reclaims both aluminium and other non-ferrous metals; the other is a high-temperature gasification (pyrolysis) system based on the Union Carbide Purox process, in which the heat for the reaction is provided by the combustion of some of the waste in pure oxygen, the product being a medium heating value gas.

(i) The scale of operation specified for a plant must be realistic. The R D F plant used as a model by Stuckenbruck and King is that at Ames, Iowa (Funk and Chantland 1975; Joensen, Hall, and Hove 1976; Joensen, Even, Hall, van Meter, and Olexsey 1979), where a single process line rated at 50 short tons per hour is used to treat 200 tons per day, 5 days per week. They assume that such a plant is capable of treating waste at its maximum capacity for a full 16 hours per 2-shift day, 7 days per week. No redundancy is allowed, nor is additional storage capacity provided for either the input waste or the product R D F.

(ii) The direct equipment cost is estimated from a list of equipment requirements and care is required to avoid the omission of significant items. For example, non-ferrous metal sorting for each of the processes costed by Stuckenbruck and King appears only as a trommel screen, with the necessary eddy-current separators (Joensen *et al.* 1976) omitted from the equipment lists. In addition, all equipment not specifically mentioned is listed as miscellaneous equipment, at a total cost of \$20–25 000. This includes motors, dust hoods, piping, controls, and control panels, each of which is a significant item of expenditure. For example, dust extraction equipment, which is now standard on transfer stations and pulverizers in Britain, will certainly be needed for the discharge from an air classifier. A single unit rated at 50 000 ft³ (1400 m³) per minute costs about £50 000. It is more than coincidence that the Ames plant encountered dust control problems, and in fact dust extractors have now been fitted (Joensen *et al.* 1979).

(iii) Significant sections of a plant are often offered on a turnkey basis by the manufacturer, and as cost estimates are only available from him, one should be wary of optimistic claims. An example is provided by the Union Carbide process, for which capital cost estimates, quoted by the company and used in different studies, increased from \$13 million in November

1972 to \$38 million in January 1976 (after correcting for inflation; see Table 18.2). This vast increase was presumably because development work revealed problems not allowed for in earlier estimates.

(iv) The factors used for equipment installation, φ_1, and for the other components of the direct plant cost, φ_2, should conform to standard practice, and major deviations should be justified explicitly. Standard chemical engineering factors are given in Table 5.2, together with those used in waste processing. The factors implied by Stuckenbruck and King are rather low. Further work is required to derive factors specific to waste processing.

(v) The indirect cost factors, φ_3, should similarly conform to standard practice. In Table 5.3, factors used in chemical engineering and waste processing are compared. The range is large and can lead to significant variations in total cost estimates. The sum of indirect cost factors used by Stuckenbruck and King is in the middle of the range, but the contingency is high at 19 per cent. The latter should be used to cover unpredictable items of cost not known at the time of the estimate, such as replacement of components which fail under testing, and *not* as an allowance for error in the estimate (Bauman 1964).

(vi) Non-plant capital costs, including working capital and start-up costs, are usually estimated as factors on the annual operating cost. Factors used for resource recovery plant are shown in Table 5.3; it is seen that those used by Stuckenbruck and King are much lower than the 4 months' operating costs recommended by Smith (1975), or the 6–8 months recommended by Schroeder and Fabuss (1978).

(vii) The basis on which the costs are estimated must be stated clearly. The estimate may be for the battery limit, including only those facilities directly involved in converting the raw material or solid waste to finished product, or it may include an element for the provision of utilities, services, and storage and handling facilities (Miller 1973). The total plant cost may be appropriate to a new or green-field site, or to an already developed site. For chemical plant, a green-field estimate will be about 40 per cent more than a battery-limit estimate (Bridgwater 1974). In most waste processing work the basis of the estimate is not made clear. Those of Stuckenbruck and King are stated to be on a green-field basis, but the R D F plant is based on the Ames plant which was built on a developed site adjacent to the municipal power station. No allowance was made for site development, access roads, administrative facilities, or electrical transformers and substations.

It is thus seen that there are several inconsistencies in the estimates of Stuckenbruck and King (1977). In Table 5.4 their estimate for the RDF plant is recalculated, giving a revised cost more than double the original. The capital cost of \$17 million is a battery-limit estimate, with storage and

Table 5.2

Components of the direct plant costs.

As factors on the delivered or installed equipment cost. The direct plant cost is given by $C_{DC} = \varphi_1\,\varphi_1\,DEC$, where

$$\varphi_2 = 1 + \sum_{i=1}^{5} f_i \qquad \text{(after equation 5.4)}$$

Component	Symbol in equation 5.4	Chemical engineering Chilton (1949); Holland et al. (1974)		Waste processing		Schulz et al. 1976[e]
				Stuckenbruck and King 1977		
		Condition	Factor	RDF plant	Pyrolysis plant	Pyrolysis plant
Installation	φ_1	Solids processing	1.45	0.04	0.07	Not available
		Mixed solids – fluid processing	1.39			
Process piping	f_1	Solids processing	0.07–0.10	a	a	0.40
		Mixed solids – fluid processing	0.10–0.30			
		Fluid processing	0.30–0.60			
Instrumentation	f_2	Little ⎰	0.02–0.05	a	a	0.20
		Some ⎱ automatic control	0.05–0.10			
		Complex ⎰	0.10–0.15			
Building[b]	f_3	Outdoor units	0.05–0.20	0.53	0.23	0.43
		Mixed indoor and outdoor units	0.20–0.60			
		Indoor units	0.60–1.00			
Utilities[c]	f_4	Minor additions	0–0.05	0	0	0.25
		Major additions	0.05–0.25			
		New site	0.25–1.00			
Services[d]	f_5	Existing plant	0–0.05	0.01	0.008	0.004
		Separated units	0.05–0.15			
		Scattered units	0.15–0.25			

(a) Included in miscellaneous equipment cost, implied factor is effectively zero.
(b) Building costs defined to include all services, including electrical, within the building (Chilton 1949).
(c) Including substation and transformer costs.
(d) Services or outside lines includes all piping, electrical works, water, and sewers beyond battery limit.
(e) Occidental waste–to–oil pyrolysis process.

handling facilities included, for a plant rated at 720 t per 16-hour day, having a single process line and no redundancy. This corresponds to a current cost of £6.1 million for a 400 t per day plant (using a scale factor of 0.8 in equation 5.5), or about £5.4 million if non-ferrous separation is omitted. This estimate is still within the range quoted above, which had a mean of £3.8 million and a standard deviation of £1.7 million.

Table 5.3

Indirect and non-plant capital cost factors.

The fixed plant cost of a plant, C_{FC}, is given by $C_{FC} = \varphi_3 C_{DC}$ where C_{DC} is the direct plant cost (Table 5.2), and $\varphi_3 = 1 + f_1 + f_2 + f_3$. The factors are expressed as a percentage of C_{DC}.

	Component	Symbol	Chemical engineering				Waste processing			
			Chilton 1949 / Holland et al. 1974	Haselbarth and Berk 1960	Midwest Research Institute 1973 Original	Midwest Research Institute 1973 Corrected[2]	Smith 1975	Stuckenbruck and King 1977	Schulz et al. 1976	Schroeder and Fabuss 1978
Indirect capital costs	Architectural and engineering fees	f_1	Straightforward plant 25–35%	6–12%	12%	28%	6.5–8.0%	5%	21%	7.5%
	Contractors overheads	f_2	Complex plant 35–50%				around 25%	10%		7%
	Contingency	f_3	Firm process 10–20%	7–14%	–	–	8–15%	19%	15%	10%
			Process subject to change 20–30%							
	Total	φ_3	30–80%	13–26%	12%	28%	39–48%	34% (RDF / Pyrolysis)	36%	25%
Non-plant capital costs[1]	Working capital		–	–	17%			RDF 5.1% / Pyrolysis 5.6%		3%
	Start-up		–	–	25%			RDF 2.6% / Pyrolysis 1.1%		20%
	Total		–	–	42%	51%	33%	RDF 7.7% / Pyrolysis 6.7%	not available	23%

1. The total capital cost C_T is given by $C_T = C_{FC} + C_{NPC}$, where C_{NPC} is the non-plant capital cost, the sum of working capital and start-up costs. Each of these is expressed as a percentage of the annual operating costs.
2. Corrected for the effect of using different interest rates for various cost categories.

Table 5.4
Revised capital cost estimate for an RDF plant.
The estimate made by Stuckenbruck and King (1977) is reworked, correcting for the inconsistencies discussed in Section 5.4.5. Costs are appropriate to a 720 t.p.d. plant in January 1976.

Item	Original estimate ($ thousand)	Basis for revised estimate	Revised estimate ($ thousand)
Processing equipment:			
(a) Shredders, air classifier, magnetic separators, conveyors, fans, and surge bins	1550	As original	1550
(b) Non-ferrous separation subsystem	25	Three eddy-current separators added (Joensen *et al.* 1976)	480[a]
(c) Miscellaneous equipment	25	Two dust control units added	150
Product handling:			
(a) Storage bin for product RDF	700	Capacity increased three-fold[b]	1690
(b) Pneumatic pipeline for RDF	155	Replace with baler and transfer handling facilities	100
Waste reception equipment	600	Overhead crane replaced by front-end loaders[c]	250
Maintenance equipment	15	As original	15
Delivered equipment cost (DEC)	3110		4230
Equipment installation	115	0.45 DEC[d]	1910
Installed equipment cost (IEC)	3225		6140
Building	1700	0.80 IEC[d]	4910
Process-piping	–	0.07 IEC[d]	430
Instrumentation	–	0.05 IEC[d]	310
Utilities	–	0.00[d]	–
Services	30	0.00[d]	–
Direct plant cost (DPC)	4955		11800
Mobile equipment	40	Includes two front-end loaders[c]	120
Indirect plant costs	1675	0.30 DPC[e]	3540
Working capital	200	} 4 months' operating costs[f]	1400
Start-up costs	100		
Land	200	Not included	–
Total capital cost	7130		16900

(a) Based on Cummings (1976) who estimated an equipment cost of $2 million for 2000 short tons per day, including glass separation. Correction assumes that 50 per cent of cost is attributable to non-ferrous metals, and uses equation 5.5 with scale factor $S = 0.8$. The estimate of $480\,000 may be compared with the $220\,000 (assuming $\varphi_1 = 1.45$) for a single aluminium separator without ancillary equipment (Schulz *et al.* 1976).
(b) Product storage capacity increased from 500 to 1500 short tons, i.e. more than 2 days' capacity, using $S = 0.8$.
(c) Waste reception assumed to be on a concrete pad, with transfer of waste to conveyors by front-end loaders.
(d) Direct plant cost factors estimated from Table 5.2. The building factor is quite high to allow for storage of untreated waste. Utilities and services are not included as the estimate is for the battery limit (including storage and handling facilities).
(e) Indirect cost factor taken from middle of range in Table 5.3, assuming a low contingency factor.
(f) Non plant costs normalized at level suggested by Smith (Table 5.3). Operating cost taken from Table 5.7.

5.4.6. Alternative methods of capital cost estimation

The preceding discussion has indicated a possible bias in published estimates of the capital costs of waste processing plants. For the purpose of comparative evaluation one may ask if there is a feasible alternative to using literature estimates.

There are several rapid methods, termed 'analogous methods', available for estimating the direct equipment cost, and these have been reviewed and improved by Allen and Page (1975). However, all of the techniques rely on correlations with historical costs for similar plant, information which is not currently available for waste processing.

An alternative rapid estimation method is the functional unit approach, developed for solid or liquid–solid processes by Bridgwater (1974). The process is split up into significant steps or functional units. The total, green-field site, capital cost is obtained from the average cost of a functional unit multiplied by the numer of such units. The method has been proposed for use in preliminary evaluation work on solid waste recovery systems (Bridgwater 1976/7). However, its value lies primarily in the comparison of processes, particularly at an early stage of development, rather than in making absolute estimates.

5.4.7. Economies of scale in capital costs

Capital cost estimates are seldom available for the exact size of plant being considered for a particular area, and thus a correction must be applied. Economies of scale are expected in the capital costs of most engineering plant. The relationship commonly postulated (e.g. Miller 1973; Holland, Watson, and Wilkinson 1974) between the costs of two plants A and B, with costs C_A and C_B and capacities W_A and W_B, respectively, is

$$\frac{C_A}{C_B} = \left(\frac{W_A}{W_B}\right)^S \qquad (5.5)$$

where S is termed the scale factor. This may be rewritten:

$$\ln C = \ln a + S \ln W \qquad (5.6)$$

where a is a constant.

Evidence for economies of scale in waste treatment or reclamation processes is lacking, most published factors being hypothetical estimates. A six-tenths power law ($S = 0.6$) is often quoted in chemical engineering, but this is mainly appropriate to gas-phase processes; an eight-tenths power law ($S = 0.8$) is more appropriate to solids-handling processes (A. V. Bridgwater, private communication 1977), and thus can be applied as a guide in waste management until such time as better information becomes available.

The use of low scale factors ($S = 0.6 - 0.7$) is a major cause for scepticism in some cost estimates for proposed waste treatment or reclamation processes.

It should be noted that S is in fact not strictly constant in value. The derivative $\{d(\ln C)/d(\ln W)\}$ increases with increasing plant capacity (Miller 1973), so that the use of S to predict costs at a capacity far removed from the original estimate may introduce considerable error.

Available information on economies of scale in waste processing is summarized in Table 5.5. Most of these factors are hypothetical estimates, rather than reflecting a statistical analysis of existing plants. Bridgwater (1977) draws heavily on the work both of the present author and of the Midwest Research Institute (1973); the latter derived their factors from those appropriate to individual unit operations, mainly in conventional applications to materials other than waste. The scale factors suggested by the present author in Table 5.5 were derived from the best available information for each process, and are fully documented in Part II. It should be noted that the scale factors for all processes tend to 1.0 for high capacities, where increases in capacity are achieved more by adding additional process lines than by expanding existing lines.

Table 5.5

Scale factors for waste processing plants

Process	Midwest Research Institute 1973	Schulz et al. 1976	Bridgwater 1977	This work (Part II)
Landfill	0.93	–	0.93	0.8
Transfer	0.93	–	–	0.85
Pulverization	–	–	–	0.85
Baling	–	–	–	0.9
Incineration: high capacity	0.78	0.65	0.9–0.95[a]	0.95[a]
low capacity			0.78	–
Modular incineration	–	–	–	1.0
Composting: high capacity	0.65	–	0.95[b]	0.95[b]
low capacity			0.65	0.65
RDF production	0.70	0.60	0.70	0.8
Suspension firing of RDF	–	–	–	0.9
Incinerator turbine	–	0.70	–	0.9
Wet pulping	0.72	0.75	–	0.9
Pyrolysis and other thermal processes:	0.78		0.78	
Occidental		0.60		0.7
Union Carbide		0.80		0.8
Andco-Torrax		0.75		0.75–0.8
Monsanto		0.60		0.7
Acid hydrolysis	–	–	–	0.8
Anaerobic digestion	–	0.60	–	0.9

(a) Critical capacity for the changeover about 10 t.p.h.
(b) Critical capacity about 450 t.p.d.

An interesting test of economies of scale in waste processing is provided by data on incinerators built in Britain during the period 1966–77 (Section 13.5). A plot of ln C versus ln W is shown in Fig. 5.3. Plants practising either energy recovery or combustion of both waste and sewage sludge are excluded. Regression analysis for all 28 plants gave $1.04 < S < 1.09$, with coefficients of determination $0.82 < R^2 < 0.92$, the variation depending on the treatment of those outliers with markedly different costs. For the regression line (1) shown in Fig. 5.3, the 95 per cent confidence interval for S is 1.05 ± 0.17. When plants with a single process line are analysed separately, the regression gives $S = 0.74$ and $R^2 = 0.52$ if the negative outlier, Bolton, is included, but $S = 1.04$ and $R^2 = 0.67$ if it is excluded. From these results a relatively high scale factor for incineration is suggested, say $S = 0.95$, but this should not be used to extrapolate costs below a capacity of about 10 tonnes per hour.

5.5. Operating cost estimates

5.5.1. The operating schedule

The comparison of operating costs for different plants requires the use of a common operating schedule. There could be 1–3 shifts per day, operation might be over 5–7 days per week, and year-round operation may be specified. As waste delivery will normally be restricted to 40 hours per week or less, care must be taken to distinguish between plant capacity as tonnes per day delivered and as tonnes per day processed. The reliability of operation is often expressed as the percentage of design capacity achievable over an extended period. Reliability will be increased by having parallel process lines or by allowing redundancy in the design.

The work of Stuckenbruck and King (1977) illustrates possible difficulties with the determination of operating schedules. For both the plants studied, RDF and gasification, 2-shift (16 hours per day) working is specified, with the third shift for maintenance, even though it is known that the gasification reactor must run continuously. Plant relaibility is stated to exceed 85 per cent during operating shifts, yet availability at full design capacity is assumed for 365 days per year for RDF, and for 328.5 days per year (90 per cent) for the gasification plant. The labour requirements are for 2-shift working, but clearly each shift will not work 7 days per week.

5.5.2. Estimation procedures

The estimation of operating costs at an early stage of planning has tended to receive less attention than capital cost estimation. If sufficient experience of similar operations in the past is available, then there is little problem. However, this is unlikely to be the case for a waste processing plant.

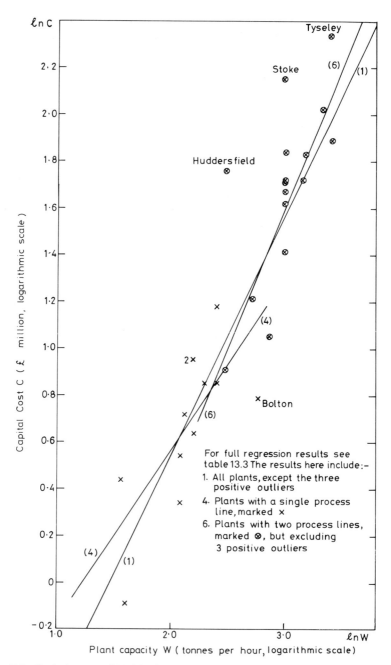

Fig. 5.3. Capital costs of UK incinerators.

A simple method of rapid estimation of operating costs has been suggested by several authors in the chemical engineering literature (Bridgwater 1976). This is a factor method, relating the component costs to certain basic variables which are estimated directly. The basic variables are:

Raw material costs, R;

Energy costs, E;

Direct labour costs, L;

Capital costs, I;

Product sales revenue, S_r.

In Table 5.6, the range of operating cost factors generally appropriate in chemical engineering are indicated, together with those suggested here as appropriate to waste processing and those used in a representative sample of applied studies.

The cost categories (a)–(e) in Table 5.6 show a measure of agreement. The raw materials cost is taken to be zero for most solid waste treatment or recovery processes but exceptions do occur. A wide range is reported for the maintenance cost (f). A sample of 40 factors, implied by cost data for waste processing, lay between $0.003\,I$ and $0.11\,I$, with a mean value of $0.041\,I$ and a standard deviation of $0.025\,I$. Part of this variability is due to accounting practice, with labour for maintenance often being included in the direct labour cost. Variations are to be expected from process to process; one study gives factors ranging from $0.027\,I$ to $0.06\,I$ with a mean of $0.038\,I$ (Schulz, Benziger, Bortz, Neamatalla, Szostak, Tong, and Westerhoff 1976). Nevertheless, over-optimistic maintenance costs are a major source of doubt in published estimates. A factor of $0.08\,I$ is suggested for a typical treatment or resource recovery process at moderate utilization rates. Further work is required to relate it to the reliability of specific unit operations, to particular processes, and to plant utilization. Indeed, a direct link of maintenance cost to the investment I may be misleading, since investment is often increased specifically to reduce maintenance costs.

The indirect cost factors, rates (l), insurance (m), overheads and administration (n), and sales expenses (q), are ignored or estimated with low values in most studies. Such an approach may be thought appropriate for facilities operated by local authorities, but the inclusion of all the attributable costs is good practice. Laboratory, royalty, and research costs should be included if appropriate; they are excluded here to simplify the discussion. Contingency on both direct and indirect costs allows for errors and omissions in the estimate. When uncertainty is being considered explicitly, the inclusion of contingency in a comparative evaluation is debatable and it is omitted here. The one significant operating cost not included by Bridgwater is for handling and disposing of the residual waste materials. This cost, denoted as residuals disposal cost D, is best estimated directly. A simple expedient is to assume a constant cost per tonne of residue or input waste.

Table 5.6
Operating cost factors

| | Source | | | | | | |
| | Chemical engineering Bridgwater 1976 | | Waste processing | | | | |
Component	Typical	Range	Systems Technology Corporation 1975	Bechtel Corporation 1975	Fairfield-Hardy (General Electric Company 1973a)	Schulz et al. 1976	'Typical' factors suggested here
Direct costs							
(a) Raw materials	R		0	0	0	0	R
(b) Energy	E		E	E	E	E	E
(c) Labour	L		L	L	L	L	L
(d) Supervision	0.2 L	0.1–0.25	0.08–0.12 {(c)+(e)}	0.15	0.12	*	0.2
(e) Payroll charge	0.25 {(c)+(d)}	0.15–0.5	*	0.30	0.22	0.25	0.4 (0.3 in U.S.A.)
(f) Maintenance	0.06 I	0.02–0.15	0.053	0.06	0.014	0.027 −0.06	0.08 (variable)
(g) Operating supplies	0.0075 I	0.005–0.01	0.004	—†	0.005	0.002 −0.014	0.008
Indirect costs							
(h) Laboratory	0.12 L	0.03–0.2	—	—	—	—	‡
(j) Royalty	0.05 {(a) to (j)}	0–0.06 S,	—	—	—	—	‡
(k) Contingency		0.01–0.10	—	—	0.15 (a) to (j) +0.015 I	—	0
(l) Rates	0.03 I	0.02–0.04	0.009	0.02	—	—	0.03
(m) Insurance	0.01 I	0.004–0.02		0.75 L +0.015 I	0.003	0.01	0.01
(n) Overhead/ administration	0.5 L+	0.4–0.8 L+	—	—	included in (k) and (r)	—	0.4 L +0.01 I
(p) Research	0.02 I	0.01–0.04 I 0.015–0.055	—	—	—	—	‡
(q) Distribution/selling	0.03 S,	0.02–0.22	—	—	0.03	—	0.1
(r) Contingency	0.1 S,	0.01–0.05	—	—	0.15	—	0
(s) Other costs	0.03 {(l) to (m)}	—	D	—	miscellaneous 0.009 I	D	D
Sum of factors to give an estimating equation	1.05 (R+E) +2.26 L +0.132 I +0.13 S,	—	E +1.43 L +0.066 I +D	E +2.25 L +0.095 I	1.15 E +1.57 L +0.049 I +0.03 S,	E 1.50 L +(0.039– 0.084) I +D	R+E +2.08 L +0.138 I +0.1 S, +D

* Included under L.
† A dash indicates that the item is not included in the operating cost estimate.
‡ Laboratory, royalty, and research costs should be included for those technologies where they are necessary. In many cases a value of zero will be appropriate, but laboratory facilities will be required for process control in more sophisticated reclamation plants. A value of zero is assumed in all

When the typical waste processing factors in Table 5.6 are summed, the operating cost C is given by:

$$C = R + E + 2.08L + 0.138\, I + 0.1S_r + D \qquad (5.7)$$

If the investment I has already been estimated, the major difficulty in using this equation lies in the estimation of L and E. Some data on manpower and energy usage are available for most systems (see Part II). In the absence of other information, Bridgwater (1976) provides general correlations for L and, with less confidence, for E, based on the functional unit approach. Estimation of S_r is discussed later.

The approach is illustrated in Table 5.7, which compares the operating cost estimates of Stuckenbruck and King (1977) for an RDF and a high-temperature gasification process, with revised estimates obtained by using the factors in Table 5.6. The inclusion of the indirect costs increases the revised estimate for the RDF plant by around 30 per cent. This estimate would be yet higher if a more realistic figure for capital investment was used. The absolute difference of the estimates is much greater for the gasification plant, due both to the higher investment and to an inconsistency in the maintenance costs quoted by Stuckenbruck and King. The basis they state is 15 per cent of capital equipment cost. The RDF value is 15 per cent of the direct, or 10 per cent of the total, capital cost. The gasification plant maintenance cost is on a pro rata basis of $2.50/ton of waste as calculated for the RDF plant. This represents only 2.1 per cent of the direct, or 1.5 per cent of the total, capital cost. At 15 per cent of direct capital, the annual maintenance cost would be around $6 million, while the revised estimate at 8 per cent of total capital is $4.3 million, each of which is much higher than the $800 000 used.

The conclusion from this discussion must be that most literature values for operating costs are rather optimistic. The method shown here produces quick and consistent estimates to use in a comparative evaluation of resource recovery and waste treatment or disposal systems. Confidence in the absolute estimates will increase with further experience and research.

5.5.3. Economies of scale

Economies of scale in operating costs are less well documented than for capital costs. Of the terms in equation 5.7, $R, E, S_r,$ and D are all directly proportional to the plant throughput, while L and I are assumed to be unchanging for a plant of given design capacity. Thus increasing plant utilization will reduce the specific operating cost, although this may be offset in part by increases in both L and in other costs such as maintenance. For plants of different design capacity, economies of scale are expected in L and I, and perhaps in E. Scale factors for L may be as low as 0.13 (Bridgwater 1976), while for $E, S_r,$ and D scale factors are about 1. In practice the term in

Table 5.7

Operating cost estimates for an RDF and a gasification plant.

The annual estimates made by Stuckenbruck and King (1977) are compared with revised estimates. obtained by applying the factors in Table 5.6 to the same input data for investment, number of men, electricity usage, product sales value, and residual disposal costs. Costs refer to January 1976

Plant type	Refuse-derived fuel	Gasification (Union Carbide Purox process)
Capacity	800 short tons per day	1000 short tons per day
Operating schedule	365 days per year	328.5 days per year
Investment, I	$7 130 000	$54 110 000
Labour force	50 men	75 men
Electricity usage	150 kWh per ton	175 kWh per ton
Produce sales value, S_r	$3 066 000 per annum	$6 110 000 per annum

	Refuse-derived fuel				Gasification (Union Carbide Purox process)			
	Original basis		Revised estimate		Original basis		Revised estimate	
Cost category	Factor	Cost ($ thousand)	Factor	Cost ($ thousand)	Factor	Cost ($ thousand)	Factor	Cost ($ thousand)
(b) Electricity $\;E$	3¢ per kWh	1310	3¢ per kWh	1310	3¢ per kWh	1730	3¢ per kWh	1730
Other utilities	–	–	10% elec.	130	–	–	10% elec.	170
(c) Labour L	$19 000 per man inclusive	950	*	950	$19 000 per man inclusive	1430	*	1430
(d) Supervision								
(e) Payroll								
(f) Maintenance	0.102 I	730	0.08 I	570	0.0154 I	820	0.08 I	4330
(g) Operating supplies	–	–	0.008 I	60	–	–	0.008 I	430
(l) Rates	–	–	0.03 I	210	–	–	0.03 I	1620
(m) Insurance	–	–	0.01 I	70	–	–	0.01 I	540
(n) Overhead/administration	–	–	0.4L + 0.01 I	320	–	–	0.4L + 0.01 I	910
(q) Distribution/selling	–	–	0.1S_r	310	–	–	0.1S_r	610
(s) Residual disposal, D	1$ per input ton	290	1$ per input ton	290	1$ per input ton	330	1$ per input ton	330
Total operating cost	E +1.56L* +0.102 I +D	3300	E +1.96L* +0.138 I +0.1S_r +D	4200	E +1.56L* +0.0154 I +D	4300	E +1.96L* +0.138 I +0.1S_r +D	12100

* Assumes that original estimate includes supervision and payroll charges at the levels given in Table 5.6 for the USA

I is often dominant, so that a good approximation is to apply the same scale factor to both capital and operating costs. Economies of scale in plant operating costs do not mean that money can necessarily be saved by increasing plant throughput, either by building a large plant or increasing utilization of a present one, as diseconomies of scale, say in the cost of transportation due to enlarging the catchment area, must also be considered (Section 6.3).

5.6. Revenues

The economic evaluation may depend critically on the revenues from the sale of recovered products or on the benefits of land reclamation. Even small changes in the revenues may affect the choice of process. For resource recovery, one needs to know the composition of the local solid waste, the recovery efficiencies of the competing processes, and the prices obtainable. Estimates of each are uncertain and subject to change with time. The use of a single deterministic value for the revenue, that is constant over time, is a weakness in most evaluations. For land reclamation, information required includes the time lag between completion of the fill and the use of the reclaimed land, whether some land will be available for use before all filling is complete, and the nature of the use proposed.

Both daily and seasonal variations in municipal solid waste composition, and variations between localities and countries, were illustrated in Table 1.2. Significant differences are evident in values for paper, plastics, other organics, metals, and glass. Variations in metal, and particularly non-ferrous metal, content have a disproportionate effect on revenues through their comparatively high prices. The organic and moisture contents together determine the calorific value of the waste and hence the potential for energy recovery. Separation of paper at source might be expected to reduce this potential considerably. Work by the U S Environmental Protection Agency suggested that separation of 35 per cent of the paper might reduce the heat content of the waste by about 9 per cent (Lowe 1974), while calculations for a rural area of Belgium indicated that separation of 20 per cent of the paper and 60 per cent of the plastics would reduce it by about 20 per cent (Naveau and Binot 1975). In Britain, local authority schemes for separate collection of paper have usually resulted in a mean co-operation rate about 1 in 3, recovering 25 per cent of the total paper (Holmes 1975*a*). Thus in practice the effect is likely to be limited.

Reliable and consistent data for recovery efficiencies of specific waste components are particularly difficult to obtain. The information available on materials is summarized in Table 5.8, and typical values are suggested. These must be used with care as recovery efficiences vary between processes, and much of the recovery equipment is still under development.

Table 5.8
Recovery of materials

Product	Recovery efficiency[a] (% by weight)			Revenue[b] (£/t of product)	Amount in 1 t of waste[c] (kg)	Revenue (£/t of waste)
	Number of observations	Range of values	Typical value			
Ferrous metals	9	75–98	90[d]	12	76	0.82
after burning	1	56	56	10		0.43
Aluminium	5	57–85	70	200	5	0.70
after burning	–	–	50	200		0.50
Other non-ferrous metals	2	67, 100	70	400	1	0.28
Glass						
Mixed fines	3	70	70	8	90	0.50
Colour sorted	3	48–55	50	12		0.54
Aggregate	–	–	Variable	0	Variable	0
Paper						
Wet-pulped fibre	3	43–50	45	15	400	2.7
Dry sorted	4	60–80	60	15		3.6
Humus (compost)	8	30–70	40[e]	3	1000[f]	1.2
Ethanol (from acid hydrolysis)	–	–	5.7[g]	220	1000[f]	12.5

(a) See Table 14.2.
(b) Prices are ex-works and are documented in Table 10.4.
(c) Table 1.3.
(d) Secondary magnetic extraction from the inorganic residue raises this to 94 per cent.
(e) Section 19.2.
(f) Efficiency based on the complete waste stream.
(g) Section 19.3.

As the form of waste-derived fuels and their efficiency of production depend entirely on the process used, the data must be derived for each process.

The prices for any secondary material product are both unstable and dependent on the local market (Levy 1974). The products tend to be bulky and of low value, so transport to users constitutes a high proportion of the price. The role of secondary materials as a buffer against short-term fluctuations in demand has led to an unstable market for recovered products (Fig. 5.4). For waste paper this has been well documented by Turner and Grace (1977), who noted a slow long-term rise in demand overlain by a well-defined short-term variation related to the business cycle. The projection of prices for recovered materials is made more complex by the novel nature of many of the products, by the uncertain quality, and by uncertain acceptability to manufacturers (Sullivan and Makar 1976). Provisional specifications for typical products have been suggested (Alter and Reeves 1975).

Prices may not be closely related to those of materials used at present

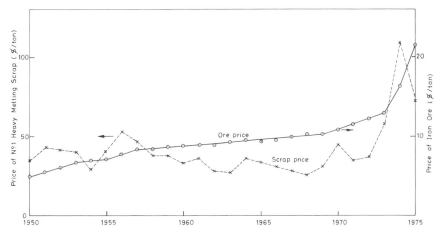

Fig. 5.4. Prices for iron ore and steel scrap in the USA.
Data taken from US Bureau of Mines, Minerals Yearbooks.

owing either to imperfect substitution or to prejudice. To take RDF as an example, its efficiency in use is less than that of coal, while new investment in RDF receiving and handling plant, increased ash handling requirements, and fears of corrosion or air emission problems each serve to reduce the price below the equivalent price of coal. Allegations of market bias against secondary materials have been substantiated in the USA, where both tax concessions and long distance freight rates favour virgin materials (US Environmental Protection Agency 1974; Goddard 1975; National Commission on Supplies and Shortages 1976; Sattin 1978). Thus, although the price of iron ore has risen steadily since 1950, steel scrap prices have fluctuated sharply with demand (Fig. 5.4). For some recovered products, current market potential is limited and new outlets are being sought, as for example the use of waste glass in aggregates (Liles 1976).

In Britain, the nationalized industries have a monopoly in the public supply of electricity or pipeline gas. Thus any electricity or gas which is surplus to requirements on-site must either be sold to them, or a royalty be paid in lieu. In the past, the Central Electricity Generating Board has only been willing to pay a price based on their marginal fuel savings rather than on the wholesale or the retail price. Unless this situation changes, prospects for gas or electricity generation from waste in Britain are poor.

It could be argued from these comments that the market price does not measure the true worth to society of a secondary product, and that a shadow price should be used instead. Recycling helps to conserve non-renewable resources, but there is debate as to whether such resources are being exploited too quickly or too slowly. The market imperfections introduce distortions in both directions (Pearce 1976). The combination of all the effects is complex, and all one can say is that, although it is likely that the market undervalues secondary materials, the evidence is not conclusive.

5.7. Economic data for the case study

The principles of economic analysis developed here are applied, in Chapter 7 and also in Part II, to a case study of some 30 options representing the current state of the art in waste disposal, treatment, reclamation, and resource recovery technology. The data used in, and the results from, the case study are summarized for convenience in Appendix A. Table A.1 summarizes the options included in the case study. In each case recovery from the inorganic fraction of the waste is restricted to magnetic metals. Additional materials recovery, of glass and non-ferrous metals, may be combined with many options. However, as such recovery is not essential to the process, it is viewed here as an incremental investment and analysed separately, three alternatives being considered.

The economic data on the processes were estimated, using the principles and framework developed here, from the literature. The assumptions required to apply the principles are outlined in Chapter 10; a few salient points are highlighted below. Full details of the data used and their derivation may be found in Part II; and cost and revenue data for each option are summarized in Tables A.2 and A.3.

The estimates were made for a plant with a design capacity of 400 t per day of waste delivery (100 000 t per annum). The expected rate of waste delivery is 300, with a range of ±40, t per day; the excess capacity provides for peak delivery rates and allows for any future increase in waste generation. Waste delivery is assumed to take place during a normal 40-hour week. Four alternative operating schedules are used, depending on the process:

    1-shift operation is used for landfill, and for most options with transfer or volume reduction prior to landfill;
    2-shift operation is specified for all waste separation plants;
    3-shift operation is used for incineration without heat recovery;
    4-shift continuous operation is specified for all high-temperature energy recovery processes or for biological processes.

Capital costs for a plant of appropriate size were estimated by analysis of historical costs and of previous estimates. Data on unit operations, or on equipment costs, are only rarely available. The assumptions made on design conception and operating standards are seldom stated explicitly, so that, for example, it is unclear how much redundancy is allowed or how many process lines are included in some of the estimates. Further uncertainty is introduced by the necessity to correct the cost estimates for inflation, to transfer costs between countries, and to adjust to a standard plant capacity. Particular care was taken in the estimation to ensure that the relative costs of different processes are of the correct order.

The resulting capital cost estimates are shown in Table A.2, together with suggested error ranges. These are expressed as

$$C = C_0 \overset{\times}{\div} (1+x) \tag{5.8}$$

where C_0 is the base cost. The notation indicates a range of costs

$$\frac{C_0}{(1+x)} \leq C \leq C_0(1+x) \tag{5.9}$$

and is becoming the accepted way of expressing the accuracy of a cost estimate, replacing the conventional $\pm 100x$ per cent. The disadvantage of the conventional method is that it implies that equal under- and over-estimates have the same significance. However, there is no limit to an over-estimate, while the limit to an under-estimate is zero since a negative value is meaningless. The actual error range is thus -100 per cent to $+\infty$ per cent. If these extremes are regarded as having equal significance, it follows that an under-estimate of $(1 + x)$ times should be of equal significance to an over-estimate of $(1 + x)$ times, as expressed in equations 5.8 and 5.9. For example, an error of -50 per cent means the estimate is one-half the actual value ($x = 1$). The equivalent positive error is twice the actual value i.e. $+100x$ per cent (100 per cent).

The standard error range for capital costs is estimated at $\overset{\times}{\div} 1.4$, i.e. $+ 40$ per cent to $- 29$ per cent. In some cases this may well be optimistic, but it is the sort of accuracy which might be expected from the order-of-magnitude estimation methods used here. With more experience of actual plants and more detailed information on the costs of particular pieces of equipment and on costs specific to a site, the error range at a pre-design planning stage may be reduced to the $\overset{\times}{\div} 1.25$ ($+ 25$ per cent to $- 20$ per cent) commonly specified in the chemical industry (Allen and Page 1975). It is interesting to compare this standard error of $\overset{\times}{\div} 1.4$ with the observed ranges of costs for convention-al waste disposal plant. For incineration, the regression results summarized in Fig. 5.3 gave the 95 per cent confidence interval on the cost of a 20 t per hour plant as £4.8 $\pm$ 0.5 million, corresponding to about $\overset{\times}{\div} 1.12$. However, for the broad cost envelope identified in Fig. 13.7, an error range of $\overset{\times}{\div} 1.35$ is indicated. In this case, estimation to $\overset{\times}{\div} 1.25$ seems plausible. For the three other conventional disposal methods, namely landfill, transfer, and pulver-ization, the observed costs show a very wide range. For example, corrected esimates for pulverization plants ranged from £0.3 to over £3 million. This variation stems from all the points discussed earlier, with major differences in design conception, operating standards and costs specific to the site. As the plants are relatively inexpensive, the costs of amenity facilities, dust control, and improved insulation to suppress noise may represent a large fraction of the total cost and be regarded as unnecessary frills. For landfill, the major cost is site preparation, which depends entirely on the specific site. To encompass the observed range of costs, an error range of $\times \atop \div$ 2.0 (+ 100 per cent to − 50 per cent) is used here. In any particular study, specification of plant requirements and site conditions will enable this range to be reduced.

Operating costs were estimated using the framework of Section 5.5. The factors used were the typical values suggested in Table 5.6, with the exception of the maintenance factor which was estimated for each process using a standard factor of 0.08 I as the guide. Raw materials costs per tonne of waste were estimated directly in the few cases where they could not be subsumed under operating supplies. Specific energy usage, as kilowatt-hours of electricity and gigajoules of fuel per tonne, was also estimated directly, the availability of information being quite good. Direct labour requirements were estimated for each case on a shift basis, with base-line values about 4 day–men for waste reception and associated tasks, 5 men per shift for separation, and 5 per shift for processing. The quantity of residue remaining for disposal is estimated directly, while the specific costs are based on a percentage of those for untreated waste landfill, plus a transport cost (Section 7.2). For each of these components of the operating costs, an accuracy of $\times \atop \div$ 1.25 is estimated.

Revenues from resource recovery are based on a waste of standard composition and calorific value (Table 1.3), with an error range of ± 10 per cent on any component. For materials, the generalized recovery efficiencies and prices of Table 5.8 are used, while the extent of recovery among the options is shown in Table A.3. For recovery of energy, the form of the fuel and its production efficiency, as the ratio of its heat content to that in the waste, are also given in Table A.3. Note that for steam production, a load factor of 75 per cent is assumed, i.e. only 75 per cent of the steam produced is actually sold. Revenues are based on the energy-specific value of the fuel displaced, discounted to allow for the additional costs of transporting, storing, and handling the waste-derived fuel (Chapter 8). The relative values used for each option are shown in Table A.3. Accuracies on the recovery efficiences are estimated at ± 5–30 per cent, the lower accuracies applying to steam and electricity production, while for the prices a range of ± 20 per cent is used.

5.8. Discussion

Much has been written on the economics of alternative processes for waste treatment, reclamation, and disposal, but the results are often difficult to compare or to use in waste management planning. The principles of sound economic evaluation have been outlined here, and a number of conventions suggested which should help to remedy this situation. These conventions may be summarized as:

(1) The purpose for which a cost estimate is derived should be clearly stated.

(2) Discounted cash flow (D C F) techniques should be used as the method of economic evaluation where the estimate is to be used in planning. Results should be presented for a range of discount rates.

(3) A standard approach to capital cost estimation should be used. This should be based on careful documentation and the use of agreed procedures as detailed below. Further research on some aspects is required.

(i) The process flowsheet should be set out in detail. Estimates should be presented for unit operations or significant process steps, so that standardization may be achieved for comparative purposes.

(ii) The design concepts and operating standards for a particular plant should be stated explicitly. While uniformity is not possible, a detailed breakdown of the estimate will allow easier comparison of options.

(iii) Estimates should be presented for a series of alternative plant operating schedules, each having associated with it an appropriate degree of redundancy and number of process lines, and an adequate storage capacity for both the input refuse and output products.

(iv) Costs specific to the site should be clearly identified so that a correction may be applied if general use is to be made of the estimate.

(v) It should be clearly stated whether the estimate assumes an already developed industrial site ('battery-limit' estimate) or a new, 'greenfield', site.

(vi) The method of cost estimation should be clearly documented and the factors used for direct and indirect costs should be stated, any deviation from 'standard' factors being carefully justified.

(4) Correction of cost estimates to the capacity of plant required should use a scale factor appropriate to the particular process. In the absence of evidence to the contrary, guidance may be taken from an eight-tenths power rule.

(5) A common method of operating cost estimation, based on the factorial approach, should be used. Further work is required to determine indirect cost factors and to relate maintenance cost factors to process flowsheets and utilization rates. Information should be given on the physical requirements, such as the number of men and the energy usage, as well as on the costs.

(6) The revenue of a particular waste processing plant will depend on local waste composition, local sale prices, and recovery efficiencies. In the absence of specific data, standard values should be assumed, but the limitations which this introduces must be remembered when interpreting

the results. To allow comparison of independent analyses and processes, assumptions must be stated explicitly.

(7) The system boundaries used to define each option must be consistent. For example, each option must refer to the same period. In addition, if waste treatment or reclamation plants in an urban area are compared with direct haul of the waste in collection vehicles to a landfill site outside the town, then costs of the additional transportation *must* be added to those of the landfill operation itself. The costs of waste transportation are discussed in the next chapter.

(8) All cost and revenue estimates made at an early stage of planning for waste management are uncertain. This uncertainty should be included explicitly in the analysis; suitable methods are demonstrated in Chapter 7.

These practices are not tiresome or trivial; they are essential to the rational discussion of the economics of waste processing.

6. THE COSTS OF WASTE TRANSPORT

6.1. Introduction

When alternative waste management technologies are to be compared, it is essential that the comparison is made on a consistent basis. Thus each option must consider all the operations on the waste which are included within the system boundary. The boundary used here (Fig. 2.2) includes not only the waste processing operation itself but also the initial delivery of the waste to the processing plant or landfill site in the collection vehicle, and the transport of any residual waste materials from the plant for final disposal.

The purpose of this chapter is to examine the economics of transporting waste materials. The discussion may conveniently be divided into three parts:

(i) The initial haul of the waste in a collection vehicle to the processing plant or disposal site. Waste must be collected, and some minimal average haul distance to a waste treatment plant is inevitable. It is proposed here that, for planning purposes, such costs be assumed constant for all types of waste transfer, treatment, or resource recovery plants. The only cases where haul costs in a collection vehicle must then be included as part of the overall disposal cost are where they differ substantially from this norm: prominent examples are direct delivery to a landfill site, where the site is generally outside the urban area and thus further away than would be a central processing plant; and local, as opposed to central, processing plants, where the haul costs will be less than for the base case. The first section thus examines the dependence of the costs of waste collection and delivery on the distance from the collection area to the waste discharge point.

(ii) The diseconomies of scale in initial waste delivery costs. As the amount of waste processed by a plant increases, so its catchment area expands and the average distance of initial waste haul will rise. The balance between the economies of scale in waste processing and the diseconomies of scale in waste transport is examined in the second section.

(iii) The costs of bulk haulage of waste from a transfer station, or of residual waste remaining after treatment or resource recovery, are examined, as a function of distance to the disposal site, in the third section.

The chapter concludes with a summary and a discussion of the use of these simple models of waste transportation. Their application is demonstrated by an example, comparing direct haul to a landfill site with indirect haul via a transfer station, as the distance to the site increases.

6.2. The cost of waste transport in a collection vehicle

6.2.1. Cost as a function of haul distance

The system boundary for waste disposal, as defined in Fig. 2.2, separates waste collection from the haul of the waste in the collection vehicle to its initial discharge point. The cost of collection itself is of concern here only in so far as it is affected by changes in the haul distance. As the haul distance and haul time increases, collection time decreases, less waste is handled per vehicle and the overall cost increases.

Several approaches to the calculation of haul cost may be identified. In the first the cost per tonne of waste for collection and haul is written as

$$C = c(d) = \frac{\text{cost per vehicle and crew}}{\text{tonnes collected per vehicle}} \qquad (6.1)$$

where the distance d enters through its effect on both the tonnes collected and the vehicle operating costs. The collection cost is that required to deliver the waste either to the end of the collection round ($d = 0$) or to a nearby point ($d = d_0$). Hence haul cost per tonne, H, may be written

$$H = h(d) = c(d) - c(d_0) \qquad (6.2)$$

An alternative method calculates the total pick-up time lost by the collection fleet in the area when the average haul distance is increased from d_0 to d, and derives from this the additional number of vehicles, ΔN_v, required to collect the same amount of waste. The haul cost, now denoted H', is written

$$H' = h'(d) = [\Delta N_v \text{ (cost per vehicle and crew)} + \text{(extra}$$
$$\text{operating costs of existing vehicles)}]/\text{(total waste}$$
$$\text{collected in the area)} \qquad (6.3)$$

This approach is used by the Department of the Environment (1976a).

Both of these methods reflect the causal mechanisms by which the haul cost is determined. It would be much simpler to derive an average cost of running a collection vehicle and to apply this to the haul operation. Typical expressions might be

$$\text{cost/tonne–minute} = \frac{\text{total cost per week of collection service}}{\substack{\text{average waste collected} \\ \times \text{length of working week}}} \qquad (6.4)$$

or

$$\text{cost/tonne–mile} = \frac{2 \times \text{hourly vehicle cost}}{\text{average speed} \times \text{average load}} \qquad (6.5)$$

where the factor 2 allows for the return trip. The second expression is used by the Greater London Council to calculate repayments to the collection authorities for haul distances greater than three miles (Patrick 1975a). The problem with these equations is that they reflect the present, or a historical, average cost over five dissimilar activities performed by the collection vehicle, namely:

The journey to and from the depot;
The actual collection or pick-up operation;
The haul to and from the waste delivery point;
The actual discharge operation;
Crew break time.

This average cost cannot be applied with confidence to any one activity, such as haul, nor can it be used where the relative times are changed, as for example when the haul time increases or the number of trips per day to the discharge point changes.

6.2.2. General form of the cost function

In order to relate the cost of collection and haul to a single variable such as haul distance, assumptions need to be made. Those used here for illustrative purposes may be summarized as:

(i) Collection is organized on the basis of solo rounds only, i.e. the collectors travel with the vehicle to its discharge point and only work productively during pick-up time.

(ii) The net length, T, of the working day is constant. This implies that the journey time to and from the discharge point and the crew break time are fixed, and that overtime is not allowed.

(iii) The number of collectors, N_c, in the team, and their loading rate, L bins per man–hour, is constant.

(iv) The number of trips per day, N_t to the discharge point is fixed.

(v) The turnround time, T_t, at the delivery point is constant.

(vi) Vehicle capacities, V, are fixed.

(vii) Vehicle life expectancy does not vary.

(viii) The average haul speed, s, is independent of distance.

(ix) The average quantity of waste per bin, W_b, is constant.

Using these assumptions, the general form of the cost function implied by equation 6.1 is shown in Fig. 6.1. The cost per tonne increases with distance, and approaches infinity at an asymptotic distance, d_a, which implies a pick-up time of zero and hence no waste collected. This type of function is used in the LGORU models for strategy evaluation (Section 3.4). However, Fig. 6.1 overstates the actual rise in unit cost with distance, as compensating changes may be made in collection practice. Assumptions (i)–(vi) all relate to variables which are, at least partially, subject to management control. For example, as the number of trips per day (assumption (iv)) decreases, successive cost functions may be drawn with increasing asymptotic distances. The reorganization of collection practice, involving also changes in the boundaries between areas served by each team of collectors and the re-routing of vehicles during pick-up, may be facilitated by the use of various mathematical modelling methods, including work study (Whittocks 1975), a scheme of the LGORU (Rutherford and Parker 1975), or computer-based design techniques (Coyle 1973). A useful review is provided by Clark (1973). In addition, the life expectancy of vehicles will decrease as haul distances rise, thus increasing the dependence of cost on distance, while the average haul speed will increase, thus reducing this dependence. The last effect is invoked by Helmenstein and Martin (1972) to justify a cost function in which haul costs rise less than proportionately with distance (Fig. 6.2).

Cost variations with collection organization, number of collectors, and vehicle capacity were explored by Green and Nice of LGORU (1967). Their results for optimum systems using different patterns of organization (assumption (i)) are shown schematically in Fig. 6.3. In a relay system each team of collectors loads continuously, with an empty vehicle available to replace the full one. In the system shown, 2 vehicles serve one team, but more complex arrangements such as 4 vehicles to 3 teams are also possible. A split team system uses, say, 6 men to load 2 vehicles, with 4 men on one and 2 on the other until the first is full, then all 6 load the second while the first discharges its load and 2 go back on its return. The aim is the same as for a relay system—to cut unproductive collection time to a minimum. Note that the cost function for an optimal split team was derived assuming that vehicles of precisely the right capacity are used for each journey time or distance, and it is therefore not applicable if an existing fleet must be used. Fig. 6.3 shows how the increasing cost function of a solo system may be offset by organizational changes. Even assuming that an optimal split team system is not possible, the combined effect is of a decreasing unit cost of haul per tonne–kilometre as the haul distance increases (cf. Fig. 6.2).

A detailed empirical study of collection costs is reported by Kemper and Quigley (1976). Haul distance was found to increase total collection time, per short ton, in one case by 3–5 min, and in the other by 0.33 min, per mile. The implied speeds were, for the first case, 10 m.p.h. on city streets and

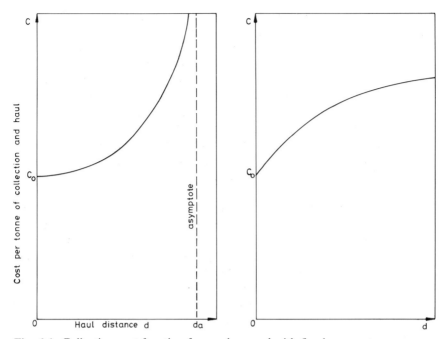

Fig. 6.1. Collection cost function for a solo round with fixed parameters.
Fig. 6.2. Collection cost function based on increasing haul speed with distance.

28 m.p.h. on interstate highways, and for the second 180 m.p.h. This absurd result was ascribed to measurement errors and a decrease in crew break time as haul time increases, assumption (ii) thus breaking down. In addition, collection time was found to decrease as the collection density, expressed as tons of waste per pick-up mile, increased. Density enters the analysis here through assumption (iii), as the loading rate per man will depend largely on the types and separation of properties. Management control is possible by varying the service, for example substituting kerbside for rear-of-house collection, or using disposable bags in place of dustbins.

Flexibility of collection organization serves to reduce the dependence of haul costs on distance in several other ways. For example, the length of the working day may be extended if driver overtime is allowed for all or part of the final trip to the discharge point and the return to depot. Turnround time at the delivery point is dependent on congestion, which can be controlled partially by long-term measures such as providing adequate traffic control and discharge bays and improving access roads across landfill sites. Vehicle capacity may be changed in the medium term to meet varying requirements.

However, it is important not to overstate the flexibility of the collection service. In practice, labour relations will often be dominant, and negotiations on bonus agreements will usually precede the implementation of any changes. This may introduce artificial constraints on haul distance if, for example, crews refuse to cross district boundaries or, for safety reasons, insist on the vehicle discharging its load before the midday break.

A general collection cost function which takes account of the inherent flexibility in organization is proposed here (Fig. 6.4). This consists of three portions, showing a decreasing unit cost of haul per tonne–kilometre at low distances, a substantial near-linear portion, and an increasing unit cost for long hauls. The validity of the linear approximation to this function, which allows the use of a constant unit cost of waste haul (pence per tonne–kilometre (p/t km), is now examined.

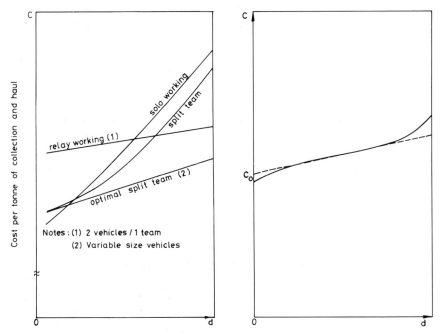

Fig. 6.3. Collection cost functions for different organizational patterns.
Fig. 6.4. Postulated general form of collection cost function.

6.2.3. Derivation of the cost function

An analytical expression for the relationship of collection cost to haul distance, using the assumptions set out in the previous section, is derived in Appendix B.1. The cost function illustrated in Fig. 6.1 may be represented in the simplest case, where the cost of a vehicle and its crew is assumed to be constant irrespective of distance, as

$$C = A(1 - Bd)^{-1} \qquad (6.6)$$
$$\approx A(1 + Bd) \qquad (6.7)$$

where A and B are constants. The minimum cost of collection, when a discharge point is available at the end of each collection round ($d = 0$), is equal to A, the ratio of total cost to the maximum amount of waste collectable. The linear approximation in equation 6.7 is valid when $Bd \ll 1$, that is the haul time is much less than the total time available for collection and haul. For short hauls, the haul cost is the product of the minimum collection cost and the fractional increase in time due to haul. From equation 6.6, the distance d_a at which the total cost approaches infinity is

$$d_a = 1/B \qquad (6.8)$$

It is shown in Appendix B.1.2 that the haul costs derived from the alternative approaches represented by equations 6.1 and 6.3 are equivalent, provided that the total number of collection vehicles, N_v, is not too small. The requirement that the number of additional vehicles, ΔN_v, must be an integer is not so restrictive as might be imagined, thanks to the flexibility in collection organization already discussed, and also to the range of vehicle capacities available on the market.

The cost function shown in equations 6.6. and 6.7 is based on the restrictive assumption that the cost of running a collection vehicle is fixed, irrespective of the haul distance and the number of trips made to the discharge point each day. A more realistic, extended cost function is also derived in Appendix B.1.3, in which the total vehicle cost, C_v, is expressed as

$$C_v = C_f + C_{op} \qquad (6.9)$$

The fixed cost, C_f, is the sum of costs for the vehicle, driver, and crew; the operating cost, C_{op}, is proportional to the number of trips to the discharge point, the cost for each trip being the sum of contributions from collection (pick-up), haul, and discharge. The operating cost of waste discharge is introduced specifically for landfill site delivery, where the uneven surface results in high tyre and maintenance costs, out of proportion to the short distances. The use of the extended cost function results in an expression similar to equation 6.7, that is

$$C \approx C_0 + Ud \qquad (6.10)$$

where C_0 is the constant cost of waste collection and U is the unit cost of waste haul, per tonne–kilometre. The analytical expression for U may be written:

$$U = \frac{2N_t\{[\{F_v + F_d + N_cF_c + MN_t(O_c + O_t)\}/s(T - N_tT_t)] + MO_h\}}{MN_cLW_b(T - N_tT_t)} \qquad (6.11)$$

The notation used is summarized both in Table 6.1 and, more comprehensively, in Table B.1.

Table 6.1

Data for the illustrative calculation (costs appropriate to 1977)

Symbol	Parameter	Value	Notes
T	Length of working day	7 h	Net of journey to and from depot, and crew break time
T_t	Turn-round time	0.25 h	Time at the delivery point
W_b	Tonnes per bin	0.017	1975–6 average waste production per capita was 345 kg/annum (Society of County Treasurers 1976). One collection per week and 0.4 bins per person assumed
V	Vehicle capacity	300 bins	Or 5 t
M	Days per working week	5	
F_v	Fixed cost of vehicle per week	£100	£25 000 capital cost, lifetime 10 years, discount rate 10%, implies a cost of £78/wk. Road licences and insurance make up the balance
F_d	Cost of driver	£110	£80/wk plus 40% on-costs
F_c	Cost of collector	£100	£70/wk plus 40% on-costs
O_h	Operating cost of haul	£0.14/km	Fuel at 70 p/gallon, 14 k.p.g.; tyres and maintenance at 9 p/km
O_c	Operating cost of collection	£1.7	6 km/pickup, 3.5 k.p.g.
O_t	Operating cost of discharge	£1	R. H. Berry (1976) estimated cost between £0.5 and £1.50. Appropriate to a landfill only
C_v	Total cost of running a vehicle	£265 + 100 N_c	Assumes two trips and 40 km haul per day
s	Average vehicle speed	20 k.p.h.	Range 10–30 k.p.h. examined
N_c	Number of collectors in a team	2–6	Variable
N_t	Number of trips per day to discharge point	1–5	Variable
L	Loading rate as bins per man-hour	See table 6.2	

The cost function for waste collection derived here defines a single curve, of the type shown in Fig. 6.1, corresponding to a fixed set of parameters. An increase in the number of trips per day, N_t, increases both C_0 and U, while an increase in the number of collectors, N_c, reduces C_0, although this is partially offset by changes in the loading rate per man. The collection policy of minimum cost thus involves the maximum number of collectors filling a vehicle which makes just one trip a day to the discharge point. This intuitive result will usually not be feasible as vehicle capacity is limited.

Two modifications to the model may be made to allow for this restriction. Constraints on capacity may be imposed, so that a cost function for given (N_t, N_c) can only be used for haul distances *greater* than the one for which exactly N_t full loads may be collected. This approach is illustrated below. An alternative method is used by LGORU in its strategy evaluation models (see also Section 3.4). The cost of running a vehicle is assumed to be proportional to the average load of waste collected, so that, as the haul distance increases and the pick-up time and average load decrease, the vehicle cost will decrease. This effect means that C_0 decreases as N_t increases, so that for short hauls the cheapest policy involves a large number of trips per day. Unfortunately, the assumption is only valid if it is further assumed that a new fleet with smaller capacity per vehicle is purchased every time the haul distance to a new discharge point increases.

6.2.4. An illustrative calculation

A worked example illustrates the use of the models to investigate the cost function for waste collection. Typical data, with costs appropriate to the first half of 1977, are summarized in Tables 6.1 and 6.2. The operating costs in particular are uncertain, as conventionally data are only provided for the complete collection operation. Loading rates per man, L, vary with the number of collectors and local variations are usually dominant: accurate measurement of L is a pre-requisite for successful modelling.

Table 6.2

The variation of loading rates and times with the number of collectors

Number of collectors	N_c	2	3	4	5	6
Loading rate per man (bins/h)[a]	L	37.5	34.7	32.2	30.0	28.2
Loading rate per team (bins/h)[a]	$N_c L$	75	104	129	150	169
Hours to fill 300 bin vehicle	t_1	4.00	2.88	2.33	2.00	1.78
Full trips per 7-hour day[b]	N_t'	1	2	2	3	3
Time over after collecting N_t' loads (h)[b]	t_2	2.75	0.73	1.85	0.25	0.92
Minimum haul distance (km)	d_l	27.5	3.7	9.3	0.8	3.1

(a) Loading rates taken from Green and Nice (1967).
(b) The number of full trips per day, and the time left over for haul and collecting additional loads, are calculated from the collection time per trip plus the turn-round time for discharge, i.e. $t_2 = T - N_t' (t_1 + T_t)$.
(c) See definition in equation 6.12. A speed of 20 k.p.h. is assumed.

In Table 6.2, the times, t_1, required by different teams to fill a standard 5-tonne vehicle are shown, together with the possible number of full trips per day, N_t', and the residual times, t_2, available for haul or for collecting an additional part load.

As noted earlier, the cost function with N_t' trips per day is only valid for hauls which take all of the available time, t_2, since otherwise the vehicle capacity is exceeded. The minimum haul distance, d_l, for which the function may be used is thus

$$d_l = \frac{t_2 s}{2 N_t'} \qquad (6.12)$$

Table 6.3 shows the asymptotic distances d_a at which the collection cost tends to infinity (equation 6.8). As the number of trips per day increases and the average haul speed decreases, so d_a decreases. The error introduced by the linear approximations of equations 6.7 and 6.10 may be shown to be 100 B^2 d^2 per cent, so that for $d \leqslant \frac{1}{2} d_a$, which from equation 6.8 becomes $d \leqslant 1/2B$, the error is less than 25 per cent, and is thus within the expected accuracy of the model. It should be noted that assuming a constant collection organization when planning delivery points is restrictive if N_t is high. For $N_t = 5$ and $s = 20$ k.p.h., d_a is 11 km; thus a delivery point must effectively be placed within 6–8 km of each collection round.

Table 6.3

Asymptotic distances.
The distances, d_a km, at which the collection cost
approaches infinity

s (k.p.h.)	1	2	N_t 3	4	5
10	33.8	16.3	10.4	7.5	5.8
15	50.6	24.4	15.6	11.3	8.6
20	67.5	32.5	20.8	15.0	11.5
25	84.4	40.6	26.0	18.8	14.4
30	101.2	48.8	31.3	22.5	17.3

The two models for collection cost, assuming, respectively, fixed and varying costs per vehicle, are compared in Table B.2. The base collection costs when $d = 0$ agree fairly well, but the simpler model consistently underestimates the unit haul costs by 9–15 per cent, owing mainly to the omission of an explicit operating cost term. The extended model will be used here.

To obtain a cost function suitable for planning, flexible collection organization must be allowed. Here an aggregate minimum cost function is constructed from individual functions calculated for different values of N_c and N_t. The calculations are contained in Table B.3 and illustrated in Fig. 6.5. The linear approximation of equation 6.10 is used, taking note both of the capacities of the vehicles which impose a minimum distance d_l (equation 6.12), and of deviations at distances greater than $\frac{1}{2} d_a$. Fig. 6.6 shows the resulting aggregate cost function. It is assumed that, for distances lower than d_l, the collection cost per tonne will remain approximately constant, as no more waste is collected and the only savings are vehicle operating costs. As d increases, it becomes economical to progressively increase the team size, although costs for 5 and 6 collectors are almost identical; at some point one less trip per day is best, accompanied by a reduction in team size. The segments of the minimum cost function deviate significantly from linearity for $N_t = 2$ and $N_c = 5$ or 6 when $d > 16$ km and for $N_t = 1$ and $N_c = 2$ when $d > 34$ km. The aggregate cost function approximates in shape to that

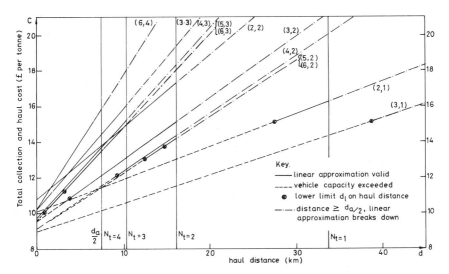

Fig. 6.5. Collection cost functions with flexible organization.
Each line is the linear approximation for specific values of (N_c, N_t).

postulated in Fig. 6.4. A linear approximation was fitted to data points from $d = 0$ to $d = 35$ km, giving $C = 10.7 + 0.178\ d$ £/t, with a coefficient of determination $R^2 = 0.93$. The 95 per cent confidence interval for the constant unit cost of haul U' is 17.8 ± 1.7 p/t km.

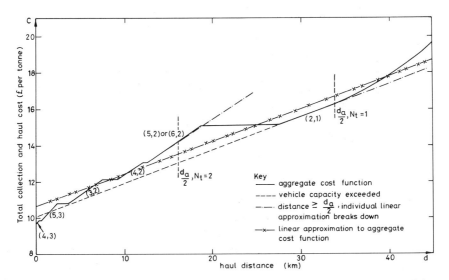

Fig. 6.6. An aggregate cost function for waste collection formed by segments of the appropriate (N_c, N_t) functions from Fig. 6.5.

It is interesting to examine the sensitivity of U' to changes in parameters other than N_c and N_t. The unit cost corresponding to $N_c = 2$ and $N_t = 1$ is within 3 per cent of the mean value of U'. Thus U' may be approximated by substituting $N_c = 2$, $N_t = 1$ into equation 6.11.

The variation of a function as its parameters change may be studied using relative sensitivity values (McCuen 1975). Writing a general function F_0 with n variables as

$$F_0 = f[F_1, F_2, \ldots, F_i, \ldots, F_n]$$

the absolute sensitivity, S, of the value of F_0 to a change in F_i is given by

$$S = \left(\frac{\partial F_0}{\partial F_i}\right)_{F_j \neq F_i} \tag{6.13}$$

S depends on the actual values of both F_0 and F_i. To compare sensitivities to different parameters, the relative sensitivity R_s, defined by

$$R_s = \frac{\partial F_0}{F_0} \Big/ \frac{\partial F_i}{F_i} = \frac{\partial F_0}{\partial F_i} \frac{F_i}{F_0} \tag{6.14}$$

is preferable. For a small range of F_i this becomes

$$R_s \approx \frac{\Delta F_0}{\Delta F_i} \frac{F_i}{F_0} \tag{6.15}$$

Thus

$$\Delta F_0 \approx R_s \frac{\Delta F_i}{F_i} F_0 \tag{6.16}$$

implying that for $R_s = 0.5$, say, a 10 per cent change in F_i will produce a 5 per cent change in F_0. The parameters with the highest R_s are those to which F_0 is most sensitive. For a linear dependence of F_0 on F_i, S is constant, and both equations 6.15 and 6.16 are exact.

Returning to the aggregate unit cost of haul, U', R_s values are shown in Table 6.4. The most sensitive parameters are all non-linear, with an order of importance (for their base values) of

$$T > L = W_b > s \approx M$$

with increases in each of these reducing the unit haul cost substantially. The effect of the turn-round time is relatively small, mainly because there is only one trip per day in this approximation to the aggregate function. The cost parameters are all linear in effect, with an order of importance

$$F_c \gg F_d \approx F_v \approx O_h \gg O_c \approx O_t$$

Attention should be focused on the parameters with highest R_s when analysing collection costs. Accurate work-study measurements are required for

Table 6.4

The relative sensitivity of the unit haul cost to the parameters.
R_s calculated from equations 6.11 and 6.14 for $N_c = 2$, $N_t = 1$, to
approximate the aggregate cost function. The base value of the
unit cost is £0.18/t km

Parameter		Linear dependence	Base value	R_s
Fixed vehicle cost	F_v	Yes	–	0.193
Cost of driver	F_d	Yes	–	0.212
Cost of collector	F_c	Yes	–	0.386
Operating cost of collection	O_c	Yes	–	0.016
Operating cost of discharge	O_t	Yes	–	0.010
Operating cost of haul	O_h	Yes	–	0.182
Average vehicle speed	s	No	10 k.p.h.	−1.635
			20	−0.818
			30	−0.545
Length of working day	T	No	6 h	−2.575
			7	−1.885
			8	−1.445
Turn-round time	T_t	No	0.1 h	0.025
			0.25	0.067
			0.5	0.150
Working days per week	M	No	4.5 days	−0.880
			5	−0.792
			5.5	−0.720
Loading rate per man	L	No	$\frac{1}{2} x_o$	−2.0
			x_o	−1.0
Average waste per bin	W_b		$2 x_o$	−0.5

the effective length of the working day, T, the loading rate per man, L, and
the average quantity of waste per bin, W_b. Otherwise, the average vehicle
speed, s, and the operating cost of haul, O_h, are most problematic, although
a 50 per cent error in the estimate of O_h will only produce an 18 per cent error
in U'. The variation of R_s with the magnitude of s emphasizes the dependence of the model on the unsatisfactory assumption of a constant average
haul speed as distance increases.

6.2.5. Discussion

A simple model of waste collection has been developed to calculate the
variation of haul cost with distance. The worked example shows how an
aggregate function can allow for changes in collection practice, but the
results must be interpreted in the light of the assumptions made. Of the eight
assumptions listed at the beginning of Section 6.2.2, only those concerned
with the number of collectors and the number of trips per day have been
relaxed. The linear approximation to the aggregate cost function is strengthened by possibilities of introducing relay or split team operation and by
the existence of flexibility in the length of the working day, either through

driver overtime or by crews taking part of their breaks during haul time. In addition, vehicle speeds will tend to increase with distance.

The model suggests that a collection cost function as shown in Fig. 6.4 is appropriate and, moreover, that a linear approximation is reasonable over an extended range, say 5–35 km. In practice, hauls of more than 20 km are uncommon, and other factors such as labour relations may provide effective upper limits.

The model produces a range of unit costs for haul of 17.8 ± 1.7 p/t km, for an average speed of 20 k.p.h. However, changes in the average speed alone, say between 15 and 30 k.p.h., give a range of 13–23 p/t km. This may be compared to typical estimates in the literature of 9 p/t mi (Crosby and Renold 1974), 20 p/t mi (Holmes 1975b) and 17–30 p/t km (Thomson 1979), which yield a cost range of 9–33 p/t km when corrected to 1977 prices.

6.3. Diseconomies of scale in initial waste delivery costs

6.3.1. A simple model of waste transport

As the amount of waste handled by a processing or disposal facility increases, so the catchment area expands and the average cost of transporting waste to the facility increases. This trend towards higher costs per tonne of waste as capacity increases is offset by the expected economies of scale in the processing or disposal costs (Sections 5.4.7 and 5.5.3). It follows therefore that there will be an optimal facility capacity, above which the total unit cost, of waste delivery plus processing, will increase. The purpose of this section is to examine the diseconomies of scale in waste delivery costs and to illustrate the calculation of optimal facility capacity. It should be stressed that the emphasis here is entirely on direct financial costs; in practice, other effects, such as increased traffic congestion around the plant, must also be taken into account.

The discussion is based on a series of simple models of waste transport to the initial discharge point, as developed in Appendix B.2. In each case, a number of simplifying assumptions are made:

(i) The plant catchment area is circular, with radius R km;

(ii) All waste transport to the plant is in collection vehicles;

(iii) The unit cost of haul, U per tonne–kilometre, is constant;

(iv) Waste production, w tonnes per capita per day, is constant.

In addition, in the simplest model it is also assumed that:

(v) Population density, p persons per hectare, within the catchment area is constant;

(vi) The plant is located at the centre of the area.

In the base case, the average unit cost of waste transport, U_a, is given by

$$U_a = \tfrac{2}{3}kUR \qquad (6.17)$$

where k is a constant, being the ratio of road to crow-fly distances. The common assumption that all waste arises at the centre of gravity of an area would imply $U_a = 0$. When the radius R is related to the total quantity of waste arising in the area, i.e. the plant throughput, W tonnes per day, equation 6.17 may be rewritten

$$U_a = bW^{\frac{1}{2}} \tag{6.18}$$

where

$$b = \tfrac{2}{3}kU\left[\frac{1}{wp\pi}\right]^{\frac{1}{2}}. \tag{6.19}$$

It can thus be seen that U_a increases with W, showing the opposite trend to the unit processing cost, U_p. If the total processing cost, C_p, is written, after equation 5.5, as

$$C_p = aW^S \tag{6.20}$$

where a is a constant and S is the scale factor, then it can be shown (Section B.2.1) that the optimum scale of a plant, W_{opt}, for which the total unit cost is a minimum, is given by

$$W_{opt} = \left[\frac{2a(1-S)}{b}\right]^x \tag{6.21}$$

where

$$x = \frac{2}{3-2S} \tag{6.22}$$

The calculation of W_{opt} is illustrated, using the typical data shown in Table 6.5, in Table 6.6. For a transfer station, the optimal scale increases from about 200 to about 600 tonnes per day (t.p.d.) with an increase in population density from 5 to 25 persons/ha, corresponding to a change from a rural to an urban area, while for an incinerator it increases from about 300 to about 1500 t.p.d. The latter result may be compared to the 500–750 t.p.d. suggested from empirical evidence by Bowen, Woodward, and Kelsey (1969), or to the 1200–2000 t.p.d. calculated by Helmenstein and Martin (1972). In the general case of $S > 0.5$, the optimum capacity is more than inversely proportional to b, being particularly sensitive to changes in the ratio of road to crow-fly distance k, and in the unit haul cost U; it is less sensitive to the rate of waste generation w or to the population density p (equation 6.19). The total cost, of waste delivery plus processing, varies little for plant capacities near the optimum; thus moderate deviations from the optimum capacity will not increase the total unit cost significantly. In practice, therefore, the choice of optimal throughput may often depend on other, non-financial, considerations, such as traffic congestion or the suitability of access roads.

Table 6.5

Data used in the diseconomy of scale calculations

Parameter	Symbol	Value	Note
Ratio of road to crow-fly distance	k	1.3	Chosen from range 1.2–1.5
Unit haul cost	U	0.18 £/t km	Derived in Section 6.2
Waste per capita	w	1.33 kg/day	Average in England is 345 kg/capita annum (Society of County Treasurers, 1976), a 5-day week for collection and processing is assumed
Population density	p	5 or 25 persons/ha	Values typical of a rural and an urban area; in England p ranges up to 50, with an overall average of 3.6 and an average for the metropolitan counties of 22
Transfer station:			
Scale factor	S	0.85	Table 5.5
Unit cost at 300 t.p.d.	U_p	£4.2/t	Tables A.4 and A.7
Incinerator:			
Scale factor	S	0.95	Table 5.5
Unit cost at 300 t.p.d.	U_p	£20/t	Table A.7

Table 6.6

Calculating the optimal scale of a processing plant
(using equation 6.21 and data in Table 6.5 to derive W_{opt} t.p.d.)

Population density p (persons/ha)	Plant type / b (equation 6.19)	a (equation 6.20)	Transfer station	Incinerator
5	0.108		160 t.p.d.	340 t.p.d.
25	0.0483		560 t.p.d.	1470 t.p.d.
Sensitivity	$b \times 1.25$		$0.71\ W_{opt}$	$0.67\ W_{opt}$
to changes in b	$b \div 1.25$		$1.41\ W_{opt}$	$1.50\ W_{opt}$

Transfer station: 9.88   Incinerator: 26.6

The discussion so far has involved average costs. For some purposes the marginal cost of transporting or processing an additional unit of waste is more relevant. Consider the decision to include an outlying town in the catchment area of a plant. If additional capacity must be provided, then this incremental investment should be compared to other waste disposal options for the outlying district. If, however, the additional waste simply increases the utilization of an existing plant, the sum of the *marginal* transport and processing costs should be compared to the costs of the alternative options. In the simple model, the marginal haul distance is always R, the radius of the catchment area (or the distance to the town), so that the marginal unit cost of haul, U_m, is given by

$$U_m = kUR \tag{6.23}$$

while the marginal cost of processing was discussed in Section 5.5.3.

6.3.2. Extending the model

The extension of the simple model by relaxing the two additional assumptions, namely those of an homogeneous population density and a central plant, is shown in Appendix B.2.2. By postulating a simple linear decrease in population density as the distance r from the centre increases, that is

$$p = p_0(1 - rp_1) \tag{6.24}$$

it is shown that, for moderate deviations from homogeneity, $Rp_1 \leqslant 0.5$, the increase in U_a is less than 15 per cent, while that in U_m is less than 25 per cent compared with the base case. Similarly, if the plant is displaced from the centre of the catchment area by less than 0.5 R, the deviation from the basic model is less than 20 per cent. The ratio of the average unit cost for an off-centre plant, U'_a, to that for a central plant depends only on the ratio of the distance from the centre to the radius of the catchment area (D/R). The relationship is shown in Fig. 6.7 for three cases, distinguished by the extent of inhomogeneity in population density.

The average distance travelled to a plant as calculated here may be compared to that when all waste is assumed to arise at the centre (Fig. 6.8). The two approaches converge for significant deviations of the plant from the centre, with a difference of less than 10 per cent for displacements of more than 1.1 R. However, if the model is applied to hauls beyond the edge of a city, then different ratios between road and crow-fly distances may be appropriate. If the road distance from the city boundary to the disposal facility is known, the model may be used to calculate transport costs to the boundary and a simple unit cost applied to the remaining journey.

6.3.3. Discussion

The simple model of waste transport derived in Appendix B.2.1. is flexible, with deviations from it being less than 20 per cent when either population density or the waste output per capita increases by 50 per cent (equations 6.18 and 6.19), when there is a moderate decrease in population density with distance, or when the plant is displaced by less than 0.5 R from the centre. These changes are all within the expected error limits of the model. A critical assumption is that of a constant unit cost of haul, which, as noted in the last section, may break down for distances greater than 30 km. For example, a plant displacement equal to a radius of 15 km implies a haul from the furthest point of 30 km, although the average haul is only 17 km. More

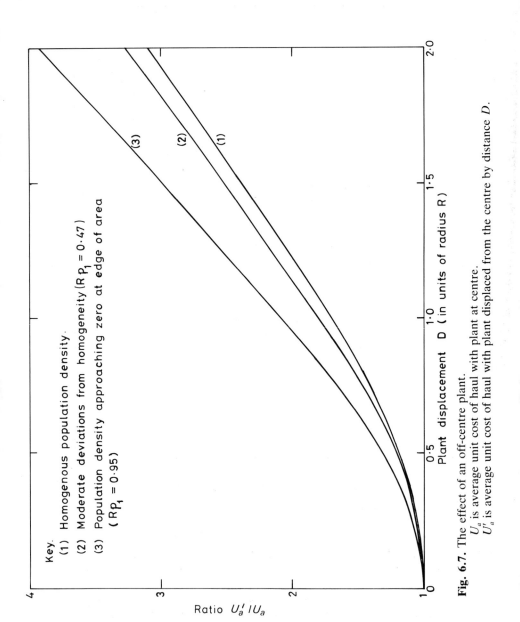

Fig. 6.7. The effect of an off-centre plant.

U_a is average unit cost of haul with plant at centre.

U'_a is average unit cost of haul with plant displaced from the centre by distance D.

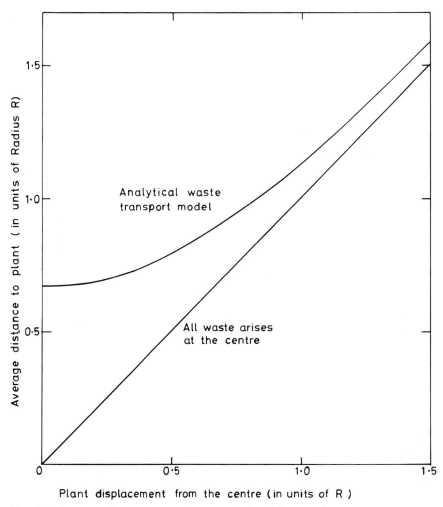

Fig. 6.8. Average distances to a plant as calculated by two alternative models.

seriously, the unit transport cost will depend on the population density. Kemper and Quigley (1976) showed a correlation of vehicle loading rates with population density, and as L changes in equation 6.11, so too will the value of the unit cost.

The primary use of the model is in the determination of optimal facility capacities (equation 6.21). The method is demonstrated for a transfer station and an incinerator in Table 6.6. Optimal capacities in the range 200–600 and 300–1500 t.p.d., respectively, were suggested by the illustrative data used; in addition, costs vary little for capacities near the optimum. With higher processing costs and lower scale factors the effect of transport costs would be less marked, although still significant, particularly at low population density. For a landfill site, with low unit costs, haul costs will dominate the disposal cost and large sites will not be economic if they rely on the direct haul of waste in collection vehicles. This is the usual rationale for the use of transfer stations, which can also be used to feed large processing plants, thus helping to realize their economies of scale. However, care is necessary in the application of the model. The optimal catchment area of a plant will depend on the cost of alternative disposal methods available in the outlying areas, and these must be considered explicitly in a particular study. Also, if one is considering an investment in additional capacity to serve an outlying district, the incremental investment should be compared to alternatives for that area.

6.4. The costs of bulk haulage

Most processing options include a bulk transport step for either all the waste or for its residue after treatment. A model is required to relate the cost to haul distance. Although attention will be restricted here to transport by road, the principles can be applied equally to barge transport, while costs of rail haul will depend more on the number of trains per day than on the tonnage or the haul distance.

Two alternative viewpoints may be put forward to relate bulk haul costs to distance. The simplest and most common is that of a constant unit cost per tonne–kilometre, while the other is of a constant cost per vehicle–day, implying a stepwise variation of cost per tonne with the number of trips per day. The cost model enables a comparison to be made.

The cost per tonne of bulk transport, C, is given by

$$C = \frac{\text{cost of the vehicle fleet}}{\text{total waste transported}}$$

$$= \frac{N_v C_v}{MW} \tag{6.25}$$

where N_v is the number of vehicles, C_v is the weekly cost of a vehicle and its driver, M is the number of working days per week, and W is the quantity of waste handled per day. The number of vehicles required is

$$N_v \geqslant N_v' = \frac{W}{N_t V} \tag{6.26}$$

where N_v is an integer, N_t is the number of trips per vehicle–day, and V is the vehicle capacity in tonnes. The cost of running a bulk haulage vehicle may be written, by analogy to equation 6.9 and B.17–B.19 for a collection vehicle, as

$$C_v = (F_v + F_d) + MN_t O_t + 2MN_t O_h d \tag{6.27}$$

where the notation is given in Table 6.7. The number of trips possible in a day may be found from the ratio of time available, T, to the time required per trip,

$$N_t \leq \frac{T}{\left(\dfrac{2d}{s} + T_t\right)} \tag{6.28}$$

Table 6.7

Data for bulk haulage (all costs at 1977 values)

Symbol	Parameter	Value	Comments
T	Length of working day	8 h	Assumes vehicle is based at the plant. Range of 7–9 h examined
T_t	Turn-round time	1 h	At plant and landfill. Range of $\frac{1}{2}$–$1\frac{1}{2}$ h examined
V	Vehicle capacity	13 t	Alternative capacities of 10, 15, 17 t examined
M	Days per working week	5	
F_v	Fixed cost of vehicle per week	£140[a]	£25 000 capital cost, lifetime 10 years, discount rate 10%, implies £78/wk. Insurance and licences at £33/wk (based on Commercial Motor, Johnson 1976). Allowance for standby vehicles and overheads at 25%[a]
F_d	Cost of driver	£110	£80/wk + 40% on-costs.
O_h	Operating cost of haul	£0.12/km	Commercial Motor cost of 15-ton tipper
O_t	Operating cost of discharge	£1	R. H. Berry (1976)
s	Vehicle speed	30 k.p.h.	Range 15–40 k.p.h. examined

(a) The fixed cost per vehicle is low compared with commercial charges for bulk haulage. A typical charge of £90/day implies F_v about £250/wk. The difference may be accounted for by the private sector's higher discount rates, more accurate accounting for overheads and profit margins.

where N_t is an integer and T_t is the turn-round time at the landfill plus the loading time at the processing plant.

These four equations, 6.25–6.28, comprise the model. Considerable simplification is possible by relaxing the integer restriction on the number of vehicles, replacing N_v in equation 6.25 by N'_v from equation 6.26. The under-estimate of C, equal to $100\,(1 - N_v/N'_v)$ per cent, will be less than 25 per cent when there are more than 5 vehicles. This condition is fulfilled when $W \geq 5\,V\,N_t$, which with $V = 13$ t is $W \geq 65\,N_t$ t.p.d. When the same vehicle fleet serves a number of plants, the restriction is applied to the combined operation. Making this approximation, and substituting 6.26 and 6.27 into 6.25,

$$C = \frac{1}{V}\left[\frac{(F_v + F_d)}{MN_t} + 2O_h d + O_t\right] \tag{6.29}$$

This cost function has three components: a fixed cost which is inversely proportional to the number of trips, a variable cost proportional to the haul distance, and a constant discharge cost. Note that C is inversely proportional to the vehicle capacity, V.

Further reduction of the model to one equation by relaxing the integer restriction on the number of trips per day, which is always a small number ($N_t \leqslant 5$), would be misleading. The use of the model may be illustrated with data given in Table 6.7.

The variable cost portion of equation 6.29 is illustrated in Fig. 6.9. In addition to the base-line, the sensitivity is shown to a range of vehicle capacities and to variations in the operating cost, O_h, of $\overset{\times}{\div} 1.25$.

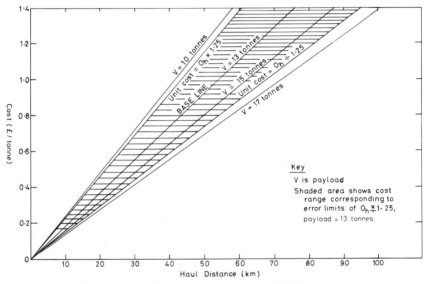

Fig. 6.9. The distance dependent component of the bulk haul cost.

The maximum haul times and distances for each number of trips per day are calculated from equation 6.28 and shown in Table 6.8 for ranges of T, T_t, and s as indicated in Table 6.7. This information is used to plot the fixed cost component of equation 6.29 against the haul time. In Fig. 6.10, the sensitivity to T_t and T is shown, with resultant shifts in the time at which a cost increment occurs. In Fig. 6.11, sensitivity to the vehicle capacities and to the level of costs is illustrated, with the size of cost increment varying at a given haul time.

In order to determine the variation of cost per tonne with distance, assumptions about average speeds need to be made. An example of such a cost function, for $s = 20$ and 30 k.p.h. and assuming fixed values of all the other parameters, is shown in Fig. 6.12. The cost is dominated by the fixed

Table 6.8

Maximum haul times and distances for bulk transport for different numbers of trips per day

Number of trips per day, N_t	Haul times (hours per single journey)					Average haul speed	Haul distances (single journey km, base time only)						First 5 km at 20, then	
T	8	8	8	7	9		15	20	25	30	35	40	30	40
T_t	1 (Base case)	½	1½	1	1									
5	0.3	0.55	0.05	0.2	0.4		4.5	6.0	7.5	9.0	10.5	12.0	6.5	7.0
4	0.5	0.75	0.25	0.38	0.63		7.5	10.0	12.5	15.0	17.5	20.0	12.5	15.0
3	0.83	1.08	0.58	0.67	1.0		12.5	16.7	20.8	25.0	29.2	33.3	22.5	28.3
2	1.5	1.75	1.25	1.25	1.75		22.5	30.0	37.5	45.0	52.5	60.0	42.5	55.0
1	3.5	3.75	3.25	3.00	4.0		52.5	70.0	87.5	105	122.5	140	102.5	135

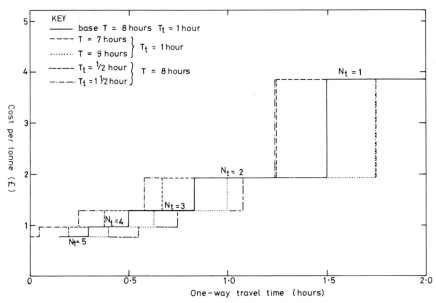

Fig. 6.10. The fixed component of the bulk haul cost, showing sensitivity to the time inputs.

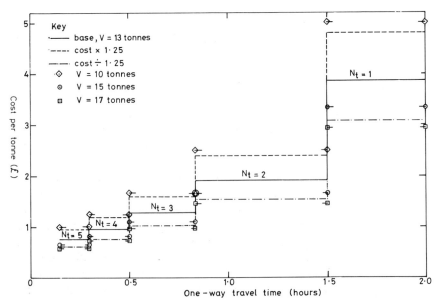

Fig. 6.11. The fixed component of the bulk haul cost, showing sensitivity to costs and payloads.

costs and, for a given haul distance, considerable savings can be made by increasing the number of trips per day. Both Fig. 6.12 and Fig. 6.10 show the flexibility this produces. In any particular study, accurate journey times should be used in preference to a general correlation with haul distance. For a given number of trips per day, the most critical parameters are the vehicle capacity and the fixed costs. For unprocessed waste, vehicle capacity may be increased by compaction, provided that legal restrictions on weight are not thereby exceeded.

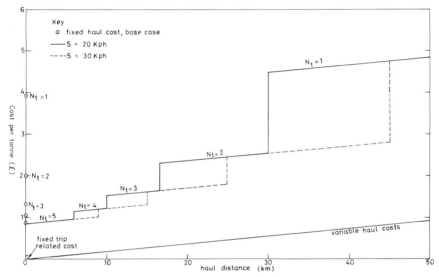

Fig. 6.12. Bulk haulage costs as a function of distance.

6.5. Discussion

Three separate models have been introduced in this chapter, with the aim of integrating the costs of transporting wastes into a discussion of the economics of waste management. The conclusions may conveniently be summarized as:

The variation in the cost of waste collection as the distance to the initial waste discharge point changes is enormously complex. No single, analytical, cost function allows adequately for the inherent flexibility in collection organization. It has been shown that the aggregate cost function may be represented approximately by a constant cost for the actual collection or pick-up operation, plus a constant unit cost per tonne–kilometre of haul; this is valid for hauls between about 5 km and 20–30 km, the upper limit depending mainly on institutional constraints such as labour relations. For the *illustrative* data used, the unit cost of haul is about 18 p/t km, although variations in the average haul speed alone produces a range of

13–23 p/t km. In any specific study, the haul cost must be derived from local data, particular attention being paid to work-study measurements of collection productivity.

The cost per tonne of transporting waste to a central processing plant increases as the catchment area becomes larger. Thus, in a given locality, economies of scale in processing costs can only be achieved at the price of diseconomies in transport costs. A simple model has been developed which provides a useful estimate of these diseconomies in a wide range of situations. Again using illustrative data, it has been shown that the optimum capacity of a plant, at which the total cost of waste delivery plus processing is a minimum, is about 200–600 t.p.d. for a transfer station, or about 300–1500 t.p.d. for an incinerator. The optimum capacity will be greatest for capital intensive plants with a low scale factor. However, the total cost varies little for capacities within several hundred tonnes per day of the optimum. If economies of scale in processing costs are to be realized by building large plants, with a capacity greater than about 800–1200 t.p.d., then attention must be paid to reducing waste delivery costs, for example by the use of transfer stations to supply waste from outlying districts.

The costs of transporting wastes in bulk by road depend critically on the number of trips which each vehicle can make per day. The variation of costs with distance is thus a step function, the cost being dominated by the fixed costs. For any given haul distance, the number of trips per day should be maximized. It may be possible to increase the number of trips by increasing haul speeds or by cutting lost time, for example by using special slave vehicles to perform the actual tipping operation at a landfill site.

We are now in a position to discuss the economics of any option for the treatment, reclamation, or disposal of waste on a fair and equitable basis. The transportation models developed here are used extensively in the next chapter, and in Part II of the book, in constructing options for dealing with the waste arising from a single source area. In any specific study, the models enable a comparison to be made, with local data, of such alternatives as:

(a) Direct delivery of the waste to the available landfill site *versus* bulk haulage from a transfer station.

(b) Simple transfer *versus* pulverization and baling, which offer potential savings both in landfill and transport costs, the latter by using higher payloads and less expensive vehicles.

(c) Two independent disposal schemes for nearby towns, *versus* the co-operative use of a single processing plant.

To demonstrate the application of the various models, the first example of direct landfill versus transfer is examined briefly. The calculations use the illustrative data from Tables 6.1, 6.2, 6.5, and 6.7. The unit cost of transfer is

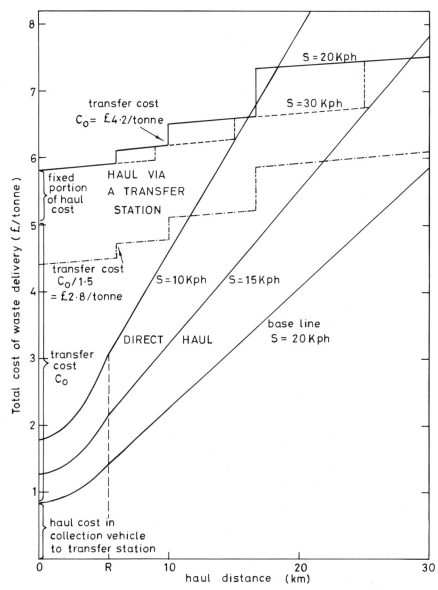

Fig. 6.13. Comparative costs of waste delivery to a landfill site by direct haul and transfer.

assumed to be £4.2/t (Tables A.4 and A.7). The transfer station is at the centre of the catchment area, which provides on average waste at 300 t.p.d. and has a population density of 25 persons/ha and a radius R of 5.4 km. The basic waste transport model gives an average haul cost to the centre of 80 p/t. The haul costs in a collection vehicle are calculated from the model for distances up to R, beyond which the constant unit cost of U p/t km is applied. The bulk haulage costs are taken from Fig. 6.12. The results are summarized in Fig. 6.13 for distances up to 30 km, which is about the upper limit of validity of the linear approximation to the direct haul cost.

The figure shows that, for the base case of $U = 18$ p/t km, direct haul is less expensive than transfer when the bulk haul speed is 20 or 30 k.p.h. and even when the transfer cost is reduced by one third to £2.8/t. For slower speeds of the collection vehicle, giving higher unit costs U, transfer becomes cheaper than direct haul, at distances between 20 and 30 km for $s = 15$ k.p.h., or between 10 and 20 km at $s = 10$ k.p.h.

It must be emphasized that this result should not be taken as proof that direct haul is normally preferable up to 30 km; a particular case must be analysed on its own merits, bearing in mind any other criteria which must be considered and any additional constraints on the direct haul distance. However, Fig. 6.13 does demonstrate the importance of the cost of transfer in the comparison, with even the lower cost of £2.8/t justifying by itself a direct haul of 15 km. Furthermore, the cost of delivery to the transfer station makes the relative direct haul cost rise less than proportionately with distance. The conventional comparison of costs for direct and indirect haul assumes that all waste arises at the centre and thus overstates the relative cost of direct haul.

7. UNCERTAINTY IN AN ECONOMIC STUDY OF OPTIONS

7.1. Introduction

The evaluation of options for the treatment, reclamation, or disposal of solid wastes requires a consideration of both transport and processing costs. The various cost estimates may be combined to yield a net present cost using discounted cash flow (DCF) analysis. The most obvious remaining feature for any economic evaluation is the uncertainty in the results. Although further work will reduce the problem for the newer technologies, uncertainty will always remain at a pre-design stage, particularly when many options are being compared. Associated with this uncertainty there is a risk that financial performance will not be achieved. Good decision making requires that best use be made of all information, including the likely error ranges in cost and revenue estimates.

The purpose of this chapter is to demonstrate two simple methods whereby uncertainty may be explicitly included in the economic analysis, and to apply the various principles developed earlier to a case study of options representing the current state of the art in waste management technology.

The first method of treating uncertainty is that of sensitivity analysis, which explores the effect, on the net present cost or overall cost per tonne of waste treated, of systematic changes in individual parameters. Sensitivity analysis may be used in two ways:

(i) To establish the relative sensitivity of the overall cost estimate to the various input parameters, and thus to focus attention on those areas where accurate estimation is vital and conversely on those where order-of-magnitude estimation is quite sufficient.

(ii) To explore the effect of different forecasts of the future, for example with regard to the quantity of waste generated or increased energy costs.

However, sensitivity analysis gives no information on either the effect of simultaneous changes in more than one parameter or the relative likelihood of a given variation in the overall cost per tonne. These criticisms are met by the complementary technique of risk analysis. Each component estimate is attributed with a probability distribution, either by estimating maximum and minimum values in addition to the mean value, or by estimating a range, e.g. $\overset{\times}{=}$ 1.25. These individual probability distributions are combined, using a simple computer program, in a DCF analysis, the result being presented as a probability distribution of the overall cost per tonne, rather than as a single apparently accurate cost.

The advantage of risk analysis is that it uses the information available on the range of the component cost estimates to produce not only a mean cost of waste disposal by that process, but also the range of costs which are likely to be encountered in practice. This is of particular importance when new and untried treatment or reclamation processes are being considered.

Both sensitivity and risk analysis are widely recommended for investment appraisal in industry (e.g. Hertz 1964, 1968; Malloy 1971; Allen 1975; Rose 1976), but use in waste management has been limited to occasional sensitivity analysis (e.g. Midwest Research Institute 1973). The computer program used here to perform both the sensitivity and the risk analysis is described in Appendix C.

7.2. The case study

The principles of economic evaluation developed here are now applied to a case study of some 30 options representing the current state of the art in waste management technology. The aim is both to demonstrate the methods and to enable an assessment to be made of the current economic status of the alternatives. For convenience, both the data used in, and the results from, the case study are collected together in Appendix A. A brief summary of the options selected is given in Table A.1: more details may be found in Part II. The cost and revenue data for the processes were discussed in Section 5.7 and are summarized in Tables A.2 and A.3.

Each option includes transport of the waste to the processing plant, processing, transport of any residual material to a landfill site, and final disposal there (Fig. 2.2). Transport of recovered materials to the point of reuse is allowed for in the revenue received. The construction of the options in terms of waste transport and residuals disposal is summarized in Table A.4.

Initial transport costs for an average 4 km haul to a central processing plant are common to each option and are thus neglected. Exceptions are direct haul to landfill, where an additional haul distance of 8 km is assumed, and modular incineration, where the total capacity of 400 tonnes per day (t.p.d.) is provided by 4 × 100 t.p.d. plants, thus reducing the average haul to about 2 km. A unit cost of 18 p/t km is assumed for haul in a collection vehicle (Section 6.2.4).

For waste transported by road from a transfer station, a haul distance of 30 km is assumed with 2 trips a day. From Fig. 6.12, a cost of £2.50/t is assumed. For rail transport a distance of 80 km and a cost of £4/t is used. When the waste is pulverized, it is assumed that a nearer landfill site at about 20 km is usable, with an additional trip per day reducing the unit cost of £1.75. For most other residues, including baled wastes, 3 trips per day to a site at 20 km distance are again assumed, but increased vehicle payloads reduce the unit cost to £1.25. Landfill costs are estimated as a percentage of those for untreated waste, taken as £2.40/t by removing the direct haul cost from that for landfill in Table A.7. For transfer by rail, an additional cost of 50 p/t is assumed for unloading the train. For residues from processing, three cases are distinguished:

(i) For mostly inorganic residues, a specific landfill cost of 50 per cent that for untreated waste is assumed. In practice, this is the most common case.

(ii) For residues containing putrescible organic materials, a cost of 70 per cent is used.

(iii) For the wet filter cake from anaerobic digestion, costs are assumed to be the same as for untreated waste.

Error ranges for both transport and landfill costs are estimated at $\overset{\times}{\div}$ 1.25, except for those options involving most transport, namely direct landfill, transfer, pulverization, and baling, where an extended range of $\overset{\times}{\div}$ 1.50 is used to allow for uncertainty in the haulage distance.

For simplicity, certain assumptions have been made in the discounted cash flow model used in the case study:

(i) The UK Treasury test discount rate of 10 per cent, current in 1977, is used. As the discount rate is a real rate of return, operating costs and revenues may be assumed to be constant over time, provided that relative prices remain unchanged (i.e. inflation is already subsumed in the calculation). The test discount rate was reassessed as 5 per cent in 1978; the effect of this reduced rate is discussed later.

(ii) Plant construction takes 3 years and the plant life is 20 years. Capital payments are made in three equal instalments over the years of construction. No subsequent capital payments or receipts are considered. All costs are discounted to the year of initial construction.

(iii) Waste output is constant.

The effect of relaxing each of these assumptions is explored later. The results of the baseline economic evaluation of options, using deterministic data, are presented in Tables A.5–A.7, which show, respectively, the breakdown of the direct operating costs of each process, the indirect, transport, and residue disposal costs, and a summary of the DCF analysis. The equivalent annual cost over each year of operation was calculated using equation 5.2. The capital charge shown in Table A.7 is equivalent to an annualized cost calculation in which the capital payments are compounded forward, at the discount rate, to the final year of construction.

7.3. Sensitivity analysis

Sensitivity analysis helps to identify the parameters that have most effect on the evaluation, and hence where accurate estimates are important. Since the net present cost shows a linear response to almost all the parameters in the simple DCF model used here, relative sensitivity, R_s, as derived in equations 6.13–6.16, provides a convenient means of summarizing the results (Table A.8). As the R_s for each parameter varies between options, either random or systematic changes in a parameter may affect the ranking of options on the criterion of least NPC. This effect may be shown in sensitivity diagrams, examples of which are given in Fig. 7.1.

From Table A.8, the most sensitive parameter is usually the investment with $0.35 < R_s < 1.35$. The sensitivity diagram in Fig. 7.1.(a) shows that uncertainty in the capital cost of options produces an overlapping which makes ranking difficult. In several cases, notably those involving heat recovery from incineration, a change in the capital cost estimate produces a more than proportional change in the NPC. Information on relative sensitivity enables one to adjust the NPC if a better capital cost estimate becomes available.

In the simple model the only components which depend on plant utilization are the energy, transport, and residue disposal costs, and the revenues. R_s is positive if the sum of these variable costs is greater than the revenues. Fig. 7.1(b) shows that a systematic increase in utilization makes the resource recovery options more competitive. Even when the NPC increases with utilization, the cost per tonne will decrease as more waste is processed. Continuous operations at 100 per cent of design capacity has already been seen to be impractical, but attention should be focused in design work on ways of increasing the utilization. However fixed costs may then increase; for example, additional investment may be necessary in storage space or redundancy, more men may be required, and maintenance costs may increase.

Net present cost is sensitive to factors affecting energy revenues, with $R_s \geq -0.6$. In Fig. 7.1(c), the effect of revenues from zero to twice the base level is shown. The importance of accurate estimates of each contributing factor, i.e. the heat content of the waste, the recovery efficiency of the process, and the price paid for the product, must be emphasized. Revenues twice those assumed in the base case reflect prices generally above current levels for conventional energy sources, but may be appropriate in the future, or if higher shadow prices for recovered energy products are thought appropriate (Section 5.6).

The other factors are of less importance. For material revenues, $-0.2 \leq R_s \leq -0.1$ for four options only, while the others, excluding the incremental options to recover additional materials, have $R_s > 0.1$. Transport

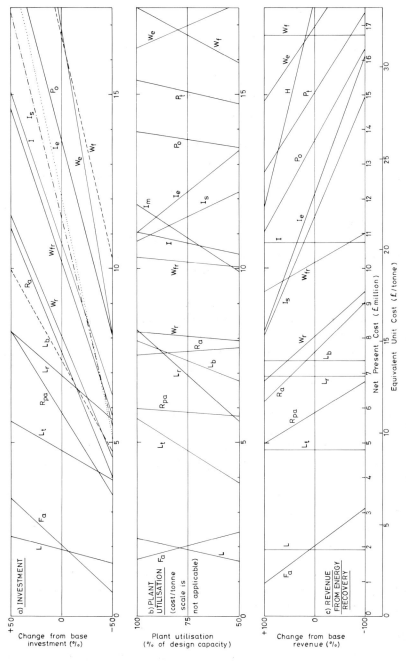

Fig. 7.1. Sensitivity diagrams. (Key in Tables A.1 or A.8.)

and landfill costs affect the landfill options considerably, but have little effect on the others. For electricity usage, $0 < R_s < 0.22$, while for fuel usage $R_s > 0.1$ for just 4 options. The effect of maintenance costs, rates, and labour costs are fairly consistent, the sensitivity to the latter being lower than may have been expected ($R_s \approx 0.1$). For those factors not shown in Table A.8, including the influence of raw materials, water supply and treatment, other utilities, and the remaining operating cost factors from Table 5.6, $R_s < 0.1$ for all options, and in most cases $R_s < 0.05$.

7.4. Risk analysis

7.4.1. Method

In risk analysis, a subjective probability distribution is attributed to each uncertain parameter. This may be specified directly as a histogram of relative frequencies or, more conveniently, may be generated from a standard distribution. Care is necessary to ensure that the distribution is appropriate to the problem (Allen 1975). If the error range is symmetrical, either of the form $C_0 \pm A$, where A is an absolute value, or of $C_0 \pm 100\,x$ per cent, a normal distribution is suitable. The skew distribution $C_0 \overset{\times}{\div} (1 + x)$ may be generated by assuming that x is normally distributed about zero, a negative value of x being interpreted as the cost $C_0/(1 + x)$ and a positive value as $C_0 (1 + x)$. In either case, the error range is assumed to correspond to $\pm 2\sigma$, where σ is the standard deviation of the normal distribution, so that there is a 95 per cent chance that the actual value lies within the range. The error ranges used in the case study are summarized in Table 7.1. The effects of alternative interpretations of the error ranges, and of changes in those ranges, are examined below.

Using Monte Carlo simulation, the probability distributions for individual estimates are combined to yield a distribution for the net present cost. The calculation is repeated using input data selected in any combination from the distributions. The selection is made by a random number so that the frequency of selection of any value is proportional to its probability. Different random numbers are used to select each parameter value, and so the parameters should be independent. If two parameters are not independent, then the same random number should be used to select both.

Sufficient repetitions should be used to reach a steady state, where the resultant NPC distribution is insensitive to a change in either the number of iterations, n, or the sequence of random numbers. In general the accuracy will increase with the square root of n. The pseudo-random numbers generated by the computer are such that supplying the same starter numbers will always give the same sequence, so that using different starters will yield an independent sample from the NPC distribution. Tests with $n = 1000$ and

Table 7.1

Error ranges in the risk analysis

Data item	Range[1]	Conditions
Investment	$\overset{\times}{\div}$ 1.4	Standard
	$\overset{\times}{\div}$ 2.0	For landfill, transfer, and pulverization
Raw materials	$\overset{\times}{\div}$ 1.25	
Electricity consumption	$\overset{\times}{\div}$ 1.25	
Fuel consumption	$\overset{\times}{\div}$ 1.25	
Water supply or treatment costs	$\overset{\times}{\div}$ 1.25	
Number of men	$\overset{\times}{\div}$ 1.25	
Maintenance factor	$\overset{\times}{\div}$ 1.25	
Transport costs	$\overset{\times}{\div}$ 1.25	Standard
	$\overset{\times}{\div}$ 1.50	For direct or indirect landfill
Residuals disposal or landfill	$\overset{\times}{\div}$ 1.25	
Plant utilization factor	± 0.10	Base value is 0.75
Materials recovery	± 5%	Standard
efficiency	± 10%	Additional materials recovery (non-ferrous metals, glass)
Price of recovered materials	± 20%	
Materials content in waste	± 10%	
Energy recovery efficiency	± 5%	Standard, base efficiency $\geqslant 0.7$
	± 25%	Electricity generation
	± 30%	Steam generation, base case is 75% of steam actually sold
	± 10%	Other cases (including ethanol)
Price of recovered energy products	± 20%	
Energy content of waste	± 10%	

1. For an explanation of the notation $\overset{\times}{\div}$ $(1 + x)$, see Section 5.7.

eight different starter pairs were performed for two options; the variation in the results was less than 2 per cent, well within the expected accuracy of the method, so $n = 1000$ was used throughout. For every option, the same pair of starter numbers was used.

The results of the risk analysis are presented in Table A.9 and summarized in Table 7.2. The mean value of the net present cost is slightly higher than for the deterministic case because the initial distributions $C_0 \overset{\times}{\div} (1+x)$ are skewed to higher costs. The main advantage of risk analysis is the information it provides on the range of costs expected. Although the cost distribution is slightly skew, its width is conveniently measured by the standard deviation s. For the net present costs in Table A.9, the standard deviations are generally between 12 and 25 per cent of the means, so that the approximate 95 per cent confidence interval ($\pm 2s$) is between 50 and 100 per cent of the mean. Thus a clear ranking of options on the criterion of least NPC will no longer be possible. The cost range shown in Table 7.2 corresponds to the 95 per cent confidence interval.

The width of the output distributions, and hence the overlap between

Table 7.2

The costs of treatment, reclamation, or disposal of municipal waste

Basic option	Specific variation	Cost range (£/t)
Landfill	Local site	3.8 ± 1.4
Landfill at a distant site	Transfer by road	9 ± 3
	Transfer by rail	14 ± 4
	Pulverization	10 ± 4
	Baling	14 ± 4
Incineration	Non-recuperative	21 ± 6
	Steam generation	22 ± 9
	Electricity generation	24 ± 10
	Modular	21 ± 5
	Modular + steam	24 ± 9
Production of a solid refuse-derived	Pulverized fuel: case (a)	4.3 ± 4.2
fuel (RDF) by dry separation	case (b)	6.3 ± 4.4
	Paper-based RDF	11 ± 3
	American RDF	15 ± 5
	Powder RDF	23 ± 8
Incineration of RDF	Suspension firing	29 ± 10
	Incinerator turbine	25 ± 10
Separation of waste by wet pulping	Fibre recovery	32 ± 9
	Incineration + electricity	33 ± 12
	Fibre + wet RDF	20 ± 6
	Wet RDF	16 ± 5
	Dried RDF	23 ± 6
Pyrolysis and other thermal process	Occidental	27 ± 8
	Union Carbide Purox	49 ± 17
	Andco–Torrax	29 ± 9
	Monsanto Landgard	31 ± 10
Biological processes	Composting	22 ± 6
	Acid hydrolysis	34 ± 11
	Anaerobic digestion	39 ± 11
Additional recovery of glass and	Separated waste	+(2.3 ± 1.0)
non-ferrous metals	Incinerator residue	+(2.8 ± 1.3)

options, is affected by the choice of variable parameters, by the error ranges used, and by the interpretation of these ranges. The effects of alternative assumptions to those used in the case study are illustrated in Table A.10. The interpretation of the error ranges is seen to be fairly critical, a decrease in the confidence interval from 95 per cent to 87 per cent increasing s by about 30 per cent. So long as the investment is included, both the mean and standard deviation appear fairly stable to changes in the number of parameters input as probability distributions. Experiments with the widths of the input distributions were directed at those parameters and options with the highest values of R_s (Table A.8). Again, the only critical parameter is the investment, with a decrease in the accuracy of an estimate from $C_0 \overset{\times}{\div} 1.4$ to $C_0 \overset{\times}{\div} 2.0$ increasing s by about 100 per cent. With other parameters, quite large changes in the assumed accuracies generally changed s by less than 10 per cent.

Risk and sensitivity analyses are not mutually exclusive. For example, in the risk analysis, plant utilization is assumed to be 0.75 ± 0.1 of the design capacity. It may be of interest to study the results for, say, a general shift in utilization to 0.90 ± 0.1. This may be achieved by repeating the risk analysis with the new data, or an approximate result may be obtained by combining the risk and sensitivity analysis results, shifting the NPC distribution by the amount indicated in the sensitivity analysis. This approximation was tested for large shifts in both plant utilization and energy prices, for an option with high R_s values (Table A.10). The shift in the means confirm those predicted by sensitivity analysis, while the standard deviations are increased by less than 5 per cent.

7.4.2. Interpretation

The consideration of uncertainty through risk analysis has led to a breakdown of the simple decision rule which ranks options in terms of least net present cost. The interpretation of the results is aided by a graphical presentation of the NPC distributions, as either relative or cumulative frequency functions. The latter are easier to interpret quantitatively (Fig. 7.2). For example, there is a 10 per cent chance that the NPC of landfill will be less than £1.6 million, and a 10 per cent chance that it will be more than £2.5 million.

The use of Fig. 7.2. in decision making must involve judgement on the acceptability of risks. Three distinct cases may be distinguished. In the simplest, there is no overlap between the cumulative frequency curves of two options. For example, with the data used in the case study, one may say with 99 per cent confidence that direct landfill to a local site is cheaper than any option with the possible exception of the use of pulverized waste as a fuel. The second case is illustrated by landfill with transfer by rail, which has a lower probability of exceeding any given NPC than has the production of American RDF and is said to dominate it probabilistically. Although rail transfer would normally be preferred on the criterion of least NPC, there is still a chance that RDF will be cheaper, and to eliminate it before more detailed study of, say, capital cost estimates, markets for RDF, and charges for rail haul, may result in an inferior decision. The third case, when the cumulative frequency curves intersect, is illustrated by landfill and the use of pulverized waste as a fuel when a higher revenue is assumed (case (a)). Although the mean cost of landfill is slightly lower, and there is a 5 per cent chance that landfill will save more than £1.6 millon, there is also a 43 per cent chance that the pulverized fuel option will save money. The choice depends on attitudes to risk; in general one might not accept a 5 per cent chance of a profit of £1 million as off-setting an equal chance of a loss of £1 million. A formal approach would seek to quantify the decision makers' utility function to transform money amounts into utility values, choosing the option which maximizes expected utility (Moore and Thomas 1976). In practice, the

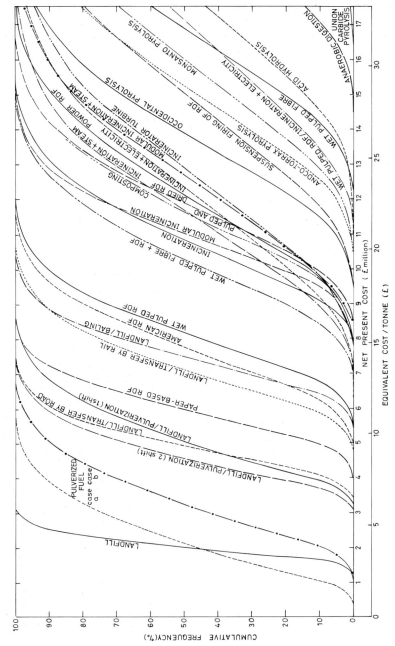

Fig. 7.2. Cumulative frequency plot of risk analysis results.

problems of estimating this function are formidable, and at a preliminary planning stage a promising option may again be eliminated prematurely.

Two further methods may aid interpretation. The first is an option ranking matrix (Table 7.3) which quantifies the overlaps in N P C. The diagonal entries correspond to the ranking based on a 90 per cent chance that the

Table 7.3. Option ranking matrix
(Key in table A.1 or A.8)

Rank	1	2	3	4	5	6	7	8	9	10	11	12	13	14	15	16	17	18	19	20	21	22	23	24	25	26	27	28	29	30
1	L 90	F_a 62	F_b 27																											
2	L 72	F_a 90	F_b 67	L_{p2} 19																										
3	L 17	F_a 73	F_b 90	L_{p2} 68	L_t 56	L_{p1} 50	R_{pa} 13																							
4		F_a 13		L_{p2} 90	L_t 87	L_{p1} 73	R_{pa} 48		L_r 11																					
5					L_t 90	L_{p1} 77	R_{pa} 54		L_r 15																					
6						L_{p1} 90	R_{pa} 80	L_b 25	L_r 41	R_a 24	W_r 11																			
7							R_{pa} 90	L_b 40	L_r 54	R_a 36	W_r 22																			
8								L_b 90	L_r 90	R_a 77	W_r 69	W_{fr} 17																		
9									L_r 90	R_a 77	W_r 69	W_{fr} 17																		
10										R_a 90	W_r 85	W_{fr} 34	I_m 12	I 21			I_s 18			I_e 15										
11											W_r 90	W_{fr} 43	I_m 22	I 30	C 15	W_{rd} 11	I_s 24	R_{po} 13	I_{ms} 12	I_e 19	D_t 13									
12												W_{fr} 90	I_m 87	I 85	C 70	W_{rd} 68	I_s 66	R_{po} 59	I_{ms} 50	I_e 55	D_t 47	P_o 28	P_t 11	D_s 20						
13													I_m 90	I 87	C 73	W_{rd} 71	I_s 69	R_{po} 63	I_{ms} 53	I_e 57	D_t 50	P_o 32	P_t 14	D_s 23	P_m 10					
14														I 90	C 77	W_{rd} 76	I_s 73	R_{po} 68	I_{ms} 57	I_e 61	D_t 53	P_o 37	P_t 18	D_s 26	P_m 13					
15															C 90	W_{rd} 90	I_s 85	R_{po} 81	I_{ms} 73	I_e 75	D_t 67	P_o 55	P_t 34	D_s 39	P_m 26	W_f 10	W_e 17			
16																W_{rd} 90	I_s 86	R_{po} 81	I_{ms} 73	I_e 75	D_t 68	P_o 55	P_t 34	D_s 39	P_m 26	W_f 10	W_e 17			
17																	I_s 90	R_{po} 87	I_{ms} 80	I_e 81	D_t 75	P_o 65	P_t 43	D_s 47	P_m 34	W_f 17	W_e 24	H 12		
18																		R_{po} 90	I_{ms} 83	I_e 84	D_t 78	P_o 70	P_t 48	D_s 51	P_m 38	W_f 22	W_e 27	H 15		
19																			I_{ms} 90	I_e 90	D_t 85	P_o 81	P_t 60	D_s 62	P_m 49	W_f 35	W_e 37	H 25		
20																				I_e 90	D_t 85	P_o 81	P_t 60	D_s 62	P_m 49	W_f 35	W_e 37	H 25		
21																					D_t 90	P_o 88	P_t 70	D_s 70	P_m 58	W_f 46	W_e 45	H 33		
22																						P_o 90	P_t 74	D_s 74	P_m 63	W_f 52	W_e 48	H 37		
23																							P_t 90	D_s 88	P_m 81	W_f 74	W_e 66	H 58	A 28	
24																								D_s 90	P_m 84	W_f 76	W_e 70	H 62	A 32	
25																									P_m 90	W_f 87	W_e 78	H 72	A 44	
26																										W_f 90	W_e 81	H 76	A 49	
27																											W_e 90	H 88	A 67	P_u 18
28																												H 90	A 70	P_u 21
29																													A 90	P_u 59
30																														P_u 90

NPC will be less than a certain value. Entries in each row give the cumulative frequency for the other options which correspond to the 90 per cent level of the diagonal element, subject to a lower limit of 10 per cent. Reading down a column gives the range of rankings possible for an option within the arbitrary 80 per cent confidence interval, the numbers indicating the *relative* likelihood of each ranking. In principle, for options below the diagonal line the relative likelihoods may be calculated from the other values, if the assumption is made that the options are independent. The full quantification of the project ranking matrix becomes complicated when an option may take many ranks. For example, to rank incineration as number 20 requires that just 6 of the 11 options to the right of I in row 14 should be cheaper. However, even without full quantification, the matrix provides a convenient method of identifying overlap.

A second method plots the means against the standard deviations (Fig. 7.3). In general, the risk as measured by the standard deviation increases with the expected cost, although in comparing individual options greater certainty may be bought at the price of a higher expected cost. This presentation makes such trade-offs clear.

7.5. Extending the case study

The results of a DCF evaluation are sensitive to two economic parameters, namely the discount rate, r, and a plant's operating life, T. Previously the choice of discount rate was seen to be controversial (Section 5.3.2) and it was concluded that results should be presented for a range. Indeed, since these calculations were made, the UK Treasury test discount rate has been reduced from 10 to 5 per cent. Results for the case study with $0 < r < 25$ per cent are shown in Fig. 7.4. As the relationship of equivalent annual cost to NPC (equation 5.2) varies with both r and T, only the unit costs are shown. These increase with r, while the NPC decreases, the effect being stronger for options with high capital costs. Changes in r have considerable effect on both absolute costs and rankings; for example, with $r < 5$ per cent production of American RDF is cheaper than rail haul to distant landfill, while for $r > 20$ per cent rail transfer is more than £5/t cheaper. However, the overall conclusions are broadly similar for discount rates in the range 5–10 per cent. Use of a low discount rate, corresponding to a social discount rate or an American municipal bond interest rate, favours the more capital intensive options for reclamation or resource recovery, while a higher discount rate, such as that derived from current commercial or municipal interest rates in Britain without correction for inflation, favours less capital intensive options for landfill. It must be emphasized that use of a nominal rate of return, uncorrected for inflation, as the discount rate is only correct if the annual cash flows include expected increases due to inflation.

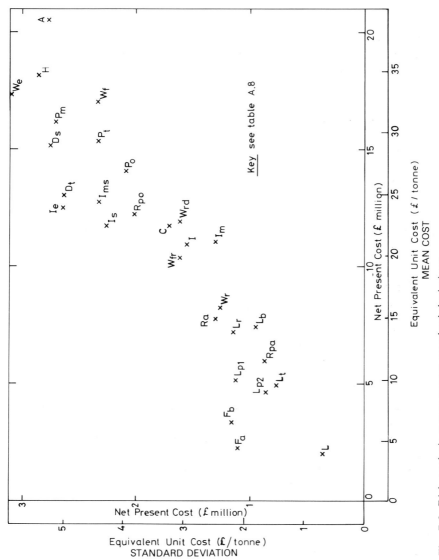

Fig. 7.3. Risk analysis means versus standard deviations.

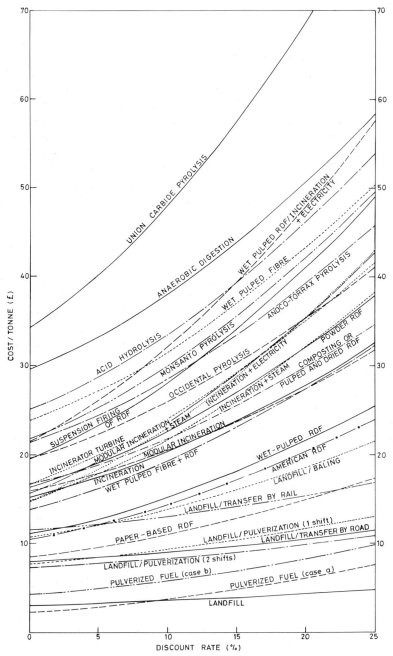

Fig. 7.4. Sensitivity to the discount rate.

The sensitivity of the case study to changes in the assumed project lifetimes is summarized in Fig. 7.5. Changes are less marked, with a range of $15 < T < 30$ years altering the unit costs by less than 10 per cent from their base values. The effect of changing T is greater for more capital intensive options, but the effect on project rankings is minimal. Although uncertainty in the lifetime of an option will introduce some additional overlapping of cost rankings, the effect will be small compared with other uncertainties.

The discounted cash flow model used so far in the case study has been very simple. To illustrate the potential of the method and to examine the sensitivity of the simple model to the assumptions, an extended DCF model was tested for several options. The sensitivity analysis is summarized in Table A.11 and the risk analysis in Table A.12. It may be concluded that:

(i) The only critical extension of scope is the inclusion of recurrent capital investments, for example in additional landfill sites. As a landfill site is unlikely to last for 20 years, and replacement sites may be either more expensive to purchase or further from the waste source, such considerations are vital for a proper discussion of direct landfill as an option either for the whole period or as an interim measure prior to a later investment, e.g. in a transfer station. The extended model may also consider the income from the sale of reclaimed land. The trial runs showed that a realistic programme of site replacement increases the cost of direct landfill by 20 per cent, while the sale of reclaimed land has only a small effect unless high shadow prices are used.

(ii) Other extensions considered were a variable construction period, changes in the waste output and relative labour or energy costs through time, and the explicit inclusion of working capital and start-up cost. While each increases the realism of the model, their effects on the net present costs are small and for many purposes the simple model will suffice. In any specific study, it would, however, be prudent to test the robustness of the results to various possible futures, by testing the effect of different forecasts of relative costs and prices, and of waste production.

The effect of different scales of operation may be examined by applying the scale factors S, listed in Table A.2, to estimates of the gross equivalent annual cost of each option. The revenue per tonne is assumed to be constant. Results, expressed as costs per tonne, are illustrated in Fig. 7.6 for average plant throughputs up to 1200 t.p.d. These must be interpreted with care. The scale factors are uncertain and the use of equation 5.5 over a wide range is questionable, so that estimates far removed from the base capacity will have substantially reduced accuracy. In addition, the high scale factors ($S > 0.85$) expected for many options are unlikely to apply at very low capacity. For incineration, a lower (design) capacity limit of 10 tonnes per hour, or about 150 t.p.d. was suggested earlier (Section 5.4.7); this is taken as the lower limit for all options, with the exception of composting, where

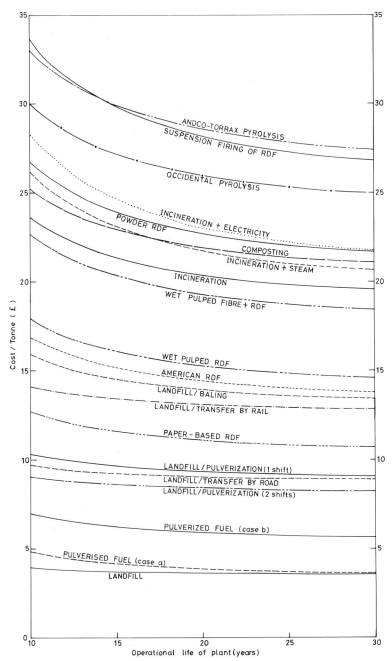

Fig. 7.5. Sensitivity to the assumed project lifetime.

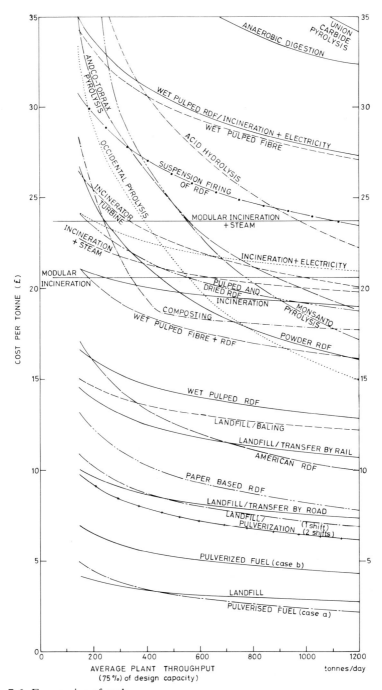

Fig. 7.6. Economies of scale.

the evidence suggests a critical capacity of about 450 t.p.d. (Section 19.2), and of modular incineration which is designed specifically for small plants, with little change in the unit costs for capacities greater than about 50 t.p.d.

From Fig. 7.6, it is clear that economies of scale can have marked effects on both absolute and relative cost estimates. The decrease in net unit cost as capacity increases is greatest for low S and high specific revenue. Thus the pyrolysis and hydrolysis options are particularly favoured by considering a large plant. This conclusion depends on the comparatively low scale factors, which are based entirely on hypothetical estimates in the literature and have not yet been confirmed by experience. As discussed earlier, the scale factors used here are generally in the range $S = 0.8 - 0.95$; guidance is taken from the calculated value of $S = 0.95$ for UK incinerators and the general value $S = 0.8$ appropriate to solid handling processes. Scale factors quoted in the literature are usually hypothetical and are often based on $S = 0.6$, which is only appropriate to gas-phase processes. Use of such low scale factors tend to bias estimates towards options with higher capital costs.

7.6. Discussion

The case study has served to demonstrate the method of economic analysis and to emphasize the importance of taking the uncertainty in the data into account explicitly. Sensitivity analysis is useful in highlighting those para-meters which have most effect on the net disposal cost and hence where accurate estimation is most important. Risk analysis attributes to each uncertain parameter a subjective probability distribution and generates a distribution for the overall net cost of disposal. The cost ranges for different options overlap extensively, so that a clear ranking is not possible. This conclusion is reinforced when the evaluation is repeated with altered dis-count rate, operating life, or plant capacity. Discounted cash flow using sensitivity and risk analysis is comparatively simple to use, and is a powerful tool for economic evaluation.

The results of the case study also enable one to assess the current econo-mic status of the options, an area of much practical significance. Some of the results are summarized in Table A.13 in the form of rankings of the options. Despite the extensive overlapping of costs and their sensitivity to many factors, certain conclusions may be drawn. A more extensive discussion of the current status of the alternative technologies for waste management is given in Part II, particularly in Chapter 21.

In general, the options may be divided roughly into two groups; the lower group have base value unit costs less than £15/t, while the upper group cost more than £20/t. The lower group contains all the landfill-based options, together with five refuse-derived fuel (RDF) options. In a specific study, attention must thus be focused on the availability of landfills, the transport distances and costs, and on the markets for a processed solid fuel.

The cheapest option in the case study, with a base cost about £4/t, is either landfill, with direct haul in a collection vehicle over an average distance 8 km more than for a central treatment plant, or the use of pulverized and magnetically separated waste directly as a fuel. The exact cost of landfill depends on the sequence of sites to be used, their costs, and their lifetimes. Replacement of the site may increase the cost by about £1/t. However, if the initial landfill will be replaced by one at a much greater distance, or if transfer will be necessary later in the period, the specific situation must be evaluated before a definite conclusion may be drawn.

The use of pulverized waste directly as a fuel is not yet proven, and is limited in its application to cement kilns or older boilers with chain grates and extensive ash handling facilities; its feasibility thus depends on further experience and on suitable industrial outlets. If an (optimistic) energy specific price (£/GJ) 40 per cent that for coal is obtainable, giving a net revenue of £2.3/t of waste (case (a)), then it is competitive with direct landfill. A net price of zero, implying that the user pays transport costs and being perhaps still optimistic (case (b)), increases the net cost to about £6/t, which still gives a margin of £2/t over indirect landfill.

If direct landfill and the use of pulverized waste as a fuel are not available, then either transfer and haul to a more distant landfill, or upgrading the RDF, should be considered. The costs of bulk transport by road depend more on the number of trips to landfill made each day than on the distance. Transfer by road to a site 30 km distant has similar costs to pulverization with transport to a site at 20 km (about £9/t). Thus, if an extra trip per day to the landfill is made possible by using a nearer site which would not be available for untreated waste, pulverization is competitive with simple transfer. Both transfer by rail to a site at 80 km and baling before landfill cost £13–14/t, substantially more than simple transfer.

Three additional RDF options are competitive with some of the landfill-based options. The cheapest (£11/t) appears to be the production of a high-grade paper-based RDF, currently being demonstrated in Britain at plants in Doncaster and Newcastle-upon-Tyne. Dry separation of waste to produce a single organic fraction containing putrescible matter gives a higher yield of a lower quality RDF, described here as American RDF. The third option produces a dewatered fuel at 50 per cent moisture from wet pulped waste. Marketing this wet fuel may not be easy and upgrading by drying raises the cost considerably. The cost differential of £3.5/t between paper-based and American-type RDF is more than accounted for by uncertainty in capital costs and in electricity consumption.

The upper group of options, with base costs greater than about £20/t, do not seem economically competitive with the options so far discussed. This conclusion may be overturned by improved cost estimates, by further developments, or by favourable markets for forms of recovered energy other than RDF. The exact ordering of the options is very dependent on the conditions chosen, and the risk analysis shows much overlapping.

All of the incineration options have mean costs of £20–24/t. Heat recovery is marginally uneconomic, but the uncertainty in the markets is considerable so that this may easily be reversed. Of the options which produce either steam or electricity, incineration of untreated waste appears generally cheaper than the more sophisticated alternatives. Modular incineration has similar costs to conventional incineration, but the conditions of the analysis weigh against it. As each module treats 12 t.p.d., and 100 t.p.d. is the maximum plant size contemplated, its particular advantages are apparent only at low capacity, where it is the cheapest of the upper group of options.

Composting has similar costs to incineration, even when the revenues are low. Wet pulping with fibre recovery is considerably more expensive than the use of the organic fraction as a fuel. Upgrading either American RDF by powdering or wet-pulped RDF by drying increases costs above those for incineration. Pyrolysis or gasification is expensive in the base case although, if economies of scale can be achieved, it may be competitive for large plants. Both acid hydrolysis and anaerobic digestion have base costs over £30/t. It should be noted that these last three technologies in particular are still not well developed, and so any conclusions drawn must remain cautious.

All of the resource recovery or reclamation options discussed above recover only magnetic metals from the inorganic fraction. Recovery of glass and non-ferrous metals has been viewed here as an incremental operation, to be undertaken if it proves to be economic. The results show a net additional cost, allowing for the reduction in landfill costs, of £2–3/t in the base case. Thus such additional recovery appears currently uneconomic, although exceptions may occur if local markets are favourable; the situation should be kept under review.

Throughout this analysis either the net present cost or its equivalent unit cost has been used as the economic criterion. However, if capital spending is restricted (Section 2.2.3), options may not necessarily be ranked in order of least net present cost. This effect may conveniently be shown as a trade-off diagram (Fig. 7.7). Capital cost may then be used as a separate, but not independent, criterion in assessment, or it may be used as a constraint to screen the options.

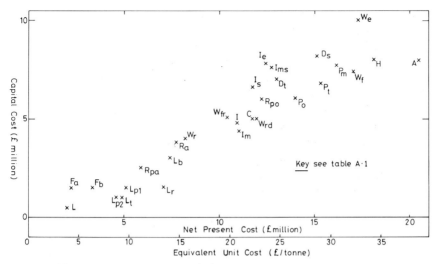

Fig. 7.7. Net present cost versus capital cost.

8. ENERGY CONSERVATION THROUGH RESOURCE RECOVERY

8.1. Introduction

Economics does not always adequately reflect the scarcity of physical resources. It is useful to have, in addition to an economic evaluation, a quantitative measure of the contribution which resource recovery from waste makes to the conservation of energy and materials. As the recovery of materials saves energy which would otherwise be used in their production, it is convenient to use energy as the unit of account. The purpose of this chapter is to develop two self-consistent measures of the energy efficiency of a process and to demonstrate the method using the same case study of options as in the complementary economic analysis.

The impact of a good or service on the total available energy resource is measured by its gross energy requirement and the techniques to determine it are commonly termed energy analysis. There are three methods in use, namely statistical, input–output, and process analysis. Statistical analysis treats the entire system making a product, using published statistics such as the census of production for data. Different technologies can be compared only if the statistics are suitably disaggregated. Input–output analysis is similar, but the source of data is the published economic input–output tables. Results are derived as the energy input per unit of financial output (e.g. MJ/£), which is known as the energy intensity of an industry or commodity group. Process analysis evaluates an individual process, and requires its materials balance and the gross energy requirements of each individual input. The latter are often derived from statistical or input–output analysis. Process analysis is the only method for comparing technologies and processes in detail.

In recent years, these techniques have been applied to many commodities and technologies; a useful text and compendium of results is available (Boustead and Hancock 1979). In August 1974, an international workshop considered the methods and conventions of energy analysis and agreed upon certain basic rules (International Federation of Institutes for Advanced Study (IFIAS) 1974). In particular, they recommended that where energy analysis is concerned with depletion of the resource base, all figures should be expressed in terms of free energy. However, they recognized that in many cases it is impossible to compute the free energy changes of actual processes, and suggested that it is sufficiently accurate in the case of intensive fuels to express figures in terms of gross enthalpy. Gross enthalpies are thus used here.

Empirical studies of energy use may be complemented by theoretical calculations of the minimum energy required to make a process operate (R. S. Berry 1976). Unfortunately the limits specified by conventional thermodynamics apply only to reversible and infinitely slow processes. Work on themodynamics in finite time is quite recent (Andresen, Berry, Nitzan, and Salamon 1977; Andresen, Salamon, and Berry 1977; Salamon, Andresen, and Berry 1977).

The application of these ideas to waste management has been restricted. Several authors have included waste collection or disposal as one component in the total life cycle of packaging containers (Hannon 1972; Berry and Makino 1974), or in an analysis of the advantages of recycling individual metals (Chapman 1974b, 1976b). Broussaud (1976) used process analysis to study the recovery of materials from incinerator residues. Other work has been largely restricted to the energy balances of recovery options, comparing the heat content of the waste-derived fuel with that of the original waste and fuels used in the process (e.g. Hecklinger 1976).

8.2. Process analysis

Process analysis is the method most appropriate to a comparison of technologies for waste management. Possible levels of the analysis are represented in Fig. 8.1, which is based on the recommendations of the IFIAS workshop. Level 1 includes only the direct inputs to the final process. An analysis would include fuels and electrical energy supplied to a process, but none of the energy for prior steps such as the generation of electricity. Level 2 includes the direct inputs to make the materials used in the process and to provide the energy at level 1. Level 3 accounts for the energy to produce capital equipment, as well as the first iteration of the requirements for input materials at level 2. Level 4 and higher levels continue the iteration; ideally this should stop where the contributions are comparable to the uncertainties in those from previous levels. Experience shows that an analysis to level 2 will include 90–95 per cent of the energy requirements to level 4, but exceptions can occur. The contribution at level 2 often exceeds that at level 1.

The quantity sought here is the amount by which the disposal of one tonne of municipal waste by each option will deplete or augment the stock of primary energy. This is subtly different from the gross energy requirement

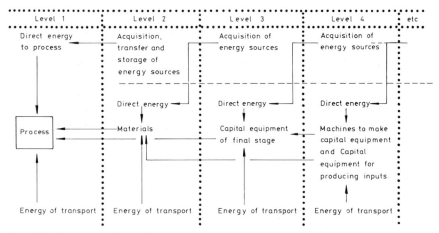

Fig. 8.1. Successive levels in a process analysis of resource requirements. (After R. S. Berry (1976).)

of a commodity being produced, as now the focus is on disposing of, rather than producing, a given material. Thus products recovered from the waste are viewed as substitutes for traditional manufacture. They contribute, directly or indirectly, to the gross energy requirement of waste disposal, reducing it by an amount equal to the quantity of primary energy saved. For example, the incineration of waste produces heat which can be used to raise steam. This steam may be credited with its heat value or, more consistently, with the primary energy to produce it from an alternative source. Iron recovered from waste is not a conventional energy source, but its use in a steel furnace needs less energy than does ore and this saving can be credited. The gross energy requirement of waste disposal can be negative, that is resource or energy recovery from waste may be a net energy source.

The level at which the analysis here is carried out depends partly on the data available. In the sense that one is interested in the energy contents of both inputs and outputs, the levels of analysis proceed in two directions. The principle is to aim for a level 3 analysis.

It is interesting to compare this framework for process analysis with that of Broussaud (1976). He compared two options for materials recovery from incinerator residue with a third, which dumped the residue after magnetic extraction of some ferrous metals and obtained the same products directly from virgin sources. The two methods are similar in principle, but that proposed here is more flexible and easier to apply in a comparison of options.

Two further problems of convention should be mentioned. The first concerns the treatment of imports. If the major energy of production is expended abroad and that of recycling is expended in a country, then one must choose to use either the full (global) energy saving, or just that part of it which occurs in the country. The problems raised here are not severe, and so global figures are used.

The second convention is that for partitioning energy in co-production processes or common services. An example is the co-processing of sewage sludge with waste, thus performing two disposal operations. A simple approach is to assign the energy of the alternative disposal method for the sludge as a credit to the process but, as such data are not available at present, where this arises here the data are adjusted to remove the sewage sludge from consideration.

8.3. Energy inputs and outputs

It is relatively straightforward to estimate the energy inputs to the waste management system. The direct energy requirements of a process are estimated directly, and evaluated to level 2. The materials supplied to the process are assigned gross energy requirements from the literature, using statistical, input–output, or process analysis results as available. The gross energy requirement of capital equipment is calculated using input–output energy intensities. The estimation of energy inputs is fully documented in Appendix D, and the resultant values are summarized in Table 8.1.

The concept of energy savings through recycling materials is rather novel,

Table 8.1
Gross energy requirements of inputs to waste management
(for full references, see Appendix D)

Item	GJ/t	MJ/unit
Diesel fuel	50.8	42.5/l
Fuel oil	47.9	$\begin{cases} 1.11/MJ \\ 45.5/l \end{cases}$
Gas	–	130/therm
Electricity	–	12/kWh
Water supply	0.009	9.2/m³
Lime	4.68	
Cover material for landfill	0.09	
Sulphuric acid	8.1	
Proprietary inorganic chemical used as an embrittling agent	20.0	
Maintenance and operating supplies		100/£(1977)
Capital investment		50/£(1977)
Effluent treatment	0.013	13/m³
Road transport		2.8/t km
Rail transport		1.2/t km
Disposal of inorganic residues	0.13	

and an explicit study of the literature had to be undertaken (Appendix E). It was assumed that the material is ready for shipment to the using facility. Allowance was made for the transportation of the product to the point of use and for all the operations made on it until it could be absorbed into the usage cycle of the virgin product. This gross energy requirement was then compared with that to produce the equivalent product using conventional routes of manufacture. Difficulties arise when the recovered product is not a perfect substitute for the conventional product. It should be noted that the values obtained for the energy savings are average values.

The estimates of typical energy savings due to recycling one tonne of various materials are summarized in Table 8.2. Substantial energy savings are apparent for all the metals, with the possible exception of the recovery of tin from tinplate and of minor components from alloys. Particular savings are seen for the electrolytically produced metals. The reclamation of glass cullet shows a small energy saving; the use of returnable glass bottles in place of the increasingly predominant disposable bottles has a much larger potential for energy saving even when the necessary collection, cleaning, and refilling are considered. Recycling paper shows substantial energy savings, particularly when credit is taken for the calorific value still remaining in the paper.

These values are used in Table 8.3 to calculate the energy savings which

Table 8.2

Typical energy savings from recycling materials
(see Appendix E and Wilson 1979*b*)

Material	Energy savings (GJ/t of product)
Metals:	
Ferrous metals	25
Aluminium	270
Copper:	
New scrap	60
Irony scrap	50
Zinc	50
Mixed non-ferrous metals	
(copper/zinc)	50
Lead	30
Nickel	160
Titanium	400
Magnesium	400
Tin (from tinplate)	low
Glass:	
As cullet	3(0–5)
By using returnable bottles	16
Paper	25

result when various materials are recovered from the solid waste stream. The calculation depends both on the quantity of the material in the waste and on the efficiency of its recovery. Information on energy savings due to the recovery of fuel products is also included in Appendix E and in Table 8.3.

Table 8.3

Energy savings due to resource recovery from solid waste
(see Appendix E)

(a) Materials

Category	Material	Primary energy saving per kg recovered (MJ)	Amount in 1 t of waste[1] (kg)	Typical recovery efficiency[2] (% by weight)	Theoretical energy saving (MJ/t of waste)	Typical energy saving (MJ/t of waste)
Inorganic	Ferrous metal:	25	76		1900	
	Normal			90		1710
	Including additional materials recovery			94		1790
	After combustion			56		1060
	Aluminium:	270	5		1350	
	Normal			70		945
	After burning			50		675
	Heavy non-ferrous metal (copper/zinc)	50	1	70	50	35
	Glass:	3	90		270	
	Mixed fines			70		190
	Colour sorted			50		135
	Aggregates	0.1	Derived	Variable	Low	Low
Organic	Paper:	25	400		10 000	
	Wet-pulped fibre			45		4500
	Dry sorted			60		6000
	Compost	11	Derived	40[3]	–	4400
	Ethanol	50	Derived	5.7[3]	–	2850

(b) Energy products

$$\frac{\text{primary energy saved}}{\text{by waste-derived fuel}} = \frac{\text{energy supplied by waste-derived fuel}}{\dfrac{\text{efficiency of production}}{\text{of conventional fuel}} \times \dfrac{\text{efficiency in use}}{\text{of conventional fuel}}} - \frac{\text{energy to}}{\begin{array}{l}\text{transport}\\\text{WDF to}\\\text{point of use}\end{array}}$$

Data for the conventional fuels

Conventional fuel	Efficiency of production	Efficiency in use[4]		
		Combustion e_2	Steam generation e_3	Overall boiler efficiency e_4
Coal	0.96	0.93	0.88	0.81
Oil	0.90	0.94	0.88	0.82
Gas	0.81	0.90	0.88	0.78
Electricity	0.30	1.0		

1. Taken from Table 1.3.
2. Taken from Table 5.8.
3. Efficiency based on the complete waste stream.
4. e_2, e_3, and e_4 defined in Section E.7.

The typical energy savings in Table 8.2 can also be used to estimate the present and potential future contribution which the recycling of materials makes to a nation's energy budget. For example, if no recycling was practised in the U K the total energy requirement would rise by about 5 per cent. If recycling were increased to its maximum potential, allowing for dissipative uses of materials, the present total energy requirements could be reduced by about 4 per cent (Wilson 1979*b*).

8.4. Energy efficiencies

So far, the discussion has centred on the gross energy requirement to dispose of waste. The waste was not assigned an energy content, although it was recognized that reclamation of energy or materials could make the gross energy requirement negative, that is the process could make a primary energy profit. It is desirable to develop a measure of the energy efficiency of a process, seen as a means of extracting the useful energy potential from waste.

Unfortunately many definitions of energy efficiency have been used. Table 8.4 shows some values, obtained by different authors, for the energy

Table 8.4

Efficiencies for the Occidental waste-to-oil pyrolysis system

Author	Description	Value (%)
Levy (1975*a,b*)	Energy yield	29,29
Levy (1975*a,b*)	Energy efficiency	36,39
Bechtel (1975)	Net thermal efficiency	46
General Electric Company (1973*a*)	Energy conversion efficiency	46.1–48.8
General Electric Company (1973*a*)	Energy yield	35
Mallan and Finney (1972)	Overall conversion efficiency	34
Poole (1975)	Net conversion efficiency	37
Preston (1976)	Net energy recovery	33
Bailie and Doner (1975):	E_1, energy in product/energy in waste	46.7
definitions as evaluated in	E_2, energy in product/energy inputs	44.6
Fig. 8.2 from Preston's data	E_2', energy in product/total energy inputs (including energy to generate electricity)	40.8
	E_3, net energy out/energy in waste	42.0
	E_3', as E_3 but including energy to generate electricity	32.3
This work	Net energy efficiency α (as E_3' but including all energy inputs to level 3)	14
	Net primary energy efficiency β (including energy savings due to ferrous metal recovery)	31
	Net primary energy efficiency (including energy savings due to recovery of ferrous metals, aluminium, and glass)	41

efficiency of the Occidental process to produce oil by pyrolysis. In Fig. 8.2 a simple representation of the energy flows for this process is shown, together with a few of the possible definitions and values of the energy recovery efficiency E. The differences arise from the treatment of the energy inputs to the process and in choice of the level of analysis (Fig. 8.1). Definitions E_2 and E_3 are at level 1, while E'_2 and E'_3 are partially at level 2, including the energy required to generate the electricity but excluding that of material inputs.

Energy flows (Preston 1976):

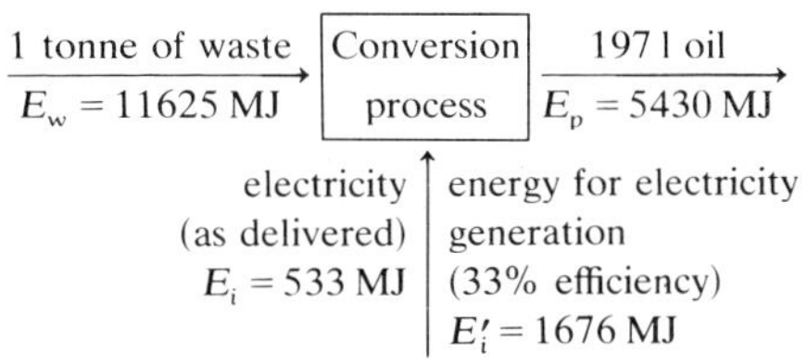

$$\underrightarrow{\text{1 tonne of waste}} \boxed{\begin{array}{c}\text{Conversion}\\ \text{process}\end{array}} \underrightarrow{\begin{array}{c}197\,\text{l oil}\\ E_p = 5430\,\text{MJ}\end{array}}$$

1 tonne of waste
$E_w = 11625$ MJ

electricity (as delivered)
$E_i = 533$ MJ

energy for electricity generation (33% efficiency)
$E'_i = 1676$ MJ

Energy recovery efficiencies (definitions after Bailie and Doner 1975);

$$E_1 = \frac{\text{energy in product}}{\text{energy in waste}} \qquad = \frac{E_p}{E_w} = 0.467$$

$$E_2 = \left\{ \begin{array}{c} \\ \\ \end{array} \right. \qquad = \frac{E_p}{E_w + E_i} = 0.446$$

$$\frac{\text{energy in product}}{\text{energy input to process}}$$

$$E'_2 = \left\{ \begin{array}{c} \\ \\ \end{array} \right. \qquad = \frac{E_p}{E_w + E'_i} = 0.408$$

$$E_3 = \left\{ \begin{array}{c} \\ \\ \end{array} \right. \qquad = \frac{E_p - E_i}{E_w} = 0.420$$

$$\frac{\text{net energy production}}{\text{energy in waste}}$$

$$E'_3 = \left\{ \begin{array}{c} \\ \\ \end{array} \right. \qquad = \frac{E_p - E'_i}{E_w} = 0.323$$

Note: E_w and E_p are gross heats of combustion

Fig. 8.2. Occidental pyrolysis—energy flows and recovery efficiencies.

Further definitions may be formulated both by including the energy savings due to materials recovered and by redefining the energy attributed to the fuel product. The latter is usually defined as its heat content, taken to mean the heat of combustion measured relative to gaseous carbon dioxide and liquid water at 25°C and 1 atmosphere pressure. The substitution equivalence (SE) corrects for the relative efficiency in a given application of the waste-derived fuel and the conventional fuel which it replaces, and is defined (Alter 1977b) by

$$SE = \frac{\text{efficiency in use of conventional fuel}}{\text{efficiency in use of waste-derived fuel}} \qquad (8.1)$$

To evaluate the primary energy saved by the use of WDF, further correction is necessary for both the efficiency of supplying the conventional fuel and for transport of the WDF to its point of use. Thus

$$\begin{aligned}
\text{primary} \\
\text{energy} \\
\text{saved}
\end{aligned} = \frac{\text{heat content of WDF} \times \text{efficiency in use of WDF}}{\begin{array}{c}\text{supply efficiency of} \\ \text{conventional fuel}\end{array} \times \begin{array}{c}\text{efficiency in use of} \\ \text{conventional fuel}\end{array}}$$

$$- \text{energy to transport WDF to point of use}$$

$$= \frac{\text{heat content of WDF}}{\begin{array}{c}\text{supply efficiency of} \\ \text{conventional fuel}\end{array}} \times \frac{1}{SE} - \begin{array}{c}\text{energy to transport} \\ \text{WDF to point of use}\end{array} \qquad (8.2)$$

Bailie and Doner (1975) attempt to provide a precise definition of the efficiency of an energy recovery process. The definition used is a modification of that for E'_2 in Fig. 8.2. In words, the efficiency factor η is the fraction of the energy input, including that to provide the direct energy for the process, which is recovered as energy product. Energy inputs or outputs via materials are not considered. The energies of the waste input and the energy products are measured as their heats of combustion. The usefulness of this efficiency factor depends on all the products of the processes which are to be compared being of the same form, that is the need to use a substitution equivalence is obviated by assuming that it remains constant. If the substitution equivalence is not considered, a process producing electricity with $\eta = 0.25$ may be considered inferior to one producing a solid refuse-derived fuel (RDF) for power generation with $\eta = 0.60$. In fact, if electricity is taken as the final product, and the generation efficiency is 33 per cent, then for the overall RDF route $\eta = 0.20$.

The problem with η is that it gives no information on the *net* energy efficiency of a process, that is on the impact of waste disposal via that process on the total supply of primary energy. In Table 8.5, three hypothetical conversion systems for waste to energy are shown. Using η, systems 1 and 2 are equivalent with values of 0.5, while that of system 3 is 0.09. However, system 2 may be obtained directly from system 3, by mixing its 1 unit of energy output with 9 units of fossil fuel, say to upgrade a gas to pipeline standard by 9:1 dilution with natural gas. To claim, as η appears to, that this operation increases the efficiency of the system, is misleading. A more useful definition is the net energy efficiency E'_3 which shows a value of zero for both systems 2 and 3.

Table 8.5

A comparison of energy efficiency η and net energy efficiency E'_3
(arbitary energy units)

	System 1	System 2	System 3
Energy in input waste	10.0	10.0	10.0
Additional energy input	1.0	10.0	1.0
Energy output	5.5	10.0	1.0
Net energy output	4.5	0.0	0.0
Efficiency η $= \dfrac{\text{energy out}}{\text{total energy in}}$	$\dfrac{5.5}{11.0} = 0.50$	$\dfrac{10.0}{20.0} = 0.50$	$\dfrac{1.0}{11.0} = 0.09$
Net efficiency (E'_3) $= \dfrac{\text{net energy out}}{\text{energy in waste}}$	$\dfrac{4.5}{10} = 0.45$	0	0

Two alternative energy efficiencies are proposed here:

α = net energy efficiency

$$= \frac{\text{GER saved by energy products} - \text{GER of inputs}}{\text{energy in waste}} \qquad (8.3)$$

β = net primary energy efficiency

$$= \frac{\begin{array}{c}\text{GER saved by energy products} + \text{GER saved by} \\ \text{material products} - \text{GER of inputs}\end{array}}{\text{energy in waste}} \qquad (8.4)$$

The gross energy requirement (GER) of each input is evaluated as far as possible to level 3. The energy efficiency α is similar to E'_3, but measures both energy inputs and outputs by reference to primary energy usage. The primary energy efficiency β takes the savings due to recycling materials into account. To compare α and β, the denominator in each case is the energy content of the waste, evaluated as its heat of combustion. Note that the maximum values of both α and β are greater than unity. The primary energy savings implied by the fuel product, evaluated by equation 8.2, may be greater than the heat content of the waste. The potential energy savings due to materials recycling are not included in the denominator of equation 8.4. Assuming a maximum value for α of 1, and that the organics are incorporated in the fuel product, the data in Table 8.3(a) suggest a maximum value for β of 1.36, although recovery of paper may increase this further.

Some problems remain with these definitions. The values for systems producing different energy outputs may not be strictly comparable. The conversion of solid RDF to gas or to oil is not directly possible and so a direct comparison can only be made assuming a common end use for the energy. This is ultimately as an energy source, whatever the energy is used for. The advantages of oil or gas over solid fuel in terms of handling, storage, and transport will not be reflected in the energy efficiency values. A useful complementary measure would be the energy-specific volume of the fuel (Eggen and Kraatz 1974). Processes that produce intermediate fuel products which may be stored before use are inherently more flexible than those which produce steam or electricity directly.

The values of α and β will depend on the precise definition of the system boundary. Consider a process requiring steam and electricity as its direct energy inputs. These may be supplied by fossil fuels or by diverting some of the product energy stream (Fig. 8.3). System (a) with fossil fuel input is the easier to analyse, as efficiencies for heat and electricity generation are well documented. The configuration (b) is probably more realistic with, for example, product gas burnt to dry incoming refuse, or steam used directly to drive fans, as in many incinerator installations. The differentiation between the two situations, or intermediate possibilities, may not always be clear in the literature. Note that α and β are not so dependent on this factor as η would be. If a process has input 10 units of waste energy, uses 3 of fossil fuel, and produces 6 of product, then $\alpha = 0.3$. If two units of product displace 2 units of fossil fuel, then α still equals 0.3. If, however, 2.5 units of product energy are required to displace the 2.0 units of fossil energy, as when inefficient on-site power generation displaces more efficient central generation, $\alpha = 0.25$. The equivalent values of η in the three cases are 0.46, 0.36, and 0.32.

8.5. The application of process analysis

These principles have been applied to the various options for waste disposal, treatment, and resource recovery as used in the case study. To show how the method works, the production of American refuse-derived fuel is taken as an example. The basic option recovers RDF and ferrous metals with a flowsheet as shown in Fig. 5.2.

The worksheet for the process analysis is shown in Table 8.6. In the first section the energy inputs are found. The factors which attribute energy requirements to each input are documented in Appendix D and summarized in Table 8.1, while the amounts of the inputs for each option were estimated from the literature (part II, Section 15.3) and summarized in Tables A.2 and A.4. The major direct energy input to RDF production is electricity. In some options oil or gas are used directly, but here such use is confined to the diesel fuel for the front-end loader at the reception pad which puts waste onto the feed conveyor. There will be various other uses of direct energy and utilities, including space heating, water supply, and waste water treatment. Rather than estimate these directly, a simple method is used, equating the

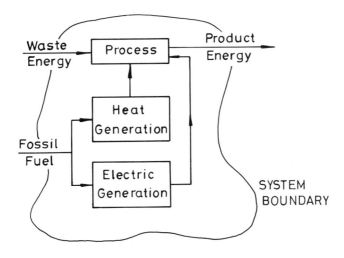

(a) Process energy supplied by fossil fuels

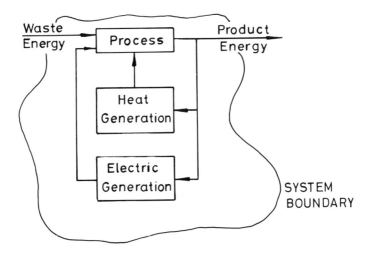

(b) Process energy supplied by the product

Fig. 8.3. Alternative configurations for utility generation.

energy requirements for other utilities to 10 per cent of the direct energy
input. When a category subsumed here, such as water supply, becomes a
major process input, it is estimated directly. This procedure is analogous to
that used in the economic analysis.

A process analysis to level 3 (Fig. 8.1) includes not only direct energy
inputs and the energy to supply them, but also the energy to supply materials

Table 8.6

Process analysis worksheet for the production of American RDF

Item	Factor	Rate of use (production)	MJ/t
Electricity	12.0 MJ/kWh	65 kWh/t	780
Diesel fuel	42.5 MJ/l	0.5 l/t	21
Other utilities	–	10% direct energy	80
Maintenance supplies	100 MJ/£	0.04 I/annum	200
Operating supplies	100 MJ/£	0.008 I/annum	41
Capital investment	50 MJ/£ 20-year life	£3.8 million	130
Residuals disposal	130 MJ/t	0.23 t/t	30
Total energy inputs	E_{IN}		1280
Ferrous metals	25 GJ/t	0.076×0.9 t/t	1710
RDF (E'_{OUT})	$\dfrac{0.69}{0.96 \times 0.81}$ (−70MJ)	8500 MJ/t	7470
Total primary energy saving	E_{OUT}		9180
Net energy efficiency	$\alpha = \dfrac{E'_{OUT} - E_{IN}}{E_W}$		0.62
Net primary energy efficiency	$\beta = \dfrac{E_{OUT} - E_{IN}}{E_W}$		0.79

E_W is the energy content of the waste (10 GJ/t).

and capital equipment. For the few options in which the consumption of raw materials is significant, their energy requirements are estimated directly. Otherwise the energy requirements of maintenance and operating supplies and of capital plant and equipment are derived by applying an energy intensity value (MJ/£) to the cost estimate. Input–output analysis shows that the energy intensity of capital investment is approximately constant, irrespective of the industry. The total energy requirement for investment is averaged over the lifetime of the plant (20 years at 75 000 t/annum). For maintenance and operating supplies this method of estimation is weaker, but it is made necessary by the present lack of data. The costs are estimated factorially from the capital investment I (Section 5.5.2) and averaged over the annual throughput. The maintenance supply factor assumes an equal contribution to maintenance costs from material and labour components.

Energy is also required for the transport of waste to the plant and for the transport and disposal of residual waste materials. For RDF production and most other processing options, it is assumed that the plant is situated centrally and the transport of untreated waste is common to all options (Section 7.2). For the residual fraction, a specific energy requirement for disposal is calculated assuming transport 20 km by road and a landfill energy requirement 50 per cent that for untreated waste (Section D.8). The amount of residuals for disposal is estimated from mass balance information (Chapter 15), referred to a standard waste composition (Table 1.3).

The second section of the worksheet evaluates the primary energy savings attributable to the process. For materials recovered, the theoretical energy savings are combined with the recovery efficiencies as shown in Table 8.3(a). For the RDF, use is made of equation 8.2. The heat content of the RDF from 1t of waste is shown in the 'rate of production' column. To evaluate the substitution equivalence of the waste-derived fuel for the conventional fuel it replaces, one must choose the appropriate fuel and application for the comparison and decide on the point of equivalence. Here it is assumed that RDF and pyrolysis oil or gas are used as supplementary boiler fuels, displacing the corresponding conventional fuel, the point of equivalence being after steam generation. Those processes which generate steam or electricity directly are assumed to displace steam from a coal-fired boiler or centrally generated electricity. Methane from anaerobic digestion is fed directly to a gas distribution network. The efficiencies assumed here for conventional fuel supply and use are shown in Table 8.3(b). The efficiencies in use of each waste-derived fuel are discussed in Part II. The boiler efficiencies of RDF and coal are derived as 0.69 and 0.81, respectively, giving $SE = 1.17$. This implies that 1.17 units of heat content in the RDF are required to replace 1 unit from coal.

For consistency, the energy to transport the waste-derived fuel to its point of use, and to handle it there, must be deducted from the energy saving. In the case of RDF, a road haul of 20 km would require about 50 MJ/t of RDF. A similar value is assumed for handling, giving a total requirement about 100 MJ/t. As American RDF is 70 per cent by weight of the input waste, the requirement is thus 70 MJ/t of waste. For oil or gas, the energy for distribution and handling is estimated as a percentage of the total energy savings from the fuel.

The worksheet in Table 8.6 concludes with the calculation of the two net energy efficiencies α and β. The values are quite high, with α at 0.62 and β at 0.79.

8.6. Discussion of the results

The results of the process analysis are summarized in Table 8.7, and in more detail in Tables A.14–A.16 which show, respectively, the energy inputs, the derivation of the primary energy savings due to fuel products, and the calculation of the net energy efficiencies for each option. Despite the many assumptions made, the results indicate the power of the technique, and allow certain general conclusions to be drawn:

(i) The two measures of energy efficiency, α, including only fuel products, and β, energy savings due to materials recovery—provide self-consistent measures of the efficiency of processes. Both α and β express the implications of the waste disposal option for the use of primary energy resources.

Table 8.7

Process analysis results.

Energy inputs and savings are MJ/t. More detailed results appear in Appendix A, Tables A.14–A.16

Option	Total energy input	Energy savings		Net energy efficiencies	
		Fuel products	Material products	α	β
Landfill	190			−0.019	−0.019
Landfill with:					
Transfer to road	460			−0.046	−0.046
Transfer to rail	560			−0.056	−0.056
Pulverization	570		1700	−0.057	0.11
Baling	630			−0.063	−0.063
Incineration:					
Non-recuperative	890		1100	−0.089	0.018
Steam generation	1400	5800	1100	0.44	0.54
Electricity generation	1800	6000	1100	0.42	0.53
Modular	3500			−0.35	−0.35
Modular + steam	3800	6800		0.30	0.30
RDF as a supplementary fuel:					
American RDF	1300	7500	1700	0.62	0.79
Powder RDF	1600	7700	1700	0.61	0.78
Paper-based RDF (UK process)	820	4000	1700	0.32	0.49
Pulverized fuel	420	8200	1700	0.78	0.95
(cement manufacture)	550	8800	1700	0.83	1.00
Incineration of RDF:					
Suspension firing	2000	5800	1700	0.38	0.55
Incinerator turbine	2100	5300	1700	0.32	0.49
Wet pulping with:					
Fibre recovery	3000		6200	−0.30	0.32
Incineration + electricity	2900	4500	1700	0.16	0.34
Fibre + wet RDF	2000	4600	6200	0.25	0.88
Wet RDF	1700	6900	1700	0.52	0.69
Dried RDF	4500	8100	1700	0.36	0.53
Pyrolysis and other thermal processes:					
Occidental	3000	4400	1700	0.14	0.31
Union Carbode Purox	3900	8300	1700	0.44	0.62
Andco–Torrax	3400	5400		0.20	0.20
Monsanto Landgard	3500	5800	1100	0.23	0.34
Biological processes:					
Composting	1400		6100	−0.14	0.47
Acid hydrolysis	5800		4600	−0.58	−0.12
Anaerobic digestion	4200	4400	1700	0.028	0.20
Additional recovery of glass and non-ferrous metals:					
From separated waste	230		1200	−0.023	0.098
From incinerator residue	250		930	−0.025	0.068

By reference to Table 8.4, which shows various efficiencies for the Occidental pyrolysis system, two observations may be made. First, the net energy efficiency, $\alpha = 0.14$, is much lower than the other measures, $0.29 < E < 0.49$. The over-estimate by the traditional efficiencies is due to their omission of some direct and indirect energy inputs. Errors also result from the failure to account for the full energy implications of using the fuel product, an effect which may in general either increase or reduce α. Secondly, the net primary energy efficiency β is significantly higher than α, with $\beta = 0.31$ or 0.41 depending on the materials recovered. Thus the indirect energy savings from materials recovery may be considerable, and β provides a more useful guide to the relative energy efficiencies of different options.

(ii) With just one exception, every resource recovery system showed net energy savings. There is little doubt that solid waste is a potential energy source.

(iii) From this preliminary analysis, the options which give the highest efficiencies, and which thus show most promise to produce or conserve energy and other resources, are some of the various RDF options, for which $0.7 < \beta < 1.0$. The highest efficiencies result from the use of pulverized and magnetically separated waste directly as a fuel, its use as a supplementary fuel for cement manufacture being particularly attractive, $\beta = 1.0$. This result rests heavily on the assumed efficiencies in use of the pulverized waste, and these need to be confirmed by experience. The production of American RDF by air classification and secondary shredding of the simple pulverized fuel results in a lower efficiency, $\beta = 0.79$. The RDF is of higher quality, but the increase in its efficiency in use is only marginal. In contrast, further upgrading to powder RDF does, on the assumptions used, increase efficiency sufficiently to compensate for the increase in process sophistication, with $\beta = 0.78$. Production of RDF from wet pulping has a lower efficiency, $\beta = 0.69$. Drying the product from 50 to 20 per cent moisture content reduces β to 0.53. On the other hand, recovery of paper fibre with the organic residues used for RDF increases β to 0.88, although α is reduced from 0.52 to 0.25. It may be expected that further development will increase the energy efficiency of RDF production.

(iv) Several options have moderate energy efficiencies, with $0.45 < \beta < 0.65$. These include the production of paper-based and dried-pulp RDF, Union Carbide gasification, steam generation from direct or suspension-fired incineration, electricity generation from direct incineration or the incinerator turbine, and composting. It should be emphasized again that neither α nor β fully reflects the quality of the products. One may feel that a lower efficiency is justified by obtaining a cleaner, storable, or more convenient fuel. The efficiency of incineration with electricity generation may be substantially increased if the waste heat can be utilized, for example as hot water at 50 °C. It may be noted that the efficiency of the Union Carbide gasification process is reduced if some of the gas is used for on-site electricity generation, which is less efficient than central generation. For steam generation, the net efficiencies assume a load factor of 75 per cent.

(v) Several resource recovery options have low energy efficiencies, with $\beta < 0.35$. Steam generation from modular incineration or from the Monsanto gasification process, and electricity generation from the incineration of wet-pulped RDF, are less efficient than for conventional incineration. Wet pulping with fibre recovery and incineration of the residue has $\alpha = -0.30$ but $\beta = 0.32$. For Torrax gasification and anaerobic digestion, $\beta \approx 0.2$. Development work on anaerobic digestion is being directed at increasing this efficiency, one suggestion being incineration of the organic residue with steam generation. Some penalty in energy efficiency may be worthwhile in return for the production of high quality methane, suitable for a distribution network. The single resource recovery option which appears to be a net energy consumer is acid hydrolysis, with $\beta = -0.12$. After accounting for ferrous metal recovery, the energy requirement for ethanol production from waste is about 70 MJ/kg, compared with 20 MJ/kg from crude oil, or 50 MJ/kg when the energy content of the ethanol is credited.

(vi) Recovery of additional materials, principally aluminium, may increase the net primary energy efficiency of many options. Recovery from a pre-sorted inorganic fraction may increase β by about 0.1, or from incineration residue by about 0.07. Thus the overall efficiency of American RDF production may be raised from $\beta = 0.79$ to 0.89.

(vii) The energy requirements of disposal options generally range from 190 MJ/t for local landfill to 630 MJ/t for baling and landfill. Recovery of ferrous metals makes either pulverization and landfill or conventional incineration net energy producers. The only major energy consumer is modular incineration, with a requirement of 3500 MJ/t.

8.7. Sensitivity analysis

In this process analysis, the data are often uncertain. Sensitivity analysis highlights those factors which affect the energy efficiencies most, and on which further work should be concentrated. In Table A.17 relative sensitivity results are shown for the net primary energy efficiency of β of seven representative options, with base values $0.2 < \beta < 0.95$. The most significant items are those affecting the energy savings due to fuel production and use, the energy savings due to paper or to ferrous metals recovery, and direct energy inputs as electricity or process heat. Of less significance are energy savings due to aluminium recovery and the energy inputs implied by maintenance supplies and capital investment. Other energy inputs and savings are relatively insignificant. Immediate priorities for further work are thus:

(i) The recovery efficiencies of the waste-derived fuels, the energy to deliver them to the point of use, their efficiencies in use and comparable values for conventional fuels.

(ii) The energy savings implied by recycling paper fibre, particularly the efficiency of separating paper from other organic wastes.

(iii) The energy savings implied by recycling ferrous scrap, and the potential for increasing it by upgrading and detinning scrap.

(iv) The direct energy inputs to the processes and their variation with the scale of the operation.

(v) The energy savings due to aluminium recovery, particularly the efficiency of recovery processes and the aluminium content in the waste.

(vi) The energy input implied by maintenance supplies involving both the estimate of maintenance costs and the estimate of the energy intensity of the maintenance supplies. Both of these components may vary from process to process.

(vii) One component of energy input not highlighted in Table A.17 but which may be of significance is the energy requirements for waste water treatment. Better data are necessary to allow assessment of this factor. In addition, water supply may become a critical factor for a few technologies if applied in arid countries.

8.8. The potential of solid waste as an energy source

It has been shown how process analysis may be used to assess the net savings of primary energy when materials and energy are recovered from waste. It is also worth looking at the overall contribution that such recovery could make to a country's energy needs. Estimates are needed of both the contribution from each tonne of waste and the total quantity of waste which may be processed economically; Britain is taken as an example.

Six options have been identified with net primary energy efficiency $0.69 < \beta < 1.0$, the potential maximum value of β being around 1.5. For illustration, a value $\beta = 0.9$ is used here. The energy content of waste is taken as 10 GJ/t (Table 1.3). Note that the total energy contribution calculated will reflect both the use of waste as an energy source and the existing energy use which is made unnecessary either in supplying other fuels or in processing raw materials.

The total quantities of waste produced in Britain have been estimated (Table 1.1) at 20 million tonnes of municipal and about 50 million tonnes of solid industrial waste per annum. It is assumed that 50 per cent of this industrial waste is similar to municipal waste, with a high paper and hence a high heat content, and can be similarly recovered. To estimate how much may be economically processed, an estimate is made that 60 per cent of the population live in conurbations of 100 000 or more people, and that these areas account for 80 per cent of the recoverable industrial waste. With these assumptions, a town of 100 000 people will generate about 95 000 tonnes a year of suitable waste, corresponding to an average plant throughput of 360 t.p.d. (for a 5-day week).

Using this information, the potential contribution of waste may be calculated at between 1 and 3 per cent of the total national energy requirement of 9.1×10^{18} J/annum (Department of Energy 1977). The contribution is modest, but nonetheless significant.

Further insight may be gained by considering an investment in resource recovery from solid waste as an investment in energy supply rather than as an alternative method of disposal. For example, one might compare the energy-specific investment (as £ per MJ of daily capacity) in resource recovery and North Sea oil. A 300 t.p.d. plant to produce a simple pulverized and magnetically separated fuel on a single shift is estimated at £1.5 million, with $\beta = 0.95$, giving £0.53 per MJ/day. Similarly, a more sophisticated plant to produce an American RDF with $\beta = 0.79$ is estimated at £3.8 million, corresponding to £1.6 per MJ/day. Investment in North Sea oil was estimated in early 1976 as $5000–10 000 per average daily barrel for larger fields, and $15 000 for some of the smaller and more remote ones (Institution of Chemical Engineers 1976). Correcting to first-half 1977 costs, this corresponds to a range of £0.58–£1.7 per MJ/day. However, this does not allow for the energy to obtain the oil.

Thus the energy-specific investment costs in resource recovery from solid waste and in North Sea oil are comparable. The economic viability of resource recovery improves if viewed as an energy source as well as a means of waste disposal.

8.9. Assessment

In the last few chapters, attention has been focused on the quantitative evaluation of options for waste management against the two criteria of economics and the use of resources as measured by the effect on primary energy supply. The results may be abstracted as a trade-off diagram, for example of net present cost versus net primary energy efficiency β (Fig. 8.4). However, selection of an option requires assessment against many criteria (Table 2.2). For illustration, a simplified assessment matrix is shown in Table A.18. Evaluations of each option from the case study are shown for five criteria, namely the net present cost, capital cost, net primary energy efficiency β, land requirements for disposal, and adequacy of the technology. Land requirements should be measured by the volume which a

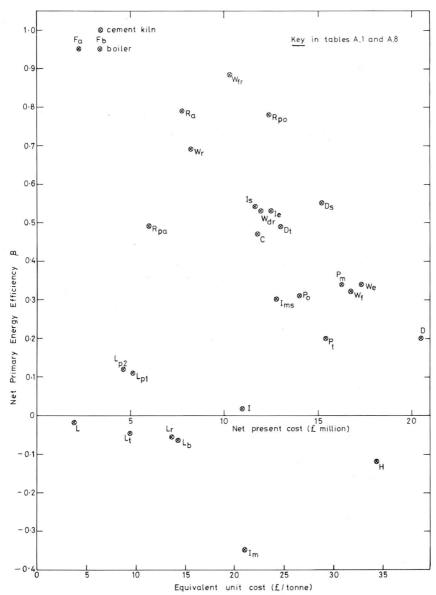

Fig. 8.4. Net present cost versus net primary energy efficiency β.

tonne of waste occupies in a landfill site following treatment but, as illustrated in Table 1.6, there is some dispute over these volumes. Many claims of volume reduction neglect the space occupied by cover material, and it is often unclear how far allowance has been made for subsequent settlement. As a substitute measure, the weight of residue for disposal is used here. Whether weight or volume is used, an underestimate will result when one of the products is a waste-derived fuel, if its use increases the quantity of ash. The adequacy of a technology is representative of criteria which are not amenable to either objective or quantitative evaluation and for which a qualitative assessment must be made.

An assessment matrix is a convenient way of summarizing results. However, as a tool to aid decision making, it must be interpreted with care. Several methods of manipulation intended to aid interpretation were identified in Section 4.2.1, where certain theoretical problems were discussed. Table A.18 serves to amplify the practical difficulties.

The simplest and least problematic modification of the matrix is to rank the options on each criterion. However, for the criteria developed here such ranking proved difficult owing both to uncertainty in the data and to differing definitions of performance. For example, the net present costs shown in the matrix are the risk analysis means and lose all the information on the spread of the distributions, while a different choice of discount rate would produce a different ranking (Table A.13). A single deterministic evaluation abstracted into an assessment matrix is an unfortunate simplification.

The problems multiply for the more sophisticated modifications. Either cardinal ranking, or normalization of the scores against each criterion to a common numerical basis, requires quantification of a single performance score against every criterion. Ranking and weighting the criteria involves political judgement, while the combination of normalized scores with criterion weights, to produce a single performance index for each option, requires that the criteria be independent. This is a significant restriction, since most of the criteria in Table 2.2 are interrelated. Net present cost and capital cost are each economic indicators; the revenue from recovered products may be introduced as a measure of dependence on unstable markets. Again, net present cost and net primary energy efficiency β are related, as they are derived largely from the same data. If markets were perfect, reflecting fully the present and future availability, production costs, and efficiency in use of commodities, then information on the energy efficiency of an option would be contained within the net present cost (Chapman 1976a). The relation of energy and economic analysis is a subject of some controversy (Webb and Pearce 1975; Common 1976; Energy Policy 1977).

The assessment matrix is a useful method of abstracting information on the performance of waste management options against many criteria. It must be remembered that not all the relevant information can be presented.

Thus its role should be as a screening tool, reducing the list of options for further, more detailed, study, rather than as a means of final selection. Screening may be used to eliminate options which fail to meet some performance standard, for example those with no potential markets for the product within 30 km, or which will not be available to commence operation in four years' time. Care is required to avoid premature elimination of an option which may, on further study, meet the standard; this is particularly true for an economic standard, such as net cost <£20/t, where uncertainty may be significant.

9. A SYSTEMS APPROACH TO WASTE MANAGEMENT PLANNING

9.1. A framework for planning

Increasing pressures on resources of land, materials, energy, and finance have combined to make waste management a complex problem at the local, regional, and national levels. The choice of methods for dealing with wastes and the long-term provision of adequate facilities are major planning problems. A systems approach seeks to provide an organized framework for planning, to gain insight into the workings of the system and to enable the planner to reach more reasoned decisions within a coherent policy, using the best available information.

The framework developed here is organized around a simple conceptual structure which formalizes planning into a series of steps. While this is an abstraction, and opinions may differ on the precise order of steps or on the relation of the ideal structure to any particular real situation, its value remains, in that it makes explicit the steps required and emphasizes inter-relationships. The distinction between political planning and the technical analysis in its support is particularly important.

The initial, and perhaps the most important, step in planning is system definition, of which three aspects may be distinguished. First, the terms of reference for the study must be set out, including local political objectives and social attitudes, national legislation and policy directives, and local government plans, finance, and structures. Secondly, the system boundary must be specified, indicating the appropriate level of planning, the types of waste, and the operations which are included. Interactions across the boundary must be taken into account. The system boundary used here includes all the operations of waste disposal, from the point where a collection vehicle leaves its round to the satisfactory disposal of the waste, or of its residue after processing, to land. Planning for waste disposal involves long-term strategic decisions with many conflicting objectives, whereas for collection it is largely a short-term operational problem. Finally, survey information is required on the quantity and types of wastes arising, including future projections, and on the availability of land.

Once the system has been defined and the assessment criteria set down, technical analysis is required. The problem is, given the expected wastes arising, to decide what kind of facilities should be built, together with their location, capacity, and time for implementation. Subdivision may be made into the evaluation and assessment of technologies, the generation of alternative strategies from the most promising options and potential locations, and the development of a plan by strategy evaluation and assessment.

This analysis may be aided by the use of mathematical models. In order to achieve a compromise between model reality and tractability, planning models focus on one or two aspects only, making simplifying assumptions in the others. For example, forecasting of future wastes arising is often neglected. In such circumstances, it is essential that the planner has an understanding of the assumptions. The model suggests plans for further study, and is not a direct planning tool. The purpose is not to *supplant* expert judgement, as a 'black box' approach would imply, but rather to *supplement* it.

Previous work in waste management has been largely restricted to the application of sophisticated operational research models to strategy evaluation. The principle is to combine technologies in such a way as to produce the least-cost plan subject to certain constraints. Unfortunately there are fundamental problems with this approach, including:

(a) Only one objective may be considered;

(b) Deterministic data on wastes arising and on facility costs are required;

(c) The capacities of facilities are not explicitly modelled.

Together these difficulties restrict the role to one of screening alternatives, for which simple models would suffice. Strategy evaluation models offer little scope for further development as practical aids to waste management planning.

The approach developed here is more pragmatic, focusing attention on the evaluation and assessment of options for dealing with wastes from a single source. A detailed analysis of the alternatives is an essential part of any planning exercise. As the system boundary is defined to include all operations on the waste, strategy evaluation has been effectively subsumed. This 'single waste flow model' is thus both a necessary and, often, a sufficient tool for planning. Although flexible enough to include several waste types from the same source, the principles have been developed here specifically for municipal wastes.

Each option is evaluated against each criterion, the results being displayed as a matrix. Assessment may be limited to displaying the matrix to best effect, so that the decision makers may more easily interpret it. Alternatively, assessment may produce a single performance index for each option against all the criteria, with interpretation reduced to choosing the option with the best score. This depends on the quantification of all performance scores and criteria weights, which in turn introduces subjective elements to the analysis. The major disadvantage is that the distinction is lost between the political planning process and the technical analysis required in its support. For such reasons, the major effort here is directed to evaluation, and in particular to the quantification of performance against the criteria of economics and the use of resources. The existence of such measures of performance is a necessary precondition for assessment. Other criteria, including technical, environmental, and political considerations, are equally important, but intangibility makes progress beyond a qualitative evaluation difficult.

9.2. Evaluation tools

Much has been written on the economics of waste processing, but little use may be made of the results until some consensus is reached on conventions. Differences in both the approach and the assumptions may lead to significant variation in the results. The conventions proposed here may be summarized under three headings:

(a) Capital cost estimates should be related to a specific process flowsheet, with breakdown into the costs of unit operations. Assumptions on design conception, operating standards, plant operating schedules, and costs specific to the site, should be clearly stated. Estimation should use a factorial method, using standard factors developed for waste processing. At present, without such conventions, it is difficult to obtain consistent estimates. Correction to the plant capacity required should use a scale factor appropriate to the particular process, but, in the absence of better information, an eight-tenths power rule may be used.

(b) Operating costs should be estimated factorially from the raw materials, energy, operating labour, capital and residue disposal costs, and the revenues. The data required are thus capital and revenue estimates plus physical information such as energy consumption. Further work is required to develop appropriate factors, for example relating maintenance costs to process flowsheets and utilization rates.

(c) Revenues should be estimated directly from local waste composition and sale prices and from expected recovery efficiencies. An evaluation of local markets is of prime importance. A social cost–benefit analysis rather than a financial appraisal requires the use of shadow rather than market prices. This approach should be examined further, but the determination of shadow prices is difficult.

The economics of waste transport has until now received limited attention. Three simple models developed here provide a basis for the integration of transport into evaluation. The cost of transport in a collection vehicle is shown, to a first approximation, to be linearly proportional to distance over the range from about 5 km to 20–30 km, the upper limit usually depending on other constraints such as labour relations. A second model considers the optimal scale of a transfer, treatment, or reclamation plant, balancing economies of scale in processing with diseconomies in transporting wastes from a larger catchment area. Finally, the costs of bulk haul are examined and a step function developed relating the cost to haul time or distance. Each model must be adapted to local conditions and increased sophistication may be added as required. Taken together, the models provide a flexible basis for the detailed comparison of waste management options, particularly those involving direct and indirect haul to landfill.

Once the options for waste management have been constructed, economic evaluation may proceed. The costs of processing, transport, and disposal are combined to give a net present cost using discounted cash flow. However, such costs are not known with certainty, a problem which is always present during planning. Good decision making requires that best use be made of all information, including the likely error ranges in cost and revenue estimates. The complementary techniques of sensitivity and risk analysis should therefore be applied to the evaluation. Sensitivity analysis is useful in highlighting those parameters which have most effect on the net present cost and hence where accurate estimates are important. The most sensitive are generally capital cost, plant utilization, and those affecting revenues. Risk analysis attributes each uncertain parameter with a subjective probability distribution and generates a distribution for the net present cost. The distributions for different options often overlap, and a clear ranking is no longer possible. This conclusion is reinforced when the evaluation is repeated with altered discount rate, operating life, or plant capacity. Discounted cash flow using sensitivity and risk analysis is comparatively simple to use, and is a powerful tool for economic evaluation.

Economics does not always adequately reflect the scarcity of physical resources. It is useful to have a separate quantitative measure of the contribution which reclamation of, or resource recovery from, waste makes to the conservation of energy and materials. As the recovery of materials saves energy which would otherwise be used in their production, it is convenient to use energy as the unit of account. The technique of process energy analysis is applied here to evaluate both the primary energy inputs to each process, and the savings implied by the use of the recovered fuel and material products. The results are expressed as two measures of net energy efficiency, differing in whether or not savings from materials recovery are included. These efficiencies enable the potential for resource conservation of different options to be compared on an equitable basis. Almost all reclamation or resource recovery options give a net energy saving. Sensitivity analysis shows that the areas where better information would have most effect on the accuracy of the results are the efficiencies in production and use of waste-derived fuels, the direct energy inputs, and the energy savings due to recycling paper and ferrous scrap. By combining estimates of energy efficiency with those for the amount of waste potentially recoverable, it is seen that resource recovery could make a modest contribution to national energy needs. Surprisingly, the energy-specific investment required for resource recovery is similar to that for North Sea Oil.

These techniques for economic and energy evaluation have been demonstrated by application to an illustrative case study. This uses the best available information, but the analysis must be repeated for any particular local situation. Nevertheless, certain general conclusions on the status of the options may be drawn (see also Chapter 21). Those which perform best in the economic evaluation are based on landfill or produce a solid refuse-derived fuel. The RDF options also show the highest net energy efficiencies. The economic comparison of these options requires detailed study, using local information on the availability of landfill space and markets for the RDF. Production of a crude RDF may even be competitive with local landfill. Other options, including incineration and pyrolysis, have both higher costs and lower energy efficiencies than those producing RDF. These conclusions may quickly be reversed by technical progress; the RDF options have been developed largely in the last five to ten years.

There are several major areas where the framework developed here could usefully be extended or strengthened by further work. These include:

(i) The development of more reliable techniques of forecasting future wastes arising.

(ii) The integration of planning for muncipal with industrial wastes, and indeed with all wastes going to land.

(iii) The development of cost factors specific to individual waste processing options. Examples include factors to relate total capital investment to delivered equipment cost, maintenance costs to investment and utilization, and both capital and operating costs to plant capacity.

(iv) The development of measures of performance on criteria other than economics or resource conservation. An example would be an index of environmental impact specific to waste management.

9.3. Postscript

There is no simple panacea which will solve all planning problems. A framework is developed here which is aimed at focusing attention on the most critical aspects. The primary problem is one of choosing the most suitable option or options and it is for this that that the analytical tools are designed. These tools are limited to the evaluation of performance against the quantifiable criteria of economics and the use of resources. The assessment of intangibles and the balancing of criteria remain firmly in the hands of the planners and the politicians.

Part II. WASTE MANAGEMENT TECHNOLOGY

10. THE CRITICAL EVALUATION OF TECHNOLOGIES

10.1. Introduction

The purpose of Part II of this book is to provide a comprehensive, up-to-date and critical review of the state of the art in waste management technology. Although a vast amount of literature has appeared on the subject, particularly over the last 10 years, it remains difficult either to see clearly the relationships between the many technologies or to obtain consistent quantitative data about them. It is hoped that this treatise will fulfil a need in both of these important respects.

The many technologies which are either currently available or have been proposed for the reclamation, treatment, or disposal of solid wastes are here rationalized under a number of headings, namely:

Landfill;
Transfer or treatment prior to landfill;
Incineration;
Separation processes;
Production of a solid refuse-derived fuel (RDF);
Direct incineration of RDF;
Wet pulping;
Pyrolysis and other thermal processes;
Biological processes.

Each chapter provides a general introduction to the technology under consideration. Particular emphasis is given to the overall objectives, to the similarities and differences between the various derivative processes, and to the relationships with other technologies. The comparison of different technologies is aided by the presentation of typical flowsheets in a standard format. The state of development of the processes and the extent of their use to date is discussed; any operating problems are highlighted. Where there have been significant recent advances in our understanding of the scientific basis of a technology, then these are reviewed in depth; one such case is the simple landfilling of wastes.

One of the major requirements in providing a critical assessment of waste management technologies is to obtain quantitative information, on materials and energy recovery and on capital and operating costs. Particular attention is given here to the compilation of these data, related to a consistent basis for comparison. Some readers may prefer to skip the more technical sections in each chapter which discuss the data, proceeding directly to the discussion at the end of the chapter.

This emphasis on consistent and quantitative data enables the methods developed in Part I of the book to be used to calculate both the overall cost of each process and also its contribution to the conservation of material and energy resources. These calculations were used as case studies in Part I and serve here as the basis of the discussion in each chapter. When the results are combined with a qualitative assessment of the state of the technology and its environmental impact, certain general conclusions may be drawn concerning the most promising options for the future.

The main text is concerned principally with municipal wastes, including domestic (household), commercial, and similar components of industrial wastes. Of course, many of the technologies are also appropriate to other types of waste. Those industrial wastes which require special care in handling and disposal are of particular public concern; they often take the form of sludges or of liquids which are unsuitable for conventional waste-water treatment. Many different technologies can be used or have been proposed to deal with such wastes. For completeness, a chapter is included on these more hazardous wastes.

10.2. A consistent basis for comparing technologies

From all the available or proposed processes which are reviewed here for the reclamation, treatment, or disposal of municipal wastes, some 30 options are selected as typical of the current state of the art, and are compared on a consistent basis. The remainder of this chapter summarizes the methods and assumptions utilized in this comparison.

10.2.1. A standard plant capacity

The standard plant size used for the comparison has a design capacity of 400 tonnes per day (t.p.d.) of waste delivery (100 000 tonnes per annum). The average rate of waste delivery is 300, with a range of ± 40, t.p.d., the excess capacity providing for peak delivery rates and allowing for any future increase in waste generation. The operating schedule depends on the process, with four principal alternatives:

(i) The plant operates 1 shift only, 5 days per week. This operating schedule is used for landfill and for some of the options with transfer or volume reduction prior to landfill.

(ii) The plant operates 2 shifts, 5 days per week, the third shift being used for maintenance. This is used for all the waste separation plants.

(iii) The plant operates 3 shifts, 5 days per week. This is used for non-recuperative incineration.

(iv) The plant operates continuously. This is used for all the high-temperature, energy-recovery processes, and for biological processes.

Any separation of the waste prior to energy recovery is on a 2-shift basis. In each case waste delivery is assumed to take place during a normal 40-hour week.

10.2.2. Estimation of capital costs

Capital costs for a plant of appropriate size are estimated by analysis of historical costs and of previous estimates. Data on unit operations, or on equipment costs, are only rarely available. The assumptions made on design conception and operating standards are seldom stated explicitly, so that, for example, it is unclear how much redundancy is allowed or how many process lines are included in some of the estimates. Further uncertainty is introduced by the necessity to correct the cost estimates for inflation, to transfer costs between countries, and to adjust to a standard plant capacity. Particular care was taken in the estimation to ensure that the relative costs of different processes are of the correct order.

All cost and revenue estimates are adjusted to prices appropriate in the first half of 1977. Capital cost estimates are adjusted using Engineering and Process Economics (E P E), and later Process Economics International (P E I), plant cost indices. These are available for up to 30 countries; values for the U K and the U S A are summarized in Table 10.1. The value of the U K index used here is E P E = 292 (P E I = 142), while that of the U S index is E P E = 163 (P E I = 109). Both these values were provisional estimates for January 1977; in the event, costs in the U K rose less quickly than expected, this value being midway between those for January 1977 and January 1978. It should be noted that correction for inflation inevitably reduces the accuracy of an estimate; this is particularly true when the base date for the original cost estimate is not clear in the literature. The best source of information on the capital costs of an existing plant is often the tender price; with a time lag of as much as five years between the original tender and the completion of the project, this introduces considerable uncertainty in a time of rapid inflation.

Transfer of costs between countries requires a location index, which measures the relative cost of identical plants when the monetary costs are converted at the exchange rate. Information on such an index is lacking, but must exist within international contracting companies. In one of the few definitive evaluations of a location index, Cran (1973) compared the capital costs of twelve types of chemical plant in the U K and the U S A, and

Table 10.1

Cost and related indices[1]

| Time | Capital costs of plant Engineering and Process Economics (EPE) indices[2] | | Index Wholesale prices | | Exchange rate | Location index |
	UK	USA	UK[3]	USA[4]	$ per £[4]	$L^x \frac{UK}{US}$ see text
1963			77.8	85.6	2.797	
1964			80.9	85.8	2.790	
1965	74.1	79.3	83.1	87.5	2.803	78.1
1966	77.3	81.9	85.8	90.4	2.790	78.6
1967	79.8	84.2	84.4	90.6	2.406	68.0
1968	83.5	89.0	93.8	92.8	2.384	66.7
1969	86.8	94.3	97.3	96.5	2.400	65.9
1970	100	100	100	100	2.393	71.4
1971	113	104	103.6	103.2	2.552	82.7
1972	126	110	107.7	107.9	2.348	80.2
1973 Jan	132	113	118.2	112.8	2.382	83.0
Apr	132	115	128.3	118.4	2.480	85.2
Jul	143	116	142.4	122.2	2.496	91.8
Oct	148	117	159.0	126.4	2.439	92.0
1974 Jan	150	119	219.2	136.2	2.277	85.6
Apr	166	123	231.3	140.7	2.433	98.0
Jul	176	140	230.6	146.5	2.376	89.1
Oct	185	143	236.9	154.0	2.334	90.1
1975 Jan	205	149	237.4	155.6	2.378	97.6
Apr	214	145	239.0	155.9	2.353	103.6
Jul	229	144	252.4	159.1	2.147	101.9
Oct	232	146	267.6	162.0	2.076	98.4
1976 Jan	245	149	273.8	162.4	2.029	99.5
Apr	261	150	305.2	164.2	1.844	95.7
Jul	276	152	324.6	166.9	1.784	96.7
Oct	283	158	348.3	167.8	1.606	85.8
1977 Jan	285	163	353.4	170.3	1.714	89.2
Apr	286	165	359.7	176.0	1.719	88.7
Jul	288	169	359.0	176.5	1.723	87.5
Oct	289	173	349.0	177.8	1.771	88.4
1978 Jan	302	176	333.1	181.1	1.935	99.0
Apr	336	182	349.2	187.0	1.851	101.9
Jul	338	185	350.0	190.8	1.932	105.3
Oct	346	191	350.3	194.7	2.090	112.9
1979 Jan	355	197	362.3	200.0	1.996	107.3
Apr	361	198	389.1	208.0	2.058	111.9
Jul	369	209	411.9	214.0	2.281	120.1
Oct	387	209	444.8	222.1	2.076	114.7
1980 Jan	404	225	501.2	230.9	2.268	121.5
Apr	412	(230)	531.4	238.0	2.266	(121.1)
Jul	(414)	(237)	529.9	244.4	2.338	(121.8)
Oct	(418)	(244)	(528.0)		2.438	(124.6)

1. Figures in brackets are extrapolations or provisional estimates.
2. EPE indices quoted up to January 1978. EPE have apparently discontinued their plant cost indices, and later values are based on the Process Economics International (PEI) indices, published quarterly since autumn 1979. After correcting for the starting date (1st quarter 1975, PEI = 100), the two sets of indices are compatible.
3. Materials and fuels purchased by manufacturing industry other than food, drink and tobacco; from Monthly Digest of Statistics.
4. From United Nations Monthly Bulletin of Statistics.

deduced that, on average, UK plant costs were 83 per cent of those in the USA. If this value is accepted then, at any time x, UK and USA plant cost may be compared using the location index L^x, corrected for changes in the exchange rate $E_{\$/£}$, and in the relative rates of inflation as measured by the EPE indices $I_£$ and $I_\$$. Thus

$$L^x\left(\frac{\text{UK}}{\text{USA}}\right) = \frac{I_£^x I_\$^{1973}}{I_\$^x I_£^{1973}} \frac{E_{\$/£}^x}{E_{\$/£}^{1973}} L^{1973}$$

$$= 30\left(\frac{I_£^x E_{\$/£}^x}{I_\$^x}\right)$$

Values of L^x are given in Table 10.1. From 1971 to 1978 the index oscillates between 80 and 104 per cent owing to short-term fluctuations in the exchange rate; the rise in the value of the pound led to a substantial increase in the index during 1979. Values prior to 1971 may be distorted by fixed exchange rates. The index may be compared to the 90–97 per cent suggested by Kay (1976). It is assumed here that a UK plant costs 90 per cent of USA costs, when compared using first-half 1977 costs and an exchange rate of $1.72/£. Thus $1 is equivalent to £0.52.

Correction of a capital cost estimate C_A for a plant of capacity W_A to the standard capacity W_0 uses equation 5.6:

$$\frac{C_0}{C_A} = \left(\frac{W_0}{W_A}\right)^S$$

where C_0 is the corrected cost estimate and S is the scale factor. The scale factor appropriate to each process is one of the items discussed in the text. When other evidence is not available, guidance is taken from a typical value for a solids-handling process, $S = 0.8$. It should be noted that the often-quoted value of $S = 0.6$ is appropriate mainly to gas-phase processes (see also Section 5.4.7).

10.2.3. Estimation of operating costs

Operating costs are estimated using the rapid estimation technique outlined in Section 5.5. Each cost component is related to the raw materials (R), energy (E), labour (L), capital investment (I), or initial waste-haul/residuals-disposal (D) cost or to the sales revenue (S_r). The factors used here are summarized in Table 10.2. The maintenance factor is estimated separately for each process, using as a guide a standard factor of 0.08 I/annum for a solids-handling process at a moderate utilization rate.

Raw materials usage per tonne of waste is estimated directly in the few cases where the costs cannot be subsumed under operating supplies. Specific energy usage, as kilowatt-hours of electricity and gigajoules of fuel per

Table 10.2

Operating cost factors

Direct costs	
(a) Raw materials	R
(b) Energy	E
(c) Labour	L
(d) Supervision	$0.2L$
(e) Payroll charge	$0.4\{(c)+(d)\}$
(f) Maintenance	$0.08I$ (variable)
(g) Operating supplies	$0.008I$
(h) Laboratory	If appropriate
(j) Royalty	If appropriate
(k) Contingency	0
Indirect costs	
(l) Rates	$0.03I$
(m) Insurance	$0.01I$
(n) Overhead/administration	$0.4L + 0.01I$
(p) Research	If appropriate
(q) Distribution/selling	$0.1S_r$
(r) Contingency	0
(s) Initial waste haul/residual waste disposal	D

Total estimating equation
Operating cost $= R + E + 2.08L + 0.138I + 0.1S_r + D$

In the case study, it is assumed that laboratory, royalty, and research costs are zero.

tonne, is also estimated directly. Other utilities, including fuel for space heating, water supply, and waste-water treatment, are estimated at 10 per cent of direct fuel costs (Bechtel Corporation 1975), unless water supply and/or treatment is a major cost when it is estimated directly. Labour requirements are estimated for each case on a shift basis, with base-line values about 4 day–men for waste reception, 5 per shift for separation, and 5 per shift for processing. These estimates in physical units are combined with the standard prices, shown in Table 10.3, to yield cost estimates. Where costs are not related to a physical basis, updating uses a wholesale price index (Table 10.1).

The other major costs of waste disposal are the initial haul of the waste to the treatment facility and the disposal of any residue from processing to a landfill site. Initial transport costs in a collection vehicle for an average 4 km haul to a central processing plant are assumed to be common to each option and are thus neglected. Exceptions are considered explicitly as they arise. The quantities of residual materials requiring landfill disposal are estimated directly and the transport costs are calculated using the methods in Chapter 6. Landfill costs are estimated as a percentage of those for untreated waste, three principal cases being distinguished.

Table 10.3
Standard prices used

Item	Unit	Unit price £	Comment
Operating labour	man–year	3500	Excludes payroll charges and supervision
Electricity	kWh	0.03	
Fuel	GJ	1.80	Average based on the price of gas and gas oil
Diesel fuel	litre	0.15	For simplicity, 1 l of diesel (calorific value
	GJ	3.90	40 MJ/l) is entered at 80 MJ/l to allow for the higher tax-inclusive price
Water supply	m³	0.1	45p/1000 gallons
Effluent treatment	m³	0.2	For dilute effluents only
Landfill cover			
Intermediate	t	0.2	
Final	t	1.5	
Lime	t	10	
Sulphuric acid	t	30	98/99% acid by the tanker load
Natural gas	GJ	1.70 ⎫	
Heavy fuel oil	GJ	1.60 ⎬ used for revenue estimation	
Coal	GJ	0.60 ⎭	

Data sources:
  Monthly Digest of Statistics, May 1977.
  Petroleum Times, 4th February 1977.
  Energy Trends, June 1977.
  Technical Data on Fuels (Rose and Cooper 1977).
  European Chemical News, 4th February 1977.
  Southern Electricity Board and Southern Gas, private communications.

(i) For mostly inorganic residues, a specific landfill cost of 50 per cent that for untreated waste is assumed. In practice, this is the most common case.
(ii) For residues containing some putrescible organic materials, a cost of 70 per cent is used.
(iii) For biologically active wastes or residues, costs are assumed to be the same as for untreated waste.

10.2.4. Estimation of revenues

Revenues from resource recovery are based on a waste of standard composition and calorific value (Table 1.3). Prices for recovered materials are shown in Table 10.4, while those for fuel products are related to conventional fuels, the ratio depending on the quality of the product. Efficiencies of recovering material products are discussed in the text. Similarly the primary energy savings from fuel products are documented in terms of the heat content of the product; the substitution equivalence, defined as the ratio of the efficiencies in use of the conventional and waste-derived fuels; the production efficiency of the conventional fuel; and the energy to transport the waste-derived fuel to the user (see also Chapter 8).

Table 10.4

Revenues from material products

Product	Ex-works price (£/t)	Comments
Ferrous metals	12	Prices fluctuate widely. Materials Reclamation Weekly (MRW) quotations in January 1977 showed a range of £10–40/t (delivered), depending on grade.
After burning	10	£27/t paid at Sheffield incinerator during 1976 (Thomas 1977)
Aluminium	200	Based on 10–12½ p/lb paid for bottle tops (David 1977) and the £120–370 from MRW
Other non-ferrous metals (Cu/Zn)	400	MRW price range £380–680/t for copper and brass, and £195–215/t for zinc (minimum quantity 2 t delivered)
Glass		
Mixed fines	8	Thomas (1977)
Colour sorted	12	Estimated
Paper	15	Prices fluctuate widely
Humus	3	Guess
Ethanol	220	BP Chemicals International, private communication

10.2.5. Uncertainty in the cost and revenue estimates

All cost and revenue estimates derived at an early stage of planning, including those derived here on a consistent basis for representative waste management technologies, will be subject to considerable uncertainty. By using such information as is available on the range of the individual estimates, methods were shown in Chapter 7 to examine the uncertainty in the overall net cost. The standard error ranges assumed here are summarized in Table 7.1; appropriate ranges for estimates of capital cost, transport cost, and energy recovery efficiencies in particular are discussed in the text. The overall results are quoted in the form $£A \pm B$/t; there is a 95 per cent chance that the cost will be in the range $£(A-B)$ to $£(A+B)$/t.

10.2.6. Discounted cash flow analysis

The data derived on a consistent basis for each option were used to calculate both the overall cost of the process and its contribution to resource conservation, using the methods developed in Part I. The costs were derived using a discounted cash flow analysis which utilized certain standard assumptions:

(i) A discount rate of 10 per cent is used.

(ii) Plant construction takes 3 years and the plant life is 20 years. Capital payments are made in three equal instalments over the years of construction.

(iii) Waste output is constant.

The effects of varying these assumptions were shown in Chapter 7 and are referred to in the discussions at the end of each chapter in Part II as appropriate.

10.2.7. Disclaimer

It must be emphasized that the calculations are made on a consistent basis for comparison, and that they therefore utilize a great many assumptions; the results must thus be interpreted as those of an illustrative case study. The case study gives a reasonable guide to the *current relative costs* of various technologies; it does not give a guide to the *absolute* cost of a particular process in a *specific local area*. Any decision to implement a waste management system must be taken in the light of an up-to-date local study in the area under consideration.

11. LANDFILL

11.1. Introduction

The only significant method for the final disposal of municipal solid waste is burial in the ground; even if treatment or reclamation processes are practised, a significant residue will remain for final disposal. Disposal of municipal waste at sea is now recognized as unacceptable, sea disposal being strictly controlled by international convention (see Chapter 20).

Landfill is the term used to describe a properly designed and controlled operation for land disposal of wastes. A landfill site should not be seen simply as a euphemism for the old open dump or uncontrolled tip. A modern landfill should conform to strict codes of practice, based on sound engineering principles. The selection and management of landfill sites is increasingly being aided by recent developments in the scientific understanding of the behaviour of waste materials in a landfill environment. A landfill site is known in American parlance as a sanitary landfill; the term 'controlled tip' was used in Britain until recently but is now being replaced by 'landfill'.

The principles of sound landfill management are based on four main criteria:

(i) Environmental nuisances such as odours, fires, vermin, insects, birds, windblown litter, and visual intrusion should be eliminated or at least kept to a minimum.

(ii) The available void space in the site should be utilized to the full by ensuring good compaction of the waste.

(iii) Problems of water pollution and gas generation should be minimized.

(iv) The management of the site should reflect the after-use for which the reclaimed land is intended.

Methods of depositing waste vary widely but, in general, good operating practice requires that waste is spread and compacted in layers, and that all exposed surfaces are covered regularly, at least at the end of each working day, with an inert material. Cover material may be excavated on-site, it may have to be purchased specifically, or certain inert wastes may be utilized. British practice is normally to deposit waste from the top of the working face, while American practice is to deposit at the bottom of the face. Some site machines, such as rubber-wheeled vehicles, are better suited to working with thin layers of refuse rather than a comparatively deep working face. The maximum depth of face recommended in the U K is 2.5 m, with a daily covering of at least 15 cm. These and other details are included in the site licence under which a landfill site is operated; model licence conditions have been published by the Department of the Environment (1976d).

Regular covering helps to reduce nuisance and to improve the visual impact of the landfill operation. Compaction helps to eliminate vermin within the landfill itself. However, supplementary methods to control nuisance are often necessary; examples include regular pest control, the use of movable litter screens and the regular collection of windblown debris from fences and trees, the planting of saplings to screen the operation, and even the use of falcons to control birds, particularly when the site is near an airfield.

Many other wastes can be co-deposited in a municipal waste landfill site. Common examples are bulky refuse, including furniture and consumer durables such as refrigerators, and condemned food or animal carcasses. In either case, these should be buried at the foot of the working face of the landfill. Hollow items should be crushed as far as possible to minimize uneven settlement of the site. Many industrial, and indeed hazardous, wastes can also be safely co-disposed with municipal wastes. Liquids are often deposited in large lagoons, but dispersal through mature refuse via trenches is the preferred method (Section 20.9; Fig. 20.5).

Landfill has been widely practised for many years, albeit with varying standards of operation. Currently it accounts for about 95 per cent of all municipal wastes in the USA, 86 per cent in England, 60–70 per cent in several other European countries and 50 per cent in Japan (Table 1.5). An extensive technical literature has developed, particularly in the USA. Specialist monographs include those of the National Center for Resource Recovery (NCRR) (1974b), of Weiss (1974), and of Noble (1976). A useful bibliography is given by Pavoni et al. (1975). A good account of British practice is given by Skitt (1979).

Despite this literature, it is hard to obtain consistent and up-to-date information on landfill. In this chapter, attention is focused on two complementary aspects:

(a) A review of recent advances in landfill science and technology;

(b) Compilation of the quantitative data required to evaluate landfill as the base-line option against which all others must be compared.

11.2. Compaction and choice of landfill site machines

Landfill space is becoming increasingly scarce near urban areas. A worked-out mineral extraction or other site which is suitable for waste disposal is a valuable asset. It is therefore in the best interests of the site operator to optimize the quantity of waste which can be deposited.

Unfortunately, the available data on waste densities in a landfill site are both scanty and confused. It is often unclear in the literature whether the density is measured on placement, after initial settling or on maturity. Similarly, it is unclear whether the densities allow for the necessary cover material. The achieved density will depend on the composition and moisture content of the waste, and will thus vary not only from place to place but also from day to day. Recently attention has focused on the comparative performance of the various machines which can be used for placing the waste in the landfill. Traditionally, either tracked (Fig. 11.1) or four-wheel drive rubber-wheeled machines (Fig. 11.2) have been used, but more recently specialist landfill compactors have been introduced (Fig. 11.3). These compactors are claimed to produce a significant increase in achieved waste densities; this claim is critically examined below.

It must first be pointed out that waste compaction is only one of the factors affecting the choice of appropriate landfill machinery. Among the alternative criteria are:

The *quantity of waste* to be handled. Smaller tracked or wheeled vehicles will normally be preferred on sites with input below about 200 tonnes of

Fig. 11.1. *Landfill operation using a tracked vehicle.* This Canadian machine is fitted with a special-purpose landfill blade. A smaller machine, common on UK sites, is shown in Fig. 12.8(a). (Photo courtesy The Harwell Laboratory.)

Fig. 11.2. *Landfill operation using a four-wheel drive rubber-tyred vehicle.* (Photo courtesy The Harwell Laboratory.)

waste per day. For inputs above about 500 t.p.d., only a large compactor is capable of coping on its own (Smith 1979).

The *availability and type of cover material*. Compactors can only spread and compact readily available cover material, stored near the working face. Either tracked or wheeled machines can economically excavate and carry cover over distances of about 100m. Obviously, if more work is done in moving cover, less time is available for placing refuse. On large sites, or where cover has to be moved longer distances, either tractor-drawn or self-loading scrapers may be used as auxiliary equipment.

Other site jobs which the machine must perform. Either tracked or wheeled machines can be used for site clearing, access road maintenance, or trench excavation. A rubber-wheeled loader can also drive on public roads if required. A compactor is not suited to these tasks.

Reliability. Steel wheels are obviously not susceptible to punctures or to track damage and may thus be more reliable. However, the use of two smaller vehicles rather than one large compactor does provide a measure of redundancy and may help to avoid problems when no machine is available to spread incoming refuse.

In general, it may be concluded that tracked or rubber-tyred machines are

Fig. 11.3. *Landfill operation using a steel-wheeled compactor.* (Photo courtesy The Harwell Laboratory.)

more flexible to cope with all the various tasks on a small landfill site, but that a compactor may handle much larger quantities of waste at the working face.

Some information on waste densities was summarized in Table 1.6. The density of directly landfilled wastes *on maturity* is often quoted in the range 0.5–0.7 t/m³. This may be compared with the densities *on placement* obtained by Bratley (1977) in a series of short, 4-day field trials in South Yorkshire. His results are summarized in Table 11.1. He himself calculated the results in terms of the average density of the combined municipal waste and its associated cover material, yielding densities between 0.7 and 1.3 t/m³. However, both landfill space and cover material are often valuable assets, the use of which should be kept to the minimum which is environmentally acceptable. A more meaningful measure is the weight of waste disposed of per unit of void space in the landfill (i.e. the volume occupied by waste *plus* cover); this measure is here referred to as the *effective density* of landfilled waste. When Bratley's results are expressed in this way (Table 11.1), they yield rather lower values, in the range 0.47–1.0 t/m³.

Bratley's results for waste densities on placement were all obtained using a novel method of deposition. The waste was deposited in cells approximately 8–12 m in width, with banks approximately 2 m in height on three sides. The collection vehicles enter at the lower level, the waste being pushed *up* a 1 in 7 slope by the site machine. Approximately 4 thin layers are

Table 11.1

Waste densities on placement in a landfill

Calculated from data given by Bratley (1977), resulting from a series of 4-day field trials at Springwell Lane landfill site, Doncaster, between May and August, 1976

Type of mobile equipment	Effective density[1] (t/m^3)	Cover material used per tonne of waste (t)	Density of waste + cover[2] (t/m^3)
Tracked machine:			
International 175C	0.47	0.49	0.70
4-wheel-drive rubber-tyred machines:			
Weatherill L86	0.67	0.37	0.91
Volvo L M841	0.56	0.37	0.77
Steel-wheeled compactors:			
Weatherill L86	0.99	0.39	1.25
Massey Ferguson 55C	0.66	0.88	1.23
Caterpillar 816	0.92	0.43	1.31
Bomag K301	0.71	0.41	1.00
Caterpillar 930	0.65	0.73	1.13
Volvo B M 846	0.63	0.96	1.24

1. $\dfrac{\text{weight of waste}}{\text{volume occupied by (waste + cover)}}$ 2. $\dfrac{\text{weight of (waste + cover)}}{\text{volume occupied by (waste + cover)}}$

required to form a complete layer 2 m deep. This technique of 'onion skinning' may be contrasted both to normal British practice, where the waste is pushed over the top of the working face, and to American practice where each day's refuse reaches to the full height of the layer being formed, the slope of the working face in either case being about 1 in 3. Onion skinning is unlikely to displace these alternative methods of working in widespread use, as it is rather time consuming in practice, and is thus best suited to relatively small sites.

The results in Table 11.1 suggest that significantly increased waste densities, about 1 t/m^3, may be obtained using certain heavy steel-wheeled compactors. However, the use of excessive cover material may obviate this advantage; for this reason four of the six compactors tested only achieved effective densities of 0.6–0.7 t/m^3. It should also be noted that Bratley's tests do not reflect compaction due to delivery vehicles running on top of the refuse; in practice this may be expected to reduce any differences between machine performance. In a deep site, with say 10 or more layers of waste, the final density of lower layers will probably be independent of the method of their initial emplacement.

The longer-term effects of increased compaction ratios are not at present known. The stabilization process may be significantly affected by excluding air and by making the waste less permeable to water. The landfill may thus decompose more slowly, delaying any after-use. On the other hand, settlement may be more even, or indeed very slight, thus aiding reclamation and reuse. If settlement of the compacted waste is only slight, then the final waste density on maturity may be little different from that using conventional deposition methods.

Despite the scarcity of hard data on waste densities, experience of landfill operations in the UK does allow certain general conclusions to be drawn:

(i) Considerable variations in density are to be expected from one site to another.

(ii) Considerable variations can be caused by differences in the amount of cover material used.

(iii) The effective density obtained depends at least as much on other factors as it does on the choice of machine. These factors include:

The skill and experience of the driver;

The mode of operation;

The rate of waste delivery.

(iv) Effective densities may be expected to fall within the following ranges:

Tracked crawler: $0.4–0.6$ t/m^3;

Rubber-tyred machine: $0.5–0.8$ t/m^3;

Steel-wheeled compactor: $0.5–1.0$ t/m^3.

Densities at the low end of these ranges probably indicate that improvements in operating practice could be made, while those at the upper end can probably only be achieved in ideal conditions, and are unlikely to be sustained in a routine operation.

(v) Placement in thin layers can give higher densities than when refuse is pushed over a relatively deep working face, but any advantage may easily be obviated if additional cover material is used.

(vi) While a compactor can yield higher densities under ideal conditions, the choice of landfill site machine should be made taking into account all the relevant factors. These include the quantity of waste, the availability and type of cover, other site jobs which the machine must perform, and reliability and costs.

(vii) With any site machine and good site management, an effective density in the range $0.5–0.8$ t/m^3 should be obtainable on placement of the waste, with a density on maturity of perhaps $0.7–1.0$ t/m^3. Any differences between machine performance will be reduced on deep sites, and by the compaction due to vehicles delivering the waste. A density on placement of 0.75 t/m^3, representing good practice, is used later in this chapter.

11.3. Landfill science

The science of landfill disposal has only recently begun to emerge as a subject worthy of serious attention. The basic principles were stated by

Bevan (1967). A landfill site may be viewed as an inelegant biological reactor, in which the waste decomposes over time. The temperature within the landfill will increase, giving rise to a fire hazard if the site is not properly managed. Settlement will occur as decomposition proceeds. Pollution problems may arise from two main sources:

(i) If water is allowed to come in contact with the waste, then an obnoxious mineralized leachate is produced.

(ii) Gases are generated from the biodegradation of the waste.

On deposition, municipal waste will contain some entrapped air. In British conditions, with an average moisture content in the waste of about 25 per cent, aerobic bacteria will multiply rapidly, and the resultant decomposition will raise the temperature in the landfill. The oxygen will be used up quickly, the aerobic bacteria being replaced by anaerobes. Anaerobic degradation of organic matter proceeds more slowly, the temperature gradually declining. If the landfill is well compacted, the peak temperature will be about 35 °C; if compaction is less efficient, allowing air ingress, temperatures may reach much higher levels, up to 60–80 °C. Anaerobic degradation is more efficient the higher the moisture content. The ultimate products of aerobic degradation of organic materials are carbon dioxide and water; anaerobic degradation produces carbon dioxide and methane in roughly equal proportions. Many intermediate chemicals occur, particularly under aerobic conditions; these include many shorter-chain aliphatic organic acids. The composition of landfill leachate depends on many factors, including the waste composition, its moisture content and the landfill age. An analysis of a 'typical' anaerobic leachate from fresh municipal waste is shown in Table 11.2.

The chemistry within a landfill site is complex. The composition of leachate is affected by such processes as:

(a) The initial solubility or leaching out of waste materials into solution;

(b) Biodegradation, which affects both carbonaceous components of the waste and also some inorganic constituents of the leachate. For example, anaerobic bacteria utilize sulphate and nitrate ions in addition to carbohydrate as their oxygen source, the reduction yielding sulphide and nitrite or ammonia;

(c) Chemical precipitation, which limits the concentration of many metal ions in solution;

(d) Acid–base reactions; domestic waste has the capacity to buffer many acid or alkaline wastes to a pH of 6–8;

(e) Complex ion formation;

(f) Chemical oxidation – reduction;

(g) Volatilization;

(h) Absorption and adsorption on various components in the waste, or on clay minerals in the intermediate cover material.

Table 11.2

Composition of landfill leachate.

These samples were taken from an experimental
landfill, 6–9 months after placement. The results
are fairly typical of an *anaerobic* leachate from
fresh municipal waste

Species	Concentration range (mg/l)
Metal ions:	
Iron	60–200
Sodium	600–900
Potassium	600–900
Other cations:	
Ammonium	400–700
Anions:	
Chloride	900–1100
Sulphate	1700–1900
Nitrate	<0.1–1.0
General organics:	
Total organic carbon	5000–10 000
Biological oxygen demand	10 000–20 000
Chemical oxygen demand	20 000–40 000
Organic Acids:	
Acetic	2200–3700
Propionic	1300–2500
n-Butyric	2400–5100
i-Butyric	200–300
	(pH units not mg/l)
pH	5.6–5.7

This complex chemistry means that municipal waste has the capacity to
attenuate the concentration of many hazardous components in leachate.
Co-disposal of hazardous wastes with municipal wastes can thus sometimes
be the *preferred* method for their management; this subject is returned to in
Chapter 20.

11.4. Water pollution

11.4.1. Background

The stages involved in the production of water pollution from a landfill site
may be summarized as:

(i) Water enters the waste. Some water will already be contained in the
waste as received, while some will be generated by biodegradation.
Additional water may come from infiltrating rainfall, liquid wastes, surface water drainage, spring issues, or by tipping direct into standing
water. Good practice requires the latter three sources to be eliminated by
proper site selection or by preliminary engineering works, for example to
divert surface water drains. In addition, the use of an impermeable top

cover and good grading to aid surface run-off from the site should mini-mize rainfall infiltration. However, in the British climate at least, some leachate production is inevitable.

(ii) The leachate leaves the landfill site. This may occur either laterally or vertically. Lateral movement may occur where impermeable intermediate cover is used, or where the permeability of the waste is reduced by high-density compaction. Care is necessary to prevent the contamination of surface water by leachate 'springs'.

(iii) The leachate passes through the rock structure beneath the site, moving first through any unsaturated zone until it reaches the water table. The concentration of contaminants may be attenuated by physical processes such as dispersion, by chemical interactions with the rock minerals and by biodegradation.

(iv) Once in the saturated aquifer, the leachate mixes with the water and travels with it to a borehole or other extraction point. The contaminated water is then combined with water coming from elsewhere and may thus enter a drinking water supply.

11.4.2. Recent research

Pollution of surface waters can be prevented by good landfill management. The various processes which can attenuate the pollution of groundwater resources in the landfill site itself, in the unsaturated zone, and in the saturated zone were studied by a 3-year research programme sponsored by the U K Department of the Environment (1978). This programme involved field investigations of 20 sites, where boreholes in and around the landfill were used to determine both the extent of any pollution plume and the attenuation of the leachate as it moved away from the site. In addition, controlled experiments were performed using field lysimeters of undisturbed sandstone, smaller blocks of undisturbed rock, laboratory columns of disturbed sand, and pilot-scale simulated landfills. Useful reviews of this and other work are provided by Mather and Bromley (1976) and by Wilson (1979a).

The presence of a significant unsaturated zone beneath a landfill site is particularly important in attenuating pollutant concentrations in landfill leachate. This point may be illustrated by the results from one of the sandstone lysimeters in the U K research programme. The concentrations of various species at the first suction probe, 40 cm below the surface, are shown in Fig. 11.4 for the first 600 days of irrigation with a synthetic leachate, which contained heavy metal ions, alkali and alkaline earth metal ions, chloride, and lower straight-chain carboxylic acids, the input concentrations being indicated on the right-hand scale (Campbell, Parker, Rees, King, and Wright 1978). This leachate is representative of that from a municipal waste landfill, with various heavy metals added.

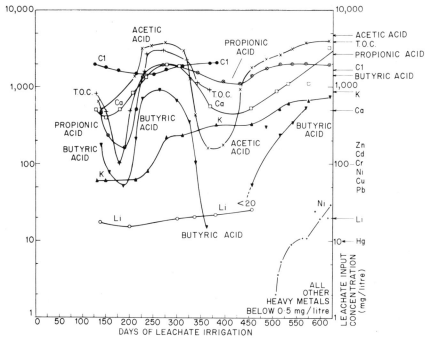

Fig. 11.4. *Attenuation of leachate components in unsaturated sandstone.* Concentration of chemical species (mg/l) in liquid extracted by a suction probe 40 cm below the surface of a sandstone lysimeter. (Reproduced by kind permission of the Department of the Environment.)

The results show that about 500 days were required for the most mobile of the heavy metal ions, nickel, to reach the probe, while there is no evidence for the breakthrough of any of the others. It is clear that precipitation, adsorption, or ion exchange are efficient attenuation mechanisms for heavy metals in Lower Greensand, while the smaller-scale monolith experiments confirm the finding for Lower Chalk and Plateau Gravels as well. The mobility of the heavy metals decreases in the order $Ni > Hg \approx Cd > Zn > Cr > Pb \approx Cu$.

In contrast with the behaviour of the heavy metals, chloride ion attained its initial concentration after 100 days. Chloride is attenuated only by dilution and dispersion, and moves at a velocity close to that of the liquid front (about 5 mm/day). Potassium attained its input concentration very slowly, presumably due to its incorporation in biomass by the microbes within the lysimeter. All the organic components show a cyclical behaviour, the decreases from near the input concentration corresponding to increased microbial activity during the summer months. The effect is most marked for acetic and butyric acids, but less so for propionic acid which is more resistant to biological attack. It is interesting that calcium follows a similar cycle, achieving a concentration in excess of that in the applied leachate when organic acid concentrations are high, presumably due to its solubilization by reaction of the rock minerals with the acids.

On the basis of this research, three hydrogeological categories have been suggested as an aid to landfill selection (Mather 1976):

(1) Those sites which provide a significant element of containment for wastes and leachates;

(2) Those which allow slow leachate migration and significant attentuation;

(3) Those which allow rapid leachate migration and insignificant attentuation.

Much recent debate has focused on the relative merits of the alternative philosophies of 'concentrate and contain' as exemplified by class 1 sites and 'attenuate and disperse' as with class 2 sites (Mather 1977).

11.4.3. Class 1 sites

Sites providing a significant element of containment are situated on relatively impermeable strata such as soft clays and marls or fine-grained compact rocks of low permeability such as slates, shales, and mudstones (Fig. 11.5(a)). A detailed site inspection using boreholes may be necessary to confirm that the poorly permeable layer is continuous beneath the whole area of the landfill. The presence of lenses of sand, gravel, or similar permeable deposits may provide preferential routes for migration of leachate, although their existence may not be apparent from a surface inspection of the site. If a head of leachate is allowed to build up at the base of the landfill, several adverse effects may occur. The liquid may fill the site, eventually overflowing the sides and polluting surface water. Alternatively, as the pressure head increases, the base of the landfill may begin to leak (Mather 1976). The saturated waste will biodegrade anaerobically, leading to the generation of methane gas. The use of local, poorly permeable materials for intermediate cover may lead to perching of leachates at different levels in the landfill and thus to the possibility of lateral seepage through the walls of the pit, and will also tend to prevent the free escape of landfill gases. This build-up of potentially explosive gas may interfere with the reuse of the site after landfilling is complete (see Section 11.5).

In view of these problems, careful management of a containment site is necessary. It is usually necessary to collect the leachate generated and to dispose of it in some way. Foul sewers may not be available at remote landfill sites, and pretreatment of the leachate may be necessary. However the liquor is dealt with, this adds significantly to the costs of running the site. In addition, care is required to limit the amount of water entering the site, either as infiltrating rainfall or as liquid waste. In dry climates, the use of a

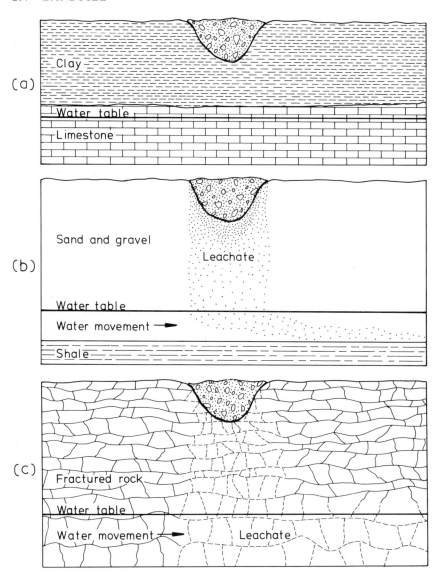

Fig. 11.5. *Classification of landfill sites.*

(a) *Class 1 or containment site.* The leachate is contained within the landfill by the impermeable clay.

(b) *Class 2 or attentuation site.* The sand and gravel allows slow leachate migration with significant attenuation. The underlying, impermeable, shale stratum protects deeper aquifers.

(c) *Class 3 or rapid migration site.* The fissured strata allow rapid leachate migration into the aquifer, with insignificant attenuation.

(Prepared by the author for the Open University, and reproduced with their permission.)

poorly permeable top cover would effectively prevent rainfall infiltration and leachate generation, although now the dry wastes would decompose only very slowly, making reuse of the site more difficult.

11.4.4. Class 2 sites

Sites allowing slow leachate migration and significant attenuation are those taking full advantage of the natural attenuation processes. Although these processes are complex and incompletely understood, it is clear that a mechanism exists which will have an effect on most if not all potential pollutants leached from landfill sites, including those derived from many hazardous wastes. An ideal site might be a dry pit in silt or fine sand through which flow is intergranular and which is underlain by a significant unsaturated zone (Fig. 11.5(b)), the nearest water abstraction point being some distance away so as to allow dilution of any residual pollution which reaches the water table. The presence of clay particles dispersed through the unsaturated zone is helpful in providing significant attenuation of metal ions. Sites on fissured strata may be acceptable if infiltration through the joints and fissures is sufficiently slow to allow time for the fissure water to diffuse into static interstitial water. This may occur for instance in the British Chalk, but is unlikely in formations such as the Carboniferous Limestone (Mather 1977).

11.4.5. Class 3 sites

Sites which allow migration of leachates at such a rate that there is insignificant attenuation will be located on a variety of geological strata, including hard calcareous rocks in which groundwater flow is mainly through fissures (Fig. 11.5(c)), and river terrace deposits with high water tables in which groundwater flow is intergranular. Such sites are normally only suitable for the disposal of relatively inert wastes, although again each site should be treated on its merits. For example, a coastal pit in fractured rock where the aquifer is already contaminated by intrusion of saline water may be acceptable for waste disposal.

11.4.6. Site selection

Attention is now directed to the choice of site for waste disposal. In any particular case, detailed site investigations are necessary; the concern here is with the general principle.

A policy of 'concentrate and contain' using a class 1 site is likely to be expensive as leachate treatment and venting of gases may well be necessary. Co-disposal of liquid wastes requires care in order to avoid overloading the site or so polluting the leachate with hazardous components that its disposal becomes a problem.

On the other hand, even an ideal 'attenuate and disperse' site involves some risk if it is situated over a valuable aquifer such as the lower Green-sand, Bunter Sandstone, or Lower Chalk. Careful management is required to avoid overloading the attenuation capacity of the unsaturated zone, for example by discharging such large volumes of liquid waste that the water table effectively rises into the base of the landfill.

On balance, a carefully selected class 2 site, using the 'attenuate and disperse' philosophy, is recommended for municipal waste landfill. In the UK, this recommendation is extended to many hazardous wastes, although some exceptions are made where a containment site is preferred (e.g. Department of the Environment 1977a). In all cases, a careful consideration of both the waste and the proposed site is required, including if possible the empirical measurement of the more important attenuation factors. It should be noted that many other countries, including the USA and West Germany, prefer the philosophy of 'concentrate and contain' for landfill disposal of wastes.

11.4.7. Use of liner materials

Some management control of the philosophy adopted at a particular site is possible. Sites allowing leachate migration may in principle be turned into containment sites by using a suitable impermeable liner material, while the attenuation capacity of a dispersal site may be increased by using a suitable permeable liner.

Many materials have been proposed for use as *impermeable* liners, including compacted or puddled native clays or chalk, bentonite and other clay sealants perhaps with a polymer additive, asphaltic or portland cement compositions, soil sealants, liquid rubber sprays, and several synthetic polymeric membranes. One of the earliest examples of a lined site was the Merstham landfill site in Surrey, England, where a chalk quarry was sealed by grading the base and progressively puddling the bottom with marly chalk.

Several recent studies have compared the available liner materials under landfill conditions, and such work is continuing. The most complete study so far published is that of Haxo (1979). The results have not been altogether favourable, the materials tending to lose compressive strength and the polymeric materials to swell. Further research and development work is required before a suitable impermeable liner material may be selected with confidence.

The successful use of impermeable liners requires careful preparation of the site and installation to avoid cracking rigid liner materials. The liner will require some protection from damage during emplacement and settlement of the landfill. Ideally it should be covered with about half a metre of sand or soil, and heavy objects which might puncture the liner should be excluded from the first layer of waste. The site needs to be graded and drains installed to allow for collection and treatment of the leachate.

The problems with the use of impermeable liner materials may be summarized briefly. Capital costs are high, around £5 per square metre (1976, installed) for some of the polymeric membranes. Little is known about the long-term behaviour of the liner materials in the hostile landfill environment, particularly with hazardous wastes. It is difficult to guarantee the integrity of the membrane after its emplacement. Bearing in mind the advantages of a site allowing slow migration and significant attenuation over a containment site for many wastes, it is clear that the indiscriminate prescription of impermeable liners for use on all sites which do not guarantee containment is at present unjustified. However, liners may be useful where a particularly sensitive aquifer is at risk, where there is insufficient unsaturated zone to allow significant attenuation, or on highly fissured strata.

The use of a *permeable* waste material to increase the attenuation capacity of a dispersal site is an interesting concept. Examples of such materials include pulverized fuel ash, concrete demolition rubble, or foundry sand. Research in this area is in progress both in the USA (Fuller, McCarthy, Alesii, and Niebla, 1976) and in the UK (Institute of Geological Sciences, private communication).

11.5. Gas generation

As the biodegradation of municipal waste in a landfill proceeds, the composition of the gas contained in the site gradually changes (Fig. 11.6). During the initial aerobic phase of degradation, available oxygen is rapidly depleted and carbon dioxide is formed. As conditions become anaerobic, carbon dioxide levels continue to be high, gradually falling as the methane concentration builds up. There is usually an early peak of hydrogen, which may reach a concentration of up to 20 per cent by volume. If there is no significant ingress of air, nitrogen levels will gradually decline to zero. After several years, an equilibrium concentration of about 50–60 per cent methane and 50–40 per cent carbon dioxide is generally attained.

In the past, landfill gas has been viewed as at best a nuisance and at worst a potential hazard. If the gas is able to escape freely to atmosphere, there may be a problem of smell associated with the presence of trace contaminants containing sulphur. If gas movement is restricted, for example by impermeable layers of cover material, a potential fire or explosion hazard may be created. Incidents have occurred affecting, for example, basements of adjoining property or buildings subsequently erected on the reclaimed site (Bromley 1979; Bromley and Parker 1979). In many cases it has been necessary to build collection facilities (such as permeable gravel trenches) into the landfill, so that the gas may be vented to the atmosphere, or even flared off, in a controlled manner; such precautions should be routine on all new large landfill sites.

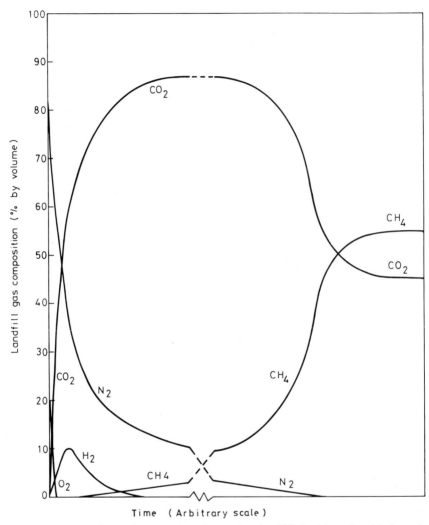

Fig. 11.6. *Gas evolution from municipal waste in a landfill site.* Note that this figure is an idealized representation of a complex situation.

With increasing shortages of energy, it is logical to view landfill gas as a potential asset and energy source. Since the concept was first developed in California in 1973, research activity has increased dramatically. Several demonstration facilities are operational in the USA, notably those at Palos Verdes (Mandeville 1976; Rice 1978), and Mountain View (Blanchet 1977; James and Rhyne 1978) in California. Research activity in the UK, for example under the Department of the Environment managed landfill programme, focuses on optimizing gas production and on its direct use as a fuel.

The original demonstration project at Palos Verdes used the relatively complex technology of molecular sieves to upgrade the raw landfill gas from about 50 per cent to about 99 per cent pure methane (from 17 MJ/m^3 to 34 MJ/m^3), for direct injection into a natural gas main. The plant suffered from considerable technical problems, notably corrosion, which have now been overcome (Rice 1978). The plant was on-stream at 90 per cent availability between January 1977 and June 1978, although the output of methane was only half the original design capacity.

The Mountain View project uses a much shallower landfill than that at Palos Verdes. The gas is again to be fed to a distribution main, but a reduction in calorific value of the mixed gases of about 2.5 per cent is permitted. The low relative volume of the landfill gas enables upgrading to a less rigorous specification, with a calorific value about 24 MJ/m^3, although molecular sieves are still necessary to achieve this upgrading. The plant started operation in mid-1978.

More recent projects have focused on the direct usage of the raw landfill gases, thus dispensing with the need for expensive molecular sieve technology. The gas could be used in a nearby industrial furnace, possibilities including both brick and cement kilns; these tend to be situated adjacent to their supply of raw materials, the worked-out pits often being used subsequently for landfill.

An interesting example is the City of Industry in California. This is a major development near Los Angeles which includes two championship golf courses, other sports facilities, and a large industrial conference centre, a 10-storey hotel being planned at a future date. Part of the 200 ha site is an old landfill site, completed in 1967. Faced with extensive site works to protect the buildings from methane gas, a feasibility study showed that collection of the gas for direct usage could provide a large percentage of the development's energy needs over a period of 8–15 years. It has been estimated that the gas recovery system will more than pay for itself in terms of energy savings. The system was scheduled for completion in late 1978 (Stearns, Wright, and Brecher 1978).

The conditions required for optimal generation of landfill gas are incompletely understood. However, it is possible to draw an analogy with the more conventional anaerobic digestion of wastes (Section 19.4), for which the required conditions are well documented. The relevant factors may be summarized as:

(i) *Temperature*, which for anaerobic digestion may be held in the mesophilic (20–40 °C) or thermophilic (50–60 °C) range. The temperature in anaerobic landfill sites is usually in the mesophilic range.

(ii) *Absence of air* is obviously necessary if anaerobic conditions are to be maintained. Air infiltration is minimized both by the use of impermeable cover and by the use of deep landfill sites. Most of the American demonstration sites are more than 30 m in depth, although Mountain View is only about 12 m deep. Some of the U K experiments are being conducted with very shallow layers of waste (2–3 m deep).

(iii) *pH* with an optimum about 6.7–7.0. Landfill leachate is normally in the range pH 6.0–8.0.

(iv) *Moisture content* for anaerobic digestion has an optimum value of about 60 per cent. Landfill sites with such a high moisture content may produce leachate problems. A minimum content about 20 per cent is necessary for biodegradation to proceed. The effect of deliberately adding water to the waste, which goes against all the accepted principles of good landfill practice, is being studied in the U K research programme.

(v) *Nutrients*, notably nitrogen, are necessary for optimum bacterial growth. The low ratio of nitrogen to carbon in municipal waste is one reason for the slow rate of degradation.

(vi) *Absence of toxic materials* is necessary for conventional anaerobic digestion. Research on the codisposal of hazardous and municipal wastes in landfill has shown the bacteria to be remarkably tolerant, presumably because the perceived concentrations are much lower than they would be in simple solution. However, particular care is required if a site is to be used for gas recovery.

The recovery of methane-rich gas from municipal waste landfill sites is an intriguing possibility which one can expect to come to fruition within a few years. The potential is greatest on deep sites, on sites where the possibility of a hazard requires the installation of gas collection and venting systems, and on sites adjacent to a potential user who can burn the gas directly in a boiler or kiln. Unfortunately, it is still too early to give any useful data either on the energy efficiency or the economics of the process. Typical of the many preliminary claims made is that sufficient methane may be produced for 10–15 years after placement to make collection worthwhile, with an overall energy recovery anywhere between 5 and 30 per cent of the heat content of the waste.

11.6. Land reclamation

If landfill is to be acceptable as a means of waste disposal, then it must be viewed also as a method of land reclamation. The planned after-use of a site should be kept clearly in mind during the landfilling operation. It is particularly important to avoid excessively uneven settlement by crushing objects such as hollow metal containers. Large accumulations of persistent hazardous materials should be avoided if there is a possibility that the land could be used for building or might otherwise be re-excavated: the problems which can arise were recently highlighted by the case of Love Canal in Niagara, where a school and housing estate had to be evacuated (Cookson 1979). In addition, the landfill of wastes in unmarked drums should be discouraged. If a site is intended for agricultural use, then hazardous wastes should be excluded from the final layer of deposited waste (see also Section 20.9).

The final restoration of a landfill site depends on the intended use. Sufficient time must be allowed for settlement before development proceeds. A depth of final cover of at least 1 m is recommended in all cases (Department of the Environment 1976d). Two recent conferences considered many aspects of the reuse of landfill sites (Midland Geotechnical Society 1979; Society of Chemical Industry 1979).

11.7. Capital costs of a landfill site

The capital cost of the landfill site includes the following elements:

Identification of a suitable site;

Proving (survey, hydrogeology, hydrology, consultancy fees);

Planning and licence applications (drawings, plans, quotations, legal fees);

Acquisition cost (may be freehold or leasehold);

Site preparation (diversion of water courses or surface drains, culverting, site grading, installation of liners and leachate-collection/surface-water-collection systems, bund and cell construction, installation of monitoring boreholes);

General site works (site office, mess room, telephone, water supply, fuel storage tank, tool store, lighting, gates and fencing, movable litter screen, fire-fighting equipment, wheel washing, weighbridge, site roads);

Mobile equipment used for handling waste and cover material, and for compaction (alternatively these may be hired);

Restoration costs (doming, clay cover, subsoil, topsoil, revegetation, trees, removal of facilities);

Residual value when site is sold (to be set against initial cost).

Many of these components of capital cost are highly dependent on the site. Some indication of the range of costs is given in Table 11.3.

The relationship of capital costs to either the total site capacity or to the daily throughput is unclear. The mobile equipment required will vary with throughput, there being some disagreement as to the capacities at which either a larger or an additional machine is needed. Large steel-wheeled compactors are claimed to be able to handle up to 1000 t of waste per day, but they are unsuitable for hauling cover material any distance across a site. Estimates of the lifetime of mobile equipment vary from 3 to 10 years. The one estimate of economy of scale in landfilling uses a scale factor $S = 0.93$ (Midwest Research Institute 1973). On the very limited evidence presented above, this appears to be high, and a value of $S = 0.8$ is tentatively suggested.

Table 11.3
Capital costs of landfill sites

| Source | Date | Throughput (t/day) | Life (years) | Capacity (10^6 t) | Capital costs (£ thousand) | | | | | |
					Land	Site preparation	General works	Mobile equipment	Miscellaneous	Total
Midwest Research 1973 Institute (MRI) 1975	1972	900	10	2.5	940					1900
						240	80	270	410	
	Nov 1973	900	10	2.5	3500					4500
Warner, Baum, and Parker 1971	1968	270	10	0.75	–	30	30	230	–	280
Sweeten 1972	1972	450	10	1.4	90	30	6	100	–	230
General Electric	1972	900	10	2.5	–		2900	1400[a]	400	4700
Company 1973a		450	10	1.2	–		1500	940[a]	330	2700
Department of the Environment 1976a	1975	250	5 / 13	0.33 / 0.85	–		100	20	70[b]	190
Colonna, McLaren, and Sano 1976	1975	45	15	0.18	–	6	30	200	12	240
		140	6	0.21	–	1	5	130	10	150
		270	25	1.8	–	370[c]	140	620	80	1200
Wilcox 1976	1975	90	5	0.12	–	30	7	50[a]	–	80
		150	5	0.20	–	110	50	50[a]	–	200
		700	25	4.6	–	90	7	130[a]	–	230
Borgese, Rossi, and Trebbi	1976	800	15	3.1	6400	–	260	850	–	7500
Association of Waste Disposal Engineers (AWDE) 1976	1976	120	8	0.25						20
		1400	7	2.5	–	490	200	–	–	690
Warwickshire County Council (private communication 1977)	1976	150	8	0.3		160		–	–	160
		500	2.3	0.3	–		90	–	–	90
West Midlands County Council 1976a	Nov 1975	500			–	–	–	50	–	50

(a) Includes cost of replacement equipment.
(b) Cost of restoration.
(c) Includes cost of 3 miles of paved road.

In order to compare options for waste management, it is necessary to use a common timescale in each case. For most capital plant, a lifetime of between 10 and 25 years can be expected. A lifetime of 20 years has been used here in the comparative evaluation. In most situations, this will mean that the option of direct delivery of waste to a local landfill must envisage the utilization of a sequence of several sites, as a landfill with capacity sufficient for 20 years is uncommon.

The comparative evaluation here assumes as a base case that a site of capacity about 2.0×10^6 m³ is available; this is sufficient to receive a waste input of 300 t.p.d. for 20 years, assuming an achieved density of 0.75/m³. The capital cost is taken as £500 000, and is assumed to include a fund sufficient to replace the mobile equipment as the need arises. In the risk analysis the error limits on this capital cost are taken as $\overset{\times}{\div}$ 2.0, i.e. the range of capital costs is £250 000–£1 000 000. The sensitivity of landfill costs to alternative assumptions about site life and the costs of replacement sites and equipment are discussed in Section 11.9.

When a landfill operation is complete, site restoration is required. The purchase of a metre of final cover, including top-soil, is expensive. Restoration costs were estimated in 1975 as £50 000 for each of two sites with capacity 330×10^3 and 850×10^3 t, respectively (Department of the Environment 1976a). The revenue from selling the restored land should be entered as a benefit to the project. However, in Britain an accounting anomaly in the system of local government finance means that only part of the revenue may be credited directly to waste disposal (Section 2.2.3).

For a standard 300 t.p.d. site, with capacity 2.0×10^6 m³, restoration costs might be £100 000; a fill depth of 8m suggests a site of about 25 ha. If this is sold after, say, 5 years, a price of £6400/h is required just to recover the investment in restoration (assuming a 10 per cent discount rate). This is very much at the high end of the price range for agricultural land in the UK (mid-1979), while for building purposes a longer stabilization period is necessary. Thus, unless a higher shadow price for the reclaimed land is appropriate (Section 5.3.4), it appears that, at best, restoration and resale of the land may break even. This should *not* be taken to imply that final restoration is uneconomic, as it is essential if landfill is to be regarded as a satisfactory means of waste disposal. It implies rather that sufficient funds should be set aside during the operation of the landfill to provide for its subsequent restoration. It is most unfortunate for the public image of waste disposal in Britain that the present cutback in local government expenditure has meant that many small landfill sites inherited from the old authorities in 1974 have never been properly restored.

11.8. Operating costs of a landfill site

The labour requirements to run a landfill site include a site foreman, equipment operators, an office/weighbridge clerk, and site labourers. A small site may have just 2 men, while a large site handling a wide variety of wastes, including hazardous liquids, may need 50. It is assumed here that the standard 300 t.p.d. site, receiving municipal waste delivered directly to the tip face by collection vehicles, requires just 3 men.

Fuel requirements must also be taken into consideration, particularly those for the operation of mobile equipment. Data on specific fuel consumption are lacking, but some estimates may be made from American cost data, using fuel prices taken from the UN Monthly Bulletin of Statistics. Thus consumption in litres/tonne of waste may be derived as 1.0 (Pathak 1974), 0.8 (fuel price 20 ¢ per gallon; Pavoni et al. 1975) and 2.5 (fuel 11.7 ¢/gallon and assuming a ratio of maintenance:fuel costs of 3:1, Stone and Conrad 1969). A mean value of 1.4 l/t is assumed here.

Maintenance requirements are largely for mobile equipment, a value of 16–18 per cent of capital cost/annum being suggested (Pavoni *et al.* 1975). If a factor of 0.18 I is applied to mobile equipment (£50 000), 0.06 I to other equipment (£50 000) and 0.02 I to the remaining investment (£400 000), then the average factor is 0.04 I.

The availability of cover material is important. In some cases, sufficient inert wastes will be delivered to provide cover or cover may be excavated on site; in others, purchase of cover will be significant. Data used by the Department of the Environment (1976*a*) suggest a requirement for primary cover of 0.11 t/t of waste and for final cover of 0.05 t/t. The data in Table 11.1 suggest rather higher requirements for primary cover, generally in the range 0.3–0.5 t/t. A metre of final cover, with a density of 0.5 t/m³, on top of 8 m of compacted waste, with a density of 0.75 t/m³, suggests a usage of 0.08 t cover per tonne of waste. A cost of 20 p/t of waste is used here for cover material, based on 0.3 t of primary cover per tonne of waste, at the nominal cost of £0.20/t, and 0.08 t/t of final cover at £1.75/t.

Direct delivery of wastes to a local landfill site will probably involve a longer journey for the collection vehicles than would delivery to a more central treatment plant. The costs of this excess haul must therefore be entered as a cost of landfill. In the comparative evaluation here, an average haul to a central treatment plant of 4 km is assumed, corresponding to a circular catchment area of radius 6 km. The landfill site is assumed to be 12 km away, giving an excess haul of 8 km. In Chapter 6, the average unit cost of transport in a collection vehicle was estimated at 18 p/t km, giving a base transport cost of £1.4/t. An error range of $\overset{\times}{\div}$ 1.5 is assumed, corresponding to a cost range of £1.0–£2.2/t.

11.9. Discussion

An economic analysis, using the methods of Chapters 5–7 and the data derived in Sections 11.7 and 11.8, yields a cost for direct delivery of waste to a local landfill site of £3.8/t, with a 95 per cent confidence interval of ± £1.4/t. If the cost of transport in a collection vehicle is subtracted, the basic cost of landfill itself is about £2.4/t.

The method of sensitivity analysis introduced in Chapter 7 enables the relative importance of the various components of the overall cost to be assessed. From the results for landfill in Table A.8, the only significant components are the capital investment cost and the cost of transport in a collection vehicle. In either case, a doubling of the base-line estimate would raise the overall net expenditure by about 40 per cent. For other cost components such as labour, maintenance, fuel, and raw materials (cover), a doubling of the estimate would raise the overall net cost by less than 8 per cent, or about £0.3/t.

This analysis is based on a site which costs £500 000 and which lasts a full 20 years. If an additional £50 000 is required to replace mobile equipment every 5 years, then the overall net cost increases by about £0.1/t. A new site every 5 years, at the same distance and with the same costs, would increase the cost by £1.0/t. An extreme case in which a new site is needed every 5 years, and the capital costs are £0.5, £1.0, £1.5, and £2.0 million respectively, for the four sites, increases the average unit cost by £2.6/t to about £6.4/t. The analysis assumes that both transport and operating costs are the same for each site; the higher capital costs for later sites could be viewed rather as an allowance for higher transport costs to a more distant site.

The benefits of land reclamation are not included in the base-line economic analysis. The costs of restoration were included to some extent as a flat rate for the purchase of final cover. If the site could be sold off after 20 years for a price of £500 000, equal to the initial capital cost, the net cost per tonne would only be reduced by £0.1. As this selling price represents a revenue of about £20 000/ha, it is clear that the effect will only be significant if high shadow prices for reclaimed land are used. A price of £100 000/ha, with the land sold off in 4 lots starting in year 10, so that 5 years are allowed for stabilization, would reduce the cost by about £0.7/t.

The results of the comparative economic analysis show that direct delivery of wastes to a local landfill is generally the cheapest option, with the possible exception of the sale of pulverized waste directly for use as a fuel. As landfill is likely to remain for some time the base-line option against which all others must be compared, it is essential that the factors which affect its economics be properly understood. Further research is required to clarify the effect of such variables as:

(a) Distance to the site;

(b) Economies of scale in landfill operation;

(c) The local hydrogeology and the philosophy adopted for leachate management. For example, the decision to line a site artificially has obvious effects on both capital costs and, through the need for leachate treatment and disposal, on operating costs;

(d) The management of the site, notably the degree of compaction and the water content of the refuse, and its effect on the stabilization and future use of the site;

(e) The collection and use of landfill gas.

Landfill of wastes obviously has a negative effect on the conservation of energy and materials. When the methods of process analysis introduced in Chapter 8 are applied, the overall primary energy requirement is found to be about 200 MJ/t, of which 140 MJ/t is attributable to the landfill. The process analysis worksheet is shown in detail in Table 11.4.

Table 11.4

Process analysis worksheet for landfill

Item	Factor	Rate of use	MJ/t
Diesel fuel	42.5 MJ/l	1.4 l/t	60
Other utilities	–	10% of fuel	6
Capital investment	50 MJ/£		
Site	10-year life	£450 000	30
Mobile equipment	5-year life	£50 000	7
Site restoration	10-year life	£50 000	3
Maintenance supplies	100 MJ/£	$0.02I$	14
Operating supplies	100 MJ/£	$0.008I$	5
Cover material	90 MJ/£	0.165 t/t	15
Transport	5.6 MJ/t km	8 km each way	45
Energy input	E_{IN}		185
Energy efficiency	$-E_{IN}/E_W{}^a$	−0.019	

(a) E_W is the heat content of the waste (10 GJ/t).

12. TRANSFER/TREATMENT PRIOR TO LANDFILL

When a landfill site is not available near a centre of population, consideration is usually given to transfer; the collection vehicles deliver waste to a central transfer station, where it is loaded into vehicles suitable for bulk transport.

One basic advantage is that the collection service has the benefit of a fixed point of waste delivery; a series of relatively small landfill sites may be used without the need to continually reorganize the routing of collection vehicles. At the transfer station, waste may be simply loaded into a vehicle, it may be compacted using a stationary ram, pulverization may be used or high-density bales may be formed. Bulk transport may be by road, rail, or barge, the first being the most common. In this chapter the three basic options of *simple transfer*, with or without compaction, *pulverization,* and *baling*, are considered in turn.

12.1. Transfer

12.1.1. Types of transfer operation

About 8 per cent of municipal waste in England was handled by transfer stations in 1975 (Society of County Treasurers and County Surveyors' Society 1976); although no later figure is available (Society of County Treasurers and County Surveyors' Society 1979) one could say with confidence that it is now well over 10 per cent. Transfer stations range from very crude arrangements to comparatively sophisticated modern engineering plants. The basic alternatives may be summarized as:

(a) The simplest system consists of an open concrete pad surrounded by an earth bund to screen the site and to give some control over windblown litter. The waste is tipped on the ground and is loaded into an open-top trailer or lorry using a front-end loader. This system is environmentally unacceptable in an urban area.

(b) A slight sophistication is to build a concrete ramp and raised apron, so that the waste can be tipped directly through loading hoppers into a waiting vehicle or container below. The operation may be enclosed in a simple building.

(c) One of the common features of all waste treatment plants is that collection vehicles tend to arrive together over comparatively short periods. Thus consideration needs to be given, even at relatively small sites, to the provision of buffer storage capacity. Otherwise, the basic advantage of transfer, that is the minimization of time lost by the collection vehicles while emptying their load, is seriously reduced. There are at least four methods of providing storage:

> The waste is discharged onto a concrete platform or floor, from which it is loaded into hoppers or onto a conveyor by a front-end loader (Fig. 12.1).

Fig. 12.1. *Waste reception on an enclosed tipping floor.* The deposited waste is moved by the front-end loaders onto conveyors, which are located on the other side of apertures in the wall separating the reception and processing halls. (Photo courtesy South Yorkshire County Council.)

> The waste is discharged into a shallow pit or bunker (about 4–5 m deep) where it is compacted by a bulldozer and pushed into hoppers or onto a conveyor.
>
> The waste is discharged into a deep bunker (between 5 and 25 m deep) from which it is loaded into hoppers by an overhead grab crane. (Fig. 12.2). This system is standard on incinerators but less common on transfer stations.
>
> The waste is discharged directly into a live-bottom bunker (i.e. onto some sort of conveyor) and is loaded into containers. Storage is thus provided not as loose waste but in enclosed containers.

(d) The waste may be loaded into open-top containers, or it may be compacted into fully enclosed containers, usually by means of a stationary compactor. Compaction may achieve higher vehicle payloads, but in Britain legal restrictions on gross vehicle weight usually negate this advantage. The choice is thus largely one of aesthetics and public health, both in transfer and in transport.

(e) A wide range of containers may be used to accept the waste. These include:

An open-top lorry;

Fig. 12.2. *Waste storage in a deep bunker.* (Photo courtesy The Harwell Laboratory.)

An open-top semi-trailer;

Containers which must be loaded on and off semi-trailers or railcars using a fork-lift truck or gantry crane (Fig. 12.3).

'Rollonoff' containers which may be loaded directly onto special-purpose vehicle.

Containers into which refuse has been compacted are usually fitted with some means of expelling their contents at the disposal site.

Fig. 12.3. *Off-loading containerized waste from a train at a landfill site.* (Photo courtesy The Harwell Laboratory.)

12.1.2. Design considerations

This great variety of options for transfer station operation makes it very difficult to discuss a 'standard' plant. The type of plant generally favoured by local authorities in Britain is relatively sophisticated; waste is discharged directly either into a hopper or into a live-bottom bunker from which it is conveyed to one of a number of stationary compactors, storage being provided in fully-enclosed containers. The containers are moved about the site by special slave vehicles, the road vehicles simply operating a shuttle service to and from the landfill.

Even within this fairly narrow definition of a 'standard' transfer operation, there is still wide scope for variations in design. For example:

Compactors vary widely in design; most employ a stationary ram which repeatedly compresses waste into the container. A variation is the pre-baling press, the container being loaded with a pre-set number of bales. Sufficient capacity must be provided to cope with peak delivery rates, as little or no primary storage is usually available. It is not uncommon for the compactors to be capable of handling the whole day's design capacity in about 2 hours. In a relatively small plant, an additional compactor may be provided to allow for down-time.

A wide variety of *hoppers* and *conveyors* are available for waste handling. Types of conveyor include vibration feeders, moving belts, plate feeders, and bucket elevators; a plate conveyor is shown in Fig. 12.4. A useful review is that by Biddulph (1976).

Traffic control is essential, particularly at larger sites. Careful consideration is necessary to ensure adequate provision of check-in facilities and unloading bays.

Weighbridges aid the efficient management of waste disposal. However, they are not provided at all transfer stations.

Dust extraction is essential to a properly controlled operation (Skitt 1972). This is one factor which strongly favours the use of a hopper or bunker for waste discharge. Dust control is very difficult when waste is discharged on a flat tipping apron.

Noise can be a serious problem where stationary compactors are used. The use of primary insulation and higher standards of building construction will reduce noise levels.

Standards of *building construction* vary widely. Provision of employee amenities differs considerably and in some cases depot facilities for the collection fleet are included in the transfer station design. The visual appearance of the building is another design variable.

The provision of *safety equipment*, including barriers, fire sprays etc., and of control facilities, which may include sophistications such as closed-circuit television and automatic devices to avoid overloading containers, is yet another source of variation.

Magnetic metals may be recovered from unprocessed waste on a conveyor belt at a transfer station. A plant has been operating since 1976 at the Benwell transfer station in Tyne and Wear, with finance provided by Material Recovery Ltd, a joint venture of the British Steel Corporation, Batchelor Robinson, and Metal Box (Material Recovery Ltd 1977). However, the efficiency of metal separation from unprocessed waste is low and such separation is assumed here to be applicable mainly to pulverized waste and other processed waste streams.

12.1.3. Capital costs for road transfer stations

All of the variations discussed above, both in the type of transfer operation

Fig. 12.4. *Plate conveyor.* This conveyor moves waste from the reception area (Fig. 12.1) to the first stage of the separation process at the Doncaster reclamation plant (Section 15.5). (Photo courtesy South Yorkshire County Council.)

and in the detailed design of the plant, combine to make the capital cost of road transfer stations extremely elastic. Even if the fairly sophisticated 'standard' concept of transfer outlined in the previous section is accepted, the basic capital cost can be quite low. It is tempting for local councillors and others to regard items, such as dust extraction, noise insulation, and employee amenities, which significantly increase the capital cost, as mere frills, and thus as a waste of public money (Hall 1975).

Some capital costs and estimates for transfer stations in Britain are shown in Table 12.1. For comparison, the costs have been adjusted to 300 t.p.d. using a scale factor of 0.85. Evidence on economies of scale is sparse, the figure chosen being between the 0.80 for a typical solids handling plant and the 0.93 used by the Midwest Research Institute (1973). Supporting evidence is provided by the data for two road transfer stations in London, and by the observation that larger plants require additional compactors, discharge bays, and weighbridges to cope with the peak rates of waste delivery.

In most of these plants, storage for the waste is provided primarily in containers rather than as incoming waste awaiting processing. Capacity is therefore sufficient to meet peak delivery rates, with 2 compactors each rated at 40 tonnes per hour (t.p.h.) needed to process 300 t.p.d., although a third is often provided to allow redundancy. The operation is usually restricted to a normal working day, any extension posing problems as no storage capacity is provided for incoming waste; in addition, there may be local objections to heavy lorries in the evening.

For road transfer the mean cost from Table 12.1 is £900 000, but the standard deviation is £760 000. Most estimates lie in the range £250 000–£750 000 for a 300 t.p.d. plant. The London costs of £2.4 million are largely due to higher design and operating standards (Ferguson 1977). Wilcox (1976) quotes a Department of the Environment estimate for 250 t.p.d. plant as £1 million (1975 prices), equivalent to £1.5 million for a 300 t.p.d. plant at 1977 prices. A capital cost of £1 million, with an error range of $\times$ 2.0 (i.e. £0.5–£2.0 million), is used here to encompass the observed variations.

12.1.4. Rail transfer

Rail transfer is less common than road transfer. In Britain, experience is confined largely to London. In 1965, the new Greater London Council (GLC) inherited three rail transfer stations using open trucks with low payloads, but these were soon discontinued for environmental reasons. Three new rail transfer stations are now operational, that at Brentford in West London coming on stream in 1977, that at Hendon in north-west London in 1979 and the third at Hillingdon during 1980.

Table 12.1
Capital costs of transfer stations in Britain

Location	Source	Stage of progress when estimate made	Completion date	Approximate date of estimate[1]	Plant throughout (t/day)	Cost (£ thousand)	Cost (£ thousand 1977)	Cost 300 t.p.d. (£ thousand 1977)
(A) Road transfer								
Chester, Cheshire	AWDE (1976)	Complete	May 1974	Oct 1973	135	176	350	680
Bournemouth, Dorset	AWDE (1976)	Planning	1978	Apr 1976	250	300	340	390
Farnborough, Hampshire	AWDE (1976)	Design	1977	Apr 1976	330	414	460	430
Grimsby, Humberside	AWDE (1976)	Tenders accepted	Dec 1976	Apr 1976	220	280	310	410
Accrington⎱Nelson⎰ Lancashire	AWDE (1976)	Design/ planning	Dec 1977	Apr 1976	150	250	280	500
Kibworth, Leicester	AWDE (1976)	Outline drawings	1979/80	Apr 1976	100	100	110	250
New Ham, London	Ferguson (1977)	Complete	1976	Jan 1974	700	2500	4870	2370
London	Patrick (1975a)	Review (not a specific plant)	–	Apr 1975	400	2250	3070	2400
Guildford, Surrey	AWDE (1976)	Complete	June 1974	Jan 1974	200	260	510	710
West Midlands	WMCC (1976a) WMCC (1976b)	Preliminary planning	– –	Nov 1975	500 200	950 630	1150 760	750 1070
(B) Rail transfer								
Brentford, London	Patrick (1975a, 1976)	Under construction	1976	July 1975	800	5200	6630	4340
Oxford	Oxfordshire C.C. (1977)	Planning	–	Jan 1977	200	600	600	850
West Midlands	WMCC (1976a)	Preliminary planning	–	Nov 1975	500	1300	1570	1020
(C) Barge transfer								
London	Patrick (1975a)	Review	–	Apr 1975	800	4–5000	5400– 6800	2400– 3000

1. For complete plants, cost is assumed appropriate to prices 6 months before completion date if better estimate is not available.
AWDE = Association of Waste Disposal Engineers.
WMCC = West Midlands County Council.

The Brentford operation is relatively sophisticated in design (Patrick 1976). It was built on land leased from British Rail adjacent to existing freight sidings. No railway works such as sidings or signalling were thus required. The basic principle is that all 800 t.p.d. of refuse are loaded onto one train, which travels overnight to the landfill site 70 km away in Oxford-shire, returning with an empty train for reloading. Each train consists of four sets of five standard freightliner wagons, each wagon carrying three containers with a maximum net weight of 15 tonnes of waste per container. The containers are owned by the GLC and the wagons by British Rail. A spare set of 5 wagons and containers is held at Brentford. In addition a full set of 60 spare containers is held for emergencies when a train fails to arrive before the day shift begins work. These containers may be transported by road if necessary.

The Brentford station has a design capacity of 800 tonnes of waste per day. There are 10 compactors working in parallel, all storage being provided in the containers. Collection vehicles discharge directly into hoppers above the compactors. Each pair of compactors is controlled by an operator, and share a wet-filter type dust extraction unit. The traffic reception and control systems are capable of handling at least 60 vehicles per hour.

Containers are loaded on and off the trains by fork-lift trucks equipped for check-weighing of the full containers. The containers are moved about on-site on semi-trailers, towed by tractors. A total of 12 semi-trailers, 3 tractors, and 2 fork-lift trucks are provided. At the landfill site containers are off-loaded by gantry crane (Fig. 12.3) and conveyed to the working face using special-purpose slave vehicles (Fig. 12.5).

The Brentford transfer station cost £5.2 million, equivalent to about £4.3 million for a 300 t.p.d. plant at 1977 prices. The total number of staff is 35. Long-term contracts have been negotiated both with British Rail and with the landfill operator.

The capital costs of a rail transfer station appear to be higher than for road transfer (Table 12.1). However, little information is available. Comparative costs for stations in London suggest a ratio for road:rail of 1:1.8. However, cost estimates made by the West Midlands County Council are lower in both absolute and in relative terms, with a cost ratio of 1:1.4. It will be assumed here that a rail transfer station costs 1.5 times as much as for road transfer, i.e. £1.5 million $\times$ 2.0 for a 300 t.p.d. plant.

12.1.5. Barge transfer

River transport of wastes is again confined in Britain to London. The 11 transfer stations existing in 1965 had been reduced by 1975 to 5, handling the same waste throughput (Patrick 1975a). Of these, 2 were felt to be unsatis-factory and were due for replacement. In all cases waste is loaded directly into open-top barges, unloading at the landfill site being by gantry crane.

Fig. 12.5. *A special-purpose slave vehicle on a landfill site.* The slave vehicle hauls the containerized waste from the rail-head, or from a transfer site near the road entrance, to the working face of the landfill. (Photo courtesy The Harwell Laboratory.)

One new station has been built, that at Cringle Dock (Ferguson 1973), where the use of pulverization has doubled the payload achieved per barge.

Little quantitative information is available on barge transfer and it is not here evaluated as a separate option.

12.1.6. Operating, transport, and landfill costs

The operating labour requirement for a typical road transfer station of standard size is about 6 men. Rail transfer uses a larger workforce, 10 men being assumed here. Electricity usage is mainly for conveyors and compactors, and is estimated at 10 kWh/t. Fuel will be used for the station vehicles required to move containers, and possibly to load wastes onto conveyors or into compactors. A consumption of 0.50 l/t is assumed (based on the 0.58 l/t for loading waste onto a conveyor at the Franklin, Ohio, resource recovery plant; Systems Technology Corporation 1975). Container handling for rail transfer is more extensive, loading onto the flat wagons being done by fork-lift truck or by gantry crane. A fuel requirement of 1.0 l/t is guessed. Maintenance is factored on investment at the low rate of 0.05 I, allowing for the low utilization of the compactors.

Bulk haulage by road is examined in detail in Part I, Section 6.4. For an assumed journey of 30 km each way, an average speed of more than 20 k.p.h. allows 2 trips per day, at a cost of £2.50/t (Fig. 6.12). If the average speed is 30 k.p.h., this cost varies little between 20 and 40 km. An increase in average vehicle pay load from 13 to 15 t would reduce the cost by about £0.3/t. Costs for rail haul are charged by train load, up to a maximum of 1400 t per train (Patrick 1976). Thus there are obvious economies of scale. Distance is only one factor in the determination of costs, others including the ease of operation of the journey and its interference with other rail traffic. In any particular case a quotation from the railway company should be used in planning. West Midlands County Council (1976a) estimated a charge of £3/t for a 500 t.p.d. plant and an 80 km journey (each way), equivalent to £4/t at 1977 prices. A cost of £4/t is used here, with an error range of $\pm$ 1.5. Costs for barge transport are similarly case dependent, with those in London being about £1.70/t for a 25 km trip (Ferguson 1973).

Landfill costs and energy requirements will be little affected by the method of waste delivery, except that unloading and site handling equipment must be provided for rail and barge haul. The transfer of containers from road vehicles to special-purpose slave vehicles designed for rough-work on landfill sites (Fig. 12.5) should also be considered; the advantages are in reduced turn-round time at the landfill and in reduced tyre and maintenance costs for expensive road vehicles. A unit cost of £2.40/t and an energy requirement of 140 MJ/t are taken from Section 11.9, with an additional £0.5 and 30 MJ/t assumed for handling waste delivered by rail or barge.

12.1.7. Discussion

The standard data suggested above were used to evaluate the economics of waste disposal via road or rail transfer. For road haul, the cost range was £9.4 $\pm$ £3.0/t, while that for rail haul was £13.6 $\pm$ £4.4/t. The base costs (not considering uncertainty) may be sub-divided as follows:

	Road	Rail
Transfer	4.2	6.2
Transport	2.5	4.0
Landfill	2.4	2.9
Total	£9.1/t	£13.1/t

In either case, the most sensitive factor affecting the overall cost estimate is the capital investment. If this could be reduced by 50 per cent, then the overall cost would be reduced by about 18 per cent.

This cost estimate for road haul is considerably higher than those for local landfill or for the direct use of pulverized waste as a fuel. In Section 6.5, the costs of direct and indirect haul via road transfer to a landfill are compared as a function of distance with the conclusion that, for the costs used here, direct haul will be less expensive so long as it is feasible. The pulverized fuel option has not yet been proven technically, and even then it will depend on the availability of a suitable local market (Sections 15.6 and 15.7). Thus in many situations it will be the cost of road transfer which is the yardstick against which other more sophisticated alternatives must be compared. The cost of rail transfer is competitive with most other options and should always be considered when suitable rail connections are available.

In terms of primary energy requirements, the process analysis yielded figures for road and rail transfer to landfill of 460 and 560 MJ/t, respectively.

12.2. Pulverization

12.2.1. Background

Pulverization of waste prior to landfill offers many advantages over the use of untreated waste. The basic principle is the use of a milling, shredding, or grinding process to reduce the particle size of the waste and to produce a material which is more homogeneous and easier to handle. The advantages claimed for pulverization may be summarized as:

It does not smell;

It is not blown about in the wind;

It does not attract or support vermin;

Fly nuisance is diminished;

Daily cover is not necessary;

The requirements for landfill space may be reduced by up to 30 per cent;

The settlement and maturing of the landfill is quicker and more even;

Because of the reduced nuisance, pulverized waste may be acceptable for deposition at sites which would be unavailable to untreated waste;

The ferrous metal content of the waste may easily be recovered;

Size reduction is a necessary first step in most reclamation or recovery processes, so a pulverization transfer station offers the flexibility to adapt to reclamation as and when the economics become favourable.

These claims need to be examined critically. While it is true that nuisance is diminished, it is optimistic to claim its complete elimination. However, the aesthetic appearance of the landfill site is undoubtedly improved, so that there are many examples where planning permission has been granted for land reclamation schemes using pulverized waste when permission might have been refused for untreated waste. A clear-cut example is a site on high ground to the leeward side of a motorway, where untreated waste would have created a hazard from litter blowing across the motorway (Loram 1976).

The savings in landfill space are not so clear cut now as they were a few years ago. Data in Table 1.6 suggest a density on maturity of 0.75–0.85 t/m³, compared with 0.5–0.7 t/m³ for untreated waste. However, modern compactor technology has increased the effective density for untreated waste to about 0.75 t/m³, so that any advantage either way is probably marginal.

Pulverization has been used quite extensively in Britain, although it accounted for only 3 per cent of municipal wastes in England in 1977–8 (Society of County Treasurers and County Surveyors' Society 1979). A survey by Loram (1976) identified some 95 plants in Great Britain, of which about 75 were still active. Thomé-Kozmiensky (1979) suggests that there are about 50 plants in France. Despite this relatively widespread usage, published data is lacking. Information on operating plants is limited to those for a 6-year demonstration project in Madison, Wisconsin (Reinhardt and Ham 1972) and the plants at Poole (Marsden 1973), Cringle Dock in London (Ferguson 1973) and Millhouses in Sheffield (Holmes 1975b; Leaver 1977); a recent USA survey of 7 plants should effectively double the available data (Savage, Trezek, Diaz, and Golueke 1979).

12.2.2. Technology

There are many types of size-reduction machines available, most being developed from mineral processing equipment (General Electric Company 1973a; Biddulph 1976). The most common methods are dry pulverization using a hammermill, or perhaps a flail mill or impact crusher, and wet pulverization using a rotary drum. In the hammermill (Fig. 12.6), the waste is fed on to a rapidly revolving rotor carrying a series of swing hammers. The waste is partly broken up by the initial impact, and is then swept round the rotor and ground against grids or wear bars. Flail mills rely more on the initial impact than on subsequent grinding. In most hammermills the output particle size is controlled by the size of the grid openings. Machines differ in their methods of coping with irreducible materials, two using a ballistic system to reject them on initial impact with the hammers, before they can enter the main part of the mill and cause jamming or hammer breakage. Loram identified eight hammermill manufacturers in the UK, seven of whom offered horizontal shaft machines and one (Tollemache) a vertical shaft mill. Detailed discussion of hammermill design is given by Franconeri (1976) and Robinson (1976).

The rotary drum method originated in Denmark and five variants, offered by three manufacturers, were identified by Loram. The waste is moistened and fed into a large, slowly rotating drum (Fig. 12.7), self-pulverization being achieved by tumbling action of the hard particles. Retention time in the container is about 3–4 h, the fine material (about 60 per cent by weight) being passed through screens and the coarse rejected at the end.

The pulverized waste produced by the two alternative methods differs considerably in appearance. When the waste is intended for landfill, dry pulverizers are usually set to produce a relatively coarse product (Fig. 12.8(a)). A typical size range is that at the Millhouses plant in Sheffield: 85 per cent < 50 mm, 95 per cent < 100 mm and 100 per cent < 250 mm (Leaver 1977). The fine product from a wet pulverizer, on the other hand, is a much

Fig. 12.6. *A hammermill.* A horizontal shaft machine. The waste enters via the conveyor on the left and is discharged at the base, on the floor below. (Photo courtesy Buhler-Miag (England) Ltd.)

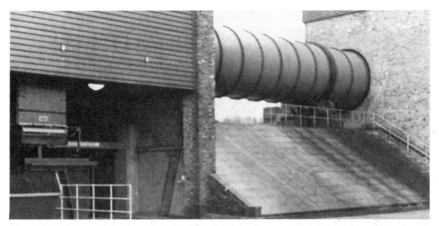

Fig. 12.7. *A rotary-drum wet pulverizer.* In this plant at High Wycombe in England, waste is fed into the drum in the building on the right, and the pulverized product is separated from the oversize rejects in the building on the left, both fractions being collected in open-top containers. (Photo courtesy The Harwell Laboratory.)

more homogeneous, fibrous material (Fig. 12.8(b)). A further difference which may be significant if reclamation of the waste is to be considered is the fate of glass bottles. The hammermill shatters glass on impact, with over 70 per cent reduced to less than 1.5 mm and over 90 per cent to less than 6 mm (Stirrup 1965). Coarse shredding with a flail mill is not quite so destructive, 60 per cent of the glass being less than 6 mm. The rotary drum, on the other hand, produces large chunks of glass, the heavy bases of bottles tending to remain intact.

In many resource recovery applications, it is desired to increase the particle size of glass while maintaining the flexibility of dry separation. One possible solution is to use a high-torque low-velocity shredder to shear rather than to shatter the incoming waste. Such devices are commonly used in clay or shale processing, and have been marketed for some years for waste processing, particularly where bulky wastes such as white goods are to be handled. The cutting edges are mounted on two counter-rotating shafts with separate motors, the direction of rotation being reversible. The size range of glass is reported as 82 per cent greater than 6 mm (Schroeder 1979). Further development work is required to adapt this equipment to primary shredding of municipal wastes.

Magnetic metals may be extracted from pulverized waste. The equipment is available, although development work is continuing (Graham 1976). The three basic alternatives are a rotating magnetic drum onto which the waste is dropped; a magnetic drum over which a conveyor belt passes; and a drum or belt-type magnet suspended over the conveyor, as shown in Fig. 12.9 (Alter and Woodruff 1977). The efficiency of separation depends on many factors

Fig. 12.8. *Pulverized waste.* The dry-pulverized waste produced by hammermills for landfill in the UK (a) is a much coarser material than wet-pulverized waste (b), although large fragments of glass are still present in the latter. The appearance of pulverized waste should be contrasted with that of untreated waste (Figs 11.1–11.3, 12.4, 12.5). (Photos courtesy The Harwell Laboratory.)

including the conveyor speed and depth of waste. Design specifications for 150 mm shredded waste are 92–95 per cent ferrous metal removal with 2–5 per cent free organics. With labels and can contents added, the recovered product may contain about 10 per cent organics. Initial operating experience at the New Orleans materials recovery plant suggests that entrapped organics may account for about 15 per cent by weight of the recovered product. They also interfere with the baling process, making marketing of the product difficult (Abert 1979*b*). Upgrading of the product, for example by air cleaning, reshredding, and magnetic extraction, may be necessary before either detinning or direct utilization in a steel furnace. A recovery efficiency of 90 per cent is assumed here for ferrous metals (Table 14.2); costs of magnetic separation are included in Table 14.3.

Fig. 12.9. *Magnetic separator.* Belt-type magnet, suspended over the end of a conveyor: non-magnetic materials drop into the chute in the centre, while magnetic metals are carried by the magnet to the separate chute on the left.

12.2.3. Capital costs

The capital costs of some pulverization plants in Britain are summarized in Table 12.2. Again a wide range of costs is observed, owing to variations in operating standards similar to those for transfer stations, and to differences in the facilities for handling the product. The mean cost is £1.4 million and the standard deviation £1.3 million for a 50 t.p.h. plant, although removal of the Cringle Dock barge transfer plant reduces the mean to £1.25 million and the standard deviation to £0.9 million. Most plants are over-designed, with equipment capable of processing the daily waste load in 6 hours or less, the only exception being the Cringle Dock plant in London which operates on

Table 12.2
Capital costs of pulverization plants in Britain

Location	Source	Stage of progress when estimate made	Completion date	Approx. date of estimate[a]	Number of process lines	Design capacity (t/h)	Design capacity (t/day)	Cost (£ thousand)	Cost (£ thousand) (1977)	Cost, 50 t.p.h. (£ thousand 1977)
(A) Hammermills										
Tollemache										
Bracknell, Berkshire	Charlesworth (1970)	Under construction	1970	1969	2	30	130	165	560	840
Alsager, Cheshire	AWDE (1976)	Complete	Oct 1970	1970	1	15		45	130	340
Ryde, Isle of Wight	AWDE (1976)	Complete	Jan 1971	1970	1	15	40–75	46	130	340
Burnley, Lancashire	AWDE (1976)	Under construction	June 1977	Apr 1976	2	80		1050	1180	810
Sheffield, South Yorkshire	Holmes (1975b)	Complete	Jan 1974	1974	1	15	90	238	420	1100
Chertsey, Surrey	DoE (1971)	Tender		1967	1	10		36	130	470
Burgess Hill, West Sussex	AWDE (1976) Millbank (1976a)	Commissioning	Aug 1976	1975	2	80	120–200	750	1020	700
Gondard										
Neston, Cheshire	AWDE (1976)	Complete	1971	1970	1	12		37	110	340
Newport, Isle of Wight	AWDE (1976)	Complete	May 1972	1971	1	(12)	60	63	160	500
Chichester, West Sussex	AWDE (1976)	Complete	Dec 1974	1973	2	40		725	1600	1910

Holmes Hazemag

Lanway										
Richborough, Kent	AWDE (1976)	Complete	Apr 1975	1974	1	40		300	530	630
Buhler-Miag										
Eastbourne, East Sussex	AWDE (1976)	Complete	1969	1968	2	12.5	25	350^d	1200^d	3600^d
Pilsley, Derbyshire	AWDE (1976)	Complete	1968	1967	1	(12.5)		160	590	1790
British Jeffrey–Diamond										
Slough, Berkshire	DoE (1971)	Tender	1972	1967	2	25		396	1450	2520
Cringle Dock, London	Millard (1974)	Complete		1971	2	50	800	2300^e	5900^e	5900^e
(B) Rotary drums										
Dano										
High Wycombe, Bucks	AWDE (1976)	Under construction	Oct 1977	Apr 1976		20	160	900	1000	2100
Droylsden, Manchester	DoE (1971)	Tender		1966	1	5		81	310	1930
Stockport, Manchester	AWDE (1976)	Outline drawings	1979	Apr 1976	2	(50)	400	2000^f	2200^f	2200^f
Vickers Seerdrum										
Glossop, Derbyshire	AWDE (1976)	Complete	1972	1971	1	10		70	180	650
Arlington, East Sussex	Skitt (1972)	Complete	1969	1968	1	7	50	40	140	680
Loughborough, Leicestershire	DoE (1971)	Tender		1968	1	9		70	250	970
John Thompson										
Poole, Dorset	Marsden (1973)	Complete	1967	1971/2	6	20	125	250	600	1250
Epsom, Surrey	DoE (1971)	Tender	1965	1965	6	9		182	690	2700

(a) For complete plants, cost is assumed appropriate to prices 1 year before completion date.
(b) Existing buildings used for part of plant.
(c) Cost £200 000 excess over tender price, owing to inflation.
(d) Secondary double-rotor mill not used in flowline.
(e) Includes cost of barge transfer facilities.
(f) Includes cost of rail transfer facilities, including remote controlled crane and side-emptying wagons.
AWDE: Association of Waste Disposal Engineers.
DoE: Department of the Environment.

two shifts. Parallel process lines are used both to provide redundancy and, in some cases, to allow bulky items to be treated. It is unclear whether sustained operation at the design capacity is feasible. For example, the larger machine at Burgess Hill, West Sussex, is rated by the manufacturers at 65 t.p.h., by Millbank (1976a) at 33 t.p.h. and by the county at 20 t.p.h., while at Cringle Dock, Ferguson (1973) reported throughput over 90 per cent of design just once in the first year of operation. Any differences in capital costs between the wet and dry processes are swamped by the other variations in Table 12.2. However, Marsden (1973) suggests that the wet process requires more capital.

The evidence for economy of scale in pulverization is again sparse. For hammermills, literature values for mineral processing, in terms of tonnes per hour, vary from $S = 0.67$ (Parkinson and Mular 1972) to $S = 0.85$ (Guthrie 1969). These would be appropriate when the size of the pulverizer itself is increased, rather than when additional process lines are added. An effective upper limit of about 70 t.p.h. on the capacity of single units for solid waste is provided by limitations on conveyor feed rates (Franconeri 1976). Operating experience with such large plants is lacking, and further development may be required. An increase in plant size is likely to be achieved by a combination of larger pulverizers and additional lines, and a scale factor of 0.8 is thus suggested and used here.

To achieve a peak throughput of 400 t.p.d. a plant size of 50 t.p.h. is specified here for single-shift or 25 t.p.h. for double-shift operation, two process lines being used in either case. Analysis is confined to dry pulverization for which there is more information. Capital costs are estimated at £1.5 million for a 50 t.p.h. plant, an increase of 50 per cent over simple transfer. For a 25 t.p.h. plant, scaling at $S = 0.8$ indicates a cost of £860 000, but this is increased to £1 million to allow for the additional storage capacity for the incoming and processed waste necessary to support double-shift operation. In each case an error range of $\overset{\times}{\div} 2.0$ is used to encompass the range of costs observed in practice.

12.2.4. Operating, transport, and landfill costs

Labour requirements for a pulverization transfer station will be higher than for a simple transfer station, and a complement of 4 men plus 4 per shift is assumed.

The power requirement for hammermill operation depends on the output particle size distribution. Data from various applications are summarized in Fig. 12.10: the uncertainty in the data is considerable. For a nominal particle size of 150 mm, a consumption in the range 5–25 kWh/t is indicated. The range of values reported in the literature is 1–91 kWh/t, that at the Millhouses plant in Sheffield being, for example, 11.5 kWh/t. A requirement of 20 kWh/t is used here for a complete pulverization transfer station. Fuel

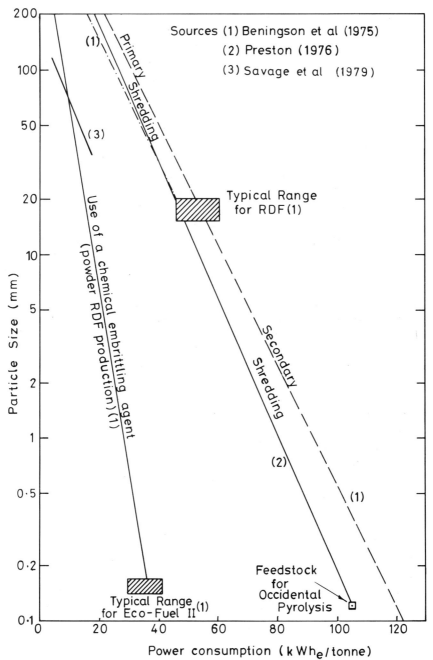

Fig. 12.10. *Electricity consumption for size reduction of solid waste.*

requirements for loading waste onto conveyors or for moving containers are assumed to be the same as for a transfer station. Water usage for wet pulverization is about 230 l/t (Loram 1976), but will depend on the initial moisture content of the waste.

Maintenance costs of pulverization are high. Detailed information on the Millhouses plant is given by Leaver (1977). This plant has a single process line rated at 15 t.p.h. During the first 3 years of operation an average of 67 t were processed in 5 h per day, with an overall availability for this restricted working day of 93 per cent. This performance was attributed in part to a careful pre-separation of bulky material and heavy metal objects, 0.5 per cent of total waste being rejected. Annual maintenance costs were calculated at about 5 per cent of capital, of which about 40 per cent was for hammer repair. Development work on the materials for hammer facing had increased the waste processed per hammer change from 18 to 22 t, reducing the wear rate and the hammer cost by about 60 per cent. An increase in throughput above the 56 per cent achieved at Millhouses (assuming an 8-hour working day) would increase maintenance costs. For a standard throughput of 75 per cent of the design capacity, costs of 0.07 I for single- and 0.10 I for double-shift operation are assumed. Two-shift operation of a pulverizer is the maximum of which it is capable, the full third shift being required for routine maintenance (Franconeri 1976).

Transport costs for pulverized waste to distant landfill will depend crucially on the vehicle payloads and on the distance (Loram 1976). If the payloads are equal to those for untreated waste but the landfill is nearer so that 3 trips per day are possible, the cost is about £1.75/t (Fig. 6.12, with distance of 20 km). Landfill costs will be reduced by the need for less cover material and easier management, a figure of 80 per cent those for untreated waste being assumed. A reduced energy requirement of 100 MJ/t is also assumed. The removal of magnetic metals will reduce the weight of the waste to be transported and landfilled; however, if wet pulverization is used the weight of the additional water (about 230 kg/t of waste input) must also be considered.

12.2.5. Discussion

The standard economic analysis using the above data for a pulverization transfer station yields overall net costs of £9.8 ± 4.2/t and £8.8 ± 3.2/t, respectively, for single- and double-shift operation. The base costs may be subdivided:

	single shift	double shift
Pulverization/transfer	6.7	5.8
Transport	1.6	1.6
Landfill	1.8	1.8
Revenue from ferrous metal recovery	−0.8	−0.8
Total	£9.3/t	£8.4/t

The overall net costs are similar to the £9.4 ± 3.0/t for road transfer. The higher processing costs (cf. £4.2/t for transfer) are offset by savings in transport and landfill, and by the sale of ferrous metals. If a nearer site is not made available by pulverization, as was assumed here, then the costs would increase by about £0.7/t. The cost differences are still small, and the relative economics of simple transfer and transfer with pulverization should be examined with local data in any specific study. This is particularly so if double-shift operation of the pulverization plant is feasible.

The costs of pulverization with subsequent landfill are dominated by the capital cost of the pulverization plant, particularly if single-shift working only is possible. A reduction in capital investment by 50 per cent would reduce the net cost by about 27 per cent.

The process analysis yields primary energy inputs of 570 and 540 MJ/t for single- and double-shift working, respectively, an increase of about 10–20 per cent over simple transfer with compaction. However, the recovery of magnetic metals gives a primary energy saving of 1700 MJ/t of waste, so that the overall net saving of primary energy is about 1150 MJ/t; net primary energy efficiency (Chapter 8) is $\beta = 0.11$.

12.3. Baling

12.3.1. Background

High-density baling of solid waste is a comparatively recent development. It has been under investigation in the USA since 1967, and several full-scale plants are now in operation. The basic principle is that the waste is compressed by three hydraulic rams into bales of weight approximately 1 t and dimensions about 1 m cubed. These bales can then be handled by fork-lift truck, transported on a flat-back vehicle and simply stacked at the landfill site (Fig. 12.11). The operation of the landfill is very much simplified and much of the nuisance is eliminated. However, the densities achieved by baling are only marginally greater than those of modern compactors on untreated waste. There is as yet no scientific understanding of the effect of baling on the degradation of the waste, although settlement, temperature, and leachate and gas generation at the Glasgow balefill site are being studied. Claims that building work may begin immediately on baled refuse landfills seem premature. A leachate will also be produced from the baling press itself.

Published information on baling is lacking, being confined to early research reports (Wolf and Sosnovsky 1972, 1977; City of San Diego 1973) and brief descriptions of new plants.

12.3.2. Technology

There are three principal variants available for the baling of municipal wastes. Two of these are manufactured by the American Hoist and Derrick

Fig. 12.11. *Balefill site.* In the foreground, the top surface of uncovered bales can be seen; the working face of the balefill is in the centre. (Photo courtesy The Harwell Laboratory.)

Company (in Britain by Harris-Economy). Their main baler processes 50–60 t of waste per hour to produce self-sustaining bales which measure 90 × 90 × 120 cm on production, but immediately expand to about 100 × 100 × 150 cm, an increase of 50 per cent by volume, with little further expansion (Millbank 1976b). However, expansion was measured by Stone and Kahle (1976) as 7.4, 28.4, and 24.6 per cent by volume after 1 hour, 1 day, and 1 week, respectively. Weight per bale is about 1.3 t, giving a density after initial springback of about 870 kg/m³. A moisture content of 25–30 per cent is required to maintain the integrity of the bales, Stone and Kahle reporting a 2 per cent breakage rate at St. Paul, Minnesota.

This baler has also been installed, inter alia, at Cobb County, Georgia (Oberman 1975), Smithtown, New York, Portland, Maine, Westboro, Maine, and Hackensack Meadowlands, New Jersey, in the USA (Anon. 1979); at Glasgow (Millbank 1976b), Leeds, and Bradford in the UK; at Bergen in Norway; at Palermo in Sicily; and at Prahran (Melbourne) in Australia. Other American Hoist machines produce lower-density, wired bales. One such plant has been installed at Chadron, Nebraska, where a 30 t.p.h. baler is handling just 20 t of waste per day; others include those at Torrington, Wyoming, Omaha, Nebraska, and Tuscaloosa, Alabama in the USA, in East Lothian and Humberside in the UK, and at Waitemata (Auckland) in New Zealand.

The third system is produced by the German company Lindemann. The waste is pulverized before it is baled, the resultant medium-density wired bales measuring about 105 × 85 × 150 cm, with a density of about 8–900 kg/m³. Equipment is available in the range 10–50 t.p.h. The first British plant using this system, at Stafford, is rated at 12.5 t.p.h. (Millbank 1976c; Skitt 1979); a larger plant at Colnbrook in Berkshire began operations in 1980, and has in fact dispensed with pre-pulverization.

12.3.3. Cost estimates

Capital cost estimates are available for a few plants. The self-sustaining bale plant at Cobb County cost $2 million in 1974, equivalent to a 1977 cost of £1.5 million; that at Glasgow cost £1.7 million, equivalent to £2 million, but this used an existing incinerator building; the Leeds plant was estimated at £2.5 million (Association of Waste Disposal Engineers 1976), equivalent to £2.5 million. An estimate made by the West Midlands County Council (1976a) was £2.5 million, equivalent to £3.1 million in 1977. The Humberside plant ordered in late 1979 had a contract value of £2.7 million. The wired bale system is possibly cheaper; Jackson, Renold, and Wilson (1975) estimated 5 plants with an aggregate capacity of 1950 t.p.d. at £3.9 million, compared with a cost of £1.3 million per self-sustaining bale system. On this basis a 400 t.p.d. plant would have cost £1.25 million in 1977. The Stafford baler was installed in an old pulverizer building. The costs were estimated (Millbank 1976c) at £60 000 for the baler and £82 000 for associated work. If this estimate is increased by 50 per cent to allow for the building, the equivalent 1977 cost for a 100 t.p.d. plant is about £250 000. The Colnbrook plant, rated at 3–400 t.p.d, was reported in 1979 as costing £2.5 million.

The self-sustaining bale system of American Hoist is selected here for further analysis. The baler is available at 50 t.p.h. design capacity, but an average throughput of only 31 t.p.h. was achieved at St. Paul (Stone and Kahle 1976). It is assumed here that a 50 t.p.h. baler operating a single shift is capable of processing an average throughput of 75 per cent of design. A capital cost of £3 million is estimated with an error range $\overset{\times}{\div}$ 1.4. As additional capacity involves the provision of extra process lines, a high scale factor of S = 0.9 is assumed. If, however, a plant of capacity, say, 500 t.p.d. is required, consideration should be given to double-shift working.

Operating cost estimates for baling must inevitably be uncertain. Labour requirements are assumed to be the same as for pulverization, that is 8 men for a single-shift operation. Energy requirements are low, about 10 kWh/t for the plant. The front-end loaders used to handle incoming waste are estimated to consume 0.5 l of fuel per tonne of waste. Maintenance is claimed to be simple and cheap; an optimistic factor of 0.06 I is thus used.

Transport costs for baled waste may be less than for untreated or pulverized waste. The bales are loaded automatically onto a flat trailer, or they may be loaded by a fork-lift truck. If loading is direct from the baler, turn-round time at the plant may be long, 14 bales taking about 25 min to produce. The payload achievable is about 17 t, an increase over the 13 t assumed for compactor-loaded containers. For a journey of 20 km each way, with three trips per day, the same as that assumed for pulverization, Fig. 6.9 and 6.11 suggest a cost of £1.25/t.

Landfill costs and energy requirements should also be reduced owing to the simpler operation. Bales are unloaded and stacked using a fork-lift truck, while minimum quantities of cover are applied by a tractor. Costs will be assumed to be 60 per cent of those for direct landfill, and 75 per cent of pulverized landfill, with an energy requirement of 100 MJ/t the same as for pulverized landfill.

12.3.4. Discussion

The preliminary cost estimates in the previous section were based on limited information, but are sufficient to allow the standard economic analysis to be meaningful. The overall net cost was calculated as £14.2 ± £3.6/t. Of this, £2.7/t is for transport and landfill, leaving a base cost of about £11.5/t attributable to the baling and transfer operation. This cost is very sensitive to the capital cost estimate; if this could be reduced from £3.0 to £1.5 million, then the overall net cost would be reduced by about £5.0/t.

Baling is the most expensive of the landfill options in the base case, although the considerable uncertainty in all the cost estimates means that a detailed local study is required before any final judgement about a specific case can be made. It should be noted in addition that the technical feasibility of baling as a reliable option for solid waste management has not yet been adequately demonstrated.

The process analysis shows that the primary energy requirement is 630 MJ/t, slightly higher than those for transfer or pulverization.

13. INCINERATION

13.1. Introduction

Incineration is a method of disposing of waste materials by their controlled combustion. Open fires have been used to burn combustible wastes for centuries. The first large-scale plant to burn municipal wastes was built in England about 1870. Since then incineration has developed into a sophisticated and environmentally acceptable technology; a typical modern plant is shown in Fig. 13.1, and a control room in Fig. 13.2. Incineration currently accounts for about 5 per cent of municipal wastes disposed of in the USA and about 10 per cent in England, but it is more widely used in many European countries (20–30 per cent) and in Japan (46 per cent); it is the dominant technology (about 70 per cent of all wastes) in both Denmark and Switzerland (Table 1.5).

The basic principles of incineration are simple. A schematic flow diagram of a modern municipal waste incinerator is shown in Fig. 13.3. The waste is

Fig. 13.1. *A modern muncipal waste incinerator.* The plant at Aarhus in Denmark. (Photo courtesy The Harwell Laboratory.)

Fig. 13.2. *Control room in a modern incinerator plant.* The large, triple line, 36 tonne per hour plant at Amagerforbraending, Copenhagen. (Photo courtesy Vølund Limited.)

charged to a refractory-lined furnace so designed as to ensure complete combustion; this is achieved by proper control of temperature, excess air, gas turbulence, and residence time in the hot zone, and of burnout time of the ash before discharge. The products of incineration are:

Gases and vapours which, after cleaning, are suitable for discharge to atmosphere;

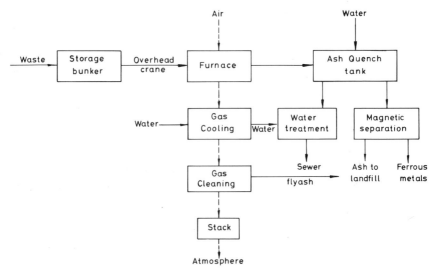

Fig. 13.3. *A schematic flow diagram for direct incineration.*

An inorganic ash which is either further processed for materials recovery, used as hardcore, or landfilled;

An aqueous effluent resulting from ash quenching and gas cooling;

Heat, which may be recovered for use as either steam or electricity.

The literature on incineration is probably more extensive than that on any other technology for waste management. Useful texts include those of Corey (1969), Cross (1972), Skitt (1972, 1979), Rubel (1974) and the National Center for Resource Recovery (1974d).

13.2. Types of incinerator

The simplest design of incinerator is a refractory-lined box to which solid wastes are fed in batches and from which the ash is periodically removed using a rake. Supplementary fuel may be necessary to preheat the furnace. A modification of the design is to add an afterburner to ensure complete combustion of the gases. This simple design is used, for example, in many small industrial incinerators to burn packaging and similar materials.

A development from this basic concept is the *multiple-chamber inciner-ator*, in which a number of combustion chambers or cells are arranged in series. A typical unit consists of six cells, the first four acting as primary combustion chambers, the fifth as an afterburner, and the sixth as the gas cleaning chamber. This design is particularly well suited to the incineration of a wide range of industrial and hazardous wastes, being both simple and flexible.

Until the early 1960s, municipal waste incineration used a similar design, with batteries of from two to six batch-type grates being arranged in parallel, sharing a common combustion chamber. However, this has now been completely superseded by the continuous grate *direct incinerator*: the waste is slowly propelled through a rectangular furnace by a moving mechanical grate, waste entering continuously at one end and the ash being discharged at the other (Figs 13.4 and 13.5).

The progress of the waste through the furnace is aided by gravity. As the waste descends it goes through the three stages of drying, combustion, and burnout. Considerable attention has been given by incinerator designers to the conditions necessary for optimum combustion:

(i) Sufficient excess air must be supplied, usually about 100 per cent. This is supplied mainly as primary air forced through the waste from below the grate.

(ii) The temperature must be controlled, a typical range being above 750 °C to ensure adequate combustion and below 1 000 °C to prevent the ash from melting and clogging the grate. The temperature is normally controlled by the addition of dilution air to the furnace as required.

(iii) Proper mixing of the gases must be achieved. This is usually ensured by continuously feeding high-pressure secondary air into the combustion chamber.

(iv) Some turbulence and mixing of the waste within the bed on the grate is also necessary. There are many proprietary variations of moving grate, all of which incorporate some method of agitating the waste (Skitt 1972). A simple classification of grates would distinguish:

Travelling grates, which consist of a series of endless chains mounted on driven rollers. Agitation is provided mainly by the vertical drop between successive grates (Fig. 13.4).

Reciprocating grates, which consist of a series of alternate fixed and moving parallel plates. The plates may be either horizontal or on an incline.

Rocking grates, which consist of a series of grate bars, some of which are hinged (Fig. 13.5).

Roller grates, consisting of a series of (usually six) large rollers at an angle of 30° to the horizontal.

Although most municipal waste incinerators now use a continuous grate design, there are numerous other types of furnace available, each of which is suited to particular applications.

There are at least two variations of the *circular grate* incinerator. In one, the solid or sludge waste is fed to the periphery of the moving hearth, being

Fig. 13.4. *The furnace hall in an incineration plant.* The small, twin line 6 tonne per hour plant at Hoersholm in Denmark. Note the vertical drops between successive travelling grates in the furnace. A waste heat boiler is fitted on top of each furnace, and in the foreground are multi-cyclone precipitators for dust removal. (Photo courtesy Vølund Limited.)

Fig. 13.5. *The furnace of a direct incinerator.* The waste is slowly propelled through the furnace by the moving mechanical grate which is here of the rocking type. Note the water-filled walls in the upper part of the furnace and the thick ash deposits on the lower, refractory-lined walls. This incinerator has been operational for more than 15 years.

guided towards the central ash discharge point by fixed ploughs. In the other, wastes are fed to the centre of a stationary hearth and are moved to the peripheral ash discharge by rotating arms. These systems were developed, respectively, for tyres and thickened sewage and for municipal waste.

The *multiple hearth* incinerator was originally designed for burning sewage sludge but has also been used for various other wastes including municipal wastes and industrial sludges, liquids, and tars. The furnace consists of a refractory-lined circular shell with refractory hearths stacked vertically. Solid or semi-solid wastes are fed through the roof and are gradually moved to lower hearths by moving arms. Liquid wastes and tars are injected through the side of the furnace. Waste flow is counter current to the flow of off-gases; the top hearths dry the sludge, the middle hearths represent the combustion zone with a temperature of 750–1000 °C, and the lower hearths serve to heat the incoming air.

The *rotary kiln* is one of the most versatile incinerator designs. It consists of a cylindrical refractory-lined shell positioned on a slight incline to the horizontal. Solid waste is fed into the upper end of the kiln and liquids or pumpable sludges are fired horizontally. The temperature in the kiln may be anywhere from 900–1650 °C, making it particularly suitable for intractable hazardous wastes such as persistent polychlorinated hydrocarbons. A rotary kiln may also be used as an after burner on a continuous grate incinerator, to ensure complete burnout of the ash.

The *fluidized bed* incinerator has been available for nearly 20 years and has found limited application mainly in burning sludges. A bed of sand or similar inert granular material is fluidized by the upward passage of air, the resultant dense turbulent medium having excellent heat transfer characteristics. The system is ideal for sludges and is used in the U K for sewage sludge incineration. Its use has also been explored for coal gasification, processed municipal waste (see Chapter 16), hospital wastes, and hazardous wastes. The operating temperature of the bed is about 900 °C.

The *liquid waste* incinerator is very commonly used in industry. A great variety of designs are available, with operating temperatures between 650 and 1650 °C. The wastes may be fired horizontally, tangentially, or vertically, either upwards or downwards. Tangentially fired designs include the cyclone and vortex incinerators. A separate after burner may be used to increase the gas residence time.

The *high-temperature slagging incinerator* is designed to operate at about 1500–1800 °C, the residue being produced as a molten slag. The 'Melt-Zit' incinerator, for example, melts the slag in a high-temperature bed of molten coke (Zinn, LaMantia, and Niessen 1970; Pavoni *et al.* 1975). The concept is similar to some of the gasification processes discussed in Chapter 18.

Many conventional industrial and power station furnaces utilize *suspension or semi-suspension firing* in which combustion takes place wholly or partially above the grate, a suspension fired boiler having only a small grate. The use of such furnaces for the incineration of processed municipal waste is discussed in Chapter 16.

13.3. Products of incineration

The gases produced by incineration consist primarily of carbon dioxide, water vapour, nitrogen, and excess oxygen, but entrapped dust particles (about 1–5 per cent of the municipal waste input by weight) necessitate cleaning before discharge. Several cleaning methods may be used, including settling chambers which remove about 40 per cent of the particulates, wet baffle screens (50 per cent), cyclones (see Fig. 13.4; 60–80 per cent), wet scrubbers (80–95 per cent), electrostatic precipitators (96–99.5 per cent), and fabric filters (99.9 per cent). The choice is determined principally by particle size and the efficiency required. For coarse particles (greater than 10 μm) any of the methods can be used, but for small particles (5 μm or less) the choice is a straight one between electrostatic precipitators and fabric filters, which are also the most expensive units. In British incinerators burning municipal wastes the electrostatic precipitator is most commonly used (Fig. 13.6). The gases entering the precipitator must first be cooled from about 1000 °C to about 300 °C. This may be achieved by a water-spray, by a steam-raising boiler, or by introducing additional air, the last having the disadvantage of increasing the amount of gas to be cleaned.

In addition to particulate removal, it may be necessary to remove acidic gases if the concentrations are in excess of permitted discharge levels. Of particular concern are hydrochloric acid, originating for municipal waste mainly from PVC, and oxides of nitrogen, sulphur, and phosphorus. The only efficient means of removal is a wet scrubber. The provision of a scrubber will usually be necessary on an incinerator handling hazardous wastes.

A related problem may be encountered if the waste contains significant amounts of volatile metals, such as lead, copper, zinc, cadmium, mercury, arsenic, or antimony. As the gas cools, metal or metal oxide fumes form, characterized by their very small particle size which is typically less than 0.1 μm. The efficient removal of such fumes requires either a high-energy scrubber or a bag filter.

The problems of gas cleaning are also relevant to furnace design. The presence of inorganic acids and molten particulate materials provides a very corrosive atmosphere. The incineration of some materials may require the use of special refractory materials in the furnace. In addition, heat recovery has been hampered by corrosion problems with water-walls and boiler tubes (Section 13.4).

Ash or clinker from a municipal waste incinerator is usually discharged onto a conveyor in a water-quench tank. Magnetic separation of the metals is commonly practised, but has a relatively low efficiency owing to oxidation of iron, a figure of 56 per cent of the input ferrous metals being suggested (Midwest Research Institute 1973). The recovered product is of low quality, the tin coating on the cans being dispersed through the metal, making detinning impracticable. Recovery of non-ferrous metals and glass from the residue is discussed in Chapter 14. Efficiency of incineration is often measured by the percentage of unburnt organics in the residue, values of less than 5 per cent free carbon and 0.3 per cent putrescibles often being specified (Skitt 1972). The weight of residue remaining for disposal is about 30 per cent of that of the incoming waste when dry, or about 40 per cent when wet. The ash was once considered inert, but concern is now expressed about the high concentrations of soluble inorganics in leachate (Schoenberger and Purdom 1976): the problem may be associated mainly with the fly-ash rather than the bottom ash (Oeltzschner and Fichtel 1979). Considerable efforts have been made to find suitable outlets for the sale of the ash as an aggregate or fill material (Collins 1978).

Fig. 13.6. *An electrostatic precipitator*. Ash is discharged at the base, and cleaned gases pass via an induced-draught fan to the stack. (Photo courtesy South Yorkshire County Council.)

Process water is used in an incinerator at four possible points; ash quenching (about 0.1 m³/t), gas cooling (2 m³/t), wet scrubbing (2 m³/t) and in some electrostatic precipitators to remove particulates from the collector plates. The effluent is corrosive (Achinger and Daniels 1970), and treatment is often necessary before discharge to sewer.

For a typical municipal waste, with composition as in Table 1.3, the overall materials balance for a modern direct incinerator may be represented approximately as follows:

Moisture and combustion products to atmosphere: 68%
Flyash: 2%
Residue (including 4.3% reclaimed as ferrous metals): 30%

13.4. Heat utilization

The heat of incineration may be utilized to raise steam, which may be used directly to drive process equipment and for heating, or indirectly to generate electricity. The heat may be recovered by water-cooled walls in the upper part of the furnace (Fig. 13.5) and/or by passing the hot gases through a heat exchanger (Fig. 13.4). Experience with heat recovery from modern municipal incinerators is limited in Britain mainly to that from four large plants, but there are some 200 such plants elsewhere in Western Europe and a further 50 in the rest of the western world, notably in Japan. It is, however, worth noting that heat recovery from the old batch-type incinerators was common in Britain between the two world wars, electricity often being generated for use in charging the municipal fleets of battery-driven vehicles.

One problem which has possibly hindered the more widespread use of heat recovery has been the corrosion of water walls and heat exchanger tubes caused by molten particulate materials and corrosive gases. The corrosive gases cause oxidation to occur on heat exchanger surfaces and the abrasive action of the ash erodes the oxidized layer, the process being continually repeated. The problems may be minimized by reducing the temperature difference between the inlet and outlet gases (thus also reducing the heat recovery efficiency), by using special materials in the most vulnerable areas, and by using special chemical cleaning processes. Useful accounts are available of corrosion problems during initial operation of the Edmonton incinerator in London (Patrick 1975b) and the Nashville incinerator in Tennessee (Avers 1975). The Coventry incinerator in England has been beset by corrosion problems, the cost of boiler repairs in the first five years of operation being about 60 per cent of the original capital cost.

High-temperature corrosion has been found particularly troublesome. Corrosion can also occur at low temperature, by condensation of corrosive liquids on surfaces when the plant shuts down or as it starts up. Frequent heating and cooling of the plant causes additional maintenance problems through excessive thermal shock, particularly on the refractory lining of the furnace. These problems can best be overcome by continuous working of the plant.

The most serious problem hindering the more widespread practice of heat recovery is undoubtedly the difficulty of ensuring a steady market. Either steam or electricity must be used as it is produced, no buffer storage being possible. Five general markets may be distinguished:

(1) The steam is used to provide heating for a housing estate, block of flats, office complex, shopping centre, or whatever. District heating schemes suffer from three major disadvantages, namely the seasonal demand, the very high capital costs, and the need to provide expensive fossil-fuel fired boilers as a standby. An example of a successful scheme is in Sheffield, England, where the incinerator provides heat to an existing district heating network (Holmes 1975c); such schemes are common in the rest of Europe.

(2) The steam is used to provide heating in winter and cooling in summer. This could provide at least a partial answer to the problem of seasonal demand in some areas. Such a facility is that at Nashville in Tennessee (Avers 1975).

(3) The steam is supplied to an industrial user. This could give a higher average load factor, and the steam distribution system and standby boilers will probably already exist. Examples include the incinerator at Coventry in England, which supplies steam for space heating and hot water to a nearby motor manufacturer (Scott and Holmes 1976); and that at Saugus, Massachusetts, which supplies steam for process use to the General Electric Company (Kelliher, Kobayashi, Howard, Stephens, DeMateo, Standrod, and Milo 1975).

(4) The steam is used to generate electricity. However, selling the electricity may still be a problem. In Britain it must be used on-site or sold to the nationalized electricity supply company. The terms of sale are likely to be unfavourable, the price being linked to the company's fuel savings and not to the market value, and continuity of supply again being required. The only incinerator in Britain generating electricity is that at Edmonton in London (Patrick 1975b).

(5) The steam is used to generate electricity, and the residual heat is used for lower quality uses. Several such combined heat–power schemes are in operation in Europe, the heat being used, for example, for district heating as in Helsinki, to raise hot water for use in greenhouses as in Hamburg (Calame 1979), or to produce distilled water as at Rijnmond in Holland (Paroubek 1979). Co-generation of electricity and process heat is particularly attractive from the viewpoint of energy efficiency.

The uncertainty in markets mean that all of the steam generated is unlikely to be sold. Mean load factors over the year were estimated by Wilson and

Swindle (1976) at between 0.25 and 0.80, with the highest values for industrial process use. A base load factor of 75 per cent is used here in evaluating heat recovery.

Information on the heat balance of steam generating incinerators is summarized in Table 13.1. The heat recovery efficiencies range from 58 to 73 per cent; a base value of 60 per cent is suggested here. This may be compared with 81 per cent for steam generation from fossil fuels. Combining this heat recovery efficiency with the average load factor of 75 per cent yields a net efficiency of only 45 per cent. However, this estimate is subject to considerable uncertainty, a range of (1 ± 0.3) times the base estimate, i.e. from 31 to 59 per cent, being suggested.

Information on the efficiency of electricity generation from incineration is limited. Hecklinger (1976) suggests an efficiency of 35 per cent from steam; combining this with a 60 per cent efficiency for steam generation yields an overall conversion of 21 per cent. This is rather higher than the 17 per cent for the Staplefield incinerator in Hamburg (Calame 1979), the 12 per cent for both the Rijnmond plant in Holland (Paroubek 1979) and the Edmonton incinerator in London (Patrick 1975b), or the 9.3 per cent projected at Bologna (Cenerini 1975). A net heat recovery efficiency of 18 ± 4.5 per cent is assumed here. This compares with an efficiency for conventional electricity generation of 30 per cent.

Table 13.1

Heat balance for incineration with steam generation
(all figures are percentages)

Item	Process Plant Association 1976	Asukata and Kitami 1974	Stabenow 1972	Eggen and Kraatz 1974	Hecklinger 1976	Holmes 1975c	Paroubek 1979
Dry exhaust gases	13.2	24.0	11.4	18.5	17.2		29.7
Moisture in exhaust gases:	19.3			13.8	13.3		
From waste			4.0				
From air			1.2				
From combustion			8.8				
Ash loss:	1.2	0.9		4.3	3.0		7.2
Combustibles in ash			2.8				
Water in ash			0.3				
Water flashed from quench tank			0.3				
Radiation and convection loss	2.0	2.1	0.4	2.0	3.3		1.8
Unaccounted losses	5.0		1.5				
Total losses	40.7	27.0	30.8	38.6	36.8	42.2	38.7
Steam generation efficiency	59.3	73.0	69.2	61.4	63.2	57.8	61.3

Heat recovery from the cooled steam remaining after electricity generation is an exciting prospect from the viewpoint of energy conservation.
Calame (1979) suggests that about 33 per cent of the heat content of the
waste can be recovered as hot water at 53 °C, to be used, for example, to heat
greenhouses. Paroubek (1979) suggests a utilization of 22 per cent of the
heat content to produce distilled water. It is suggested here that utilization
of the waste heat by combined heat–power generation could save a further
20 per cent of the heat content of the waste.

13.5. Capital costs

The economics of incineration depend critically on the operating schedule of
the plant. Four alternative patterns are in use in Britain, being one, two, or
three shifts per day, five days per week, and continuous working. One- or
two-shift working means that the furnace must heat up and cool down each
day, with consequent loss of performance, thermal stress on the equipment,
and increased risk of corrosion. Heat utilization probably necessitates continuous working. Here it is assumed that a non-recuperative incinerator
operates 3 shifts, 5 days per week; a twin-stream, 20 t.p.h. plant is specified,
allowing some excess capacity over the 400 t.p.d. design. A heat recovery
plant operates continuously, and the smaller capacity of 16 t.p.h. is used.

Capital costs for the majority of direct incinerators in Britain are summarized in Table 13.2. The updated costs are plotted against the design
capacity in Fig. 13.7, showing considerable scatter about an approximate
straight line through the origin. There are six plants for which the costs lie
beyond the general range indicated in the figure. Of these, high estimates for
the four recent plants at Huddersfield, Stoke, Tyseley, and Sheffield may be
due in part to errors in updating the costs, which, contrary to the assumption
used, may already have included some allowance for inflation during construction. The high estimate for Edmonton (off the scale in Fig. 13.7) may be
attributed to electricity generation. The low estimate for the Bolton plant is
difficult to verify as it has a much greater capacity than other non-
recuperative incinerators with a single process line.

The use of a straight line through the origin to fit the data in Fig. 13.7
presumes that the capital cost per unit of design capacity is constant. To test
for economy of scale, equation 5.6 is used, i.e.

$$\ln C = \ln a + S \ln W$$

where C is the cost (£ million), W is the design capacity (tonnes per hour), S
is the scale factor, and a is a constant. The data for non-recuperative
incinerators (parts (a) and (b) of Table 13.2) are shown in Fig. 5.3 as a plot of
$\ln C$ versus $\ln W$. Regression analysis results using equation 5.6 are summarized in Table 13.3. When all the data are analysed together, $1.04 < S < 1.09$

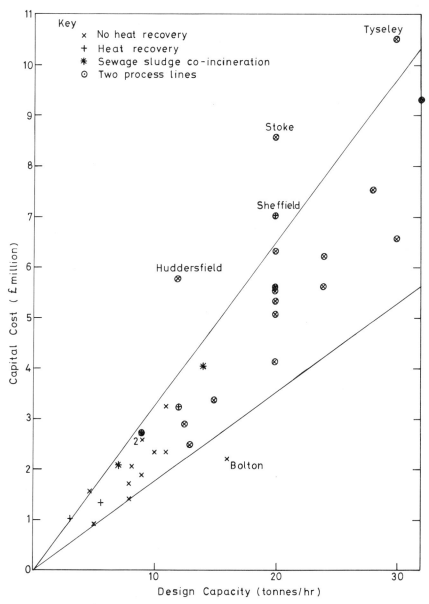

Fig. 13.7. *Capital costs of British incinerators.* Corrected to first-half 1977 prices.

Table 13.2

Capital costs of British incinerators[1]

Location	Completion date	Approximate date of estimate[2]	Plant throughput (t/h)	Cost (£ thousand)[2]	Cost (£ thousand) standard capacity 1977	Comments
(a) *Single process line*						
Exeter, Devon	Jan 1970	1968	8.3	590	2050	
Basingstoke, Hampshire	Nov 1969	1968	9	540	1890	
Southampton, Hampshire	Dec 1974	1972	11	1400	3240	
Winchester, Hampshire	Oct 1972	1971	9	1000	2580	
Folkestone, Kent	1974	1971	4.8	600	1550	
Blackburn, Lancashire	Feb 1972	1969	11	700	2350	
Bolton, Lancashire	Jan 1971	1968	16	630	2200	
Middleton, Manchester	May 1968	1966	8	370	1400	
Rochdale, Manchester	Mar 1973	1972	8	740	1710	
Rhondda, Mid Glamorgan		1971	9	1000	2580	Cyclone gas cleaning
Telford, Shropshire	Apr 1976	1973	10	1150	2350	
Lichfield, Staffordshire	Mar 1971	1967	5	250	910	Cyclone gas cleaning
(b) *Twin process lines*						
Avonmouth, Avon	June 1972	1969	30	1960	6590	
Derby, Derbyshire	1970	1966	15	890	3360	Cyclone gas cleaning
Dawsholm, Glasgow	Aug 1970	1967	24	1700	6220	
Portsmouth, Hampshire	Jun 1976	1973	20	3100	6320	
Blaby, Leicester	May 1974	1971	20	1600	4130	

Gateshead, Tyne and Wear (T & W)	Feb 1973	1970	20	1900	5550	
South Tyneside, T & W	1972	1969	20	1500	5050	
Sunderland, T & W	1972	1969	20	1660	5580	
Tynemouth, T & W	Oct 1971	1969	20	1580	5320	
Dudley, West Midlands	Jun 1970	1966	12.5	760	2870	
Perry Barr, West Midlands	Sept 1971	1968	24	1600	5600	
Tyseley, West Midlands	1977	1974	30	6000	10 500	
Huddersfield, West Yorkshire	Mar 1975	1972	12	2500	5790	
(c) Heat recovery						
Edmonton, London	May 1971	1967	5 × 14	10 420	38 000	Electricity generation
Mansfield, Nottinghamshire		1969	1 × 5.5	400	1350	District heating
Sheffield, South Yorkshire	Sept 1976	1974	2 × 10	4000	7000	District heating
Coventry, West Midlands	1975	1972	3 × 12	3420	7600	Steam to a factory. Actual cost £4 140 000
Otley, West Yorkshire	Feb 1974	1971	1 × 3	400	1030	Not yet commissioned. Steam was intended for heat treatment of sewage sludge
Swindon, Wiltshire	1973	1971	2 × 6	1250	3230	
(d) Sewage sludge co-combustion						
Stockton, Cleveland	Jul 1976	1972	2 × 16	4000	9300	Commissioned after several years delay
Havant, Hampshire	Oct 1974	1971	1 × 14	1440	4000	
Altrincham, Manchester	Feb 1973	1971	2 × 4.5	1050	2700	
Redhill, Surrey	Apr 1973	1970	1 × 7	700	2040	Not yet commissioned

1. Information taken from a variety of sources, principally the Sumner report (Department of the Environment 1971), the Association of Waste Disposal Engineers (1976), the Process Plant Association (1976), and the journal Solid Wastes.
2. Costs are based on tender.

and $0.82 < R^2 < 0.92$. R^2 increases, and thus the goodness of fit increases (R^2 = 1 for a perfect fit), as the outliers identified above are eliminated from the analysis. To test for differences between plants with single and twin process lines, further analyses were carried out. For a single process line R^2 is low, while $S = 0.74$ or 1.04 depending on whether or not the Bolton plant is used. With all the data except the 3 positive outliers, the 95 per cent confidence interval for S is 1.04 ± 0.17; while for the cost at 20 t.p.h. capacity (ln W = 3.0), ln $C = 1.57 \pm 0.11$, so that $C = £4.8$ million $\overset{\times}{\div} 1.12$.

Table 13.3
Regression analysis on the capital costs of British incinerators without heat recovery
Equation estimated is $\ln C = \ln a + S \ln W$

Case	Data used	Number of plant n	Coefficient of determination R^2	ln a	S	ln C when ln W = 1.5	2.0	3.0
1	All plant, excluding 3 positive outliers[a]	25	0.88	−1.54	1.04		0.54	1.57
2	As 1, but excluding Bolton	24	0.92	−1.56	1.05		0.55	1.60
3	All plant, including outliers	28	0.82	−1.62	1.09		0.56	1.65
4	1 process line only	12	0.52	−0.92	0.74	0.19	0.56	
5	As 4, but excluding Bolton	11	0.67	−1.51	1.04	0.04	0.56	
6	2 process lines only, excluding 3 outliers[a]	13	0.86	−1.98	1.19		0.40	1.60
7	2 process lines only, including outliers	16	0.55	−1.23	0.97		0.72	2.18

(a) The three positive outliers are the plants at Huddersfield, Stoke, and Tyseley.

From this analysis, it is clear that, if economies of scale in the capital cost of incineration exist at all, they are small ($S \approx 1$), although for low capacity (below 10 t.p.h.) the data are rather limited. The results suggest that S may be lower for a single process line, but this depends critically on a single plant (Bolton). Dawson (1970) analysed the net running costs of 21 incinerators in California, obtaining (with W measured as the annual tonnage processed) $0.83 < S < 0.90$. Tanner (1975) examined the capital costs of Swiss incinerators, finding that the cost was proportional to capacity up to 600 t.p.d. (i.e. $S = 1.0$). Wilcox (1976) concluded from several published correlations of cost and capacity that evidence for economy of scale is strong below 500 t.p.d., being ambiguous for larger capacities. Bowen et al. (1969) suggest that imaginative design may negate economies of scale for plant as small as 3.5–5 t.p.h., while an optimum size of 500–750 t.p.d. is suggested, above which increased transport costs would dominate economies of scale. Scale factors quoted or used by other authors include $S = 0.78$ (Midwest Research Institute 1973), 0.70 (Schulz et al. 1976), 0.78 up to 10 t.p.h. and 0.90–0.95 over 10 t.p.h. (Bridgwater 1977), and 0.67 up to 2200 t.p.d. and 0.87 for higher capacities (Ward and Schoenenberger 1979). On the present analysis of UK incinerator costs and supporting evidence from the literature, a scale factor for incineration of $S = 0.95$ is suggested, but its use should be restricted to plants with capacity greater than about 10 t.p.h. The base cost for a 20 t.p.h. non-recuperative incinerator is taken as £4.8 million The 95 per cent confidence interval calculated above indicated an error range of $\overset{\times}{\div}$ 1.12, while the broad cost envelope identified in Fig. 13.7 suggests $\overset{\times}{\div}$ 1.35. The standard error range of $\overset{\times}{\div}$ 1.40 is used here, with the effect of the narrower range of $\overset{\times}{\div}$ 1.25 being examined later.

In Fig. 13.7 it is seen that the costs of incinerators with heat utilization are generally above average, but the other variations in the data may swamp this effect. The addition of the boiler will not raise the cost as much as might be expected, as it will replace the spray cooling tower otherwise necessary. Waterwalls reduce the furnace temperature and so lower the ratio of excess air required, thus reducing the size of the gas cleaning equipment. Estimates of the relative costs of heat recovery and non-recuperative incinerators are summarized in Table 13.4.

Table 13.4

Relative costs of incineration with and without heat recovery.
(Incineration without heat recovery = 1.0)

Source	Basis of estimates	Steam generation Refractory furnace	Steam generation Waterwall furnace	Electricity generation
Day and Zimmerman Associates (1968)	Total plant costs excluding building	1.60 1.70	1.20 1.25	
Belcher and Pépé (1969)	Total plant costs (Edmonton incinerator)			1.36
Fife (1970)	Equipment costs (tenders for Chicago Northwest plant)		1.70 1.71 1.47	
Jones and Henry Engineers (1970)	Total plant costs Installed equipment costs	1.16 1.36	1.23 1.51	
Niessen *et al.* (1970)	Total plant costs		1.37	
Midwest Research Institute (1973)	Total plant costs	1.25		1.90
Short (1973)	Equipment costs	1.02		
Squires and Fisher (1974)	Installed equipment costs	1.57	1.33	
West Midlands County Council (1976a)	Total plant costs		1.27	
Holmes (1975c)	Total plant costs	1.25		

For steam generation, a waterwall furnace with a boiler or heat exchanger for gas cooling is cheaper than a refractory furnace with separate boiler. (In addition to the data in Table 13.4, Rayman and Scott (1972) gave a cost ratio of 1.36 from tenders for the Coventry plant). The ratios based on equipment alone tend to be higher than those for total plant costs, as many building costs are common to any incinerator. An average value for the ratio of total plant costs of 1.35 is used here. This is appropriate to the incinerator itself, and does not include costs for steam distribution or standby fossil-fuel boilers. Steam distribution increases the capital costs by a factor of 1.05–2.26 depending on the application (Wilson and Swindle 1976). A factor of 1.3 is used to allow for modest provision of such facilities. The total capital cost of incineration with heat recovery as steam is thus taken as 1.7 times that of a non-recuperative incinerator of the same capacity. For a 16 t.p.h. plant the base cost is thus £6.6 million, with an error range taken as $\overset{\times}{\div}$ 1.40.

For electricity generation there is less information available (Table 13.4). The estimate used for simple incineration by Belcher and Pépé (1969) is high; the investment in the Edmonton incinerator implies a 1977 cost for a 20 t.p.h. plant ($S = 0.95$) of £11.6 million, an increase of 140 per cent over the base case used here. A cost increment for electricity generation over simple incineration of 100 per cent is assumed, giving a cost of £7.8 million for a 16 t.p.h. plant, with the error range again taken as $\overset{\times}{\div}$ 1.40.

13.6. Operating costs

Labour requirements for an incinerator rated at 16–20 t.p.h. are estimated at 4 men plus 6 per shift, with 7 per shift for a heat recovery plant. Total complements are thus 22 and 32 men, for plants with and without heat recovery.

Energy use in a modern incinerator is principally as electricity. Watson and Burnett (1972) gave data for 12 British plants, with a mean value of 29.0 and a standard deviation of 8.3 kWh/t. For steam generation, Schultz et al. (1976) quote 77 kWh/t. For electricity generation Patrick (1975b) gave 71.5 kWh/t for Edmonton while Asukata and Kitami (1974) gave 77–135 kWh/t for Japan. Electricity usage is here assumed at 30, 60, and 80 kWh/t for simple incineration, incineration with steam generation, and incineration with electricity generation. In some plants steam is used to drive process equipment directly, thus reducing electricity requirements. For a plant generating electricity, process requirements are assumed to be supplied by self-generation, reducing the net electricity for sale. A residual consumption of 9 per cent of the process requirement is entered in the economic analysis to maintain consistency in the estimation of other utilities (normally 10 per cent of direct energy use).

Maintenance costs for incineration are poorly documented. Achinger and Daniels (1970) gave detailed costings for six incinerators, with maintenance factors ranging from 0.02–0.06 I and a mean of 0.035 I. Maintenance on the Derby incinerator in 1975–6 cost £91 000 (Process Plant Association 1976), which is 0.034 of the updated investment. This excludes the wages of maintenance personnel; assuming equal contributions from maintenance labour and materials, and no external maintenance contracts, this is equivalent to about 0.07 I. The Coventry incinerator encountered severe corrosion problems. About £1 million was spent on boiler repairs in the period 1975–9, with a further £1 million for major works approved in autumn 1979. This expenditure was in addition to normal maintenance work. The total maintenance cost was probably in excess of 0.1 I/annum, even when an updated investment cost is used. A fairly optimistic maintenance factor of 0.07 I is used here for all three incineration options.

The quantity of ash produced by incineration is about 0.4 wet tonnes per tonne of waste, which is reduced by magnetic extraction of ferrous metals to about 0.35 t/t for disposal. Specific transport costs to a site at 20 km distance are assumed to be the same as for baled waste, with a higher pay load than for untreated waste. Landfill costs and energy requirements are assumed to be 50 per cent of those for untreated waste. The total cost of residue disposal is thus £2.45/t of residue, a value which is also used for other largely inorganic residues.

13.7. Discussion

The information presented here for a standard plant treating an average of 300 tonnes of waste per day yields the following results in the economic analysis:

Simple incineration	£20.8 ± 6.0/t
Steam generation	£22.3 ± 8.5/t
Electricity generation	£23.6 ± 10.0/t

Insufficient information was available to evaluate the combined generation of electricity and heat as a separate option.

The general level of costs is higher than for all the landfill-based options and also for several of the refuse-derived fuel options. The very wide range of the overall cost estimates should be noted; no definitive judgement on the relative costs of the three alternatives is possible. The costs in each case are sensitive to the estimate of capital cost and, in the heat recovery options, to the revenues. For example, if the accuracy of the capital cost estimate could be increased from $C_0 \overset{\times}{\div} 1.40$ to $C_0 \overset{\times}{\div} 1.25$, then the error range for simple incineration would be reduced to ± £4.0/t. A reduction in the capital cost estimates by 25 per cent would reduce the overall costs per tonne by between 20 and 30 per cent. If favourable markets for steam or electricity exist locally, then incineration with heat recovery would become more competitive.

This economic analysis suggests that incineration may not be one of the more promising waste management options for the future; however, the technology is largely proven and the uncertainties in the costs are such that it should always be considered as a possibility in preliminary planning work.

Heat recovery from incineration is one of the major options available for the utilization of solid waste as a resource. The results of the process analysis are thus of particular interest. For the three cases of simple incineration, steam generation, and electricity generation, respectively, the analysis yields primary energy inputs of 900, 1400, and 1800 MJ/t, with a saving due to ferrous metals recovery of 1100 MJ/t. To evaluate the primary energy savings implied by steam generation, the heat provided by sale of 75 per cent of the steam is assumed to displace steam from a coal fired boiler with efficiency 81 per cent, the efficiency of coal production being taken as 96 per cent (Table 8.3(b)). The 4.5 GJ of heat supplied per tonne of waste thus saves 5.8 GJ of primary energy per tonne. The 1.8 GJ/t of energy supplied as electricity is compared with 30 per cent efficient central generation, giving a primary energy saving of 6 GJ/t. The net energy efficiencies α are thus -0.09, $+0.44$, and $+0.42$, while the net primary energy efficiencies β are $+0.02$, $+0.54$, and 0.53 for the three cases.

Co-generation of electricity and heat offers the prospect of substantial increases in energy efficiencies, if a market for the low-temperature heat can be found. It was suggested earlier that, in addition to 18 per cent of the heat content recovered as electricity, a further 20 per cent could be recovered as, say, hot water at 50 °C. Assuming that the additional energy inputs are matched by the primary energy requirements to produce the heat by alternative means, and that 75 per cent of the heat can be utilized on average throughout the year, then the energy efficiencies for combined generation of power and heat are approximately $\alpha = 0.57$ and $\beta = 0.68$.

Under the assumptions under here, there is little to choose between generation of steam or electricity as means of saving energy, unless a use can be found for the waste heat from electricity generation. This conclusion is sensitive to both the load factor for steam use, with the suggested error range of ± 30 per cent giving $\beta = 0.54 \pm 0.17$, and to the efficiency of electricity generation, a range of ± 25 per cent giving $\beta = 0.53 \pm 0.15$. The net primary energy efficiency β may be increased by 0.07 by recovering additional materials, particularly aluminium, from the residue (Section 14.6).

13.8. Modular incineration

13.8.1. Background

This chapter has so far concentrated on the continuous grate direct incinerator, which is the normal option for the incineration of municipal wastes. Other types of incinerator design were reviewed in Section 13.2, and the incineration of processed waste will be returned to in Chapter 16. One further alternative which has recently been proposed is the subject of this section. This is a simple batch-loaded incinerator which utilizes a two-stage combustion process. Waste is loaded into the primary furnace where it is burnt in an oxygen-deficient atmosphere, the majority of the organic materials being decomposed into small volatile molecules. The gases are passed at 800 °C to a secondary combustion chamber where they are burnt at a temperature of 1000–1200 °C. The exhaust gases are claimed to be clean enough for direct discharge to the atmosphere, after air cooling to 800 °C.

This system is typified by the American Consumat incinerator, manufactured in Britain by Robert Jenkins Systems. The Consumat has been installed for municipal waste disposal in the U S A, but its use in Britain has so far been limited largely to commercial and hospital wastes; a small municipal plant rated at 18 t.p.d. has been ordered for the Orkney Islands in Scotland.

The incinerator is supplied in modular form, each module having a capacity up to 1 t.p.h. This enables small plants to be built, a maximum size of 100 t.p.d. being suggested for a municipal waste plant. The incinerators are free standing, with a short steel stack, the proposed arrangement being around the perimeter of a waste reception building, in which the waste is tipped on the floor and fed into the charging hoppers by a front-end loader. Two-shift operation is suggested, with automatic controlled burn-down of the incinerators each evening enabling the cool ash to be unloaded before work commences the next day. Heat recovery is possible using a plug-in modular boiler on each unit, the design allowing the boiler to be bypassed when steam is not required, avoiding the need for expensive steam-dumping equipment.

13.8.2. Quantitative data

Economic data for this system is available only from literature which is supplied by the manufacturer, and which is based on limited commercial experience (Robert Jenkins Systems 1976); thus some care must be taken in its use. It is assumed that 4 plants will be used to provide a peak capacity of 400 t.p.d. The average transport cost to the plants will be about half that for a central plant; for an area of radius 6 km the saving is about 2 km haul, or about 36 p/t of waste.

Each plant consists of 8 modules, which may operate for $12\frac{1}{2}$ hours per day, at a design capacity of 1 t.p.h. Each module costs £70 000 installed (mid-1976), with civil engineering and building work estimated at £240 000 for the complete plant. This low estimate is attributed to the self-contained incinerators which stand outside; it includes site preparation, the waste reception building, roads, drainage, plumbing, and electrical work. A weighbridge is not provided, nor are office or amenity facilities. To allow for these, the estimate is increased by 50 per cent, while £50 000 is added for three front-end loaders, including one spare. The total capital cost estimate per plant is thus £970 000, or £1.1 million on a 1977 cost basis. For four plants, capital requirements are thus £4.4 million.

Each plant is operated by 2 men per shift. Here, an additional man is assumed as an office–weighbridge clerk on the day shift. Thus 20 men are required for the four plants. Electricity usage is given as 17 kWh/t, while fuel usage, as auxiliary fuel in both the primary and secondary combustion chambers, is about 20 therms of gas per tonne. Fuel usage by the loaders will be higher than for a transfer station, and is estimated at 1.0 l/t. Water usage is about 50 l/t. Annual maintenance costs are claimed to be only 0.02 of installed equipment costs. Here the low, but more realistic, estimate of 0.04 of total capital cost is used. Residue from the incinerators is claimed to be about 30 per cent of the input waste, and transport and disposal costs are assumed as for standard incineration.

The heat recovery module is claimed to cost £60 000 per unit, or £480 000 per plant (mid-1976, installed). No piping or steam distribution costs are included. To allow for minimal distribution costs, this estimate is increased by 50 per cent, to give a 1977 cost of £800 000. Electricity usage is 5 kWh/t. A heat recovery efficiency of 100 per cent is assumed by the company. Efficiency may be higher than for conventional incineration, and a value of 70 per cent is assumed here, together with a load factor of 75 per cent. It is claimed that no additional men are required, but an extra man per shift is included here.

13.8.3. Discussion

The standard economic analysis results in a cost of £21.0 ± 5.0/t, or £24.2 ± 8.8/t with steam generation. These compare with £20.8 ± 6.0/t and £22.3 ± 8.4/t for conventional incineration, and suggest that there is little to choose economically between the options. When the technology has been adequately demonstrated, modular incineration may become attractive for small plants, even when compared with the cheaper treatment options. In addition, the transport economies resulting from the use of several local plants rather than one central plant may in some cases be considerably greater than the 36 p/t assumed here. Steam generation does not appear attractive as an independent option, particularly as continuous supply is not possible, but the flexibility of adding individual modules as required might make it economic as an incremental investment, perhaps after a plant has been built.

The process analysis shows relatively high energy inputs of 3500 and 3800 MJ/t for modular incineration without and with steam generation. Net energy efficiencies are $\alpha = \beta = -0.35$ and $+0.30$, respectively. The use of a supplementary fuel for incineration makes the process much more energy intensive than simple incineration, even if a higher steam generation efficiency is assumed as here.

14. PHYSICAL SEPARATION OF WASTE

14.1. Introduction

The majority of the processes used or proposed for the reclamation or recovery of municipal waste utilize some means of physically separating the components of the waste. It is useful to distinguish between:

Primary separation of waste components, for example to produce a mainly organic and a mainly inorganic fraction.

Secondary separation of particular components, for example the magnetic separation of ferrous metals from the inorganic fraction.

Tertiary separation, used to upgrade separated fractions. An example is the separation of glass from contaminants such as ceramics, stone, and bone.

Many properties of the components may be exploited to separate waste. Those most commonly used include particle size, bulk density or specific gravity, magnetic susceptibility, electrical conductivity, and colour; however, other properties are also important in some processes, examples including resilience, brittleness, malleability, shape, cross-sectional area, inertia, sliding friction, and surface conditions. A partial listing of unit processes and possible applications is given in Table 14.1. Many of the processes are developments from those used in mineral processing.

In this chapter, methods of separating the inorganic from the organic fraction of municipal waste are first considered. The organic fraction is usually processed further for energy recovery, the exact methods depending on the particular process being used; the various options are looked at in subsequent chapters. Prospects and technologies for the recovery of organic materials are reviewed here.

The nature of the inorganic fraction is virtually independent of the overall process being used for waste reclamation. It may simply be landfilled or it may be processed further for materials recovery. In the comparative evaluation presented here, only the recovery of magnetic metals is included in the basic options. The recovery of additional materials, principally non-ferrous metals and glass, from the inorganic fraction is regarded as an incremental

Table 14.1

Physical separation methods potentially applicable to municipal waste

| Properties of material exploited | | Unit process | Environment | Examples of types of equipment | Examples of possible applications |
Primary	Secondary				
Particle size		Screening	Dry	Trommel	(a) Primary separation of untreated waste
			Wet	Vibratory	(b) Secondary separation into several fractions
			Wet	Vibratory	(c) Separation of fine particles from intermediate products
	Resistance to breakage/ pulping	Selective size reduction/ screening	Dry	Centrifugal Hammermill/screen	(d) Fibre recovery in wet pulping
			Semi-wet	Wet pulverization/screen	Separation of metals (malleable) from glass and ceramics (brittle)
			Wet	Wet pulper/cyclone	Separation of fibres from plastics and other non-pulpables or non-reduceables
Bulk density/specific gravity		Sink/float	Wet	Drum Cone	Secondary separation of organic (float) from inorganic (sink)
		Heavy-media	Wet	Aqueous suspension of ferrosilicon or magnetite	Separation of different plastics Tertiary separation of organics from glass and metals glass from metals different metals ceramics from glass
			Dry	Ferrofluid levitation Fluidized bed	
		Mineral jig	Wet		Secondary separation of organics, aluminium, and other non-ferrous metals
		Cyclone	Dry	Cyclone De-entrainment chamber	De-entrainment of solid particles from airstream (after air classifier)
			Wet	Hydrocyclone	Separation of glass from wet-pulped waste

Physical property	Technique	Dry/Wet	Equipment/type	Application
Aerodynamic drag (function of cross-section area, mass of particle, Reynolds number, shape, etc.)	Air classifier	Dry	Vertical Zig-zag Horizontal Cross-flow Impulse Rotary drum	Primary separation of (shredded) waste into dense and light fractions Secondary separation of putrescible organic materials from heavier inorganics Tertiary separation of paper into heavy and light fractions
Fluid drag	Wet elutriation	Wet	Rising current or hydraulic classifier	Secondary separation of dense and light fractions Tertiary separation of glass from light (organic) contaminants
Inertia	Vibrating tables	Dry Wet	'Stoner' or air table 'Wiffley table'	Secondary separation of dense and light fractions
Aerodynamic drag, inertia, resilience, sliding friction	Ballistic separator	Dry	High speed projection Projection on to suitable target/surface	Separation of organic/inorganic materials Separation of heavy and resilient/light and inelastic particles
Superficial hydrophobicity	Froth flotation	Wet		Tertiary separation of fine glass from ceramics, stone, bone, etc.
Magnetic susceptibility	Magnetic separation	Dry	Electromagnetic drum, head pulley, or overband magnet	Separation of magnetic metals
	Electrodynamics (eddy-current)	Dry	Linear induction motor, static permanent magnets, or rotary drum	Separation of aluminium
Electrical conductivity	Electrostatic	Dry	High intensity magnetic separator Drum type	Tertiary separation of clear from coloured glass aluminium from non-conductors paper from plastics different plastics
Transparency	Electronic sorting	Dry	Single particle at a time systems, perhaps with several channels operating in parallel	Separation of glass from ceramics or stones on basis of transparency
Colour	Optical sorting	Dry		Tertiary separation of glass into colours

Note: further information is given by Drobny, Hull, and Testin (1971) and by Douglas and Birch (1976).

investment, to be treated on its own merits. In this chapter the various unit processes are considered and two alternative flowsheets for recovery are evaluated; an additional process which utilizes incinerator residue as its raw material is also considered.

14.2. Separation of inorganic and organic fractions

There are three broad alternatives for the primary separation of municipal waste into a mainly organic and a mainly inorganic fraction. These may be distinguished largely in terms of the initial methods used to reduce the particle size of the waste materials, that is:

Wet pulverization;
Wet pulping;
Dry separation, often involving size reduction in a hammermill or similar device.

14.2.1. Wet pulverization

This method was discussed in Section 12.2; the untreated waste is moistened and fed into a large, slowly rotating drum, in which self-pulverization is achieved by the tumbling action of the hard components. Waste is normally separated into two fairly crude fractions. The fine fraction is passed through screens at the end of the drum. This contains about 60 per cent of the waste by weight and is a fairly fibrous, mainly organic material (Fig. 12.8(b)) but it does contain a lot of glass. The coarse fraction which passes out of the end of the drum is mainly inorganic, but also contains, for example, sheets of plastics and objects such as shoes.

An interesting Japanese development of the rotary drum pulverizer aims to increase the efficiency of separating the inorganic from the organic fraction (Ito and Hirayama 1975). The drum is divided into two sections with internal rotating scrapers in each. Dry waste enters the first stage where glass and other brittle materials are pulverized and screened out, together with other fine materials including most of the putrescible organics. Water is added before the second section, which operates as a standard wet pulverizer, separating paper fibre from remaining materials. A pilot plant rated at 1 tonne per hour (t.p.h.) was operated between 1976 and 1979, and a demonstration plant rated at 10 t.p.h. began operation in Yokohama City in 1979.

This 'semi-wet selective pulverizing classifier' is the central feature of most Japanese work on resource recovery from municipal waste. The complete demonstration plant, nicknamed 'Stardust '80', will include various options for upgrading the three separated waste fractions (Nomoto, Torisu, Hirayama, and Ito 1979):

(1) The first fraction includes 90–95 per cent of the putrescible organics,

80–90 per cent of the glass and about 30 per cent of the (mainly flimsy) paper in the waste; its overall composition is about 90 per cent organic. This will be evaluated both for composting (Takeuchi, Hirayama, and Ito 1979) and for anaerobic digestion.

(2)The intermediate fraction contains about 50 per cent of the paper content of the waste, and has an overall composition of about 85 per cent paper. This will be evaluated for upgrading and recovery of the paper fibres (Yoda, Miyazaki, and Machida 1979).

(3) The residual fraction contains 75–95 per cent of the plastics and 85–90 per cent of the metals in the waste. Its composition is about 80 per cent organic and 20 per cent metals. It will be evaluated for extraction of ferrous metals and pyrolysis of the residue (Andoh, Ishii, Hirayama, and Ito 1979).

14.2.2. Wet pulping

In the wet pulper, waste is introduced as an aqueous slurry (3–10 per cent solids) and is reduced in size by a segmented blade rotating at very high speed. The processed waste passes out of the bottom of the pulper, while materials not pulpable or friable are rejected ballistically by the rotating blades to the outer portions of the pulper drum where they are removed. The pulped waste is largely organic in content; most of the remaining inorganics, which consist mainly of fine glass particles, are removed in a liquid cyclone. Various alternative uses for the pulped organic fraction have been proposed, including fibre recovery, dewatering for sale as a fuel or for incineration on site, and drying to give a higher-grade fuel for sale. These options are considered in Chapter 17.

14.2.3. Dry separation

This is the method of primary separation most commonly used or proposed for solid waste recovery and/or reclamation. The major unit processes are:

    Size reduction;
    Screening;
    Air classification;
    Magnetic separation.

A basic flowsheet for dry separation is shown in Fig. 14.1(a), but there are almost an infinite number of variations possible. The waste is first pulverized and magnetic metals are removed (Section 12.2.2). The actual separation is achieved by air classification; the mixed waste falls through an air stream in which light materials are entrained. The efficiency of separation depends on aerodynamics, much effort over the last 10 years having gone into developing suitable equipment for use with municipal waste. Many variations are possible, the most common being a vertical zigzag classifier (Boettcher 1972; Colon 1976; Senden and Tels 1979), others including horizontal, vertical,

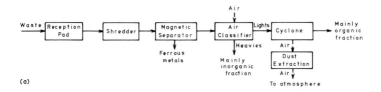

(a)

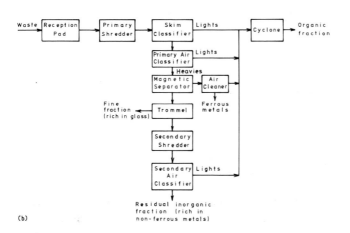

(b)

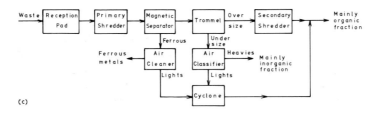

(c)

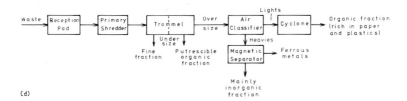

(d)

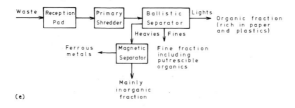

(e)

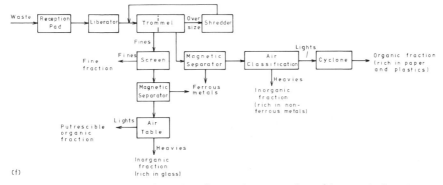

Fig. 14.1. *Dry separation of municipal waste into organic and inorganic functions.*
(a) Basic flowsheet
(b) Process modifications to improve separation of organics
(c) Use of screen to reduce load on air classifier
(d) Use of screen to produce two (or more) mainly organic fractions
(e) Replacement of air classifier with ballistic separator
(f) Replacement of primary shredding by screening.

cross-flow, and impulse-type (National Center for Resource Recovery 1972), a conical rotating classifier (Holmes 1979), and an inclined rotary drum classifier (Grubbs, Paterson, and Fabbus 1976). An example of an air classifier is shown in Fig. 14.2.

Experience of the application of air classification to waste separation is still limited, so that detailed information on costs, performance, reliability, and efficiency of separation is scarce at present. The best documented performance data available are probably those for the Raytheon rotary drum classifier; tests at feed rates of 15–60 t.p.h. on pulverized waste in the size range 40–300 mm yielded an ash content in the light fraction of between 12 and 26 per cent. The efficiency of separation was particularly sensitive to changes in feed rate, air velocity, and particle size (Grubbs and Coulombe 1978). For example, separation is more efficient for larger particle sizes. This is presumably due to the shattering of glass in hammermills, the fine glass fragments becoming entrapped by the light organic components of the waste; this phenomenon is not so pronounced for coarser shredding, as for example in a flail mill (Section 12.2.2).

Numerous modifications of the basic flowsheet in Fig. 14.1(a) have been proposed. One of the most common is to move the magnetic separator after the air classifier, applying only to the heavy fraction (cf. Fig. 5.2). The efficiency of incorporating combustible organic materials in the light fraction can be improved at the expense of additional process sophistication, an example being shown in Fig. 14.1(b). A preliminary skim classifier removes some light material before the air classifier, and a secondary air classifier removes any residual organics from the heavy fraction after further

Fig. 14.2. *Air classifier.* The novel type of classifier used at the Doncaster waste sorting plant (Section 15.5). Waste enters via a high-speed conveyor, and separation is effected in the cylindrical section of the classifier. Light materials are removed from the base of the disengagement chamber on the right. (Photo courtesy South Yorkshire County Council.)

processing. This flowsheet is used at the 1800 t.p.d. Monroe County plant in New York (Table 15.1; Schroeder 1979).

The process flowsheets discussed so far include most organic materials in the light fraction, which contains about 65–80 per cent by weight of the original waste. Use of screening prior to air classification can remove much material with a higher ash content, producing a better quality product. It has indeed been claimed that the oversize fraction from a trommel screen can be designed to be largely organic, so that only the undersize fractions need to be air classified. The original Continental Can process, and its development by Combustion Engineering (Smith, 1976; Smith and von Steiger 1979; Fig. 14.1 (c)), produce a similar product to the conventional flowsheets above, whereas the development by R.E.G. Associates discards the finest fraction and air classifies an intermediate fraction, producing an organic product containing 50–55 per cent by weight of the waste, with an ash content reduced from about 20 to about 12 per cent. A 45 t.p.h. plant using this flowsheet has been built at Madison, Wisconsin (Table 15.1). Screens can also be designed and used in such a way that the light fraction from the subsequent air classifier (about 20–40 per cent of input waste) consists mainly of paper and plastics (Fig. 14.1 (d)). This is the principle both of the Byker refuse-derived fuel plant in England (Section 15.5) and of the Buhler-Miag Compo+Pell (compost plus pelletized fuel) process (Wyss 1979).

An interesting variation on the general theme of dry separation is the Swedish PLM process, which replaces the air classifier with a ballistic separator (Fig. 14.1(e)). The shredded waste is fed onto an oscillating, inclined, perforated surface. Light and flexible particles are thrown upwards, while rigid and heavy particles move down the inclined surface; fine materials pass through the perforated screen. It is claimed that the light fraction (40–50 per cent of input waste) consists of about 80 per cent of paper and plastics (Hansen 1979).

Primary shredding of waste is a high energy consumer; it tends to shatter glass and entrap organic contaminants within tin cans; and it contaminates paper with putrescible wastes. These disadvantages have led to the development of a number of processes where the initial shredding is replaced by a 'waste liberator' which merely opens paper and plastic bags full of waste (Fig. 14.1(f)). The primary classification is then achieved by screening, for example in a trommel. Oversize wastes may be processed to remove cardboard boxes or bundled newspapers, they may be pulverized and recycled through the trommel, or they may simply be landfilled. The fines and putrescible materials are screened out, so that the light fraction from air classification of the intermediate sized wastes is again predominantly paper and plastics. Research has been carried out in West Germany, France, and England; a flowsheet similar to that in Fig. 14.1(f) is being used in the Doncaster demonstration plant (Section 15.5). The trommel screen at the Doncaster plant is shown in Fig. 14.3.

It is obvious from this discussion that many variations on the theme of dry separation are possible, depending largely on the composition of the input waste and on the desired products. Early research in the USA, for example at the Bureau of Mines (United States Bureau of Mines; Sullivan, Stanczyk, and Spendlove 1973), was directed at recovering several organic fractions for materials recovery, while later work has aimed more at producing a single stream for use as a solid refuse-derived fuel (American RDF; Section 15.3). In Europe, research has been directed at producing a fraction rich in paper and plastics, which may be used either as an RDF (paper-based RDF; Section 15.5), or as separation technology is developed, as a source of recovered paper.

14.3. Recovery of organic materials

14.3.1. Paper

The prospects for the recovery of paper from the organic fraction of waste are improving. Considerable research has been directed at the upgrading of paper-rich fractions obtained from semi-wet selective pulverization, for wet pulping (Chapter 17), and from some variants of dry separation. Several of the dry processing schemes considered above (Fig. 14.1(d), (e), (f)) produced a mixed paper and plastics fraction. Further separation of this material is difficult (Milgrom 1975), although some success has been achieved

Fig. 14.3. *Trommel screen*. The trommel screen used at Doncaster for primary separation of the waste into 3 fractions. In figure (a) an external view is shown; note

on the research scale with air classification (Colon 1976), with electrostatic separation (Kispert, Sadek, Anderson, and Wise 1975; Henstock 1976), and with selective crushing/air-classification devices (Cavanna, Almarez, Cristobal, and Ramfrez 1978; Hoberg and Julius 1979). Direct utilization of the paper and plastics mixture, apart from its use as a fuel, is possible; one process mixes the dried material with its own weight of wood particles to form a wallboard (Elopak Group 1976).

At least two dry separation processes claim to produce a paper-rich fraction which is not substantially contaminated with plastics. The Babcock Kraus-Maffei (BKMI) system (Fig. 14.4(a)) incorporates several novel features in the flowsheet, including a low-energy cutting roller crusher, protected by a ballistic separator which removes contrary objects such as paving slabs or cast metal. The horizontal cross-flow air classifier is claimed to produce three fractions, namely a heavy fraction, a medium-weight fraction consisting of heavy paper and board, and a light fraction. The latter is further separated into paper and plastic-rich fractions in the cyclone, by a mechanical device which takes advantage of the different tensile strengths; the efficiency of separation is claimed to be greater than 80 per cent. An approximate mass balance from waste containing 47 per cent paper, 10 per cent plastics and 5 per cent ferrous metals is given as (Steier 1979):

Ferrous metals	5%
Heavy paper and board	20%
Light paper	10%
Plastic sheeting	5%
Composting plant input	60%

A 15 t.p.h. plant at Landskrona in Sweden was due to start operation in 1979. No quantitative data on costs or product quality is yet available.

The Swedish company Fläkt also have a process designed primarily for paper recovery (Fig. 14.4(b)). Primary separation uses a fairly standard flowsheet, a trommel screen after the flail mill removing a fair proportion of the plastics in the oversize fraction. The light fraction from the vertical zigzag air classifier is shredded again; empirical observation on the size distribution of this material led to the use of a trommel screen to achieve what is claimed to be efficient separation into fine impurities, clean paper (< 100 mm) and plastics (> 100 mm). The paper fraction is further upgraded using a Fläkt flash dryer, as widely used in the pulp industry. Secondary air classification separates the product into largely chemical fibres (heavy

---

the three separate conveyors below the screen for removing the products, and also the ducts at the top which lead to a central dust extraction unit. An internal view is seen in figure (b): note the large rectangular holes in the foreground for the medium-sized fraction. The device at the top was used to remove rags, but has since been discarded. (Photo courtesy South Yorkshire County Council.)

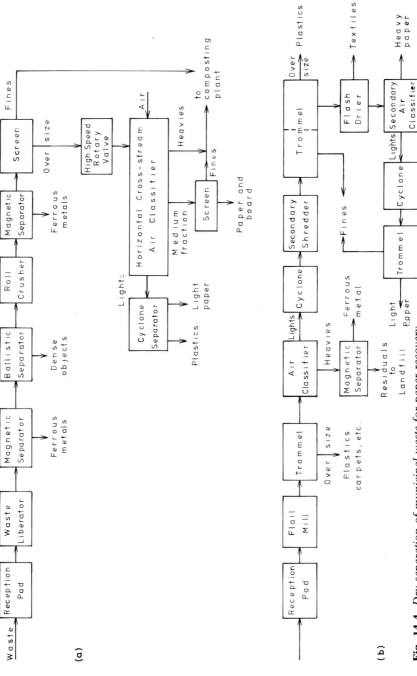

Fig. 14.4. *Dry separation of municipal waste for paper recovery*
(a) Babcock Krauss-Maffei separation system
(b) Fläkt system

fraction) and largely mechanical fibres (light fraction). An approximate materials balance for waste containing 22 per cent paper, 3 per cent ferrous metals, 6 per cent plastics and 37 per cent putrescible organic materials is given as (Smulders 1979):

Ferrous metals	2.8%
Light paper	7.3%
Heavy paper	6.0%
Plastics	3.6%
Fine residue	31%
Heavy particles to landfill	38%
Moisture to atmosphere	11%

The overall recovery efficiency for paper implied by these figures is 60 per cent, but claims as high as 75 per cent have been made. The process has been tested on a 5 t.p.h. pilot plant in Sweden (Cederholm 1978); a 25 t.p.h., 500 t.p.d. plant at Wijster in Holland began commissioning late in 1979 (Smulders 1979); a 12.5 t.p.h. plant in Stockholm was due to begin operations in the summer of 1980, and is shown in Fig. 14.5. Little quantitative detail of the process is yet available, although the energy inputs, at about 80 kWh of electricity and 600 MJ of heat per tonne, appear quite high (Cederholm 1978). However, it is fair to say that this currently represents one of the best developed technologies for separation of reasonable quality paper fibres from mixed waste.

14.3.2. Other organic materials

If the technology for paper recovery from mixed municipal waste has not yet

Fig. 14.5. *The Fläkt plant for paper recovery from municipal waste at Lovsta, Stockholm.* This photograph shows the plant about 6 months before operations were scheduled to begin. In the foreground is the overhead railway used to transfer incoming waste from the adjacent municipal incinerator. The two cyclones associated with the air classifiers are visible on the roof, while the flash drier is on the right.

been adequately proven, that for plastics recovery can only be described as primitive. Both the BKMI and Fläkt systems described above claim to produce saleable plastic fractions, but both developers have been more interested in the paper product. In general, much further research and development work is required if a mixed soiled plastic waste is to be acceptable for recycling. Ideally, the component plastics should be separarated; methods explored, largely on the laboratory scale, including sink-float, hydrocyclone, and electrostatic separation (Bahr 1979). Alternatively, the mixed waste may be used in a lower-grade application, for example as a filler in insulating board manufacture (Menges and Haberstroh 1979) or for moulded articles such as fence posts (Aoyagi 1975).

Either the putrescible organic fraction of municipal waste, or a mixed fraction including also paper, may be utilized as a feedstock for the reclamation of new materials; examples include composting or the cultivation of earthworms to produce a fertilizer (Chapter 19).

14.4. Recovery of inorganic materials

Materials recovery from the largely inorganic fraction(s) produced by any of the primary separation methods can follow a variety of routes, using unit operations taken mainly from mineral processing. Three typical flowsheets are shown in Fig. 14.6.

14.4.1. Secondary separation

Secondary separation of the residue into remaining organic materials, a glass-rich fraction, and a metal-rich fraction is included in some primary separation schemes (e.g. Figs. 14.1(b), (f)). The methods used for this separation typically combine one or more of the following:

(i) Magnetic separation.

(ii) Screening, with the oversize material containing most of the metals and the fines most of the glass.

(iii) A mineral jig which separates waste particles by specific gravity, with light particles floating off and heavy particles sinking, an efficient separation into two or three fractions being achieved.

(iv) A rising current or hydraulic classifier which operates on a similar principle.

(v) A heavy-media separator, in which choice of a medium of correct density, and of the correct particle size of the feedstock, allows efficient separation of organics from glass and metals, of glass from metals, of different metals, or of ceramics from glass. Heavy media often consist of an aqueous suspension of fine magnetite, ferrosilicon, or other dense material. The magnetite or ferrosilicon may be recovered for reuse by magnetic separation. An interesting development is 'ferrofluid levitation'

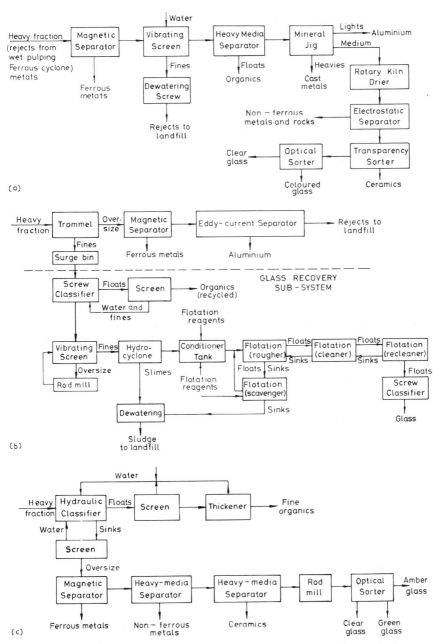

Fig. 14.6. *Materials recovery from the mainly inorganic fraction of municipal waste.*
(a) The flowsheet used at Franklin, Ohio (Cummings 1976)
(b) A simplified flowsheet of the Occidental process (Morey *et al.* 1976)
(c) The Aachen process (Hoberg and Schulz 1977).

in which the apparent specific gravity of the suspension is varied by the application of a magnetic field. The Dutch State Mines have developed a cyclone technique using either water or a heavy medium as the operating fluid; the use of centrifugal rather than gravitational forces allows a much more efficient density separation for small particles, 0.5 mm or less (Absil, Reeves, Basten, and Dalmijn 1979). Another form of heavy medium is a dry fluidized bed; a device for the separation of aluminium and other non-ferrous metals from incinerator residue was developed by the Warren Spring Laboratory in England (Miles and Douglas 1972).

14.4.2. Non-ferrous metals

Tertiary separation of the inorganic waste components is usually aimed at the recovery of non-ferrous metal or glass fractions for recycling. The three basic alternatives for non-ferrous metals are (Bourcier and Dale 1978a):

① *Heavy-media* separation, which is best suited to a particle size range of 2.5 to 5 cm. Hydrocyclone methods could extend the range down to 0.3 cm.

② *Electrodynamic* or *eddy-current* separation, in which a magnetic field is induced in pieces of metal, the effect being strongest for aluminium. The optimum size range for separation is about 4–10 cm, although some designs claim to handle sizes down to 1.2 cm. Various proprietary devices have been developed, including a linear induction motor (Alter, Natof, and Blayden 1976), a series of static permanent magnets (Spencer and Schlömann 1975) and a rotary drum separator also using permanent magnets (Schlömann 1976).

③ *Electrostatic* separation, in which efficient separation of metals from non-conductors is achieved because the metals lose a static electrical charge more quickly. The technique has also been proposed for the separation of paper from plastics.

14.4.3. Glass

The approach adopted for separating glass also depends critically on the particle size of the feedstock, which in this case is controlled by the method used for primary separation. Initial pulverization of waste tends to shatter glass, a hammermill reducing 90 per cent, and a flail mill 60 per cent, to less than 6 mm (Section 12.2.2). Wet pulverization and flowsheets utilizing a primary screen before size reduction (e.g. Fig. 14.1(f)) tend to produce larger pieces of glass, typically in the size range 15–40 mm.

For glass with a particle size greater than about 6 mm, the unit operations which can be utilized include:

(a) A rising current or hydraulic classifier to separate (heavy) glass from (light) organics;

(b) Vibrating tables to achieve a similar function;

(c) Heavy-media separation to remove ceramics;

(d) An electronic sorter which examines each particle separately, and uses transparency to differentiate ceramics and stones from glass;

(e) A similar electronic sorter, set to differentiate particles optically into two or three fractions, either flint (clear) and coloured glass, or flint, amber, and green glass;

(f) A high-intensity magnetic separator, which yields two fractions, coloured and flint glass.

The Doncaster RDF demonstration plant in England (Section 15.5) includes glass recovery. The fraction screened from the incoming waste, in the size range 15–40 mm, is separated by two vibrating 'air tables' or 'stoners', into light, mainly putrescible wastes and a heavy glass-rich fraction. This passes to a rising current separator (Fig. 14.7), where the sinking glass is collected by the rotating wheel and discharged into a separate chute from the light material, which simply overflows a weir. The glass is partially dewatered in helical conveyors and taken to two electronic sorters (Fig. 14.8); the first is described as a single-channel, bulk transparency sorter and the second as a six-channel optical sorter. The aim is to produce a mixed glass cullet at least 99.7 per cent and preferably 99.9 per cent pure, but no performance tests have yet been made.

For glass with a particle size less than 6 mm, separation is usually by froth flotation (Heginbotham 1978). A typical flowsheet is shown in Fig. 14.6(b). The sequence of operations may be summarized as:

A screw classifier to remove light organics;

A rod mill for reduction to a uniform (< 1 mm) particle size;

Removal of remaining organic slimes;

Addition of chemical reagents;

A series of flotation tanks, in which the quality of the floating glass is gradually increased and the sinking fraction is recycled;

The sinking fraction from the initial flotation tank is dosed with more reagent, the floating product being recycled and the sinks being rejected.

The product glass is a very fine mixed cullet. It may be difficult to dewater completely, and upgrading is only possible using the relatively untried technique of high-intensity magnetic separation to yield clear and coloured glass.

14.4.4. Operating experience

It must be emphasized that much of the technology discussed here for waste separation has not yet been demonstrated on a commercial scale. Pilot tests of both aluminium and glass recovery at Franklin in Ohio during 1976 were disappointing (Section 14.5). Both aluminium (eddy-current) and glass (froth flotation) recovery modules have been installed at the National Center for Resource Recovery's New Orleans demonstration plant (Abert 1979b). Problems elsewhere in the plant have delayed commissioning of the

Fig. 14.7. *Rising current separator.* The glass-rich fraction enters a continuously flowing water bath, in which a large paddle-wheel rotates. The heavy glass sinks and is lifted by the sectioned wheel, being deposited into the central chute at the top. Light organic materials overflow the weir and pass down the belt in the foreground. (Photo courtesy South Yorkshire County Council.)

glass recovery system. Aluminium recovery has been intermittent, and efficiency has been low owing to inefficient operation of screening devices earlier in the flowsheet. Aluminium and glass recovery systems are included in several other USA plants at present in construction or start-up, notably those at Monroe County, New York, and Milwaukee, Wisconsin; glass recovery is included in the Doncaster plant in the UK. However, these modules are not vital to the running of the overall plants, and considerable

Fig. 14.8. *Glass purification at Doncaster.* The glass is partially dewatered in helical conveyors and then passes to two electronic sorters in series. The figure shows a helical conveyor in the centre and an electronic sorter on the left. (Photo courtesy South Yorkshire County Council.)

delays may be anticipated before teething problems are overcome and significant operating experience is accumulated. The quality of initial samples of recovered aluminium delivered to the Reynolds Metals Company from five USA plants was reported to be promising (Bourcier and Dale 1978*b*).

14.4.5. Quantitative data

Much of the available information on separation efficiencies of materials from mixed municipal waste is based on design estimates (Table 14.2). While differences will exist between processes, it is at present only realistic to apply general values to all processes. The values suggested and used here are included in Table 14.2: it should be noted that the efficiency for magnetic metal recovery, 90 per cent of that in the input waste, is the only one backed by significant operating experience, although even in this case considerable problems do still exist (Section 12.2.2).

Information on the quality of recovered materials comes mainly from experimental work. To provide a basis for quality control and the negotiation of contracts, Alter and Reeves (1975) proposed standard specifications

Table 14.2

Recovery efficiencies of materials from solid waste

	Material							
	Ferrous metals		Non-ferrous metals		Glass		Paper	
Source	Untreated waste	Incinerator residue	Aluminium	Others	Mixed fines	Colour sorted	Wet-pulped fibre	Dry sorted
Midwest Research Institute (1973)	89.5	55.7		66.7	70.0	–	45.5	–
Smith (1975)	90.6	–	–	–	–	–	–	–
St. Louis plant (Shannon, Fiscus, and Gorman 1975)	75	–	–	–	–	–	–	–
Franklin plant (Systech 1975)	98.0	–	–	–	–	–	42.6	–
Landman and Darmstadt (1975)	90	–	80	–	–	48	–	–
Kispert et al. (1975)	95	–	85	–	–	55	–	–
Mantellini (1975)	95	–	–	–	–	–	–	60
Preston (1976)	94.3	–	57.1	–	69.7	–	–	–
Schulz et al. (1976)	95	–	70	100	70	50	50	–
Smulders (1979)	–	–	–	–	–	–	–	60
Steier (1979)	–	–	–	–	–	–	–	64
Hoberg and Schulz (1977)	–	–	–	–	–	–	–	80
Typical value used here	90	56	70		70	70	50	45	60

which could be met by current technology. Results of detailed evaluations of products from the U S B M process are available (Sullivan and Makar 1976).

So far, discussion has centred on the unit operations which separate the waste into different fractions, but materials handling (Biddulph 1976) and storage are also important. Storage of the organic products from separation may be a problem (Hickman 1976), particularly if the putrescible fraction is included. In general, mechanical retrieval of the organic fraction from a storage bin is necessary, either a live-bottom or live-centre bin (Fisher 1976) being used. Further development may still be necessary in the light of operational problems with bridging above the level of the drag-conveyors (Hagerty 1977).

Cost estimation for resource recovery plants ideally requires information on the costs of the unit operations. Unfortunately, such information is lacking, and that available (Table 14.3) is not consistent. For example, the capital cost estimates made by the National Center for Resource Recovery for the plant at New Orleans reflect partly gifts and loans of equipment, rather than costings for a commercial plant. It is not clear how far supplementary equipment, such as conveyors, motors, dust extractors, and storage bins, are included in the estimates. For some equipment, estimates are based on conventional applications, and considerable modification may be required for waste treatment.

14.5. Additional recovery of materials

14.5.1. Processes

Two alternative processes for the recovery of materials from the inorganic fraction of separated municipal waste are evaluated in this section. The flowsheets are shown in Fig. 14.6(a) and (b), the processes being demonstrated at Franklin, Ohio, and (with some modifications) at Monroe County, New York, respectively.

The Franklin process is the more sophisticated of the two alternatives.

Table 14.3

Capital costs of unit operations

(all costs are £ thousand (1977) for installed equipment)

			National Center for Resource Recovery (NCRR) (1974c)	Kispert et al. (1975)	Source		Stuckenbruck and King (1977)
					Schulz et al. 1976		
					General data	Occidental system	
Item	Plant capacity	t.p.d.	680	910	910	910	730
		t.p.h.	43	60	38	38	45
Weighbridge			43	–	–	50	140
Primary shredding			530	750	860	460	200
Magnetic separation[d]			19	58	140	13	150
Ferrous metal baler[d]			47	–	–	–	–
Trommel screen for primary separation			130	130	–	–	–
Air classification			230	230	570	90	180
Secondary shredding			–	210	290	–	200
Storage bin for RDF			–	600[a]	–	–	400[b]
Rising current and heavy-media separation			140	–	170	–	–
Roll crushing and electrostatic separation of aluminium from glass			100	460[c]	110	190	–
Rod mill			–	–	–	240	–
Froth flotation of glass			–	–	180	140	–
Colour sorting of glass			180	790	250	–	–
Electrostatic separation of plastics			–	310[c]	–	–	–

(a) Capacity of bin is 900 t.
(b) Capacity of bin is 450 t.
(c) Estimated using installation factor 1.45 (Table 5.2).
(d) The complete ferrous metal extraction system, including conveyors and product baler, at the Benwell transfer station cost £260 000 (Material Recovery Ltd, 1977).

The desired products are aluminium, other non-ferrous metals and colour-sorted glass. However, the early performance of the demonstration plant was poor (Hagerty 1977). The aluminium-rich fraction from the mineral jig was only 60 per cent pure, but this has now increased to about 80 per cent (Bourcier and Dale 1978b). The clear (flint) glass was 96 per cent pure optically, but was contaminated with an excessive amount of stones and ceramics. In addition, the yield of glass was much lower than expected. About 25 per cent of the glass in the input waste was lost to the organic fraction in wet pulping. Of the glass entering the recovery process, only 46 per cent was recovered, giving an overall 35 per cent yield compared with the 50 per cent design. It is assumed here that design performance is achievable.

The Occidental process recovers aluminium and fine glass. Aluminium recovery was originally envisaged using a linear induction motor, but the Monroe County plant will use an alternative design of eddy-current separator, using permanent magnets and developed by the Raytheon Service Company. Glass separation is by froth flotation. The plant was due to start operations in 1979–80.

14.5.2. Quantitative data

Information on both of these processes is based on design estimates by the developers. Installed equipment costs for the Franklin process were estimated by Cummings (1976) as $2 million for a plant with a raw waste input of 1800 t.p.d. If a scale factor of $S = 0.8$ is assumed, together with a Lang factor $f_L = 3.1$ (equation 5.3) and an equipment installation factor $\varphi_1 = 1.45$ (equation 5.4), each of which is appropriate to a typical solids handling plant, then a 1977 capital cost of about £800 000 is estimated for a plant handling 400 t.p.d. of raw waste input. Schulz et al. (1976) gave a detailed cost estimate for the Occidental process (Table 14.3), the installed equipment cost for additional materials recovery being about $1 million for a 900 t.p.d. plant. For a 400 t.p.d. plant, this is equivalent to a total capital cost of about £700 000.

For both plants, residual ferrous metals are recovered, and it is estimated that a further 4 per cent is removed in addition to the 90 per cent removed by the primary magnetic separator. Manpower is assumed to be one man for product handling, plus two men on each of two shifts. Electricity requirements for the Occidental process are given as 8 kWh/t of input waste for aluminium separation and 3 kWh/t for glass recovery (Preston 1976). A total requirement of 12 kWh/t is assumed here in each case. Water usage is substantial for the froth flotation process, and a consumption of 0.5 m³/t is taken. A similar quantity of waste water is produced, and this is assumed to be suitable for direct discharge to sewer. Annual maintenance costs were estimated by Cummings in 1974 as 12.5 per cent and in 1976 as 8.8 per cent of delivered equipment costs, i.e. as 8.3 per cent and 7 per cent of total capital costs. A standard requirement of 0.08 I is assumed here. The residual materials in each case are landfilled, but there is an incremental saving as less residue is produced than in the basic process. However, this saving could be reversed if the residue contains much water. If it is assumed that all the glass is in the inorganic fraction and that there is no additional water in the residue, net reduction in landfill requirements are 0.05 and 0.07 t/t for the Franklin (colour sorting) and the Occidental (froth flotation) process, respectively.

14.5.3. Discussion

The standard economic analysis yields cost estimates for additional materials recovery of £2.27 ± £1.10/t of waste and £2.30 ± £0.96/t for the Franklin and the Occidental processes, respectively. The costs were effectively identical for all the conditions examined. An error range on the product prices of ± 50 per cent increased the standard deviation by about £0.1/t. For a large plant processing 1200 t of waste per day, the net cost is reduced to about £1.4/t; breakeven would then require revenues from the recovered materials about twice the base level. The overall estimates are very sensitive to those for capital cost; a 50 per cent reduction in capital would reduce the net costs by between 55 and 65 per cent, to about £1/t in the base case.

It is concluded that, on the costs and prices assumed here, the recovery of additional materials from the dense, mainly inorganic fraction separated from municipal waste is at present uneconomic. This conclusion could readily be overturned by favourable local conditions or by future developments, the factors favouring economic recovery including:

Reductions in capital cost;

Favourable local markets;

Higher concentrations of glass and non-ferrous metals in the waste stream;

Increased efficiency of separation;

A large-scale operation.

In the short term, the performance of the demonstration plants will be watched with interest to see if the technology is capable of achieving reliably the results claimed for it.

The process analysis also gives similar results for the two options; energy inputs of 230 MJ/t of untreated waste and primary energy savings from recovered materials of 1200 MJ/t, of which 950 MJ/t is attributable to aluminium, yield a net primary energy efficiency $\beta = 0.10$. Thus additional recovery of inorganic materials from municipal waste would significantly increase the contribution of a reclamation process to the overall conservation of energy and material resources.

14.6. Materials recovery from incinerator residue

In addition to magnetic separation, which is already widely practised, more comprehensive recovery of materials from incinerator residues has been explored. The unit operations and the flowsheets are similar to those for other inorganic waste fractions. The United States Bureau of Mines (USBM) process is the best documented (Sullivan and Stanczyk 1971; Fabuss, Spencer, and Schroeder 1975; Sullivan and Makar 1976), a simplified flowsheet being shown in Fig. 14.9. Preliminary separation is achieved by a trommel screen to remove massive metals, and a mineral jig to separate any remaining organic materials. The resultant fraction is crushed and screened, the oversize being processed by heavy-media separation for non-ferrous metal recovery and the undersize by froth flotation and high-intensity mag-

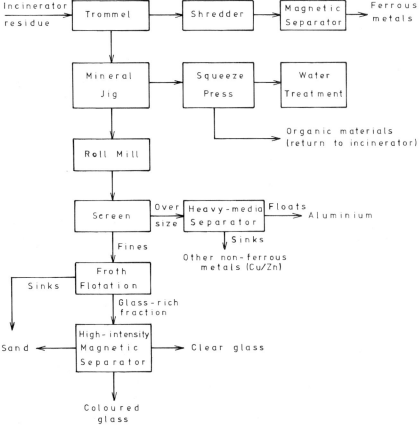

Fig. 14.9. *Materials recovery from incinerator residue.* A simplified flowsheet based on the USBM process.

netic separation for glass recovery. Pilot-scale tests gave an aluminium fraction 97 per cent pure and a non-ferrous mixture containing 55 per cent copper and 35 per cent zinc (Sullivan and Makar 1976). The French Bureau de Recherches Géologique et Minières have a similar process (Broussaud 1976). Both the Warren Spring Laboratory (Miles and Douglas 1972) and the Dutch State Mines (Absil *et al.* 1979) systems recover just the metals; the former uses a fluidized bed and the latter heavy-medium cyclones for final separation.

The USBM process is well documented and is evaluated here. Materials balance information is shown in Table 14.4, as given in the literature and as calculated here. The yield of aluminium is reduced compared with that from raw waste due to oxidation during combustion.

Table 14.4

Materials balance for incinerator residue recovery.
The USBM process is used as a model. Percentage by weight of dry residue

			Source			
	Sullivan and Stancyzk (1971)	Fabuss *et al.* (1975)	Broussaud (1976)	Theoretical[a]	Calculated here	
Product					Recovery efficiency[b]	Recovered products
Ferrous metals	30.5	14.6	15.0	25.3	0.56	14.2
Aluminium	1.6	1.25	0.4	1.7	0.50	0.8
Copper/zinc	1.2	0.63	0.4	0.3	0.67	0.2
Glass	47.5	30.0	9–18	30.0	0.70	21.0
Ash/sand	19.2	37.9	66–75	42.7[c]	–	63.8[c]
Organics	–	15.6	–	–	–	–
Total	100.0	100.0	100	100.0	–	100.0

(a) Theoretical value is calculated from waste composition in Table 1.3; the residue is assumed to be 30 per cent by weight (dry) of the original waste and to contain all the metals and glass.
(b) Recovery efficiencies from Table 14.2, except for aluminium where the yield is reduced by oxidation.
(c) Calculated by difference.

An 8 t.p.h. plant operating 2 shifts, 5 days per week is assumed to be capable of handling the residue from a 400 t.p.d. incinerator. A proposed demonstration plant at Lowell in Massachusetts was abandoned when the incinerator was closed because it could not meet improved standards for air emission. The capital cost for this 27 t.p.h. plant was estimated at $4.75 million (Fabuss *et al.* 1975), which is equivalent to a 1977 cost for an 8 t.p.h. plant of £1.1 million ($S = 0.8$). This is reduced to £1 million here to reflect the saving in magnetic separation and ash handling equipment on the incinerator.

Energy usage was given as 2.5 kWh of electricity per tonne of input waste and 1 therm of gas per tonne. Water usage and discharge to sewer after treatment may be cut by recycling to a minimum of $0.5m^3/t$. Labour requirements are estimated as for materials recovery from the inorganic fraction, at 1 man plus 2 on each of 2 shifts. It is assumed that 60 per cent of the residue after processing is given away as an aggregate, at a net disposal cost of zero, while the remaining 40 per cent (filter cake from water treatment) is disposed of to landfill. The reduction in landfill requirements is from 0.35 to 0.08 (plus flyash, say 0.02) t/t, a net saving of 0.25 t/t. No credit is taken for ferrous metals recovery as such recovery is assumed to be normal on all incinerators.

The standard economic analysis yields an incremental net cost for material recovery from incinerator residues of £2.8 ± £1.4/t of input waste. The process analysis shows an energy input of 250 MJ/t, with a saving due to the material products of 930 MJ/t, of which 680 MJ/t is attributable to aluminium. This yields an incremental net primary energy efficiency $\beta = 0.068$. This would increase the net primary energy efficiency of incineration with steam or electricity generation to $\beta = 0.60$.

By comparison with the previous section, material recovery from incinerator residue is seen to cost slightly more than that from the separated inorganic fraction of unburnt waste, with a rather lower return in terms of increased net primary energy efficiency. However, the error limits on the cost estimates show considerable overlap, so that no firm conclusion on the relative merits of the alternative approaches can be drawn.

15. REFUSE-DERIVED FUELS

15.1. Introduction

The concept of selling a solid fuel produced by physical processing of municipal waste is relatively recent, dating back only to about 1970. Such a fuel is here termed a refuse-derived fuel or RDF, the term waste-derived fuel or WDF being used in a more generic sense to include *any* derived fuel, including oil, gas, steam, or electricity. However, these two terms are often used interchangeably in the literature.

Despite its recent development, a great many processes have already been proposed for RDF production and use. Several commercial and demonstration plants are in operation, both in the USA and in Europe. In most cases, the sale of RDF for use as a supplementary fuel to replace coal in conventional industrial or power station boilers is envisaged. Many of the boilers are quite old, using chain grates which are suited to handling high-ash fuels. Many process variations are designed to upgrade the fuel so that wider markets become available. An attractive use for RDF is as a supplementary fuel in a cement kiln; the high ash content is here a positive advantage as it forms part of the final product. Processes which envisage the combustion of RDF in special purpose facilities, rather than as a supplementary fuel in existing facilities, are examined in the next chapter.

In Section 14.2, three alternative general methods were distinguished for the primary separation of municipal waste into its organic and inorganic components. All three methods may be adapted to RDF production:

(a) Wet pulverization produces a fairly fine, fibrous organic fraction, contaminated with glass. The moisture content is higher than for the input waste, typically in the range 40–60 per cent. The manufacturers of the Dano pulverizer in the UK have been carrying out tests using an oily sludge rather than water as the wetting agent, the product being termed variously 'enriched-pulverized refuse' and 'multi-source fuel'. Preliminary results and burning trials were quite promising (Jones 1977; Tottman, Tittle, and Jones 1979), and it is understood that development work is continuing.

(b) Wet pulping produces a water slurry containing the organic fraction. Either the rejects from fibre recovery or the entire organic process stream may be dewatered and sold as an RDF. Various options are examined in Chapter 17.

(c) Dry separation may be adapted to produce various qualities of RDF, depending primarily on the extent of separation of inorganic materials and of the putrescible components from the paper and plastics in the organic fraction. The options for RDF production examined in this chapter are all based on dry separation.

15.2. An overview of RDF processes

15.2.1. RDF production

The simplest process for the production of an RDF by dry separation involves pulverization of the waste in a hammermill and the separation of ferrous metals by magnetic extraction. The particle size range required may be more stringent than when the pulverized waste is intended for landfill. If this is the case, the pulverizer may be designed to produce a finer product, or alternatively the product may be screened and the oversize material pulverized again.

The first RDF demonstration plant at St. Louis in Missouri originally produced a simple pulverized product, but problems were encountered both with excessive wear in the system feeding RDF into the boiler and with overloading of the bottom ash hoppers; an air-classifier was added to the separation system to overcome these problems (Bendersky, Shannon, Gorman, Park, and Holloway 1975).

A similar process is, however, being developed in Britain by Imperial Metal Industries (IMI) in co-operation with the West Midlands County Council; preliminary operating experience was reported as being very encouraging (Marshall and Harvey 1977; Marshall 1978). The IMI process is based on a proprietary feed system and the use of stoker fired chain-grate boilers with extensive ash handling facilities.

The Portland cement manufacturers Blue Circle have pioneered the use of twice-pulverized waste, with a particle size less than 50 mm, as a supplementary fuel in cement kilns. A one-year trial was completed successfully and further investment in the process has been made.

Most of the proposed systems for RDF production include air classification to separate heavy inorganic components from the now largely organic RDF. The incorporation of one or more screens early in the flowsheet can be used either to avoid the need for air classification of the entire process stream (e.g. Fig. 14.1(c)), or to remove the putrescible materials before air classification, so that the RDF contains mainly paper and plastics (Figs 14.1(d), (e), (f)). In some cases, bundled newspapers and cardboard are hand-picked from the incoming waste. In general, American processes incorporate most organics into the RDF, while those developed in Europe separate mainly paper and plastics. A typical European RDF is shown in Fig. 15.1(a). Significant differences between processes may also stem from the extent of materials recovery from the inorganic fraction and also of RDF upgrading.

15.2.2. Upgrading the product

Various methods may be used to upgrade the RDF product:

(a) Secondary shredding of the RDF is common, with the final particle size depending on user requirements. Suspension firing of the RDF in a pulverized-coal boiler requires a particle size less than 30 mm, while some applications may require particle sizes about 15 mm. These products are often referred to as fluff-RDF (Fig. 15.1(b)).

(b) Storage of RDF is a serious problem, particularly if the putrescible fraction is contained in the fuel. Mechanical retrieval of the RDF from a storage bin is necessary, using for example a live-bottom or live-centre bin (Fisher 1976). Such bins are both very expensive and seem to require further development, at least for use with the cruder fuels (Hagerty 1977). The simplest alternative is to bale the waste. Once again, available baling machines need to be adapted to the particular RDF product.

(c) A rather more satisfactory solution to RDF storage is the formation of fuel pellets or briquettes (Fig. 15.1(c)). However, for RDF these processes are relatively untried and further development work is required (Wogrolly 1975; Cohen and Parrish 1976). A series of tests using animal feed pelletizing equipment have been conducted by the NCRR (Alter and Arnold 1978). A proprietary process to produce fuel pellets has been developed by Bühler-Miag and Asthall Holdings, and is being demonstrated at the Eastbourne pulverizer plant in England (Stuart 1979; Wyss 1979). Pelletizers are incorporated in the two UK demonstrations plants at Doncaster and Tyne and Wear (Section 15.5; Skitt 1979).

(d) A proprietary process has been developed to produce a powder-RDF, with particle size less than 1 mm. The system utilizes a chemical embrittling agent prior to size reduction in a ballmill. The powder-RDF is claimed to be both stable in storage and suitable for co-firing with heavy fuel oil.

15.2.3. RDF utilization

Compared with the information on RDF production, comparatively little has yet been published on its utilization. Considerable capital investment will be required for RDF receiving, storing, and firing facilities, while additional ash handling and gas cleaning equipment may be necessary. The demonstration plant at St. Louis was studied in detail; little change occurred in emissions to air (Kilgroe, Shannon, and Gorman 1975), but bottom ash generation was significantly increased (Fiscus, Gorman, and Kilgoe 1976).

Fig. 15.1. *European refuse-derived fuels.* These products consist mainly of paper and plastics. (a) shows the air classifier light fraction at Doncaster. (b) shows the RDF from the Eastbourne plant after secondary shredding, while (c) shows the same product after pelletization. (Photo (a) courtesy South Yorkshire County Council; photos (b) and (c) courtesy Buhler-Miag (England) Ltd.)

Extensive tests on boiler corrosion and deposits from firing solid waste, either alone in an incinerator (Krause, Vaughan, and Miller 1973, 1974; Krause, Vaughan, and Boyd 1975) or as a supplementary fuel in a coal-fired power station (Krause, Vaughan, and Boyd 1976; Krause, Vaughan, Cover, Boyd, and Oberacker 1977) have been performed by the Battelle Columbus Laboratory in conjunction with the US Environmental Protection Agency. The results show that the initial corrosion rate of a typical boiler tube alloy is similar in co-firing to that when coal is burnt alone, but is an order of magnitude less than when waste is burnt alone. Chloride corrosion from the RDF may be offset by co-firing with high-sulphur coal, the RDF also tending to reduce sulphur dioxide emissions both by dilution and by sulphate particulate formation. Further tests are being performed on long-term corrosion rates.

Preliminary results of a series of trials on the co-firing of pelletized RDF with coal in a spreader-stoker, semi-suspension fired boiler are encouraging. At coal:RDF ratios up to 1:2 by volume, minor adjustments allowed satisfactory performance of the boilers. Both fly ash and bottom ash generation increased significantly, but little change occurred either in emissions to air or in rates of corrosion (Degler and Wiles 1979).

The first two years of operation of the Ames RDF plant have been documented (Joensen *et al*. 1979). Problems were encountered with excessive bottom ash generation, but boiler efficiency, particulate and gaseous emissions, and corrosion rates were all little changed.

Further experience of satisfactory performance over an extended period is necessary before the doubts of potential users of RDF can be overcome. The largest potential market in Britain is provided by the Central Electricity Generating Board; their reaction is guarded, as the most suitable plants are also the least efficient (Millbank 1976*e*).

15.2.4. RDF options

The remainder of this chapter examines in more detail five alternatives for the production and use of RDF; namely:

A typical American system;

The production of powder RDF;

A typical European process, the RDF consisting mainly of paper and plastics;

A system producing a simple pulverized fuel;

A system producing pulverized fuel for firing in a cement kiln.

15.3. American RDF

15.3.1. Background

The production of RDF for sale as a supplementary boiler fuel was pioneered in the USA. Many variations have been proposed, but the basic flowsheet is that of Fig. 5.2 (see also Section 14.2 and Figs 14.1(a) and (b)). The distinctive feature is that the RDF contains most of the organic materials, including the putrescible fraction. This product is here termed 'American RDF'. Useful listings of alternative processes are those of the National Center for Resource Recovery (1974*a*), of Jackson (1974), and of the Bechtel Corporation (1975), while a bibliography has been compiled by Ball, Beltz, Smith, Engdahl, and Reid (1978).

Operating experience is limited largely to that from the demonstration plant at St. Louis and from the first small commercial plant at Ames in Iowa, which began production in November 1975. The information available at the end of 1980 on 11 plants, which were at some stage of operation, or of initial start-up, is summarized in Table 15.1. All the plants have experienced some sort of teething problems, as one might expect for a new technology. Among these, the following are worth noting:

(a) Several plants are unable to market the RDF;

(b) Most plants have had major problems in handling and conveying materials.

Table 15.1

Plants for the production of American R D F.
Principal sources of information: Schwegler (1978), Hagerty (1977), Alvarez (1979), Abert (1979a), updated by numerous private communications during a visit to the USA in October, 1980.

Location	Design capacity (t.p.d.)	Status	Comments
Ames, Iowa	180	Operational since 1975	Problems encountered with dust control, R D F storage, and excessive ash production in boilers. Disc screens installed to remove fine materials from R D F to overcome boiler slagging problems. New dump-grate installed in suspension fired boiler. Floor of R D F storage bin replaced twice. Dust collection system added.
Baltimore County, Maryland	350–1450	Operational since 1976	Processed about 600 t.p.d. in 1977–8. No market has been found for R D F (Willey and Bassin 1978).
Chicago, Illinois	900	Closed	Start-up problems in the air-lock system and in meeting particle size requirements for the product R D F. Abandoned within 1 year.
Lane County, Oregon	450	Start-up began in 1978	Start-up problems with uneven feed to the air classifier and plugging in conveyors from the classifier to storage hoppers. No market has yet been found for R D F. Dust control facilities added. Explosion in Nov. 1979.
Madison Wisconsin	360	Operational since summer 1980	Unique flowsheet producing higher quality R D F (p 272). Working satisfactorily at design capacity.
Milwaukee, Wisconsin	1450	Start-up began in 1977	Start-up problems restricting capacity to about 50 per cent design. Rotary disc screen installed to remove fines from R D F in attempt to eliminate boiler slagging problems. Conveyor belts also widened to increase capacity. Market for R D F insufficient.
Monroe County, New York	1800	Start-up began in 1979	Problems with materials handling and conveying at many points in the complete flowsheet.
New Orleans, Louisiana	600	Start-up began in 1978	Designed for materials recovery. No market for R D F. Materials handling problems.
Niagara Falls, New York	1800–2700	Start-up began in 1980	Owned by Hooker Chemical Corporation. Project includes two new boilers to produce electricity for use on site.
St. Louis, Missouri	180	Operation ceased	Demonstration project. Proposed 7200 t.p.d. scheme abandoned by Union Electric. One conclusion was need for dust control equipment.
Tacoma, Washington	450	Operational since 1979	Developed from existing pulverization transfer station. No market as yet for R D F.

(c) The RDF has a high ash content and may overload ash handling facilities on suspension fired boilers;

(d) The incorporation of fine materials in the RDF may cause boiler slagging problems. At least two facilities have added a screen to remove such materials from the product;

(e) The RDF may cause problems in storage;

(f) Dust control equipment must be provided.

Any firm assessment of this process for resource recovery from solid waste must await at least a few years' operating experience from these early facilities.

15.3.2. Capital costs

The difficulties of estimating the capital costs of American RDF production plants were discussed in some detail in Section 5.4 as an example of the general problem for any new technology. Some of the capital cost estimates found in the literature have been summarized in Table 15.2. The estimates are divided into those from general literature studies and those from design studies for particular planned or operating plants. The many designs have been classified into two broad categories, the basic process recovering RDF and ferrous metals, while additional materials recovery includes glass and/or non-ferrous metals.

Table 15.2

Capital cost estimates for American RDF production plants.

Study group or plant location	Reference	Approximate date of estimate	Number[a] of process lines	Design capacity[a] t.p.d.	Design capacity[a] t.p.h.	Basic process[b] ($ million 1977)	Additional materials recovery[c] ($ million 1977)	Common basis[d] (£ million 1977)
Part A: Literature Studies								
National Centre for Resource Recovery (NCRR)	NCRR (1974c)	1974	1	900	57	–	7.4	1.9
	Smith (1975)	Jan 1974				7.1	–	
	Stallings (1974)	1974				5.8	8.4	
Midwest Research Institute (MRI)	MRI (1973)	1971	1	900	57	11.9	–	4.4
	MRI (1975)	Dec 1973				15.6	–	
	Smith (1975)	Jan 1974				15.9	–	
	Franklin et al. 1974	1974				–	18.8	
General Electric Company (GEC)	GEC (1973a)	1972	2	900	57	–	20.5	5.3
	GEC (1973b)	1973				–	25.0	
	Smith (1975)	Jan 1974				19.2	–	
United States Bureau of Mines (USBM)	Phillips (1977)	Apr 1976	1	900	64	–	15.9	3.3
Combustion Power Company	GEC (1973a)	1972	3	900	n.a.	–	5.2	1.2

Table 15.2—cont.

Study group or plant location	Reference	Approximate date of estimate	Number of process lines	Design capacity t.p.d.	t.p.h.	Basic process[b] ($ million 1977)	Additional materials recovery[c] ($ million 1977)	Common basis[d] (£ million 1977)
Smith, 'plant X'	Smith (1975)	Jan 1974	2	1450	91	21.2	27.4	4.0
GEC, St. Louis-type plant	GEC (1973a)	1973	3	900	n.a.	16.4	–	4.5
Columbia University	Schulz (1973)	1973	n.a.	1400	n.a.	13.1	–	4.4
	Schulz (1975)	1974	n.a.	900	42	12.6	14.6	
	Schulz et al. (1976)	1975	n.a.	900	42	11.7	–	
Bechtel Corporation	(1975)	1974	2	900	91	–	14.6	2.3
Stuckenbruck and King	(1977)	Jan 1976	1	730	45	–	7.8	2.2
Bidwell and Mason	(1975)	1975	n.a.	1500	n.a.	£3.1	–	1.1
Horner and Shifrin	(1973)	1971	2	1330	83	12.3	–	2.5
Schroeder and Fabuss	(1978)	1977	1	900	64	15.0	–	3.7
Part B: Planned or operating plants[e]								
Albany, New York	Hopper (1975)	1974	n.a.	540	n.a.	8.0	–	3.3
Ames, Iowa*	Funk and Chantland (1975)	1974	1	180	45	–	7.4	2.0
Baltimore County, Maryland*	McKewen (1976)	Oct 1975	2	1450	100	11.1	–	2.0
Bridgeport, Connecticut	Hopper (1975) NCRR (1976) Morey et al. (1976)	1974	n.a.	1400–1600	n.a.	–	38.4	5.9
Chicago, Illinois	NCRR (1976) Suloway (1977)	1975	2	900	145	21.4	–	2.8
East Bridgewater, Massachusetts*	NCRR (1976)	1973	n.a.	450	n.a.	15.5	–	7.4
Housatonic Valley, Connecticut	Hopper (1975)	1974	n.a.	1360	n.a.	29.1	–	5.8
Madison, Wisconsin*	Hopper (1975)	1974	n.a.	180	n.a.	4.6	–	4.7
Milwaukee, Wisconsin*	Bielicki (1977)	1975	2	1450	90	20.2	–	3.8
Monroe County, New York*	Carlson et al. (1976)	1975	n.a.	1800	125	–	33.7	4.1
Montgomery County, Maryland	Hopper (1975)	1974	n.a.	1100	n.a.	21.2	–	5.0
Montgomery County, Ohio	Hopper (1975)	1974	n.a.	550	n.a.	–	19.9	6.8
New Britain, Connecticut	Hopper (1975)	1974	n.a.	1600	n.a.	29.1	–	5.0
St. Louis, Missouri	Klumb (1976)	1974	n.a.	7200	n.a.	–	93.0	4.9

Summary of the common-basis costs		Number of points	Mean cost (£m)	Standard deviation (£m)
	Part A	13	3.1	1.4
	Part B	14	4.5	1.7
	Part A + B	27	3.8	1.7

(a) n.a. not available.
(b) Basic process recovers ferrous metals and RDF.
(c) Additional materials recovery includes glass and/or non-ferrous metals.
(d) Common basis of 25 t.p.h. (or 400 t.p.d.) for the basic process. Additional materials recovery assumed to increase cost by 25 per cent. Adjustment of capacity uses equation 5.5, $S = 0.8$. For details of transfer costs from \$ to £, see Section 10.2.2.
(e) Operating plants marked with an asterisk. Some of the projects have not progressed beyond the planning stage, while in others the eventual plant built does not produce American RDF.

To compare the estimates, correction is made to a 400 t.p.d. (25 t.p.h.) plant using the basic process. From the literature studies a relative cost ratio of 1.2 is deduced for additional materials recovery compared with the basic process. Evidence for economy of scale is sparse, with a value of $S = 0.8$ for a typical solids handling process being the best guide for all the RDF processes; this is much higher than the 0.70 used by the Midwest Research Institute (1973) or the 0.60 used by Schulz *et al.* (1976). Schroeder and Fabuss (1978) use a value of 0.47 up to 900 t.p.d. and 1.0 for larger plants; however, the lower value contradicts their quoted range of scale factors for mechanical handling plants of 0.7–0.9. The sharp transition at 900 t.p.d. is because this is assumed to be the upper limit for a single process line; however, operating experience at throughputs about 60 t.p.h. (2-shift operation) is very limited, and in practice even relatively small plants will usually have parallel process lines to allow some redundancy.

The normalized cost estimates in Table 15.2 show a wide range, from £1–£7.4 million, with a mean of £3.8 million and a standard deviation of £1.7 million. The estimates from literature studies are significantly lower than those for planned or operating plants. A cost of £3.8 million for the basic process is assumed here, and error ranges of $\times \atop \div 1.4$ and $\times \atop \div 2.0$ are explored.

15.3.3. Other data

Information on the efficiency of RDF production and use, and on electricity consumption, is summarized in Table 15.3. It is estimated here that the RDF represents 70 per cent by weight and 85 per cent by heat content of the input waste. The heat content of the RDF is thus about 12 MJ/kg. Materials recovery, including ferrous metals, reduces the residual fraction from 30 per cent by weight. RDF efficiency in use is quoted between 68 and 100 per cent. A value of 69 per cent overall efficiency of steam generation (e_4 in Table E.5) is estimated here, which may be compared with an efficiency from coal of 81 per cent (Table 8.3(b)), giving a substitution equivalence of 1.17. The price paid for RDF is based on the energy-specific price of coal, adjusted for the substitution equivalence and for the additional costs of using RDF. Thus the costs of transport, of handling, storage, and firing at the boiler plant, and of additional ash disposal are not calculated explicitly, but are allowed for by a 30 per cent reduction in the revenue expected. The overall revenue is thus $70/1.17 = 60$ per cent that of coal, i.e. £0.36/GJ.

Electricity usage in the process depends on the particle size of the RDF (Fig. 12.10). An average size of 15–20 mm requires perhaps 50–60 kWh/t for size reduction. An overall consumption of 65 kWh/t is assumed here.

Labour requirements are probably similar to incineration on a shift basis. Thus, 4 men plus 6 shift are assumed here, giving a complement of 16 men

Table 15.3

American RDF production efficiency and electricity consumption data

Source	Reference	RDF production % by weight	RDF production % by heat content	RDF efficiency in use%	Electricity usage (kW/t) RDF and ferrous metals	Electricity usage (kW/t) RDF and additional materials recovery
St. Louis	Shannon et al. (1975)	79.8	82.3	–	33	–
demonstration plant	Bendersky et al. (1975)	77.0	79.6	<79	–	–
	Kilgroe et al. (1976)	–	–	68–80	–	–
	Fiscus et al. (1977)	80.6	85	–	29	–
Ames, Iowa plant	Joensen et al. (1979)	84 (78)*	–	–	52	–
Continental Can Combustion	Smith and von Steiger (1979)	77	95.5	74	14	–
Engineering process		55	73	–	–	–
Madison plant	private communication					
Monroe County plant	Schroeder (1979)	65–70	–	–	–	–
American Can (Americology) process	Bielicki (1977)	65.0	–	–	–	–
Union Electric process	Klumb (1976)	80	–	–	–	–
General Electric Company study	(1973a)	63.2	86.6	–	83	–
Midwest Research Institute	(1973)	–	100.0	–	–	–
Bechtel Corporation	(1975)	77.5	92.8	–	–	84
Columbia University	Schulz (1975)	–	–	–	61	83
	Schulz et al. (1976)	72.5	86.2	–	60	–
Stuckenbruck and King	(1977)	–	100.0	–	–	165
Hecklinger	(1976)	–	94.7	69.7	33	–
Eggen and Kraatz	(1974)	–	69.0	69.4	–	–
Pfeffer	(1978)	57	–	–	–	–
Used in this work		70	85	69	65	77

*After retrofitting of disc screens to remove fines from the RDF.

for 2-shift operation. Maintenance costs are difficult to assess owing to the lack of operating experience. The two pulverizers will have high maintenance requirements, while other equipment may be less troublesome once any teething problems have been overcome. A fairly optimistic value of 0.08 I is assumed for 2-shift operation, at a utilization of 75 per cent; this contrasts sharply with the value of 0.027 I used by Schulz et al. (1976) for a plant operating continuously with 90 per cent availability, or with the 0.05 I used by Schroeder and Fabuss (1978) for a two-shift operation at 90 per cent utilization.

15.3.4. Discussion

The standard economic analysis yields a mean cost for production of American RDF of £14.8/t, with a 95 per cent confidence interval of ± £5.0/t. If the accuracy of the capital cost estimate (£3.8 million) decreases from $\overset{\times}{\div}$ 1.4 to $\overset{\times}{\div}$ 2.0, which is more in line with the range in Table 15.2, then the cost is £15.6 ± 11.0/t (Table A.10). The overall net cost is also very sensitive to the estimate of capital, a reduction from £3.8 million to, say, £2.5 million reducing the mean cost by about £5/t. Under some conditions American RDF production is competitive with landfill via rail haul or baling, and a reduction in the capital cost would further increase its attractiveness.

The process analysis for American RDF is discussed in detail in Section 8.5. The worksheet in Table 8.6 shows an energy requirement of 1300 MJ/t, with a primary energy saving from RDF utilization of 7500 MJ/t and from ferrous metals of 1700 MJ/t. The net energy efficiencies are thus $\alpha = 0.62$ and $\beta = 0.79$. Additional recovery of non-ferrous metals and glass can increase β to 0.89. These efficiencies compare favourably with those of incineration with heat recovery, where $\beta = 0.54$ or 0.60.

15.4. Powder RDF (Eco-Fuel II)

15.4.1. Background

Combustion Equipment Associates and their research partners Arthur D. Little Inc. have developed a process which reduces the RDF to a fine powder known as Eco-Fuel II (Beningson, Rogers, Lamb, and Nadkarni 1975; Beningson 1979). The flowsheet has been modified considerably during development (Fig. 15.2). Production of the crude RDF is currently by initial screening, with oversize materials recycled through a flail mill, followed by magnetic separation and air classification using hot combustion gases from the process heater. The partially dried light fraction passes to a secondary trommel which removes any fine incombustible material. A proprietary inorganic chemical 'embrittling agent' is added in the trommel, the aim being to destroy the fibre strength of cellulosic materials. The treated RDF then passes to a ballmill where it is dried and fine ground at a temperature of 100–200 °C. The ballmill product is screened into three fractions, the oversize rejects passing to landfill or for aluminium recovery, the middle fraction returning to the ballmill and the fine fraction (< 1 mm) forming the product Eco-Fuel II. The process has been licensed to the German firm Mannesmann Veba Unwelttechnik (MVU); they have modified the flowsheet to be more appropriate to European refuse, replacing the ballmill by drying and fine pulverization.

The powdered fuel can be pelletized or briquetted for easier handling and storage, and may be suitable for co-firing in oil or gas fired boilers. Particle

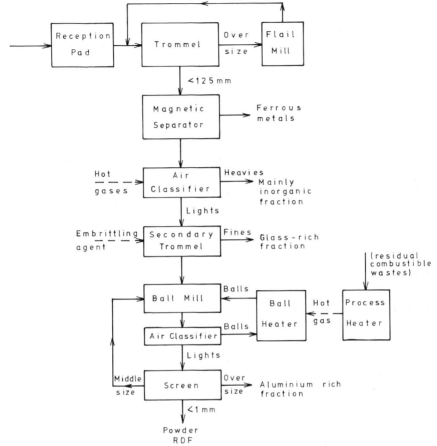

Fig. 15.2. *Powder RDF.*

size is less than 1 mm, density is about 500 kg/m³ compared with less than 100 kg/m³ for American RDF, ash content is reduced from 20 to 10 per cent, moisture content is reduced to about 2 per cent, and heat content is increased to about 16 MJ/kg.

An 1100 t.p.d. plant at East Bridgewater, Massachusetts, has been modified to produce Eco-Fuel II and performance tests were carried out in March 1979 (Beningson 1979). A 1650 t.p.d. plant at Bridgeport, Connecticut, began start-up in late 1979. A 2700 t.p.d. plant for Newark, New Jersey, is planned. Technical problems have been mainly concerned with materials handling, but financial problems threaten the future of the project.

In Europe, MVU have operated a 5 t.p.h. pilot plant. An industrial sized plant capable of handling 500 t.p.d. will be incorporated in the Ruhr Resource Recovery Centre (RZR) at Herten (Sonnenschein 1979).

15.4.2. Quantitative data

About 80 per cent of the heat content in the waste is recovered in the powder RDF, contained in about 50 per cent of the original weight. The efficiency in use of the fuel will be higher than for American RDF owing to lower moisture and ash contents, a value of 75 per cent being suggested here (compared with 69 per cent). The substitution equivalence for coal is thus $81/75 = 1.08$. The higher-grade powder RDF should also command a higher energy-specific price and an increase from 60 to 80 per cent that of coal is assumed. If the powder fuel does indeed prove to be suitable for co-firing with oil or gas, then its energy-specific value will be considerably higher than this.

Electricity usage in the process is similar to that for American RDF as the chemical treatment reduces the requirement for size reduction (Fig. 12.10), and 65 kWh/t is assumed here. Recent information confirms this value for the modified European process, but suggests that a value of 100 kWh/t may be more appropriate to the parent process. In addition, diesel fuel is used at a rate of 0.9 l/t (Beningson et al. 1975), presumably for input waste and product handling. The standard value of 0.5 l/t is used here. The nature and quantity of the inorganic chemical used is proprietary information, the only indication being that the quantity may be as low as 0.5 per cent by weight. A value of 5 kg chemical per tonne of waste is thus used here. The cost of the chemicals is difficult to assess, Schulz et al. (1976) suggesting about $0.70/t. The assumption is made that the chemicals cost the equivalent of 25 kWh/t of electricity, that is 75 p/t of waste or £150/t of chemical. The energy requirement for the chemical is guessed at 20 MJ/kg, based on data given by Smith (1969).

Capital costs for the three USA plants were given by the National Center for Resource Recovery (1978) as $10–12 million for 1100 t.p.d. at East Bridgewater, $53 million for 1650 t.p.d. at Bridgeport and either $25 million for 900 t.p.d. or $70 million for 2700 t.p.d. at Newark. The low cost for the East Bridgewater plant may be appropriate to the original design, which did not include upgrading of the RDF to Eco-Fuel II. The costs for Newark suggest a high scale factor of 0.94; however, both costs include an unspecified amount for boiler conversion which is independent of the scale of waste processing, so a lower value of $S = 0.8$ is used here. The data for Bridgeport and Newark suggest a capital cost for a 400 t.p.d. plant in 1977 of £8.9 million and £7.9 million, respectively, while that for East Bridgewater is much lower at £2.8 million. Schulz et al. (1976) used a capital cost 70 per cent higher than for American RDF, but still less than that used for many other fuel recovery options. A perhaps rather optimistic cost of £6.0 million for a 400 t.p.d. plant is assumed here, compared with £3.8 million for American RDF.

Labour requirements are assumed to be 25 per cent, or 2 per shift, greater than for American RDF, giving a complement for double-shift operation of 20 men. Maintenance costs are entirely unknown and 0.08 *I* is assumed. The products, apart from 50 per cent by weight of fuel, are ferrous metals (6.8 per cent), a residue of about 20 per cent by weight, and a discharge, mainly water vapour, to the atmosphere.

15.4.3. Discussion

The standard economic analysis suggests a mean cost for powder RDF production of £23.3/t of waste, with a 95 per cent confidence interval of ± £7.8/t. Its competitiveness is aided by low discount rates or large plants, but on the data used here, the additional investment over that for American RDF is not covered by the increased revenues from the higher-quality product. If powder RDF could be used as a substitute for heavy fuel oil rather than for coal, with an energy-specific price of, say, 80 per cent that of oil, the revenue would increase by about £6/t of waste. Thus even for an optimistic assumption, powder RDF has a higher mean net cost than American RDF, although this difference is swamped by the uncertainty in the estimates.

The process analysis shows that the energy requirements for powder RDF production are about 300 MJ/t of waste higher than for American RDF, while the primary energy saving from the RDF is increased by 200 MJ/t of waste. Thus the net energy efficiencies are reduced only marginally, with $\alpha = 0.61$ and $\beta = 0.78$. Note that this conclusion is sensitive to the energy requirement for the chemicals used.

15.5. Paper-based RDF

15.5.1. Background

Several processes under development in Europe recover an RDF that consists mainly of paper and plastics (Section 14.2; Figs 14.1(d), (e), and (f); Fig. 15.1). Some of the alternative approaches are listed in Table 15.4. About half the processes are aimed directly at the recovery of materials; in most other cases RDF is seen as an intermediate option, pending development of technologies and markets for recovering paper and plastics. In this section the two demonstration plants in England are selected as typical examples of paper-based RDF production. Although the technologies differ considerably, they are evaluated here as a single option. Sufficient quantitative information to compare the options in Table 15.4 is not yet available; hopefully, this situation will soon be remedied for the other commercially available systems, including the Fläkt and BKMI processes for paper recovery (Section 14.3.1).

Initial research and development work in the UK was performed by the Warren Spring Laboratory (Douglas and Birch 1976). A demonstration

Table 15.4

European processes for recovery of paper-based RDF and/or paper

Developer	Reference	Current status	Comments
Aachen University	Hoberg and Schulz (1977)	Pilot plant	Flowsheet similar to Fig. 14.1(f). Mixed paper and plastics product evaluated for paper recovery.
Babcock Krauss–Maffei Industrieanlagen (BKMI), W. Germany	Steier (1979)	First commercial plant at Landskrona, Sweden, 15 t.p.h. operational 1979	Process R–80. Aims at recovery of paper. Flowsheet in Fig. 14.4(a). See discussion in Section 14.3.1.
Bureau de Recherches Géologiques et Minières (BRGM), France	Clin and Gony (1979)	Pilot plant 2 t.p.h.	Revalord process. Flowsheet similar to Fig. 14.1(f). Aim is comprehensive recovery of materials.
Bühler-Miag, Switzerland	Wyss (1979) Stuart (1979)	Deomonstration plant at Eastbourne, England, 15 t.p.h. operational 1979	Compo + Pell process. Flowsheet similar to Fig. 14.1(d), with subsequent fine shredding, drying, and pelletizing of the RDF.
ENADIMSA, Spain	Cavanna et al. (1976), (1978)	Demonstration plant in Tarragona Province, 15–20 t.p.d., was planned to be operational in 1977 but not mentioned in 1978 report	Flowsheet similar to Fig. 14.1(b), but aiming at comprehensive recovery of materials. Designed for waste with high (approximately 50 per cent) putrescible organic content.
Fläkt, Sweden	Cederholm (1978) Smulders (1979)	Commercial plants at Wijster, Holland, 25 t.p.h., 1979–80; and Stockholm, Sweden, 12.5 t.p.h., 1980	Flowsheet in Fig. 14.4(b), discussion in Section 14.3.1. Aims at recovery of upgraded paper fractions.
Forni Impianti Industriali, Milan, Italy	Mantellini (1975)	Pilot plant, 10 t.p.h.	Aims at comprehensive recovery of materials.
PLM, Sweden	Hansen (1979)	Pilot plant, 10 t.p.h. Plants being offered commercially	Brini system. Flowsheet for primary separation in Fig. 14.1(e). Paper and plastic product upgraded by drying and pelletizing for use as fuel. Also evaluated for paper recovery.
Sociétè d'étude et d'ingénière (Soceting), France	Holmes (1979)	Pilot plant, 8 t.p.h.	Waste conditioned in silos and dried before being air classified. Light fraction pelletized directly for use as fuel.
TNO/Esmil–Habets, Holland	Holmes (1979) Colon (1976)	Pilot plant, 15 t.p.h.	Aims at paper fibre recovery. Product from basic flowsheet (Fig. 14.1(a)) screened and air classified again.
Tyne and Wear County Council, England	Jackson (1979)	Demonstration plant at Byker, Newcastle-upon-Tyne, 30 t.p.h., operational 1979–80.	Flowsheet in Fig. 15.3(b). Primary separation as in Fig. 14.1(d). Produces pelletized RDF. See discussion in text.
Warren Spring Laboratory, England	Douglas and Birch (1976) South Yorkshire County Council (1979)	Demonstration plant at Doncaster, 10 t.p.h., operational 1979–80.	Flowsheet of demonstration plant in Fig. 15.3(a). Primary separation similar to Fig. 14.1(f), simplified from original. Produces pelletized RDF. See discussion in text.

plant, funded partially by the Department of the Environment, has been built at Doncaster in South Yorkshire; commissioning began in September 1979 and the plant was expected to be fully operational some time in 1980. The flowsheet, shown in Fig. 15.3(a), is a somewhat simplified version of the original, but still preserves the essential features. The waste reception and feeding systems were shown in Figs 12.1 and 12.4. Primary separation of the waste uses a rotary trommel screen (Fig. 14.3) without any preliminary size reduction; a screw liberator to release waste contained in plastic or paper bags has not in fact been installed, as plastic bags are not used for refuse collection in the Doncaster area and paper bags were found to burst naturally. The intermediate fraction from the trommel screen, with a size range of 40–200 mm, is magnetically separated before air classification (Fig. 14.2). The light fraction (Fig. 15.1a) will be a largely free from putrescible organic materials, these being mainly less than 40 mm in size. The glass-rich fraction is further processed for recovery (Section 14.4.3). The oversize fraction also contains much paper (Fig. 15.4), and the recovery of this, using a laser technique, is being investigated.

A second demonstration plant in England aims to achieve a similar RDF product by a more conventional processing route (Fig. 15.3(b)). The waste is shredded coarsely in a hammermill before passing to a trommel screen to remove both under- and over-size fractions. The material between 12 and 150 mm in size is fed to a rotating cone air classifier, the light fraction again consisting mainly of paper and plastics. This plant, at Byker in Tyne and Wear, also began commissioning in 1979.

These two plants utilize rather different technologies but are viewed here as variations on a theme. The RDF product in each case will be shredded and pelletized; the performance of the pelletizing equipment and the marketability of the fuel are particular points which will be watched with considerable interest. The Doncaster plant is in some ways the more ambitious project, the flowsheet including additional recovery of glass, paper, and board, and perhaps even compost from the putrescible fraction for use in local land reclamation programmes. (Thomas 1977; South Yorkshire County Council 1979). However, these are probably best viewed at this stage as 'frills' to be developed when the principle of RDF production has been demonstrated. In the long term, either plant could be adapted to paper recovery from the paper and plastic fraction if this should prove to be a viable alternative to pelletizing for use as a fuel.

15.5.2. Quantitative data

Quantitative information for either of these plants is still rather speculative. The costs are likely to be broadly similar, so they are treated here as a single option. The only products are assumed to be a pelletized RDF, ferrous metals, and a residue for landfill.

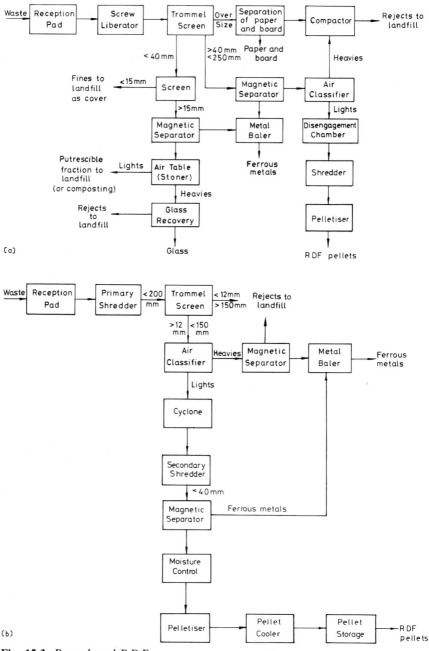

Fig. 15.3. *Paper-based RDF.*
(a) Doncaster plant
(b) Byker plant.

Fig. 15.4. *Oversize material from the trommel screen at Doncaster.* Recovery of paper from this fraction is being investigated. (Photo courtesy South Yorkshire County Council.)

The capital costs of the plants were originally estimated in 1976 at about £1.5 million each, while the final costs are about £3 million at Doncaster and £3.7 million at Byker. Millard (1977) estimated the costs at about £2.5–£3.0 million. As both demonstration plants were initially designed to handle an average 300 t.p.d. (only one line rated at 10 t.p.h. has actually been installed at Doncaster, although space has been provided for a second line), the costs may be used directly for our standard 2-line 25 t.p.h., 400 t.p.d. design capacity plant. A cost of £2.5 million at mid-1977 prices is estimated for use here. While this may be optimistic for the present plants, the capital costs of demonstration facilities always include some development costs, in this case particularly for the air classifier and fuel pelletizer. In addition, both plants include sufficient capacity in their stationary compactors to act as normal transfer stations if there should be teething problems. Thus some reduction in capital costs for future facilities could occur owing to 'learning'. It should be noted that this cost estimate of £2.5 million appears rather low compared with the £3.8 million for American RDF.

Operating labour is estimated at 4 day–men plus 6 on each of two shifts, giving a total of 16 men. Electricity usage in the original Warren Spring pilot plant was relatively low, and a figure of 35 kWh/t was used in the case study here. However, the addition of the fuel pelletizer will significantly increase consumption (Alter and Arnold 1978) and a figure of 50 kWh/t may turn out to be more appropriate at Doncaster; the use of a primary pulverizer at Byker may increase consumption still further, a figure of about 80 kWh/t perhaps being reasonable. Maintenance costs are again assumed to be 8 per cent of capital investment per annum.

Design estimates for RDF production (Millard 1977) envisaged that the Byker plant will recover about 30 per cent by weight of input waste, compared with about 20 per cent at Doncaster, the difference being due to variations in the composition of the waste in the two areas. The calorific value was estimated at about 14 MJ/kg for Byker and as high as 17 MJ/kg for Doncaster. Here, the RDF product is assumed to be 30 per cent by weight of the waste input, with a heat content of 15 MJ/kg. The RDF thus contains about 45 per cent of the heat content in the waste. The RDF is estimated to have an efficiency in use of 70 per cent, giving a substitution equivalence of 1.15 when compared with coal, and an energy-specific value 70 per cent that of coal (these values compare to an efficiency in use of 69 per cent and an energy-specific value 60 per cent that of coal for American RDF).

Recovery of 6.8 per cent by weight of ferrous metals leaves a balance of 63 per cent of the waste for landfill disposal. This residue is assumed to have similar transport costs but higher landfill costs than other dense but more inert residues; the landfill cost is 70 per cent that of untreated waste and the energy requirement is 100 MJ/t.

15.5.3. Discussion

The standard economic analysis based on this information yields an overall net cost for paper-based RDF production of £11.3 ± £3.4/t of waste. This is less than the cost of landfill with rail haul or baling, and at low discount rates or for a large plant the mean cost approaches that for road transfer to a landfill at 30 km. An increase in electricity consumption from 35 to a more realistic 50–80 kWh/t would increase the mean cost to about £12–£13/t.

These costs are less than for American RDF which has a mean cost of £14.8/t. The major source of this difference is in the capital costs used. An increase in the capital cost of the paper-based RDF plant from £2.5 to £3.0 million would increase the mean cost to about £13.1/t, or at the higher electricity consumption, to £13.5–£14.5/t. It should be remembered that the 27 estimates for the cost of an American RDF plant in Table 15.2 showed a mean of £3.8 million, but also a standard deviation of £1.7 million. If the capital cost for paper-based RDF could be reduced to, say, £1.5 million, then the mean net cost, even with the higher electricity usage, would be reduced to about £10/t. This may be compared with a mean net cost of £9.4/t for transfer and road haul to a distant landfill; the difference in these mean costs is statistically insignificant.

The results of this comparative evaluation are very promising. The preliminary conclusion must be that the production of paper-based RDF is potentially able to compete in cost terms with distant landfill if suitable markets are available, although obviously the technology has yet to be proven in operation.

Process analysis shows an energy requirement for paper-based RDF of 820 MJ/t of waste, although increased electricity consumption could increase this to about 1000–1400 MJ/t. The energy savings from the RDF are only 4000 MJ/t, compared with 7500 MJ/t for American RDF, so that the net energy efficiencies are relatively low, with $\alpha = 0.32$ and $\beta = 0.49$ (increased electricity consumption would give $\alpha = 0.26$–0.30 and $\beta = 0.43$–0.47). This compares unfavourably with $\beta = 0.79$ for American RDF.

15.6. Pulverized waste as a fuel

15.6.1. Background

The simplest form of RDF is ordinary pulverized waste with only the magnetic metals removed. Pulverized waste was fired directly into power station boilers in the early stages of the St. Louis demonstration project, but was abandoned because of excessive wear in the RDF feed system to the boiler and excessive ash production. A similar concept has been developed with more success by Imperial Metal Industries (IMI) in co-operation with the West Midlands County Council (Marshall and Harvey 1977; Marshall 1978).

Waste from a transfer station is delivered to a pulverization plant near the entrance to the IMI works. The pulverized waste, with a particle size 90 per cent < 75 mm, is stored in containers and transported about 2 km to the works power plant. There it is tipped onto an inclined slat conveyor and blown through burners in the rear wall of the boiler. The proprietary feed system is a key feature of the process. Some combustion occurs in suspension, while the chain grate allows considerable time for complete burn-out of the remaining materials. This process is only applicable to chain-grate stoker fired boilers; this is a significant restriction as such units are becoming obsolete and relatively few remain, the IMI boilers dating from 1930–5. However, if such a boiler is available, then its conversion to RDF co-firing might prove an attractive alternative to its replacement with a modern boiler.

The IMI project was first conceived during 1974 and a five-year agreement with the county council was signed in 1975. The council agreed to provide up to 50 000 t of waste per annum and to make a payment of £2/t for the first 15 000 t of waste delivered in each of the first two years, all additional waste being accepted free of charge. It should be noted that the disposal cost to the council is not, however, negligible, as delivery from an existing transfer station is required, IMI being unwilling to accept delivery direct from collection vehicles. The first boiler was converted during 1975 and extensive trials and development work on the fuel feed system carried on through 1976. The second boiler was converted during 1977.

15.6.2. Quantitative data

Little quantitative information is available on the use of pulverized waste directly as a fuel. Here it is assumed that the fuel preparation costs are identical to those for pulverization in Section 12.2. Two options are evaluated in the economic analysis, differing in the assumptions made concerning the price of the fuel:

Case (a) assumes an energy-specific value 40 per cent that of coal, compared with 60 per cent for American RDF. This is perhaps optimistic.

Case (b) assumes a net price of zero, that is the pulverized fuel is provided free to the user who only pays for its transport. This may also be considered optimistic, but is probably less than the price effectively paid by IMI who run their own pulverizer. To maintain consistency in the risk analysis, the error range on the mean price of zero was taken as ± £1.6/t (in place of the assumption used elsewhere of ± 20 per cent).

The pulverized fuel contains 93 per cent of the original waste by weight; it is assumed here to contain 95 per cent of the original heat content. Eggen and Kraatz (1974) suggest that the efficiency in use of pulverized fuel is very little different from that of the higher-grade American RDF (Table E.5), although the higher ash content will increase the amount of residue for subsequent disposal. An efficiency in use of 68 per cent, compared with 69 per cent for American RDF and 70 per cent for paper-based RDF, is taken here.

15.6.3. Discussion

The results from the economic analysis show that direct use of pulverized waste as a fuel may be very competitive if its use can be shown to be technically feasible and suitable markets found. For case (a), the net cost of £4.3 ± 4.2/t is comparable to £3.8 ± 1.4/t for direct landfill at a local site, and the risk analysis shows a 40 per cent chance of achieving a lower net cost than that for landfill (Fig. 7.2.). Double-shift working of the pulverization plant reduces the cost by about £1/t, while a discount rate of 5 per cent makes single-shift pulverized fuel production the cheapest option. In case (b), with a lower price for the fuel, net costs are increased to £6.3 ± 4.4/t, which is still lower than any of the indirect landfill options.

This optimistic analysis is supported in part by the financial arrangements for the IMI project. IMI are presumably able to make a small operating profit by accepting waste free of charge and pulverizing it on site. Their pulverizer will be comparatively cheap to run, as no facilities to receive collection vehicles and no employee amenity facilities had to be provided, all the necessary services being already available on site. Even so, the price paid for the fuel is probably intermediate between cases (a) and (b) examined above. Thus one may conclude that the direct use of pulverized waste as a fuel is economically attractive, provided that (i) its technical reliability is proven and (ii) a suitable local market for the fuel can be found.

The process analysis shows that the direct use of pulverized waste as a fuel is also attractive from the viewpoint of resource and energy conservation. The energy requirement for pulverization is 420 MJ/t, and that for transport to the user about 50 MJ/t, while the primary energy savings from the fuel are about 8300 MJ/t; thus the net energy efficiencies are estimated at $\alpha = 0.78$ and $\beta = 0.95$. If the efficiency in use is indeed not increased substantially by upgrading the fuel, then the energy efficiency of the simple pulverized fuel option will be much higher than for other RDF options; $\beta = 0.95$ here, while for American RDF $\beta = 0.79$ or for paper-based RDF $\beta = 0.49$.

15.7. Cement manufacture

An interesting alternative to the use of RDF in a steam generating boiler is its use in cement manufacture. The process is particularly attractive because the ash content of the waste is incorporated in the cement product, so that little residue remains for disposal. Thus minimal pre-processing of the waste may actually be an advantage rather than a liability. The use of waste to replace up to 20 per cent of the coal or oil is likely to have only marginal effects on gaseous emissions, and cement kilns already have electrostatic precipitators and tall stacks. As cement kilns operate at about 1450 °C, there is scope for the co-combustion of some industrial, and perhaps even some hazardous, wastes.

In Britain, Blue Circle have conducted trials with municipal waste at three plants. In all cases the pulverized waste from a hammermill was screened at 50 mm, the oversize fraction (20 per cent by weight) being separated magnetically and pulverized again. Two of the trial plants, at Westbury (Knights 1976) and Shoreham (Millbank 1976a) use the wet process for cement making, with coal as the fuel. The specific energy consumption of this process is relatively high. A later series of trials, at Plymstock, aimed to establish the feasibility of the concept in a more modern oil fired dry-process kiln (Haley 1979). A full-scale processing facility was installed at the Westbury works during 1979, and a 10-year contract has been signed with the local authority for the disposal of up to 80 000 t of waste per year.

Here this process is regarded as an extension of the simple pulverized fuel option, extending the potential for marketing the product at the expense of some increase in cost. The higher capital costs for secondary pulverization may be offset in part by a higher price for the product, reflecting the lack of an ash for disposal. No separate economic analysis is attempted. Knights (1976) provided general correlations between the charges necessary to cover costs and the quantity of waste delivered to the cement works. These charges varied with the form of the delivered waste:

	50 000/annum	100 000/annum
Crude waste	£5.3/t	£2.0/t
Pulverized waste	£4.3/t	£0.6/t
Prepared waste (< 50 mm)	£1.4/t	−£1.0/t

The energy efficiency of the process may be somewhat different from that of the simple pulverized fuel. A smaller particle size is necessary, and so an increase in electricity consumption of 10 kWh/t is assumed, increasing the energy requirement by 130 MJ/t. The efficiency in use of the fuel may also increase, particularly as there is no ash loss. Such losses are between 3 and 7 per cent (Table E.5), and an increase in efficiency from 68 to 73 per cent is thus assumed here. This increases the primary energy saving from fuel use by 600 MJ/t so that the net energy efficiences are raised by 0.05 to $\alpha = 0.83$ and $\beta = 1.00$.

15.8 Summary

From this discussion of various processes for the production of a solid refuse-derived fuel to be used as a supplementary fuel, several important points deserve emphasis:

(1) All of the processes have been developed over the last 10 years and have yet to be proven in large-scale commercial use over an extended period.

(2) The choice of RDF production process must be based on a careful study of local markets for the fuel and on the composition of the local waste. Long-term contracts for the sale of the fuel should be negotiated at an early stage.

(3) The use of pulverized waste directly as a fuel, either in a chain-grate stoker fired boiler or, with some additional size reduction, in a cement kiln, appears on the information available at present to be most attractive both economically and from the viewpoint of resource conservation. Indeed, this is the only option which seems to be capable of competing in cost terms with landfill at a local site.

(4) Upgrading the RDF should be undertaken only for sound marketing reasons. The choice between American RDF, containing most of the organic fraction of the waste, and European paper-based RDF is com-

plex, and further experience is required before a judgement can be made. The paper-based RDF may have some cost advantage, while American RDF gives a higher efficiency of energy recovery. Either system may be competitive in cost terms with transfer and bulk haul to a distant landfill.

(5) Upgrading the RDF to a powder fuel appears expensive, but this is a relatively high-grade fuel and this advantage may compensate for the relative complexity of the process.

(6) Many other RDF production processes, based on dry separation, wet pulping, or wet pulverization, are under development. The most promising options in the long term may turn out to be ones which were not highlighted here.

(7) Many of the operational problems to date can be attributed to problems in the apparently simple tasks of conveying, handling, and storing materials. More development work is required in these basic areas which have hitherto tended to be taken for granted.

16. INCINERATION OF REFUSE-DERIVED FUELS

The last chapter considered various options for the production of a solid refuse-derived fuel and its use as a supplementary energy source in an industrial or utility boiler or in a cement kiln. A prepared RDF can also be incinerated in a purpose-built facility. The use of a higher-grade fuel enables more advanced incinerator technologies to be utilized than for untreated waste, but the basic disadvantage of incineration still remains—the heat is recovered as steam or electricity which must be used immediately following its generation.

Any form of RDF is suitable for incineration. Two alternative approaches are considered in this chapter, namely suspension or semi-suspension firing of RDF using furnaces designed for fuels with a moderate to low ash content, and fluidized bed combustion.

16.1. Suspension firing of RDF

16.1.1. Background

Simple incineration of untreated waste requires that the material should remain on a grate within the furnace for an extended period in order to allow burn-out of the ash. If the waste is upgraded by reduction to a smaller and more uniform particle size and by removal of most of the incombustible inorganic components, a furnace can be used in which combustion occurs mainly in suspension above the grate. Waste with a maximum particle size of 100 mm may be burnt by semi-suspension (spreader-stoker) firing, in which about 20–40 per cent of the fuel is consumed on the grate. Furnaces of this type are used with low-grade fuels such as bark or coffee grounds. Full suspension firing is used with high-grade fuels such as pulverized coal; as almost all the combustion occurs in suspension, only a small grate is provided. Maximum particle size for suspension firing is about 30 mm.

There has been little experience to date with either semi-suspension or suspension firing of prepared waste, other than as a supplementary fuel, a notable exception being the incinerator at Hamilton, Ontario. This has been burning about 500 t of shredded refuse per day in a semi-suspension fired furnace since 1972.

Two plants are currently beginning operation in the U S A. The 900 t.p.d. day plant at Akron, Ohio, will use the steam from a semi-suspension fired incinerator to serve an existing district heating and cooling scheme. The plant began commissioning in the summer of 1979 (Abert 1979a). The 680 t.p.d. plant at Albany, New York, will produce R D F and transport it about 15 km to a new semi-suspension fired incinerator, which will provide steam for heating and cooling government office buildings. The R D F is a simple pulverized fuel, with magnetic metals removed and a nominal particle size of 75 mm. Commissioning began in May 1980 (Mahoney 1978).

16.1.2. Mass burning versus suspension firing

Two papers at the same conference have compared incineration of untreated waste, sometimes referred to as mass burning (M B), with suspension firing of prepared waste (S F); the conclusions which they reached on the relative economics were exactly opposite. Cohan, Fernandes, Maguire, and Shenk (1975) assumed that the waste is burnt alone, with capital costs 30–40 per cent higher for S F than for M B, but their conclusions favoured S F as the cheaper option. Standrod and Dodt (1975) assumed that prepared waste is used with a supplementary fuel such as coal, so that only the costs attributable to waste processing are relevant for semi-suspension firing (S S F) or S F. The capital costs of M B were now the highest, but the overall costs made it the cheapest option. These two papers emphasize the care which must be taken when interpreting published cost data. In these cases sufficient information is given on the assumptions and on the breakdown of the costs to compare the evaluations in detail; small changes in the assumptions would reverse the conclusions. Here just a few assumptions are compared to clarify the relative costs of S F and M B.

Capital costs are probably higher for S F. Although requirements for ash handling and gas cleaning equipment are lower (the latter owing to the reduced ratio of excess air required), and furnace costs may also be reduced, this is more than offset by the costs of waste separation. A cost increase over a conventional steam generating incinerator of 25 per cent is assumed here, giving a capital cost for suspension firing of £8.2 million for a 16 t.p.h. plant. This estimate includes some allowance for steam distribution.

Labour requirements are assumed by Cohan et al. to be invariant, either between processes or with scale (from 700–1500 t.p.d.), while an increase of 30 per cent for S F over M B is assumed by Standrod and Dodt. Here it is assumed that 5 men on each of 2 shifts operate the preparation plant, while the incinerator shift complement is reduced from 7 to 5, giving an overall increase in complement from 32 to 34.

Energy usage is assumed by Cohan *et al.* to decrease marginally from MB to SF, while Standrod and Dodt assume a threefold increase, largely due to production of the RDF. From Fig. 12.10, size reduction of the waste to 30 mm requires about 50 kWh/t. An increase for SF over the 60 kWh/t for MB seems inevitable, and a value of 90 kWh/t is assumed here.

Maintenance requirements are assumed by Cohan *et al.* to be constant at 0.03 I, while Standrod and Dodt used 0.014 I for MB, 0.048 I for SSF, and 0.078 I for SF. Corrosion problems with the boilers may be reduced with SF, owing to the removal of metals from the waste. A maintenance requirement of 0.07 I is assumed here, based on 0.07 I for MB and 0.08 I for RDF preparation.

Residuals for disposal from MB and SF are taken to be equal, although from MB they will consist mainly of ash and from SF of inorganic rejects from separation. The ferrous metals recovered from SF will command a higher price than those from MB.

Steam generation efficiency from waste is assumed by Cohan *et al.* to be 63 per cent from MB and 74 per cent from SF, as the boilers used in the latter case are more efficient. In contrast, Standrod and Dodt assume that MB is 17 per cent more efficient than SF, because some of the heat content of the waste is lost with the inorganic fraction in SF. If 85 per cent of the heat content is in the RDF, and the steam generating efficiency is increased to 70 per cent, then the overall conversion of waste to steam is 60 per cent, the same as for MB.

16.1.3. Discussion

When the standard economic analysis is applied to these data for suspension firing of RDF, the overall net cost is estimated at £28.8 ± £10.4/t of waste. This may be compared both with £22.3 ± £8.6/t for the incineration of untreated waste with heat recovery as steam, and with £14.8 ± £5.0/t for the production of American RDF and its sale for use as a supplementary fuel. The increase in mean cost compared with direct incineration results from the additional process sophistication, which does not produce increased returns in terms of energy recovery. The overall cost is very sensitive to the estimate of capital cost; if this could be reduced to a similar figure to that for direct incineration, then the mean net cost would be reduced to about £23/t.

In comparing suspension firing with direct incineration, it must be remembered that SF is a new technology which remains to be demonstrated for wastes.

The process analysis shows an energy requirement of 2000 MJ/t of waste, an increase of 580 MJ/t over direct incineration. The energy saving from steam is unchanged, but that from more efficient recovery of ferrous metals is increased by 650 MJ/t. The net energy efficiency, α, is thus reduced from

0.44 to 0.38, while the net primary energy efficiency, β, is increased from 0.54 to 0.55.

16.2. Incinerator turbine

16.2.1. Background

An alternative method of burning prepared waste is in a fluidized bed (Section 13.2). A plant aimed at the incineration of about 350 t.p.d. of RDF, and a similar quantity of sewage sludge (20 per cent solids), in Duluth, Minnesota, began commissioning in 1979 (Huang, Sanneman, and Johnson 1979).

A novel system utilizing fluidized combustion of RDF has been under development by the Combustion Power Company in the USA since 1967. The hot gases from the incinerator are used, after cleaning, to drive a gas turbine for electricity generation (Fig. 16.1). This system is often known as the CPU-400, as 400 short tons per day is the capacity of currently available gas turbines. A 70 t.p.d. pilot plant has been operated sporadically in California since 1973.

The fluidized sand-bed is operated at 760 °C, although gas-phase combustion above the bed raises the temperature to about 850 °C. Combustion efficiency in the fluidized bed is excellent, making such incinerators well adapted to burning sludges. Thus, this system could be used to burn a

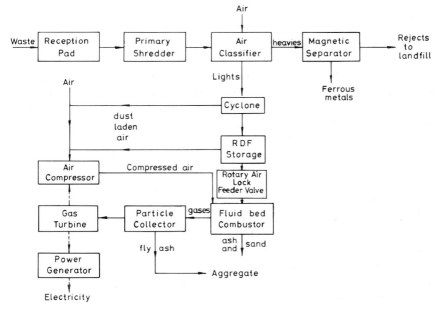

Fig. 16.1. *Combustion power incinerator turbine.*

combination of RDF and undewatered (6 per cent solids) sewage sludge. The hot gases from the reactor are used directly to drive a gas turbine which in turn drives a compressor and an electric generator. The compressor supplies air to the fluidized bed. The critical problem with the system is gas cleaning prior to the gas turbine, which is necessary to prevent corrosion. The turbines are designed for an inlet gas temperature of 950 °C, so the gases must not be cooled prior to cleaning (an electrostatic precipitator requires a temperature of about 300 °C). The original design used cyclone separators, but these did not perform adequately, and were replaced with a moving granular bed filter (R. A. Chapman 1975). Attention is now being concentrated on developing this filter for advanced coal burning processes, and work on the system as a waste disposal option has been suspended (Gage and Chapman 1977).

16.2.2. Quantitative information

Information is limited to results from pilot study tests (Chapman and Wocasek 1974; R. A. Chapman 1975) and some literature evaluations (Bechtel Corporation 1975; Schulz et al. 1976). Data are summarized in Table 16.1, together with those assumed here. The American feedstock is assumed to contain 70 per cent by weight of the input waste; of this fuel some 20 per cent is carried over by the gases from the reactor. It is claimed that no sand needs to be added to the fluid bed, as equilibrium is attained with ash from the waste. The ash is assumed to be given away for use as an aggregate. Overall efficiency of the process, as (heat content of electricity)/(heat content of waste) is 16 per cent, which compares with the 18 per cent expected from conventional incineration and subsequent electricity generation. The evaluation uses a net efficiency of 12.6 per cent (350 kWh/t) after supply of process requirements of 100 kWh/t, with a residual electrical usage of 9 kWh/t to allow for other utilities. Capital costs are claimed to be of the same order as for incineration with steam generation, and £7.0 million $\times \atop =$ 1.4 is used here. The waste preparation plant operates 2 shifts, while the reactor/turbine runs continuously. The reactor system is of modular design, with a maximum module size of 360 t.p.d., and thus a high scale factor of, say, $S = 0.95$. For the overall process, including waste preparation with a scale factor about 0.8, $S = 0.9$ is assumed. Labour requirements are assumed to be the same as for suspension firing of RDF. Maintenance costs are expected to be high; Schulz et al. (1976) take a value of 0.06 I, compared with 0.027 I for RDF production or 0.037 I for incineration with steam generation. A factor of 0.10 I is assumed here.

16.2.3. Discussion

The standard economic analysis shows that the incinerator turbine has an overall net cost of £24.7 ± £10.0/t, compared with conventional incineration with electricity generation which has a net cost of £23.6 ± £10.0/t. The lower generation efficiency is offset by the claimed reduction in capital cost. This relatively promising result must be regarded with some scepticism as the technology remains to be demonstrated. The incentive for further development work is limited as the process does not seem to offer any advantage over conventional incineration with electricity generation.

The process analysis gives an energy requirement of 2100 MJ/t, an increase of 330 MJ/t over incineration. The energy savings implied by electricity production are reduced by 670 MJ/t, while those from ferrous metal and aggregate recovery are increased by 660 MJ/t. Thus the net energy efficiencies α and β are both reduced, with values of 0.32 and 0.49, respectively, compared with 0.42 and 0.53 for incineration.

Table 16.1
The Combustion Power incinerator turbine

Item of data	Bechtel 1975	Schulz et al. 1976	Gage and Chapman 1977	Assumed here
Material balance (kg/t of waste):				
Ferrous metals	67	67		68
Aluminium	6	5	122	–
Rejects to landfill	152	50		232
Ash and sand	150	200	163	150
Exhaust gases	625	675	725	550
Energy balance (kWh/t):				
Electricity used	85	110	–	100
Electricity generated	820	489	–	450
Net generation	735	379	–	350
Captial cost (£ million 1977):				
900 t.p.d.	16.9	13.5	–	–
400 t.p.d.	8.1	6.5	–	7.0
Number of men:				
900 t.p.d.	52	46	–	
400 t.p.d.				30
Maintenance	0.06I	0.06I	–	0.10I

17. WET PULPING

17.1. Introduction

Wet pulping is one of the three basic alternatives for primary separation of waste into its organic and inorganic components (Section 14.2). The organic fraction is produced as an aqueous slurry containing about 3–7 per cent solids. As the utilization of this material presents rather different problems, and opportunities, from those associated with a solid refuse-derived fuel from dry separation, the various processes based on wet pulping are considered in a separate chapter.

Wet pulping has been developed in the USA, largely by the Black-Clawson Company, a subsidiary of Parsons and Whittemore Inc. The process is based on technology widely used in the paper industry. A demonstration plant at Franklin in Ohio operated for several years from 1971, processing up to 45 t of waste in an 8-hour day.

A simplified flow diagram of the Franklin plant is shown in Fig. 17.1. The waste is fed as a wet slurry (about 3–10 per cent solids) into the 'hydra-pulper'. A segmented blade rotates at very high speed, reducing most of the organic materials to a fine pulp and shattering glass. The processed waste passes out of the bottom of the pulper and into a cyclone, which removes most of the glass and other grit; the non-pulpable or friable materials are rejected ballistically by the rotating blade and are removed from the periphery of the hydrapulper drum.

In the Franklin plant, the slurry from the hydrapulper cyclone (3 per cent solids) is fed to a fibre recovery system, where larger particles (2 mm) are screened in a selectifier, further grit is removed by centrifugal cleaners, and the very short fibres are taken out by a run-down screen. The resultant fibre product is dewatered to about 15–20 per cent solids in a hydradenser screw press, and then to about 45–50 per cent solids in a cone press. Fibre recovery is about 45 per cent of the paper content of the waste (see Table 14.2), although the product is contaminated with oil, grease, and bacteria. The rejects from the fibre recovery system are similarly dewatered, sewage sludge being added before the second dewatering (cone press) stage. The resultant wet RDF is incinerated in a fluidized bed with no heat recovery.

Since the Franklin plant began operating in 1971, the developers have

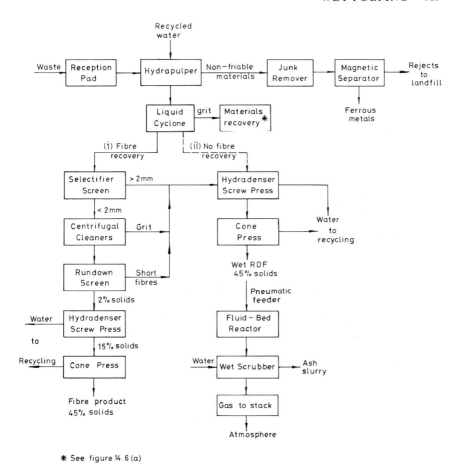

* See figure 14.6 (a)

Fig. 17.1. *Wet pulping.* Based on the flowsheet used at Franklin (Systech 1975).

switched their attention from fibre to energy recovery. The fibre recovery system is bypassed, the whole cyclone process stream being dewatered by a screw press and then a cone press. No sewage sludge addition is suggested. The resultant wet RDF has a moisture content of about 50 per cent.

The prospects for selling this fuel directly appear to be poor as a special boiler is required. It is suggested rather that it is either incinerated on site, or upgraded by drying. An 1800 t.p.d. plant has been built at Hempstead, New York, with a specially designed semi-suspension fired moving-grate furnace to raise steam for electricity generation (Landman and Darmstadt 1975). This plant began commissioning in 1978 but was closed during 1980 following con-tractual, political, and operational problems. A similar 2700 t.p.d. plant is planned for Dade County, Florida. In Japan, an adaptation of a bark boiler, with a water-cooled pinhole grate, has been in use at Ryusenen since

1975 (Narisoko and Kanai 1976). A three-stage rotary drying process has also been proposed, to reduce the moisture content of the fuel to 20 per cent or less. This product, known as wet-pulped fibrous fuel No. 2, may be pulverized and pelletized, is more homogeneous than American RDF, and is similar in quality to powder RDF (Schulz *et al.* 1976). However, no commercial plant to produce this dried RDF has yet been constructed.

17.2. Information from the Franklin demonstration plant

The Franklin demonstration plant has been well documented, with an excellent technical, environmental, and economic evaluation of its performance from 1971 to 1974 by the Systems Technology Corporation (Systech) (1975), in addition to earlier papers (Neff 1972; Kohlepp 1974) and reports on the materials recovery plant (see Section 14.5; Cummings 1974, 1976). Some of the information in the Systech report is summarized in Table 17.1. The economic evaluation was based on physical data determined at Franklin and used to scale the plant up to 450 and 900 t per 20-hour working day. The smaller plant is assumed to be equivalent to the standard 400 t per 16-hour day plant studied here. Further increase in capacity requires duplication of equipment; scale factors derived from the capital costs of each sub-system are 0.9. Independently calculated scale factors for operating costs also average 0.90 for the plant, although for sub-systems the range is from 0.53 to 1.0. Values of S quoted elsewhere include 0.72 (Midwest Research Institute 1973) and 0.75 (Schulz *et al.* 1976).

The sub-systems identified in Table 17.1 are not independent. The dewatering of the rejects from fibre recovering was included with pulping and separation in the economic (but not in the technical) evaluation, in order to facilitate analysis of the RDF or heat recovery options. If fibre recovery is removed, the throughput of both the dewatering and incineration sections will increase, thus increasing electricity consumption. Fuel usage is primarily for the front-end loader on the waste reception pad; the value derived at Franklin of about 0.5 l/t has been used throughout this study. Some fuel usage will also be necessary for reheating the reactor, but this should be minimized by continuous operation. However, continuous operation is inconsistent with the low labour requirement for incineration. A total labour force of 12 also appears low. Water usage and water treatment requirements were high at Franklin, owing to the integration of the plant with a neighbouring water treatment plant. When fibre recovery is not in operation, a closed loop operation is possible with no discharge of water, except for the ash slurry from the wet scrubber on the incinerator. The one test of such operation took 10 days to reach equilibrium; recycling of the process water to the hydrapulper increased the slurry from 3 to 7 per cent solids, and raised the solids content of the RDF produced to 50 per cent.

Table 17.1
Wet pulping of solid waste
(data from Systech (1975))

Item	Units	Sub-system						Total plant
		Waste reception	Pulping	Separation	Dewatering	Incineration	Fibre recovery	
Capital cost, 450 t.p.d. 22.5 t.p.h.	$ million, 1977	1.46		5.68		4.36	2.53	14.0
Operating Labour (450 t.p.d. 260 day/a)	number of men	2		8.25		0.25	1.5	12
Fuel usage	l/t	0.58		0		(0)	0	0.58
Electricity consumption	kWh/t	0	32	62		62	12	168
Materials balance								
Organics in slurry	Dry weight kg/input tonne of waste (29% moisture)		434		237		256	–
To materials recovery			107					107
Ferrous metals			68					68
Reclaimed fibre							121	121
Waste with fibre							17	17
Rejects to landfill		53	44					97
Waste to water					19	8	40	67
(Biological oxygen demand)				(19)		(6)	(53)	(72)
(Suspended solids)				(21)			(90)	(118)
Emissions to atmosphere						229		229
Water supply								
normal operation	m³/t			6.5	0	3.2	4.0	13.6
Closed loop (without fibre recovery)				0.3	0	6.4	–	6.7
Maintenance costs (450 t.p.d.)	Annual as fraction of capital cost	0.050		0.059		0.036	0.068	0.052
Scale factors 450–900 t.p.d.:	Dimensionless							
Capital costs		0.895		0.897		0.898	0.893	0.90
Operating costs		0.53		0.92		0.93	1.00	0.90

Some further experience with closed loop operation is necessary, particularly with regard to the build-up of bacteria and pathogens. With fibre recovery, some net production of waste water is inevitable, and treatment needs to be provided.

17.3. Options based on wet pulping

Five options based on wet pulping are evaluated here, each of which may be supplemented by additional materials recovery from the cyclone rejects stream. These are:

(i) Fibre recovery with no heat recovery from the incinerator, as at Franklin;

(ii) No fibre recovery and incineration of the dewatered R D F to generate electricity, as at Hempstead;

(iii) Production of dewatered R D F, with fibre recovery;

(iv) Production of dewatered R D F;

(v) Production of dried R D F at 20 per cent moisture.

The data used are summarized in Table 17.2. The capital costs of plants (i), (iii), and (iv), based on the Systech data, are £7.4, £5.1, and £3.8 million, respectively, at first-half 1977 prices. The contract price for the Hempstead plant (type (ii)) was originally $55 million for 1800 t.p.d. (Hopper 1975), but had risen to $73 million by 1978 (National Center for Resource Recovery 1978); this is approximately equivalent to £10 million for a 400 t.p.d. plant (using $S = 0.9$). Schulz et al. (1976) quoted a plant producing dried R D F at $13.5 million for 900 per 24-hour day. Correcting to 400 t per 16-hour day, this is equivalent to £5.5 million. By comparison with the Systech estimate for a dewatered R D F plant, this implies £1.7 million for the 3-stage rotary drier, which appears to be high. It is assumed that the dewatered and dried R D F plants cost, respectively, £4 and £5 million, with other costs as above.

Each plant is assumed to operate 2 shifts, 5 days per week, with the exception of the incinerator modules in options (i) and (ii) which run continuously. Labour requirements are assumed to be 4 day–men, plus 5 per shift for dewatered R D F production, 1 for fibre recovery or R D F drying, 3 for incineration, and 1 for electricity generation.

Electricity consumption is based on that at Franklin. The requirements for dewatering and incineration at Franklin reflected a low throughput following the fibre recovery system. It is assumed that energy for separation and dewatering is increased by about 10 per cent, giving a total requirement for dewatered R D F production of 100 kWh/t. However, an increase in throughput of the incinerator by a factor of 1.5 would increase its energy requirement to about 90 kWh/t, steam and electricity generation facilities raising this further to about 130 kWh/t. The electricity generation option

Table 17.2

Options based on wet pulping. A summary of data and results

Item	Option				
	Fibre recovery plus fluid-bed incineration (Franklin)	Incineration plus heat recovery as electricity (Hempstead)	Fibre recovery plus dewatered RDF	Dewatered RDF	Dried RDF
Capital cost, 400 t.p.d., 25 t.p.h. (£ million 1977)	7.4	10.0	5.1	4.0	5.0
Operating labour (number of men)	28	30	16	14	16
Electricity consumption (kWh/t)	170	(150)	110	100	100
Net cost from the economic analysis (£/t)	32.3±8.8	32.8±11.8	19.7±6.2	15.6±4.8	22.6±6.2
Energy requirement (MJ/t)	3000	2900	2000	1700	4500
Energy savings from recovered materials (MJ/t)	6200	1700	6200	1700	1700
Energy savings from recovered fuel (MJ/t)	0	4500	4600	6900	8100
Net energy efficiency α	−0.30	0.16	0.25	0.52	0.36
Net primary energy efficiency β	0.32	0.34	0.88	0.69	0.53

would thus use about 220 kWh/t; this contrasts with the 90 kWh/t quoted by Landman and Darmstadt (1975) for the Hempstead plant. The estimate based on Franklin is likely to be high, as the fluid bed uses a compressed air blower not used at Hempstead. However, feeding R D F to the incinerator, gas cleaning, ash handling, steam raising, and electricity generation all use power; an additional requirement of 50 kWh/t, giving a total of 150 kWh/t, is assumed here, although this is supplied from on-site generation. In addition to the front-end loader for waste handling, fuel is necessary for the rotary drier in option (v). The requirement is given by Schulz *et al.* (1976) at about 2.2 G J/t.

The heating value of the dewatered R D F is given by Systech as 90 per cent of that in the input waste, or 60 per cent if fibre recovery is in use. The efficiency of steam production from this fuel is assumed to be 50 per cent when burnt alone, compared with 60 per cent for untreated waste at 25 per cent moisture. Electricity generation from the steam is assumed to be only 30 per cent efficient, compared with 35 per cent from conventional inciner- ators or 42.5 per cent from modern fossil fuel boilers (Hecklinger 1976), because of lower steam temperature (Landman and Darmstadt 1975). The overall conversion of waste to electricity is thus only 13.5 per cent efficient compared to 18 per cent from conventional incineration. The net generation is 8 per cent, or 225 kWh/t.

Dewatered R D F is assumed to command an energy-specific price of 50 per cent that of coal, compared with 60 per cent for American R D F, owing to its high moisture content. On drying to 20 per cent moisture the price is increased to 70 per cent that of coal, while the boiler efficiency on co- combustion with coal is raised from 60 to 70 per cent (compared with an efficiency from American R D F of 69 per cent). The dried R D F is thus assumed to be equivalent to paper-based R D F.

Water usage is only substantial when fibre recovery is used or if the incinerator uses a wet scrubber for gas cleaning. With fibre recovery, a requirement of 5 m³/t is assumed, which is half that used at Franklin, while a similar quantity requires treatment, this taking place on site before dis- charge to sewer.

Maintenance costs based on experience at Franklin were included in Table 17.1, ranging from 0.036 *I* for the incinerator to 0.5–0.7 *I* for the other sub-systems. The factor for incineration is much lower than the 0.07 *I* used here (Section 13.6) and an overall factor of 0.06 *I* is thus taken. This may be compared with the 0.034 *I* used by Schulz *et al.* (1976); both factors are optimistic in view of the severe maintenance problems at Hempstead.

Each option recovers ferrous metals from the hydrapulper rejects, with 100 kg/t remaining for disposal. In addition, 110 kg/t are rejected by the cyclone, and are either sent to landfill or for materials recovery. The R D F represents 720 kg/t at 25 per cent moisture, or 900 kg/t at 50 per cent moisture.

17.4. Discussion

The results of the standard economic and process analyses for the options based on wet pulping are included in Table 17.2. The five options are discussed in turn:

(i) The original system as demonstrated at Franklin, including fibre recovery and incineration of the residues without heat recovery, is seen to be very expensive, with an overall net cost of £32 ± £9/t of waste. The revenue from fibre recovery is only about £2.7/t of waste. The net energy efficiency α is negative since there is no fuel product, while the net primary energy efficiency is also low, $\beta = 0.30$.

(ii) The modified system at present being demonstrated on a large scale, 1800 t.p.d., at Hempstead is also expensive. All the organic fraction is dewatered and incinerated for electricity generation. The overall net cost of £33 ± £12/t is very sensitive to the high estimate of capital cost. If this could be reduced from £10 million to, say, £7 million, the mean net cost would be about £22/t, which is competitive with that of electricity generation from conventional incineration. The overall energy efficiency β is, however, only 0.34, compared with 0.53 for conventional incineration.

(iii) This system is similar to that demonstrated at Franklin, except that the dewatered rejects from fibre recovery are marketed directly as a fuel. The overall net cost is £20 ± £6/t, which is cheaper than for conventional incineration, while the net primary energy efficiency is very high, $\beta = 0.88$.

(iv) This is the simplest system, the organic process slurry simply being dewatered and marketed as a wet RDF at 50 per cent moisture content. In common with the previous option, the main doubt over this system is the marketability of the RDF product. If a reasonable price for the product can be obtained, 50 per cent that of coal per megajoule of heat content, then the overall net cost is estimated at £16 ± £5/t. This is competitive with other options for RDF production or for landfill at a distant site. The net primary energy efficiency is reasonable, $\beta = 0.69$.

(v) Upgrading the wet RDF by drying to about 20 per cent moisture will increase the marketability of the product. However, the additional process sophistication and energy inputs do not break even at the relative prices and fuel qualities assumed here. The overall net cost is increased to £23 ± £6/t, while β is reduced to 0.53.

In summary, wet pulping provides a flexible processing technique which allows fibre and/or energy recovery. However, all the options are capital intensive and the two basic products, dewatered fibre or RDF, both present marketing difficulties. The cheapest option would be the production of dewatered RDF, if the fuel could be sold at a reasonable price. This option would be competitive with other systems for RDF production and also with some options for landfill at a distant site. Combined fibre recovery and dewatered R D F production would increase the mean cost by about £4/t, but the net primary energy efficiency is also increased, from $\beta = 0.69$ to 0.88, which makes it one of the most efficient resource recovery options. Upgrading the R D F by drying both increases the net cost and reduces the efficiency β. Incineration of the wet RDF on site is very capital intensive and, unless the capital can be reduced, yields very high net costs. The first commercial plant at Hempstead has encountered severe difficulties, and it is not certain that the plant will reopen. The continued availability of options based on wet pulping must therefore be in some doubt.

18. PYROLYSIS AND OTHER THERMAL PROCESSES

18.1. Introduction

The thermal processing of organic materials without complete combustion has been practised for many centuries. The carbonization of wood to give charcoal was widespread throughout the ancient world. The carbonization of coal to produce town gas and coke was one of the foundations on which the industrial revolution was built. The destructive distillation of wood, and later of by-products from the coal-gas industry, provided the basic feedstocks for the chemical industry before the development of petrochemicals.

In the last 10 years, interest in these processes has once again increased, in response to the growing shortage of fossil fuels. Over 100 processes have been proposed for coal gasification, in preparation for the new generation of gas works when natural gas supplies become scarce. Similarly, over 150 processes have been proposed for the conversion of municipal wastes, plastics, tyres, wood, agricultural wastes, and other sources of 'biomass' into useful fuels. However, most of these processes have only been tested on the laboratory or small pilot-plant scale. Experience on a near-commercial scale is very limited, the pyrolysis of tyres being probably the most advanced.

Thermal processes may be subdivided into a number of distinct categories. The term 'pyrolysis' is often used as a generic term to describe alternatives to incineration, but such usage is not strictly accurate. The major alternatives are shown schematically in Fig. 18.1 and the terms are explained below:

Combustion is the reaction of organic or other compounds with air to produce heat and combustion products, normally carbon dioxide and water. Complete combustion of waste is termed incineration (see Chapter 15).

Pyrolysis is the thermal decomposition of organic materials in the absence of oxygen. The products are solids, liquids, and gases, the relative yields depending on process conditions. *Destructive distillation* describes a pyrolysis optimized to produce liquid products, while *carbonization* produces mainly solid products, specifically carbon.

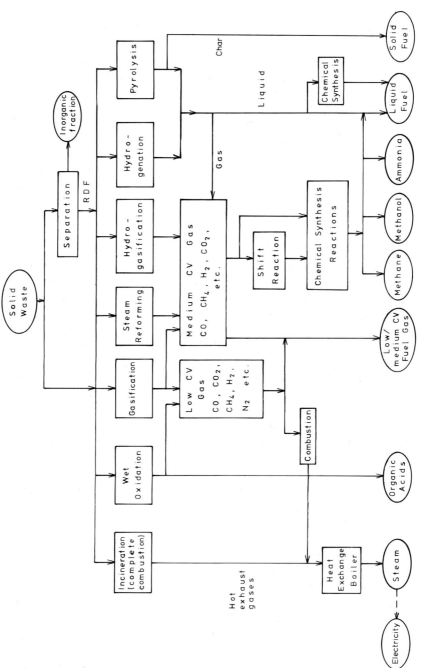

Fig. 18.1 *Thermal processes for the reclamation of solid waste.* Note that byproducts are omitted in this simplified, schematic representation.

Gasification is sometimes used to describe the reaction of organic com-pounds with less oxygen or air than would be required for complete combustion, when some pyrolysis also occurs. The terms *starved-air incineration* and *partial oxidation* are synonymous with gasification.

Steam reforming is the reaction of organic compounds with steam to yield principally carbon monoxide and hydrogen.

Hydrogasification and *hydrogenation* are the pyrolysis of organic com-pounds in a hydrogen-rich atmosphere under such conditions as to yield predominantly gases and liquids, respectively.

Wet oxidation is the reaction of a wet slurry containing organic com-pounds with oxygen at a high temperature and pressure. The products are a low-heating-value gas and a solution containing organic acids, which may be separated and recovered.

18.2. Products of thermal processes

When municipal waste, or a solid refuse-derived fuel, is used as the feed-stock for thermal processing, a mixture of solid, liquid, and gaseous frac-tions are produced, depending on the process conditions. A large number of reactions may occur and many of these take place simultaneously; the major reactions are summarized in Fig. 18.2. The relative yields of the various products may be controlled by manipulating this complex chemistry, largely through control of the environment within the reactor. The theory of pyrolysis, a consideration of which is important if process conditions are to be optimized, is discussed for example by Lewis (1976) and by H. T. Wilson (1977).

One of the main controlling parameters is temperature. As a refuse-derived fuel is heated in the absence of oxygen, the reactions may be summarized as:

At low temperatures the RDF is dried, moisture being driven off.

Between 100 °C and about 300 °C, water, carbon dioxide, ketones, acids, and other highly oxygenated hydrocarbons are given off.

Above 300 °C, primary char formation begins. Flammable vapours are released consisting mainly of the light gases carbon monoxide, carbon dioxide, hydrogen, methane and ehtylene. A condensible 'oil' is formed consisting mainly of highly oxygenated compounds.

Above 500 °C, secondary reactions occur. The primary products react further with each other and with the feed. The major products are carbon monoxide, hydrogen, and methane.

Above 1500 °C, the inorganic residue forms a molten slag which may be drained from the reactor.

The major products are now considered in turn, together with the condi-tions necessary to optimize their production.

Reaction	Heat of reaction Exothermic	Endothermic
Destructive distillation		
$(C_6H_{10}O_5)_n \longrightarrow$ High and moderate molecular weight liquids (oxygenated tars and oils) + low molecular weight organic acids, ketones, and aromatics + char + CO_2 + H_2O		X
Carbonization		
$(C_6H_{10}O_5)_n \longrightarrow 6n\ C + 5n\ H_2O$	X	
Pyrolysis		
$C + 2H_2O \longrightarrow CO_2 + 2H_2$		X
$C + H_2O \longrightarrow CO + H_2$		X
$C + CO_2 \longrightarrow 2CO$		X
$C + 2H_2 \longrightarrow CH_4$	X	
$CO + H_2O \longrightarrow CO_2 + H_2$ (water–gas shift reaction)	X	
$CO + 3H_2 \longrightarrow CH_4 + H_2O$	X	
$2CO + 2H_2 \longrightarrow CH_4 + CO_2$	X	
$CO_2 + 4H_2 \longrightarrow CH_4 + 2H_2O$	X	
Combustion (heat source in gasification processes)		
$C + O_2 \longrightarrow CO_2$	X	
$C + \frac{1}{2}O_2 \longrightarrow CO$	X	
$CO + \frac{1}{2}O_2 \longrightarrow CO_2$	X	
$H_2 + \frac{1}{2}O_2 \longrightarrow H_2O$	X	
$CH_4 + 2O_2 \longrightarrow CO_2 + 2H_2O$	X	
Steam reforming		
$(C_6H_{10}O_5)_n + nH_2O \longrightarrow 6n\ CO + 6nH_2$		X
$CO + H_2O \longrightarrow CO_2 + H_2$	X	
Hydrogasification (hydrogen may be formed by gasification of char or by shift reaction from carbon monoxide)		
$(C_6H_{10}O_5)_n + 12n\ H_2 \longrightarrow 6nCH_4 + 5nH_2O$	X	
Hydrogenation		
$(C_6H_{10}O_5)_n + 6nH_2 \longrightarrow 6n(CH_2) + 5nH_2O$ (higher molecular weight hydrocarbons)	X	
Wet oxidation (equation not quantitative; other products formed)		
$(C_6H_{10}O_5)_n + O_2 + H_2O \longrightarrow CH_3CO_2H + C_2H_5CO_2H + (CO_2H)_2 + CH_3OH + CO_2 + H_2O$		

Fig. 18.2. *Major chemical reactions utilized in thermal processes.* For the sake of clarity, organic waste is represented as cellulose, $(C_6H_{10}O_5)_n$. Many reactions have been greatly simplified. Most reactions are reversible.

(1) A solid char consisting mainly of carbon is produced by most processes. This is a low-grade fuel, and is often burnt to provide heat for the pyrolysis reactions. An alternative use would be as activated carbon, for example in water treatment. At high operating temperatures, and particularly if some oxygen is introduced, the char is completely gasified in the reactor.

(2) The ash or slag produced as a residue may be either landfilled or used as an aggregate.

(3) The liquid product separates into two fractions. An aqueous solution, containing various highly oxygenated compounds including methanol, acetic acid, acetone, and formaldehyde, is produced by most processes. This liquor will require treatment before disposal to sewer.

(4) The second liquid fraction is a tarry oil, which also consists mainly of oxygenated hydrocarbons. The production of oil is maximized by a low operating temperature, about 500 °C, and by a short residence time in the reactor. The properties of pyrolytic oil are discussed in Section 18.6.

(5) The gaseous products are those which have been suggested most widely for use as a waste-derived fuel. The composition and yield of the gas varies greatly, depending on process conditions. Optimum yields of carbon monoxide, hydrogen, and methane occur at about 1000 °C. The calorific value varies between about 4 and 20 MJ/m^3 for natural gas, depending mainly on the extent of product dilution with combustion gases or with nitrogen from combustion air.

Pyrolysis oil or gas are waste-derived fuels for which the principal use is co-combustion with fossil fuels in conventional boilers, cement kilns, or similar applications. Combustion on site to raise steam for sale is probably the most realistic option for the very low calorific value gases. The higher-grade pyrolysis gases may be upgraded further for direct use as a fuel or for use in chemical synthesis. The ratio of hydrogen to carbon monoxide is first increased by a water–gas shift reaction

$$CO + H_2O \rightarrow H_2 + CO_2$$

to form 'synthesis gas'. Examples of the use of synthesis gas include:

(i) Methanation to produce substitute natural gas (Snyder, Brehany, and Mitchell 1975)

$$CO + 3H_2 \rightarrow CH_4 + H_2O$$

(ii) Production of methanol (Stiles 1977)

$$CO + 2H_2 \rightarrow CH_3OH$$

(iii) Production of higher alcohols

(iv) The Haber process to produce ammonia (Mathematical Sciences Northwest 1974)

$$N_2 + 3H_2 \rightarrow 2NH_3$$

(v) Fischer-Tropsch synthesis of hydrocarbons

$$nCO + 2nH_2 \rightarrow (CH_2)_n + nH_2O$$

or

$$2nCO + nH_2 \rightarrow (CH_2)_n + nCO_2$$

These reactions utilize a variety of catalysts, temperature, and pressures. The processes are all used, with conventionally derived feedstocks, in the chemical industry.

18.3. Basic process characteristics

The environment within the thermal reactor controls the course of the competing pyrolytic reactions, and its manipulation allows the yield of any desired product to be maximized. A number of basic process characteristics which affect the reactor environment are discussed in this section.

18.3.1. Method of heat transfer

Pyrolysis or other thermal processes require the supply of heat to the reactor. Various alternative heating schemes are illustrated schematically in Fig. 18.3. These may be summarized as:

External heating, in which heat from a combustion reaction is transferred through the walls of the reactor (Fig. 18.3(a)). The rate of heating is usually low.

Direct heating by oxidation of the char or partly pyrolysed waste. The hot combustion gases heat the feedstock as they pass through the reactor (Fig. 18.3(b)). The addition of air or oxygen often results in complete gasification of the char. The product gases are diluted with carbon dioxide and, if air is used, with nitrogen.

Internal heating with pyrolysis products. Some of the pyrolysis products are burnt externally to preheat other products which are recirculated through the reactor (Fig. 18.3(c)). The pyrolysis gases are not diluted with combustion products, and liquids or char can be recycled to be further pyrolysed if required.

Internal heating with steam (steam reforming). Some of the pyrolysis products are burnt externally to superheat steam which is passed through the reactor (Fig. 18.3(d)).

Internal heating with synthesis gas. Some of the pyrolysis products, usually the char, are gasified externally in the presence of steam and air to yield a hot synthesis gas, rich in hydrogen, which is passed through the reactor (Fig. 18.3(e)). This mode of heating is common in hydrogenation or hydrogasification processes.

Internal heating with an inert heat carrier. Some of the pyrolysis products are burnt to heat a liquid or solid which is mixed with the RDF, heating and pyrolysing it. The heat carrier is separated from the other products on leaving the reactor and recycled (Fig. 18.3(f)). Various inert heat carriers have been proposed including molten metals and salts, steel or ceramic balls, and sand.

(a)

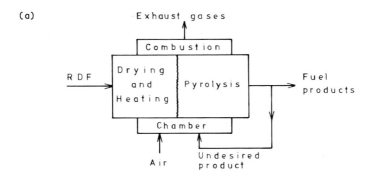

(b)

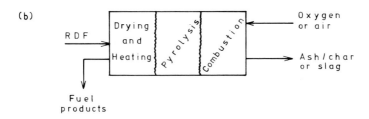

(c)

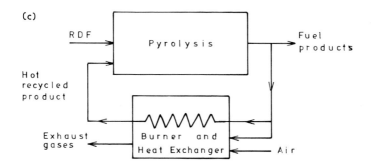

(d)

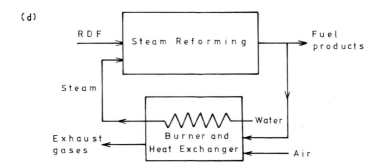

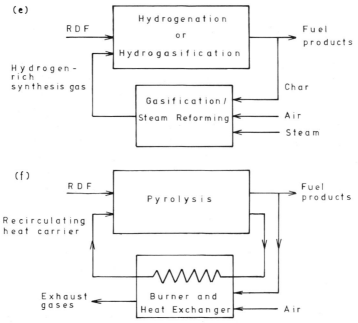

Fig. 18.3. *Alternative methods of effecting the thermal degradation of waste.* Differentiation is made in terms of the mode of heat transfer. The representations are purely schematic and should not be taken as defining either the types of reactor or the direction of evolved gas flow.

    (a) external heating
    (b) direct heating by oxidation
    (c) internal heating with pyrolysis products
    (d) internal heating with steam
    (e) internal heating with synthesis gas
    (f) internal heating with inert heat carrier

18.3.2. Evolved gas flow

The gaseous environment within the reactor is determined largely by the relative movement of the product gases and the solid feedstock. Four basic alternatives can be distinguished:

Counter-current flow, in which the gases are carried against the flow of feed and can thus react with fresh RDF.

Co-current flow, in which the gaseous and solid intermediate products are carried together, so that their chemical interaction is encouraged.

Cross-flow, in which the gases flow at right angles to the solid feed. If the bed is narrow, the gaseous products are quickly removed from the reactor, thus minimizing the opportunity for further reaction.

Mixed flow, as for example in a fluidized bed where fresh feed and solid products are mixed throughout the reactor.

18.3.3. Other process variables

Many other factors influence the course of pyrolytic reactions. Among these
are:

The *temperature profile* within the reactor. A slow rate of heating the
RDF and high reactor temperatures will encourage thermodynamic control of the reactions, that is the more stable gaseous products will pre-
dominate. A high rate of heating and a low reactor temperature will
favour kinetic control so that, for example, yields of the unstable, in-
termediate-molecular-weight, tars and oils will be maximized.

The *particle size* of the feedstock; this is important in determining the rate
of heat transfer to the inner regions of the particles and thus in controlling
the residence time of the solid RDF in the reactor. Some processes utilize
untreated waste as the feedstock, but most require either pulverization
and removal of magnetic metals or the production of a higher-grade
RDF.

The *operating pressure*; in most processes this is about ambient. A high
internal pressure can be used, for example, to increase the yield of oil in
hydrogenation.

Catalysts; these are commonly used in the chemical industry to direct the
course of thermal processes. Relatively few catalytic processes have yet
been explored for municipal waste feedstocks.

18.4. Types of reactor

Reactors for thermal treatment of waste are designed to combine the
various process variables in such a way that the yield of a certain desired
product is maximized. The great complexity of process variables is reflected
in the wide variety of reactor designs in the literature. However, it is possible
to classify the designs into three generic types:

Vertical-flow reactors;
Horizontal-flow reactors;
Dilute-phase reactors.

These are now examined in turn.

18.4.1. Vertical-flow reactors

One of the most common designs is the vertical-shaft reactor. The reactor is
a simple cylinder made of steel, or of steel lined with refractory material.
The RDF enters at the top of the shaft and char and/or ash is removed at the
bottom. Many gasification processes use this design, air or oxygen being
introduced at the bottom to burn the char and perhaps also to convert the
ash into a molten slag. The radial temperature profile in a vertical-shaft
reactor is difficult to control, particularly if external heating is used. In an
internally heated reactor, the profile will become more even as the particle

size of the RDF is reduced. The rate of heating the feedstock is usually low and solid residence times are of the order of hours. An inherent advantage of the vertical shaft is simplicity, there being no moving parts in the hot zone.

An adaptation of the vertical shaft is the cross-flow reactor. Preheated gases are forced through the falling bed of refuse at right angles to the direction of flow. The reaction time for both the product gases and for the solid feed will be relatively short.

A rather different concept of vertical-flow reactor is the multiple hearth. A similar design is used in incineration and in composting. The RDF enters at the top of the reactor and is gradually moved to lower hearths by the action of a rotating plough. Gases flow upward through the reactor, mixing with the solids which are being continuously agitated. Solid residence times are again long.

18.4.2. Horizontal-flow reactors

Another common design is the rotary kiln, which consists of a cylindrical steel drum, perhaps refractory lined, inclined at a few degrees from the horizontal. Solid RDF enters at one end and is moved through the hot zone by the slowly rotating drum. Almost any mode of heating or pattern of gas flow may be used. The tumbling action of the drum improves heat transfer, particularly in externally heated reactors. However, the rate of heating is still relatively low.

Various horizontal-shaft reactors have been proposed. The solid feedstock may be conveyed through the reactor by a conveyor belt, moving grate, or vibratory chute, or by a moving bed of molten metal or inorganic salts. Mechanical means of conveying the solids may prove unreliable at high operating temperatures.

18.4.3. Dilute-phase reactors

There are various reactor designs where the solid RDF is dispersed in a gaseous or other fluid medium. The low density of solids in the reactor gives excellent heat transfer and low residence times. Extensive pre-treatment of the RDF to give a small particle size is necessary if full advantage is to be taken of these characteristics.

These reactors may be conveniently classified by the relative movement of gases and solids:

(1) Counter-current flow is used in the free-fall reactor where the solid RDF slowly falls through an upcoming, preheated gas stream.

(2) Co-current flow is used in the entrained bed or transport reactor where the solid RDF is blown into the reactor by a stream of preheated gas. Heat transfer may be achieved, for example, by mixing with a gas stream containing hot char.

(3) Mixed flow is used in a fluidized bed reactor. One variant uses a circulat-

ing sand bed, the sand being preheated in a separate reactor by the combustion of entrained char particles.

18.5. Thermal processes developed for municipal waste

A great variety of pyrolytic processes have been proposed for the reclamation of municipal waste. However, relatively few of these have reached the pilot plant stage, and none has yet been successfully demonstrated on a large commercial scale. Useful listings of the alternative options are given by Huang *et al.* (1975), Tanner (1975) and Jones (1978), but no detailed, critical comparison has yet been published.

A selection, including most of the better developed processes, is shown in Table 18.1. The intention is more to illustrate the variety of process options available, rather than to short-list the most promising options for further development.

In subsequent sections, the four processes which have reached the most advanced stage of development, and for which most quantitative data are available, are discussed and evaluated in some detail. In each case a demonstration plant has been built, and in one case several small commercial plants are in operation. These processes include just one true pyrolysis, the other three being gasification reactions:

The *Occidental* flash-pyrolysis process utilizes a high-quality RDF and an entrained bed reactor to achieve rapid reaction at the relatively low temperature of 500 °C the product is a pyrolytic oil.

The *Union Carbide Purox* process uses pulverized waste in a vertical shaft reactor. Heat is provided by combustion of the char at the base of the reactor in a stream of pure oxygen. The high temperature (1600 °C) melts the ash. The main product is a medium-heating-value gas.

The *Andco–Torrax* process is similar, only the waste is introduced to the vertical shaft without pre-treatment and air is used as the source of oxygen for combustion. The product gas has a low heating value; the small commercial plants built in Europe burn the gas on site to raise steam.

The *Monsanto Landgard* process utilizes pulverized waste and a rotary kiln reactor. Part of the waste is again combusted using introduced air and the low-calorific-value gas is burnt on site to raise steam. The largest pyrolysis plant so far built, designed to process 900 t of waste per day, uses this system but has been plagued with operating problems.

It should be emphasized that when pyrolysis eventually emerges as a viable option for municipal waste reclamation, the leading processes may not include any of these four American processes. This is particularly the case since recent development work has been most intense in Europe, and also in Japan. Before discussing these processes in detail, it is thus worth looking briefly at a few of the better developed European pyrolysis systems.

Table 18.1
A Selection of Thermal Processes for the Reclamation of Municipal Waste

Process description	Originator	Process name	Type of reactor	Mode of heating	Direction of gas flow	Other process features	Scale of operation (tonnes/day)	Major products	References
Pyrolysis	Pollution Control (Denmark)	Destrugas	Vertical shaft	External	Co-current		18	Gas, char	Jensen (1977)
	Foster–Wheeler Power Products (UK)	Cross-flow	Vertical shaft	Internal with product gas	Cross-flow		1	Gas, oil or char	H. T. Wilson (1977)
	Kiener (Germany)	Kiener	Rotary drum	External with combustion gases	Co-current	Low temperature, gases cracked in second reactor, product used in gas engine	(120)	Gas or electricity	Lenz (1979)
	Babcock Krauss–Maffei (Germany)	BKMI	Rotary kiln	External, fired by product gas	Co-current	Low temperature, gases cracked in second reactor	10	Gas	Schmidt (1979)
	Mannesmann Veba (Germany)	MVU (GMU)	Rotary kiln	External	Co-current	Moderate temperature	4	Oil	Bracker (1979)
	Resource Sciences (US)	Pyrotek	Horizontal kiln	Radiant tube heaters inside kiln	Co-current	Solids moved on vibrating conveyor	240	Gas, char	Bechtel (1975)
	Ebara Corporation (Japan)	Two-bed	Fluidized bed	Internal with product gas and hot sand	Mixed flow	Moderate temperature, second reactor heats sand by combustion of some product gas	5 (30)	Gas	Andoh et al. (1979)
	West Virginia University (US)	–	Fluidized bed	Internal with product gas and hot sand	Mixed flow		4	Gas	Alpert et al. (1972)
	Occidental (US)	–	Entrained bed	Internal with product gas and hot char	Co-current	Low temperature, short residence time	(180)	Oil	Section 18.6
Gasification (partial oxidation, starved-air incineration)	Andco/ Carborundum (US)	Torrax	Vertical shaft	Direct by partial oxidation in air	Counter-current	High temperature, ash produced as molten slag	180	Gas (steam)	Section 18.8
	Hitachi Shipbuilding and Engineering (Japan)	–	Vertical shaft	Direct by partial oxidation in air and steam	Counter-current	Non-slagging. Rotary grate	20	Gas (steam)	Mori (1979)
	Saarberg– Fernwärme	SFW–Funk	Vertical shaft	Direct by partial oxidation in pure	Counter-current	Non-slagging	15	Gas	Heinrich (1979)

Process	Organization	Trade name	Reactor	Heating	Flow	Notes	Scale	Product	Reference
	Corporation (US) BSP/Envirotech (US)	—	Multiple hearth	Direct by partial oxidation in air	Counter-current		130	Gas	Shelton (1978)
	Monsanto (US)	Landgard	Rotary kiln	Direct by partial oxidation in air	Counter-current		900	Gas (steam), char	Section 18.9
	Devco (US)	Pyrolator	Rotary kiln	Direct by partial oxidation in air	Counter-current	Solids moved through kiln by internal chain	110	Gas, char	Bechtel (1975)
	Battelle Northwest (US)	—	Molten salt	Direct by partial oxidation in air	Counter-current		Small	Gas	Hammond and Mudge (1975)
Steam reforming	Wright–Malta Corporation (US)	—	Rotary kiln	External	Co-current	Gases fired in gas-turbine, exhaust gases used for heating	Small	Gas (electricity)	Hooverman and Coffman (1977)
Hydrogenation	US Bureau of Mines	—	Sparged reactor	External, or internal by recycling of some products or by synthesis gas	Co-current	Uses high pressure, sodium bicarbonate catalyst. Hydrogen produced by reaction $CO + H_2O$	Small	Oil	Appell et al. (1970) Steffgen (1974)
Hydrogasification	US Bureau of Mines	—	Vertical reactor	Internal by hot synthesis gas	Co-current		Small	Gas	Steffgen (1974)
	Battelle Columbus Laboratory (US)	Syngas	Free fall reactor	Internal by hot synthesis gas	Counter-current		Small	Gas	Felderman et al. (1976)
Wet oxidation	University of California, Berkeley (US)	—	(Laboratory batch reactor)	External	–	Wet slurry heated with oxygen under pressure, yield of organic acids 45% by weight	Small	Organic acids	Goluecke and McGauhey (1970, 1971)
	Ciba–Geigy (Switzerland)	—	Gas–liquid exchange column	Direct by partial oxidation in air	Co-current	Developed for chemical process waste waters, primarily as a detoxification method	Commercial	Steam (organic acids)	Anderau (1977)
	Ontario Research Foundation (Canada)	Wetox	Multi-compartmental horizontal autoclave	Direct by partial oxidation in air	–	Developed for sewage sludge and industrial waste waters	Commercial	Steam (organic acids)	Laughlin and Cadotte (1979)

Note: scales of operation shown in brackets refer to planned or otherwise unproven plants.

One of the earliest processes to be used for municipal wastes was the Destrugas process developed by Pollution Control Limited in Denmark. A 5 t.p.d. pilot plant in Kalundburg has operated since 1971. Pulverized waste enters the top of a vertical ceramic retort, heat being supplied through the walls. The main product of the reaction at 800–1000 °C is a medium-heating-value gas containing about 45 per cent hydrogen and 10 per cent methane, with a heat content of 17 MJ/m³ (Jensen 1977). A second pilot plant has been built in Japan, and a 100 t.p.d. plant is planned in Bavaria. However, little quantitative information is yet available on the Destrugas process.

In Britain, work has been carried out at the Warren Spring Laboratory on several indirectly heated systems (Douglas, Webb, and Power 1976). The favoured design is the cross-flow system, in which prepared waste passes down a vertical reactor between two vertically located grates in opposition. Hot recycled product gases are blown through the bed from the upstream to the downstream grate, pyrolysing the feed. The process may be adapted to produce a fuel oil, medium-heating-value gas, or char. The process has been licensed to Foster Wheeler Power Products through the National Research and Development Corporation (H. T. Wilson 1977). Foster Wheeler have been operating a small 1 t.p.d. pilot plant, but plans to build a larger-scale pilot plant with financial assistance from the Department of the Environment have now been shelved.

Considerable research work has been carried out in the last few years in West Germany, a total of 18 projects being financed at least partially by the federal government (Barniske 1979). Four of the better developed processes for municipal wastes are included in Table 18.1:

Both the *Kiener* and the *BKMI* processes utilize an externally heated rotary drum or kiln for low-temperature carbonization at 450–550 °C. The product gas is cracked in a subsequent reactor, the energy required to raise the temperature to 1000–1100 °C being provided by partial combustion in air. The Kiener process uses a coke-bed reactor while BKMI uses a thermal cracker. After gas cleaning, the gases have a relatively low calorific value, about 7 MJ/m³. The Kiener process envisages using the gas to run an engine for electricity generation. Both processes have so far only been operated on a pilot scale.

The *MVU* process also uses an externally heated rotary kiln, but the pyrolysis temperature is 700 °C and the primary product is an oil, which is quenched from the crude gas by fuel oil. The remaining gas is used to heat the reactor. An oil yield of 50 per cent of the organic feedstock is claimed; the composition is more than 98 per cent aromatic compounds, but detailed information on the quality and utilization of the oil has not yet been made available. Testing has been carried out in a small, 200 kg/h, pilot plant.

The *SFW–Funk* process is another vertical-shaft gasification system, the reactor temperature being 800–1000 °C and the combustion taking place in pure oxygen with added steam. A 1 t.p.h. pilot plant is operational. The product gas has a calorific value of 8–11 MJ/m^3 and contains about 25–35 per cent H_2, 25–40 per cent CO, 5–10 per cent CH_4, and 15–25 per cent CO_2.

18.6. The Occidental process

18.6.1. Background

The Occidental Petroleum Company have developed a low-temperature flash-pyrolysis system, designed to maximize the yield of oil. A 180 t.p.d. demonstration plant at El Cajon, near San Diego in California, was due to begin operation during 1978 (Carbe 1976). However, commissioning of the plant was suspended after a few months pending a comprehensive review of the process (Schwegler 1978).

Much has been written on the Occidental process, particularly when it was still in the early stages of development. The most authoritative reports are those of Preston (1976) and Levy (1975*a*, *b*).

A simplified flowsheet is shown in Fig. 18.4. The central feature is the vertical entrained bed reactor, into which the fine-ground fluff RDF is blown by preheated product gas. Heat for the reaction is provided by hot char particles, which are blown into the reactor at about 750 °C. Heat transfer in the reactor is excellent, the combination of the low residence time and low operating temperature (with an average about 500 °C) giving optimum conditions for the formation of pyrolytic oils.

The feedstock for the pyrolysis reactor is an up-graded American RDF. The light fraction from the air classifier is dried to 3 per cent moisture and screened to reduce the inorganic content from 10 to 4 per cent. The organics from the undersize material (< 1.2 mm) are separated by an air table, and rejoin the oversize fraction. The remaining fines are passed to the glass recovery section of the materials recovery system (Fig. 14.6(b)). The organics are fine ground, the product RDF being 80 per cent less than 1.2 mm.

The product gas leaving the reactor at about 500 °C is separated from the entrained char in a cyclone, and is then cooled rapidly to 80 °C to prevent further cracking of the high-molecular-weight oils. Cooling is achieved by spraying oil into the gas stream in a decanter from which the product is removed. The remaining gases are cleaned and used to supply both process heat, for example for drying the RDF, and the hot transport gas to convey waste and char into the reactor. The major by-product is a highly contaminated aqueous fraction from the oil decanter.

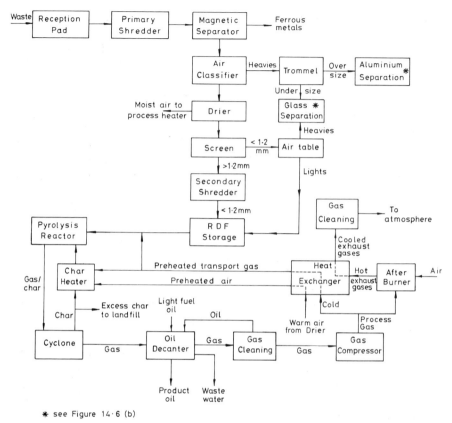

* see Figure 14·6 (b)

Fig. 18.4. *Occidental pyrolysis.*

18.6.2. Quantative data

Published information on the materials and energy balance of the Occidental process is not entirely consistent, presumably because it was produced while development work continued. For example, early flowsheets used water cooling, producing a larger aqueous fraction for disposal to sewer. The materials balance used here is:

Ferrous metals, 68 kg/t;

Recovered oil, 220 kg/t (170 l/t);

Water for disposal, 19 kg/t;

Residue for disposal to land (including excess char and additional materials which may be recovered), 280 kg/t;

The balance of about 410 kg/t is discharged to the atmosphere as combustion gases.

The yield of oil is adjusted to the 47 per cent recovery by heat content given by Preston (1976).

The pyrolytic oil has a heating value about 21 MJ/kg, or about 50 per cent that of a residual heavy fuel oil. It is viscous, fairly soluble in water, acidic and thus corrosive to mild steel, and polymerizes at high temperature. The preferred product contains 14 per cent by weight of water, added to reduce the viscosity, and is stored or pumped at 70 °C, about 30 °C higher than for a residual fuel oil. It is not miscible with fuel oil, but test burning of mixtures was successful (Preston 1976). The ash content is about 0.5 per cent. The efficiency in use of pyrolytic oil for steam generation was calculated by Hecklinger (1976) as 83.6 per cent compared with 82 per cent for conventional oil (Table E.5). This appears rather optimistic and here a substitution equivalence of 1.05 is used. Storage and distribution are assumed to reduce the overall efficiency in use of the oil by 10 per cent. The price of pyrolytic oil is calculated here from the energy-specific price of fuel oil, with a 20 per cent reduction to allow for transport and handling charges.

A small quantity of highly contaminated waste water is produced by the pyrolysis process. This has a chemical oxygen demand of about 10 per cent by weight. Pre-treatment of this liquor will be necessary before disposal to sewer; a cost of £0.50, and an energy requirement of 50 MJ, per tonne of input waste is assumed here.

About 47 per cent of the heat content of the waste is recovered as oil. The energy inputs to the process are quite high, including 2.5 l of a light fuel oil per tonne (i.e. about 100 MJ/t) to quench the reaction products, and at least 143 kWh/t of electricity. The latter value is quoted by Preston (1976), but is inconsistent with his own data for the requirements of size reduction which are shown in Fig. 12.10. An average particle size of 1 mm requires 80 kWh/t, compared with the 66 kWh/t he used for feed preparation including air classification, the air table, and magnetic separation. Assuming 10 kWh/t for these other operations, a total electricity consumption of 170 kWh/t is calculated. Of this about 90 is for feed preparation, 70 for pyrolysis, and 7 for the afterburner.

A pyrolysis plant must be operated continuously to achieve satisfactory performance. A design capacity of 400 t.p.d., 5 days per week, may thus be provided by a 300 t.p.d. plant operating 7 days per week. The project budget for the 180 t.p.d. demonstration plant was $14.4 million in 1976 (Preston 1976), which included funds for the first year of operation. Published estimates for a commercial 900 t.p.d. plant are about $25–29 million (1977). Assuming that the process can be made to work satisfactorily, one would expect some cost reduction in a commercial plant owing to learning, so that a cost of $27 million for a 900 t.p.d. plant may be reasonable. For a high-temperature process involving substantial gas handling a relatively low scale factor may be appropriate, and $S = 0.7$ is assumed. A 300 t.p.d. plant is thus estimated at \$12.5 million or £6.6 million. This estimate includes the cost of additional materials recovery (Section 14.5) and is thus further reduced to £6.0 million. It must be emphasized that this estimate is tentative, and in view of the problems with the current demonstration plant it may also be rather optimistic.

Manpower requirements are estimated at 4 day–men plus 5 men per shift for feedstock preparation and 5 per shift for the pyrolysis section. Thus with 2-shift operation for waste preparation and 4 for pyrolysis the total complement is 34. Maintenance costs for pyrolysis may be expected to be relatively high as it is a complex process involving corrosive products. A standard, and perhaps optimistic, factor of 0.08 I is used here for all the pyrolysis processes.

18.6.3. Discussion

The Occidental pyrolysis process is technologically sophisticated and has not yet been successfully demonstrated on a medium scale. In view of the problems with the demonstration plant, any quantitative estimates of costs or of contributions to resource conservation must be very tentative. On the basis of the data available during the development of the process, the standard economic analysis suggests an overall net cost of about £27 ± £8 per tonne of waste. The total revenue from sale of products is only about £6 per tonne of waste. The use of a low scale factor ($S = 0.7$) means that the process appears rather more competitive for a larger plant. At 1200 t of waste per day the mean net cost is about £15/t, which is less than for incineration but is still more than landfill or RDF production (Fig. 7.6).

Process analysis suggests an energy requirement about 3000 MJ/t of waste, with primary energy savings from oil and ferrous metals of 4400 MJ/t and 1700 MJ/t, respectively. Thus the net energy efficiencies are relatively low, with $\alpha = 0.14$ and $\beta = 0.31$. Recovery of non-ferrous metals and glass from the inorganic fraction would increase β to 0.41.

The combination of process problems in the development plant, a low energy efficiency, and probably also a relatively high net cost, do not make the prospects for the Occidental process particularly bright.

18.7. The Union Carbide Purox process

18.7.1. Background

The Union Carbide Corporation have developed a high-temperature gasification process which yields a medium-heating-value gas and a molten slag. Pulverized and magnetically separated waste enters the top of a vertical-shaft reactor and is successively dried and pyrolysed as it descends. The heat for the reaction at 1650 °C is provided by combustion in 95 per cent pure oxygen of the char and partly pyrolysed waste which reaches the base of the reactor. The product gas leaves the top of the reactor and the molten slag forms a granular product on quenching with water. A flowsheet is shown in Fig. 18.5. The process has been developed through a small pilot plant (Anderson 1974) to a 180 t.p.d. demonstration plant (Fisher, Kasbohn, and Rivero 1976) which has been operating at their South Charleston, West Virginia, plant since 1974. Several commercial plants were being planned in the USA (Klass 1977), but no contracts have yet been signed. Indeed, it appeared in early 1980 that the entire process was being redesigned, with the intention of producing a lower calorific value gaseous product for on-site utilization. This section discusses only the original concept of the Purox process.

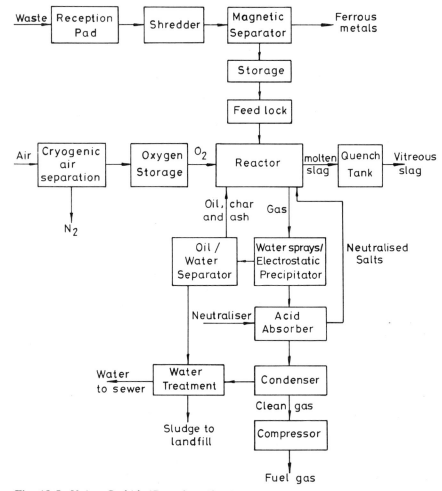

Fig. 18.5. *Union Carbide 'Purox' gasification.*

The process may utilize untreated waste but, after initial operation, pulverization and magnetic separation facilities for feed preparation were added to the demonstration plant. The gases leaving the reactor are cleaned by water sprays and an electrostatic precipitator which removes oil and char for recycling to the reactor. The gases then pass through an acid absorber from which neutralized salts are bled back to the reactor, and finally water is removed in a condenser.

18.7.2. Quantitative data

The process uses about 200 kg oxygen per tonne of waste. This is produced on site by cryogenic air separation. Each tonne of waste yields about:

    68 kg of ferrous metals;
    150 kg of fused slag;
    280 kg of waste water;
    700 kg of gas.

The waste water contains about 50 g COD/l (chemical oxygen demand per litre) and the process now includes on-site treatment, in a Unox oxidation plant, to reduce this to 0.2 g/l for disposal to sewer. The fused slag may be used as an aggregate, and a net disposal cost of zero is assumed here.

The product gas contains about 25 per cent H_2, 10 per cent hydrocarbons, 40 per cent CO and 25 per cent CO_2 by volume. It has a heat of combustion about 13 M J/m³ at standard temperature and pressure; although this is lower than the 34 M J/m³ for methane, Purox gas has a similar heat release per unit volume of combustion products and hence a similar flame temperature (Eggen and Kraatz 1974). Indeed the efficiency of Purox gas to raise steam may be greater than that of methane, a substitution equivalence of 0.94 being suggested from Table E.5; a substitution equivalence of 1.0 is assumed here. The product gas contains between 67 and 83 per cent of the heat content in the waste, the average of eight literature values being 77 per cent; 75 per cent is used here.

Various suggestions have been made for the utilization of the product gas other than by combustion in a steam raising boiler (Section 18.2). However, only the basic process making Purox gas will be examined here. The sale of the gas may present problems owing to its high energy-specific volume and hence high pumping and storage costs. In Britain, pipeline transport to an external customer would require negotiation with the British Gas Corporation who have a monopoly in pipeline supply. To allow for these difficulties, the revenue from the product gas per GJ of heating value is taken as 70 per cent that of natural gas, while the energy requirement for distribution is assumed to be 10 per cent of the heat content of the gas.

Capital costs for the Purox process are only available from the Union Carbide Corporation. Their estimates as quoted by different authors are shown in Table 18.2; it may be observed that they have increased with time.

Table 18.2

Capital cost estimates for the Union Carbide Purox gasification process

Source of estimate	Date of estimate[a]	Capacity (short tons per day)	Capital cost ($ million)		
			Gasification sub-systems[b]	Complete gasification plant[c]	Estimate reduced to common basis[d]
General Electric Company (1973*a*)	5.11.72	1000		9.8	12.9
Schulz (1973)	4.1.74	2000		22.4	16.8
Seattle (1974)	(May 1974)ᐟ	1500	23.3		21.4
Seattle[e]	1.8.74	1500	16.1		13.6
Bechtel Corporation (1975)	1974	1000		27.0	27.7
Schulz (1975)	(May 1975)	1000	18.0	19.2	20.5
Seattle (1975)	(June 1975)	1500	32.0		26.3
Snyder *et al.* (1975)	(November 1975)	1750		38.0[f]	25.0[f]
Schulz *et al.* (1976)	1975	1000		22.9[g]	20.9[g]
Bodner (1976)	1976	700	20.0		29.1
Stuckenbruck and King (1977)	January 1976	1000	34.7		38.0

(a) Where date of estimate is not available, the date of publication is given in brackets.
(b) Cost of gasification plant without waste reception or preparation facilities.
(c) Cost of gasification plant with waste reception but no preparation facilities.
(d) First-half 1977 cost for the gasification sub-system of a 1000 short ton per day plant. Capacity correction uses equation 5.5 and scale factor $S = 0.8$. Reception and storage facilities are assumed to represent 10 per cent of the total plant cost.
(e) Mathematical Sciences Northwest 1974.
(f) Includes cost of piping gas to customers.
(g) Estimate for plant with shredded waste feed to the reactor. Reception, storage, and preparation facilities assumed to be 20 per cent of the total plant cost.

This is presumably due to problems encountered during development, e.g. the need to introduce waste water treatment. The most recent of ᵤₑ estimates, that of Stuckenbruck and King (1977), is equivalent to $38 million at mid-1977 prices for a 900 t.p.d. pyrolysis plant including oxygen production and waste water treatment, but not including refuse preparation facilities or indirect project costs. Their total plant cost is equivalent to $59 million. The plant is of modular design, with a module size of 300 t.p.d. for pyrolysis and 450 t.p.d. for oxygen production and waste water treatment. Economies of scale are therefore likely to be small with $0.75 < S < 0.9$; $S = 0.8$ is used here (Schulz *et al.* 1976). A 300 t.p.d. plant may thus be estimated at £13 million (1977).

Manpower requirements are estimated at 4 day–men, plus 4 per shift for feed preparation and 7 per shift for pyrolysis, the increase over the Occidental process being due to oxygen production and waste water treatment. The total complement is thus 40 men. Electricity consumption is quite high. Early estimates were about 130 kWh/t (General Electric Company 1973a) but more recent estimates are about 200 (Schulz et al. 1976) to 220 kWh/t (Stuckenbruck and King 1977); 200 kWh/t is assumed here.

18.7.3. Discussion

The Union Carbide process is technologically sophisticated and very capital intensive. No commercial plant has yet reached construction, although several plants have been planned. It is interesting that considerable attention has been paid to the use of the gas for chemical synthesis, an option which would increase the capital required still more. With the developmental data currently available, the standard economic analysis yields a net cost of £49 ± £17 per tonne of waste. The revenues total about £10/t of waste, compared to £23/t to meet the capital charge at a 10 per cent discount rate. If the current, lower, discount rate of 5 per cent is used, then the mean net cost is reduced to about £34/t. An increase in scale to 1200 t.p.d. would yield a similar reduction in cost. However, in all these cases the Purox process remains the most expensive of all the options examined here. If the high capital cost could be reduced by 40 per cent, to about £8 million at 1977 prices, then the mean net cost would be reduced to about £28/t. It is interesting to compare these results with those of Schulz et al. (1976), who ranked the Purox process as one of the cheapest. This optimistic result was based mainly on a gross underestimate of capital costs (see Table 18.2).

Process analysis suggests an energy requirement of 3900 MJ/t, with primary energy savings of 8300 MJ/t from the gas and 1700 MJ/t from ferrous metals and the aggregate produced. The net energy efficiencies of $\alpha = 0.44$ and $\beta = 0.62$ are about twice those for other pyrolysis processes, and are higher than for most other options with the exception of those producing a solid RDF.

The high electricity consumption of the Purox process has led to proposals to reduce costs by using a gas turbine to generate electricity (Schulz 1975). With 24 per cent turbine efficiency and 96 per cent generator efficiency (General Electric Company 1973a), the efficiency of electricity generation from the gas is 23 per cent, neglecting the energy requirements implied by additional capital and maintenance costs. To provide 200 kWh/t of electricity, 3100 MJ/t of gas is thus required, reducing the quantity for sale to 4400 MJ/t. The saving of 2400 MJ/t in centrally generated electricity is achieved only by reducing the primary energy saving from the fuel product by 3400 MJ/t. Thus the net energy efficiencies are reduced by 0.1. This result may be regarded as general if central generation of electricity is to be substituted by less efficient on-site generation.

18.8. The Andco–Torrax process

18.8.1. Background and operating experience

This high-temperature gasification process is similar to Purox. Untreated waste is fed into the top of a vertical-shaft furnace, the heat for the reaction being provided by the combustion of char and partly pyrolysed waste in preheated air. The product gas is diluted not only with carbon dioxide from combustion but also with nitrogen from the air; its heating value is about 4–8 MJ/m^3, roughly half that of Purox gas and a sixth that of methane. Several other proprietary processes are similar to Torrax, including some which are labelled as high-temperature starved-air incineration, e.g. the American Thermogen Melt-Zit process (Zinn *et al.* 1970; Pavoni *et al.* 1975).

The Torrax process has been developed since 1969, initially by a company jointly owned by Andco Incorporated and the Carborundum Company. Andco acquired rights to exploit the process in most of the world in 1976. A total of six plants have been built or are under construction (Table 18.3), including four commercial plants in Europe, with capacities between 170 and 400 t.p.d. The gasifier at the Luxembourg plant is shown in Fig. 18.6, while a view of the external equipment at the Frankfurt plant is shown in Fig. 18.7.

The flowsheet used in all these plants is shown in Fig. 18.8. The pyrolysis

Table 18.3

Operating experience with the Andco–Torrax process

Location	Capacity (t per day)	Date of initial operation	Use for product steam	Comments	Status Autumn 1979 (see text)
Orchard Park, Buffalo	70	1971–76	None	Demonstration Plant	Operations completed
Luxembourg	200	September 1976	Electricity	Steam combined with that from two existing 200 t.p.d. incinerators for electricity generation	Process modifications. Under testing
Grasse, France	170	October 1977	Process steam	Steam sold to perfume industries. Some used to generate electricity for process use	Plant failed to meet performance standards. Closed
Frankfurt, W. Germany	200	July 1978	Electricity	On site of existing incinerator	Plant closed pending modifications
Creteil, France	400	September 1979	Electricity	Two process lines in parallel	Commissioning due to begin
Hamamatsu City, Japan	75	Mid-1980 (projected)		Complex includes two new 150 t.p.d. incinerators	Under construction

Fig. 18.6. *The gasifier in the Andco–Torrax plant at Luxembourg.* In the foreground the feed and distribution system for the hot air can be seen, with the hearth area of the gasifier immediately behind. (Photo courtesy Andco Incorporated.)

Fig. 18.7. *The Andco–Torrax plant at Frankfurt.* The gasifier and control room are inside the building. On the right hand side of the figure, the recuperative towers for preheating input air can be seen in front of the secondary combustion chamber. Moving towards the left one can see the heat recovery boiler, electrostatic precipitator, and induced draught fan for feeding the cleaned gases to the common stack. (Photo courtesy Andco Incorporated.)

gas is burnt in a secondary combustion chamber, the hot exhaust gases being used partly to heat combustion air but mainly (85–90 per cent) to raise steam. The efficiency of overall steam generation from waste is between 67 and 69 per cent (Legille, Berczynski, and Heiss 1975). The use for the steam at the various plants is indicated in Table 18.3.

A useful account of the very considerable operating problems encountered in the first few years of the commercial plants is given by Rudblom (1979). These problems may be summarized as:

(a) Slag flow rates were much higher than expected and far exceeded the handling capacities of the original systems for quenching and transporting the granular product.

(b) Air leaks into the top of the reactor occurred and a mechanical seal had to be developed.

(c) Gross channelling of the refuse in the gasifier occurred, the hot gas thus having an easy pathway, by-passing the unreacted material. These problems were reduced by substantial redesign and rebuilding, the Luxembourg plant for example coming back on line in spring 1979. Satisfactory performance has yet to be demonstrated.

(d) Noise pollution caused by fans and other equipment led to the closure of the Frankfurt plant in early 1979. Large, acoustically insulated, structures and sophisticated noise suppression devices have now been added.

(e) Corrosion has occurred both in the boilers and in the recuperative towers for preheating combustion air. The air temperature can only be raised to 600 °C rather than the required 1000 °C. Raising the air temperature by combustion of natural gas or oil has been adopted, but this reduces the oxygen content of the air and so lowers the effective capacity of the gasifier.

(f) The dust in the product gas had led to blockages in the recuperative towers. At the Grasse plant, natural gas burning had to be adopted.

The plant at Luxembourg is the only one which was operating in autumn 1979. The Grasse plant was closed in July 1979 as it had failed to meet performance specifications on both refuse capacity and energy consumption. The Frankfurt plant was closed in Feburary 1979 for the addition of noise suppression equipment, and to await an evaluation of gasifier modifications at Luxembourg aimed at the elimination of refuse channelling. The other two plants were not yet operational.

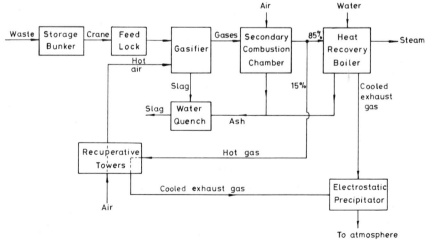

Fig. 18.8. *Flowsheet for Andco–Torrax gasification.*

Steam is an inflexible product because it must be used as it is produced. Process modifications have been proposed in the USA to produce instead a low-grade gas for external consumption (Page 1976), but so far no commercial development has been reported. The pyrolysis gas passes through a cyclone which separates the char from the remaining gas, of which only a portion passes to a secondary combustion chamber to provide heat for the process air, while the rest is available for sale. The gas contains a proportion of high-molecular-weight compounds which would condense at low temperature, so it must be pumped above 290 °C if a sophisticated gas cleaning and condensing system is to be avoided. It is suggested that the char should be ground and reinjected into the gas before burning at the user's facility. About 93 per cent of the heat content of the waste is recovered in fuel products, with a distribution of gas 54 per cent, oils 12 per cent, and char 18 per cent (Page 1976). However, Schulz *et al.* (1976) quote a heat content of 48 per cent in the gas, which is their sole product.

18.8.2. Quantitative data

Preliminary performance information on the commercial Torrax plants is only just becoming available. Such economic information as has been published is based on extrapolations from the demonstration plant, and is thus likely to be optimistic. When the system was intitially evaluated here, the only source of data available was Schulz *et al.* (1976) who costed the modified gas-export system. Recently, data for the basic steam generating system have been given by Marks, Bohn, and Melan (1979). The results in Appendix A and elsewhere in the book thus refer to the Torrax process producing gas for sale; the economics and energy efficiencies of the two alternatives are now compared.

The capital cost for the Torrax process estimated by Schulz *et al.* (1976) was about 75 per cent of the average for other pyrolysis systems, resulting in an estimate here of £6.8 million for a plant with nominal capacity of 400 t.p.d. This may be low as the Purox system, which it most closely resembles, was grossly underestimated by Schulz. The scale factor is taken as 0.75 after Schulz. Marks *et al.* (1979) present data for steam generating plants with capacities from 230 to 1350 t.p.d. Their scale factors apparently vary from 0.5 to 1.0. When allowance is made for the basic module size of about 300 t.p.d., an average scale factor in the range 0.75–0.8 may be deduced. When the costs are corrected to mid-1977 levels, our standard plant is estimated at about £9 million. A higher capital cost for steam generation is in fact to be expected, as additional plant including the secondary combustion chamber and steam condensers must be provided.

Labour costs were estimated here at 4 day–men, plus 5 per shift, giving the low total of 24 men, owing to the lack of waste preparation facilities. This compares well with the 30 men, including administrative staff, estimated by

Marks for a 450 t.p.d. plant. A standard annual maintenance cost factor, 8 per cent of capital, is assumed; the 4 per cent estimated by Marks appears rather optimistic, particularly in the light of early operating experience.

Electricity consumption has been estimated variously as 138 kWh/t by Schulz, 70 kWh/t by Legille *et al.* (1975) and 90 kWh/t by Marks *et al.* (1979). Figures of 140 and 90 kWh/t for the gas-export and steam generating options, respectively, are used here. Supplementary fuel usage for gas export was given by Page (1976) as 0.7 GJ/t. Design values for steam generation include the 2.8 m³ of natural gas (about 100 MJ) per tonne and 300 MJ/t given by Marks, and the 10 l oil (about 400 MJ) per tonne given by Rudblom (1979). However, as noted above, fuel consumption in the commercial plants has been far in excess of design, that at Luxembourg being about 50 l oil (about 2 GJ) per tonne. Design improvements in future plants should reduce this figure, and a value of 1.5 GJ/t is used here.

The Torrax process produces about 200 kg/t of slag, which is assumed here to be sold as an aggregate. The gas-export system produces about 80 kg/t of char and the steam generating system a similar quantity of flyash; in either case this is assumed to be landfilled.

The product gas from the gas-export system is assumed to contain 60 per cent of the heat content of the waste, but to command an energy-specific price only 50 per cent that of natural gas, to allow for the high distribution costs and for the substitution equivalence which is taken as 1.1. The effective efficiency in use of the gas is reduced by 20 per cent to allow for distribution losses. The efficiency of steam generation is taken as 68 per cent, compared with 60 per cent for incineration; the average load factor for steam utilization is again taken as 75 per cent.

18.8.3. Discussion

The projected information for a gas-exporting plant yields, in the standard economic analysis, a net cost of £29 ± £9/t of waste. The higher capital cost of the steam generating option is offset by the increased revenue, the net effect on the overall cost being slight. The mean net cost is reduced to about £25/t if a discount rate of 5 per cent is used, and to about £20/t for a larger, 1200 t.p.d. plant.

Process analysis gives energy requirements about 3400 and 3800 MJ/t for the gas-export and steam generating options, respectively, with primary energy savings of 5400 and 6600 MJ/t. The net energy efficiencies ($\alpha = \beta$) are relatively low, at 0.20 and 0.28, respectively.

It must be emphasized once again that these results are based on limited data; any firm conclusion on the Andco–Torrax process must await satisfactory operating experience over a sustained period from the current commercial plants.

18.9. The Monsanto Landgard process

18.9.1. Background and operating experience

This gasification process utilizes a rotary kiln reactor, shredded waste entering one end and passing slowly along. The heat for the reaction is again provided by burning the waste which reaches the end of the kiln, using air and supplementary fuel oil. The product gas has a low heating value and is fed to an afterburner to raise steam. The solid residue consists of a mixture of ash and char; the kiln temperature is too low to reduce it to a molten slag.

The process was developed, by Monsanto Enviro-Chem Systems, in a 30 t.p.d. plant at St. Louis, Missouri, and is currently being demonstrated in a 900 t.p.d. plant at Baltimore, Maryland, although the plant has experienced severe problems since commissioning began in 1975. Indeed, Monsanto withdrew from the project early in 1977. A 9 t.p.h. plant has also been operated in Japan (Hamabe, Tsugeno, and Nozu 1975).

The flowsheet for the Baltimore plant is shown in Fig. 18.9 (Sussman 1974, 1975). The waste is pulverized to a nominal 100 mm size and then stored. The pyrolysis kiln is about 30 m long and 6 m in diameter, rotates at 1 revolution per minute, and has a waste retention time of about 20 minutes. The product gas contains about 69 per cent N_2, 11 per cent CO_2, 7 per cent H_2, 5 per cent hydrocarbons, and 2 per cent O_2 by volume and has a heating value about 3–4 MJ/m^3. It presents poor prospects for direct sale unless, for example, the plant is alongside a conventional steam generating boiler. Overall efficiency of steam generation was estimated at 60–61 per cent from pilot plant operation, and in this respect the Baltimore plant has performed as expected (Sussman 1975). Thus the efficiencies of steam generation from waste incineration or gasification are about equal. The residue from the kiln is separated by flotation. The light fraction is screened to remove unburnt organics, with the fine char being thickened and dewatered to 50 per cent solids in a vacuum filter. The dry char contains about 50 per cent free carbon but is contaminated with inorganic salts. The use of the material in waste waster treatment and similar applications has been suggested (Stevenson, Leckie, and Eliassen 1973). Currently it is landfilled and a disposal requirement of 160 kg/t is assumed. The heavy fraction from flotation is magnetically separated; the residue represents about 150 kg per input tonne and contains 65 per cent glass. It may be processed for glass and non-ferrous metals recovery, sold as an aggregate, or, as assumed here, landfilled.

Sussman (1975) detailed the problems encountered at Baltimore, which can be attributed mainly to scaling up from 30 to 900 t.p.d. In the kiln itself, the combustion reaction is very rapid, producing a local temperature up to 1400 °C, compared with the design value of 800 °C. One result is the vaporization of both organic and inorganic salts, which subsequently condense giving a particulate loading in the gas about 2.5 times that expected. The

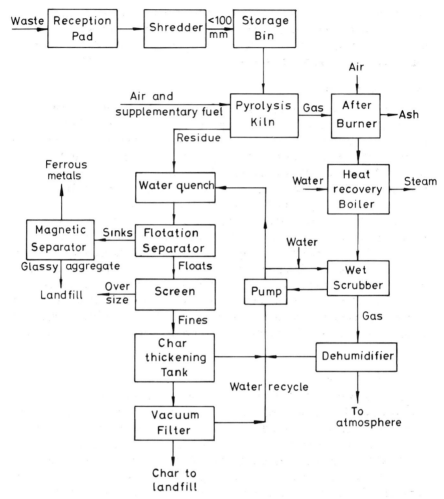

Fig. 18.9. *Monsanto 'Landgard' gasification.* Based on the original flowsheet for the Baltimore plant.

particle size distribution changed, from mainly larger than 10 μm to mainly less than 0.5 μm, so that the wet scrubber resulted in no net decrease in particulate loading. A wet electrostatic precipitator and a high stack have now been installed. Other problems were mechanical, notably in the residue removal conveyor. When an irregularity occurred in the kiln feed rate, large chunks of residue were discharged, immediately stopping the conveyor. The kiln takes 14 hours to cool so that the conveyor may be repaired, and a further 14 hours to heat up to operating temperature, so that down-time was considerable. The excessive thermal stress caused the refractory lining in the kiln to crack, and chunks of refractory caused similar malfunction. Both the refractory lining and the residue conveyor have been replaced. Modifications of the plant were completed in 1979, and by mid-1980 the plant was routinely processing 500 t of waste per day (cf. design of 900 t.p.d.).

18.9.2. Quantitative data

The Baltimore plant was originally estimated to cost $15 million (1972), but Sussman (1975) quoted a modified plant replacement cost of $28 million, equivalent to a 1977 cost of $31 million. A relatively low scale factor of 0.7 is assumed, the same as for the Occidental process. For a 300 t.p.d. plant, a cost of £7.7 million is thus suggested. Operating labour at Baltimore is quite low, about half that for waterwall incineration (Sussman 1975), although Schulz et al. (1976) give similar labour requirements for incineration and all the pyrolysis processes. Here a complement of 4 day–men, plus 4 per shift for waste preparation and 5 per shift for gasification, is assumed, giving a total of 32 men. Electricity usage was quoted by Sussman (1974) as 84 kWh/t, based on the pilot plant. A requirement of 100 kWh/t is used here to allow for the additional process equipment. Auxiliary fuel usage is about 1.1. G J/t. Water usage is minimal even with a wet scrubber in use as process water is recycled. It is assumed that 75 per cent of the available steam is sold. Despite experience at Baltimore, a standard maintenance factor of 0.08 l is assumed.

18.9.3. Discussion

Based on data from the Baltimore demonstration plant, the standard economic analysis yields a net cost of £31 ± £10/t of waste. The expected economies of scale are again considerable, a 1200 t.p.d. plant showing a mean net cost about £17/t. Process analysis shows an energy requirement of 3500 M J/t, with primary energy savings of 5800 M J/t from the steam and 1100 M J/t from ferrous metals. The net energy efficiencies are thus $\alpha = 0.23$ and $\beta = 0.34$. The savings are similar to those from either incinerations or suspension firing, while the energy requirements are increased, resulting in lower efficiencies.

It must be emphasized in conclusion that the Baltimore demonstration plant has not operated satisfactorily and that Monsanto have abandoned the development of this process. Thus the above results must be treated with caution.

18.10. Summary

From this discussion of thermal processes for the reclamation of solid wastes, a number of points have emerged:
(a) Although the concept of thermal conversion of solid wastes into useful

fuels is highly promising, much additional research and development work remains to be done before processes based on it can be recommended for general use.

(b) A great many processes have been proposed for the thermal treatment of municipal or similar wastes. However, operating experience at a useful scale is strictly limited.

(c) The term 'pyrolysis' is often used as a generic term to describe alternatives to incineration. However, 'pyrolysis' should strictly be applied only to thermal degradation of organic materials in the absence of air. When some of the waste is combusted in oxygen or air, then the term 'gasification' is more appropriate.

(d) The most common product from thermal processing is a low- to medium-heating-value gas. The more dilute gases are best suited to combustion *in situ* to generate steam. The higher-quality gases may be sold for use as a supplementary fuel, or may be used as a feedstock for chemical synthesis.

(e) Pyrolytic oil is a low-quality product containing mainly highly oxygenated compounds. It is viscous, corrosive, and tends to polymerize on storage. A higher-quality oil may be produced by chemical synthesis, using either gas or oil as feedstock, or from hydrogenation of waste.

(f) The reactions which may occur during thermal processing of organic wastes are extremely complex. Control may be exercised via many process variables, including the mode of heat transfer, the direction of evolved gas flow, the rate of heating, the particle size of the solid feedstock, the operating pressure, or the use of catalysis. More fundamental research is required if the yields of desired products are to be optimized.

(g) The great multiplicity of reactor designs may be classified into three main types, namely vertical-flow, horizontal-flow, and dilute-phase reactors.

(h) From a detailed examination of four of the processes currently at the most advanced stage of development, the main conclusion is that it is not possible to make any firm assessment of costs at present.

(i) The only system in commercial use is the Andco–Torrax gasification process. Four small plants have been built in Europe, but have experienced considerable problems. After three years of continual modifications, the first plant at Luxembourg appeared at last to be operating moderately well.

(j) Both the Monsanto Landgard and the Occidental systems have experienced severe operating problems in their demonstration plants. The Union Carbide Purox process has been 'commercially available' for several years, but no customers have yet materialized.

(k) From such preliminary economic information as is available, all of the processes appear to be at least as expensive as incineration, although they may be more competitive for large plants or if the discount rate is low. The costs for the Union Carbide process are much higher than for any other option examined here.

(l) The process analysis suggests that the net primary energy efficiencies are low, in the range $\beta = 0.2 - 0.35$, with the exception of the Union Carbide process, for which $\beta = 0.6$.

19. BIOLOGICAL PROCESSES

19.1. Introduction

Biological processes for the reclamation of wastes again have their origins in ancient history. Early agriculture often relied on the return of animal manures to the land to act as a fertilizer and to add humus to the soil. The Chinese have practised the composting of crop residues and night soil (human faeces) for many centuries. Anaerobic digestion of human sewage and animal wastes to produce methane gas has been applied in many parts of the world at least since the beginning of this century.

Biological processes are obviously restricted in their application to the organic fraction of municipal wastes. For this reason, operating experience is much more extensive in those countries where the waste is largely organic. In industrialized countries the vegetable and putrescible content of municipal waste is generally about 15–30 per cent, while the paper content is about 25–45 per cent. In less developed countries, or countries such as Israel where materials are scarce, the vegetable and putrescible content may be over 70 per cent (Table 1.2).

The various alternative biological processes are shown schematically in Fig. 19.1. Landfill can be viewed as a simple and inefficient method of composting and/or anaerobic digestion. As discussed in Chapter 11, considerable interest is now being shown in its potential for methane production. The more specific biological processes all require pre-treatment of the waste, either to reduce the particle size and remove magnetic metals, or preferably to remove most of the inorganic materials.

Composting is the aerobic degradation of organic materials to yield a stable humus-like product, for use primarily as a soil conditioner. The degradation is most efficient with putrescible wastes; paper and wood degrade more slowly, usually over a period of several months.

Cellulose, the major constituent of paper, may be hydrolysed using acid or enzymatic catalysis, to yield glucose. The glucose may in turn be fermented to yield either ethanol or yeast (single-cell protein). Alkaline hydrolysis may be used either to remove the lignin sheathing and thus to increase the solubility and reactivity of cellulose, or else to yield a mixture of low-molecular-weight organic acids. It should be noted that hydrolysis does

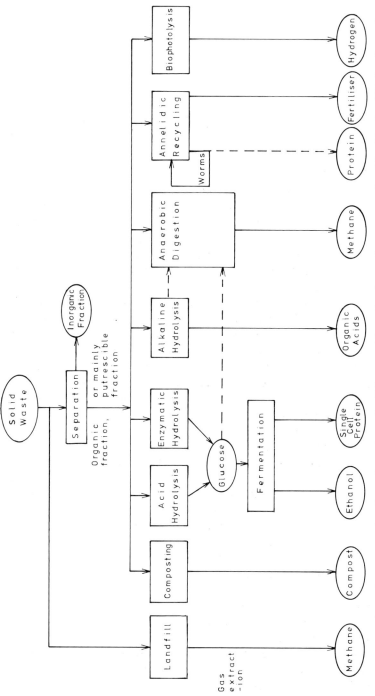

Fig. 19.1. *Biological processes for the reclamation of solid waste.* Note that byproducts are omitted in this simplified, schematic representation.

not reclaim any useful products from non-cellulosic components of municipal waste.

Anaerobic digestion of organic materials in the absence of air yields a mixture of methane and carbon dioxide. The reactivity of the organic fraction of municipal waste is low, and a large undigested residue is usually produced. This problem may be alleviated to some extent by the pre-hydrolysis of cellulosic materials.

Organic wastes may be used as the feedstock for a rapidly expanding population of red earthworms. The process of annelidic recycling effectively turns the waste into a rich fertilizer in the form of worm castings; excess worms can be dried and used as a high-protein supplement in animal food. The first commercial scale annelidic recycling facility began operating in Canada in 1970, treating food-processing wastes. The system is under intensive development in Japan, and at least eleven small plants are processing between 10 and 30 t.p.d. of biodegradable wastes (Rossi 1979). A rather similar concept being developed in Spain is to utilize putrescible wastes to breed fly larvae for use as a protein supplement in animal food (Cavanna et al. 1978).

A possible route for biological reclamation of wastes which has received little attention is biophotolysis. This is the sunlight or ultra-violet induced enzymatic reduction of water inside the cells of plant material to produce hydrogen gas.

The remainder of this chapter examines in turn the three major biological options, namely composting, hydrolysis, and anaerobic digestion.

19.2. Composting

19.2.1. Principles

Composting of municipal wastes has had a chequered history over the past four decades. Most plants operating in industrialized countries have experienced difficulty in marketing the product. Compost is a low-grade fertilizer, and is valued mainly as a soil conditioner.

The successful practice of composting must be based on a sound understanding of the microbiology of the process. This has been the subject of much research, good reviews being given for example by Gotaas (1956), Gray and Biddlestone (1973) and Golueke (1977). In the early stages of composting, mesophilic organisms (mainly bacteria) multiply, the temperature in the active mass rising rapidly. Above 40 °C, the mesophiles die and thermophilic organisms (mainly actinomycetes and fungi) take over. By 60 °C the thermophilic fungi have died off and the reaction is kept going by the spore-forming species of bacteria and actinomycetes. The attainment of temperatures around 60 °C is necessary to ensure the destruction of pathogenic organisms. At about this stage, the rapidly degradable vegetable and putrescible components of waste become used up and the reaction rate slackens. The rate of heat generation becomes less than the rate of heat loss from the surface, and the mass begins to cool down. As the temperature decreases, the various types of organism in turn slowly attack the cellulose and lignin components of the waste. After ambient temperatures have been achieved once more, a further period of curing or maturing is required. This additional maturation is necessary to allow remaining cellulose and lignin to degrade. The use of immature compost actually takes nutrients from the soil and may damage plants.

The composting of organic wastes is a dynamic and extremely complex ecological process. The temperature, pH, and food availability change rapidly, with consequential changes in the numbers and species of organisms present. The rate of degradation towards the final stable product is controlled by a number of interrelated environmental factors, including:

Particle size and structural strength of the feedstock;
Availability of nutrients;
Moisture content;
Aeration and agitation;
pH;
Size of composting heap.

The optimum values of the major composting parameters are summarized in Table 19.1.

19.2.2. Practice

A simplified flow diagram for composting municipal waste is shown in Fig. 19.2. The four basic steps are preparation, digestion, curing, and finishing. *Preparation* usually involves separating the organic and inorganic fractions; although this could be done after digestion, the compost would then have become contaminated with potentially toxic metals. In most published work manual separation is assumed, together with magnetic extraction of ferrous metals and size reduction of the remaining materials. Air classification can obviously be used to replace hand separation. Preparation of the waste may also require the addition of nutrients, principally nitrogen, to feed the micro-organisms and so speed decomposition. Sewage sludge is often used as a convenient source of nutrients.

Digestion is the critical step in which most of the microbiological action takes place; it includes the mesophilic, thermophilic, and cooling phases as outlined above. The simplest method of digestion is to pile the prepared waste in windrows about 1.5–2 m high and about 2–2.5 m wide. The windrows must be regularly turned to ensure adequate aeration; this is most efficiently achieved using a purpose-built turning machine (Fig. 19.3). According to Golueke (1977), a well managed and mechanized windrowing operation can achieve digestion in as little as two weeks. During this time the

Table 19.1

Factor affecting the rate of composting

Factor	Comments
Particle size and structural strength of feedstock	Particle size should be small enough to give adequate surface area for microbial attack, but not so small that little void space remains between particles. Materials which lose their structural strength when wet should not be composted alone as the lack of void space would impede air movement. Optimum size is 1–4 cm for mechanical plants with forced aeration, or 4–8 cm for windrows and natural aeration.
Availability of nutrients	Nitrogen is the major nutrient required by the micro-organisms. An optimum ratio of carbon to nitrogen (C/N) is about 30:1. Municipal waste has a C/N about 60:1, so that nutrients need to be added, usually in the form of sewage sludge.
Moisture content	Water is required by micro-organisms, a minimum level of 30 per cent being necessary. The optimum level is the maximum achievable without filling the pore spaces with water and thus impeding air movement, and is usually about 50–60 per cent.
Aeration and agitation	Adequate aeration is necessary for the composting process. An optimum air flow of 2–6 m^3/day/kg of volatile solids is required during the thermophilic stage. Regular agitation aids aeration and exposes fresh material to attack, but too much agitation leads to excessive heat loss and compression of the heap.
pH control	pH changes from acid to alkaline during composting. However, deliberate pH control usually has little effect on the process.
Heap size	A minimum heap size is necessary, particularly in windrowing, to provide thermal insulation. The maximum size is determined by the prevention of overheating. Optimum size for windrows is about 1.5m high and 2.5m wide.

windrows should be constructed on a paved surface to facilitate the movement of turning equipment.

Many proprietary mechanical digesters have been developed to increase the rate of decomposition by agitation and forced aeration; typical retention times are about 3–6 days. About 30 systems have been listed by Breidenbach (1971) and by Gray, Biddlestone, and Clark (1973). However, these may be classified into three broad categories:

(1) Rotating drum digesters are basically lengthened versions of a wet pulverizer (Section 12.2). An example is the Dano system which has been used quite extensively in Europe and Japan.

(2) Tank digesters spread the waste in tanks with a perforated base through which air enters, mechanical agitation being provided by moving arms. Examples include the Fairfield–Hardy system, with a circular tank in which waste enters at the periphery and is gradually moved to a central discharge, and the Metro–Waste process which uses rectangular tanks and batch digestion.

(3) Silo digesters resemble multiple-hearth incinerators, consisting of a number of tiers. Waste enters the top deck and is gradually moved to lower

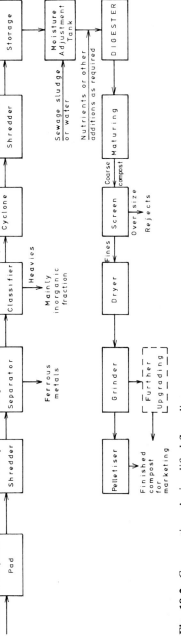

Fig. 19.2. *Composting.* A simplified flow diagram.

Fig. 19.3. *The windrow method of composting.* The compost is being turned, homogenised and aerated by a purpose built Compo-S T A R 4000 turning machine. (Photo courtesy Buhler-Miag (England) Ltd.)

decks, for example by ploughs which also provide agitation and aeration. More recent silo methods include the Varro process of Ecology Inc., and the Peabody–Holmes process.

Curing is necessary after initial degradation to allow the decomposition of remaining cellulose and lignin. The time allowed depends on the proposed use, with an ideal of about three months. Windrows are commonly used for curing, although the Varro process, for example, claims to accomplish curing in the bottom two decks of an 8-deck silo digester. Such claims are probably best regarded with some scepticism.

The *finishing* of the compost depends both on its pre-processing and on the use. Screening, to remove remaining inorganics, drying, grinding, and pelletization are commonly used, the product being marketed in bags or in bulk. Glass in the compost may be a problem, but grinding at least reduces the size of offending particles. The Varro process (General Electric Company 1973*a*) includes several options for more sophisticated finishing, for example by separation in an air cyclone to produce a fine compost suitable for water spraying. Other uses proposed for compost include as a fertilizer base, in wallboard production, as an aggregate in building blocks, or as an artificial roughage in cattle feed (Herschel Shosteck Associates 1972). Its primary use remains, however, as a soil conditioner. Its fertilizer content is low (about 1 per cent nitrogen, 0.25 per cent phosphorus, and 0.25 per cent potassium), and concern has been expressed both on pathogen survival and on the levels of toxic metals. However, by proper control of digestion and the use of modern methods for pre-separation of the waste, these problems can largely be overcome. An ideal pre-separation is one which does not involve initial pulverization of the waste; this enables small, dry-cell batteries to be removed from the compostable fraction by magnetic separation, *before* any contamination from the heavy metals in the batteries has occurred.

Over 200 composting plants have been used worldwide for municipal wastes, but many of these have now been abandoned. In Britain, the available data need careful interpretation as rotary-drum pulverizers are sometimes classified as composting plants. Only one operational plant is actually producing compost. This is the Dano rotary drum plant at Wanlip in Leicestershire. The plant was first built in 1967 and has recently been renovated (Millbank 1976*d*). The product is marketed countrywide under the tradename 'Lescost'. Although many of the more sophisticated mechanical digesters were designed and demonstrated in the United States, no composting plant is now operational in that country. Composting currently accounts for up to 10–15 per cent of municipal waste disposal in several European countries, notably Switzerland, Austria, and France (Table 1.5). Its use has been declining, but there does appear to have been some resurgence in the last couple of years; at least five plants were being built in Sweden and Denmark in the period 1978–80. Most operational plants in less developed countries, such as those in Mexico, use windrowing systems. However, this is the main market being exploited by manufacturers of mechanical systems. For example, Peabody–Holmes are building two composting plants in Libya with silo digesters and a combined capacity of 900 t.p.d.; the total contract, including incinerators for the residues, was worth £30 million (Peabody–Gallion Corporation 1976).

Many authors have tended to dismiss windrowing as inefficient, wasteful of land, and likely to create a public nuisance through foul odours. However, Golueke (1977) points out that mechanical systems are very capital intensive, do not completely eliminate odours, and require only a little less land, thanks to recent improvements in windrowing techniques and the need in either case for a long period of maturing. As composting seems mainly to have a future in smaller rural communities, or in less developed countries with a waste high in putrescible materials, where capital is scarce and land is often plentiful, windrowing seems to be the most promising option. However, in arid areas where humus is in short supply, windrows might tend to dry out rapidly. In such circumstances, the advantages of mechanical digesters might be more obvious.

19.2.3. *Quantitative information*

Most published information on composting plants concerns relatively sophisticated mechanical systems developed in the USA, which have had limited practical application (Table 19.2). This discussion is therefore directed mainly to mechanical rather than windrowing methods of digestion.

The claimed capital costs of the seven processes listed vary between £2 million and £7 million at mid-1977 costs for a plant with design capacity of 360 t.p.d. The rotary drum plant at Salzburg in Austria which opened in 1978 was reported to have cost about £4 million, for a capacity of 3–400 t.p.d. (Lutz 1979). The 250 t.p.d. windrowing plant ordered for Eskilstuna in Sweden in 1979 had a contract value of £3 million. These costs may be compared with the £3.8 million estimated in Section 15.3 for the production of American RDF, which is similar to the feedstock preparation required here. An estimate of £5 million is made here for a plant with a design capacity of 400 t.p.d.; this corresponds to the replacement cost quoted by Millbank (1976d) for the Dano plant in Leicestershire.

Economies of scale in capital costs are comparatively well documented. From the data in Table 19.2 two scale factors emerge, namely 0.6 up to about 400 t.p.d. and 0.9–1.0 at higher capacities. Factors of 0.65 and 0.95 are used here, with a critical capacity for the changeover of 450 t.p.d.

It is assumed that curing and finishing operate one shift only, with waste preparation on two shifts and the digesters working continuously. The labour force of 30 men is made up of 8 day–men, 5 per shift for preparation and 3 per shift for digestion. Energy requirements are quite high, but are poorly documented. Schulz et al. (1976) give a usage of 28 kWh of electricity and 330 MJ of heat per tonne for the Varro process, equivalent to 120 kWh/t if the heat is supplied by electricity. The Salzburg plant is reported to use 45 kWh/t (Lutz 1979). Otherwise, data are given for the connected power only, which ranges from 500 to 3500 kW, that for the Varro process being high. If a loading of 2000 kW is used at full power for an average of 40 h/week, the usage is about 50 kWh/t. From Fig. 12.10, the power consumption for size reduction to 40 mm is about 40 kWh/t. It is assumed here that energy is supplied as electricity to the process at a rate of 60 kWh/t, with an additional 1.5 l/t of diesel fuel for handling incoming waste and the windrows used for curing the compost. Maintenance requirements of composting are difficult to assess, and a standard factor of 0.08 I/annum is used.

The materials balance of composting is complicated by the addition of sewage sludge in many processes (Table 19.2). Owing to lack of data, the effect of the sludge is here neglected. It is assumed that one tonne of waste produces 0.40 t of compost, 0.07 t of ferrous metals, and 0.30 t of inorganic rejects, the balance being discharged to the atmosphere, mainly as carbon dioxide and water. The residue is disposed of, with costs as for incinerator residue.

The revenue from selling compost is difficult to assess; a price of £3/t of compost is assumed here, giving a revenue of £1.20/t of waste.

Table 19.2

Data on composting systems

Manufacturer	Type of digester	Source	Capital costs[a] Original (million)	Capital costs[a] Adjusted (£ m 1977)	Scale factor Critical capacity x t.p.d.	Scale factor Low capacity x >	Scale factor High capacity x <	Number of men	Connected power (kW)	Sewage sludge Added (t/t)	Compost produced (t/t of waste)
Fairfield-Hardy	Circular tank	General Electric Company (GEC) 1973a Drobny, Hull, and Testin 1971	$4.2 $3.0[b]	3.6 5.5[b]	360	0.6 – 0.72	0.9 – 1.1	32	1900	0.25	0.30
Metro-Waste	Rectangular tank	Drobny et al. 1971 Pavoni et al. 1975	$2.0	1.7	360	0.4 – 0.5	1.0	30	1500	n.a.	n.a.
International Disposal Corporation (Naturizer)	Silo	Drobny et al. 1971 Pavoni et al. 1975	$4.0	3.4	360	0.6	1.0	45	820	n.a.	n.a.
Ecology (Varro)	Silo	GEC 1973a Schulz et al. 1976	$9.0 $5.7[b]	7.1 3.4	540 n.a.	0.6 n.a.	1.0 n.a.	40 20	3500 [c]	0 0	0.50 0.50
Geochemical–Eweson	Rotary drum	GEC 1973a	$3.8[b]	6.9[b]	140	0.92	0.97 – 0.99	4	n.a.	0.33	0.60
Dano[d]	Rotary drum	Association of Waste Disposal Engineers 1976 Millbank 1976d	£1.25 (1967)	5.0	n.a.	n.a.	n.a.	n.a.	n.a.	0.30	0.65
Conservation International	Windrowing (with grinding)	GEC 1973a	$2.7	2.1	n.a.	0.82	n.a.	20	450	0	0.60

n.a.: not available.
(a) 360 t.p.d. plant.
(b) Installed equipment costs given, standard factor of 3.10/1.45 = 2.14 used (Section 5.4).
(c) 28 kWh of electricity + 330 MJ of heat/t of waste.
(d) Data is for the Wanlip plant in Leicestershire which processes 40 000 t of waste/annum.

19.2.4. Discussion

Using the available data for mechanical digestion processes, the standard economic analysis yields a net cost for composting of £22 ± £6/t of waste. The net cost is relatively insensitive to the price of compost. On the basis of this analysis composting is comparable in cost with incineration, but more expensive than landfill or the production and sale of a refuse-derived fuel.

The process analysis yields an energy input to composting of 1400 MJ/t. The energy savings from materials recovery are uncertain as the energy to supply humus is not easy to evaluate. It is credited here (Section E.6) with its heat content, assumed to be the same as for untreated waste, and with the energy to obtain and transport peat. The saving is thus 11 GJ/t of compost, or 4400 MJ/t of waste. Coupled to a ferrous metal saving of 1700 MJ/t, net energy efficiencies for composting are thus $\alpha = -0.14$ and $\beta = 0.47$.

The limitations of the data on which this analysis was based must be emphasized. It should be noted in particular that windrowing systems could in favourable circumstances yield a rather lower net cost per tonne. The local conditions which might indicate that composting is worth considering as a waste disposal option include:

A shortage of humus in the soil, as for example in an arid area;

A high organic content in the waste, making less sophisticated pre-treatment necessary;

A plentiful supply of land;

The availiabity of cheap labour.

This evaluation has considered composting of all the organic materials in the waste. Alternatively, composting may be applied as a unit operation to the putrescible fraction, such as that from the separation flowsheets in Figs 14.1(d)–(f). The first commercial plants using each of the paper separation processes highlighted in Section 14.3.1 are designed to compost the residual organic materials. Composting is also being considered for incorporation in the Doncaster sorting plant (Thomas 1977) and is used for fine material screened from dry pulverized wastes at the Caister-on-Sea plant in Norfolk (Singh 1976). The intention in the latter cases is to use the compost in land reclamation or as a cover material for landfill.

19.3. Hydrolysis

19.3.1. Introduction

Cellulose can by hydrolysed, using an acid, alkali, or enzyme as catalyst, to yield sugars

$$(C_6H_{10}O_5)_n + nH_2O \rightarrow nC_6H_{12}O_6$$

which can in turn be fermented to yield ethanol

$$C_6H_{12}O_6 \rightarrow 2C_2H_5OH + 2CO_2$$

or other products which include single-cell protein (SCP) and low-molecular-weight organic acids. Municipal waste contains cellulose mainly as paper, and interest has been shown primarily in two variations, acid hydrolysis to yield ethanol and enzymatic hydrolysis of yield SCP. Attention here is focused primarily on acid hydrolysis for which most information is available.

Enzymatic hydrolysis has been developed in recent years by the University of California at Berkeley (Golueke and McGauhey 1971) and by the US Army Research and Development Command at Natick (Spans 1976). Comprehensive reviews are given by Das and Ghose (1973), Humphrey (1974) and Rogers (1976). The basic process features may be outlined:

(1) The feedstock must be mainly cellulosic, and must be ground to a very fine particle size.

(2) Hydrolysis occurs at low temperatures (30–60 °C) in a solution containing 5–10 per cent solids. Retention times are about 48–64 h. Resultant sugar solutions must be dilute (2.5–5.0 per cent) to prevent inhibition of the enzymatic reaction.

(3) Recovery of the enzyme for reuse is difficult; much is lost by absorption on the non-cellulosic fraction of the substrate.

(4) Sterile conditions must be maintained to prevent the loss of enzyme or sugar.

Alkaline hydrolysis has received comparatively little attention (Bell and Jones 1977). Under mild conditions, the cellulose is rendered more soluble and reactive by the removal of the lignin sheathing. Some depolymerization of cellulose itself may also occur. More vigorous conditions yield a mixture of low-molecular-weight organic acids, including acetic, oxalic, lactic, and formic acids, and methanol. The method could potentially yield a product such as oxalic acid in commercial quantities.

19.3.2. Acid hydrolysis

Acid hydrolysis of cellulose was discovered in the last century and was used commercially for ethanol production from wood in the USA during the two world wars. Saeman (1945) studied the reaction kinetics, showing that two first-order reactions occur, the first being hydrolysis to fermentable sugar and the second a breakdown of the sugar into non-fermentable products on continued exposure to hot acid. As both reactions are kinetically controlled, there is an optimum time for maximum fermentable sugar yield at any given temperature and acid concentration. The wartime process used a temperature of 180 °C at an acid concentration of about 0.5 per cent H_2SO_4, with a reaction time of about 3–5 h.

Porteous (1967, 1969) extrapolated Saeman's data for wood cellulose, predicting a maximum sugar yield of 55 per cent under optimum conditions of 230 °C, 0.4 per cent H_2SO_4, and reaction time 1.2 min. Using this information, Porteous proposed a continuous process for the hydrolysis of municipal waste. His colleagues at Dartmouth College, New Hampshire, carried out experimental work in both batch and flow reactors, obtaining maximum yields of 52–54 per cent at 230 °C, 1 per cent H_2SO_4, and about 1 min residence time (Fagan 1969; Fagan, Converse, and Grethlein 1970; Fagan, Grethlein, Converse, and Porteous 1971; Converse, Grethlein, Karandikar, and Kuhrtz 1973; Grethlein 1975). To achieve these maximum sugar yields, the cellulose must have appropriate chemical reactivity for reaction. Brenner, Rugg, and Rogers (1977) reported a series of experiments with different methods of preparing the paper feed stock. Their maximum yield of 49 per cent was achieved by using a very short reaction time (10–20 s) and wet pulped waste which had been subject to a 10 megarad radiation dose. Without irradiation the best yield was only 37 per cent. They also reported plans to build a 1 t.p.d. continuous flow pilot plant.

A simplified flowsheet for the acid hydrolysis of municipal waste is shown in Fig. 19.4. The waste preparation system suggested here produces an RDF rich in paper; the technology for plastics removal is not well developed (Section 14.3.2). The RDF is mixed with hot water and acid at 230 °C and injected into the tubular flow reactor. The reaction is quenched by flash cooling to 100 °C, either in a multi-stage system which maximizes heat recovery (Porteous 1969) or in a single stage (Fagan *et al.* 1970). Control of the reaction time may be a problem, as a reaction will begin during the mixing or heating of the reactants and will continue during cooling, particularly if this is achieved slowly. To obtain maximum sugar yield, recycling of some of the reaction products is necessary (Fagan 1969). The remaining slurry is neutralized with calcium carbonate, filtered, and evaporated to produce a 12 per cent sugar solution, which is the recommended concentration for ethanol fermentation. Neutralization of sulphuric acid with lime may present difficulties because of the formation of insoluble calcium sulphate. The fermentation is carried out for 20–24 h at 40 °C, the resulting solution being distilled or rectified to yield a 95 per cent ethanol solution.

19.3.3. Quantitative data

Fagan (1969) wrote a computer program to simulate the performance of the hydrolysis system under different conditions. The economics were found to be sensitive to the reaction temperature, residence time, acid concentration, recycle rate, and solid to liquid ratio. Cost estimates are given in most of the Porteous and Fagan papers. The size of plant studied which is most appropriate here is 250 t (dry weight) per day; this is equivalent to a weekly throughput of 2300 t of waste as delivered at 25 per cent moisture.

Capital costs were estimated from equipment lists at £1.4 million (Porteous 1971) and £2.4 million (Porteous 1975), equivalent to £4.2 and £3.4 million at 1977 prices; an average of £3.8 million is taken here. Of this, 17 per cent or £650 000 is the cost of waste reception and feedstock preparation facilities. The production of RDF by dry separation was estimated in Chapter 15 at £3.8 million for American RDF or £2.5 million for paper-based RDF. The reason for this substantial difference was not clear. Neither system included plastics removal from the product. An intermediate value of £3.3 million is suggested and used here; when this is substituted, the overall capital cost becomes £6.5 million.

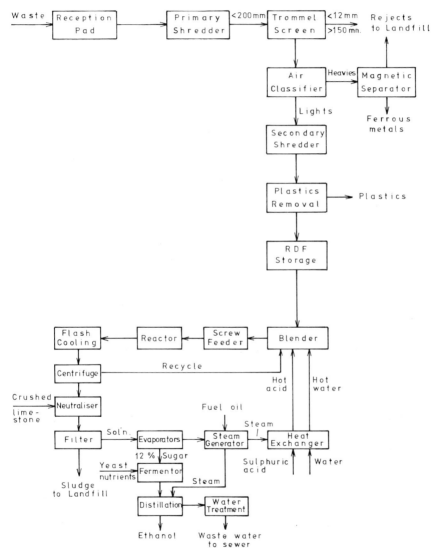

Fig. 19.4. *Acid hydrolysis.*

However, this may still be an underestimate as the original estimate (Porteous 1971) did not include provision for handling and storage facilities for ethanol, sulphuric acid, limestone, fuel oil, or unreacted residue, and used a Lang factor f_L (ratio of total plant cost to delivered equipment cost, equation 5.3) of only 2.67. Using a factor $f_L = 3.63$, for a typical solids–fluids processing plant (Holland et al. 1974), and allowing £400 000 for the additional facilities, the estimate for the hydrolysis and fermentation sections of the plant is increased from £3.1 to £4.6 million, giving a total plant cost of about £8 million; this estimate is used here. A scale factor of 0.8 was estimated for RDF production, while for hydrolysis and fermentation a lower factor of 0.7 may be appropriate; however, a cautious overall factor of 0.8 is suggested.

The reaction yield is taken to be 50 per cent of the maximum available sugar, a value which may be optimistic. With 40 per cent paper in the waste, or 31 per cent on a dry weight basis (Table 1.3), and 75 per cent cellulose content in the paper, the net sugar yield is thus 129 kg/t of waste. Ethanol yields obtained by Converse et al. (1973) were 85–94 per cent of the maximum, but commercial fermentation of molasses only yields 80 per cent. Using a 90 per cent yield, the net yield of ethanol (on 100 per cent basis) is 57 kg/t of waste. A single waste hydrolysis plant, processing 75 000 t of waste per annum, would thus produce over 4000 tonnes of industrial ethanol per annum, which would be competing in a market where UK sales (excluding in-house use by the producing industry) have averaged about 140 000 tonnes per annum over the last 10 years (Annual Abstract of Statistics, 1966–76). Widespread use of waste hydrolysis would thus require the development of substantial new markets for ethanol if a significant decrease in price was to be avoided.

The overall mass balance of the process given by Porteous (1971) suggests that about 440 kg/t of dry solids remain for disposal to land, with about 180 kg/t for disposal to sewer after removal of the fermentable sugar. More detailed mass balances are given by Fagan (1969) and by Converse et al. (1973). The residue for landfill disposal contains about 25–30 per cent moisture by weight, and it is assumed that, after extraction of ferrous metals, 500 kg/t remain. This is assumed to have a transport cost as for other dense residues, but a higher landfill cost, 70 per cent of that for untreated waste (cf. the residue from production of paper-based RDF). The waste water produced is a major problem, Porteous suggesting a biological oxygen demand (BOD) content of 5 g/l. The capital cost estimated by Porteous in 1971 included water treatment facilities, although this may have been omitted from his (lower) 1975 estimate. It is assumed that the discharge of about 5 m³/t is charged at the standard rate of 20 p/m³. Water usage in the process is also about 5 m³/t.

When the optimum concentration of 0.4 per cent H_sSO_4 is used, the process requires theoretical quantities of 19 kg H_2SO_4/t of waste and an equimolar amount of $CaCO_3$ for neutralization. The amount of acid is doubled by Porteous (1969) to allow 'costing latitude', although experimental work gave optimal yields for 1 per cent H_2SO_4. It is optimistically assumed here that 40 kg/t of each is used. This results in production of about 55 kg/t (dry weight) of $CaSO_4$ sludge, increasing the total residue for land disposal to about 600 kg (wet weight)/t of waste. The theoretical heat requirement for the hydrolysis reaction and for distillation is about 1.4 GJ/t (Porteous 1969). To allow for combustion inefficiency and heat losses this is increased by 50 per cent, giving a requirement about 2.1 GJ/t. Electricity usage for preparation of RDF is about 50–80 kWh/t, not including plastics separation; an overall requirement of about 130 kWh/t is suggested.

Labour requirements for separation were estimated (Chapter 15) at 4 men, plus 6 on each of 2 shifts. For the hydrolysis and fermentation processes, 2 additional day–men plus 5 men on each of 4 shifts is assumed, giving a total complement of 38 men. Maintenance is estimated at a standard factor of 0.08 l/annum.

19.3.4. Discussion

All the available approaches for hydrolysis of the cellulosic fraction of municipal waste are at an early stage of development. Any quantitative assessment must thus be regarded as extremely tentative. With this proviso, the data presented above yield, in the standard economic analysis, an overall net cost for acid hydrolysis of £34 ± £11/t of waste. This cost is quite sensitive to the price of ethanol; the total revenue is about £13/t of waste, more than for any of the other options examined. If the capital cost could be reduced from £8 million to £4 million, the net cost would be reduced to about £20/t.

The process analysis indicates an energy requirement of 5800 MJ/t, which is only partially offset by the primary energy savings of 1700 MJ/t from ferrous metals and 2900 MJ/t from ethanol, so that the net energy efficiencies are both negative, with $\alpha = -0.58$ and $\beta = -0.12$. Of the options studied here which involve some form of resource recovery from waste, acid hydrolysis appears to be the only net energy consumer.

19.4. Anaerobic digestion

19.4.1. Principles and operating experience

The production of methane at pipeline quality from organic wastes has been the goal of much academic research; a useful review of some 200 references is that of Hobson, Bousfield, and Summers (1974). Anaerobic digestion may be viewed as either a three- or four-stage process. If a substantial part of the organic feedstock is cellulosic, then a preliminary hydrolysis must occur.

The three basic steps are then conversion of glucose, other carbohydrates, proteins, and fats, into short-chain fatty acids by so-called acidogenic bacteria; conversion of these acids into acetate and bicarbonate by acetogens; and final conversion into methane and carbon dioxide by methanogens.

Anaerobic digestion has been widely applied since the beginning of this century to waste water treatment and animal manures; a typical sewage sludge digester is illustrated in Fig. 19.5. Interest in a possible application to municipal wastes is more recent; a first international conference was held recently (Wheatley and Stafford 1979). Laboratory work has been carried out by a number of organizations, notably the Institute of Gas Technology in Chicago (Ghosh and Klass 1976, 1977), the Dynatech Corporation (Kispert *et al.* 1975; Kispert, Sadek, and Wise 1976; Wise, Sadek, Kispert, Anderson, and Walker 1975), the University of Illinois (Pfeffer 1974; Pfeffer and Liebman 1976), University College, Cardiff, and the Catholic University of Louvain in Belgium (Naveau, Nyns, Binot, and Delafontaine 1979). Larger-scale tests using a redundant 400 m³ sewage digester at Franklin, Ohio, have been reported (Swartzbaugh, Miller, and Wiles 1977; Jarvis, Swartzbaugh, Walter, and Wiles 1978), while a 45–90 t.p.d. pilot plant at Pompano Beach, Florida (Pfeffer, 1978), began start-up in November, 1978.

A typical flowsheet is shown in Fig. 19.6. Any separation method may be used, the organic fraction being mixed with sewage sludge before digestion. Successful operation of the digester requires control of five parameters:

Fig. 19.5. *Anaerobic digester for sewage sludge.* This plant is in Helsinki, Finland.

(i) Temperature, which may be held in either the mesophilic (40 °C) or thermophilic (60 °C) range, the latter giving higher methane yields and hence a shorter retention time (Pfeffer and Liebman 1976).

(ii) The maintenance of anaerobic conditions.

(iii) pH, with an optimum range of 6.7–7.0 achieved by use of sodium bicarbonate or lime.

(iv) Nutrients, necessary for optimum bacterial growth, are supplied by the sewage sludge.

(v) Toxicity of the input waste, which may be reduced by careful separation of inorganic materials, by chemical precipitation within the digester, and by dilution.

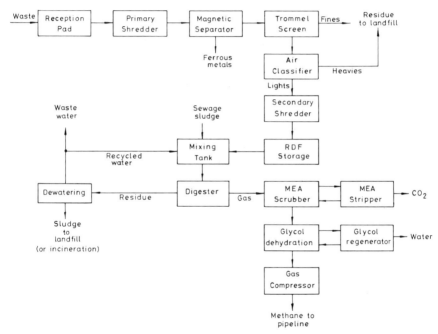

Fig. 19.6. *Anaerobic digestion.*

Even if these conditions may be established and maintained, it remains to be demonstrated that municipal waste may be successfully digested on the large scale. An early 75-day test at Franklin proved disappointing, with only 7.5 per cent destruction of the volatile solids in the waste. The problem was caused by stratification of the wet-pulped material in the digester, with ash settling and plastics floating, each trapping organic materials (Swartzbaugh *et al.* 1977). Subsequent trials used either a mechanical agitator, or a gas draft tube agitator, to replace the original recirculation pump in the digester. Short-term tests showed satisfactory digestion of a slurry containing 4 per cent solids, with 45–50 per cent destruction of the volatile solids in the waste. However, some stratification still occurred, with a gradual build-up of scum on the surface. The long-term viability of the system has yet to be proven (Jarvis *et al.* 1978).

Most studies have used a single digester, but recent work suggests that separation of the acidogenic and methanogenic processes may aid the stability of the system (Keenan 1976). The addition of a preliminary hydrolysis stage, to convert the cellulose to glucose or to remove the lignin sheathing and thus render the cellulose more prone to enzymatic hydrolysis in the digester, may significantly increase the yields from the overall process (Fig. 19.1; Ghosh and Klass 1977; Klee and Rogers 1977).

Experimental evidence for the advantages of multi-stage digestion is provided by recent Japanese work (Ishida, Odawara, Gejo, and Okumura 1979). They show that the liquefaction and gasification processes are both highly pH dependent, with optimum ranges of 5.2–6.3 and 7.5–8.2, respectively. The conventional range of pH 6.7–7.0 for the combined process is thus an uneasy compromise. Their advanced process, consisting of the three sequential steps alkaline pre-treatment, liquefaction, and gasification, was tested in a 25 l digester in semi-continuous mode over a 54-day period. Compared with a conventional one-step process, total retention time was reduced from 14 to 8 days; methane production increased from 240 to 340 litres per kilogram of volatile solids; methane concentration in the product gas increased from 42 to 75 per cent; and maximum volatile solid loading increased from 5.5 to 9.4 kg/m^3 per day.

The gas from the digester contains about 50 per cent CO_2 and trace amounts of H_2S which must be removed, for example by scrubbing with monoethanolamine (MEA). The methane is dried by glycol dehydration, the product being of pipeline quality. Both MEA and glycol are regenerated and recirculated.

The undigested material remaining in the digester must be dewatered and disposed of. This is a critical problem, and has been studied by Pfeffer and Liebman (1976). They used both vacuum filtration and centrifugation for dewatering, the latter giving a sludge containing up to 30 per cent solids. This sludge presents a disposal problem, landfill being made difficult by the high biological activity. Incineration has been suggested, partly for disposal and partly to raise the energy efficiency of the process. The use of the residue as a filler in panelboard production shows some promise (Walters, Pfeffer, and Chow 1977). The effluent remaining after dewatering is of very poor quality, and on-site treatment is probably necessary.

19.4.2. Quantitative information

Several of the laboratory studies included computer simulation of the process economics. Capital costs have been estimated at $14 million (1972) for a

1450 t.p.d. plant (Ghosh and Klass 1976), \$22.2 million (1974) for 900 t.p.d. (Kispert *et al*. 1975) and \$14.3 million (1973) for 900 t.p.d., including residue incineration (Pfeffer and Liebman 1976). The digesters have estimated retention times up to 10 days, with each digester handling about 100 t of input waste per day (Hitte 1976). Thus the overall scale factor is high, with $S = 0.9$ assumed here. Using this factor, the above estimates are equivalent, for a 400 t.p.d. plant on a 1977 cost basis, to £3.5, £6.6, and £5.1 million, respectively. In each case, the waste preparation system uses dry separation to produce an American RDF. The estimates for those parts of the plant which prepare and store the RDF are £0.7, £1.7, and £1 million, respectively, which may be compared with the estimate in Section 15.3 of £3.8 million. If this figure is substituted, and an average value is used for the digestion, gas cleaning, and residue disposal subsections, a total plant cost about £8 million is suggested.

The mass and energy balances for the process are complicated by the addition of sewage sludge. It is assumed that the sludge solids are 60 per cent digestible (Kispert *et al*. 1975). The heat content of the methane recovered is then calculated as 37.5 per cent (Pfeffer and Liebman 1976), 35 per cent (Schulz *et al*. 1976), 42 per cent (Hecklinger 1976) or 47 per cent (Ghosh and Klass 1976) of that in the input waste. A value of 40 per cent is assumed here. The methane is of pipeline quality, so a price just 10 per cent less than that for natural gas is assumed, with an energy supply efficiency (including distribution losses) of 90 per cent. Initial waste separation produces ferrous metals, plus 230 kg/t of rejects for landfill disposal. The sludge from dewatering contains between 180 (Kispert *et al*. 1975) and 310 (Ghosh and Klass 1976; Pfeffer and Liebman 1976) kg of dry solids per tonne, with a solid content of about 25 per cent. The quantity of sewage sludge disposed of by the process is about 40 kg dry solids per tonne, so that the net production of sludge is reduced to about 250 kg/t. It is optimistically assumed that 1 t of wet sludge per tonne of waste remains to be disposed of, that landfill is an acceptable means of disposal, and that the costs are similar to those for untreated waste. Waste water generation is about 0.5 m³/t (Kispert *et al*. 1975), but pre-treatment facilities are not included in the cost estimate and an arbitrary cost of 50 p/t is assumed, together with an energy requirement of 100 MJ/t.

Electricity usage in the process is quoted at about 60 kWh/t, but this is lower than the 65 kWh/t used in Section 15.3 for RDF preparation, and so an overall requirement of 90 kWh/t is assumed. Process heat is used both in the digester and for the regeneration of monoethanolamine. A requirement of 1.5 GJ/t is assumed, midway between the 1 GJ/t of Pfeffer and Liebman (1976) and the 2 GJ/t of Schulz *et al*. (1976). Water usage is minimized by recirculation and by the water in the sewage sludge. Chemicals are used at several points in the process; an alkali is used for pH control in the digester and additional nutrients may be added; MEA for acid gas removal is recirculated, losses amounting to about 20 g/t of waste (Kispert *et al.* 1975); glycol for dehydration of the methane is recirculated. The only substantial chemical cost would be nutrients, and it is assumed here that the sewage sludge contains adequate amounts. Thus chemical costs are subsumed under operating supplies.

Manpower requirements for anaerobic digestion are taken to be the same as for acid hydrolysis, that is a total complement of 38 men. A standard maintenance factor of 0.08 *I*/annum is assumed.

19.4.3. Discussion

The data derived above are once again based on extrapolations from small-scale development studies; they must thus be regarded as very tentative. When the standard economic analysis is applied, the overall net cost, £39±£11/t of waste, is high. Process analysis gives an energy requirement of 4200 MJ/t, with primary energy savings from the methane gas of 4400 MJ/t and from ferrous metals of 1700 MJ/t, resulting in low net energy efficiencies of $\alpha = 0.03$ and $\beta = 0.20$.

Current research is aimed largely at increasing the energy efficiency of the process. Incineration of the residue would substantially increase the capital requirements and would multiply the marketing problems by producing steam for sale. More promising are developments related to a fundamental understanding of the microbiology of the process, which should in time enable the yield of methane to be increased and the quantity of undigested residues to be reduced. Optimization of process conditions may require separation of digestion into two or more steps, and this increase in process sophistication could increase capital requirements, tending to negate the advantages of increased revenue from gas sales. However, a final judgement on process economics must await further technical research and development work.

20. HAZARDOUS WASTES

20.1. Introduction

Although this book has been concerned primarily with municipal wastes, including domestic (household), commercial, and similar components of industrial wastes, much of the material is also relevant to other industrial wastes. Those industrial wastes which require special care in handling and disposal are of particular public concern. These 'hazardous' wastes are the subject of this chapter.

The definition of hazardous wastes is problematical. In the UK, the Deposit of Poisonous Wastes Act (1972) avoided the issue by listing those wastes which were considered to be non-hazardous or otherwise exempt from its provisions. A recent directive of the European Economic Community (Council of the European Economic Community 1978) lays a general obligation on member states to ensure the safe disposal of hazardous wastes and to give priority to their prevention and recovery. The directive is accompanied by a list of toxic or dangerous substances selected as requiring priority consideration (Table 20.1).

The quantities of wastes generated by industry are generally not known with any certainty. In Britain, this situation should eventually improve as more Waste Disposal Authorities carry out surveys as required under Section 2 of the Control of Pollution Act. A preliminary estimate of the quantity of hazardous wastes generated in Britain is about $4–5 \times 10^6$ t/annum (Wilson 1979a). It is impossible at present to break this estimate down in any detail, although the majority (perhaps about 80 per cent) appears to be in the form of sludges or of liquids which are unsuitable for discharge to sewer. Such materials are inherently more difficult to handle than solid wastes.

The great majority of hazardous wastes generated in Britain are either disposed of to land or at sea, in shallow coastal waters. A few per cent are incinerated, treated chemically or encapsulated prior to landfill disposal. The dominant position of land disposal, including landfill and the lagooning of liquids or sludges, is due mainly to its low cost. Other methods of treatment or disposal will generally be restricted to the top end of the market, to wastes which either are difficult to landfill or which have a high recovery value.

Table 20.1

The EEC list of hazardous wastes

1	Arsenic; arsenic compounds
2	Mercury; mercury compounds
3	Cadmium; cadmium compounds
4	Thallium; thallium compounds
5	Beryllium; beryllium compounds
6	Chrome VI compounds
7	Lead; lead compounds
8	Antimony; antimony compounds
9	Phenols; phenol compounds
10	Cyanides, organic and inorganic
11	Isocyanates
12	Organic-halogen compounds, excluding inert polymeric materials and other substances referred to in this list or covered by other directives concerning the disposal of toxic or dangerous waste
13	Chlorinated solvents
14	Organic solvents
15	Biocides and phyto-pharmaceutical substances
16	Tarry materials from refining and tar residues from distilling
17	Pharmaceutical compounds
18	Peroxides, chlorates, perchlorates, and azides
19	Ethers
20	Chemical laboratory materials, not identifiable and/or new, whose effects on the environment are not known
21	Asbestos (dust and fibres)
22	Selenium; selenium compounds
23	Tellurium; tellurium compounds
24	Aromatic polycyclic compounds (with carcinogenic effects)
25	Metal carbonyls
26	Soluble copper compounds
27	Acids and/or basic substances used in the surface treatment and finishing of metals

A general approach may be outlined to the problem of deciding how to deal with any particular hazardous waste arising. The options are arranged in a hierarchy, and each is examined in turn until an environmentally acceptable solution is found:

(1) Can the waste be reduced or even eliminated by modifying the production process or changing the product design?

(2) Does the waste have the potential for recovery of its constituent materials or energy content?

(3) Is the waste acceptable for landfill, and can a suitable site be found within a reasonable distance?

(4) Can the hazard be removed by decomposing the waste, either thermally, chemically, or biologically?

(5) Can the waste be immobilized by solidification or encapsulation so that land disposal becomes acceptable?

(6) Is the waste acceptable for disposal at sea?

This approach provides a framework which may be expanded as necessary to suit particular groups of wastes. An example of such a decision tree, developed for tarry and distillation wastes and other chemical based residues, is shown in Fig. 20.1. Note that it is assumed that the waste must arise.

These various alternatives are now examined in more detail, land disposal being left to the end.

20.2. Waste reduction

The ideal way to solve a waste disposal problem is to alter the production process so that less waste or a less noxious waste is generated. An example is the metal finishing industry, which operates a wide range of specialized processes for the surface treatment of metals and other materials to protect them against corrosion, to improve their properties, or to enhance their appearance. In Britain, the industry uses about 120×10^6 t/annum of rinsing water which is discharged to sewer after precipitation of the toxic metal components, often as the hydroxides. At least 100 000 t of these sludges are disposed of annually. The Department of the Environment's (1976g) code of practice recommends that the quantities of waste be reduced by reducing water consumption, by modifying the rinsing technique, by reusing water, by modifying component design, by segregating concentrated solutions such as plating baths for separate treatment, and by segregating process effluents as far as possible to facilitate the recovery of metals.

In some cases, the difficulties of waste disposal are such as to force manufacturers to use substitute materials. An example is the use of polychlorinated biphenyls. Ten years ago PCBs were widely used in many industries, but the environmental problems in using and disposing of these very stable and persistent materials have restricted their use to certain dielectric applications only (Department of the Environment 1976f).

20.3. Recovery

Recovery of resources is obviously a preferred method of waste management, but unfortunately it is severely limited in practice by economic considerations. Recovery is aided by keeping waste streams segregated and as concentrated as possible. In some cases the recovered product may be reused directly in the process. Examples are copper and nickel recovery from metal finishing processes; the recovery of oils, fats, and plasticizers by solvent extraction from filter media such as activated carbon and clays; and acid recovery by spray roasting, ion exchange, or crystallization. In other cases, the recovered product is of lower quality than the original, or is a distinct by-product. Examples include the 'laundering' of waste solvents and oils, and the processing of waste caustic from petroleum refining for recovery of saleable sodium sulphide and cresylic acid. Wastes with a high

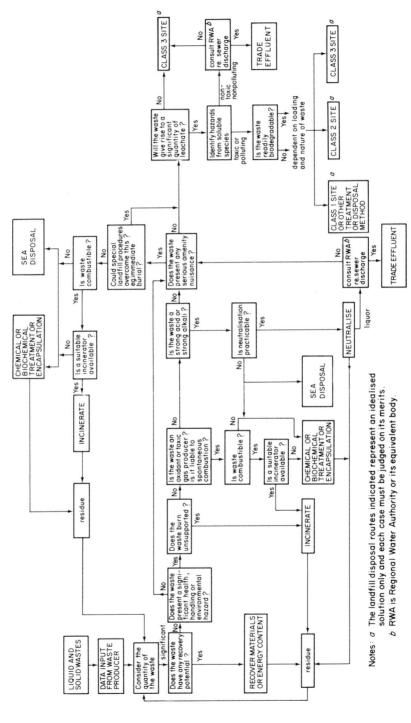

Fig. 20.1. *Decision-making guidelines for a class of potentially hazardous wastes.* Developed from the Department of the Environment's code of practice for tarry and distillation wastes and other chemical based residues (Department of the Environment, 1977a).

Notes: *a* The landfill disposal routes indicated represent an idealised solution only and each case must be judged on its merits.
       b RWA is Regional Water Authority or its equivalent body.

calorific value, such as oils, solvents, and liquid tarry wastes, may also be used as a fuel suplement to recover their energy content. One interesting idea is to use oily wastes instead of water when wet pulverizing domestic refuse to produce a multi-source fuel (Section 15.1). Yet another possibility is the use of one firm's waste as another's raw material. Examples include the use of phthalic anhydride manufacturing residues as feedstock for maleic anhydride production, phosphoric acid from an electronics firm in detergent manufacture, and formic acid waste to replace hydrochloric acid in industrial boiler descaling. A recent development is the Waste Materials Exchange which publishes details of available wastes to facilitate such co-operation; a useful review of some 20 such schemes, operating in 16 countries in Europe, N. America, and Australasia, is given by Wolbeck (1980).

20.4. Incineration

Thermal treatment by incineration is the obvious way of destroying the toxicity of certain hazardous and combustible wastes. It is the recommended method of disposing of chlorinated hydrocarbons, oils, and solvents which cannot be recovered, oil contaminated with cyanide, acid tars, and formulated pesticides if they cannot be used. Considerable flexibility in operation is required to handle a wide range of industrial wastes, including liquids and pumpable sludges, thermoplastic solids, conventional solids such as cardboard and wood, and drummed material.

Several of the incinerators described in Section 13.2 are suitable for hazardous wastes; examples include the multiple chamber, rotary kiln, and liquid waste types, a typical installation being illustrated in Fig. 20.2. A general purpose incinerator for hazardous wastes must be fitted with a wet scrubber to remove noxious acidic gases. This requirement may be dispensed with for ship-borne incinerators, as the acidic gases will be absorbed by the sea. Incineration at sea is perhaps the most environmentally sound option for some classes of organic wastes. Its use is now subject to international convention; it must be shown that destruction of the toxic components in the waste is more than 99.9 per cent complete under the conditions attained within the incinerator (Anon. 1978).

Some hazardous wastes may pose problems in an incinerator. Among points to note are the following:

(1) Adequate operating conditions must be provided to ensure the complete combustion of the toxic components. The four criteria which are relevant here are temperature, residence time, excess air, and turbulence. A distinction should be made between conditions adequate for complete pyrolysis (destruction of the original compound) and complete combustion (oxidation of all organic materials to carbon dioxide and water). Most chlorinated hydrocarbons require temperatures of about 1000–1200 °C,

Fig. 20.2. *A rotary kiln incinerator for hazardous wastes.* This is perhaps the most versatile incinerator design for intractable wastes. The French plant illustrated here is typical of several centralized treatment centres for hazardous wastes in Europe. In the foreground are storage tanks for liquid wastes and facilities for feeding wastes into the rotary kiln. In the background is the afterburner chamber which ensures the complete combustion of product gases. (Photo courtesy The Harwell Laboratory.)

for at least 1 second at 100 per cent excess air, to ensure complete combustion.

(2) Compounds containing volatile metals such as lead, cadmium, zinc, copper, mercury, and arsenic pose problems as the fumes formed tend to be of very small particle size and difficult to remove. A high-energy wet scrubber has been used to remove lead, copper, and zinc, but even then it may be difficult to dispose of the scrubber water. The efficient removal of mercury and perhaps also cadmium requires a bag filter, which has many disadvantages for use on an incinerator. Materials containing substantial concentrations of these metals are probably best not incinerated.

(3) Some materials may damage the incinerator structure unless special refractory liners are used; examples include explosives, acids and alkalis, low-melting-point inorganic halides, fluorides, and compounds of titanium or vanadium.

(4) Some materials require special precautions to protect the operators. Very toxic or pathogenic wastes may present difficulties in ensuring safe handling prior to incineration. Similarly, strongly odiferous materials such as

mercaptans may be difficult to feed into the incinerator without creating a public nuisance. Materials of very low flashpoint should be mixed with other materials before incineration.

Incineration is not limited in its application to thermal decomposition. Waste heat from an incinerator may be used to evaporate aqueous wastes or to thicken sludges, prior to incineration or some other form of treatment or disposal. An incinerator can also be used to calcine non-combustible inorganic wastes, rendering them more refractory and thus less likely to leach out of a landfill site.

20.5. Chemical treatment

Many methods of chemical treatment have been suggested to detoxify hazardous wastes. Among the better developed options are:

Neutralization of strong acids and bases.

Oxidation, which is recommended for aqueous solutions containing cyanide. Hypochlorite oxidizes the cyanide to cyanate, while chlorine yields carbon dioxide and nitrogen. Wet air oxidation of concentrated organic effluents from the chemical industry was included in Table 18.1.

Reduction is the recommended method for concentrated wastes containing hexavalent chromium, which may be reduced to non-toxic trivalent chromium using sulphur dioxide or metabisulphite under acidic conditions.

Alkaline hyrolysis is an effective detoxification method for certain pesticides, including some organophosphorus and carbamate compounds.

Acid hydrolysis is less generally applicable, but may be useful, for example, for some dithiocarbamate fungicides. As these contain metal atoms, their incineration in any quantity may present problems.

Exhaustive chlorination of residues from chlorinated hydrocarbon manufacture has been developed on a commercial scale by Hoechst in Germany. The main product is carbon tetrachloride, so that 'chlorolysis' could be classed as a reclamation process.

The most extensively practised method of 'chemical treatment' in the U K is the *cracking of oil–water emulsions*. The recovered oil is used generally as a low-grade fuel.

A large number of other more or less exotic methods of chemical treatment have been investigated, mainly on the small research scale. Examples applicable to organic, and particularly to chlorinated organic, materials include:

Reduction with metallic sodium, either molten or in a suitable solvent;

Photolytic degradation using ultra-violet light or sunlight;

Microwave-plasma-induced free radical decomposition;

Catalytic dechlorination using nickel boride;

Catalytic hydrodechlorination, in which chlorine atoms are progressively replaced by hydrogen;
Oxidation with ozone in solution.

A useful review is that of Wilkinson, Kelso, and Hopkins (1978).

20.6. Biological treatment

Biological or biochemical degradation may be a practical detoxification method for some hazardous organic wastes. Aerobic treatment processes, such as activated sludge, percolating filters, and oxidation lagoons may be used for industrial liquid wastes with a high biological oxygen demand. Considerable attention has been given to the isolation of suitable micro-organisms to degrade such difficult wastes as phenols, oils, pharmaceuticals, and pesticides. An example is the work of Münnecke (1978), who isolated a crude enzyme extract, from a mixed microbial culture grown on parathion, which could hydrolyse in addition eight other organophosphorus insecticides. This enzyme was successfully used, in the laboratory, in a continuous flow column reactor for pesticide waste water treatment.

If biological treatment of a hazardous waste is contemplated, care is required to ensure that other components in the waste neither poison the organisms nor render the residue unfit for landfill disposal.

20.7. Solidification and encapsulation

A third line of defence for dealing with very toxic wastes if their recovery or decomposition is not possible is some form of chemical or physical fixation. The idea generally is to render the toxic component in as stable or insoluble a form as possible so that ultimate disposal to land or sea is less likely to result in its passing into solution, so reducing the risk of its transfer to living organisms. Simple examples include:

Chemical precipitation of metals from solution, usually as the hydroxide or sulphide. So long as acids are kept segregated, the metal ions are relatively immobile in such sludges.

The *dewatering of sludges* prior to disposal, for example by pressure or vacuum filtration, by centrifugation, or by freezing and thawing prior to filtration.

Other methods aim to solidify or encapsulate liquids or sludges, thus making them easier to handle and dispose of. Encapsulation was originally developed for the treatment of radioactive wastes, the materials used including cement, bitumen, and glass. Much recent research has focused on developing cheaper methods which could be applied to other hazardous wastes, and several hundred proprietary processes now exist, mostly designed for specific applications. A useful compendium–textbook has recently been published (Pojasek 1979).

Stabilization technologies may be subdivided into a number of categories, which are now considered in turn:

(i) *Vitrification*. The waste is incorporated in a glass block. This process is expensive, and has been limited in application to high-level radioactive wastes.

(ii) *Cement-based processes*. The most widely used waste solidification processes are based upon calcium-containing hydraulic cements. The cementitious and pozzolanic reagents are added to a waste slurry and the mixture sets to the solid form in a few days. A number of proprietary processes have been developed which are based upon calcium silicate or alumino silicate hydration reactions. Products vary from friable, soil-like materials to rock-like, monolithic solids. All may be used to fix pollutants homogeneously in the matrix. The systems producing monolithic block may also be used to encapsulate discreet packages of waste.

The products of this group of solidification systems can be described as inorganic polymers and are largely successful in treating inorganically-based wastes. There is evidence that some organic pollutants can be contained in moderate concentrations and it is possible to improve the performance of these systems in relation to organic materials as shown by a recent patent but, in general, they do not work with high levels of organics in the waste. They should not be used where the primary requirement is to retain organic contaminants.

It is thought that a number of mechanisms may operate in these systems which contribute to the fixation of pollutants:

1. Ionic incorporation of cations in channels formed in the lattices of the hydrated minerals.

2. Replacement of aluminium in the inorganic polymer structures by other species in a high oxidation state, e.g. Iron III. Divalent atoms can be involved but require the presence of additional positive charges to achieve overall electro-neutrality. These may be supplied by ionically bound cations.

3. Adsorptive behaviour of finely divided alumino silicates, such as fly ash.

4. Ion exchange of sodium, potassium in the fly ash for other cations.

5. Bulk effect of pollutant phase being trapped in the 3-dimensional cementitious system, particularly, for example, in creched air entrainment sites.

In addition to these chemical aspects, the physical properties of the products are most important in considering the degree of isolation of the 'fixed' pollutants from the environment. In a landfill situation, a solid with low permeability and sufficient mechanical strength to resist the compressive forces to which it may become subjected will represent a relatively small surface area to percolating water, thereby reducing the risk of leaching.

Proprietary variations of cement-based solidification processes include Sealosafe (Stablex) first developed in the UK, Chemfix and Stoncrete (USA), Petrifix (France) and Tezuka Kosan (Japan). The largest waste stabilization plant in the world is shown in Fig. 20.3 while an example of a stabilized waste after treatment is illustrated in Fig. 20.4.

Fig. 20.3. *Waste solidification plant.* Polymer Tower for the Waste Management and Land Reclamation Centre, Thurrock, Essex, England. The plant is capable of treating 400 000 tonnes of liquid, solid and semi-solid wastes per annum. The treated waste, Stablex, is transferred in the form of a slurry into tankers for transport to the landfill site and hardening. Blocks of Stablex are shown in the foreground. (Photo courtesy The Stablex Group.)

(iii) *Lime-based processes.* The chemical principles utilized here are similar to those in the cement-based processes. Lime is mixed with a fine-grained, siliceous material, such as pulverized fuel ash or cement-kiln dust, and the wet slurry to form a hardened material sometimes known as pozzolanic concrete. The method is again restricted in application mainly to inorganic wastes.

(iv) *Thermoplastic techniques.* The dried waste is mixed with a molten organic material, such as bitumen, paraffin wax, or polyethylene, at elevated temperature, and placed in a container where it solidifies

Fig. 20.4. *A toxic sludge after stabilization using the Chemfix process.* The treated waste is shown being discharged into a lagoon, immediately after processing in the mobile Chemfix plant. The stabilized waste sets solid in about 24 hours. (Photo courtesy Wimpey Waste Management Ltd.)

as it cools These processes are very efficient for a restricted range of mainly inorganic contaminating species, but also tend to be very expensive.

(v) *Organic polymer techniques*. These are typified by the urea–formaldehyde process and the water-extensible polyester process. The monomer and the waste sludge are first mixed, a catalyst or curing agent is then added and thoroughly dispersed, and the mixture is placed in a container and allowed to set. Waste particles are simply trapped within the polymer structure, there being no chemical interaction. Some liquid may escape during the setting process. The processes are best suited to inorganic contaminants in a water-based waste; as the catalysts used tend to be strongly acidic, some metal ions may escape encapsulation by dissolution in the water which is not trapped.

(vi) *Encapsulation (coating) techniques*. There are many variations on the general theme of binding a waste sludge and then encapsulating it in a coating or jacket of some kind. One approach is to use a polybutadiene binder and a thin polyethylene jacket. The method is especially suited to very soluble inorganic contaminants, but is extremely expensive.

In summary, solidification technologies for industrial wastes have developed rapidly over the last 10 years. The various processes are applicable to a wide range of inorganic contaminants, although any particular waste will always require testing to check both its compatibility with the process and the efficiency of its stabilization. The relatively cheap and well developed cement-based processes will probably achieve the most widespread application, the more expensive organic techniques being reserved for specialized applications. Fixation may represent the best environmental option for some wastes containing highly toxic metals such as mercury, cadmium, lead, arsenic, and antimony.

20.8. Sea disposal

Disposal of wastes at sea is now subject to international conventions which make it an offence to dump, or to load for the purpose of dumping, any material on the sea without a licence from the competent authority, and except in accordance with the conditions of that licence. The licensing authority, which in England and Wales is the Ministry of Agriculture, Fisheries, and Food (MAFF), must in effect consider a comprehensive environmental impact assessment for each application before a licence can be granted. Licences are only granted when sea disposal represents the best environmental option, or when there is no appreciable danger to the marine environment.

The Oslo Convention applies to the North Sea and the north-east Atlantic (Her Majesty's Government 1972), while the London Convention applies worldwide (Her Majesty's Government 1976). Both conventions specify in detail the factors to be considered before a licence is granted, and in addition list materials for which dumping should be prohibited and others for which special care is required. The prohibited substances are mercury, cadmium, and their compounds, organohalogen compounds, some carcinogens, persistent floatable plastics and (Oslo only) organosilicon compounds. For the materials to be treated with special care, including arsenic, lead, copper, zinc, cyanides, fluorides, and pesticides, licences issued for wastes containing more than 0.1 per cent must be notified at once to the Commissions and hence to all parties to the conventions. The concentration is regarded by many countries as the upper limit but Britain takes a more flexible attitude; 13 such licences were notified during 1976.

Shallow sea dumping may be the best environmental option for the disposal of certain dilute aqueous wastes containing acids or alkalis and readily biodegradable materials such as phenols. Licences for some 900 000 t of such wastes were issued by MAFF in 1977. The major producing industries are coal carbonization, oil refining, petrochemicals, and pharmaceuticals.

Deep sea disposal is a much more expensive and limited method than shallow sea dumping. The wastes must be sealed in drums and encapsulated in concrete. Until March 1980, about 2000 t of wastes a year were licensed in Britain for deep sea disposal. However, most of these were solid cyanide-containing residues from heat treatment processes, and such dumping has now ceased.

20.9. Land disposal

Landfill is currently the most widely practised method for disposing of hazardous wastes. Recent research results suggest that a properly selected and managed landfill site may represent an acceptable disposal route for perhaps the majority of such wastes. However, landfill is obviously not applicable to all wastes, and each case should be judged on its merits. In general, three factors need to be considered when assessing the suitability of a specific waste for disposal at a particular landfill site:

(1) Problems in handling the waste on the landfill site;

(2) Possible adverse effects on the subsequent use of the reclaimed land;

(3) The potential for polluting either surface or ground water resources.

20.9.1. Handling problems

Handling problems impose some constraints on the types of waste which may be safely landfilled. Examples include:

(a) Flammable liquids which burn unsupported at less than 40 °C present a fire risk and should only be landfilled in minimal quantities (Department of the Environment 1977b).

(b) Highly odiferous materials including mercaptans, organic sulphides, thiophen derivatives, isonitriles, and amines are liable to cause a public nuisance if landfilled.

(c) The mixing of incompatible wastes should be avoided. Strong acids produce noxious fumes on contact with many anions, notably sulphide, while strong alkalis liberate ammonia from ammonium salts. Similarly strong oxidants should not be co-disposed with organic wastes. The mixing of organic solvents with tarry wastes may cause a fire or explosion. Acid wastes aid the mobility of heavy metal ions in landfill.

(d) Highly toxic compounds must be presented for landfill in such a way that there is no hazard to the operators.

20.9.2. Future use of the site

Concentrating wastes which present handling difficulties in particular areas of a site may introduce further problems. If the deposit is likely to remain intact for a substantial period, there is clearly a risk of later disturbance during redevelopment or excavation. In extreme cases, such as that at 'Love Canal' in Niagara, New York, the health of people living or working on reclaimed sites may be adversely affected (Cookson 1979). Such situations should be avoided, by one of three methods:

(1) Dispersing the waste along the working face of the landfill, if this can be done safely;

(2) Finding an alternative method of disposal;

(3) Accepting the long-term sterilization of the land and keeping careful records so as to prevent future disturbance.

In addition, when redevelopment for agricultural use is likely, disposal of metal bearing or other phytotoxic wastes should be terminated at the maximum depth to which the roots of crops would penetrate, allowing for the addition of topsoil or other cover material. Wastes containing 'spent oxide' from old town gas works are notorious for preventing revegetation of reclaimed landfill sites.

A particular handling problem arises with drummed wastes. In many industries it has been traditional to use empty drums to contain liquid or sludge wastes prior to disposal. These drums present problems in landfill management both through creating voids when they collapse and by blighting future reuse of the site; if an unidentified drum of waste is uncovered, then it must be treated *as if* it contained either an extremely toxic material such as cyanide or a potentially flammable, explosive, or reactive material, such as metallic sodium. Drums should preferably be emptied, washed out, and either reused or crushed after emptying and incorporated in the landfill. However, this can only be done safely in the light of information from the waste producer and under competent supervision. The practice of drumming wastes should be discouraged.

20.9.3. Water pollution

In Chapter 11, two alternative policies for the management of a landfill site were outlined, with regard to the prevention of water pollution. It was seen that a policy of 'attenuate and disperse' may, if properly managed, be as acceptable environmentally as the superficially safer policy of 'concentrate and contain'. Cumulative research results on attenuation of leachates from hazardous waste landfill sites suggest that this conclusion may be extended from municipal wastes to some hazardous wastes (Department of the Environment 1978). However, for some other wastes a containment site may be preferred; in any particular case, careful consideration of both the waste and of the proposed disposal site is required, based if possible on empirical measurement of the more important attenuation factors (Wilson and Waring 1980).

It must be remembered that water pollution potential is only one of the factors to be taken into account when selecting landfill policy. The segregation of chemical wastes into a special-purpose, completely sealed, containment site, as favoured for example in the USA and in West Germany, depends for its safety on continued supervision, perhaps for many years after the active life of the site has ceased, to prevent the accumulation and overflow of leachates. In addition, such supervision is also required to prevent any interference with or excavation of the site in the future, as any hazards associated with handling the wastes are likely to persist; the policy could be termed one of storage rather than of disposal. An extreme example of such storage is the use of an underground salt mine, such as that in the state of Hessen in West Germany

An alternative policy, favoured for example in the UK, is to co-dispose hazardous wastes and municipal wastes; an immediate dilution/dispersal of the hazard is thus achieved, and in addition interactions within the landfill may serve to detoxify the hazardous waste, or at least to attenuate any potential for water pollution. Dispersal of liquid industrial wastes through trenches in relatively mature domestic waste is illustrated in Fig. 20.5. Examples of possible detoxification mechanisms in co-diposal include:

The *neutralization* of acid wastes. Research is currently in progress to quantify the buffering capacity of municipal waste.

Biodegradation of certain hazardous organic wastes.

Degradation of cyanide containing wastes; the possible mechanisms include volatilization as hydrogen cyanide, hydrolysis to form ammonium formate, conversion to thiocyanate, and aerobic biodegradation (Department of the Environment 1978).

Attenuation mechanisms include:

Precipitation of metal ions. Oxidizing conditions lead to the precipitation of iron as ferric hydroxide, with the co-precipitation of heavy metal ions.

Anaerobic conditions result in the reduction of sulphate to sulphide, with the consequent precipitation of many heavy metals as the insoluble sulphides.

Adsorption or *absorption* of organic liquids such as halogenated solvents and oils on municipal waste. Field observations suggest that there is no free drainage of oil from solid wastes at a concentration of 5 per cent weight for weight (Department of the Environment 1978).

Fig. 20.5. *Liquid wastes being dispersed through trenches in a landfill site.* At the Pitsea landfill site in England, acidic wastes and oxidizing wastes are discharged directly from tankers into separate trenches (as illustrated here), while most compatible wastes are dispersed via a common trench system. (Photo courtesy Cleanaway Ltd, formerly Redland Purle Ltd.)

20.10. Discussion

The safe and economic disposal of increasing quantities of hazardous wastes is a problem facing most industrial countries. Currently most of these wastes are deposited on land, and for financial reasons alone this situation is likely to continue for some time to come. Recent research on the behaviour of hazardous wastes in landfill sites has shown that, with proper management and site selection, most wastes can be satisfactorily disposed of in this manner. In many cases a policy of 'attenuate and disperse' for leachate management may be environmentally preferable to the more cautious 'concentrate and contain'. However, each individual case must be treated on its merits.

Other methods of managing hazardous wastes are likely to be restricted to those wastes which either have a high value for recovery or which are unwelcome at a landfill site. Among the latter may be included flammable materials which burn unsupported; materials with a strong odour or which produce toxic gases; strong oxidants, acids, or alkalis; concentrated persistent toxic substances; and other materials hazardous to the operators.

The science of hazardous waste management is just beginning to emerge from the Dark Ages. Much remains to be done to further our understanding of the behaviour of waste materials in the environment. Particular objectives of future research should include:

Identification and measurement of the critical attenuation factors for particular wastes;

The selection and management of landfill sites to optimize such attenuation;

Development of alternative recycling, treatment, and disposal processes for difficult wastes;

Interpretation of the results to provide practical guidance which can be applied by waste managers.

21. THE STATE OF THE ART IN WASTE MANAGEMENT TECHNOLOGY

21.1. Comparing technologies

The aim of Part II of this book has been to provide a comprehensive and critical review of alternative waste management technologies. Having considered each group of technologies in turn, this final chapter provides an overall assessment of the current state of the art, as seen in 1980, and speculates on future trends.

From the wide range of technologies reviewed, some 30 options were selected as typifying the state of the art and were evaluated in considerable detail. The methods developed in Part I of the book were used to estimate both the overall costs of each process and also its contribution to the conservation of energy and material resources. The results are summarized in Table 21.1, and provide the basis for the discussion in this chapter.

The limitations of the quantitative data in Table 21.1 have been discussed in some detail elsewhere, but the basic caveats and assumptions are worth repeating:

(i) The comparative evaluation is based on the best available information in the open literature. It should be viewed as an illustrative case study; it is thus useful as a general guide to *relative* costs and energy efficiencies, but the results should *not* be applied directly to any particular, local, situation.

(ii) A few emerging technologies are not included in the evaluation, because of a scarcity of published quantitative information. Examples include European processes for dry separation of paper, which are here regarded as a derivative of the paper-based RDF option; and Japanese developments based on their semi-wet selective pulverizing classifier.

(iii) The absence of quantitative information on criteria other than economics and resource conservation does not imply in any way that these are unimportant; for example, both capital costs and the weight of residue remaining for landfill disposal are included in Table A.18. The state of development of the technology is typical of the many criteria which cannot adequately, or even usefully, be quantified.

Table 21.1

Comparative evaluation of waste management technologies

Basic technology	Specific variation	Major recovered product[a]	Cost range (£/t)[b]	Net primary energy efficiency β	State of development[c]
Landfill	Local site	Land	3.8 ± 1.4	− 0.02	1
Landfill at a distant site	Transfer by road	Land	9 ± 3	− 0.05	1
	Transfer by rail		14 ± 4	− 0.06	1
	Pulverization		10 ± 4	0.11	1
	Baling		14 ± 4	− 0.06	2
Incineration	Direct incineration using a moving metal grate	—	21 ± 6	0.02	1
		Steam	22 ± 9	0.54	1*
		Electricity	24 ± 10	0.53	1*
	Modular, using small local plants	—	21 ± 5	− 0.35	2
		Steam	24 ± 9	0.30	2
Production of a solid refuse-derived fuel (RDF) by dry separation	Pulverized fuel: case (a)	RDF	4.3 ± 4.2	0.95	2
	case (b)		6.3 ± 4.4		
	Paper-based RDF		11 ± 3	0.49	2/3
	American RDF		15 ± 5	0.79	2
	Powder RDF		23 ± 8	0.78	2
Incineration of RDF	Suspension firing	Steam	29 ± 10	0.55	2
	Incinerator turbine	Electricity	25 ± 10	0.49	4
Separation of waste by wet pulping	Fibre recovery	Paper	32 ± 9	0.32	3
	Incineration	Electricity	33 ± 12	0.34	2
	Fibre + wet RDF	Paper + RDF	20 ± 6	0.88	3
	Wet RDF	RDF	16 ± 5	0.69	3
	Dried RDF	RDF	23 ± 6	0.53	3
Pyrolysis and other thermal processes	Occidental	Oil	27 ± 8	0.31	3
	Union Carbide Purox	Gas	49 ± 17	0.62	3
	Andco–Torrax	Gas (steam)	29 ± 9	0.20	2
	Monsanto Landgard	Steam	31 ± 10	0.34	3
Biological processes	Composting	Compost	22 ± 6	0.47	1*
	Acid hydrolysis	Ethanol	34 ± 11	− 0.12	5
	Anaerobic digestion	Methane	39 ± 11	0.20	4
Additional recovery of glass and non-ferrous metals	Separated waste	Aluminium	+(2.3 ± 1.0)	+(0.10)	2
	Incinerator residue	and glass	+(2.8 ± 1.3)	+(0.07)	4

(a) Ferrous metals also recovered by most technologies.
(b) Costs at mid-1977 levels in the U.K.
(c) 1. Many years of operating experience. An asterisk denotes that technical problems still exist.
2. Commerical plants becoming operational in period 1976–80.
3. Demonstration plants (> 100 t.p.d.) operational in period 1971–80.
4. Pilot plant operational.
5. Laboratory scale only.

(iv) In each case, recovery of materials from the inorganic fraction of the waste is restricted to magnetic metals. Recovery of glass and non-ferrous metals is viewed as an incremental investment and analysed separately.
(v) All costs and prices are estimated at mid-1977 values in the UK.
(vi) The estimates refer to a plant with design capacity 400 t.p.d. of waste delivery (100 000 t per annum). The expected rate of waste delivery is 300 ± 40 t.p.d. the excess capacity allowing flexibility.

21.2. Landfill versus RDF

21.2.1. General comparison

On the three criteria highlighted in Table 21.1, namely the net cost of waste disposal using a technology, its contribution to the conservation of energy and material resources as measured by the net primary energy efficiency β, and its state of development, two broad groups of technologies emerge as the current 'front-runners'. The first group involve the landfilling of all or most of the waste, either directly or after minimal pre-treatment. The second group utilize some fraction of the waste as a solid refuse-derived fuel (RDF) for co-combustion with coal, usually in existing industrial or electrical utility boilers.

The landfill options are all fairly economical, and most have been practised for many years, although there have been considerable recent advances both in environmental standards and in landfill science and technology. The major disadvantages of landfill lie both in its poor public image and in its waste of valuable resources, although it can have positive benefits when used for land reclamation.

The RDF options combine a fairly competitive cost with a high degree of resource conservation, the net primary energy efficiency β ranging from 0.5 to 1.0 (in theory, full materials recovery could yield a maximum value of β, which is the ratio of net primary energy outputs to the heat content of the input waste, of about 1.5). The drawbacks to RDF production and use are twofold: the technology has been developed over the last 10 years, and has still to be adequately proven over an extended period of routine operation; in addition, markets for the fuel products are still being explored, and in some cases the scarcity of suitable boilers may restrict the applicability of the technology to fairly specific geographical areas.

21.2.2. Local landfill

Landfill of untreated wastes at a local site will often be the cheapest option for the disposal of municipal wastes if a suitable site is available. It is important to include in the comparison of options not only the disposal costs, but also the transport costs to deliver the wastes in collection vehicles (Chapter 6). In the case study, a landfill site about 12 km from the centre of population was postulated, compared to 4 km for most central treatment plants. The mean cost was about £4/t, of which about £1.5/t is attributable to the incremental transport cost. The exact cost of landfill depends on many factors, including:

Distance to the site;

Site preparation and other capital costs;

Lifetime of the site.

When landfill is being compared with treatment plants with an expected life of 15–20 years, it is probable that a sequence of small sites will have to be evaluated to provide a similar lifetime. To compare an incinerator with 20-year lifetime with a landfill which will be filled in just 2 years is nonsense. In the case study, various alternative assumptions regarding replacement sites increased the mean net cost by between £1 and £3/t.

In the past, landfill sites have often been little more than open dumps, posing significant public health risks through fires, vermin, and insects. Implementation of modern codes of practice have gone a long way to eliminating such nuisances. Proper site management requires that the waste should be well compacted in layers, and covered each day. This has in turn led to advances in machine technology, particularly the heavy steel-wheeled compactor. Recent research has laid the foundations of landfill science, which aims at understanding the behaviour of waste materials in a landfill environment. Of particular importance are the generation of a noxious mineralized leachate which may pollute water resources; the generation of a gas rich in methane, which may present a hazard, hindering redevelopment of the site, or which may be harnessed as an energy source; and the overall rate of stabilization of the fill, which again affects future use of the reclaimed land.

Landfill of wastes will probably remain as a major disposal route for some time to come. A properly selected and managed landfill site can provide a satisfactory solution, but the political problems of obtaining such sites near urban areas are likely to increase.

21.2.3. Pulverized waste as a fuel

The only option in the case study potentially capable of competing in economic terms with local landfill is the direct use of pulverized and magnetically separated waste as a fuel. The technical feasibility of this approach remains to be proven over an extended period, and the fuel is limited in its application to older boilers with chain grates and extensive ash handling facilities, or to cement kilns. The quality of feedstock required in the latter case is rather higher, a double pulverization being used to achieve a particle size less than 50 mm, but the high ash content is a positive advantage, the ash being incorporated in the cement product. Thus preparation of a pulverized RDF for cement kiln firing is one of the few options which produces little or no residual waste for landfill disposal.

The net cost of disposing of waste by producing a pulverized fuel depends critically on the price which can be obtained for the product. If an (optimistic) energy-specific price (£/GJ) 40 per cent that for coal is obtainable, giving a net revenue of £2.3/t of waste (case (a)), then it is competitive with direct landfill. A net price of zero, implying that the user pays transport costs and being perhaps still optimistic (case (b)), increases the mean cost to about £6/t, which still gives a margin of £2/t over indirect landfill. However, it must be stressed that the 95 per cent confidence interval on these costs is wide, the cost range for case (a) being, for example, £4.3 ± £4.2/t. Any specific study must focus attention on local markets and prices obtainable for the fuel.

The direct use of pulverized waste as a fuel has a very high net energy efficiency, $\beta = 0.95$–1.0, the higher value applying to cement manufacture. This result depends critically on the assumed efficiencies in use of the pulverized waste, and these need to be confirmed by experience.

21.2.4. Distant landfill

If local landfill or the use of pulverized waste as a fuel are not available, then either bulk haulage of the waste to a more distant landfill or upgrading the RDF should be considered.

Four basic options for distant landfill were included in the case study. The waste may simply be transferred from collection vehicles and compacted into containers for haul by road or by rail. Alternatively it may be pulverized before shipment to the landfill site, the claimed advantages including higher vehicle payloads, easier management of the landfill site, less environmental nuisance, and a more rapid and even stabilization of the site, making future redevelopment both earlier and less troublesome. Claims regarding savings of landfill space are still controversial, particularly since the advent of steel-wheeled compactors on normal landfills. Recently, a fourth alternative has emerged, namely medium- or high-density baling of wastes prior to shipment for landfill. The advantages claimed here include higher payloads, cheaper vehicles, higher landfill densities, easy placement of the waste, and the complete elimination of many environmental nuisances. However, the first commercial plants using baling technology have only come on line since about 1975, and extensive operating experience has still to be accumulated.

The costs of bulk haulage of waste were discussed in Chapter 6. The increase in costs with distance to the landfill sites follows a series of steps, the principal determinant being the number of trips possible per day. In the case study, road haul to a site at 30 km was postulated, there being 2 trips by each vehicle in a working day. It was assumed that pulverization could make a nearer site, at 20 km distance, available, thus enabling an extra trip to be made each day. Rail haulage costs depend less on distance than on the ease of the trip for the railway company.

On the basis of the case study there is little to choose between simple transfer of wastes to road and pulverization prior to transfer, the cost range being about £9 ± £3/t. Comparison of simple transfer with direct haul shows the latter to be cheaper for distances up to 20–30 km, under the costs and conditions assumed here, and in the absence of other constraints such as trade union objections to such long hauls in collection vehicles. Both rail haul and baling are rather more expensive, at about £14 ± £4/t. Clearly the uncertainty in the costs is such that there is no substitute for a detailed, local, comparison of all the options, taking into account the numerous relevant criteria.

21.2.5. Upgraded RDF

A very wide range of technologies has been developed over the last 5–10 years to produce a more or less sophisticated solid fuel from municipal wastes. The options differ markedly in the production methods, state of development, quality, and form of RDF, and hence its marketability, costs, and net energy efficiencies.

There are three basic approaches to the primary separation of waste into its organic and inorganic fractions, and all three have been adapted to the production of an RDF from the mainly organic fraction. The most widely applied is dry separation, generally using some combination of the unit operations pulverization, screening, air classification, and magnetic separation. Three variations on the theme were selected for evaluation in the case study:

(1) Production of a single organic fraction, containing most of the putrescible materials in addition to the paper and plastics. Such a fuel is here termed American RDF. Upgrading before use may involve further size reduction, baling, or pelletization. Storage of loose RDF may present problems. There has been limited commercial experience with several variations on this theme, and in all cases considerable technical difficulties have been encountered in the early stages.

(2) Further upgrading of American RDF to produce a powdered fuel, claimed to be suitable for co-firing with oil. It is evaluated here as a substitute merely for pulverized coal in suspension fired boilers. A demonstration plant has operated and a large commerical plant began start-up in late 1979.

(3) Production of at least two organic fractions, with the paper and plastics being utilized as RDF and the putrescible materials either landfilled or composted. Many variations on the theme of paper-based RDF have been developed, mainly in Europe. The case study utilizes data from the two, rather different, demonstration plants in the UK which were beginning operations in 1979–80. Both of these plants aim to produce a pelletized fuel. Several proprietary processes are aimed at producing a paper

product suitable for direct recycling, examples including the Swedish Fläkt and German Babcock Krauss–Maffei systems. Here paper recovery is viewed as a potential long-term alternative to RDF production, to be undertaken when the separation technology is better developed and marketing problems overcome; both the UK demonstration plants are designed for eventual conversion to paper recovery. However, those processes aimed directly at paper production should be included in any specific study when suitable data emerges from the commercial plants now beginning operations.

A second approach to primary separation of wastes is based on the well developed technology of wet pulverization in a rotary drum. Normally water is added to the wastes, self-pulverization being achieved by the tumbling action of hard materials. The largely fibrous fine fraction, containing per-haps 30–50 per cent moisture, is separated by screening. Two interesting developments of this technology in the direction of resource recovery should be mentioned here, although the current lack of quantitative data precluded their inclusion in the case study. The first involves the replacement of water by an oily waste; large quantities of oil–water emulsions are landfilled in the UK at present. The resultant 'enriched pulverized fuel' has been evaluated by the Central Electricity Generating Board and the results are encourag-ing. The second is a Japanese innovation, called the semi-wet selective pulverizing classifier. Here the drum is subdivided into two sections, with internal rotating scrapers in each. The waste enters the first section dry, fine particles, putrescible materials, and shattered glass being screened out. The second section operates in the traditional semi-wet mode, the fine fraction now being mainly paper. A demonstration plant began operation in 1979, the complete project including at least 4 sub-systems for upgrading the three initial fractions. The paper-rich fraction is being upgraded for fibre recovery rather than RDF production.

The third approach to primary separation is based on wet pulping of wastes, the organic fraction being produced as a wet slurry. Five options for utilizing this material are included in the case study, namely:

(a) Processing for fibre recovery, the residual materials being dewatered and incinerated. This is the original concept as demonstrated between 1971 and 1974.

(b) Dewatering and incineration for electricity generation. A large commercial plant began start-up in 1978 but was closed in 1980.

(c) Fibre recovery and dewatering of the residuals for sale as a wet (50 per cent moisture) RDF.

(d) Dewatering and sale as a wet RDF.

(e) Upgrading the RDF by drying to 20 per cent moisture. This material resembles paper-based RDF, but is probably more consistent in composi-tion.

No significant operating experience has been accumulated for the production, or more particularly the use, of these fuel products.

Of the RDF options included in the case study, paper-based RDF production at £11 ± £3/t appears to be the cheapest. However, its modest advantage over American-based RDF at £15 ± £5/t is based largely on an (optimistically) low electricity consumption and also a rather lower capital cost, the justification for which is not readily apparent. American RDF production has a much higher net primary energy efficiency than paper-based RDF, $\beta = 0.79$ compared with $\beta = 0.49$. The reduction, from pulverized fuel ($\beta = 0.95$) to American RDF to paper-based RDF, is due to the decreasing proportion of the heat content of the refuse incorporated in the fuel, with only a marginal increase in the efficiency in use of the RDF to compensate. However, the increasing quality of the fuel should make marketing easier, paper-based RDF having potentially a relatively wide application. It should be noted that, in the case study, paper-based RDF production is economically competitive with landfill of wastes at a distant site.

Production of wet-pulped RDF at 50 per cent moisture content is fairly competitive from both an economic (net cost £16 ± £5/t) or resource conservation ($\beta = 0.69$) viewpoint, but the marketability of the fuel must remain very questionable. Combining fibre recovery with residual RDF production increases the mean net cost by about £4/t, but β is also increased to the very attractive 0.88, which is, in the case study, second only to the pulverized fuel options. It should be noted that direct utilization of the residual materials after fibre recovery is both much cheaper and more efficient than the original concept of incineration. Upgrading American RDF by powdering was estimated to increase the net cost to £23 ± £8/t, the energy efficiency remaining relatively unchanged at $\beta = 0.78$ thanks to the higher efficiency in use of the product. However, this evaluation assumed that the powder RDF could only be used as a coal substitute. If, on the other hand, co-combustion with oil does prove feasible, then an increase in revenue of about £6/t of waste could be achieved.

In summary, rapid technological progress over the last decade has thrown up a whole range of RDF options which appear potentially competitive in economic terms with landfill at distant sites, while at the same time achieving high efficiencies of resource conservation. Future progress should be watched with care, and a selection of RDF options should be considered in any comparative evaluation of waste management technologies for a particular locality.

21.3. Incineration and other technologies

The remaining options examined in the case study all had base costs greater than about £20/t, and thus seem relatively uncompetitive when compared with the landfill and R D F technologies already discussed. However, it must be emphasized that this is a very general conclusion, based on current information; it may be reversed by improved cost estimates, by further developments in technology, by favourable markets for forms of recovered energy other than R D F, or by other local factors. The uncertainty in costs is such that it would be wrong to eliminate these technologies before due consideration has been given to all the available information; in addition, economics is just one of the criteria to be taken into account.

21.3.1. Incineration

Incineration is a well established technology for the treatment of municipal wastes, with over a century of operating experience. Modern direct incinerators have been in use for about 20 years, the early plants now approaching the end of their operating life. The proportion of wastes disposed of by incineration varies widely between countries, from a low of 5 per cent in the USA and 10 per cent in England, to a high of about 70 per cent in Denmark and Switzerland. In most European countries and in Japan, heat recovery is normally practised, the steam being used typically for district heating or electricity generation. However, both steam and electricity must be used as they are produced, and this leads to marketing difficulties, more especially in summer. There are still some technical problems with incineration, in particular corrosion in heat recovery boilers and increasingly stringent emission standards for the effluent gases.

In the case study, direct incineration without heat recovery had a cost range of £21 ± £6/t, while both steam and electricity generation had a wider range, £22 ± £9/t and £24 ± £10/t, respectively. The overall costs are very sensitive to the capital investment, a reduction of 25 per cent reducing the net costs per tonne by 20–30 per cent. In addition, even a fairly small increase in revenues from steam or electricity sales would increase competitiveness. Both of the heat recovery options are moderately efficient from a resource conservation viewpoint, with β about 0.55 ± 0.15: the utilization of the waste heat from electricity generation, for example as hot water at 50 °C, could increase the base value of β to about 0.7.

The mean net costs of incineration appear to be higher than those for the production of most forms of solid refuse-derived fuel; in addition the net primary energy efficiency β is generally lower. However, the uncertainty in both the economic and the energy analyses are great, and it is not possible to make any general judgement on the relative merits of the processes. Given that incineration is a proven technology and that favourable market conditions for steam and electricity do exist in many countries, it would be wrong not to include incineration in the initial list of possible options to be considered in preliminary planning work.

Various developments in municipal waste incineration have been proposed in recent years. The preparation of the waste into an RDF before incineration allows the use of more sophisticated furnaces. Examples include:

(1) Firing of the RDF in suspension in a boiler with only a small grate. In the case study this option increased mean net costs by about £7/t, while increasing the net primary energy efficiency only marginally.

(2) Firing of the RDF partly in suspension and partly on a grate, using modifications of boilers designed for other low grade fuels such as bark or coffee grounds. The fuel may be pulverized and magnetically extracted waste, or wet-pulped waste dewatered to 50 per cent moisture content. The latter case was evaluated, with the heat being used for electricity generation as in a large plant at present beginning operations in the USA. The net cost was estimated at £33 ± £12/t, the energy efficiency being relatively low, $\beta = 0.34$.

(3) Firing of the RDF in a fluidized bed. This technology has many advantages for liquid or sludge wastes, but a small particle size is preferred for solid feedstocks. The case study evaluated the incinerator turbine, in which the off-gases are used to drive a gas-turbine for electricity generation. However, it should be noted that problems were encountered in cleaning the gases without lowering their temperature, and development work is in abeyance. The net cost was estimated as £25 ± £10/t, with an energy efficiency $\beta = 0.49$.

Based on these three examples, it may be concluded that upgrading of the waste before incineration does not appear particularly attractive at present, the increased process sophistication, and therefore capital costs, not being matched sufficiently by compensating increases in revenues and in net energy efficiency.

An interesting development is the modular incinerator which is a simple, batch-loaded unit utilizing a two-step combustion process. The exhaust gases are claimed to be suitable for direct discharge to air without prior cleaning. The particular advantage of this concept is that it is specifically designed for small quantities of waste, and can thus be contemplated by communities producing between 10 and 100 tonnes of waste per day, for which the only other economic option is probably landfill. The case study suggests that modular incineration has costs similar to those for the conventional process, but it is not really suitable for an urban area producing 300 or more tonnes of waste per day. The first plant ordered in the UK, for the Orkney Islands, illustrates its proper application. However, it must be stated that modular incineration is very expensive compared with local landfill, the technology has not yet been adequately proven for municipal wastes, and the supplementary fuel consumption results in a very poor energy efficiency, even if steam generation and utilization is feasible.

21.3.2. Other thermal processes

Thermal processing of organic materials without complete combustion, to produce fuel products—solid, liquid, or gaseous—has been undergoing a revival over the last 10 years, with some 150 processes at some stage of development. Despite this activity, much fundamental work remains to be done to understand the complex chemistry and to optimize process conditions to yield the desired products. Operating experience on a meaningful scale has been limited; the few large-scale plants treating municipal wastes have all been plagued with operating problems.

The term 'pyrolysis' is often used in a generic sense to describe alternatives to incineration. However, 'pyrolysis' should strictly be applied only to the thermal degradation of organic materials in the absence of air. When some waste is combusted in oxygen or air to provide heat for the reaction, the term 'gasification' is more appropriate. Pyrolysis typically yields either an oil or a medium-heating-value gas as the principal product. Gasification typically yields a fuel gas, diluted with combustion products and, if air is used, with nitrogen. Marketing a low-calorific-value gas would be difficult, so combustion on site to raise steam is a feature of many process designs. Pyrolytic oil is not quite so attractive a product as one might have hoped; it is viscous, corrosive, and tends to polymerize on storage. Most pyrolysis products could be upgraded into a variety of chemicals or fuels by chemical synthesis.   Much work remains to be done to demonstrate the adequacy of thermal processing technologies. Several small commercial plants have been built using the Andco–Torrax process, but in the autumn of 1979 only one plant was operational, and that was still being debugged after three years of continual modifications. The data used in the case study to evaluate four American processes must be seen in this context, as it is too early to draw any firm conclusions. On present evidence, pyrolysis and gasification appear expensive, although they could become competitive with incineration for large plants if claimed economies of scale materialize. Net primary energy efficiencies appear generally low, the exception being an oxygen gasification process producing a medium-heating-value gas. Thermal processing is a highly promising technology for the future and developments should be watched with interest.

21.3.3. Biological processes

Biological processing of organic wastes is not a new concept. The major reclamation routes may be summarized as:

(1) Composting is the aerobic degradation of organic materials to yield a stable, humus-like product, primarily for use as a soil conditioner.

(2) Anaerobic degradation, in the absence of air, yields a gas rich in methane. Traditional processes use a wet slurry of wastes, but landfill

may be regarded as solid-phase anaerobic digestion. Landfill gas is increasingly being viewed as a useful energy source.

(3) Hydrolysis of the cellulosic component yields sugars, which can be fermented to yield chemicals such as ethanol, or used as a food source for the production of single-cell protein (yeast).

(4) The waste may be used as a food source for the cultivation of, for example, red earthworms or fly larvae. The products are either a fertilizer (e.g. worm castings) and/or protein (dried worms or larvae).

Considerable operating experience has been accumulated worldwide with the composting of municipal wastes, but problems have been encountered in marketing the product. Practice appears to be reverting to windrow methods of composting, perhaps aided by forced aeration, in preference to the more capital intensive 'high-rate' alternatives. The case study suggests a net cost of composting of about £22 ± £6/t, with a net primary energy efficiency (assuming that the compost could be used as an energy source) of $\beta = 0.47$. Composting is likely to be important in the future chiefly in arid areas where humus is required for soil enrichment, or for the putrescible fraction of separated waste.

Neither anaerobic digestion nor hydrolysis represent available technologies for the reclamation of municipal waste. Current pilot and demonstration plants for digestion yield only a low conversion of organics to methane, a large, biologically active, residue remaining for disposal by landfill or incineration. The result, in the case study, is a high net cost, £39 ± £11/t, plus a low energy efficiency, $\beta = 0.2$. Recent research on the mechanism of anaerobic digestion promises substantial improvements in the efficiency of the process, albeit at the expense of additional sophistication.

Hydrolysis of the cellulosic components of waste is at present only a research technique, developed at the laboratory scale. Catalysis may be by acidic, alkaline, or enzymatic means; the ultimate products may include ethanol, organic acids, and single-cell protein. Much projected information has been published on the acid hydrolysis of refuse to yield ethanol; these data were evaluated in the case study to yield a net cost of £34 ± £11/t and a net primary energy efficiency of $\beta = -0.12$. The high energy inputs were not matched by the energy value attributed to ethanol as presently produced from oil.

21.3.4. Additional recovery of glass and non-ferrous metals

All of the resource recovery technologies evaluated in the case study included only the magnetic separation of ferrous metals from the inorganic fraction of the waste. Recovery of additional materials, principally non-ferrous metals and glass, is best viewed as an optional extra, to be undertaken if justified on its own merits. The technology for separating and purifying these additional materials is still being developed, and only limited operational experience is available. The recovery of non-ferrous metals, principally aluminium, obviously, depends on the presence of sufficient quantities of such metals in the waste; development work has been most intense in the USA where aluminium cans account for up to 1–2 per cent of the waste. Glass recovery is most efficient for larger particle sizes, above about 5 mm; one problem is that the hammermills commonly used for primary pulverization of the incoming waste tend to shatter glass into tiny fragments.

In the case study, two processes for the recovery of non-ferrous metals and glass from separated waste and one from incinerator residue were evaluated. The incremental net costs, over and above the cost of the basic technology, were about £2–3 ± £1/t of raw waste. Incremental energy efficiencies were about $\beta = 0.1$. Thus, additional recovery of inorganic materials appears currently uneconomic, but can substantially increase the net primary energy efficiency of resource recovery from waste. This economic assessment could be reveresed for a large plant if net revenues were doubled; thus materials recovery could prove economic, either now or in the (near) future, if local markets are favourable, and the situation should be kept under review.

21.4. Future trends

Technological development in the fields of waste reclamation, treatment, and disposal has been rapid over the past decade, and the rate shows little sign of slackening. Many of the new technologies described here will reach commercial maturity in the 1980s, while others will doubtless fall by the wayside.

For the next decade, the predominant technology will probably continue to be landfill, with significant contributions from incineration and the production of solid refuse-derived fuels. As the shortage of fuels begins to bite, competition for land use near urban areas continues to grow, and environmental issues move further towards the centre of the political arena, the pressure to restrict the use of landfill in favour of reclamation or resource recovery will increase. On the other hand, economic problems will limit the funds available for capital investment; this will tend to favour landfill, and also to swing the balance away from its traditional alternative, incineration, towards the newer, less capital intensive RDF technologies. One interesting development which will receive increasing attention is the recovery and utilization of methane-rich gas from landfill sites.

The technology for separating municipal waste is in its infancy. With an increasing number of operational plants, progress to date should be consolidated over the next few years. The penetration of RDF technologies into the total solid waste disposal market depends on several factors, including:

(1) Reliability of the technology in practice;

(2) The development of improved, robust equipment for conveying, handling and storing waste and fractions separated therefrom;

(3) Costs proving to be competitive with landfill at least when no suitable local site is available;

(4) The development of markets for the product fuel, particularly in the electricity generating industry;

(5) The development of alternative markets, for example for separated paper and plastics;

(6) The attitudes of governments to financing development work and in ensuring that market forces do not discriminate against products recovered from waste.

Incineration technology stands at a cross-roads; on the one hand it is a proven, efficient means of energy recovery from waste, at a time when energy resources are becoming scarce; on the other hand, it is capital intensive, appears increasingly expensive when compared with other options, and faces growing competition from refuse-derived fuel production. In Britain, the prospects for investment in new incinerators look bleak; in other European countries and in Japan, where district heating is common place, its future is probably assured, although requirements for gas cleaning may become more stringent and therefore both more difficult and more expensive to meet. One interesting concept, which marries the strengths of RDF and incineration, is the production of storable RDF pellets for incineration in district heating boilers during the winter months, thus ensuring full utilization of the steam produced.

Composting is the only other reclamation process with significant operating experience. Its future probably lies in those countries where climatic conditions require humus to bring the land to productive use, and also as an adjunct to separation processes, treating the putrescible fraction of the waste. Marketing the product is likely to get more difficult rather than easier, as environmental concern increases over trace levels of heavy metals in soil. This problem can be alleviated by careful separation of wastes, for example removing batteries from the compostable fraction before pulverization of the waste.

Research and development work will continue on a wide range of thermal and biological processes for waste reclamation. If progress in the 1980s matches that on separation and RDF technology in the 1970s, then the prospects for the reclamation of municipal solid wastes will look rather different, and hopefully even more promising, in 1990 than they do in 1980.

Appendixes

A. DATA AND RESULTS FROM THE CASE STUDY OF WASTE MANAGEMENT TECHNOLOGIES

Table A.1
Options examined in the case study

Option	Symbol used in graphical presentation of results	Description
Landfill	L	Direct landfill of untreated waste with transport to a local site in a collection vehicle
Landfill with:		Indirect landfill with the waste delivered initially to a transfer point, from which it is transported in bulk to a distant landfill
Transfer to road	L_t	The waste is compacted into containers for road transport
Transfer to rail	L_r	The waste is compacted into containers and loaded onto a train
Pulverization	L_{p1} L_{p2}	The dry waste is pulverized in a hammermill and loaded, after extraction of ferrous metals, into containers for road transport. The plant may operate 1 or 2 shifts per day
Baling	L_b	The untreated waste is compressed into high-density bales which are transported on flat trailers
Incineration:		Controlled combustion to produce a sterile ash for landfill and gases for discharge to air
Non-recuperative	I	A conventional direct incinerator in which a moving metal grate slowly propels the waste through the furnace and the gases are cleaned in an electrostatic precipitator
Steam generation	I_s	As above with the waste heat used to raise steam for direct use in heating
Electricity generation	I_e	As above, with the steam used to generate electricity
Modular	I_m	A starved air incinerator using two combustion chambers, the gases being suitable for discharge without cleaning. The modular design allows local plants to be built, thus saving transport costs. Steam generation may be added if a suitable market is available
Modular + steam	I_{ms}	
RDF as a supplementary fuel:		The waste is processed to produce a solid refuse-derived fuel (RDF) for use as a supplementary fuel in an industrial or utility boiler. Each option involves dry separation of the organic and inorganic fractions, using some combination of pulverization, air classification, magnetic separation, and screening
American RDF	R_a	The approach widely developed in the USA in which most of the organic fraction is incorporated in the RDF

Table A.1—cont.

Option	Symbol used in graphical presentation of results	Description
Powder RDF	R_{po}	The fine powder is produced by chemical treatment to destroy the fibre strength, followed by drying and grinding in a ball mill. This 'Eco-Fuel II' may be suitable for co-firing in oil or gas fired boilers
Paper-based RDF	R_{pa}	European variants produce an RDF containing mainly papers and plastics. The prototypes taken here are the two demonstration plants being built in the UK
Pulverized fuel	F_a F_b	Pulverized fuel is used directly as a fuel either in a chain-grate boiler or in a cement kiln. Two options differ in the price assumed for the fuel
Incineration of RDF:		Incineration using a prepared fuel
Suspension firing	D_s	The RDF is burnt mainly in suspension in a furnace with a small grate, the heat being used to raise steam
Incinerator turbine	D_t	The RDF is burnt in a fluidized bed incinerator with the cleaned exhaust gases used to drive a gas turbine for electricity generation
Wet pulping with:		The waste is converted to an aqueous slurry which enters a 'hydrapulper', where the organics are pulped and inorganics are rejected by centrifugal action
Fibre recovery	W_f	The organics are processed for fibre recovery, the rejects being burnt, after dewatering, in a fluidized bed incinerator
Incineration + electricity	W_e	The organic slurry is dewatered and burnt in a semi-suspension fired moving grate furnace to raise steam for electricity generation
Fibre + wet RDF	W_{fr}	The rejects from fibre recovery are dewatered and sold directly as an RDF
Wet RDF	W_r	The entire organic slurry is dewatered and sold as an RDF
Dried RDF	W_{rd}	The wet RDF is upgraded by a three-stage rotary drying process which reduces the moisture content from 50 per cent to 20 per cent
Pyrolysis and other thermal process:		Thermal decomposition in the absence or near absence of air. The mix of solid, liquid, and gaseous fuel products depends on the conditions chosen. The options chosen are representative of the more developed variants
Occidental	P_o	Low-temperature flash pyrolysis of a fluff RDF to produce a heavy fuel oil
Union Carbide Purox	P_u	A high-temperature process in which the heat of reaction is provided by the combustion of some refuse in pure oxygen at the base of a vertical-shaft reactor. Produces a medium-heating-value gas from pulverized waste input. Electricity may be self-generated
Andco–Torrax	P_t	A similar high-temperature process, but with untreated waste input and combustion in preheated air. The low-heating-value gas may be difficult to market, or may be used to raise steam for sale
Monsanto Landgard	P_m	A rotary kiln is used for pyrolysis of pulverized waste in a starved-air atmosphere. The low-heating-value gas is burnt in a secondary combustion chamber to raise steam
Biological processes:		
Composting	C	The waste is separated into inorganic and organic fractions, the latter being composted in windrows or a high-rate mechanical digester. The product is a humus for use as a soil supplement

Table A.1—cont.

Option	Symbol used in graphical presentation of results	Description
Acid hydrolysis	H	The cellulose content of the organic fraction of the waste is hydrolysed using acid catalysis to yield ethanol
Anaerobic digestion	A	The separated organic fraction of the waste is slurried in water and digested in the absence of air to yield, after gas purification, high-purity methane. A substantial biologically active residue is left for landfill disposal
Additional recovery of glass and non-ferrous metals:		All the above options assumes that only ferrous metals are recovered from the inorganic fraction of the waste. Recovery of non-ferrous metals and glass are analysed as incremental options, to be undertaken if merited in their own right
Separated waste/Franklin		Uses a vibrating screen, heavy-media separator, mineral jig, electrostatic separator, and an optical sorter to separate aluminium, other non-ferrous metals, and colour-sorted glass. This system is being demonstrated at Franklin, Ohio
Separated waste/Occidental		Uses a trommel screen, with eddy-current separation of aluminium from the oversize fraction, and froth flotation separation of crushed fine glass from the undersize
Incinerator residue		Uses a trommel screen, mineral jig, and heavy media separator to recover aluminium, other non-ferrous metals, and crushed fine glass from incinerator residue

Table A.2
Summary of cost data

Option	Capital cost (£m)	Accuracy ± × (1 + x)	Scale factor	Operating schedule—number of shifts: Preparation x_1	Reactor x_2	Number of men: Breakdown	Total	Raw materials[a] cost (£/t)	Energy and utilities (kWh/t)[b]	(GJ/t)	Water supply[c] (m³/t)	Water treatment[c] (m³/t)	Maintenance factor	Residue (t/t)
Landfill	0.5	2.0	0.8	1	–	$1 + 2x_1$	3	0.2	0	0.11	–	–	0.04	0
Landfill with:														
Transfer to road	1.0	2.0	0.85	1	–	$3 + 3x_1$	6	–	10	0.04	–	–	0.05	1.0
Transfer to rail	1.5	2.0	0.85	1	–	$3 + 7x_1$	10	–	10	0.08	–	–	0.05	1.0
Pulverization:														
1 shift	1.5	2.0	0.8	1	–	$4 + 4x_1$	8	–	20	0.04	–	–	0.07	0.93
2 shifts	1.0	2.0	0.8	2	–	$4 + 4x_1$	12	–	20	0.04	–	–	0.10	0.93
Baling	3.0	1.4	0.9	1	–	$4 + 4x_1$	8	–	15	0.04	–	–	0.06	1.0
Incineration:														
Non-recuperative	4.8	1.4	0.95	–	3	$4 + 6x_2$	22	–	30	0	2.1	0.2	0.07	0.35
Steam generation	6.6	1.4	0.95	–	4	$4 + 7x_2$	32	–	60	0	–	–	0.07	0.35
Electricity generation	7.8	1.4	0.95	–	4	$4 + 7x_2$	32	–	(80)	0	–	–	0.07	0.35
Modular	4.4	1.4	1.0	2	2	$4 + 8x$	20		17	2.2			0.04	0.20

American RDF	3.8	1.4	0.8	2	4	$4 + 6x_1$	16	—	63	0.04	—	—	0.08	0.23
Powder RDF	6.0	1.4	0.8	2	—	$4 + 8x_1$	20	0.75	65	0.04	—	—	0.08	0.20
Paper-based RDF	2.5	1.4	0.08	2	—	$4 + 6x_1$	16	—	35	0.04	—	—	0.08	0.63
Pulverized fuel, cases (a) and (b)	1.5	2.0	0.8	1	—	$4 + 4x_1$	8	—	20	0.04	—	—	0.08	0
Incineration of RDF:														
Suspension firing	8.2	1.4	0.9	2	4	$4 + 5x_1 + 5x_2$	34	—	90	0.04	—	—	0.07	0.35
Incinerator turbine	7.0	1.4	0.9	2	4	$4 + 5x_1 + 5x_2$	54	—	(100)	0.04	—	—	0.10	0.23
Wet pulping with:														
Fibre recovery	7.4	1.4	0.9	2	4	$4 + 6x_1 + 3x_2$	28	—	170	0.04	5	5	0.06	0.21
Incineration + electricity	10.0	1.4	0.9	2	4	$4 + 5x_1 + 4x_2$	30	—	(150)	0.04	—	—	0.06	0.21
Fibre + wet RDF	5.1	1.4	0.9	2	4	$4 + 6x_1$	16	—	110	0.04	5	5	0.06	0.21
Wet RDF	4.0	1.4	0.9	2	—	$4 + 5x_1$	14	—	100	0.04	—	—	0.06	0.21
Dried RDF	5.0	1.4	0.9	2	—	$4 + 6x_1$	16	—	100	2.24	—	—	0.06	0.21
Pyrolysis and other thermal processes:														
Occidental	6.0	1.4	0.7	2	4	$4 + 5x_1 + 5x_2$	34	—	170	0.14	—	£0.5	0.08	0.20
Union Carbide Purox	13.0	1.4	0.8	2	4	$4 + 4x_1 + 7x_2$	40	—	200	0.04	—	—	0.08	0
Andco–Torrax	6.8	1.4	0.75		4	$4 + 5x_2$	24	—	140	0.74	—	—	0.08	0.08
Monsanto Landgard	7.7	1.4	0.7	2	4	$4 + 4x_1 + 5x_2$	32	—	100	1.14	—	—	0.08	0.31
Biological processes:														
Composting	5.0	1.4	0.65/0.95	2	4	$8 + 5x_1 + 3x_2$	30	—	60	0.12	—	—	0.08	0.30
Acid hydrolysis	8.0	1.4	0.8	2	4	$4 + 5x_1 + 6x_2$	38	1.6	130	2.14	5	5	0.08	0.60
Anaerobic digestion	8.0	1.4	0.9	2	4	$4 + 5x_1 + 6x_2$	38	—	90	1.54	0.5	—	0.08	d
Additional recovery of materials:														
Franklin	0.8	1.4	0.8	2	—	$1 + 2x_1$	5	—	12	0	—	—	0.08	−0.05
Occidental	0.7	1.4	0.8	2	—	$1 + 2x_1$	5	—	12	0	0.5	0.5	0.08	−0.07
Incinerator residue	1.0	1.4	0.8	2	—	$1 + 2x_1$	5	—	2.5	0.1	0.5	0.5	0.08	−0.25

(a) Normally subsumed under operating supplies.
(b) Figure in brackets indicates that electricity is self-generated.
(c) Normally subsumed under other utilities, estimated at 10 per cent of direct fuel costs.
(d) Anaerobic digestion produces 0.23 t/t inorganic residue and 1 t/t wet filter cake.

Table A.3
Summary of revenue data

Option	Ferrous metal[a]	Organic material	Fuel product[b]	Heat recovery efficiency[c] Gross (per cent)	Net (per cent)	Accuracy (±x%)	Fuel displaced[b]	Relative cost of WDF (%)	Revenue from WDF (£/GJ)	(£/tonne of waste)
Landfill										
Landfill with:										
Transfer to road										
Transfer to rail										
Pulverization										
1 shift	F									
2 shift	F									
Baling										
Incineration:										
Non-recuperative	B									
Steam generation	B		Steam	60	45	30	Av	90	1.60	7.20
Electricity generation	B		E	18	15.1	25	E	67	5.56	8.39
Modular										
Modular + steam			Steam	70	52.5	30	Av	90	1.60	8.40
RDF as a supplementary fuel:										
American RDF	F		Solid	85		5	Coal	60	0.36	3.06
Powder RDF	F		Solid	80		5	Coal	80	0.48	3.84
Paper-based RDF	F		Solid	45		10	Coal	70	0.42	1.89
Pulverized fuel:										
Case (a)	F		Solid	95		5	Coal	40	0.24	2.28
Case (b)	F		Solid	95		5	Coal	0	0	0
Incineration of RDF:										
Suspension of firing	F		Steam	60	45	30	Av	90	1.60	7.20
Incinerator turbine	F		E	16	12.4	25	E	67	5.56	6.89
Wet pulping with:										
Fibre recovery	F	Paper								
Incineration + electricity	F		E	13.5	8.1	25	E	67	5.56	4.50
Fibre + wet RDF	F	Paper	Solid	60		10	Coal	50	0.30	1.80
Wet RDF	F		Solid	90		5	Coal	50	0.30	2.70
Dried RDF	F		Solid	90		5	Coal	70	0.42	3.78
Pyrolysis and other thermal processes:										
Occidental	F		Oil	47		10	Oil	75	1.20	5.60
Union Carbide Purox	F		Gas	75		5	Gas	70	1.20	9.00
Andco–Torrax			Gas	60		10	Gas	45	0.80	4.80
Monsanto Landgard	B		Steam	60	45	25	Av	90	1.60	7.20
Biological processes:										
Composting	F	Humus								
Acid hydrolysis	F	Ethanol								
Anaerobic digestion	F		Methane	40		10	Gas	90	1.50	6.00

Additional recovery of materials:[d]	Residual ferrous metal	Al	Other non-ferrous metal	Glass Mixed fines	Colour sorted
Franklin	1	1	1	0	1
Occidental	1	1	0	1	0
Incinerator residue	0	B	1	1	0

(a) F indicates recovery from untreated waste, B recovery from residue after burning.
(b) E is electricity, Av is an average fuel (Table 10.3).
(c) Heat recovery efficiency is ratio of heat content in WDF to heat content in waste. Net value allows for consumption of electricity in the process when it is supplied by self-generation, and for a steam load factor of 75 per cent.
(d) 1 indicates recovery, B a reduced yield after burning, and 0 no recovery.

Table A.4
Transport and residue disposal in the options

	Initial waste transport		Residuals disposal — transport				Residuals disposal — landfill			Residuals disposal — totals	
Option	Distance (km)	Cost (£/t)	Amount for disposal (t/t)	Distance (km)	Cost (£/tonne of residue)	Cost (£/tonne of waste)	Per cent of raw waste landfill cost	Cost (£/tonne of residue)	Cost (£/tonne of waste)	Cost (£/tonne of residue)	Cost (£/tonne of waste)
Landfill	+8	1.40	0								
Landfill with:											
Transfer to road			1.0	30	2.50	2.50	100	2.40	2.40	4.90	4.90
Transfer to rail			1.0	80	4.00	4.00	100+	2.90	2.90	6.90	6.90
Pulverization			0.93	20	1.75	1.60	80	1.92	1.80	3.70	3.40
Baling			1.0	20	1.25	1.20	60	1.44	1.45	2.70	2.70
Incineration:											
Non-recuperative			0.35	20	1.25	0.44	50	1.20	0.42	2.45	0.90
Steam generation			0.35							2.45	0.90
Electricity generation			0.35							2.45	0.90
Modular	−2	−0.36	0.30							2.45	0.75
Modular + steam	−2	−0.36	0.30							2.45	0.75
RDF as a supplementary fuel:											
American RDF			0.23							2.45	0.60
Powder RDF			0.20							2.45	0.50
Paper-based RDF			0.63	20	1.25	0.79	70	1.68	1.06	2.90	1.85
Pulverized fuel			0							–	0
Incineration of RDF:											
Suspension firing			0.35							2.45	0.90
Incinerator turbine			0.23							2.45	0.60
Wet pulping with:											
Fibre recovery											
Incineration + electricity											
Fibre + wet RDF			0.21							2.45	0.50
Wet RDF											
Dried RDF											
Pyrolysis and other thermal processes:											
Occidental			0.20							2.45	0.50
Union Carbide Purox			0							–	0
Andco–Torrax			0.08							2.45	0.20
Monsanto Landgard			0.31							2.45	0.75
Biological processes:											
Composting			0.30							2.45	0.75
Acid hydrolysis			0.60	20	1.25	0.75	70	1.68	1.01	2.90	1.75
Anaerobic digestion			0.23							2.45	0.60
			1.0	30	2.50	2.50	100	2.40	2.40	4.90	4.90
Additional recovery of materials:											
Franklin			−0.05							2.45	−0.12
Occidental			−0.07							2.45	−0.17
Incinerator residue			−0.25							2.45	−0.60

Table A.5
Direct operating costs
(£ thousand/annum)

Option	Raw material	Electricity	Fuel	Water supply treatment	Other utilities	Labour	Supervision	Payroll	Maintenance	Operating supplies	Direct operating cost
		Energy and utilities									
Landfill	15	0	15	–	1.5	11	2.1	5.0	20	4.0	73
Landfill with:											
Transfer to road	0	23	5.4	–	2.8	21	4.2	10	50	8.0	124
Transfer to rail	0	23	1.1	–	3.3	35	7.0	17	75	12	182
Pulverization											
1 shift	0	45	5.4	–	5.0	28	5.6	13	105	12	220
2 shift	0	45	5.4	–	5.0	42	8.4	20	100	8.0	234
Baling	0	34	5.4	–	3.9	28	5.6	13	180	24	294
Incineration:											
Non-recuperative	0	68	0	19	6.8	77	15	37	336	38	596
Steam generation	0	135	0	–	19	112	22	54	462	53	851
Electricity generation	0	0	0	–	18	112	22	54	546	62	814
Modular	0	38	297	–	34	70	14	34	176	35	698
Modular + steam	0	50	297	–	35	98	20	47	304	61	911
RDF as a supplementary fuel:											
American RDF	0	146	5.4	–	15	56	11	27	304	30	595
Powder RDF	56	146	5.4	–	21	70	14	34	480	48	874
Paper-based RDF	0	79	5.4	–	8.4	56	11	27	200	20	405
Pulverized fuel, cases (a) and (b)	0	45	5.4	–	5.0	28	5.6	13	105	12	220
Incineration of RDF:											
Suspension of firing	0	203	5.4	–	21	119	24	57	574	66	1070
Incinerator turbine	0	0	5.4	–	23	119	24	57	700	56	984
Wet pulping with:											
Fibre recovery	0	383	5.4	113	39	98	20	47	444	59	1210
Incineration + electricity	0	0	5.4	–	35	105	21	50	600	80	897
Fibre + wet RDF	0	248	5.4	113	25	56	11	27	306	41	831
Wet RDF	0	225	5.4	–	23	49	9.8	24	240	32	608
Dried RDF	0	225	302	–	53	56	11	27	300	40	1010
Pyrolysis and other thermal processes:											
Occidental	0	383	19	38	40	119	24	57	480	48	1210
Union Carbide Purox	0	450	5.4	–	45	190	28	67	1040	104	1880
Andco–Torrax	0	315	100	–	42	84	17	40	544	54	1200
Monsanto Landgard	0	225	154	–	38	112	22	54	616	62	1280
Biological processes:											
Composting	0	135	16	–	15	105	21	50	400	40	783
Acid hydrolysis	120	293	289	113	58	133	27	64	640	64	1800
Anaerobic digestion	0	203	208	38	41	133	27	64	640	64	1420
Additional recovery of materials:											
Franklin	0	27	0	–	2.7	18	3.5	8.4	64	6.4	130
Occidental	0	27	0	11	2.7	18	3.5	8.4	56	5.6	132
Incinerator residue	0	5.6	14	11	1.9	18	3.5	8.4	80	8.0	150

Table A.6
Indirect, transport, and residue disposal costs
(£ thousand/annum)

Option	Direct operating costs	Indirect operating costs					Transport in collection vehicle[a]	Residue disposal		Total operating cost
		Rates	Insurance	Overheads	Selling	Total		Transport	Landfill or total	
Landfill	73	15	5.0	9.2	0	29	105	0	0	207
Landfill with:										
Transfer to road	124	30	10	18	0	58	0	188	180	550
Transfer to rail	182	45	15	29	0	89	0	300	218	789
Pulverization										
1 shift	220	45	15	26	6.2	92	0	120	135	567
2 shift	234	30	10	27	6.2	73	0	120	135	562
Baling	294	90	30	41	0	161	0	94	109	658
Incineration:										
Non-recuperative	596	144	48	79	3.2	274	0		68	938
Steam generation	851	198	66	111	57	432	0		68	1350
Electricity generation	814	234	78	123	66	501	0		68	1380
Modular	698	132	44	72	0	248	−27		56	975
Modular + steam	911	228	76	115	63	482	−27		56	1420
RDF as a supplementary fuel:										
American RDF	595	114	38	60	29	242	0		45	882
Powder RDF	874	180	60	88	35	363	0		38	1270
Paper-based RDF	405	75	25	47	20	168	0		140	713
Pulverized fuel										
Case (a)	220	45	15	26	23	110	0		0	329
Case (b)	220	45	15	26	6.2	92	0		0	312
Incineration of RDF:										
Suspension firing	1070	246	82	130	60	518	0		68	1650
Incinerator turbine	984	210	70	118	58	455	0		45	1480
Wet pulping with:										
Fibre recovery	1210	222	74	113	26	436	0		38	1680
Incineration + electricity	897	300	100	142	40	582	0		38	1520
Fibre + wet RDF	831	153	51	73	40	317	0		38	1190
Wet RDF	608	120	40	60	26	246	0		38	890
Dried RDF	1010	150	50	72	35	307	0		38	1360
Pyrolysis and other thermal processes:										
Occidental	1210	180	60	108	48	396	0		53	1660
Union Carbide Purox	1880	390	130	186	74	780	0		0	2660
Andco–Torrax	1200	204	68	102	36	410	0		15	1620
Monsanto Landgard	1280	231	77	122	57	487	0		56	1830
Biological processes:										
Composting	783	150	50	92	15	307	0		56	1150
Acid hydrolysis	1800	240	80	133	100	553	0		131	2480
Anaerobic digestion	1420	240	80	133	51	504	0	188	225	2330
Additional recovery of materials:										
Franklin	130	24	8.0	15	12	59	0		−9	179
Occidental	132	21	7.0	14	9.3	51	0		−13	171
Incinerator residue	150	30	10	17	9.6	67	0		−45	171

(a) Transport costs relative to the base case of a central plant.

Table A.7
The baseline DCF analysis of options.
All costs are £ thousand/annum unless otherwise stated

Option	Total operating cost	Materials revenue (£/tonne of waste)	Energy revenue (£/tonne of waste)	Total revenue	Capital charge	Equivalent annual cost	Equivalent cost (£/tonne of waste)	Net present cost (£ thousand)
Landfill	207	0	0	0	65	272	3.63	1920
Landfill with:								
Transfer to road	550	0	0	0	130	680	9.06	4780
Transfer to rail	789	0	0	0	194	983	13.1	6920
Pulverization								
1 shift	567	0.82	0	62	194	700	9.33	4920
2 shift	562	0.82	0	62	130	630	8.40	4430
Baling	658	0	0	0	389	1050	14.0	7360
Incineration:								
Non-recuperative	938	0.43	0	32	622	1530	20.4	10 800
Steam generation	1350	0.43	7.20	572	855	1630	21.8	11 500
Electricity generation	1380	0.43	8.39	661	1010	1730	23.1	12 200
Modular	975	0	0	0	575	1550	20.6	10 900
Modular + steam	1420	0	8.40	630	985	1780	23.7	12 500
RDF as a supplementary fuel:								
American RDF	882	0.82	3.06	291	493	1080	14.5	7620
Powder RDF	1270	0.82	3.84	350	778	1700	22.7	12 000
Paper-based RDF	713	0.82	1.89	203	324	834	11.1	5870
Pulverized fuel								
Case (a)	329	0.82	2.28	233	194	291	3.88	2050
Case (b)	312	0.82	0	62	194	445	5.93	3130
Incineration of RDF								
Suspension firing	1650	0.82	7.20	602	1060	2110	28.2	14 900
Incineration turbine	1480	0.82	6.89	578	908	1810	24.1	12 700
Wet pulping with:								
Fibre recovery	1680	3.52	0	264	959	2380	31.7	16 700
Incineration + electricity	1520	0.82	4.50	399	1300	2410	32.2	17 000
Fibre + wet RDF	1190	3.52	1.80	399	661	1450	19.3	10 200
Wet RDF	890	0.82	2.70	264	518	1150	15.3	8060
Dried RDF	1360	0.82	3.78	345	648	1660	22.5	11 700
Pyrolysis and other thermal processes:								
Occidental	1660	0.82	5.60	482	1778	1950	26.0	13 700
Union Carbide Purox	2660	0.82	9.00	737	1680	3610	48.1	25 400
Andco–Torrax	1620	0	4.80	360	881	2140	28.6	15 100
Monsanto Landgard	1830	0.43	7.20	572	998	2250	30.0	15 800
Biological processes:								
Composting	1150	2.02	0	152	648	1640	21.9	11 600
Acid hydrolysis	2480	0.82	12.54	1000	1040	2520	33.6	17 700
Anaerobic digestion	2330	0.82	6.00	512	1040	2860	38.1	20 100
Additional recovery of materials:								
Franklin	179	1.56	0	117	104	166	2.21	1170
Occidental	171	1.24	0	93	91	168	2.24	1180
Incinerator residue	171	1.28	0	96	130	205	2.73	1440

Table A.8
Relative sensitivity
(R_s values, as defined by equations 6.13–6.16)

Option	Key to graphs	Investment	Labour costs	Electricity costs	Fuel costs	Maintenance factor	Rates factor	Transport costs[a]	Residual disposal or landfill	Plant utilization	Material recovery	Energy recovery
Landfill	L	0.418	0.080	0	0.061	0.073	0.055	0.386*	0	0.502	0	0
Landfill with:												
Transfer to road	L_t	0.350	0.064	0.036	0.009	0.074	0.044	0.276	0.265	0.586	0	0
Transfer to rail	L_r	0.362	0.074	0.025	0.012	0.076	0.046	0.305	0.221	0.564	0	0
Pulverization												
1 shift	L_{p1}	0.552	0.083	0.071	0.008	0.150	0.064	0.172	0.193	0.365	−0.079	0
2 shift	L_{p2}	0.457	0.139	0.079	0.009	0.159	0.048	0.190	0.214	0.405	−0.088	0
Baling	L_b	0.710	0.056	0.035	0.006	0.172	0.086	0.090	0.104	0.235	0	0
Incineration:												
Non-recuperative	I	0.809	0.105	0.049	0	0.220	0.094	–	0.044	0.086	−0.019	0
Steam generation	I_s	1.040	0.143	0.091	0	0.283	0.121	–	0.041	−0.183	−0.018	−0.297
Electricity generation	I_e	1.160	0.134	0	0	0.315	0.135	–	0.039	−0.294	−0.017	−0.327
Modular	I_m	0.648	0.094	0.027	0.211	0.114	0.085	−0.017*	0.036	0.258	0	0
Modular + steam	I_{ms}	0.973	0.115	0.031	0.184	0.171	0.128	−0.015*	0.032	−0.088	0	−0.319
RDF as a supplementary fuel:												
American RDF	R_a	0.939	0.108	0.149	0.005	0.281	0.105	–	0.042	−0.046	−0.051	−0.191
Powder RDF	R_{po}	0.943	0.086	0.095	0.003	0.282	0.106	–	0.022	−0.028	−0.033	−0.152
Paper-based RDF	R_{pa}	0.802	0.140	0.104	0.007	0.240	0.090	–	0.166	0.058	−0.066	−0.153
Pulverized fuel												
Case (a)	F_a	1.329	0.200	0.170	0.020	0.361	0.155	–	0	−0.529	−0.191	−0.529
Case (b)	F_b	0.869	0.131	0.111	0.013	0.236	0.101	–	0	0.000	−0.125	0 (b)
Incineration of RDF:												
Suspension firing	D_s	0.999	0.117	0.105	0.003	0.271	0.116	–	0.032	−0.116	−0.026	−0.230
Incinerator turbine	D_t	1.112	0.137	0	0.003	0.387	0.016	–	0.023	−0.249	−0.031	−0.257
Wet pulping with:												
Fibre recovery	W_f	0.771	0.086	0.177	0.002	0.187	0.093	–	0.016	−0.143	−0.100	0
Incineration + electricity	W_e	1.026	0.090	0	0.002	0.249	0.124	–	0.016	−0.016	−0.023	−0.126
Fibre + wet RDF	W_{fr}	0.872	0.080	0.188	0.004	0.211	0.106	–	0.026	0.048	−0.164	−0.084
Wet RDF	W_r	0.865	0.089	0.216	0.005	0.209	0.105	–	0.033	0.047	−0.048	−0.159
Dried RDF	W_{rd}	0.745	0.070	0.149	0.200	0.181	0.090	–	0.023	0.185	−0.033	−0.154
Pyrolysis and other thermal processes:												
Occidental	P_o	0.823	0.127	0.216	0.011	0.246	0.092	–	0.027	0.050	−0.028	−0.194
Union Carbide Purox	P_u	0.964	0.081	0.137	0.002	0.288	0.108	–	0	−0.045	−0.015	−0.168
Andco-Torrax	P_t	0.850	0.082	0.162	0.051	0.254	0.095	–	0.007	0.069	0	−0.151
Monsanto Landgard	P_m	0.915	0.103	0.110	0.075	0.274	0.103	–	0.025	−0.019	−0.013	−0.216
Biological processes:												
Composting	C	0.815	0.133	0.090	0.011	0.244	0.091	–	0.034	0.052	−0.083	0
Acid hydrolysis	H	0.850	0.110	0.128	0.126	0.254	0.095	–	0.052	0.040	−0.022 c	−0.336
Anaerobic oxgestion	A	0.749	0.097	0.078	0.080	0.224	0.084	0.066	0.079	0.154	−0.019 c	−0.142
Additional recovery of materials												
Franklin		1.289	0.219	0.179	0	0.385	0.144	–	−0.054	−0.508	−0.632	0
Occidental		1.114	0.216	0.177	0	0.333	0.125	–	−0.076	−0.330	−0.498	0
Incinerator residue		1.308	0.178	0.030	0.073	0.391	0.147	–	−0.200	−0.486	−0.424	0

(a) Transport costs marked with an asterisk are for haul in a collection vehicle; otherwise for bulk haulage.
(b) In the pulverized fuel option, case (b) assumes a net price of zero for the fuel, so $R_s = 0$. Obviously this price will vary with the price of conventional fuel.
(c) Ethanol is here classified as an energy product.

Table A.9
Results of the risk analysis

Option	Net present cost (£ thousand)			Equivalent unit cost (£/tonne)			Operating cost (£ thousand)			Revenue (£ thousand)		
	Base	Mean	s	Base	Mean	s	Base	Mean	s	Base	Mean	s
Landfill	1920	2000	360	3.63	3.79	0.69	207	215	31	0	0	0
Landfill with:												
Transfer to road	4780	4960	770	9.06	9.39	1.5	550	565	69	0	0	0
Transfer to rail	6920	7180	1160	13.1	13.6	2.2	789	812	100	0	0	0
Pulverization												
1 shift	4920	5170	1130	9.33	9.80	2.1	567	588	88	62	62	8
2 shift	4430	4630	860	8.40	8.77	1.6	562	580	76	62	62	8
Baling	7360	7500	950	14.0	14.2	1.8	658	670	72	0	0	0
Incineration:												
Non-recuperative	10 800	11 000	1560	20.4	20.8	3.0	938	955	120	32	32	4
Steam generation	11 500	11 700	2260	21.8	22.3	4.3	1350	1380	160	572	577	110
Electricity generation	12 200	12 500	2640	23.1	23.6	5.0	1380	1410	190	661	666	120
Modular	10 900	11 100	1300	20.6	21.0	2.5	975	991	95	0	0	0
Modular + steam	12 500	12 800	2330	23.7	24.2	4.4	1420	1450	150	630	635	130
RDF as a supplementary fuel:												
American RDF	7620	7790	1300	14.5	14.8	2.5	880	898	100	291	292	34
Powder RDF	12 000	12 200	2040	22.7	23.3	3.9	1270	1300	160	350	351	42
Paper-based RDF	5870	5980	870	11.1	11.3	1.7	713	724	72	203	204	23
Pulverized fuel												
Case (a)	2050	2260	1100	3.88	4.29	2.1	329	346	79	233	233	26
Case (b)	3130	3350	1170	5.93	6.34	2.2	312	328	99	0	62	8
Incineration of RDF:												
Suspension firing	14 900	15 200	2760	28.2	28.8	5.2	1650	1680	200	602	607	110
Incinerator turbine	12 700	13 000	2640	24.1	24.7	5.0	1480	1510	210	578	580	96
Wet pulping with:												
Fibre recovery	16 700	17 000	2340	31.7	32.3	4.4	1680	1710	180	264	265	35
Incineration + electricity	17 000	17 300	3100	32.2	32.8	5.9	1520	1550	230	399	402	63
Fibre + wet RDF	10 200	10 400	1620	19.3	19.7	3.1	1190	1210	120	399	401	43
Wet RDF	8060	8230	1270	15.3	15.6	2.4	890	907	96	264	265	30
Dried RDF	11 700	11 930	1620	22.5	22.6	3.1	1360	1380	130	345	346	41
Pyrolysis and other thermal processes:												
Occidental	13 700	14 000	2090	26.0	26.6	4.0	1660	1680	170	482	484	62
Union Carbide Purox	25 400	25 900	4430	48.1	49.2	8.4	2660	2710	350	737	739	94
Andco–Torrax	15 100	15 400	2330	28.6	29.2	4.4	1620	1650	190	360	362	51
Monsanto Landgard	15 800	16 200	2710	30.0	30.6	5.1	1830	1860	210	572	577	110
Biological processes:												
Composting	11 600	11 800	1710	21.9	22.3	3.2	1150	1170	140	152	152	20
Acid hydrolysis	17 700	18 100	2850	33.6	34.3	5.4	2480	2530	230	1000	1010	140
Anaerobic digestion	20 100	20 300	2770	38.1	38.8	5.5	2330	2370	230	512	514	66
Additional recovery of materials:												
Franklin	1170	1200	290	2.21	2.27	0.55	179	182	22	117	118	16
Occidental	1180	1210	250	2.24	2.30	0.48	171	174	19	93	94	13
Incinerator residue	1440	1180	350	2.73	2.80	0.67	171	175	27	96	97	13

s is the standard deviation.

Table A.10
The effect of changing the assumptions in the risk analysis

Assumptions	Example option	Case	Base case (B)	Net present cost mean	s
Interpretation of the error ranges	American RDF	1.50 σ (86.6%) confidence		7890	1700
		2.0 σ (95.4%) interval	B	7790	1300
		2.5 σ (98.8%)		7740	1060
Number of distributions	American RDF	All those in Table 7.1	B	7790	1300
		All except the revenue factors		7780	1270
		Investment, labour and electricity usage, and residue disposal costs		7830	1260
		Investment only		7700	1320
		Revenue factors with or without plant utilization		7610	170
		Plant utilization only		7620	24
Width of the input distributions	American RDF	[×]⁄_÷ 1.25		7720	880
		[×]⁄_÷ 1.4	B	7780	1300
		[×]⁄_÷ 2.0		8210	2880
(a) Investment	Incineration	[×]⁄_÷ 1.25		10 870	1040
		[×]⁄_÷ 1.4	B	10 950	1560
	Pulverized fuel, case (a)	[×]⁄_÷ 1.4		2100	520
		[×]⁄_÷ 2.0	B	2260	1100
	Landfill	[×]⁄_÷ 1.4		1950	230
		[×]⁄_÷ 2.0	B	2000	360
(b) Energy recovery efficiency	Incineration with steam generation	⁺⁄_− 10%		11 760	2200
		⁺⁄_− 30%	B	11 740	2260
	Incineration with electricity generation	⁺⁄_− 10%		12 470	2600
		⁺⁄_− 25%	B	12 460	2640

(c) Revenues from recovered materials		Price	Recovery efficiency			
	Composting	± 20%	± 5%	B	11 780	1710
		± 50%	± 10%		11 780	1730
	Wet pulping with recover of fibre and wet RDF	± 20%	± 5%	B	10 410	1620
		± 50%	± 10%		10 400	1670
	Additional material recovery Franklin model	± 20%	± 10%	B	1200	292
		± 50%	± 10%		1200	338

(d) Transport	Landfill	[×]⁄_÷ 1.25		1990	338
		[×]⁄_÷ 1.5	B	2000	364
	Landfill with transfer to road	[×]⁄_÷ 1.25		4940	731
		[×]⁄_÷ 1.5	B	4960	772
	Landfill with transfer to rail	[×]⁄_÷ 1.25		7150	1090
		[×]⁄_÷ 1.5	B	7180	1160
	Landfill with pulverization (1 shift)	[×]⁄_÷ 1.25		5160	1110
		[×]⁄_÷ 1.5	B	5170	1130
	Landfill with baling	[×]⁄_÷ 1.25		7490	945
		[×]⁄_÷ 1.5	B	7500	954

Shift in base value of a parameter (a) Plant utilization	Incineration with electricity generation	0.75 ± 0.10	B	12 460	2640
		0.90 ± 0.10		11 740	2680
		Shift predicted by sensitivity analysis		{ − 733 11 730	
(b) Energy price	Incineration with electricity generation	Base ± 20%	B	12 460	2640
		1.5 × base ± 20%		10 450	2770
		Shift predicted by sensitivity analysis		{ −2040 10 420	

s is the standard deviation.

Table A.11
Sensitivity analysis for the extended DCF model.

Extension					Landfill		Incineration with electricity generation		American RDF	
					NPC (£ thousand)	(£/tonne)	NPC (£ thousand)	(£/tonne)	NPC (£ thousand)	(£/tonne)
Base case					1910	3.63	12 200	23.1	7620	14.4
(i) Delay in construction		1 year					11 700	24.7	7290	15.5
Delay cost £270 000/a		2 year					11 200	26.6	6980	16.6
(ii)										
Recurring investment (£ thousand).										
Year	5	10	15	20						
Replace vehicles	50	50	50		1970	3.73	12 200	23.2	7670	14.5
Replace ⎫	50	500	50				12 400	23.5	7820	14.8
equipment ⎭	50	1000	50				12 500	23.8	7980	15.1
Replace landfill		500	500		2170	4.12				
site		500	1000		2270	4.31				
	500	500	500		2430	4.61				
	1000	1500	2000		3300	6.26				
Land reclamation				−500	1850	3.51				
(sale value)				−1000	1790	3.40				
				−1800	1700	3.21				
		−500	−500	−800	1560	2.95				
Replace site		500	500	−500	2110	4.00				
and reclaim		500	1000	−500	2210	4.19				
land	500			−800	2070	3.93				
(iii)										
Growth in waste production		1% per annum			2010	3.37	11900	19.9	7590	12.7
(iv)										
Growth in relative cost of labour		1% per annum			1930	3.66	12 300	23.4	7700	14.6
(v)										
Growth in relative cost/value of energy		2% per annum			1940	3.67	11 400	21.6	7540	14.3
(vi)										
Working capital		4 months operating costs			1970	3.74	12 600	23.8	7860	14.9
(iii)–(vi) combined		as above			2100	3.53	11 500	19.2	7810	13.1
As above + waste growth		2% per annum			2200	3.31	11 000	16.6	7770	11.7
As above + energy cost growth		5% per annum			2140	3.59	10 100	16.9	7670	12.9

Table A.12
Risk analysis for the extended DCF model

		Landfill		Incineration with electricity generation		American RDF	
Extension		NPC (£ thousand)	(£/tonne)	NPC (£ thousand)	(£/tonne)	NPC (£ thousand)	(£/tonne)
Base case	Mean	1990	3.77	12 500	23.6	7790	14.8
	s	340	0.64	2640	5.0	1300	2.5
(1) Delay in construction, average 1 year	Mean			12 000	25.4	7470	15.9
histogram: 0 1 2 3	s			2480	5.3	1260	2.7
Relative chances (RC) 6 8 3 1							
(ii) Recurring investment: Landfill £500 000 years 5,10,15	Mean	2560	4.86	12 800	24.2	8040	15.2
Others £50 000 years 5,15: £500 000 year 10	s	400	0.76	2670	5.1	1350	2.6
(ii)(a) Same recurring investments years input as histograms:	Mean	2590	4.90	12 800	24.3	8060	15.3
	s	400	0.75	2610	5.0	1320	2.5
(iii)–(vi) As in Table A.11.	Mean	2200	3.69	11 620	19.5	7920	13.3
	s	390	0.66	2750	4.6	1380	2.3

year RC   year RC   year RC

year	RC	year	RC	year	RC
4	4	8	1	13	1
5	15	9	8	14	4
6	1	10	15	15	5
		11	2	16	1

Table A.13
Option ranks

		Conditions							
		Risk analysis				Discount rate		Waste throughput	
Option	Deterministic base case (and means from risk analysis)	90% confidence level	ranges (Table 7.3)	Plant utilization 100%	Revenues twice base level	5%	25%	150 t.p.d.	1200 t.p.d.
Landfill	1	1	1–3	2	2	2	1	1	2
Landfill with:									
Transfer to road	5	5	3–8	6	7	=5	5	5	6
Transfer to rail	8	9	4–12	11	10	=8	7	8	9
Pulverization									
1 shift	6	6	3–11	5	6	=5	6	6	5
2 shift	4	4	2–8	4	4	4	4	4	4
Baling	9	8	6–12	9	=11	=8	9	9	10
Incineration									
Non-recuperative	13	14	10–25	15	21	13	14	=13	19
Steam generation	15	17	10–28	13	13	14	18	15	20
Electricity generation	19	20	10–28	14	14	16	22	=17	23
Modular	14	13	10–25	19	24	15	12	12	22
Modular + steam	20	19	11–28	16	15	=19	21	16	26
RDF as a supplementary fuel:									
American RDF	10	10	6–16	8	8	=8	10	11	8
Powder RDF	18	18	11–28	20	18	=19	17	20	13
Paper-based RDF	7	7	3–11	7	5	7	8	7	7
Pulverized fuel									
Case (a)	2	2	1–4	1	1	1	2	2	1
Case (b)	3	3	1–7	3	3	3	3	3	3
Incineration of RDF:									
Suspension firing	23	24	12–29	23	22	23	24	22	25
Incinerator turbine	21	21	11–28	17	16	21	20	19	21
Wet pulping with:									
Fibre recovery	26	26	15–29	27	28	27	26	24	27
Incineration + electricity	27	27	15–30	26	27	26	=28	=25	28
Fibre + wet RDF	12	12	8–24	12	=11	12	=13	=13	14
Wet RDF	11	11	6–21	10	9	11	11	10	11
Dried RDF	17	16	11–27	21	17	=17	=15	=17	=17
Pyrolysis and other thermal processes:									
Occidental	22	22	12–28	22	19	22	19	23	12
Union Carbide Purox	30	30	27–30	30	30	30	30	30	30
Andco–Torrax	24	23	12–29	24	26	24	23	=25	=17
Monsanto Landgard	25	25	13–29	25	25	25	25	27	15
Biological processes:									
Composting	16	15	11–27	18	20	=17	=15	21	16
Acid hydrolysis	28	28	17–30	28	23	28	27	28	24
Anaerobic digestion	29	29	23–30	29	29	29	29	29	29
Additional recovery of materials									
Franklin	1	1	1–3	1	1	1	2	2	1
Occidental	2	2	1–3	2	2	2	1	1	2
Incinerator residue	3	3	1–3	3	3	3	3	3	3

Table A.14
Energy requirements for waste management technologies
(MJ/tonne of waste)

Option	Electricity	Other fuels	Water supply/ effluent treatment	Other utilities	Raw materials	Maintenance supplies	Operating supplies	Capital investment	Transport[a]	Landfill or residuals disposal	Total
Landfill	0	60	–	6	15	14	5	40	45*	0	190
Landfill with:											
Transfer to road	120	21	–	14	–	33	10	33	84	140	460
Transfer to rail	120	43	–	16	–	50	16	50	96	170	560
Pulverization											
1 shift	240	21	–	26	–	70	16	50	52	93	570
2 shift	240	21	–	26	–	67	10	33	52	93	540
Baling	180	21	–	20	–	120	32	100	56	100	630
Incineration:											
Non-recuperative	360	0	19	36	–	220	51	160	–	46	890
Steam generation	720	0	–	72	–	300	70	220	–	46	1430
Electricity generation	960	0	–	96	–	370	83	260	–	46	1810
Modular	200	2640	–	290	–	110	47	140	–11*	39	3470
Modular + steam	260	2640	–	290	–	200	80	250	–11*	39	3760
RDF as a supplementary fuel:											
American RDF	780	21	–	80	–	200	41	130	–	30	1280
Powder RDF	780	21	–	80	100	320	64	200	–	26	1580
Paper-based RDF	420	21	–	44	–	140	26	83	–	98	820
Pulverized fuel	240	21	–	26	–	70	16	50	–	–	420
(cement manufacture)	360	21	–	38	–	70	16	50	–	–	550
Incineration of RDF:											
Suspension of firing	1080	21	–	110	–	390	89	270	–	46	2010
Incinerator turbine	1200	21	–	120	–	470	74	240	–	30	2140
Wet pulping with:											
Fibre recovery	2040	21	110	210	–	290	78	240	–	27	3020
Incineration + electricity	1800	21	–	180	–	400	100	330	–	27	2870
Fibre + wet RDF	1320	21	110	130	–	210	54	170	–	27	2040
Wet RDF	1200	21	–	120	–	160	43	130	–	27	1700
Dried RDF	1200	21	2440	370	–	200	53	160	–	27	4470
Pyrolysis and other thermal processes:											
Occidental	2040	140	50	220	–	320	64	200	–	26	3040
Union Carbide Purox	2400	21	–	240	–	690	130	430	–	0	3910
With self-generation	0	21	–	240	–	690	130	430	–	10	1510
Andco–Torrax	1680	800	–	250	–	390	92	220	–	10	3400
Monsanto Landgard	1200	1240	–	240	–	410	82	250	–	40	3470
Biological processes:											
Composting	720	64	–	78	–	270	53	160	–	39	1380
Acid hydrolysis	1560	2350	110	390	510	430	85	270	–	94	5800
Anaerobic digestion	1080	1690	100	280	–	430	85	270	84	170	4170
Additional recovery of materials:											
Franklin	140	0	–	14	–	43	8	26	–	–7	230
Occidental	140	0	12	14	–	38	7	23	–	–9	230
Incinerator residue	30	130	12	16	–	53	10	33	–	+35	250

(a) Transport energy requirements marked with an asterisk are for haul in a collection vehicle; otherwise for bulk haulage.

Table A.15
Primary energy savings from waste-derived fuels

Option	Fuel product[a]	Heat recovery efficiency[b] (%)	Efficiencies in use WDF	Efficiencies in use Conventional fuel	Substitution equivalence	Efficiency of producing the conventional fuel	Transport of WDF to user (MJ/tonne of waste)	Primary energy savings (MJ/tonne of waste)
Landfill								
Landfill with:								
Transfer to road								
Transfer to rail								
Pulverization								
1 shift								
2 shift								
Baling								
Incineration:								
Non-recuperative								
Steam generation	Steam	45	–	–	1.0	78	0	5800
Electricity generation	E	18	–	–	1.0	30	0	6000
Modular								
Modular + steam	Steam	53	–	–	1.0	78	0	6800
RDF as a supplementary fuel:								
American RDF	Solid	85	69	81	1.17	96	70	7500
Powder RDF	Solid	80	75	81	1.08	96	50	7700
Paper-based RDF	Solid	45	70	81	1.15	96	30	4000
Pulverized fuel	Solid	95	68	81	1.19	96	93	8200
(cement manufacture)	Solid	95	73	81	1.11	96	93	8800
Incineration of RDF:								
Suspension firing	Steam	45	–	–	1.0	78	0	5800
Incinerator turbine	E	16	–	–	1.0	30	0	5300
Wet pulping with:								
Fibre recovery								
Incineration + electricity	E	13.5	–	–	1.0	30	0	4500
Fibre + wet RDF	Solid	60	60	81	1.35	96	60	4500
Wet RDF	Solid	90	60	81	1.35	96	90	6900
Dried RDF	Solid	90	70	81	1.15	96	70	8100
Pyrolysis and other thermal processes:								
Occidental	Oil	47	78	82	1.05	90	10%[c]	4400
Union Carbide Purox	Gas	75	78	78	1.0	81	10%[c]	8300
With self-generation	Gas	44						4900
Andco-Torrax	Gas	60	71	78	1.1	81	20%[c]	5400
Monsanto Landgard	Steam	45	–	–	1.0	78	0	5800
Biological processes:								
Composting								
Acid hydrolysis								
Anaerobic digestion	Methane	40	78	78	1.0	81	10%[c]	4400

(a) E is electricity.
(b) Ratio of heat content of WDF to heat content of waste. Value for electricity generation is gross, and for steam generation is net, allowing for 75 per cent load factor.
(c) Oil and gas distribution costs estimated as a percentage of the total primary energy saving.

Table A.16

Process analysis results
(Energy inputs and savings are MJ/tonne of waste)

Option	Total energy input	Fuel	Ferrous metals	Other inorganics	Organic materials	Total	α	β
					Primary energy savings from products		*Net energy efficiencies*	
Landfill	190					0	−0.019	−0.019
Landfill with:								
Transfer to road	460					0	−0.046	−0.046
Transfer to rail	560					0	−0.056	−0.056
Pulverization								
1 shift	570		1700			1700	−0.057	0.11
2 shift	540		1700			1700	−0.054	0.12
Baling	630					0	−0.063	−0.063
Incineration:								
Non-recuperative	890		1100			1100	−0.089	0.018
Steam generation	1400	5800	1100			6900	0.44	0.54
Electricity generation	1800	6000	1100			7100	0.42	0.53
Modular	3500					0	−0.35	−0.35
Modular + steam	3800	6800				6800	0.30	0.30
RDF as a supplementary fuel:								
American RDF	1300	7500	1700			9200	0.62	0.79
Powder RDF	1600	7700	1700			9400	0.61	0.78
Paper-based RDF	820	4000	1700			5800	0.32	0.49
Pulverized fuel	420	8200	1700			9900	0.78	0.95
(cement manufacture)	550	8800	1700			10 500	0.83	1.00
Incineration of RDF:								
Suspension firing	2000	5800	1700			7500	0.38	0.55
Incinerator turbine	2100	5300	1700	15		7100	0.32	0.49
Wet pulping with:								
Fibre recovery	3000		1700		4500	6200	−0.30	0.32
Incineration + electricity	2900	4500	1700			6200	0.16	0.34
Fibre + wet RDF	2000	4600	1700		4500	10 800	0.25	0.88
Wet RDF	1700	6900	1700			8600	0.52	0.69
Dried RDF	4500	8100	1700			9800	0.36	0.53
Pyrolysis and other thermal processes:								
Occidental	3000	4400	1700			6200	0.14	0.31
Union Carbide Purox	3900	8300	1700	15		10 100	0.44	0.62
With self-generation	1500	4900	1700	15		6600	0.34	0.51
Andco–Torrax	3400	5400		20		5400	0.20	0.20
Monsanto Landgard	3500	5800	1100			6900	0.23	0.34
Biological processes:								
Composting	1400		1700		4400	6100	−0.14	0.47
Acid hydrolysis	5800		1700		2900	4600	−0.58	−0.12
Anaerobic digestion	4200	4400	1700			6200	0.028	0.20
Additional recovery of materials:					*Aluminium*			
Franklin	230		76	180	950	1200	−0.023	0.097
Occidental	230		76	190	950	1210	−0.023	0.098
Incinerator residue	250		0	260	680	930	−0.025	0.068

Table A.17

Sensitivity analysis: relative sensitivity of β for several options

Item	β_0	Pulverized fuel	American RDF	American RDF with additional materials recovery	Wet pulping with fibre and wet RDF	Incineration and steam generation	Occidental pyrolysis	Anaerobic digestion
		0.95	0.79	0.89	0.88	0.54	0.31	0.20
Electricity		−0.025	−0.099	−0.10	−0.15	−0.13	−0.66	−0.54
Other fuels		−0.002	−0.003	−0.002	−0.002	–	−0.043	−0.85
Water supply/effluent treatment		–	–	–	−0.013	–	−0.016	−0.050
Other utilities		−0.003	−0.010	−0.010	−0.015	−0.013	−0.070	−0.14
Raw materials		–	–	–	–	–	–	–
Maintenance supplies		−0.007	−0.025	−0.027	−0.024	−0.054	−0.099	−0.20
Operating supplies		−0.002	−0.005	−0.005	−0.006	−0.012	−0.020	−0.041
Capital investment		−0.005	−0.016	−0.018	−0.019	−0.042	−0.066	−0.14
Transport		–	–	–	–	–	–	−0.042
Landfill or residuals disposal		–	−0.004	−0.003	−0.003	−0.008	−0.008	−0.085
Total energy inputs		−0.044	−0.16	−0.17	−0.23	−0.26	−0.98	−2.09
Ferrous metals		0.18	0.22	0.20	0.19	0.20	0.55	0.86
Aluminium				0.11				
Other inorganic materials				0.02				
Organic materials (paper)					0.51			
Fuel product		0.86	0.95	0.84	0.52	1.06	1.43	2.23

Table A.18
Assessment matrix

Option	Net present cost (equivalent unit cost, £/tonne)	Capital cost (£ million)	Net primary energy efficiency β	Weight for disposal to land (tonne/tonne)	Adequacy of technology[a]
Landfill	3.8	0.5	−0.02	1.0	Proven
Landfill with:					
Transfer to road	9.4	1.0	−0.05	1.0	Proven
Transfer to rail	13.0	1.5	−0.06	1.0	Proven
Pulverization					
1 shift	9.8	1.5	0.11	0.93	Proven
2 shift	8.8	1.0	0.12	0.93	Proven
Baling	14.2	3.0	−0.06	1.0	Commercial
Incineration:					
Non-recuperative	20.8	4.8	−0.02	0.35	Proven
Steam generation	22.3	6.6	0.54	0.35	Proven*
Electricity generation	23.6	7.8	0.53	0.35	Proven*
Modular	21.0	4.4	−0.35	0.30	Commercial
Modular + steam	24.2	7.6	0.30	0.30	Commercial
RDF as a supplementary fuel:					
American RDF	14.8	3.8	0.79	0.23[b]	Commercial
Powder RDF	23.2	6.0	0.78	0.20[b]	Commercial
Paper-based RDF	11.3	2.5	0.49	0.63[b]	Demonstration
Pulverized fuel					
Case (a)	4.3	1.5	0.95–1.0	0[b]	Demonstration
Case (b)	6.3				
Incineration of RDF:					
Suspension firing	28.8	8.2	0.55	0.35	Commercial
Incinerator turbine	24.7	7.0	0.49	0.23	Development
Wet pulping with:					
Fibre recovery	32.3	7.4	0.32	0.21	Demonstration
Incineration + electricity	32.8	10.0	0.34	0.21	Commercial
Fibre + wet RDF	19.7	5.1	0.88	0.21[b]	Demonstration†
Wet RDF	15.6	4.0	0.69	0.21[b]	Demonstration†
Dried RDF	22.6	5.0	0.53	0.21[b]	Demonstration†
Pyrolysis and other thermal processes					
Occidental	26.6	6.0	0.31	0.20	Demonstration
Union Carbide Purox	49.2	13.0	0.62	0	Demonstration
Andco–Torrax	29.2	6.8	0.20	0.08	Commercial
Monsanto Landgard	30.6	7.7	0.34	0.31	Demonstration
Biological processes:					
Composting	22.3	5.0	0.47	0.30	Proven*
Acid hydrolysis	34.3	8.0	−0.12	0.60	Research
Anaerobic digestion	38.8	8.0	0.20	1.23	Development
Additional recovery of materials:					
Franklin	2.3	0.8	0.10	−0.05	Demonstration
Occidental	2.3	0.7	0.10	−0.07	Demonstration
Incinerator residue	2.8	1.0	0.07	−0.25	Development

(a) Proven—in use for a number of years. An asterisk indicates that technical problems still exist.
  Commercial—plants have been sold and are now coming on line.
  Demonstration—full-scale demonstration plants planned or in use (≥100 t/day). Those marked with a dagger are developments from demonstration plants.
  Development—pilot plant is/has been operated.
  Research—laboratory-scale work.
(b) The combustion of a solid refuse-derived fuel or RDF in a conventional boiler will increase the quantity of ash requiring disposal. The weight for disposal to land in this table excludes such ash contained in the RDF. When RDF is burnt in a cement kiln the ash is incorporated in the product.

B. MODELS OF WASTE TRANSPORT

In this appendix, the derivations of two of the models of waste transport introduced in Chapter 6 are documented in more detail. In Section B.1 the relationship of collection cost to haul distance is examined, while Section B.2 considers the diseconomies of scale in transporting waste to a central processing plant.

B.1. Waste transport in a collection vehicle

B.1.1. The simple model

The aim here is to derive an analytical expression for the relationship shown in Fig. 6.1, between total cost of waste collection and haul, and the haul distance from the collection round to the waste discharge point, using the assumptions set out in Secton 6.2.2. For convenience the notation is summarized in Table B.1.

Equation 6.1 states that the total cost per tonne, C, of waste collection and haul to the discharge point, is the ratio of the total cost of running a vehicle, C_v, to the total quantity of waste collected, W_v, each week, that is

$$C = \frac{C_v}{W_v} \tag{B.1}$$

W_v is given by the product of the time available for collection and the tonnes of waste collected per unit time. Thus

$$W_v = (T_c M)(N_c L W_b) \tag{B.2}$$

where M is the number of days in the working week, N_c is the number of collectors in each team, L is the loading rate in bins per man–hour, and W_b is the average quantity of waste per bin.

The time available for collection each day, T_c is that not used for either haul or discharge of the waste:

$$T_c = T - N_t(T_t + T_h) \tag{B.3}$$

where T is the effective length of the working day, N_t is the number of trips to

Table B.1

Notation for collection cost derivation

Symbol	Explanation
C	Total cost per tonne of collection and haul
C_o	Collection cost per tonne
C_f	Fixed cost of a vehicle and collection team per week
C_{op}	Operation cost of a vehicle per week
C_v	Total cost of a vehicle and collection team per week
d	Haul distance
d_o	Base distance used to define collection operation
d_a	Asymptotic distance where C approaches infinity
d_l	Lower haul distance below which capacity limits on the vehicle are exceeded
F_c	Fixed cost of a collector per week
F_d	Fixed cost of a driver per week
F_v	Fixed cost of a vehicle per week
H	Haul cost per tonne
H'	Haul cost per tonne calculated from changes in vehicle numbers
L	Loading rate as bins per man-hour
M	Number of days per working week
N_c	Number of collectors in a team
N_t	Number of trips per day to the discharge point
N_t'	Number of full loads which may be collected in the working day
N_v	Number of vehicles required for collection $(d = d_o)$
ΔN_v	Additional number of vehicles required to collect the same amount of waste when haul distance is increased
O_c	Operating cost of collection per load
O_h	Operating cost of haul per kilometre
O_t	Operating cost of discharging a load at a landfill site
s	Average haul speed
T	Length of working day, after deduction of time for journey to and from the depot and for crew breaks
T_c	Time available for collection per day
T_h	Time used for haul, per round trip
T_{ho}	Haul time when distance is d_o
T_t	Turn-round time at the discharge point
t_1	Time to fill the vehicle to capacity
t_2	Time remaining after collecting and discharging N_t' full loads in day
U	Unit cost of haul, per tonne–kilometre
U'	Unit cost of haul for the aggregate cost function
V	Vehicle capacity in bins
W_a	Total waste collected per week in the area
W_b	Average tonnes of waste per bin
W_v	Waste collected per vehicle per week
A, B, G, J, K	Constants defined in the text

the discharge point each day, and T_t is the turn-round time at the discharge point.

The time for the return journey, T_h, is obtained from the haul distance and average speed s:

$$T_h = \frac{2d}{s} \tag{B.4}$$

Assuming as a first approximation that C_v, the cost of a vehicle and its crew, is constant, substitution of B.2–B.4 into B.1 gives

$$C = \frac{C_v}{MN_cLW_b} \frac{1}{\left\{T - N_tT_t - \left(\frac{2N_t}{s}\right)d\right\}}$$

$$= \frac{C_v\left\{1 - \frac{2N_t}{s(T - N_tT_t)}d\right\}^{-1}}{MN_cLW_b(T - N_tT_t)}$$

$$= A(1 - Bd)^{-1} \tag{B.5}$$

where

$$A = \frac{C_v}{MN_cLW_b(T - N_tT_t)} \tag{B.6}$$

and

$$B = \frac{2N_t}{s(T - N_tT_t)} \tag{B.7}$$

For the assumptions used, A and B are both constants.

The minimum cost of collection, C_0, when a discharge point is available at the end of each collection round, is obtained by substituting $d = 0$ into equation B.5; $C_0 = A$, the ratio of total cost to the maximum amount of waste collectable. Using the more general form of equation 6.2, the haul cost is

$$H = c(d) - c(d_0)$$

$$= A\left[\frac{1}{(1 - Bd)} - \frac{1}{(1 - Bd_0)}\right]$$

$$= \frac{AB(d - d_0)}{(1 - Bd)(1 - Bd_0)} \tag{B.8}$$

Equation B.5 may be expanded:

$$C = A(1 + Bd + B^2d^2 + \ldots) \tag{B.9}$$

which may be approximated by

$$C \approx A(1 + Bd) \tag{B.10}$$

When $Bd \ll 1$, that is the haul time is much less than the total time available for collection, the unit haul cost per tonne–kilometre is AB. Thus for short hauls, the haul cost is given by the product of the minimum collection cost and the fractional increase in time due to haul. From equation B.5 the distance d_a at which the cost approaches infinity is

$$d_a = \frac{1}{B} \qquad (B.11)$$

B.1.2. An alternative derivation

Under certain conditions this derivation from equation 6.1 is equivalent to that based on the additional number of vehicles required when haul distance is increased from d_0 to d; the fleet size is increased from N_v to $N_v + \Delta N_v$ vehicles. Equation 6.3 may be rewritten, assuming a constant cost per vehicle, C_v, as

$$H' = \frac{\Delta N_v C_v}{W_a} \qquad (B.12)$$

where W_a is the total waste collected in the area each week. The additional number of vehicles, ΔN_v, is the smallest integer greater than the ratio of the collection time lost by haul to the new collection time per vehicle.

$$\Delta N_v \geq \frac{N_v N_t (T_h - T_{h0})}{T_c} \qquad (B.13)$$

where T_{h0} is the haul time when the distance is d_0. On substitution of equations B.3, B.4, and B.7, B.13 becomes

$$\Delta N_v \geq \frac{N_v \left(\dfrac{2N_t}{s}\right)(d - d_0)}{\left(T - N_t T_t - \dfrac{2N_t}{s} d\right)}$$

$$= \frac{N_v B(d - d_0)}{(1 - Bd)} \qquad (B.14)$$

Similarly, the total number of vehicles, N_v, required for collection when the haul distance is d_0 is given by the ratio of the total waste in the area to the waste which can be collected by one vehicle:

$$N_v \geq \frac{W_a}{MN_c L W_b \left(T - N_t T_t - \dfrac{2N_t}{s} d_0\right)}$$

which on substitution of equations B.6 and B.7 yields

$$N_v \geq \frac{A W_a}{C_v (1 - Bd_0)} \qquad (B.15)$$

Unless N_v and ΔN_v are very small numbers, the relaxation of the integer restriction on the number of vehicles, by the replacement of the inequality signs in equations B.14 and B.15 with equalities, is unlikely to be a serious approximation. Any errors will be within the general accuracy of the model, while in practice both N_v and ΔN_v may be varied within limits by changes in collection practice, and the capacities of new vehicles may be chosen to meet requirements. Thus one may substitute equations B.14 and B.15 into B.12, giving

$$H' = \frac{AB(d - d_0)}{(1 - Bd)(1 - Bd_0)}$$

(B.16)

Comparing equations B.16 and B.8, $H = H'$ and the two approaches are equivalent.

B.1.3. Extending the cost function

The simple model derived so far has used a constant cost for a collection vehicle and its crew. This assumption is now relaxed, and an extended cost function is derived. One may write the vehicle cost as the sum of fixed and operating costs:

$$C_v = C_f + C_{op}$$

(B.17)

where the fixed cost may be broken down into contributions from the vehicle, driver, and crew:

$$C_f = F_v + F_d + N_c F_c$$

(B.18)

and the operating cost into collection, haul, and discharge:

$$C_{op} = MN_t(O_c + 2O_h d + O_t)$$

(B.19)

Note that the operating cost expression is simplified by assuming that the pick-up cost, O_c, is independent of the amount collected. The operating cost of waste discharge, O_t, is introduced specifically for landfill site delivery, where the uneven surface results in high tyre and maintenance costs, out of proportion to the short distances.

Substituting equations B.17–B.19 into B.6:

$$A = \frac{F_v + F_d + N_c F_c + MN_t(O_c + O_t) + 2MN_t O_h d}{MN_c L W_b (T - N_t T_t)}$$

$$= \frac{G + Jd}{K}$$

(B.20)

where the constants G, J, and K are given by

$$G = F_v + F_d + N_c F_c + MN_t(O_c + O_t)$$

(B.21)

$$J = 2MN_t O_h$$

(B.22)

$$K = MN_cLW_b(T - N_tT_t) \qquad \text{(B.23)}$$

and

$$C_v = G + Jd \qquad \text{(B.24)}$$

With equation B.5 this yields

$$C = \frac{(G + Jd)}{K}(1 + Bd)^{-1} \qquad \text{(B.25)}$$

which may be approximated, using B.10, as

$$C \approx \frac{G}{K} + \frac{1}{K}(GB + J)d \qquad \text{(B.26)}$$

The minimum cost of collection, when $d = 0$, is

$$C_0 = \frac{G}{K} \qquad \text{(B.27)}$$

and the haul cost is

$$H = \frac{(GB + J)}{K}d \qquad \text{(B.28)}$$

$$= Ud$$

where the unit cost of haul, U, becomes, on substitution of equations B.7 and B.21–B.23,

$$U = \frac{2N_t\left[\dfrac{\{F_v + F_d + N_cF_c + MN_t(O_c + O_t)\}}{s(T - N_tT_t)} + MO_h\right]}{MN_cLW_b(T - N_tT_t)} \qquad \text{(B.29)}$$

B.1.4. Applying the model

The model as developed above must be applied with care. For example, capacity constraints on the weight of waste which may be collected on each trip need to be superimposed on the basic equations; the rationale is explained in Section 6.2.3. The application of the model is illustrated with a worked example in Section 6.2.4.

The two models for collection costs, assuming, respectively, fixed and varying costs per vehicle, are compared in Table B.2. The base collection costs, when $d = 0$, agree fairly well, but the simpler model consistently underestimates the unit haul costs by 9–15 per cent, owing mainly to the omission of an explicit operating cost term. The calculations for the worked example in Section 6.2.4 are shown in Table B.3.

B.2. Models for waste delivery to a processing plant

The purpose of this section is to develop a series of models of waste delivery

Table B.2
A comparison of the simple and extended models

With collection costs defined as the cost when $d = 0$, the collection costs and unit haul costs are calculated from equations B.10 and B.26, respectively. The calculation assumes that s $= 20$ k.p.h. and $N_c = 3$. All costs are in £

				N_t			
Item	Equation	1	2	3	4	5
A	B.6	9.67	10.07	10.47	10.91	11.38
B	B.7	0.0148	0.0308	0.0480	0.0667	0.0870
G	B.21	523.5	537.0	550.5	564.0	577.5
J	B.22	1.40	2.80	4.20	5.60	7.00
K	B.23	58.27	56.11	53.95	51.79	49.63
Collection costs:						
Simple model	A	9.70	10.07	10.47	10.91	11.38
Extended model	G/K	8.98	9.57	10.02	10.89	11.64
% difference	a	+7.9	+5.2	+2.6	+0.18	−2.2
Haul costs:						
Simple model	AB	0.144	0.310	0.503	0.727	0.990
Extended major	GB/K	0.133	0.294	0.490	0.726	1.012
model[b] minor	J/K	0.024	0.050	0.078	0.108	0.141
total		0.157	0.344	0.568	0.834	1.153
% difference	a	−8.5	−10.0	−11.4	−12.8	−14.1

(a) % difference $= 100 \times \dfrac{\text{cost from simple model} - \text{cost from extended model}}{\text{cost from extended model}}$

(b) The unit haul cost from the extended model consists of two components, the major one being analogous to that from the simple model, and the minor one arising from the explicit consideration of operating costs.

Table B.3
The variation in collection costs with organizational changes

N_c	N_t	G (equation) (B.21)	J (B.22)	K (B.23)	Time for haul t_2 (h) (Table 6.3)	Minimum distance d_l (km) (equation) (6.12)	Collection cost $= \dfrac{G}{K}$ (£) (B.27)	Unit haul cost $= \dfrac{GB + J}{K}$ (£) (B.28)
2	1	423.5	1.40	42.02	2.75	27.5	10.08	0.183
	2	437	2.80	40.46	−1.50	−	10.80	0.402
3	1	523.5	1.40	58.27	3.87	38.7	8.98	0.157
	2	537	2.80	56.11	0.73	3.7	9.57	0.344
	3	550.5	4.20	53.95	−2.39	−	10.20	0.568
4	1	623.5	1.40	72.27	4.42	44.2	8.63	0.147
	2	637	2.80	69.60	1.84	9.2	9.15	0.322
	3	650.5	4.20	66.92	−0.74	−	9.72	0.529
5	1	723.5	1.40	84.04	4.75	47.5	8.61	0.144
	2	737	2.80	80.93	2.50	12.5	9.11	0.315
	3	750.5	4.20	77.81	0.25	0.8	9.65	0.517
6	1	823.5	1.40	94.68	4.97	49.7	8.70	0.144
	2	837	2.80	91.18	2.94	14.7	9.18	0.313
	3	850.5	4.20	87.67	0.92	3.1	9.70	0.514
	4	864	5.60	84.16	−1.12	−	10.27	0.751

to a transfer, treatment, reclamation, or disposal facility. The application of the models is discussed in Section 6.3.

B.2.1. The basic model

A number of simplifying assumptions are made in each case:
    (i) The plant catchment area is circular with radius R.
    (ii) All waste transport to the plant is in collection vehicles.
    (iii) The unit cost of haul, U per tonne–kilometre, is constant.
    (iv) Waste production per capita, w, is constant.
In addition, in the basic model, it is further assumed that:
    (v) Population density, p, within the area is constant.
    (vi) The plant is located at the centre of the area.
Using Fig. B.1, the waste arising, δW, in a small segment of the catchment area is

$$\delta W \approx wpr\, \delta r\, \delta \theta$$

from which the total waste W is

$$W = \int_0^{2\pi} \int_0^R wpr\, \mathrm{d}r\, \mathrm{d}\theta$$
$$= wp\pi R^2 \tag{B.30}$$

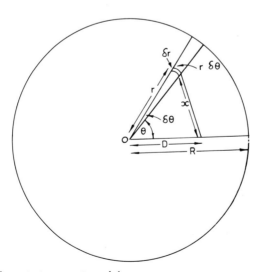

Fig. B.1. Ideal waste transport model.

The total amount of transport, T tonne–kilometres, which is required to concentrate this waste at the centre, is given by

$$T = \int_0^{2\pi} \int_0^R wpr^2 \, dr \, d\theta$$

$$= \frac{2\pi wpR^3}{3} \tag{B.31}$$

The average haul distance per tonne is waste is

$$\bar{d} = \frac{T}{W} = \tfrac{2}{3}R \tag{B.32}$$

and the average unit cost of waste transport, U_a, is thus

$$U_a = \tfrac{2}{3}kUR \tag{B.33}$$

where k is a constant, the ratio of road to crow-fly distances. The usual assumption of all waste arising at the centre of an area would imply $U_a = O$. Substituting for R from equation B.30 above, U_a may be related to the plant throughout, W:

$$U_a = bW^{\frac{1}{2}} \tag{B.34}$$

where

$$b = \tfrac{2}{3}kU\left[\frac{1}{wp\pi}\right]^{\frac{1}{2}}. \tag{B.35}$$

Hence U_a increases with W, showing an opposite trend to the unit processing cost. The total processing cost, C_p, may be written, after equation 5.5 (Sections 5.4.7 and 5.5.3), as

$$C_p = aW^S \tag{B.36}$$

where a is constant and S is the scale factor, from which the unit cost is

$$U_p = \frac{C_p}{W} = aW^{-(1-S)} \tag{B.37}$$

The total unit cost of processing and transport, U_T, is thus

$$U_T = U_a + U_p$$
$$= bW^{\frac{1}{2}} + aW^{-(1-S)} \tag{B.38}$$

For turning points,

$$\frac{dU_T}{dW} = \tfrac{1}{2}bW^{-\frac{1}{2}} - (1-S)aW^{-(2-S)}$$

$$= 0$$

The optimum scale of a plant, W_{opt}, for which the total unit cost is a minimum, is thus

$$W_{opt} = \left(\frac{2a(1-S)}{b}\right)^x \tag{B.39}$$

where

$$x = \frac{2}{3-2S} \tag{B.40}$$

The calculation of W_{opt} is illustrated in Section 6.3.1.

This discussion has focused on average haul costs. In some circumstances, the marginal haul cost is more relevant. From Fig. B.1, it can be seen that the marginal haul distance for an additional unit of waste is always R, the radius of the catchment area, so that the marginal unit cost of haul, U_m, is

$$U_m = kUR \tag{B.41}$$

B.2.2. Extending the model

This simple model may be extended by relaxing two assumptions, those of homogeneous population density and a central plant. Population density might be expected to decline with distance from the city centre. If a linear decrease is postulated,

$$p = p_0(1 - rp_1) \tag{B.42}$$

then substitution in equations B.30 and B.31 gives

$$W = \frac{wp_0\pi R^2}{3}(3 - 2p_1R)$$

and

$$T = \frac{wp_0\pi R^3}{6}(4 - 3p_1R)$$

from which

$$U_a' = kU\frac{T}{W}$$

$$= \frac{kUR}{2}\left(\frac{4 - 3p_1R}{3 - 2p_1R}\right) \tag{B.43}$$

This reduces to equation B.33 when $p_1 = 0$. Equation B.43 is obviously valid only when $R < 1/p_1$, at which distance the population density becomes zero. The proportional decrease in U_a', compared with U_a for the case of homogeneous density, is

$$\Delta U_a = \frac{U_a - U_a'}{U_a} = \frac{p_1R}{4(3 - 2p_1R)} \tag{B.44}$$

For values of population density at the edge of the catchment area of $0.5\,p_0$, $0.25\,p_0$, and zero, corresponding ΔU_a are 0.0625, 0.125, and 0.25. However as the density decreases, so larger catchment areas are required for the same waste throughput W. Substitution of R in terms of W involves the solution of a cubic equation which was here done numerically. For a given W, $1 \leqslant U'_a/U_a \leqslant R'/R$, while for the marginal costs, $U'_m/U_m = R'/R$. Results are given in Fig. B.2. for $p_1 = 0.02$ and 0.04 in the range $W = 0$–1000 t.p.d. For values of $p_1 R < 0.5$, the increase of U'_a over U_a is less than 15 per cent, while for U'_m the increase is less than 25 per cent.

These results indicate that, for moderate deviations from homogeneous population density, the simple model gives adequate results. If a particular situation necessitates a correction, the use of equation B.42 should suffice, so long as $p_1 R < 0.5$. A more sophisticated approach is possible, but does

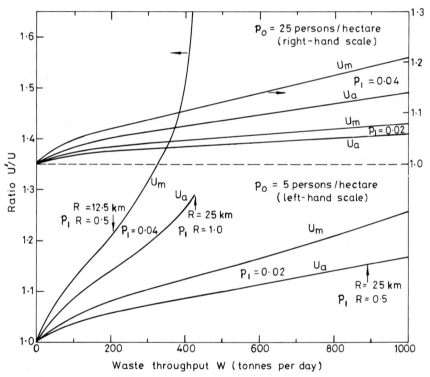

Fig. B.2. *The effect of inhomogeneous population density on the average unit costs of waste transport.*
  U' is the unit cost when p $=$ p$_0$ (1-rp$_1$)
  U is the unit cost when p $=$ p$_0$
  Subscript 'a' denotes average unit cost
  Subscript 'm' denotes marginal unit cost
  R is radius of catchment area.

not seem appropriate given the general accuracy of either the model or the data. An example of what can be done is the use of an empirical urban density function, such as that proposed by Clark (1951),

$$p = p_0 e^{-mr} \tag{B.45}$$

to account for the spatial variation beyond the central business district of a city. Data given by Newling (1966) for 46 urban areas in the USA gave $25 < p_0 < 500$ persons/ha, and $0.04 < m < 0.75$ per km. When equation B.45 is substituted in equations B.30 and B.31:

$$W = \frac{2\pi p_0 w}{m^2} \{1 - (1 + mR)e^{-mR}\} \tag{B.46}$$

and

$$U_a = \frac{kU}{m} \left\{ 2 - \frac{m^2 R^2 e^{-mR}}{1 - (1 + mR)e^{-mR}} \right\} \tag{B.47}$$

Results are shown in Table B.4 for $p_0 = 100$ persons/ha and $0.1 < m < 0.5$. Waste production is dominated by the high population density near the centre, while, for higher values of m, $p \approx 0$ when $r \geqslant 15$ km. Equation B.45 was not designed for use near the centre, p_0 being estimated to give the best fit of the equation to the spatial data. Several modifications have been proposed to overcome this difficulty, an example being,

$$p = p_0 e^{mr - nr^2} \tag{B.48}$$

(Newling 1969), which allows p to rise initially with increasing r, before beginning to fall.

Table B.4

The effects of inhomogeneous population density.

Using the exponential function $p = p_0 e^{-mr}$ (B.45), with $p_0 = 100$ persons/ha.

m (1/km)	Radius (km)											
	5		10		15		20		25		30	
	W	U_a	W	U_a	W	U_a	W	U_a	W	U_a	L	U_a
0.1	1750	75	2210	142	3710	202	4980	254	5970	300	6670	338
0.2	550	71	1250	127	1670	169	1990	196	2010	214	2060	224
0.3	410	67	750	112	870	137	912	149	924	154	927	155
0.4	310	64	480	98	513	112	521	116	522	117	522	117
0.5	240	60	321	85	334	92	334	93	334	94	334	94
Marginal unit cost U_m	–	117	–	234	–	351	–	468	–	585	–	702

W in tonnes per day.

U_a, U_m in pence per tonne-kilometre.

Attention is now turned to the assumption of a central plant. If the plant is displaced from the centre of the circle by a distance D, referring to Fig. B.1,

$$T = \int_0^{2\pi} \int_0^R wprx \, dr \, d\theta$$

$$= 2wp \int_0^\pi \int_0^R r(r^2 + D^2 - 2rD \cos \theta)^{\frac{1}{2}} \, dr \, d\theta \qquad (B.49)$$

This integral has been solved numerically, and the average unit costs calculated, using W from equation B.30. The ratio of the average unit cost for an off-centre plant to that for a central plant depends only on the ratio of the distance from the centre to the radius of the catchment area (D/R), the relationship being shown in Fig. 6.7. For displacements less than $0.5 \, R$, deviation from the central plant model is less than 20 per cent.

The effects of non-homogeneous population and an off-centre plant can be combined, and cases are also included in Fig. 6.7. The effects reinforce one another, although the extent of this synergism is small unless the density becomes very low, as in curve (3) of Fig. 6.7.

C. FLOWSHEETS FOR THE DCF COMPUTER PROGRAM

The computer program for the discounted cash flow sensitivity and risk analysis was developed from that of Professor D. H. Allen (private communication 1976). The program is written in modular form, with control from one of two subroutines (SENS or RISK). The principal subroutines specific to waste disposal are those which input and manipulate the resource recovery data and which calculate the annual operating costs and revenues and the yearly cash flows. For simplicity, the sensitivity and risk analysis flowsheets are shown independently, although each share many of the subroutines.

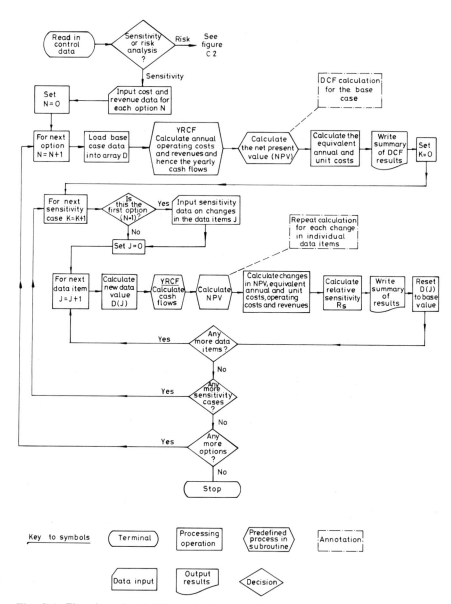

Fig. C.1. Flowsheet for DCF sensitivity analysis.

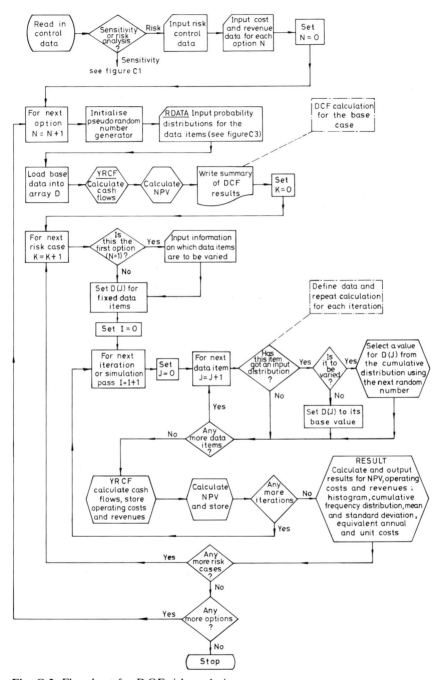

Fig. C.2. Flowsheet for DCF risk analysis.

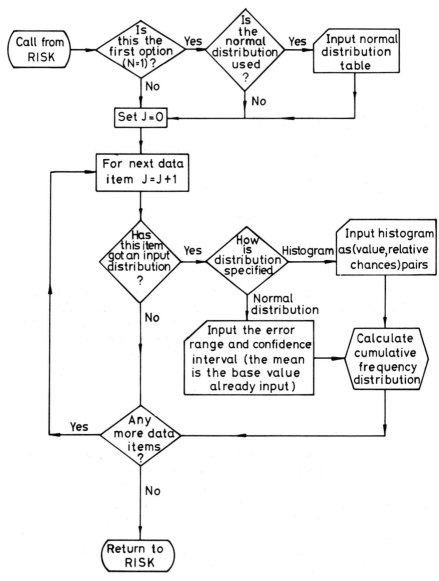

Fig. C.3. Flowsheet for subroutine R D A T A—inputs the probability distributions for the risk analysis.

D. THE GROSS ENERGY REQUIREMENTS OF INPUTS AND OUTPUTS TO THE WASTE MANAGEMENT SYSTEM

D.1. Introduction

Here the gross energy requirements assigned to both the inputs to and the residual waste outputs from waste management systems are documented. The aim of the process analysis is a comparative evaluation of the primary energy implications of alternative waste management technologies (Chapter 8). As far as possible the process inputs are evaluated at level 3 (Fig. 8.1). The primary energy savings implied by recovered products are documented in Appendix E.

D.2. Direct energy inputs

Direct energy inputs are credited with a value that includes not only the heat content, but also the energy invested to bring the energy to the point of use. The values used are taken from Chapman, Leach, and Slesser (1974), and are generally appropriate to the U K in 1971–72 (Table D.1). The exception is electricity where the efficiency, including losses in generation and transmission, is taken as 30 per cent, which is about the current U K average. Thus $3.33\,\text{kWh}_t = 1.0\,\text{kWh}_e$, where subscript t denotes thermal (i.e. primary energy) and subscript e denotes electricity.

D.3. Material inputs

The raw materials input to the various processes are evaluated using gross energy requirements from the literature (Table D.2). The energy requirement for landfill cover is assumed to be the same as for sand, approximately 100 M J/t.

Table D.1

Gross energy requirements of some fuels.
Data source: Chapman, Leach, and Slesser (1974),
except for electricity

Fuel	GJ/t	MJ/unit
Coal: supplied to the cement industry	26.7	–
industrial average	29.7	–
Motor spirit	52.4	38.9/l
Diesel fuel	50.8	42.5/l
Fuel oil	47.9	45.5/l
		1.11/MJ
Gas	–	130/therm
Electricity	–	12/kWh

Table D.2

Gross energy requirements for assorted materials

Material	Unit	MJ/unit	Source
Water supply	m³ (t)	9.2	Casper *et al.* (1975) (UK 1968)
Lime	t	4680	Chapman (1973)
Sand (used as a model for	t	72	Casper *et al.* (1975) (UK 1968)
landfill cover)		104.4	Broussaud (1976) (France)
Sulphuric acid	t	8100	Berry *et al.* (1975)
Proprietary inorganic chemical	t	20 000	Guess, based on Smith (1969)
used as embrittling agent			
(Section 15.4)			

D.4. Maintenance and operating supplies

The major material inputs will generally be operating and maintenance supplies. Few data are available on the physical quantities used, and in most cases an estimate will have to be made from the monetary expenditure. A factorial method of operating cost estimation is introduced in Section 5.5. On this system, operating supplies are estimated at 0.008 I/annum, where I is the capital cost, while maintenance varies around 0.08 I/annum. Of the maintenance expenditure, approximately 40 per cent (Black 1970) to 50 per cent (Walton 1968) is attributable to materials, the balance being labour; a value of 50 per cent is used here.

Once a cost estimate has been made, the primary energy implications need to be estimated. Both statistical and input–output methods produce energy intensity (MJ/£) data for industry or commodity groups, although the former should yield more accurate results (Casper, Chapman, and Mortimer 1975). When an energy intensity has been determined, the value may need to be corrected for time or transferred between countries. The assumptions made here are that the energy inputs do not change with time or between countries, so that correction may be achieved simply by using a cost index and a monetary location index (Chapter 10).

For maintenance and operating supplies, the published energy analyses are difficult to interpret as no well-defined industry or commodity group is involved. Some data for related categories are given in Table D.3. The British data are corrected to £(1968) using the index of wholesale prices for basic materials and fuels purchased by manufacturing industry (Table 10.1). The American data for 1963 are compared with British data for the same year using the monetary exchange rate of 2.79$/£ then current. Self-consistency is quite good, with the statistical energy intensities being some-what higher than those from input–output analysis. An approximate aver-age of 360 MJ/£(1968) is equivalent to 95.5 MJ/£ (1977). An energy intensity value of 100 MJ/£ is used here; it is emphasized that this is a rough estimate only and so it is essential to examine the sensitivity of the process analysis results to it.

Table D.3
Energy intensities of some sectors relevant to maintenance and operating supplies

		Source				
	Statistical analysis UK, 1968 (MJ/£) Casper	Input–output analysis				
		Wright (1974) (US, 1963)		Wright (1975) (UK, 1963)	Wright (1975) (UK, 1968)	
Category	et al. (1975)	(MJ/$)	(MJ/£ 1963)[1]	(MJ/£ 1963)	(MJ/£ 1968)[2]	(MJ/£ 1968)
Lubricating oils, greases	1960	–	–	–	–	–
Paint	537	145	405	374	310	260
Iron castings	532	148	414	448	372	414
Nuts, bolts, and screws	291	86	240	193	160	182
Pumps etc.	212	56	156	150	125	136

1. Conversion from 1963 $ to £ at exchange rate of 2.79.
2. Updating UK costs from 1963 to 1968 using index of wholesale prices (Table 10.1), relative value 1.21.

D.5. Capital investment

In an energy analysis to level 3 (Fig. 8.1), the gross energy requirement of a process includes the energy requirement of the capital employed. If the energy cost per unit output is sought, this energy requirement is distributed over the total output during the project life. The energy requirements of capital investment are again conveniently estimated using energy intensity values. From input–output analysis, Wright (1974) obtained:

US 1963 mean 165.7 MJ/£, standard deviation 44.1 MJ/£;

UK 1963 mean 158.8 MJ/£, standard deviation 11.8 MJ/£.

where comparison of USA/UK figures uses the monetary exchange rate of 2.79$/£. The values are closely grouped, which should make the possibilities of serious error smaller than for maintenance and operating supplies. Casper *et al.* (1975) from their statistical analysis of 1968 UK data derived the values shown in Table D.4, which are again closely grouped, but higher than the input–output data. For capital equipment an average value of 220 MJ/£(1968) appears reasonable. However, the prices used here are producers prices, that is at the factory gate. Delivery, installation, and construction costs are not included. Wright (1975) gives an input–output value for road transport of 84 MJ/£(1968), while construction costs (Table D.4) are around 140 MJ/£. An overall energy intensity of capital investment of 180 MJ/£(1968) is thus suggested. When this value is updated using the Engineering and Process Economics plant cost index (Table 10.1), it is equivalent to 51.5 MJ/£(1977). A value of 50 MJ/£ is thus used here. Transfer to the USA is achieved using a location index, 1$ = £0.52 (Section 10.2.2), giving 26 MJ/$.

Table D.4

Energy requirements of capital investment

Category	MJ/£1968
Construction and earth moving equipment	273
Mechanical handling equipment	222
Pumps, valves, and compressors	212
Industrial engines	238
Mining machinery	253
Miscellaneous machinery	194
Industrial plant and steelwork	194
General mechanical engineering	261
Electrical machinery	221
Construction (private)	130
Construction (public)	143
All capital (input–output)	131 [±9.8]

Data sources: Casper *et al.* (1975). Comparative input–output figures from Wright (1974) updated from 1963–8 at 1.21 (wholesale price/EPE index, Table 10.1).

D.6. Waste water treatment

As shown in Fig. 2.2, the boundary of the waste management system specifically includes any energy requirements associated with treating discharges to air or water to an acceptable standard. It is assumed that data on energy use in the process include the energy requirements of electrostatic precipitators or other necessary devices for air pollution control, while those for water treatment are usually not included whether or not on-site treatment is necessary to upgrade the residue for discharge to sewer. In addition to on-site treatment costs, those of treatment in the sewerage works before the waste can be discharged to a river must also be included.

Reliable data on the energy requirements of waste water treatment are not available at present. The energy requirement is linked to the concentration of contaminants in the effluent, to the treatment method used, and to the discharge standard. The data which do exist are generally average values. Davidson, Ross, Chynoweth, Michaels, Dunnette, Griffis, Stirling, and Wang (1975) gave an energy intensity for waste water treatment in industry of 210 MJ/\$ (1968), implying an energy requirement of about 8 MJ/m³. Sachs and Berry (1976) derived an average energy requirement for sewage treatment in Chicago of 5 MJ/m³, which compared with 3.5 MJ/m³ for water supply. The energy requirements of water supply in the UK are higher (Table D.2), and applying the ratio of treatment to supply energy above would yield an approximate GER for treatment of 13 MJ/m³.

These average values may be contrasted with other data. Neff (1972) gave the electrical requirements of reducing biological oxygen demand (BOD) in an effluent as 3.0 MJ_e/kg BOD. Prather and Young (1976) examined the electrical energy for treatment of a petroleum refinery effluent with a design loading of 350 mg/l BOD and 800 mg/l COD. The results suggest a requirement of 4.4 MJ_e or 15 MJ_t/m³. As an example, the Franklin demonstration plant of the Black–Clawson wet sorting system (Chapter 17) produced 72 kg BOD/t of waste, contained in 10.6 m³ of water (Systems Technology Corporation 1975), implying a concentration of 7g/l. The average value of 13 MJ/m³ implies an energy requirement of 140 MJ/t; 3.0 MJ_e/kg BOD gives 720 MJ_t/t; the 15 MJ/m³ of Prather and Young, increased tenfold to allow for a twentyfold increase in concentration, suggests 1600 MJ/t; the estimated treatment cost of 0.28 \$/t and the energy intensity value above implies a requirement of only 60 MJ/t. For this case at least, waste water treatment may have a significant energy requirement, but correct evaluation must await more information. In the process analysis here, an average value of 13 MJ/m³ is used, with *ad hoc* estimation for those systems which produce small quantities of a highly contaminated effluent.

D.7. Transport

Transport may enter the analysis of waste management systems at three separate points (Fig. 2.2): delivery of waste in a collection vehicle, transport for recovered products to the point of reuse, and bulk haulage of waste or residual materials after processing to distant landfill. The energy implications of transport of the recovered materials is included in the energy savings due to recovery (Appendix E). The bulk haulage of waste may be considered as a typical transport operation. In Table D.5 some literature estimates of the energy requirements per tonne–kilometre of freight transport are summarized. The direct energy estimates are in reasonable agreement with each other, and are lower than the energy analysis estimates. The values of Leach and Slesser (1972) and of Mortimer (1974) are not, however, directly comparable, the former being for specific cases while the latter are averages for 1968. The process analysis by the Advisory Council on Energy Conservation (1977) is the most comprehensive study; in this case at least, specific allowance was made for the return journey after discharge of the load. The values used in this analysis are, for road transport 2.8 MJ/t km, and for rail transport 1.2 MJ/t km, each appropriate to the single journey distance. Energy requirements for waste transport in a collection vehicle are, in the absence of more relevant data, assumed to be double those for other road transport to allow for the lower payload.

Table D.5
Energy requirements of transport

Source	Basis	Road (MJ/t km)	Rail (MJ/t km)
Mortimer (1974)	Statistical analysis, average for the UK, 1968	2.7 ± 0.1	1.4 ± 0.2
Leach and Slesser (1972), revised by Mortimer (1974)	Direct energy costs, UK 1971–2	1.7	0.58
Hirst (1973)	USA, average direct energy, 1970	2.0	0.47
Midwest Research Institute (1974)	USA, direct energy	1.8	0.58
Broussaud (1976)	France, energy analysis	3.0	0.86
Advisory Council on Energy Conservation (1977)	Process analysis UK		
	Tipper work Waste tipping (bulk movements)	1.4–2.5	
	8–10 t payload	1.7–3.2	
	12–15 t payload	1.3–2.5	
	Freightliner (train)		0.5–1.6

D.8. Residuals disposal

The residue from a resource recovery system is dense and relatively easy to handle compared with raw refuse. It is assumed that the energy requirement for the landfill of raw waste (Table 11.4; 140 MJ/t) is appropriate also to compacted refuse from a transfer station. For pulverized or baled waste this is reduced by 30 per cent to 100 MJ/t. For a fairly inert residue from resource recovery, 50 per cent or 70 MJ/t is used. Transport by road has an energy requirement of 2.8 MJ/t km, the distance being that for a single trip. Standard distances of 20 km for pulverized or baled waste or the residue after processing and 30 km for untreated waste are used, reflecting possible differences in the ease of obtaining sites. For disposal of residual wastes remaining after processing, the energy requirement is thus $20 \times 2.8 = 56$ MJ/t for transport $+ 70$ MJ/t for landfill, $= 130$ MJ/t total.

E. ENERGY CONSERVATION THROUGH RECYCLING MATERIALS

E.1. Introduction

The recycling of materials may have a significant impact on the use of primary energy resources since the utilization of a secondary material often uses less energy than does production from virgin sources. Many estimates have been made of the energy savings through recycling individual materials. However, thes estimates are often at variance with each other and may be difficult to compare owing to differences in the exact system being considered. For example, the energy to produce steel ingots from new scrap is obviously less than that for a similar quantity of ferrous scrap contained in municipal waste as collected in a dust-cart.

The purpose of this Appendix is to critically review the literature in order to suggest estimates of the energy savings due to recycling one tonne of a given material. The estimates are developed here specifically for use in deriving the energy efficiency of alternative options for the disposal, treatment, or reclamation of solid wastes (Chapter 8). However, other applications where such estimates are useful include (Wilson 1979b):

(i) Pinpointing the materials of most concern from an energy conservation point of view, and conversely focusing attention on those cases where the energy savings are marginal and where particular care is necessary in planning a recycling programme so as not to increase net energy consumption.

(ii) Assessing the national or global potential of recycling materials as a means of conserving energy supplies.

The aim here is to estimate the gross energy savings due to recycling one tonne of various materials. It is assumed that the material has already been separated from other components of the waste stream and is ready for shipment to the using facility. Allowance is made for the transportation of the product to the point of use and for all the operations made on it until it may be absorbed into the usage cycle of the virgin product. This gross energy requirement is then compared with that needed to produce the equivalent product using conventional routes of manufacture. For example, ferrous metal scrap is assumed to be used for making steel ingots, and the energy requirement for this process should thus be compared with those for traditional processes to obtain the same product. Difficulties arise when the recovered product is not a perfect substitute. In principle, process analysis results are the most relevant but other literature values are considered where appropriate. It should be noted that the values obtained for the energy savings are average values. The energy saving for an additional tonne of material recycled (the marginal value) may or may not be closely related to the average value.

It is useful to distinguish between different types of scrap. The common categories are:

Home scrap, which arises and is consumed within the manufacturing facility;

New scrap, which is generated while the material is being fabricated into finished products at other plants, an example being steel scrap from a motor car body plant;

Old (or *post-consumer*) *scrap*, which arises when the product has served its designated purpose.

Levels of recycling for home and new scrap are already fairly high for most materials, while levels for old scrap vary from moderate to very low.

E.2. Metals

Literature estimates of the gross energy requirements of production of the five most common metals—steel, aluminium, copper, zinc, and lead—are summarized in Table E.1. Not all the estimates are independent as most authors use those of others quite freely. The general agreement is good, considering the differences which one would expect to arise between countries, with the grade of mineral ore, with the production technology and with the methods of analysis. Note that the census and input–output analysis methods do not distinguish between secondary and primary production and thus yield average values. The effect is most noticeable for data on aluminium production in the U K.

The energy requirements for steel production from primary materials show some agreement. Distinction is made between the production of 'crude' steel, that is the steel furnace product cast into ingots or rolled into slabs, and finished steel. The primary metal cycle for the two classes requires 15–50 and 45–80 G J/t, respectively. An international comparison of crude steel production in seven countries (the six major E E C countries plus the U S A) showed a range of average gross energy requirements from 15.2 to 23.8 G J/t. This variation was explained by differences in the furnace technology used, by the age of the steelmaking facilities and also by the amount of scrap, which varied from 306 to 632 kg/t of crude steel. This was made up of about 200–250 kg of recycled home scrap, the balance being purchased

Table E.1

Energy requirements for metals production from virgin ore and scrap metal. (All figures are GJ/t)

Author	Date	Type of Analysis	Steel Crude	Steel Finished	Steel From scrap	Aluminium Virgin	Aluminium Scrap	Copper Virgin	Copper Scrap	Zinc Virgin	Zinc Scrap	Lead Virgin	Lead Scrap
Atkins	1973	Process (USA)	37			259	9.2	130		76		31	
Batelle Institute	1975	Process (USA)				284		149		92			
Berry and Fels	1972 1973	Census (USA)		54		291							
Berry and Makino	1974	Process (USA)		54	26	261	9.5	51	7.8				
Bravard et al.	1972	Process (USA)		56	23	259		61	7.0				
Broussaud	1976	Process (France)	17	45	8.4	262	14						
Chapman P. F.	1975	Census (UK)	37	47		96	–	45					
Chapman P. F.	1975	Best Estimates		48	23	328	11	72	9.0	72		25	
Chapman P. F.	1974	Process (UK)				328	15	80	23	67	9.0	54	7.2
Critoph	1975 a, b	Process (UK)	38										
Franklin et al.	1975	Literature (US)		57	6.7	292	11						
Hannon	1972	Statistical (USA)		65		372							
INCPEN	1975	Process (UK)		53	30								
Kellogg	1976	Estimates (USA)			15		14	21	21	21	20	12	11
A D Little/Battelle Columbus	1978	Process (USA)			24		17						
Makhijani and Lichtenberg	1972	Statistical (USA)	50	79		267		83		58		51	
Midwest Research Institute	1974			58	7.9	308	13	83					
Roberts	1974	Process (World Average)		58	29	284	7.2	59	7.2	40	7.2	34	7.2
Waller[1]	1976	Process (UK)	23–49		20–26								
Wright	1975	Input–Output U.K. 1968		23		52		68					
Wright	1974	USA, 1963	13	25		97		88		42		51	

1. Detailed results are given for three types of steel furnace using either imported or domestic (UK) ore, with scrap charges 0–100 per cent.
INCPEN: Industry Committee for Packaging and the Environment.

$G = 10^9$

$M = 10^6$

2590000000

1356000000

– 1356000000

scrap (Long 1977). The routine use of scrap in steel production makes more difficult the calculation of a base-line 'virgin material' energy requirement.

For steel production from scrap, energy requirements range from 7 to 36 GJ/t. Again several factors contribute to this wide variation in estimates:

(i) The end product may be assumed to be hot blast furnace metal, crude steel, or finished steel.

(ii) Some convention is required for the energy content attributed to the scrap. For example, Waller (1976) ascribes an energy content of zero to purchased scrap but that for finished steel to home scrap, with a 50–50 use of the two assumed.

(iii) The energy requirement depends on the steelmaking technology. For example, a recent study compared steel production from scrap using an electric arc furnace, open hearth furnace, and a cupola, estimating the gross energy requirements as 10, 24, and 36 GJ/t of product, respectively (Little and Battelle 1978).

It is clear from this discussion that the use of scrap in the production of steel saves energy, but that the amount of that saving depends on many circumstances including the quality of the scrap, the steelmaking technology and the conventions used in analysis. Further research is required to establish reasonable figures suitable for various applications. A current best estimate of the energy saving due to recycling one tonne of ferrous scrap, for example that recovered from municipal waste, is *25 GJ/t*, based on a requirement for virgin materials of about 50 GJ/t and for scrap of about 25 GJ/t.

Aluminium production from primary and secondary materials has energy requirements of 240–380 and 7–17 GJ/t, respectively (Table E.1). The lower values from statistical or input–output analyses reflect the average production mix in a country. The differences in the energy requirements of production from virgin ore may be accounted for in terms of the efficiency of electricity generation, the alloy composition, and the form of output product assumed. The process analysis of Chapman (1974a) yielded a gross energy requirement of 56 GJ (electrical) plus 94 GJ (thermal) per tonne, which, with an electricity efficiency of 30 per cent, gives a value of 280 GJ/t. With 10 GJ/t for secondary production, this yields an energy saving due to recycling of *270 GJ/t*.

The gross energy requirement (GER) of copper production from ore depends principally on the ore grade (G per cent) available, the following relationship being derived by Chapman (1974a):

$$GER = \frac{52.5}{G} + 27.5 \text{ GJ/t copper}$$

which on correction to an electrical efficiency of 30 per cent becomes:

$$GER = \frac{45.4}{G} + 25.7 \text{ GJ/t copper}$$

An ore grade of 0.5–2 per cent gives 120 GJ/t<GER<48 GJ/t, encompassing the range in Table E.1; an exception is the value of Berry and Fels (1972) which is for finished metal. The energy requirement increases rapidly as the ore grade falls below 1 per cent, so that the primary energy implications of recovering copper include a surrogate or substitute measure of the resource conservation potential, as the more scarce the resource becomes, the lower is the ore grade which may be mined economically. For secondary production of copper, energy requirements fall into two ranges, either 7–9 GJ/t or 20–23 GJ/t. The former figures are appropriate to clean scrap while the latter refer to 'irony' old scrap, with a copper content of perhaps 20–60 per cent (Chapman 1974b; Little et al. 1978).

The energy saving from recycling copper thus depends both on the ore grade currently available and on the quality of the scrap. If it is anticipated that lower ore grades will become necessary in the future, a calculation based on the current ore grade will undervalue recycling. An ore grade of 1 per cent corresponds to a gross energy requirement of 70 GJ/t. For new scrap, the energy requirement is about 10 GJ/t, giving an energy saving of about *60 GJ/t*. Copper may be recovered from municipal waste as a mixture of 'other non-ferrous metals', which contains about 55 per cent copper and 35 per cent zinc (Sullivan and Makar 1976). The energy requirement to recover copper from such a mixture is about 20 GJ/t, so that for this type of old scrap the energy saving is about *50 GJ/t* of copper.

The gross energy requirements of zinc production from ore or from scrap are relatively poorly documented. The values in Table E.1 are similar to those for copper and the energy savings from recycling zinc may as a first approximation be taken as the same as for copper. Thus one tonne of mixed copper and zinc from municipal waste represents an energy saving of about *50 GJ*.

For lead, the available data suggest energy requirements from virgin sources and from scrap of 25–55 GJ/t and 7–12 GJ/t respectively. Taking average values of 40 and 10 GJ/t, the energy saving due to recycling lead is estimated at about *30 GJ/t*.

E.3. Glass

The energy requirements for glass manufacture from virgin materials, as derived by various authors, are summarized in Table E.2. Agreement is only fair, most values being in the range 16–32 MJ/t. Most of the analyses refer to glass bottles, but this is not always so. Hannon (1972) provides the following breakdown for the production of glass containers from virgin materials:

	GJ/t
Material acquisition	2.1
Transport (400 km)	0.3
Manufacture	18.0
Total	20.4

Thus 90 per cent of the energy requirement is in manufacture, which in turn is dominated by the energy to melt the raw materials. There is some evidence that the use of recycled glass cullet may lower the temperature required in the furnace slightly, the reduction in fuel consumption due to each additional 10 per cent of cullet used being given as 1.5 per cent by the Industry Committee for Packaging and the Environment (INCPEN) (1975) and as 2.5 per cent by Shelley (1977). Each tonne of cullet recycled may thus save 2 GJ/t from materials acquisition plus about 3.5 GJ/t by reducing fuel consumption. This suggested energy saving of about 5 GJ/t of cullet appears to contradict the often expressed view that recycling glass does not save energy. However, this view is usually based on the energy requirement to separate glass from mixed waste (Hannon 1972; Makhijani and Lichtenberg 1972; Midwest Research Institute 1974), which is considered separately in this study. Nevertheless, since the suggested saving of about 5 GJ/t is well within the uncertainty range for glass manufacture from virgin materials, 16–32 GJ/t, it is perhaps prudent to conclude that although glass appears to represent a potential indirect energy source once it has been collected together, further research to confirm the exact value of this energy saving is required. A conservative value of *3 GJ/t* is used here for the energy saving due to recycling glass cullet.

Table E.2
Energy requirements for glass production from virgin materials

Author	Date	Type of analysis	GJ/t
Berry and Makino	1974	Process (USA), bottles	9.1
Casper *et al.*	1975	Statistical (UK 1968), plate glass	23
Hannon	1972	Statistical (USA), bottles	20
INCPEN	1975	Bottles	18
Makhijani and Lichtenberg	1972	Statistical (USA):	
		Plate glass	29
		Bottles	32
Midwest Research Institute (USEPA 1973)	1972	Direct energy (USA)	16

INCPEN: Industry Committee for Packaging and the Environment.
USEPA: US Environmental Protection Agency.

The relatively small energy saving from recycling glass cullet may be contrasted with that from reusing returnable glass bottles. For example, Hannon (1972) calculated the energy requirement for an 8-trip bottle of capacity 16 fluid ounces (0.47 l) as 3.4 MJ/trip, compared with 8.2 MJ/trip for a non-returnable bottle. As his non-returnable bottles weighed 0.3 kg, this represents an energy saving of 16 GJ/t of non-returnable glass bottles. Thus the use of returnable glass bottles is much more attractive from the point of view of energy savings than the recovery and reuse of non-returnable bottles as cullet.

E.4. Paper

The energy requirements to produce paper from virgin materials or from recycled paper products are summarized in Table E.3. The overall agreement in the requirements for virgin materials is poor. This can be attributed in part to the differences in energy requirements for finished paper, as given for example by Berry and Makino (1974), and for producing pulp, as given for example by Goddard (1975) or Hunt and Franklin (1973). In addition,

Table E.3

Energy requirements for paper manufacture

Author	Date	Type of analysis	Grade of paper	Gross energy requirements (GJ/t)	
				Virgin materials	Recycled pulp
Berry and Makino	1974	Process USA	Unbleached kraft	47	
			Boxboard	39	
			Corrugated boxes	41	
			Folding boxes	48	
			Set-up boxes	53	
			Sanitary food containers	48	
			Fibre cans and drums	48	
			Groundwood pulp	7.6	1.7
Chapman	1975	Statistical UK, 1968	UK industry average (value is sensitive to the energy requirement used for imports)	27	
INCPEN	1975	Process UK	Packaging containers	71	
Makhijani and Lichtenberg	1972	Statistical USA	USA industry average	25	
Wright	1974	Input–output	USA pulp industry—1963	28	
			USA Paper industry—1963	61	
	1975		UK paper and —1963	43	
			board industry—1968	37	
Goddard	1975	Direct energy only	Newsprint (groundwood)	20	5.5
			Bleached kraft	6.7	5.5
			Semi-chemical process	13	5.5
			Sulphite process	28	5.5
Hunt and Franklin	1973	Direct energy, including that to generate electricity	Corrugating medium	14	5.5
			Printing paper	24	10
			Type of pulp:		
			Unbleached kraft	18	5.5
			Bleached kraft	24	10
			Groundwood	20	5.5
			Semi-chemical	13	5.5
			Sulphite	28	10

not all the figures are based on full energy analyses, Hunt and Franklin for example including only direct energy inputs and the energy required to generate electricity.

Recycled paper substitutes for the virgin material as pulp. Four main types of wood pulp may be distinguished, namely kraft, semi-chemical, groundwood, and sulphite. Kraft pulp is produced by chemical methods using an alkaline solution of caustic soda and sodium sulphide. Kraft is the lowest-cost chemical pulp and produces the strongest fibres. A wide variety of trees can be used, especially those with a high resin content such as pine or Douglas Fir. Yields are 40–50 per cent by weight. Kraft pulps are principally used in paperboard and coarse paper grades; unbleached grades are used in packaging and bleached grades in packaging boards and a number of paper grades including printing grades and tissues. Direct energy requirements for kraft pulp production are quoted as 18 and 24 MJ/t for unbleached and bleached grades, respectively, by Hunt and Franklin (1973) but as 6.7 MJ/t by Goddard (1975). The discrepancy arises because some of the wood fibre entering a kraft mill is burned in the chemical recovery furnace to provide energy to run the process. Hunt and Franklin regard this fibre as a primary fuel in its own right, whereas Goddard sees it rather as a raw material for paper production, reducing the energy requirement for the process. The former interpretation is more consistent with the principles of process energy analysis.

Semi-chemical pulp is produced by using a mild chemical treatment on chipped wood followed by mechanical separation of the wood fibres. The yield is high, but the fibres are not so strong and flexible as kraft pulp. The pulp is made mainly from hardwoods and is used for corrugating medium in paperboard boxes. The direct energy requirement is about 13 MJ/t of pulp.

Groundwood pulp is the lowest-quality pulp and is produced mechanically by grinding action to separate wood fibres from resinous binders. It is used for newsprint and some printing papers. The gross energy requirement is given by Berry and Makino (1974) as 7.6 MJ/t, in contrast to a direct energy requirement of 20 MJ/t given by Goddard (1975) and by Hunt and Franklin (1973), the latter value being higher than that for kraft pulp because it is assumed that power is supplied as electricity.

Sulphite pulp is produced by heating low-resin woods such as spruce with sulphurous acid and a basic salt. The pulp is of good quality and goes into printing grades of paper such as business papers and into tissue. The direct energy requirements are high at 28 MJ/t.

When paper is reused, some of the fibres are damaged by reprocessing so that its quality decreases. Thus much waste paper is incorporated in a lower grade of product than the original. High-grade waste papers such as printers' waste, tabulating cards, computer printouts, and tissues are generally used as pulp substitutes in the fine-paper sector. Bulk waste paper grades such as old newspapers, used corrugated boxes, kraft paper, and mixed paper and board are consumed mainly in the newsprint and packaging sectors. They are simply repulped with almost no chemical treatment required. However, it is possible to upgrade bulk grades to higher quality uses by deinking and bleaching. This process involves chemical digestion and requires both more energy and more waste paper per tonne of pulp produced. Direct energy requirements per tonne of pulp are about 5.5 MJ for repulping and 10 MJ for deinking and bleaching (Goddard 1975; Hunt and Franklin 1973), although Berry and Makino (1974) quote a much lower figure of 1.7 MJ/t for repulping. Waste paper consumption per tonne of pulp is given as 1.1 t for repulping and 1.4 t for deinking and bleaching (Hunt and Franklin 1973) or as 1.5–2.0 t for repulping (Berry and Makino 1974).

It is clear from this discussion that the energy savings from recycling paper both depend on the specific grade of waste paper, the recycling process, and the virgin pulp displaced, and are also uncertain due to discrepancies in the available information. For waste paper recycled as newsprint or packaging, energy savings per tonne of pulp are variously given (Table E.3) as 6 MJ or 14 MJ for groundwood pulp, 12 MJ for unbleached kraft, and 7 MJ for semi-chemical pulp. As about 1.1 t of waste paper are required to produce a tonne of pulp, an energy saving of about 10 MJ/t of waste paper is indicated, although the process analysis of Berry and Makino (1974) suggests a lower figure of about 5 MJ/t. For waste paper recycled as higher-quality paper, suggested savings are 1.2 MJ (Goddard 1975) or 14 MJ (Hunt and Franklin 1973) for bleached kraft and 22 MJ or 18 MJ for sulphite pulp. The higher value for kraft pulp is used here as it is more consistent to regard the by-product pulp used in the virgin material process as a fuel input. As kraft pulp dominates sulphite pulp in terms of volume, and about 1.4 t of waste paper is required to displace 1 t of pulp, an energy saving of about 10 MJ/t of waste paper is again indicated.

In contrast to the other materials discussed so far, paper is also a source of energy, although aluminium and to a lesser extent iron will oxidize on combustion and thus contribute a small amount to the heat content of solid waste (Table 1.3). The energy requirements in Table E.3 do not include the energy content of the paper itself. Energy analyses generally include the calorific value of chemical feedstocks, but apparently not of timber feedstocks. It was concluded above that recycling one tonne of waste paper implies an energy saving of about 10 GJ. Paper in municipal waste has an average calorific value of about 13 GJ/t at 25 per cent moisture content (Kaiser 1975) while dry paper has a calorific value of about 18 GJ/t. Thus it appears that direct energy recovery from waste paper is more attractive from an energy conservation viewpoint than recycling as paper. However, recycled paper still has a calorific value. The definition of gross energy requirement of a process includes the calorific value of the products. Thus, the gross energy saving due to recycling one tonne of waste paper is the sum of the energy savings from recycling, about 10 GJ/t, and the calorific value still in the paper, about 15 GJ/t, that is a total of about *25 GJ/t*. This gross energy saving should be compared with the potential 15 GJ/t if the paper is efficiently converted to energy or with zero if the paper is simply landfilled.

E.5. Plastics

The manufacture of plastics from virgin raw materials, normally crude oil or natural gas, is very energy intensive. Gross energy requirements were calculated by Berry, Long, and Makino (1975) for the production of four different plastics in the Netherlands, UK, and USA. The results are summarized in Table E.4 and are in the range 90–170 GJ/t. Substantial international differences were observed, due largely to the different chemical synthesis routes possible, that adopted depending on local circumstances. With such high energy requirements, the potential benefits from recycling are obvious.

Table E.4

Gross energy requirements to produce plastics

All figures in GJ/t, taken from Berry *et al.* (1975).

	Country		
Plastic	The Netherlands	UK	USA
Polythene	95	104	163
Polypropylene	–	171	157
PVC	92	88	88
Polystyrene	133	96	124

Clean scrap of a single plastic, such as that generated in fabricating plastic packages, can often be reused simply by grinding and adding to the virgin plastic. The energy savings from such recycling has been suggested as 80 per cent (Industry Committee for Packaging and the Environment 1975). When heat depolymerizes the product, as with polystyrene, the clean scrap needs to be substituted in the manufacturing process. If the scrap is dirty, or contains more than one type of plastic, recycling is more difficult. Development of technology to separate plastics from other waste, to separate different types of plastics or to reuse mixed plastics is in its infancy (Aoyagi 1975; Bahr 1979). As the prospects for the recovery or recycling of post-consumer plastic waste are currently poor, no attempt has been made to quantify any possible energy savings.

E.6. Materials derived from waste

In addition to recovery of the metals, glass, and paper contained in municipal or in similar industrial wastes, various other products may be reclaimed by processing the waste. Examples include the use of the inorganic residue from processing as an aggregate and the conversion of the organic fraction into material products.

The inorganic residue from a solid waste resource recovery process is often suggested as a source of aggregate. As such it would directly displace conventional products such as sand and gravel, which have a gross energy requirement calculated variously as about 72, 83, or 104 MJ/t (Chapman, 1973; Makhijani and Lichtenberg 1972; Broussaud 1976). An energy saving of about *100 MJ/t* is thus suggested here.

The materials which may be derived from the organic fraction of municipal waste include compost, ethanol, methanol, ammonia, methane, and organic acids. Compost and ethanol are considered here as typical examples, being the only ones produced by the options included in the case study of Chapter 8.

The primary energy savings from compost depend on its use. As a soil conditioner it may be viewed as a substitute for peat, which has an energy content as a fuel and is transported relatively long distances. In wallboard production it substitutes for wood chip or plaster, and in building blocks for an aggregate. It may also be used directly as a fuel, but other processes are better suited to refuse-derived fuel production. Here the compost is credited with its heat content, taken as 10 GJ/t, the same as for unprocessed waste, and with the energy saved by not digging and transporting peat. An average distance of 200 km indicates a transport requirement about 500 MJ/t (Section D.7), and this is doubled to allow for extraction. Thus the energy savings to be credited to compost are about *11 GJ/t*.

Industrial ethanol is normally produced from crude oil via naptha and ethylene, the hydration being indirect via the sulphate ester or by direct addition under catalysis. The energy requirement to produce ethylene, not including the heat content of the oil feedstock, is about 17 GJ/t (Smith 1969; Berry *et al.* 1975). This is assumed to increase to about 20 GJ/t for ethanol production. To this should be added its heat content of 30.2 GJ/t (Rose and Copper 1977), giving a total gross energy requirement for ethanol of *50 GJ/t*.

E.7. Waste-derived fuels

The recovery of a fuel product from solid waste may take various routes, including the direct generation and sale of steam or electricity, or the production of a gaseous, liquid, or solid waste-derived fuel (WDF) as a substitute for a conventional fuel. The energy saving due to a fuel product is the primary energy required to provide the conventional fuel which would give an equivalent amount of useful heat or work. If the substitution equivalence (SE) of a waste-derived fuel is defined as its relative efficiency compared with the conventional fuel it replaced (equation 8.1),

$$SE = \frac{\text{efficiency in use of conventional fuel}}{\text{efficiency in use of waste-derived fuel}}$$

then the energy saving may be written (equation 8.2)

$$\frac{\text{primary}}{\text{energy}} = \frac{\text{heat content in WDF}}{\text{efficiency of producing}} \times \frac{1}{\text{SE}}$$
$$\text{saved} \qquad \text{conventional fuel}$$

$$-\text{energy to transport WDF to point of use}$$

The efficiences are defined in terms of useful calorific output per unit of energy input. Efficiencies of supply of coal, gas, and oil in the United Kingdom are 0.955, 0.811, and 0.896, respectively, including delivery to the user (Chapman *et al.* 1974). For electricity, a supply efficiency of 0.30 is assumed (Section D.2).

The fuel efficiency is dependent on the exact conditions prevailing. A common application of the waste-derived and conventional fuels must be defined, and this is commonly steam or electricity generation. The appropriate value of the substitution equivalence is discussed for each process in Part II of the text, but it is convenient to discuss the more general data here.

Eggen and Kraatz (1974) compared the performance of several waste-derived and conventional fuels, with a common end use of steam generation, while Hecklinger (1976) calculated the efficiencies of steam and electricity generation from six waste-derived fuels. Their results are compared in Table E.5. The efficiencies do not take account of energy inputs. The combustion efficiency e_2 is derived from combustible losses, either due to incomplete combustion (L_b) or to inerts in the fuel (L_i), and vaporization losses (L_w), which are due to any moisture in the fuel and to the product water being formed as vapour and not as the liquid assumed in the definition of the heat of combustion. The steam generation efficiency e_3 is derived from losses due to the exhaust gases (L_x) and a miscellaneous loss term (L) which includes radiation and boiler blowdown losses. The overall boiler efficiency e_4 is the product of e_2 and e_3. An independent check on the efficiencies for conventional fuels is provided by Kempe's Engineers Yearbook (1974)

The agreement between the figures for comparable fuels in Table E.5 is good. For conventional fuels, values for e_2 of 0.90, 0.94, and 0.93 are used here for gas, oil, and coal, respectively, with a common value for e_3 of 0.88. Note that values of e_3 for waste-derived fuels vary considerably, so that

Table E.5

The performance of selected waste-derived and conventional fuels

		Fuel																	
		Waste-derived fuels												Conventional fuels					
		Incineration of raw waste		RDF a[a]	RDF b[b]		Pyrolysis and other thermal processes							Natural gas		Fuel oil		Coal	
							To oil	Gas[c]	Gas[d]	Gas[e]	Union Carbide		Anaerobic digestion						
Item	Symbol	1	2	1	1	2	2	1	1	2	1	2	2	1	3	1	3	1	3
Energy in fuel/energy in waste	e_1	1.0	1.0	0.947	0.69	0.852	0.528	0.94	0.94	0.861	0.75	0.777	0.417	–	–	–	–	–	–
Combustible losses	L_b	0.028	0.030	0.020	0.020	0.072	0	0	0	0	0	0	0	0	0	0	0	0.010	0.03
Vaporization losses	L_i	0.015	–	0.015	0.015	–	0	0	0	0	0	0	0	0	0	0	0	0.015	0
Combustion efficiency	L_w	0.138	0.133	0.134	0.130	0.128	0.076	0.147	0.077	0.056	0.047	0.077	0.110	0.10	0.10	0.053	0.06	0.045	0.04
$(1 - L_b - L_i - L_w)$	e_2	0.819	0.837	0.831	0.835	0.800	0.924	0.853	0.923	0.944	0.953	0.923	0.890	0.90	0.90	0.947	0.94	0.930	0.93
Excess air (%)	–	100	100	20	20	30	10	7.5	7.5	80	7.5	15	5	7.5	7.5	7.5	7.5	20	20
Stack temperature (°C)	–	260	260	260	260	175	175	260	260	300	260	175	175	260	260	260	260	260	260
Exhaust gas losses	L_x	0.185	0.172	0.122	0.121	0.080	0.069	0.119	0.111	0.190	0.095	0.067	0.066	0.098	0.10	0.097	0.10	0.111	0.10
Miscellaneous losses[f]	L	0.02	0.033	0.02	0.02	0.023	0.020	0.02	0.02	0.049	0.02	0.018	0.018	0.02	0.02	0.02	0.02	0.02	0.02
Steam generation efficiency[g] $(1 - L_x - L)$	e_3	0.795	0.795	0.858	0.859	0.897	0.911	0.861	0.869	0.761	0.885	0.915	0.916	0.882	0.88	0.883	0.88	0.869	0.88
Overall boiler efficiency $(e_2 + e_3 - 1)$	e_4	0.614	0.632	0.689	0.694	0.697	0.836	0.714	0.792	0.705	0.838	0.837	0.806	0.782	0.78	0.830	0.82	0.799	0.81
Efficiency of waste to steam $(e_1 e_4)$	e_5	0.614	0.632	0.652	0.479	0.594	0.441	0.671	0.744	0.607	0.629	0.650	0.336	–	–	–	–	–	–
Efficiency of electricity generation from steam	e_6	–	0.35	–	–	0.425	0.425	–	–	0.35	–	0.425	0.425	–	–	–	–	–	–
Efficiency of waste to electricity $(e_5 e_6)$	e_7	–	0.221	–	–	0.252	0.188	–	–	0.212	–	0.276	0.143	–	–	–	–	–	–

Sources of data: 1. Eggen and Kraatz (1974)
2. Hecklinger (1976)
3. Kempe's Engineers Yearbook (1974)

(a) Shredding and magnetic separation only (pulverized fuel).
(b) American processing as in Fig 5.2.
(c) Un-named air gasification process.
(d) As (c) but with the product gas scrubbed and dried.
(e) Monsanto 'Landgard' process.
(f) The miscellaneous losses, including radiation losses, are not calculated by Eggen and Kraatz (source 1) for each fuel, but their general figure of 1½–2 per cent is used here to allow comparison.
(g) The losses in steam generation are expressed as fractions of the total energy in the fuel.

calculations of the substitution equivalence should usually assume equivalence after steam generation, (e_4) rather than after combustion (e_2). A typical value of substitution equivalence implied by the data in Table E.5 would be that of American RDF, where $e_4 = 0.69$, while for coal $e_4 = 0.81$, giving a value of $SE = 1.17$. The efficiencies of electricity generation from steam (e_6) given by Hecklinger (1976) fall into two groups, 0.35 for untreated waste or waste-derived fuel burnt alone and 0.425 for WDF burnt in 10–20 per cent combination with conventional fuels. The latter figure may be taken as typical also of conventional fuels burnt alone. The lower value for firing waste alone arises from the lower temperature and pressure of the steam generated.

The energy to transport the waste-derived fuel to its point of use, and to handle it there, must be deducted from the energy saving. For solid fuels, a haul of about 20 km by road is assumed, giving an energy requirement of 56 MJ/t. This is doubled to allow for handling, so that the total requirement is taken as 100 MJ/t of RDF. For oil or gas products, distribution and handling is estimated as a percentage of the total energy savings from the fuel, with a value in the range of 10–20 per cent.

E.8. Summary

The estimates of typical energy savings due to recycling one tonne of various materials are summarized in Table 8.2. Substantial energy savings are apparent for all the metals examined, with particular savings for electrolytically produced metals such as aluminium. Recycling of metals is already at a moderate level in most countries, although for these larger-volume metals at least there is still much potential for increased recycling (Grace 1978). The reclamation of glass cullet shows a small energy saving once it has been collected, although some care needs to be taken to ensure that the energy costs of collection do not offset this saving. The use of returnable glass bottles in place of the increasingly predominant disposable bottles has a much larger potential for energy saving even when the necessary collection, cleaning, and refilling are considered. Recycling paper shows substantial energy savings, particularly when credit is taken for the calorific value still remaining in the paper.

REFERENCES

Note

To update the information given in this book, the author would recommend the services of the Waste Management Information Bureau of the Harwell Laboratory. A modest annual subscription secures not only the monthly abstract journal but also an initial four free searches in the extensive, keyworded, computer data bank, which contains (1981) some 20,000 documents. Further information, and a complimentary copy of the Waste Management Information Bulletin, may be obtained from The Manager, WMIB, Harwell Laboratory, Oxon. OX11 0RA, England.

Abert, J. G. (1979a). State and tendencies of recycling in North America. *Proc. int. Recycling Congr., Berlin* (ed. K. J. Thomé-Kozmiensky) Vol. 1, pp. 18–25. Springer-Verlag, Berlin.

—— (1979b). Separation processes at Recovery 1, New Orleans, Louisiana, USA. *Proc. int. Recycling Congr., Berlin* (ed. K. J. Thomé-Kozmiensky) Vol. 2, pp. 892–8. Springer Verlag, Berlin.

——, Alter, H., and Bernheisel, J. F. (1974). The economics of resource recovery from municipal solid waste. *Science, N.Y.* **183**, 1052–8.

Absil, J. H., Reeves, P. C., Basten, A. T., and Dalmijn, W. L. (1979). Resource recovery from US incinerator residue by water only cyclone process and heavy medium cyclone process. *Proc. int. Recycling Congr., Berlin* (ed. K. J. Thomé-Kozmiensky) Vol. 1, pp. 553–8. Springer Verlag, Berlin.

Achinger, W. C. and Daniels, L. E. (1970). An evaluation of seven incinerators. *National Incinerator Conference, Cincinnati* pp. 32–64. American Society of Mechanical Engineers (ASME), New York.

Advisory Council on Energy Conservation (1977). *Freight transport—short and medium term considerations.* Department of Energy, Energy paper No. 24. HMSO, London.

Aerojet-General Corporation and Engineering Science Inc. (1969). A systems study of solid waste management in the Fresno area. US Public Health Service (PHS) Office of Solid Waste Management Programs, Washington, Report No. SW-5d, PHS publication No. 1959.

Allen, D. H. (1975). Calculating the risks in project evaluation. International Symposium on Cost Engineering, Paper F, Utrecht, Holland.

—— and Page, R. C. (1975). Revised technique for predesign cost estimating. *Chem. Engng, Albany* **82**, 142–50.

Aller, R. F. (1979). Methane production from urban solid wastes. *Proc. int. Recycling Congr., Berlin* (ed. K. J. Thomé-Kozmiensky) Vol. 2, pp. 816–22. Springer Verlag, Berlin.

Alpert, S. B., Ferguson, F. A., and others (1972). Pyrolysis of solid waste: a technical and economic assessment. Report by Stanford Research Institute for West Virginia University, as part of a programme for the Environmental Protection Agency (EPA), Washington. Issued by the National Technical Information Service (NTIS), Springfield, Virgina as Report No. PB 218 231.

Alter, H. (1977a). European materials recovery systems. *Environ. Sci. Technol.* **11**, 444–8.

—— (1977b). Energy conservation and fuel production by processing solid wastes. *Environ. Conserv.* **4**, 11–19.

—— and Arnold, J. (1978). Preparation of densified refuse-derived fuel on a pilot scale. *Proc. Sixth Mineral Waste Utilization Symp., Chicago* pp. 171–7. US Bureau of Mines and IIT Research Institute.

—— and Reeves, W. R. (1975). Specifications for materials recovered from municipal refuse. Environmental Protection Agency, Washington, Report No. EPA-670/2-75-034. Issued by National Technical Information Service, Springfield, Virginia as Report No. PB 242 540.

—— and Woodruff, K. L. (1977). Magnetic separation: recovery of saleable iron and steel from municipal solid waste. Environmental Protection Agency, Washington, Report No. EPA/530/SW-559.

——, Natof, S., and Blayden, L. C. (1976). Pilot studies processing MSW and recovery of aluminium using an eddy current separator. *Proc. Fifth Mineral Waste Utilization Symp., Chicago* pp. 161–8. US Bureau of Mines and IIT Research Institute.

Alvarez, R. J. (1979). Energy from thermal processing and status, incineration of municipal refuse in the United States. *Proc. int. Recycling Congr., Berlin* (ed. K. J. Thomé-Kozmiensky) Vol. 1, pp. 419–24. Springer Verlag, Berlin.

Anderau, B. (1977). Thermische Verfahren zur Entsorgung Von Chemieabfällen. Berichtsband der VFWL-Tagung über Industriefeuerungen und Beseitigung von Betriebsabfällen in Industrie und Gewerbe (VFWL-Schrift Nr. 109.). VFWL, Spanweidstr. 3, CH-8006, Zurich.

Anderson, J. E. (1974). The oxygen refuse converter—a system for producing fuel gas, oil, molten metal and slag from refuse. *Nat. Incinerator Conf., Miami* pp. 337–46. American Society of Mechanical Engineers, New York.

Anderson, L. E. and Nigam, A. K. (1967). A mathematical model for the optimization of a wastes management system. Report ORC 67–25. Operations Research Center, University of California, Berkeley.

Andoh, N., Ishii, Y., Hirayama, Y., and Ito, K. (1979). Disposal of municipal refuse by the 'two-bed pyrolysis system'. *Proc. int. Recycling Congr., Berlin* (ed. K. J. Thomé-Kozmiensky) Vol. 1, pp. 575–80. Springer Verlag, Berlin.

Andresen, B., Salamon, P., and Berry, R. S. (1977). Thermodynamics in finite time: extremals for imperfect heat engines. *J. Chem. Phys.* **66**, 1571–7.

——, Berry, R. S., Nitzan, A., and Salamon, P. (1977). Thermodynamics in finite time. I. The step-Carnot cycle. *Phys. Rev.* **A15**, 2086–93.

Annual Abstract of Statistics. Central Statistical Office, HMSO, London.

Anon. (1978). Ocean dumping convention amended to provide rules on incineration. *Int. Environ. Reporter* **1**, 362–3.

—— (1979). Report on baling. Balers, balefills provide solutions. *National Waste News* (USA), June, pp. 14–19.

Aoyagi, T. (1975). Disposal and recycling of plastics in Japan. First International Conference on Conversion of Refuse to Energy, Montreux, Switzerland, pp. 79–84.

Appell, H. R., Wender, I., and Miller, R. D. (1970). Conversion of municipal refuse to oil. *Proc. third annual North-Eastern Regional Anti-Pollution Conference on Reuse and Recycle of Wastes, Univ. of Rhode Island* pp. 225–31. Technomic Publishing Co., Westport, Conn.

Arrow, K. J. (1976). The rate of discount for long-term public investment. In *Energy and the environment—a risk–benefit approach* (ed. H. Ashley, R. L. Rudman, and C. Whipple). Pergamon Press, New York.

Association of Waste Disposal Disposal Engineers (A W D E) (1976). Development project information service—review of recent current projects. [Available from the secretary, A W D E, Lancashire County Council, Preston.]

Asukata, R. and Kitami, S. (1974). Present situation and future trends of Japanese refuse incineration plants with power generation. *Nat. Incinerator Conf., Miami* pp. 127–42. American Society of Mechanical Engineers, New York.

Atkins, P. R. (1963). *Aluminum—a manufactured resource.* Aluminum Can Company of America.

Avers, C. (1975). Technical/economic problems in energy recovery incineration. International Symposium on Energy Recovery from Refuse, University of Louisville, Kentucky.

Bahr, A. (1979). The sorting of plastic waste. *Proc. int. Recycling Congr., Berlin* (ed. K. J. Thomé-Kozmiensky) Vol. 2, pp. 1202–7. Springer Verlag, Berlin.

Bailie, R. C. and Doner, D. M. (1975). Evaluation of the efficiency of energy resource recovery systems. *Resource Recovery Conserv.* 1, 177–87.

Baker, J. S. (1963). A cooperative municipal refuse disposal program, Prince George's County Maryland. Municipal Technical Advisory Service, College of Business and Public Administration, University of Maryland.

Ball, D. A., Beltz, P. R., Smith, P., Engdahl, R. B., and Reid, W. T. (1978). Annotated bibliography on supplemental firing of municipal solid waste in electric utility boilers. Electric Power Research Institute Report No. E P R I - R P-687.

Ballam, C. J. and Collins, W. G. (1975). Economic advantages of using aerial photography for mapping potential tipping sites. *Solid Wastes* 65, 485–95.

Barghoorn, M. and Gössele, P. (1979). The practical execution of the analysis of domestic solid waste. *Proc. int. Recycling Congr., Berlin* (ed. K. J. Thomé-Kozmiensky) Vol. 1, pp. 231–6. Springer Verlag, Berlin.

Barniske, L. (1979). Status report on the research programme 'New processes of thermal waste treatment'. *Proc. int. Recycling Congr., Berlin* (ed. K. J. Thomé-Kozmiensky) Vol. 1, pp. 67–73. Springer Verlag, Berlin.

Battelle Institute (1975). Energy use patterns in metallurgical and non-metallic mineral processing. Reports to U S Bureau of Mines, issued by N T I S as report Nos P B 245 759 and P B 246 357.

Bauman, H. C. (1964). *Fundamentals of cost engineering in the chemical industry.* Reinhold, New York.

Bechtel Corporation (1975). Fuels from municipal refuse for utilities: technology assessment. Report for Electric Power Research Institute. Issued by National Technical Information Service, Springfield, Virginia as Report No. P B 242 413.

Belcher, C. A. and Pépé, P. D. (1969). The G L C plant at Edmonton. *Conf. Incineration of Municipal and Industrial Waste, Brighton.* Institute of Fuel, London.

Bell, C. F. and Jones, C. J. (1977). *The production of useful chemicals from cellulose containing wastes.* Report issued by the Harwell Laboratory, No. A E R E - M2897.

Bendersky, D., Shannon, L. J., Gorman, P. G., Park, W. R., and Holloway, J. R. (1975). St. Louis refuse fuel demonstration plant—technical and economic performance. First International Conference on Conversion of Refuse to Energy, Montreux, Switzerland, pp. 7–13.

Beningson, R. M. (1979). RDF—approach to solid waste disposal. *Proc. int. Recycling Congr., Berlin* (ed. K. J. Thomé-Kozmiensky) Vol. 1, pp. 942–7. Springer Verlag, Berlin.

——, Rogers, K. J., Lamb, T. J., and Nadkarni, R. M. (1975). Production of Eco-Fuel II from municipal solid waste. First International Conference on Conversion of Refuse to Energy, Montreux, Switzerland, pp. 14–21.

Berman, E. B. (1973a). A model for selecting, sizing and locating regional solid waste processing and disposal facilities. The Mitre Corporation, Bedford, Massachusetts, Report M73-111.

—— (1973b). Solid waste management planning: tailoring the choice to the economic environment. The Mitre Corporation, Report No. M73-84.

—— (1976). Resource recovery regional design analysis for the eastern Massachusetts region. The Mitre Corporation, Report No. MTR-3221.

Berry, R. H. (1976). Waste disposal management in Lancashire—a case study. Unpublished M.Sc. thesis, Warwick University.

—— (1978). Forecasting in waste disposal. *Local Govt Stud.* **4**, 61–9.

Berry, R. S. (1976). Thermodynamics and energy use in materials supply. In *Materials technology—1976* (ed. A. G. Chynoweth and W. M. Walsh). American Institute of Physics Conference Proceedings No. 32.

—— and Fels, M. F. (1972). The production and consumption of automobiles. A report to the Illinois Institute for Environmental Quality.

—— —— (1973). The energy cost of automobiles. *Science and Public Affairs*, December, p. 11.

—— and Makino, H. (1974). Energy thrift in packaging and marketing. *Technology Rev.* **76**.

——, Long, T. V., and Makino, H. (1975). An international comparison of polymers and their alternatives. *Energy Policy* **3**, 144–55.

Bevan, R. E. (1967). *Notes on the science and practice of the controlled tipping of refuse.* Institute of Public Cleansing, London.

Biddulph, M. W. (1976). Principles of recycling processes. *Conserv. Recycling* **1**, 31–54.

Bidwell, R. and Mason, S. A. (1975). Fuel from London's refuse: an examination of economic viability. First International Conference on Conversion of Refuse to Energy, Montreux, Switzerland, pp. 596–601.

Bielicki, L. C. (1977). The economics of recovering recyclable materials from urban wastes. *Symp. Clean Fuels from Biomass and Wastes, Orlando, Florida* pp. 279–90. Institute of Gas Technology, Chicago.

Black, J. H. (1970). Operating cost estimation. In *Cost and optimization engineering* (ed. F. C. Jelen) pp. 338–54. McGraw-Hill, New York.

Blanchet, M. J. (1977). Treatment and utilization of landfill gas. Mountain View project feasibility study. Environmental Protection Agency, Washington, Report No. EPA/530/SW-583.

Bodner, R. M. (1976). Dutchess County, N.Y., moves towards pyrolysis. *Waste Age* **7**, 48.

Boettcher, R. A. (1972). Air classification of solid wastes—performance of experimental units and potential applications for solid waste reclamation. Environmental Protection Agency, Washington, Report No. WPCRS-SW-30C.

Bolton, R. L. and Klein, L. (1971). *Sewage treatment—basic principles and trends* (2nd edn). Butterworth, London.

Bond, R. G. and Straub, C. P. (ed.) (1973). *Handbook of environmental control.* Vol. II: *Solid waste.* Chemical Rubber Company Press, Cleveland, Ohio.

Borgese, D., Rossi, C., and Trebbi, G. (1976). A technical and economic overview on the use of solid waste in power plant boilers. *Nat. Waste Processing Conf., Boston* pp. 141–50. American Society of Mechanical Engineers, New York.

Borough of Hove (1974). *Refuse pulverization plant.*

Bourcier, G. F. and Dale, K. H. (1978*a*). The technology and economics of the recovery of aluminium from municipal solid wastes. *Resource Recovery Conserv.* **3**, 1–18.

—— —— (1978*b*). Aluminium scrap recovered from full-scale municipal refuse processing systems. *Proc. of the Sixth Mineral Waste Utilization Symposium, Chicago,* pp. 178–87. US Bureau of Mines and IIT Research Institute.

Boustead, I. and Hancock, G. F. (1979). *Handbook of industrial energy analysis.* Ellis Horwood, Chichester.

Bowen, I. G., Woodward, G. P. B., and Kelsey, G. D. (1969). The economics of municipal refuse incineration. *Conf. Incineration of Municipal and Industrial Waste, Brighton.* Institute of Fuel, London.

Bracker, G. P. (1979). Pyrolytical resource recovery. *Proc. int. Recycling Congr., Berlin* (ed. K. J. Thomé-Kozmiensky) Vol. 1, pp. 695–9. Springer Verlag, Berlin.

Bratley, K. J. (1977). A description of comparative performance tests of mobile plant on a major landfill site. *Solid Wastes* **67**, 57–80.

Bravard, J. C., Flora, H. B., and Portal, C. (1972). Energy expenditures associated with the production and recycle of metals. Oak Ridge National Laboratory, Report ORNL-NSF-EP-24.

Breidenbach, A. W. (1971). Composting of municipal solid wastes in the United States. Environmental Protection Agency, Washington, Report No. SW-47r.

Brenner, W., Rugg, B., and Rogers, C. (1977). Utilization of waste cellulose for production of chemical feedstocks via acid hydrolysis. *Symp. Clean Fuels from Biomass and Wastes, Orlando, Florida* pp. 201–12. Institute of Gas Technology, Chicago.

Bridgwater, A. V. (1974). The functional unit approach to rapid cost estimation. *Cost Engineer* **13**, 1–8.

—— (1976). Rapid methods of estimating operating costs in the chemical process industries. Design Congress, Institute of Chemical Engineering, Birmingham Paper C1.

—— (1976/7). New techniques for estimating costs of waste recovery schemes. *Resource Recovery Conserv.* **2**, 181–92.

—— (1977). Technological economics applied to waste recovery and treatment processes. *Effluent Water Treatment J.* **17**, 223–9.

Bromley, J. (1979). Gas generation and the problems it creates in land reclamation. *Conf. Reclamation of Contaminated Land, Eastbourne* Paper D4. Society of Chemical Industry, London.

—— and Parker, A. (1979). Methane from landfill sites. *International Environment and Safety* August, pp. 9–11.

Brookes, J. E. and Green, J. A. (1968). Refuse disposal in South Hampshire. Local Government Operational Research Unit Report C38.

Broussaud, A. (1976). Indirect energy savings generated by urban refuse recovery. *Proc. Fifth Mineral Waste Utilization Symp., Chicago* pp. 153–60. US Bureau of Mines and IIT Research Institute.

Brusset, H. and Rocherolles, G. (1979). General survey of the quantities of solid waste and sludge produced in Europe and their processing costs. *Proc. int.*

Recycling Congr., Berlin (ed. K. J. Thomé-Kozmiensky) Vol. 1, pp. 217–24. Springer Verlag, Berlin.

Bugler, J. (1975). Bedfordshire brick. In *The politics of physical resources* (ed. P. J. Smith). Penguin Books, Harmondsworth.

Buss, T. F. (1973). The Landgard system for resource recovery and solid waste disposal. Third Annual Environmental Engineering and Science Conference, University of Louisville, Kentucky. Data reproduced by Pavoni *et al.* (1975).

Calame, R. (1979). The functional use of the heat generated by a refuse incineration plant, as exemplified by the RIP Hamburg Staplefield. *Proc. int. Recycling Congr., Berlin* (ed. K. J. Thomé-Kozmiensky) Vol. 1, pp. 425–31. Springer Verlag, Berlin.

Campbell, D. J. V., Parker, A., Rees, J. F., King, J. W., and Wright, S. J. (1978). Uffington lysimeters: operation and results (part 3). Department of the Environment Report No. WLR 42, London.

Carlson, D., Spencer, D., and Christensen, H. (1976). Monroe County resource recovery project. *Proc. Fifth Mineral Waste Utilization Symp., Chicago* pp. 196–203. US Bureau of Mines and IIT Research Institute.

Casper, D. A., Chapman, P. F., and Mortimer, N. D. (1975). Energy analysis of 'The report on the census of production, 1968'. Open University research report ERG-006.

Cavanna, M. M., Riano, E., Almaraz, J. S., and Ramirez, H. G. (1976). Latest developments in processing Spanish urban raw refuse. *Proc. Fifth Mineral Waste Utilization Symp., Chicago* pp. 141–5. US Bureau of Mines and IIT Research Institute.

——, Almaraz, J. S., Cristobal, F. P., and Ramfrez, H. G. (1978). Upgrading products from raw refuse for marketing. *Proc. Sixth Mineral Waste Utilization Symp., Chicago* pp. 261–6. US Bureau of Mines and IIT Institute.

Cederholm, C. (1978). Test results and application in commercial municipal solid waste plants. *Proc. Sixth Mineral Waste Utilization Symp., Chicago* pp. 188–95. US Bureau of Mines and IIT Research Institute.

Cenerini, R. (1975). Heat from domestic refuse: cost–benefit analysis. First International Conference on Conversion of Refuse to Energy, Montreux, Switzerland, pp. 434–8.

Chapman, P. F. (1973). Energy costs of producing copper and aluminium from primary sources. Open University research report ERG-001.

—— (1974a). The energy costs of producing copper and aluminium from primary sources. *Metals Materials* **8**, 107–11.

—— (1974b). Energy conservation and recycling copper and aluminium. *Metals Materials* **8**, 311–19.

—— (1975). The energy costs of materials. *Energy Policy* **3**, 47–57.

—— (1976a). Energy analysis: a review of methods and applications. *Omega* **4**, 19.

—— (1976b). Estimating the efficiency of recycling. *Recycling and Waste Disposal* **1**, 43–6.

——, Leach, G., and Slesser, M. (1974). The energy costs of fuels. *Energy Policy* **2**, 231–43.

Chapman, R. A. (1975). Development of a solid-waste fired gas turbine system. First International Conference on Conversion of Refuse to Energy, Montreux, Switzerland, pp. 343–8.

—— and Wocasek, F. R. (1974). CPU-400 solid waste fired gas turbine development. *National Incinerator Conf., Miami* pp. 347–57, American Society of Mechanical Engineers, New York.

Charlesworth, H. (1970). Pulverization of refuse comes to Easthampsted R.D.C. Rural District Review, March.

Charnes, A. and Cooper, W. W. (1963). Deterministic equivalents for optimizing and satisficing under chance constraints. *Oper. Res.* **11**, 18–39.

Chilton, C. H. (1949). Cost data correlated. *Chem. Engng, Albany* **56**, 97–106.

City of San Diego (1973). Baling solid waste to conserve sanitary landfill space—a feasibility study. Report No. E P A - S W - 44d-73, issued by National Technical Information Service, Springfield, Virginia as P B 214 960.

Clark, C. (1951). Urban population densities. *J. R. Statistical Soc.* **A114**, 490–6.

Clark, R. M. (1973). Solid waste: management and models. In *Models for environmental pollution control* (ed. R. A. Deininger) Chapter 14. Ann Arbor Science Publishers, Michigan.

Clayton, K. C. and Huie, J. M. (1973). *Solid waste management—the regional approach*. Ballinger Publishing Company, Cambridge, Mass.

Clifford, J. S. and McRoberts, T. S. (1976). Review of materials usage and constraints on recycle. Conference on Use and Reuse of Materials, Queen Mary College, London.

Clin, F. and Gony, J. N. (1979). A French process for household refuse recovery. *Proc. int. Recycling Cong., Berlin* (ed. K. J. Thomé-Kozmiensky) Vol. 2, pp. 878–86, Springer Verlag, Berlin.

Cohan, J. J., Fernandes, J. H., Maguire, M. E., and Shenk, R. C. (1975). Prepared vs unprepared refuse fired steam generators. First International Conference on Conversion of Refuse to Energy, Montreux, Switzerland, pp. 407–15.

Cohen, M. and Parrish, C. (1976). Densified refuse-derived fuel. *National Center for Resource Recovery Bull.* **6**, 4–9.

Collins, R. J. (1978). Promising applications for municipal incinerator residues. *Proc. Sixth Mineral Waste Utilization Symp., Chicago* pp. 211–21. U S Bureau of Mines and I I T Research Institute.

Colon, F. J. (1976). Recycling of paper. *Conservation and Recycling* **1**, 129–36.

Colonna, R. A., McLaren, C., and Sano, E. (1976). Decision-makers guide in solid waste management. Environmental Protection Agency, Washington, Report No. E P A - S W - 500, issued by National Technical Information Service, Springfield, Virginia as Report No. P B 258 266.

Common, M. (1976). The economics of energy analysis reconsidered. *Energy Policy* **4**, 158–65.

Converse, A. O., Grethlein, H. E., Karandikar, S., and Kuhrtz, S. (1973). Acid hydrolysis of cellulose in refuse to sugar and its fermentation to alcohol. Environmental Protection Agency, Washington, Report No. E P A - 670/2-73-11, issued by National Technical Information Service, Springfield, Virginia as Report No. P B 221 239.

Cookson, C. (1979). The spoiling of America. *New Sci.* 21 June, pp. 1015–17.

Corey, R. C. (ed.) (1969). *Principles and practices of incineration*. Wiley-Interscience, New York.

Council of the European Economic Community (1978). Council directive of 20th March, 1978 on toxic and dangerous waste. *Official Journal of the European Communities L84*, 31 March, 43–7.

Coyle, R. G. (1973). Computer-based design of refuse collection systems. In *Models for environmental pollution control* (ed. R. A. Deininger) Chapter 14. Ann Arbor Science Publishers, Michigan.

Cran, J. (1973). Location index compares costs of building process plants overseas. *Process Engineering*, April, 109–11.

Critoph, R. (1975). A computer model of energy and material flows in the U K iron and steel industry. School of Transportation, University of Southampton.

Crosby, J. G. and Renold, J. (1974). Where to put solid wastes—a preliminary study into the economics of coordinating solid waste disposal with land reclamation and mineral extraction. Local Government Operational Research Unit, report C.168, prepared for West Yorkshire County Council.

Cross, F. C. (1972). *Handbook on incineration*. Technomic Publishing Company, Westport, Conn.

Cummings, J. P. (1974). Glass and aluminium recovery sub-system—Franklin, Ohio. *Proc. of the Fourth Mineral Waste Utilization Symp., Chicago* pp. 106–15. U S Bureau of Mines and I I T Research Institute.

—— (1976). Glass and non-ferrous metal recovery sub-system at Franklin, Ohio. *Proc. Fifth Mineral Waste Utilization Symp., Chicago* pp. 175–83. U S Bureau of Mines and I I T Research Institute.

Cunningham, R. T. and Voglar, M. J. (1975). The Kirlees experiment. Institute of Solid Wastes Management autumn meeting, Bradford. *Solid Wastes* **65**, 613–18.

Das, K. and Ghose, T. K. (1973). Economic evaluation of enzymic utilization of waste cellulosic materials. *J. appl. Chem. Biotechnol.* **23**, 829–36.

David, R. (1977). Price up for milk bottle tops. *Financial Times*, 28 February.

Davidson, J., Ross, M., Chynoweth, D., Michaels, A. C., Dunnette, D., Griffis, C., Stirling, J. A., and Wang. D. (1975). Energy needs for pollution control. In *The energy conservation papers* (ed. R. H. Williams). Ballinger, Cambridge, Mass.

Davies, D. R. (1975). A regional approach to waste management. *77th Annual Conf. Institute of Solid Wastes Management, Brighton*. Institute of Solid Wastes Management, London.

Dawson, R. (1970). The economics of regional planning for solid waste management. Ph.D. thesis, University of California, Berkeley.

Day and Zimmerman Associates (1968). Special studies for incinerators in Washington D C. Environmental Protection Agency, Office of Solid Waste Management Programs, Public Health Service, P H S Publication No. 1748.

Degler, G. H. and Wiles, C. C. (1979). Co-firing densified refuse derived fuel in a spreader stoker fired boiler. *Proc. int. Recycling Congr., Berlin* (ed. K. J. Thomé-Kozmiensky) Vol. 2, pp. 1271–6, Springer Verlag, Berlin.

Department of Energy (1977). *Digest of U K Energy Statistics 1977*. HMSO. London.

Department of the Environment (1971). *Report of the working party on refuse disposal* (the 'Sumner report'). HMSO, London.

—— (1976a). *Reclamation, treatment and disposal of wastes—an evaluation of options*. Waste management paper No. 1. H M S O, London.

—— (1976b). *Waste disposal surveys*. Waste management paper No. 2. H M S O, London.

—— (1976c). *Guideline for the preparation of a waste disposal plan*. Waste management paper No. 3. H M S O, London.

—— (1976d). *The licensing of waste disposal sites*. Waste management paper No. 4. H M S O, London.

—— (1976e). *The relationship between waste disposal authorities and private industry*. Waste management paper No. 5. H M S O, London.

—— (1976f). *Polychlorinated Biphenyl (P C B) Wastes—A Technical Memorandum on Reclamation, Treatment and Disposal Including a Code of Practice*. Waste Management Paper No. 6. H M S O, London.

—— (1976g). *Metal finishing wastes—a technical memorandum on arisings, treatment and disposal including a code of practice.* Waste Management Paper No. 11. HMSO, London.

—— (1977a). *Tarry and distillation wastes and other chemical based residues—a technical memorandum on arisings, treatment and disposal including a code of practice.* Waste Management Paper No. 13. HMSO, London.

—— (1977b). *Solvent wastes (excluding halogenated hydrocarbons)—a technical memorandum on reclamation and disposal including a code of practice.* Waste Management Paper No. 14. HMSO, London.

—— (1978). *Cooperative programme of research on the behaviour of hazardous wastes in landfill sites.* HMSO, London.

—— (1979). *Local authority waste disposal statistics 1974–5 to 1977–8.* Waste Management Paper No. 22. HMSO, London.

Department of the Environment and the Welsh Office (1970). Capital programmes. DoE Circular 2/70, WO circular 116/70. HMSO, London.

—— (1976a). The balancing of interests between water protection and waste disposal. Circular DoE 39/76, WO 53/76. HMSO, London.

—— (1976b). Capital programmes. Circular DoE 66/76, WO 89/76. HMSO, London.

—— (1977). The Town and Country Planning Act 1971 (Part II as amended by the Town and Country Planning (Amendment) Act 1972) and the Local Government Act 1972): Memorandum on structure and local plans. Circular DoE 55/77, WO 82/77. HMSO, London.

Department of the Environment and other departments (1977). The governments expenditure plans (Cmnd 6721)—implications for local authority expenditure 1976–9. Circular DoE 37/77. HMSO, London.

—— (1978). The governments expenditure plans (Cmnd 7049). Implications for local authority expenditure 1978/82. Circular DoE 28/78. HMSO, London.

—— (1979). The governments expenditure plans (Cmnd 7439): implications for local authority expenditure 1979/83. Circular DoE 15/79. HMSO, London.

Devroede, R. (1979). Method followed to determine the number, the location, and the kind of urban wastes processing works in the French speaking part of Belgium. *Proc. int. Recycling Congr., Berlin* (ed. K. J. Thomé-Kozmiensky) Vol. 1, pp. 130–4. Springer Verlag, Berlin.

Diering, B. (1979). A contribution to recycling of organic solids, reclamation from solid wastes and cost reduction in construction of sewage plants. *Proc. Int. Recycling Congr., Berlin* (ed. K. J. Thomé-Kozmiensky) Vol. 2, pp. 1101–8. Springer Verlag, Berlin.

Dorfman, R. (1972). Conceptual model of a regional water quality authority. In *Models for managing regional water quality* (ed. R. Dorfman, H. D. Jacoby, And H. A. Thomas) pp. 42–83. Harvard University Press.

—— and Jacoby, H. D. (1972). An illustrative model of river basin pollution control. In *Models for managing regional water quality* (ed. Dorman *et al.*) pp. 84–141.

Douglas, E. and Birch, P. R. (1976). Recovery of potentially re-usable materials from domestic refuse by physical sorting. *Resource Recovery Conserv.* **1**, 319–44.

——, Webb, M., and Power, C. (1976). Developments leading to the design of an urban refuse pyrolysis unit for gas production. *Proc. Fifth Mineral Waste Utilization Symp., Chicago* pp. 241–50. US Bureau of Mines and IIT Research Institute.

Drobny, N. L., Hull, H. E., and Testin, R. F. (1971). Recovery and utilization of municipal solid waste. US Public Health Service Publication No. 1908.

——, Qasim, S. R., and Valentine, B. W. (1971). Cost effectiveness analysis of waste management systems. *J. Environ. Sys.* **1**, 189–210.

Eggen, A. C. W. and Kraatz, R. (1974). Relative value of fuels derived from solid wastes. *National Incinerator Conf., Miami* pp.19–32. American Society of Mechanical Engineers, New York.

Elopak Group (1976). Municipal waste into particle board. *Solid Wastes* **66**, 20.

El-Shaieb A-M. (1968). Optimal activity locations. Operations Research Center, report No. ORC-68-3, University of California, Berkeley.

Energy Policy (1977). The economics of energy analysis revisited. Letters from M. Webb and D. W. Pearce, M. Common, and P. F. Chapman. *Energy Policy* **5**, 158–61.

Energy Trends (1977). June issue. Department of Energy, London, published monthly.

Engineering and Process Economics. EPE plant cost indices international (ed. J. Cran). Published quarterly, 1976–9. Elsevier Scientific Publishing Company, Amsterdam.

Engineering Science Inc. & Grunwald, Crawford and Associates (1971). Merced County solid waste management study, phase I. Final report to Merced County Association of Governments. Issued by NTIS as report No. PB 203 542.

Erlenkotter, D. (1975). Capacity planning for large multilocation systems: approximate and incomplete dynamic programming approaches. *Man. Sci.* **22**, 274–85.

Esmaili, H. (1972). Facility selection and haul optimization model. *J. sanit. Engng. Div., Proc. Am. Soc. civ. Engrs.* **98**, 1005–20.

European Chemical News (1977). Market Prices, February. [Published weekly.]

Fabuss, B. F., Spencer, D. B., and Schroeder, R. L. (1975). Processing residues for profit. First International Conference on Conversion of Refuse to Energy, Montreux, Switzerland, pp.497–502.

Fagan, R. D. (1969). The acid hydrolysis of refuse. M. Eng. thesis, Thayer School of Engineering, Dartmouth College, New Hampshire.

——, Converse, A. O., and Grethlein, H. E. (1970). The economic analysis of the acid hydrolysis of refuse. *Proc. third annual North Eastern Regional Antipollution Conference on Reuse and Recycle of Wastes, University of Rhode Island* pp.124–41. Technomic Publishing Co., Westport, Conn.

——, Grethlein, H. E., Converse, A. O., and Porteous, A. (1971). Kinetics of the acid hydrolysis of cellulose found in paper refuse. *Environ. Sci. Technol.* **5**, 545–7.

Feldman, H. F., Felton, G. W., Nack, H., and Alderstein, J. (1976). Syngas process converts waste to SNG. *Hydrocarb. Process. Petrol. Refin.* **55**.

Ferguson, J. (1973). Appraisal of the performance of Cringle Dock solid wastes pulverization plant. *Solid Wastes* **63**, 649–67.

—— (1977). Design features of Jenkins Lane solid waste transfer station. *Solid Wastes* **67**, 232–50.

Fife, J. A. (1970). Design of the northwest incinerator for the City of Chicago. *National Incinerator Conf., Cincinnati* pp. 249–60. American Society or Mechanical Engineers, New York.

Financial Statistics. Central Statistical Office, HMSO, London, [Published monthly.]

Fiscus, D. E., Gorman, P. G., and Kilgroe, J. D. (1976). Bottom-ash generation in a coal-fired power plant when refuse-derived supplementary fuel is used. *National Waste Processing Conf., Boston* pp. 438–90, American Society of Mechanical Engineers, New York.

——, ——, Schrag, M. P., and Shannon, L. J. (1977). St. Louis Demonstration Final

Report: Refuse Processing Plant Equipment, Facilities and Environmental Evaluations. Report to the USEPA, Washington, Report No. EPA-600/2-77-155a. Issued by National Technical Information Service, Springfield, Virginia as Report No. PB 272 757.

Fisher, C. D. (1976). Live-center bin. *National Waste Processing Conf., Boston* pp. 465–70. American Society of Mechanical Engineers, New York.

Fisher, T. F., Kasbohm, M. L., and Rivero, J. R. (1976). The Purox system. *Symp. Clean Fuels from Biomass, Sewage, Urban Refuse and Agricultural Wastes, Orlando, Florida* pp. 447–59. Institute of Gas Technology, Chicago.

Franconeri, P. (1976). Selection factors in evaluating large solid waste shredders. *National Waste Processing Conf., Boston*, pp. 233–48. American Society of Mechanical Engineers, New York.

Franklin, W. E., Bendersky, D., and Park, W. R. (1974). Energy recovery systems for municipal solid waste—a technical/economic review and forecast. *Second National Conf. Energy and the Environment.* American Institute of Chemical Engineers, Dayton, Ohio.

——, ——, ——, and Hunt, R. G. (1975). Potential energy conservation from recycling metals in urban solid wastes. In *The energy conservation papers* (ed. R. H. Williams), Ballinger, Cambridge, Mass.

Fuertes, L. A. (1973). Social and economic aspects of solid waste haul and disposal. M.Sc. dissertation, Mass. Inst. of Tech.

——, Hudson, J. F., and Marks, D. H. (1974). Solid waste management: equity trade-off models. *J. Urban Planning Dev. Div., Proc. Am. Soc. Civ. Eng.* **100** (UP2), 155–71.

Fuller, W. H., McCarthy, C., Alesii, B. A., and Niebla, E. (1976). Liners for disposal sites to retard migration of pollutants. In *Residual management by land disposal*, USEPA Report No. 600/9-76-015, pp. 112–26.

Funk, H. D. and Chantland, A. O. (1975). Solid waste for power generation in a small city. First International Conference on Conversion of Refuse to Energy, Montreux, Switzerland, pp. 268–74.

Fürmaier, B. (1979). Necessity and possibilities of waste treatment and waste recovery for reuse: shown by the domestic waste disposal program of Bavaria. *Proc. int. Recycling Congr., Berlin* (ed. K. J. Thomé-Kozmiensky) Vol. 1, pp. 145–51. Springer Verlag, Berlin.

Gage, S. J. and Chapman, R. A. (1977). Environmental impact of solid waste and biomass conversion to energy processes. *Symp. Clean Fuels from Biomass and Wastes, Orlando, Florida* pp. 465–82. Institute of Gas Technology, Chicago.

Garbe, Y. M. (1976). Demonstration of pyrolysis and materials recovery in San Diego, California. *Waste Age* **7**, 82–5.

General Electric Company (GEC) (1973a). *Solid waste management—technology assessment.* General Electric Company, Schenectady, New York. [Updated 1974.]

——, (1973b). Preliminary design of a solid waste separation plant: final report. State of Connecticut Department of Environmental Protection, Hartford, Connecticut.

Ghosh, S. and Klass, D. L. (1976). Substitute natural gas from refuse and sewage sludge by the biogas process. *Symp. Clean Fuels from Biomass, Sewage, Urban Refuse and Agricultural Wastes, Orlando, Florida* pp. 123–82. Institute of Gas Technology, Chicago.

—— —— (1977). Two-phase anaerobic digestion. *Symp. Clean Fuels from Biomass and Wastes, Orlando, Florida* pp. 373–416. Institute of Gas Technology, Chicago.

Goddard, H. C. (1975). *Managing solid wastes—economics, technology and institutions*. Praeger, New York.

Golueke, C. G. (1977). *Biological reclamation of solid waste*. Rodale Press, Emmaus, Pennsylvania.

—— and McGauhey, P. H. (1970). Comprehensive studies of solid waste management—first and second annual reports. Sanitary Engineering Research Laboratory, University of California, Berkeley. Issued by National Technical Information Service, Springfield, Virginia as a Report No. PB 218 265.

—— —— (1971). Comprehensive studies of solid waste management—third annual report. Report to Environmental Protection Agency Washington, No. EPA/530/SW-10rg.

Gotaas, H. B. (1956). *Composting: sanitary disposal and reclamation of organic wastes*. World Health Organization Monograph Series No. 31, WHO, Geneva.

Grace, R. P. (1978). Metals recycling–a comparative national analysis. *Resources Policy* **4**, 249–56.

Graham, W. O. (1976). Marketing and equipment design, municipal solid waste ferrous metal recovery. *National Waste Processing Conference, Boston* pp. 385–408. American Society of Mechanical Engineers, New York.

Gray, K. R. and Biddlestone, A. J. (1973). Composting: process parameters. *Chemical Engineer* No. 270, February, pp. 71–6.

——, ——, and Clark, R. (1973). Review of composting—part 3: processes and products. *Process Biochem.* **8**, 11–15, 30.

Green, J. A. (1969). Predicting future quantities of refuse. Local Government Operational Research Unit, Report No. T.20.

—— and Nice, R. W. (1967). Thinking about refuse collection. Local Government Operational Research Unit, Report No. T.9.

Green, R. (1979). Waste management in Japan. Proceedings of the conference Elmia-Avfall '79, Jönkoping, Sweden, pp. 336–90. [Available from Elmia A. B., Jönkoping.]

Grethlein, H. E. (1975). Acid hydrolysis of refuse. *Biotechnol. and Bioeng. Symp. No. 5* (ed. C. R. Wilkie), pp. 303–18. Interscience, New York.

Grossman, D., Hudson, J. F., and Marks, D. H. (1974). Waste generation models for solid waste collection. *J. envir. Engng Div., Proc. Am. Soc. civ. Engng,* **100**, 1219–30.

Grubbs, M. R. and Coulombe, E. J. (1978). Evaluating rotary drum air classification of shredded solid waste. *First World Recycling Congr., Basle,* Paper 5, Day 2. Exhibitions for Industry Ltd., Oxted, Surrey, England.

——, Paterson, M., and Fabuss, B. M. (1976). Air classification of municipal refuse. *Proc. Fifth Mineral Waste Utilization Symp., Chicago* pp. 169–74. US Bureau of Mines and IIT Research Institute.

Guthrie, K. M. (1969). Data and techniques for preliminary capital cost estimating. *Chem. Engng, Albany* **76**, 114–42.

Haddix, G. F. (1975). Regional solid waste planning models—two cases. *Comput. Urban Soc.* **1**, 179–93.

—— and Wees, M. (1975). Solid waste planning models with resource recovery. 47th National joint meeting of the Operations Research Society of America and The Institute of Management Sciences, Chicago.

Hagerty, D. J. (1977). Current American alternatives in resource recovery. *Solid Wastes* **67**, 251–67.

Haley, C. (1979). Use of domestic refuse as a fuel in cement manufacture. *Proc. int.*

Recycling Congr., Berlin (ed. K. J. Thomé-Kozmiensky), Vol 1, pp. 312–17. Springer Verlag, Berlin.

Hall, B. J. (1975). Transfer stations and associated equipment. *Solid Wastes* **65**, 555–62.

Halmø, T. M. (1976). The content of nutrients in household waste. Proc. Conf. Elmia-Avfall '76. Jönkoping. Sweden, pp. 7:1–7:14.

Hamabe, I., Tsugeno, T., and Nozu, S. (1975). Pyrolyzing test of municipal waste in Japan. First International Conference on Conversion of Refuse to Energy, Montreux, Switzerland, pp. 244–9.

Hammond, V. L. and Mudge, L. K. (1975). Feasibility study of use of molten salt technology for pyrolysis of solid waste. Environmental Protection Agency, Washington Report No. 670/2-75-014. Issued by National Technical Information Service, Springfield, Virginia as Report No. P B 238 674.

Hannon, B. (1972). System energy and recycling. A study of the beverage industry. Illinois University. Issued by N T I S as Report No. P B 233 183.

Hansard (1977). 17 February, pp. 318–19.

Hansen, B. (1979). Process for the recovery from household waste of solid fuel (d-R D F), or alternatively secondary paper, and their reuse. *Proc. int. Recycling Congr., Berlin* (ed. K. J. Thomé-Kozmiensky) Vol. 2, pp. 936–41. Springer Verlag, Berlin.

Hansen, J. A., Tjell, J. C., and Christensen, T. H. (1979). Danish research related to solid waste, sludge and soil management. Proceedings of the conference Elmia-Avfall '79, Jönkoping, Sweden, pp. 502–24.

Hardy, W. E. and Grissom, C. L. (1976). An economic analysis of a regionalized rural solid waste management system. *Am. J. Agric. Econ.* **58**, 179–85.

Harrington, J. J. (1969). Systems analysis: a key aspect of modern management and planning. *Mod. Govt. natl. Devel.* **57**.

Harvey, D. J. and O'Flaherty, T. G. (1972). An analysis of solid waste transportation and disposal alternatives. *I N F O R* **11**, 187–200.

Haselbarth, J. E. and Berk, J. M. (1960). Chemical plant cost breakdown. *Chem. Engng, Albany* **67**, 158.

Haxo, H. E. (1979). Liner materials exposed to municipal solid waste leachate. Proceedings of the Fifth Annual Research Symposium, Municipal Solid Waste: Land Disposal, Orlando, Florida. Environmental Protection Agency, Washington, Report No. E P A-600/9-79-023a.

Hecklinger, R. S. (1976). The relative value of energy derived from municipal refuse. *National Waste Processing Conf., Boston* pp. 133–40. American Society of Mechanical Engineers, New York.

Heginbotham, J. H. (1978). Recovery of glass from urban refuse by froth flotation. *Proc. Sixth Mineral Waste Utilization Symp., Chicago* pp. 230–40. U S Bureau of Mines and I I T Research Institute.

Heinrich, F. (1979). The gasification of municipal and industrial waste in accordance with the S F W—Funk process. *Proc. int. Recycling Congr., Berlin* (ed. K. J. Thomé-Kozmiensky) Vol. 1, pp. 588–94, Springer Verlag, Berlin.

Hekimian, K. J. (1972). A systems engineering approach to environmental quality management, with emphasis on solid waste management. Ph.D. thesis, University of Southern California, University Microfilm No. U M-73-7252.

Helmenstein, S. and Martin, F. (1972). Planning criteria for refuse incinerator system. *Combustion* **45**, 11–17, (1974). [Translation from the German.]

Helms, B. P. and Clark, R. M. (1971) Selecting solid waste disposal facilities. *J. sanit. Engng Div., Proc. Am. Soc. civ. Engrs.* **97**, 443–51.

Henstock, M. E. (1976). Modern techniques for recycling. *Conserv. Recycling*, **1**, 83–90.

Her Majesty's Government (HMG) (1972). Convention for the prevention of marine pollution by dumping from ships and aircraft (The Oslo Convention). HMSO, London, Miscellaneous No. 21.

—— (1976). Convention on the prevention of marine pollution by dumping of wastes and other matter (The London Convention). HMSO, London, Treaty Series No. 43.

Herschel Shosteck Associates (1972). An overview of potential markets for municipal compost—a preliminary study. Report for Environmental Protection Agency, Washington. Issued by NTIS as Report No. PB 229 568.

Hertz, D. B. (1964). Risk analysis in capital investment. *Harv. Business Rev.* **42**, 95–106.

—— (1968). Investment policies that pay off. *Harv. Business Rev.* **46**, 96–108.

Hickman, W. B. (1976). Storage and retrieval of prepared refuse. *National Waste Processing Conference, Boston* pp. 455–64. American Society of Mechanical Engineers, New York.

Hill, M. (1968). A goals-achievement matrix for evaluating alternative plans. *J. Am. Inst. Planners* **34**, 19–29.

Hillier, F. S. and Lieberman, G. J. (1967). *Introduction to operations research*. Holden-Day, San Francisco.

Hirst, E. (1973). Energy intensiveness of passenger and freight transport modes 1950–1970. Oak Ridge National Laboratory Report No. ORNL-NSF-EP-44.

Hitte, S. J. (1976). Anaerobic digestion of solid waste and sewage sludge into methane. *Compost Sci.* **17**, 26–30.

Hoberg, H. and Julius, J. (1979). Possibilities for the final purification of recovered materials. *Proc. int. Recycling. Congr., Berlin* (ed. K. J. Thomé-Kozmiensky) Vol. 2, pp. 866–70. Springer Verlag, Berlin.

—— and Schulz, E. (1977). The Aachen process for treating household refuse. *Aufbereitungs-Technik* **18**, 1–5. [In German.]

Hobson, P. N., Bousfield, S., and Summers, R. (1974). Anaerobic digestion of organic matter. *CRC Critical Reviews in Environmental Control* **4**, 131–91.

Holland, F. A., Watson, F. A., and Wilkinson, J. K. (1974). How to estimate capital costs. *Chem. Engng, Albany* **81**, 71–6.

Holmes, J. R. (1975*a*). *The recovery of useful material from refuse*. The Institution of Municipal Engineers, London, Monograph No. 27 on Protection of the Environment.

—— (1975*b*). The Millhouses refuse pulverization transfer station, Sheffield. *J. Instn Municipal Engrs* **102**, 237–44.

—— (1975*c*). Refuse into energy in the City of Sheffield refuse incineration department. Autumn meeting of the Institute of Solid Wastes Management, Bradford. *Solid Wastes* **65**, 576–81.

—— (1979). Municipal waste processing. In *Developments in environmental control and public health 1* (ed. A. Porteous) Chapter 3, pp. 63–105. Applied Science Publishers, London.

Hooverman, R. H. and Coffman, J. A. (1977). Rotary kiln gasification of biomass and municipal wastes. *Symp. Clean Fuels from Biomass and Wastes, Orlando, Florida* pp. 213–36. Institute of Gas Technology, Chicago.

Hopper, R. E. (1975). A nationwide survey of resource recovery activities. Environmental protection Agency, Washington, Report No. EPA/530/SW-142.

Horner and Shifrin Inc. (1973). Solid waste as a fuel for power plants. Issued by NTIS as Report No. PB 220 316.

Huang, C. J., Dalton, C., *et al.* (1975). *Energy recovery from solid waste* Vols 1 and 2. National Aeronautics and Space Administration, Washington, Report Nos. NASA-CR-2525 and 2526. Issued by National Technical Information Service, Springfield, Virginia as Report Nos. N75-20830 and 25292.

Huang, W. C., Sanneman, F. H., and Johnson, J. A. (1979). Incineration of municipal sewage sludge in fluidized bed reactor system fired with refuse-derived fuel—a co-disposal alternative. *Proc. int. Recycling Congr., Berlin* (ed. K. J. Thomé-Kozmiensky) Vol. 1, pp. 343–8. Springer Verlag, Berlin.

Hudson, J. F., Grossman, D. S., and Marks, D. H. (1975). Analysis models for solid waste collection. Massachusetts Institute of Technology, report for Environmental Protection Agency, National Environment Research Center, No. EPA-670/2-75-026a. Issued by National Technical Information Service, Springfield Virginia as Report No. PB 239 117.

Humphrey, A. E. (1974). Current developments in fermentation. *Chem. Engng, Albany* **81**, 98–112.

Hunt, R. G. and Franklin, W. E. (1973). Environmental effects of recycling paper. Forest Products and the Environment, *Am. Inst. Chem. Eng. Symposium Series* 133, **69**, 67–78.

Industry Committee for Packaging and the Environment (INCPEN) (1975). Packaging and the energy equation. Recycling and Waste Disposal, September, 15–18.

Institution of Chemical Engineers (1976). Report of the research committee working party on materials and energy resources. Institution of Chemical Engineers, Rugby.

—— (1977). A new guide to capital cost estimation. Prepared in conjunction with the Association of Cost Engineers. Institution of Chemical Engineers, Rugby.

International Business Machines Corporation (IBM) (1973). *Mathematical Program System Extended (MPSX), Mixed Integer Programming (MIP), program description* (2nd edn).

International Federation of Institutes for Advanced Study (IFIAS) (1974). Energy analysis. Workshop Report No. T6, Stockholm.

Ishida, M., Odawara, Y., Gejo, T., and Okumura, H. (1979). Biogasification of municipal waste. *Proc. int. Recycling Congr., Berlin* (ed. K. J. Thomé-Kozmiensky) Vol. 2, pp. 797–802. Springer Verlag, Berlin.

Ito, K. and Hirayama, Y. (1975). Resource recovery from municipal refuse by semi-wet selective pulverizing system. First International Conference on Conversion of Refuse to Energy, Montreux, Switzerland, pp. 354–9.

Jackson, D. R., Renold, J., and Wilson, R. (1975). Alternatives in waste disposal. Local Government Operational Research Unit, Report No. C212, for South Yorkshire County Council.

Jackson, D. W. (1979). Recovering ferrous metal and producing a pelletised waste derived fuel. Proceedings of the conference Elmia-Avfall '79, Jönkoping, Sweden, pp. 15–26.

Jackson, F. R., (1974). Energy from solid waste. Noyes Data Corporation, Park Ridge, New Jersey.

Jackson, P. M., Moar, L. J., and Ulph, A. M. (1975). An economic study of domestic waste management. *Solid Wastes* **65**, 276–82.

James, S. C. and Rhyne, C. W. (1978). Methane production, recovery and utilization from landfills. *Symp. Energy from Biomass and Wastes, Wash.* pp. 317–24. Institute for Gas Technology, Chicago.

Jarvis, C. E., Swartzbaugh, J. T., Walter, D. K., and Wiles, C. C. (1978). A biogasification mixing study: conversion of municipal solid waste to methane. *Symp. Energy from Biomass and Wastes, Wash.* pp. 677–95. Institute of Gas Technology, Chicago.

Jensen, P. K. (1977). Refuse refineries. *Conserv. Recycling* **1**, 201–7.

Joensen, A. W., Even, J., Hall, J. L., van Meter, D., and Olexsey, R. (1979). Economic and technical evaluation of the Ames, Iowa, solid waste recovery system. *Proc. int. Recycling Congr., Berlin* (ed. K. J. Thomé-Kozmiensky) Vol. 2, pp. 903–8, Springer Verlag, Berlin.

——, Hall, J. L., and Hove, M. (1976). Processed solid refuse as a supplementary fuel at the City of Ames, Iowa. National Waste Processing Conference, Boston, pp. 49–58. American Society of Mechanical Engineers, New York.

Johnson, J. (1976). *Commercial motor tables of operating costs* (60th edn). I P C Business Press, London.

Jones, B. (1977). Heat and energy from waste. *Recycling and Waste Disposal* **2**, 208–13.

Jones, J. (1978). Converting solid wastes and residues to fuel. *Chem. Engng, Albany* **85**, 87–94.

Jones and Henry Engineers Ltd., (1970). Proposal for a refuse disposal system in Oakland County, Michigan. Public Health Service publication No. 1960.

Kaiser, E. R. (1975). Physical-chemical character of municipal refuse. International Symposium on Energy Recovery from Refuse, University of Louisville, Kentucky.

Kay, S. R. (1976). Location index. *Engng Process Econ.* **1**, 327.

Kazanowski, A. D. (1968). Cost-effectiveness fallacies and misconceptions revisited. In *Cost-effectiveness—economic evaluation of engineered system* (ed. J. M. English) Chapter 8. Wiley, New York.

Keenan, J. D. (1976). Multiple staged methane recovery from solid wastes. *J. environ. Sci. Health* **A11**, 525–48.

Kelliher, W. J., Kobayashi, R., Howard, A. H., Stephens, W. C., DeMatteo, M., Standrod, S. E., and Milo, J. F. (1975). The Boston North-shore system—A case study of a multi-community, privately financed refuse disposal and energy recovery system. First International Conference on Conversion of Refuse to Energy, Montreux, Switzerland, pp. 513–24.

Kellogg, H. H. (1976). The role of recycling in conservation of metals and energy. *J. Metals* **28**, 29–32.

Kempe's Engineers Yearbook (1974). (ed. C. E. Prockter) (79th edn). Morgan-Grampian, London.

Kemper, P. and Quigley, J. M. (1976). *The economics of refuse collection.* Ballinger Publishing Company, Cambridge, Mass.

Kilgroe, J. D., Shannon, L. J., and Gorman, P. G. (1975). Emissions and energy conversion from refuse processing and mixed fuel boiler firing. First International Conference on Conversion of Refuse to Energy, Montreux, Switzerland, pp. 190–6.

——, ——, —— (1976). Environmental studies on the St. Louis—Union Electric refuse firing demonstration. *Symp, Clean Fuels from Biomass, Sewage, Urban Refuse and Agricultural Wastes, Orlando, Florida* pp. 413–26. Institute of Gas Technology, Chicago.

Kispert, R. G., Sadek, S. E., and Wise, D. L. (1976). An evaluation of methane production from solid waste. *Resource Recovery Conserv.* **1**, 245–55.

——, ——, Anderson, L. C., and Wise, D. L. (1975). Fuel gas production from solid waste. Dynatech Research and Development Company report No. 1258, National Science Foundation Report No. N S F-R A N N-74-268.

Klass, D. L. (1976). Wastes and biomass as energy resources: an overview. *Symp. Clean Fuels from Biomass, Sewage, Urban Refuse and Agricultural Wastes, Orlando, Florida* pp. 21–58. Institute of Gas Technology, Chicago.

—— (1977). Biomass and wastes as energy resources: 1977 update. *Symp., Clean Fuels from Biomass and Wastes, Orlando, Florida* pp. 1–28. Institute of Gas Technology, Chicago.

Klee, A. J. (1971). The role of decision models in the evaluation of competing environmental health alternatives. *Man. Sci.* **18**, B52–B67.

—— (1972). The utilization of expert opinion in decision making. *Am. Inst. Chem. Engng J.* **18**, 1107–15.

—— and Rogers, C. J. (1977). Biochemical routes to energy recovery from municipal wastes. *Pac. Chem. Engng Congr. (Proc)* **2**, 759–64.

Klumb, D. L. (1976). The Union Electric Company's 8000 ton per day solid waste utilization system. *Symp. Clean Fuels from Biomass, Sewage, Urban Refuse and Agricultural Wastes, Orlando, Florida* pp. 77–88. Institute of Gas Technology, Chicago.

Knights, D. (1976). Domestic refuse disposal via cement kilns. *Solid Wastes* **66**, 320–6.

Kohlepp, D. H. (1974). The dynamics of recycling. 78th National meeting of the American Institution of Chem. Engineers, Salt Lake City, Utah.

Krause, H. H., Vaughan, D. A., and Boyd, W. K. (1975). Corrosion and Deposits from Combustion of Solid Waste. Part 3—Effects of Sulphur on Boiler Tube Metals. *J. Engng Pr. Trans. Am. Soc. Mech. Eng.* Ser. A. **97**, 448–52.

——, ——, —— (1976). Corrosion and Deposits from Combustion of Solid Waste. Part 4—Combined Firing of Refuse and Coal. *J. Engng Pr. Trans. Am. Soc. Mech. Eng.* Ser. A. **98**, 369–74.

——, ——, and Miller, P. D. (1973). Corrosion and Deposits from Combustion of Solid Waste. *J. Engng Pr. Trans. Am. Soc. Mech. Eng.* Ser. A. **95**, 45–52.

——, ——, —— (1974). Corrosion and Deposits from Combustion of Solid Waste. Part 2—Chloride Effects on Boiler Tube and Scrubber Metals. *J. Engng Pr. Trans. Am. Soc. Mech. Eng.* Ser. A. **96**, 216–22.

——, ——, Cover, P. W., Boyd, W. K., and Oberacker, D. A. (1977). Corrosion and deposits from combustion of solid waste. Part 5—Firing of refuse with high-sulphur coal. *J. Engng Pr. Trans. Am. Soc. Mech. Eng.* Ser. A. **99**, 449–55.

Kreiter, B. G. (1979). Research and development in the Netherlands in the field of analysis and treatment of municipal solid wastes Proc. Conf. Elmia-Avfall '79, Jönkoping, Sweden pp. 583–601.

Kühner, J. (1974). Centralization and decentralization for regional solid waste management: toward Paretian environmental analysis. Ph.D. thesis, Harvard University.

—— and Harrington, J. J. (1973). Mathematical models for developing regional solid waste management policies. Optimization in Civil Engineering Conference, University of Liverpool. Reprinted in *Engng Optimization* **1**, 237–56 (1975).

——, —— (1974). Large-scale mixed integer programming for investigating multi-party public investment decisions: application to a regional solid waste management problem. 45th National joint meeting of the Operational Research Society of America and The Institute of Management Sciences, Boston.

——, —— (1975a). Mathematical modelling for regionalization of resource recovery. International Conference on Mathematical Models for Environmental Problems, Southampton University.

——, —— (1975b). Discussion on: Solid waste management: equity trade-off models, Fuertes *et al.* (1974), *J. urban Planning Dev. Div., Proc. Am. Soc. civ. Engng* **101**, (UP2), 235–9.

—— and Heiler, B. (1973). Regional planning models for solid waste management. In *Models for environmental pollution control* (ed. R. A. Deininger) Chapter 16. Ann Arbor Science Publishers, Michigan.

Landman, W. J. and Darmstadt, W. J. (1975). Energy recovery from hydrapulping at Hempstead. First International Conference on Conversion of Refuse to Energy, Montreux, Switzerland, pp. 589–95.

Lang, H. J. (1948). Simplified approach to preliminary cost estimates. *Chem. Engng, Albany* **55**, 112–13.

Laughlin, R. G. W. and Cadotte, A. P. (1979). A process for energy recovery from sewage sludge and industrial waste streams. *Proc. int. Recycling Congr., Berlin* (ed. K. J. Thomé-Kozmiensky) Vol. 2, pp. 803–9. Springer Verlag, Berlin.

Leach, G. and Slesser, M. (1972). Energy equivalent of network inputs to food producing processes. Unpublished report, available from M. Slesser, Dept. of Pure and Applied Chemistry, University of Strathclyde, Glasgow.

Leaver, J. F. (1977). An analysis of the performance and maintenance of a modern refuse pulveriser. *Solid Wastes* **67**, 296–313.

Legille, E., Berczynski, F. A., and Heiss, K. G. (1975). A slagging pyrolysis solid waste conversion system. First International Conference on Conversion of Refuse to Energy, Montreux, Switzerland, pp. 232–7.

Lenz, S. (1979). Pyrolysis, a link between waste disposal and energy supply. *Proc. int. Recycling Congr., Berlin* (ed. K. J. Thomé-Kozmiensky) Vol. 1, pp. 640–5. Springer Verlag, Berlin.

Levy, S. J. (1974). Markets and technology for recovering energy from solid waste. Environmental Protection Agency, Washington, Report No. EPA/530/SW-130.

—— (1975*a*). San Diego County demonstrates pyrolysis of solid waste to recover liquid fuel, metals and glass. Environmental Protection Agency, Washington, Report No. EPA-530/SW-80d.2.

—— (1975*b*). The conversion of municipal solid waste to a liquid fuel by pyrolysis. First International Conference on Conversion of Refuse to Energy, Montreux, Switzerland, pp. 226–31.

Lewis, F. M. (1976). Thermodynamic fundamentals for the pyrolysis of refuse. *National Waste Processing Conference, Boston* pp. 19–48. American Society of Mechanical Engineers, New York.

Lichfield, N., Kettle, P., and Whitbread, M. (1975). *Evaluation in the planning process*. Urban and Regional Planning Series Vol. 10. Pergamon Press, Oxford.

Liles, K. J. (1976). Lightweight structural concrete aggregate from municipal waste glass. *Proc. Fifth Mineral Waste Utilization Symp., Chicago* pp. 219–22. US Bureau of Mines and IIT Research Institute.

Little, A. D. Inc. and Battelle Columbus Laboratories (1978). Study for US Bureau of Mines. Reported in *Materials Reclamation Weekly*, 13 May, p. 16.

Long, T. V. (1977). International comparisons of industrial energy use. Proceedings of the NSF-Mitre Workshop on Long-Run Energy Demand.

Loram, R. G. (1976). Refuse pulverization—a review of a decade of progress. *Solid Wastes*, **66** 580–603.

Lowe, R. A. (1974). Energy conservation through improved solid waste management. Environmental Protection Agency, Washington, Report No. EPA/530/SW-125.

Lutton, R. J., Regan, G. L., and Jones, L. W. (1979). Design and construction of covers for solid waste landfills. Report for the Environmental Protection Agency, Washington, No. E P A -600/2-79-165.

Lutz, W. (1979). Operating experience at the waste material and sedimented sludge composting plant at Siggerviesen, Salzburg. Proceedings of the conference Elmia-Avfall '79, Jönkoping, Sweden, pp. 257–84.

McCuen, R. H. (1975). The anatomy of the modelling process. International Conference on Mathematical Models for Environmental Problems, Southampton University.

McDonald, P. I. (1976). Environmental impact of waste disposal sites: methods of assessment. *Solid Wastes* **66**, 509–14.

McKewen, T. D. (1976). Maryland resource recovery facility. *Waste Age* **7**, 80–3.

Mahoney, P. F. (1978). A N S W E R S: Albany New York solid waste energy recovery system. City-State partnership solid waste energy recovery. *Proc. Sixth Mineral Waste Utilization Symp., Chicago*, pp. 158–63. US Bureau of Mines and I I T Research Institute.

Makhijani, A. B. and Lictenberg, A. J. (1972). Energy and well being. *Environment* **14**, 11–18.

Mallan, G. M. and Finney, C. S. (1972). New techniques in the pyrolysis of solid wastes. Garrett Research and Development Co. Inc., Report G R&D 72–035.

Malloy, J. B. (1971). Risk analysis of chemical plants. *Chemical Engineering Progress* **67**, 68–77.

Mandeville, R. T. (1976). Fuel gas from landfill. *Symp. Clean Fuels from Biomass, Sewage, Urban Refuse and Agricultural Wastes, Orlando, Florida* pp. 197–204. Institute of Gas Technology, Chicago.

Manne, A. S. (ed.) (1967). *Investment for capacity expansion: size, location and time phasing*. Mass. Institute of Technology Press, Cambridge, and Allen and Unwin, London.

Mantellini, G. (1975). Dry system recycling plant. First International Conference on Conversion of Refuse to Energy, Montreux, Switzerland, pp. 602–7.

Marks, D. H. and Liebman, J. C. (1970). Mathematical analysis of solid waste collection. U S Public Health Service, Office of Solid Waste Management report No. S W-5rg, P H S publication No. 2104.

—— —— (1971). Location models—solid waste collection example. *J. Urban Planning and Dev. Div., Proc. Am. Soc. civ. Engng* **97** (U P1), 15–30.

Marks, S. D., Bohn, D., and Melan, C. (1979). Recent developments in a slagging process for conversion of refuse to energy. *Proc. int. Recycling Congr., Berlin* (ed. K. J. Thomé-Kozmiensky) Vol. 1, pp. 601–8. Springer Verlag, Berlin.

Marsden, A. (1973). Pulverization and tipping of municipal wastes. *Chemical Engineer* No. 270, February, pp. 80–5.

Marshall, A. H. (1974). *Financial management in local government*. Allen and Unwin, London.

Marshall, J. E. (1978). *Experience with solid waste as a supplementary fuel*. I M I Energy Systems, P O Box 216, Witton, Birmingham B6 7BA, England.

—— and Harvey, K. (1977). The use of refuse as a supplementary fuel. *Solid Wastes* **67**, 5–23.

Material Recovery Ltd. (1977). Recovering tinplate from domestic refuse. *Iron and Steel International* **50**, 373–4.

Materials Reclamation Weekly. Distinctive Publications Ltd., Croydon.

Mathematical Sciences Northwest Inc. (1974). Feasibility study: conversion of solid waste to methanol or ammonia. Report for the City of Seattle Department of Lighting.

Mather, J. D. (1976). Hydrological guidelines for the selection of landfill sites. In: Department of the Environment (1976d), op. cit.

—— (1977). Attenuation and control of landfill leachates. 79th Annual Conference of the Institutes of Solid Wastes Management, Torbay, 1977. Reported in *Solid Wastes* **67**, 362–78.

—— and Bromley, J. (1976). Research into leachate generation and attenuation at landfill sites. Land Reclamation Conference, Thurrock.

Menges, G. and Haberstroh, E. (1979). Reprocessing of mixed and contaminated plastic wastes by foaming and sintering. *Proc. int. Recycling Congr., Berlin* (ed. K. J. Thomé-Kozmiensky) Vol. 2, pp. 1193–98, Springer Verlag, Berlin.

Merrett, A. J. and Sykes, A. (1963). *The finance and analysis of capital projects*, Appendix, Table B. Longmans, London.

Midland Geotechnical Society, The (1979). The engineering behaviour of industrial and urban fill. Proceedings of a symposium at the University of Birmingham. [Available from Department of Civil Engineering, University of Birmingham, England.]

Midwest Research Institute (M R I) (1973). Resource recovery: the state of technology. Report for the President's Council on Environmental Quality. Issued by National Technical Information Service, Springfield, Virginia as Report No. P B 214 149.

—— (1974). Resource and environmental profile analysis of nine beverage container alternatives. Environmental Protection Agency, Washington, Report No. E P A/530/S W-91c.

—— (1975). Baseline forecasts for resource recovery, 1975–1990. Issued by National Technical Information Service, Springfield, Virginia as Report No. P B 245 924.

Miles, J. E. P. and Douglas, E. (1972). Recovery of non-ferrous metals from domestic refuse. *Surveyor* **140** (4200), 36–8.

Milgrom, J. (1975). The present state of recycling thermoplastics—and future trends. *Solid Wastes* **65**, 533–42.

Millard, R. (1974). Regional refuse disposal—does it work? 76th Annual Conference of the Institute of Solid Wastes Management, Scarborough. Reported in *Solid Wastes* **64**, 471–85.

—— (1977). Energy from waste and its potential use as a fuel. 79th Annual Conference of the Institute of Solid Wastes Management, Torbay. Reported in *Solid Wastes* **67**, 390–403.

Millbank, P. (1976a). Built-in flexibility at Burgess Hill. *Surveyor* **147** (4382), 15.

—— (1976b). High density waste goes to ground in Glasgow. *Surveyor* **148** (4408), 15.

—— (1976c). Staffordshire opts for wired-up wastes. *Surveyor* **147** (4381), 7.

—— (1976d). Leicester composting—an exception to the rule. *Surveyor* **148** (4396), 13.

—— (1976e). CEGB stay cool on refuse as fuel. *Surveyor* **147** (4369), 13–14.

Miller, C. A. (1973). Current concepts in capital cost forecasting. *Chem. Engng Prog.* **69**, 77–83.

Mishan, E. J. (1975). *Cost–benefit analysis* (2nd edn). Unwin University Books, London.

Mitre Corporation (1976). Wrapping up the solid waste management problem: a model for regional solid waste management planning. Report No. M-76-207. Also available are a Users guide, Report No. M T R-3222; programmers manual, M T R-3224; and documentation of operational and exercise runs, M T R-3219.

Monthly Digest of Statistics. Central Statistical Office. H M S O, London.

Moore, P. G. and Thomas, H. (1976). *The anatomy of decisions*. Penguin Books, Harmondsworth.

Morey, B., Griffin, T. D., Gupta, A. K., and Hopkins, I. J. T. (1976). Resource recovery from refuse. *Proc. Fifth Mineral Waste Utilization Symp., Chicago* pp. 184–94. US Bureau of Mines and IIT Research Institute.

Mori, T. (1979). Integrated system for solid waste disposal with energy recovery and volumetric reduction by new pyrolysis furnace. *Proc. int. Recycling Congr., Berlin* (ed. K. J. Thomé-Kozmiensky) Vol. 1, pp. 609–14, Springer Verlag, Berlin.

Morris, P. A. (1974). Decision analysis expert use. *Man. Sci.,* **20**, 1233–41.

—— (1977). Combining expert judgements: a Bayesian approach. *Man. Sci.* **23**, 679–93.

Morse, N. and Roth, E. W. (1970). Systems analysis of regional solid waste handling. Public Health Service, Office of Solid Waste Management Programs, Report No. SW-15c, PHS Publication No. 2065.

Mortimer, N. D. (1974). The energy costs of road and rail transport UK 1968. Open University research report ERG 004.

Münnecke, D. M. (1978). Detoxification of pesticides using soluble or immobilized enzymes. *Process Biochem.* **13**, 14–16, 31.

Narisoko, M. and Kanai, N. (1976). Hydropulped municipal waste-firing incinerator for the Ryusen-en Corporation. *IHI Engineering Review* **9**, 68–80.

Nash, C., Pearce, D., and Stanley, J. (1975*a*). Criteria for evaluating project evaluation techniques. *J. Am. Inst. Planners* **41**, 83–9.

——, ——, —— (1975*b*). An evaluation of cost–benefit anlysis criteria. *Scot. J. Polit. Econ.* **22**, 121–34.

Nash, C. A. (1973). Future generations and the social rate of discount. *Environ. Planning* **5**, 611–17.

National Center for Resource Recovery (NCRR) (1972). Materials recovery system—engineering feasibility study. National Center for Resource Recovery, Washington.

—— (1974*a*). *Resource recovery from municipal solid waste: a state of the art study.* Lexington Books, Mass.

—— (1974*b*). *Sanitary landfill: a state of the art study.* Lexington Books, Mass.

—— (1974*c*). *Cost analysis for the New Orleans resource recovery and disposal program.* National Center for Resource Recovery, Washington.

—— (1974*d*). *Incineration: a state of the art study.* Lexington Books, Mass.

—— (1976). Status of resource recovery systems. *Solid Wastes Management/ Resources Recovery J.* **19**, 40–1.

—— (1978). Resource recovery activities—a status report (as of March 1978). *National Center for Resource Recovery Bulletin* **8**, (insert).

National Commission on Supplies and Shortages (1976). *Government and the nation's resources.* Chapter 8, on Recycling, reprinted by Environmental Protection Agency as Report No. SW-601.

Naveau, H. P. and Binot, R. (1975). Influence of separate collection on calorific power of urban solid wastes. First International Conference on Conversion of Refuse to Energy, Montreux, Switzerland, pp. 56–60.

——, Nyns, E. J., Binot, R., and Delafontaine, M. (1979). Recycling of effluents and organic residues into methane by anaerobic digestion—new perspectives. *Proc. int. Recycling Congr., Berlin* (ed. K. J. Thomé-Kozmiensky) Vol. 2, pp. 738–8. Springer Verlag, Berlin.

Neff, N. T. (1972). Solid waste and fibre recovery demonstration plant for the City of Franklin, Ohio: an interim report. Environmental Protection Agency, Washington, Report No. EPA-530/SW-47d.i.

Nejat, Z. (1979). Energy recovery from solid waste in the city of Teheran. *Proc. int. Recycling Congr., Berlin* (ed. K. J. Thomé-Kozmiensky) Vol. 1, pp. 189–94. Springer Verlag, Berlin.

Newling, B. E. (1966). Urban growth and spatial structure. *Geogrl Rev.* **56**, 213–25.

—— (1969). The spatial variation of urban population densities. *Geogrl Rev.* **59**, 242–52.

Nice, R. W. and Selby, M. J. P. (1969). Cooperative refuse disposal in the U K. Third annual Israel Conference on Operations Research.

Niessen, W. R., Chensky, S. K., Dimitriou, A. N., Field, E. L., Le Mantle, C. R., and Zinn, R. E. (1970). Systems study of air pollution from municipal incineration, Vols 1–3. Issued by National Technical Information Service, Springfield, Virginia as Report Nos. P B 192 378–80.

Nigam, A. K. (1970). Optimal strategies in capacity expansion. Operations Research Center, Report No. O R C-70-20, University of California, Berkeley.

Noble, G. (1976). *Sanitary landfill design handbook.* Technomic Publishing Company, Westport, Conn.

Nemoto, M., Torisu, M., Hirayama, Y., and Ito, K. (1979). Development of semi-wet selective pulverizing system (second report). *Proc. int. Recycling Congr., Berlin* (ed. K. J. Thomé-Kozmiensky) Vol. 2, pp. 1009–14. Springer Verlag, Berlin.

Oberman, M. A. (1975). High density solid waste baler is installed in Cobb County, Georgia. *Waste Age*, **6**, 46–8, 75.

Oeltzschner, H. and Fichtel, K. (1979). The problems of the utilization of solid residues from thermal waste treatment. *Proc. int. Recycling Congr., Berlin* (ed. K. J. Thomé-Kozmiensky) Vol. 1, pp. 512–17. Springer Verlag, Berlin.

Oxfordshire County Council (1977). Waste disposal—site for rail transfer station. Report to the environmental committee, 18 July.

Page, F. J. (1976). Torrax—a system for recovery of energy from solid waste. *National Waste Processing Conference, Boston*, pp. 109–16. American Society for Mechanical Engineers, New York.

Panagiotakopoulos, D. (1976). Multi-commodity multi-transformed network flows, with an application to residuals management *Man. Sci.* **22**, 874–82.

Parker, C. and Portlock, P. (1974). Waste disposal planning. Local Government Operational Research Unit, Report No. T.51.

Parkinson, E. A. and Mular, A. L. (1972). *Mineral processing equipment costs and preliminary capital cost estimations.* The Canadian Institute of Mining and Metallurgy, special Vol. 13.

Paroubek, Z. A. (1979). Waste handling Rijnmond energy production of a large-scale waste incineration plant. *Proc. int. Recycling Congr., Berlin* (ed. K. J. Thomé-Kozmiensky) Vol. 1, pp. 432–8. Springer Verlag, Berlin.

Pathak, A. A. (1974). Optimal configuration of a regional solid waste management system. Operations Research Center, Report No. O R C 74–16, University of California, Berkeley. Issued by National Technical Information Service, Springfield, Virginia as Report No. P B 233 360.

Patrick, P. K. (1975a). Solid waste disposal in Greater London—the first ten years. *Public Health Engr.*, **18**, 173–7.

—— (1975b). Operational experience in energy recovery through incineration. International Symposium on Energy Recovery from Refuse, University of Louisville, Kentucky.

—— (1976). Greater London's plans for rail haul of solid wastes. *Solid Wastes* **66**, 150–7.

Pavoni, J. L., Heer, J. E., and Hagerty, D. J. (1975). *Handbook of solid waste disposal—material and energy recovery.* Van Nostrand Reinhold, New York.

Peabody–Gallion Corporation (1976). Two composting plants sold to Libya. Press release, 4 March. 6 St. James Street, London.

Pearce, D. W. (1975). The social cost of noise. Report to the Organisation for Economic Cooperation and Development, Paris, Report No. U/ENV/N/75.3.

—— (1976). *Environmental economics.* Longmans, London.

Pedersen, S. D. (1979). The potential in Denmark for substituting natural resources by waste incineration products. *Proc. int. Recycling. Congr., Berlin* (ed. K. J. Thomé-Kozmiensky) Vol. 1, pp. 528–32. Springer Verlag, Berlin.

Peters, M. S. and Timmerhaus, K. D. (1968). *Plant design and economics for chemical engineers.* McGraw Hill, New York.

Petroleum Times (1977). Current prices. **81**, 4 February. [Published weekly.]

Pfeffer, J. T. (1974). Reclamation of energy from organic waste. Environmental Protection Agency, Washington, Report No. EPA/670/2-74-016. Issued by National Technical Information Service, Springfield, Virginia as Report No. PB 231 176.

—— (1978). Methane from urban solid wastes—the RefCOM project. *Process Biochem.* **13**, 8–11.

—— and Liebman, J. C. (1976). Energy from refuse by bioconversion, fermentation and residue disposal processes. *Resource Recovery Conserv.* **1**, 295–313.

Phillips, T. A. (1977). An economic evaluation of a process to separate raw urban refuse into its metal, mineral and energy components. US Bureau of Mines Information Circular 8732.

Pojasek, R. B. (ed.) (1979). *Toxic and hazardous waste disposal*, Vol. 1: *Processes for stabilization/solidification.* Ann Arbor Science Publishers, Ann Arbor, Michigan.

Poole, A. (1975). The potential for energy recovery from organic wastes. *The energy conservation papers* (ed. R. H. Williams). Ballinger, Cambridge, Mass.

Popovich, M. L., Duckstein, L., and Kisiel, C. C. (1973). Cost-effectiveness analysis of disposal systems. *J. envir. Engng Div., Proc. Am. Soc. civ. Engng* **99** (EE5) 577–91.

Porteous, A. (1967). Towards a profitable means of municipal refuse disposal. ASME annual conference, Pittsburg, paper 67 WA/PID-2. Reprinted in: *Incinerator and Solid Waste Technology* pp. 397–415. American Society of Mechanical Engineers.

—— (1969). The recovery of industrial ethanol from paper in waste. *Chemistry and Industry,* December, pp. 1763–70.

—— (1971). A new look at solid waste disposal. *Public Cleansing* **61**, 152–70.

—— (1975). An assessment of energy recovery methods applicable to domestic refuse disposal. *Resources Policy* **1**, 284–94.

Powell, M. J. D. (1964). A method for minimizing a sum of squares of non-linear functions without calculating derivatives. *Comput. J.* **7**, 303–7.

Prather, B. V. and Young, E. P. (1976). Energy for wastewater treatment. *Hydrocarb. Processing Petrol Refin.* **55**, 88–91.

Preston, G. T. (1976). Resource recovery and flash pyrolysis of municipal refuse. *Waste Age* **7**, 83–98.

Price, C. (1973). To the future: with indifference or concern?—The social discount rate and its implication in land use. *J. Agric. Econ.* **24**, 393–8.

Process Economics International. The PEI plant cost indexes. Published quarterly since Autumn 1979. Chemecon Publishing Company, London.

Process Plant Association (1976). A symposium on the supply of incineration plant—a technical review of plant design, performance and future developments in relation to other methods of waste disposal. Available from P P A, 197 Knightsbridge, London.

Randol, R. (1975). Resource recovery plant implementation: guides for municipal officials—financing. Environmental Protection Agency, Washington, Report No. E P A/530/S W-157.4.

Rao, D. (1975). A dynamic model for optimum planning of regional solid waste management. Ph.D. thesis, Clarkson College of Technology, University Microfilm No. U M-75-16, 942.

Rayman, N. and Scott, P. J. (1972). Design of a refuse incineration plant for the City of Coventry, England. *National Incinerator Conference, New York*, pp. 166–77. American Society of Mechanical Engineers, New York.

Rees, R. (1973). The economics of investment analysis. Civil Service College Occasional Paper No. 17. H M S O, London.

Reinhardt, J. J. and Ham, R. K. (1972). Final report on a milling project at Madison, Wisconsin, between 1966 and 1972. Environmental Protection Agency, Washington, report prepared by the Heil Company, Milwaukee, Wisconsin.

Resource Planning Associates (1974). Financial methods for solid waste facilities. Environmental Protection Agency, Washington, Report No. E P A/530/S W-76c. Issued by National Technical Information Service, Springfield, Virginia as Report No. P B 234 612.

Rice, F. C. (1978). Commercial production of pipeline quality gas at the Palos Verdes landfill. *Symp. Energy from Biomass and Wastes, Wash.* pp. 345–52. Institute for Gas Technology, Chicago.

Robert Jenkins Systems (1976). Consumat-destroys the waste, then burns the smoke. Brochure, R J S Ltd., Whortley Road, Rotherham, Yorkshire.

Roberts, F. (1974). Energy consumption in the production of materials. *Metals and Materials* **8**, 167–73.

Roberts, K. J. (1972). Forecasting the useful life of tip sites. Local Government Operational Research Unit, Report No. T.6.

Robinson, W. D. (1976). Shredding systems for mixed municipal and industrial solid wastes. *National Waste Processing Conference, Boston*, pp. 249–60. American Society of Mechanical Engineers, New York.

Rogers, C. J. (1976). Problems and potential associated with the production of protein from cellulosic wastes. *Resource Recovery Conserv.* **1**, 271–7.

Rose, J. W. and Cooper, J. R. (ed.) (1977). *Technical data on fuel* (7th edn). British National Committee of the World Energy Conference.

Rose, L. M. (1976). *Engineering investment decisions—planning under uncertainty.* Elsevier, Amsterdam.

Rossi, B. A. (1979). Asian recycling aims at energy savings. *Proc. int. Recycling Congr., Berlin* (ed. K. J. Thomé-Kozmiensky) Vol. 1, pp. 170–4. Springer Verlag, Berlin.

Rossman, L. A. (1971). A general model for solid waste management facility selection. M.Sc. dissertation. Department of Civil Engineering, University of Illinois, Urbana.

Rubel, F. N. (1974). *Incineration of solid wastes.* Noyes Data Corporation, Park Ridge.

Rudblom, L. (1979). Pyrolysis of waste-operation experiences. The Andco–Torrax system. Proceedings of the conference Elmia-Avfall '79, Jönkoping, Sweden, pp. 84–110.

Rutherford, J. and Parker, C. J. (1975). Refuse collection in Thanet. Local Government Operational Research Unit, Report No. C.192.

Sachs, E. S. and Berry, R. S. (1976). Resource analysis: water and energy as linked resources. Progress report presented to the annual meeting of The Illinois Water Resources Center by the University of Chicago Resource Analysis Group.

Saeman, E. F. (1945). Hydrolysis of cellulose and decomposition of sugar in dilute acid at high temperature. *Ind. Engng Chem. analyt. Edn*, **37**, 43–52.

Sakiyama, T., Takamatsu, H., and Nishizaki, H. (1979). Resource recovery from municipal solid wastes. *Proc. int. Recycling Congr., Berlin* (ed. K. J. Thomé-Kozmiensky) Vol. 1, pp. 60–6. Springer Verlag, Berlin.

Salamon, P., Andresen, B., and Berry, R. S. (1977). Thermodynamics in finite time II. Potentials for finite time processes. *Phys. Rev.* **A15**, 2094–2102.

Sattin, B. M. (1978). Barriers to the use of secondary metals. *Proc. Sixth Mineral Waste Utilization Symp., Chicago* pp. 370–80. US Bureau of Mines and IIT Research Institute.

Savage, G. M., Trezek, G. J., Diaz, G. F., and Golueke, C. G. (1979). Field studies of municipal solid waste size reduction equipment. *Proc. int. Recycling Cong., Berlin* (ed. K. J. Thomé-Kozmiensky) Vol. 2, pp. 1003–8. Springer Verlag, Berlin.

Schlömann, E. (1976). Rotary drum metal separator using permanent magnets. *Resource Recovery Conserv.* **2**, 147–58.

Schlottmann, A. (1977). New life for old garbage—resource and energy recovery from solid wastes. *J. environ. Econ. Mgmt.* **4**, 57–67.

Schmalensee, R., Ramanathan, R., Ramm, W., and Smallwood, D. (1975). Measuring external effects of solid waste management. Environmental Protection Agency, Washington, Report No. EPA/600/5-75-010. Issued by National Technical Information Service, Springfield, Virginia as Report No. PB 243 407.

Schmidt, R. (1979). State of development of a rotary kiln pyrolysis process. *Proc. int. Recycling Congr., Berlin* (ed. K. J. Thomé-Komiensky) Vol. 1, pp. 646–50. Springer Verlag, Berlin.

Schneider, W., Strott, J., Van Wickeren, P., and Kranz, E. (1974). Forecasting and optimization in municipal refuse disposal. *Battelle Frankfurt Information Bulletin* No. 19, pp. 51–56.

Schoenberger, R. J. and Purdom, P. W. (1976). Long term chemical leaching from incinerator residue. *National Waste Processing Conference, Boston*, pp. 489–97. American Society of Mechanical Engineers, New York.

Schroeder, R. L. (1979). Processing techniques critical for effective resource recovery. *Proc. int. Recycling Congr., Berlin* (ed. K. J. Thomé-Kozmiensky) Vol. 1, pp. 975–80. Springer Verlag, Berlin.

—— and Fabuss, B. M. (1978). Resource Recovery Plant Cost. First World Recycling Congress, Basle, Paper I, 2.

Schultz, G. P. (1967). Managerial decision making in local government: facility planning for solid waste collection. Ph.D. thesis, Cornell University, Ithaca, New York.

—— (1969). Facility planning for a public service system: domestic solid waste collection. *J. Reg. Sci.* **9**, 291–307.

Schulz, H. W. (1973). Resource recovery from municipal solid waste. Proceedings of the Bioconversion Energy Research Conference, Massachusetts University, Amerhurst, pp 15–30; National Science Foundation. Issued by National Technical Information Service, Springfield, Virginia as Report No. PB 231 149.

—— (1975). Costs/benefits of solid waste reuse. *Environ. Sci. Technol.* **9**, 423–7.

——, Benziger, J. B., Bortz, B. J., Neamatalla, M., Szostak, R. M., Tong, G. and Westerhoff, R. P. (1976). Resource recovery technology for urban decision makers Prepared for the National Science Foundation by Urban Technology Center, Columbia University, New York. Issued by National Technical Information Service, Springfield, Virginia as Report No. P B 252 458.

Schwarz, F. and Collins, J. H. (1974). The disposal of waste on land-aspects of strategic planning, monitoring and enforcement relevant to potential computer applications. Part I I c of: A study of waste disposal, waste recovery and pollution control systems as they affect or are the responsibility of local authorities. A report for the I B M (U K) Scientific Centre, by the International Systems Corporation of Lancaster, (I S C O L Ltd.).

Schwegler, R. E. (1978). *Solid waste facts.* Institute for Solid Wastes, American Public Works Association, Chicago. [Published annually.]

Scott, P. J. and Holmes, J. R. (1974). The capacity and principal dimensions of refuse storage bunkers in modern incineration plants. *National Incinerator Conference, Miami* pp. 51–86. American Society of Mechanical Engineers, New York.

—— —— (1976). Heat utilisation at Coventry waste reduction unit. *Chartered Municipal Engineer* **103**, 29–37.

Seattle, City of (1974). Seattle's solid waste . . . an untapped resource. A report to the City by the Departments of Engineering and Lighting, Seattle.

—— (1975). Solid waste to methanol/ammonia conversion plants. Draft Environmental Impact Statement.

Senden, M. M. G. and Tels, M. (1979). Influence of the stage geometry on the performance of multistage zig-zag classifiers at low particle concentrations. *Proc. int. Recycling Congr., Berlin* (ed K. J. Thomé-Kozmiensky) Vol. 2, pp. 988–96. Springer Verlag, Berlin.

Shannon, L. J., Fiscus, D. E., and Gorman, P. G. (1975). St. Louis refuse processing plant-equipment, facility and environmental evaluations. Environmental Protection Agency, Washington, Report No. E P A-650/2-75-044.

Shelley, S. V. (1977). Glass recycling—A state of the art report. *Recycling and Waste Disposal* **2**, 60–1.

Shelton, R. D. (1978). Stagewise gasification in a multiple-hearth furnace. In *Solid wastes and residues—conversion by advanced thermal processes* (ed. J. L. Jones and S. B. Rodding) American Chemical Society Symposium Series 76. American Chemical Society, Washington.

Shields, L. R. (1972). Long-term planning in refuse disposal strategy. M.Tech. dissertation, Operational Research Dept., Brunel University.

Shiga, M. (1975). Separate collection of household refuse in Tokyo. First International Conference on Conversion of Refuse to Energy, Montreux, Switzerland, pp. 61–6.

Shin, K. C. (1979). Possibilities and limitations of refuse treatment for gaining raw materials and energy. *Proc. int. Recycling Congr., Berlin* (ed. K. J. Thomé-Kozmiensky) Vol. 1, pp. 26–31.

Short, W. (1973). Alternative methods of incineration. Institute of Fuel Symposium, London, 25 September.

Singh, R. (1976). Pulveriser transfer station at Caister starts trials. *Munic. Engng*, **153**, 1869.

Skelly, M. J. (1968). Planning for regional refuse disposal systems. Ph.D. thesis, Cornell University, University Microfilm No. U M-69-7307.

Skitt, J. (1972). *Disposal of refuse and other waste.* Charles Knight, London.

—— (1979). *Waste disposal management and practice.* Charles Knight, London.

Smith, F. A. (1975). Resource recovery plant cost estimates: a comparative evaluation of four recent dry shredding designs. Environmental Protection Agency, Washington, Report No. EPA-530/SW-163.

Smith, H. (1969). The cumulative energy requirements of some final products of the chemical industry. *Trans. (World Power Conference)* **18**(E), 71–89.

Smith, J. (1979). Choice of landfill site machines. *Natn. Ass. Waste Disposal Contractors News* August, pp. 16–17. National Association of Waste Disposal Contractors, London.

Smith, M. L. (1976). The CRRC approach to urban solid waste processing. *Proc. Fifth Mineral Waste Utilization Symp., Chicago* pp. 204–14. US Bureau of Mines and IIT Research Institute.

——and von Steiger, H. (1979). The Combustion Engineering approach to municipal solid waste energy recovery. *Proc. int. Recycling Congr., Berlin* (ed. K. J. Thomé-Kozmiensky) Vol. 1, pp. 324–30.

Smulders, C. T. A. L. (1979). The sorting plant at VAM, Holland. *Proc. int. Recycling Congr., Berlin* (ed. K. J. Thomé-Kozmiensky) Vol. 2, pp. 899–902.

Snyder, N. W., Brehany, J. J., and Mitchell, R. E. (1975). East Bay solid waste energy conversion system. First International Conference on Conversion of Refuse to Energy, Montreux, Switzerland, pp. 428–33.

Society of Chemical Industry (1979). *Conference on the Reclamation of Contaminated Land, Eastbourne.* Society of Chemical Industry, London.

Society of County Treasurers and County Surveyors's Society (SCT) (1976). Waste disposal statistics 1975–76. [Available from the Hon. Treasurer, Society of County Treasurers, P.O. Box 13, County Hall, Newcastle-upon-Tyne.]

—— (1979). Waste disposal statistics 1977–78. [Available from the Society of County Treasurers, County Hall, Truro, Cornwall, TR1 3BD. Published annually since 1974–5. Also available are Waste disposal statistics based on estimates, published annually since 1977–8.]

Solid Wastes. Monthly journal of the Institute of Solid Wastes Management, London.

Sonnenschein, H. W. (1979). Fuel recovery from municipal solid waste. *Proc. int. Recycling Congr., Berlin* (ed. K. J. Thomé-Kozmiensky) Vol. 2, pp. 948–51. Springer Verlag, Berlin.

South Yorkshire County Council (1979). The Doncaster Project. Brochure. South Yorkshire County Council Environment Department, Barnsley.

Spans, L. A. (1976). Enzymatic hydrolysis of cellulosic wastes to fermentable sugars for alcohol production. *Symp. Clean Fuels from Biomass, Sewage, Urban Refuse and Agricultural Wastes, Orlando, Florida* pp. 325–48. Institute of Gas Technology, Chicago.

Spencer, D. B. and Schlömann, C. (1975). Recovery of non-ferrous metals by means of permanent magnets. *Resource Recovery Conserv.* **1**, 151–65.

Squires, D. M. and Fisher, M. J. (1974). Incineration with heat recovery. Course on Utilisation of Domestic Refuse, University College, Cardiff.

Stabenow, G. (1972). Performance of the new Chicago Northwest incinerator. *Natnl Incinerator Conf., New York*, pp. 178–94. American Society of Mechanical Engineers, New York.

Stallings, J. W. (1974). The economics of resource recovery. *Second Natnl Conf. Energy and the Environment.* American Institute of Chemical Engineers, Dayton, Ohio.

Standrod, S. E. and Dodt, J. P. (1975). Refuse management: three forms of burning for energy recovery. First International Conference on Conversion of Refuse to Energy, Montreux, Switzerland, pp. 416–21.

Stearns, R. P., Wright, T. D., and Brecher, M. (1978). Recovery and utilization of methane gas from a sanitary landfill—City of Industry, California. *Symp. Energy from Biomass and Wastes, Wash.* pp. 325–44. Institute for Gas Technology, Chicago.

Steffgen, F. W. (1974). Clean fuels from solid organic wastes. *Proc. Fourth Mineral Waste Utilization Symp., Chicago* pp. 13–21. US Bureau of Mines and IIT Research Institute.

Steier, K. (1979). Operating experiences with a large-scale refuse sorting plant. *Proc. int. Recycling Congr., Berlin* (ed. K. J. Thomé-Kozmiensky) Vol. 2, pp. 887–91. Springer Verlag, Berlin.

Stern, H. I. (1973). Regional interindustry solid waste forecasting model. *J. environ. Eng. Div., Proc. Am. Soc. Civ. Engng* **99**(EE6), 851–72.

Stevenson, M. K., Leckie, J. O., and Eliassen, R. (1973). Preparation and evaluation of activated carbon produced from municipal refuse. Environmental Protection Agency, Washington, Report No. EPA/670/2-73-10. Issued by National Technical Information Service, Springfield, Virginia as Report No. PB 221 172.

Stiles, A. B. (1977). Methanol, past, present and speculation on the future. *Am. Inst. Chem. Eng. Journal* **23**, 362–75.

Stirrup, F. L. (1965). *Public cleansing: refuse disposal.* Pergamon Press, Oxford.

Stone, R. and Conrad, E. T. (1969). Landfill compaction equipment efficiency. *Public Works,* May, pp. 111–13.

—— and Kahle, R. (1976). Evaluation of solid waste baling and landfilling. *The American Public Works Association Reporter,* **43** (10).

Stuart, M. (1979). The energy scheme that is pure rubbish. *The Guardian,* London, 21 August, p. 2.

Stuckenbruck, L. C. and King, C. F. (1977). Recovery of energy and other resources from solid waste—an economic systems evaluation. *Engng Process Econ.* **2**, 27–43.

Sullivan, P. M. and Makar, H. V. (1976). Quality of products from Bureau of Mines resource recovery systems and suitability for recycling. *Proc. Fifth Mineral Waste Utilization Symp., Chicago* pp. 223–33. US Bureau of Mines and IIT Research Institute.

—— and Stanczyk, M. H. (1971). *Economics of recycling metals and minerals from urban refuse.* US Bureau of Mines Report No. TPR 33.

——, Stanczyk, M. H., and Spendlove, M. J. (1973). *Resource recovery from raw urban refuse.* US Bureau of Mines Report No. RI 7760.

Suloway, M. (1976). Chicago's refuse disposal system—organization and financing. *Symp. Clean Fuels from Biomass, Sewage, Urban Refuse and Agricultural Wastes, Orlando, Florida* pp. 437–46. Institute of Gas Technology, Chicago.

—— (1977). Chicago's new refuse disposal installation. *Symp. Clean Fuels from Biomass and Wastes, Orlando, Florida* pp. 303–11. Institute of Gas Technology, Chicago.

Sussman, D. (1974). Baltimore demonstrates gas pyrolysis, interim report. Environmental Protection Agency, Washington, Report No. EPA-530/SW-75d.i.

—— (1975). Recent applications of pyrolysis. International Symposium on Energy Recovery from Refuse, University of Louisville, Kentucky.

—— (1976). Resource recovery plant implementation: Guides for municipal officials—accounting format. Environmental Protection Agency, Washington, Report No. EPA/530/SW-157.6.

Swartzbaugh, J. T., Miller, J. W., and Wiles, C. E. (1977). Operating experience with large scale digestion of urban refuse with sewage sludge. *Symp. Clean Fuels from Biomass and Wastes, Orlando, Florida* pp. 353–72. Institute of Gas Technology, Chicago.

Sweeten, J. M. (1972). Design of a solid waste management system for the Eastern Appalachia Health Region of N. Carolina. Environmental Protection Agency, Washington, Report No. EPA-530/SW-80-of. Issued by National Technical Information Service, Springfield, Virginia as Report No. PB 214 089.

Systems Technology Corporation (Systech) (1975). A technical, environmental and economic evaluation of the 'Wet Processing System for the Recovery and Disposal of Municipal Solid Waste'. Report to Environmental Protection Agency, Washington, No. EPA/530/SW-109c. Issued by National Technical Information Service, Springfield, Virginia as Report No. PB 245 674.

Tabasaran, O. (1979). Main research topics in the Department of Waste Management of the University of Stuttgart and a report on current investigations of practical interest concerning landfill gas. Proceedings of the conference Elmia-Avfall '79, Jönkoping, Sweden, pp. 535–57.

Takeuchi, R., Hirayama, Y., and Ito, K. (1979). A new composting system. *Proc. int. Recycling Congr., Berlin* (ed. K. J. Thomé-Kozmiensky) Vol. 2, pp. 1070–5. Springer Verlag, Berlin.

Tanner, R. K. (1975). Will the classical refuse incineration method of refuse disposal be superseded by pyrolysis? First International Conference on Conversion of Refuse to Energy, Montreux, Switzerland, pp. 214–19.

Thomas, G. A. (1977). The Doncaster project. *Recycling and Waste Disposal* **2**, 62–4.

Thomé-Kozmiensky, K. J. (1979). Energy and material recycling. *Proc. int. Recycling Congr., Berlin* (ed. K. J. Thomé-Kozmiensky) Vol. 1, pp. 1–12. Springer Verlag, Berlin.

Thomson, P. (1979). Ph.D. thesis in preparation, University of Aston in Birmingham.

Tintner, G. and Sengupta, J. K. (1972). *Stochastic economics—stochastic processes, control and programming*. Academic Press, New York.

Tottman, J. D., Tittle, K., and Jones, B. (1979). The combined firing of coal and waste derived fuel in steam raising plant. *Proc. int. Recycling Congr., Berlin* (ed. K. J. Thomé-Kozmiensky) Vol. 1, pp. 301–6, Springer Verlag, Berlin.

Turner, R. K. and Grace, R. P. (1977). Forecasting the market demand for waste paper. *Long Range Forecasting* **10**, 30–6.

UK Parliament (1978). The nationalised industries. White paper presented to parliament by the Chancellor of the Exchequer by Command of Her Majesty, March, 1978. Cmnd. 7131. HMSO, London.

United Nations Monthly Bulletin of Statistics.

United States Bureau of Mines. *Minerals Yearbook.*

US Environmental Protection Agency (USEPA) (1973). First report to Congress on resource recovery and source reduction. Environmental Protection Agency, Washington, Report No. EPA/530/SW-118.

—— (1974). Second report to Congress on resource recovery and source reduction. Environmental Protection Agency, Washington, Report No. EPA/530/SW-122, 112 pp.

—— (1975). Third report to Congress on resource recovery and waste reduction. Environmental Protection Agency, Washington, Report No. EPA/530/SW-161.

University of Louisville (1970). Louisville, Kentucky—Industrial Metropolitan Region solid waste disposal study, Vols 1 and 2. Inst. of Ind. Research (Speed Scientific School).

Vasan, K. S. (1974). Optimization models for regional public systems. Operations

Research Center, Report No. ORC-74-6, University of California, Berkeley. Issued by National Information Service, Springfield, Virginia as Report No. PB 231 309.

Victor, P. A. (1972). *Pollution: economy and environment*. University of Toronto Press and Allen and Unwin, London.

Walker, W. E. (1968). Adjacent extreme point algorithm for the fixed charge problem. Center for Environmental Quality Management and Department of Operations Research, Ithaca, New York.

——(1973). A heuristic adjacent extreme point algorithm for the fixed charge problem. The Rand Corporation, Report No. P-5042.

—— (1976). A heuristic adjacent extreme point algorithm for the fixed charge problem. *Man. Sci.* **22**, 587–96.

——, Aquilina, M., and Schur, D. (1974). Development and use of a fixed charge programming model for regional solid waste planning. The Rand Corporation, Report No. P-5307.

Waller, R. F. (1976). Primary energy requirements for the production of iron and steel in the U.K. Open University research report ERG 011.

Walsh, H. G. and Williams, A. (1969). Current issues in cost–benefit analysis. Civil Service College Occasional Paper No. 11, HMSO, London.

Walters, C. S., Pfeffer, J. T., and Chow, P. (1977). Production of panel-board from residue left from the fermentation of organic waste for methane. *Forest Prod. J.* **27**, 12–20.

Walton, P. R. (1968). Sources of error in operating-cost estimates. *Chem. Engng, Albany* **75**, 150–2.

Ward, L. O. and Schoenenberger, R. J. (1979). Anatomy of regional solid waste resource recovery projects. *Proc. int. Recycling Congr., Berlin* (ed. K. J. Thomé-Kozmiensky) Vol. 1, pp. 89–95. Springer Verlag, Berlin.

Warner, A. J., Baum, B., and Parker, C. H. (1971). *Plastics solid waste disposal by incineration or landfill*. Manufacturing Chemists Association.

Waste Management Advisory Council (WMAC) (1976). First Report. HMSO, London.

Watson, L. (1974). Evaluating alternative waste disposal strategies using a computer based model. Joint ISCOL (International Systems Corporation of Lancaster) and Redland Purle Ltd. Conference, Waste disposal—planning the way ahead, London, 14–15 May.

Watson, R. H. and Burnett, J. M. (1972). Recent developments and operating experience with British incinerator plant. *National Incinerator Conference, New York* pp. 155–65. American Society of Mechanical Engineers, New York.

Webb, M. and Pearce, D. W. (1975). The economics of energy analysis. *Energy Policy* **3**, 318–31.

Wenger, R. B. and Rhyner, C. R. (1972). Evaluation of alternatives for solid waste systems. *J. environ. Sys.* **2**, 89–108.

Weiss, S. (1974). *Sanitary landfill technology*. Noyes Data Corporation, Park Ridge, New Jersey.

Wersan, S., Quon, J., and Charnes, A. (1971). Mathematical modelling and computer simulation for designing municipal refuse collection and haul services. Northwestern Univ., Environmental Protection Agency, Washington, Report No. SW-6rg. Issued by National Technical Information Service, Springfield, Virginia as Report No. PB 208 154.

West Midlands County Council (1976a). Waste disposal plan. Report to the Environmental Services and Consumer Protection Committee, 18 February.

—— (1976*b*). Waste disposal plan—first progress report, September.

Weston, Roy, F., Inc. (1971). A mathematical model to plan and evaluate regional solid waste systems. Report for New York State Department of Environmental Conservation, West Chester, Pennsylvania.

Wheatley, B. I. and Stafford, D. A. (ed.) (1979). *First Int. Symp. Anaerobic Digestion*. University College of Wales, Cardiff.

Whipple, W. (1975). Principles of determining a social discount rate. *Water Resour. Bull.* **11**, 811–19.

Whittocks, A. L. (1975). Controlled financing in refuse collection. *Publ. Financ. Account.* **2**, 186–9.

Wilcox, J. (1976). Urban waste: economic aspects of technological alternatives. International Symposium on Economics of Materials Recycling, Bellagio, Italy. Reprinted in *Solid Wastes* **67**, 149–66 (1977).

Wilkinson, R. R., Kelso, G. L., and Hopkins, F. C. (1978). State-of-the-art report: pesticide disposal research. Midwest Research Institute report to the Environmental Protection Agency, Washington. Issued by National Technical Information Service, Springfield, Virginia as Report No. P B 284 716.

Willey, C. R. and Bassin, M. (1978). The Maryland Environmental Service/Baltimore County resource recovery facility, Texas, Maryland. *Proc. Sixth Mineral Waste Utilization Symp., Chicago*, pp. 280–5. U S Bureau of Mines and I I T Research Institute.

Wilson, D. C. (1977*a*). Strategy evaluation in the planning of waste management to land—a critical review of the literature. *Appl. Math. Modelling* **1**, 205–17.

—— (1977*b*). *Strategy evaluation in the planning of waste management to land—a comprehensive review of the literature*. Atomic Energy Research Establishment, Harwell Report No. R-8769, H M S O, London.

—— (1979*a*). Recent developments in the management of hazardous wastes. In *Developments in Environmental Control and Public Health—1*, (ed. A. Porteous), pp. 107–57. Applied Science, London.

—— (1979*b*). Energy conservation through recycling. *Energy Research*, **3**, 307–23.

—— and Waring, S. (1980). The safe landfilling of hazardous wastes. *Third Int. Congr. Industrial Waste Waters and Wastes, Stockholm* Session III, Paper 3. International Union of Pure and Applied Chemistry.

Wilson, H. T. (1977). Pyrolysis—a further option for waste treatment. *Chart. mech. Engr* **24**, 35–8.

Wilson, M. J. and Swindle, D. W. (1976). The markets for and the economics of heat energy from solid waste incineration. *Resource Recovery Conserv.* **1**, 197–206.

Wise, D. L., Sadek, S. E., Kispert, R. G., Anderson, L. C., and Walker, D. H. (1975). Fuel gas production from solid waste. *Biotechnol. bioeng. Symp. No. 5* (ed. C. R. Wilke) pp. 285–301. Interscience, New York.

Wogrolly, E. G. (1975). Briquetting of waste for solid fuel. First International Conference on Conversion of Refuse to Energy, Montreux, Switzerland, pp. 573–9.

Wohlfarter, A. and Striedlinger, H. (1979). A solution to the recycling of useful components gained from municipal refuse. *Proc. int. Recycling Congr., Berlin* (ed. K. J. Thomé-Kozmiensky) Vol. 2, pp. 871–7. Springer Verlag, Berlin.

Wolbeck, B. (1980). Waste Material exchanges. *International Solid Wastes Congress, Wembley, London, June 1980*. International Solid Wastes Association, % 28 Portland Place, London, W1N 4DE.

Wolf, K. W. and Sosnovsky, C. H. (1972). High pressure compaction and baling of solid waste. Environmental Protection Agency, Washington, Report No. S W-

32d. Issued by National Technical Information Service, Springfield, Virginia as Report No. PB 213 596.

—— —— (1977). High pressure compaction and baling of solid waste. In *Handbook of solid waste management* (ed. D. G. Wilson) pp. 136–49. Van Nostrand Reinhold, New York.

Wright, D. J. (1974). Goods and services—an input-output analysis. *Energy Policy* **2**, 307–15.

—— (1975). The natural resource requirements of commodities. *Appl. Econ.* **7**, 31–9.

Wyss, F. J. (1979). Energy recycling through refuse pelletizing. *Proc. int. Recycling Congr., Berlin* (ed. K. J. Thomé-Kozmiensky) Vol. 2, pp. 952–7. Springer Verlag, Berlin.

Yoda, T., Miyazaki, T., and Machida. O. (1979). Making pulp from municipal refuse. *Proc. int. Recycling Congr., Berlin* (ed. K. J. Thomé-Kozmiensky) Vol. 2, pp. 1176–81. Springer Verlag, Berlin.

Zinn. R. E., LaMantia, C. R., and Niessen, W. R. (1970). Total incineration. *National Incinerator Conference, Cincinnati*, pp. 116–27. American Society of Mechanical Engineers, New York.

INDEX

Notes.
1. Main references are indicated by bold type **269** ff.; references to data on a subject are given in italics *168*; references which include a photograph are in sans serif 220.
2. All technologies included in the case study of options for waste management are marked with an asterisk*. The appropriate section or chapter in Part II is indicated in bold type. However, the comparative tables, graphs and discussion in Part I, and the tables of data and results in Appendix A, are *not* indexed, for each individual technology. The appropriate references may be found under 'case study'.
3. All items of data, which are either input to, or produced by, the economic or energy analysis of options in the case study, are indicated by a dagger. The main references for each are listed, including any significant discussion for individual technologies in Part II. However, in many cases the item is mentioned for *every* technology, and listing of all such references is not attempted. The appropriate tabulations in Appendix A are included.